Financial Behavior

FINANCIAL MARKETS AND INVESTMENTS SERIES

H. Kent Baker and Greg Filbeck, Series Editors

Portfolio Theory and Management
Edited by H. Kent Baker and Greg Filbeck

Public Real Estate Markets and Investments
Edited by H. Kent Baker and Peter Chinloy

Private Real Estate Markets and Investments
Edited by H. Kent Baker and Peter Chinloy

Investment Risk Management
Edited by H. Kent Baker and Greg Filbeck

Private Equity: Opportunities and Risks
Edited by H. Kent Baker, Greg Filbeck, and Halil Kiymaz

Mutual Funds and Exchange-Traded Funds: Building Blocks to Wealth
Edited by H. Kent Baker, Greg Filbeck, and Halil Kiymaz

Financial Behavior

PLAYERS, SERVICES, PRODUCTS, AND MARKETS

H. KENT BAKER

GREG FILBECK

and

VICTOR RICCIARDI

OXFORD
UNIVERSITY PRESS

OXFORD
UNIVERSITY PRESS

Oxford University Press is a department of the University of Oxford. It furthers the University's objective of excellence in research, scholarship, and education by publishing worldwide. Oxford is a registered trade mark of Oxford University Press in the UK and certain other countries.

Published in the United States of America by Oxford University Press
198 Madison Avenue, New York, NY 10016, United States of America.

Library of Congress Cataloging-in-Publication Data
Names: Baker, H. Kent (Harold Kent), 1944- editor. | Filbeck, Greg, editor. |
Ricciardi, Victor, editor.
Title: Financial behavior : players, services, products, and markets /
[edited by] H. Kent Baker, Greg Filbeck, and Victor Ricciardi.
Description: New York City : Oxford University Press, 2017. | Series:
Financial markets and investments series | Includes index.
Identifiers: LCCN 2016036009 | ISBN 9780190269999 (hardcover)
Subjects: LCSH: Investments—Psychological aspects. | Investments—Decision making. |
Finance—Psychological aspects.
Classification: LCC HG4515.15 .F56 2016 | DDC 332.601/9—dc23
LC record available at https://lccn.loc.gov/2016036009

Contents

List of Figures

List of Tables

Acknowledgments

The simpler you say it, the more eloquent it is.
—August Wilson

Publishing a book requires the involvement of many people. Although acknowledging everyone who participated in the process would be difficult, we would like to single out the following individuals. First, we greatly appreciate the helpful comments of the anonymous reviewers of our book proposal that helped us fine-tune our proposal.

Second, the chapter authors merit special thanks because without them this book would not have been possible. We firmly believe that every writer needs an editor, because self-editing can be difficult and often leads to missed mistakes. Our task as editors is to help our authors convey content in the most effective manner possible. The difference between the right word and nearly the write word can be enormous. As Arthur Plotnik once said, "You write to communicate to the hearts and minds of others what's burning inside you, and we edit to let the fire show through the smoke." We also adhere to the notion expressed by E. B. White that "The best writing is rewriting." Therefore, based on our edits and comments, most authors rewrote their chapters at least twice. They did so without complaint—at least without any complaints expressed directly to us. Perhaps J. Russell Lynes was correct: "No author dislikes to be edited as much as he dislikes not to be published."

Third, our partners at Oxford University Press performed in the same highly professional manner that they have throughout the Financial Markets and Investments Series. Scott Parris, Anne Dellinger, and Cathryn Vaulman helped steer the book through the early stages of the process while David Pervin and Emily MacKenzie played important roles later in the process. Special thanks also go to Rajakumari Ganessin (Project Manager), Carole Berglie (Copyeditor), and Claudie Peterfreund (Indexer). These are just a few of the people who played important roles in this book project.

Fourth, we appreciate the research support provided by our respective institutions: the Kogod School of Business at American University, the Behrend College at Penn State Erie, and the Business Management Department at Goucher College.

Finally, we thank our families for their encouragement and support and dedicate the book to them: Linda and Rory Baker; Janis, Aaron, Kyle, and Grant Filbeck; and Jaymie, Kristin, and Julianna Lunt.

Acronyms and Abbreviations

AAII	American Association of Individual Investors
ACA	Affordable Care Act of 2010
ACT	acceptance and commitment therapy
ADL	activity of daily living
AFS	Academy of Financial Services
AHEAD	Asset and Health Dynamics among the Oldest Old
AI	appreciative inquiry
AICPA	American Institute of CPAs
AIM	Affect Infusion Model
AMH	adaptive market hypothesis
APD	antisocial personality disorder
AUM	assets under management
BLS	Bureau of Labor Statistics
BM	book-to-market
CALIS	Covariance Analysis of Linear Structural
CAPM	capital asset pricing model
CBOE	Chicago Board Options Exchange
CCAPM	consumption CAPM
CD	certificate of deposit
CEA	Council of Economic Advisers
CEO	chief executive officer
CF/P	cash flow-to-price
CFA	Chartered Financial Analyst
CFO	chief financial officer
CFP	Certified Financial Planner
CFTC	Commodity Futures Trading Commission
COT	commitment of trader
CPA	Certified Public Accountant
CPI	consumer price index
CPT	Cumulative Prospect Theory
CRD	Central Registration Depository
CRM	customer relationship management

D/P	dividends-to-price
DB	defined benefit
DBT	dialectical behavioral therapy
DC	defined contribution
DJIA	Dow Jones Industrial Average
E/P	earnings-to-price
EFFH	extended functional fixation hypothesis
EMH	efficient market hypothesis
EPS	earnings per share
ETF	exchange-traded fund
FCA	Financial Conduct Authority
FCAA	Financial Counseling Association of America
FDNA	Financial DNA Assessment
FEARS	Financial and Economic Attitudes Revealed by Search
FINRA	Financial Industry Regulatory Authority
FMH	fractal market hypothesis
FPA	Financial Planning Association
FPSB	Financial Planning Standards Board
FPSM	Financial Planning Strategy Modes
FTA	Financial Therapy Association
GAO	Government Accountability Office
GDP	gross domestic product
GNH	gross national happiness
GWAS	genome-wide association studies
HFT	high-frequency trading
HNWI	high net worth individuals
HO	homeowners insurance
HRS	Health and Retirement Study
HWM	high water mark
IAFP	International Association for Financial Planning
IAPD	Investment Adviser Public Disclosure
IAR	Investment Advisor Representative
IARD	Investment Adviser Registration Depository
IBCFP	International Board for Standards and Practices for Certified Financial Planners
IBD	independent broker-dealers
ICAPM	intertemporal capital asset pricing model
ICFP	Institute of Certified Financial Planners
IOC	immediate or cancel
IPO	initial public offering
IPS	investment policy statement
IRA	Individual Retirement Account
IRS	Internal Revenue Service
KMV	key mediating variable
LOP	law of one price

M&A	merger and acquisition
MBS	mortgage-backed security
MEC	modified endowment contract
MFO	multi-family office
MI	motivational interviewing
MMF	money market fund
MMH	mood maintenance hypothesis
MPT	modern portfolio theory
MRI	magnetic resonance imaging
MS	mortality salience
MVO	mean-variance optimization
NAIC	National Association of Insurance Commissioners
NAPFA	National Association of Personal Financial Advisors
NASD	National Association of Securities Dealers
NBBO	national best bid and offer
NEFE	National Endowment for Financial Education
NEST	National Employment Savings Trust
NFCC	National Foundation for Credit Counseling
NFIP	National Flood Insurance Program
NLSY	National Longitudinal Survey of Youth
NPV	net present value
NYSE	New York Stock Exchange
OCIE	Office of Compliance Inspections and Examinations
OECD	Organization of Economic Cooperation and Development
OPT	option pricing theory
PCL	[Hare] Psychopathy Checklist
PFS	Personal Financial Specialist
PMI	Purchasing Managers' Index
QDIA	qualified default investment alternative
RCT	randomized control trial
Red FD	Regulation Fair Disclosure
Reg NMS	SEC Regulation National Market Systems
REIT	real estate investment trust
RIA	Registered Investment Adviser
SAA	strategic asset allocation
SAD	seasonal affective disorder
SCF	Survey of Consumer Finances
SEC	Securities and Exchange Commission
SEO	seasoned equity offering
SIP	Securities Information Processor
SML	security market line
SOA	Society of Actuaries
SRO	self-regulatory organization
SSRN	Social Science Research Network
SVI	Google Search Volume Index

SWF	sovereign wealth fund
TAA	tactical asset allocation
TBW	Taylor, Bean & Whitaker Mortgage Corporation
TMT	terror management theory
UHNW	ultra-high net worth
UX	user experience
VIX	CBOE Volatility Index

About the Editors

H. Kent Baker, CFA, CMA, is a University Professor of Finance in the Kogod School of Business at American University. Professor Baker is an author or editor of 26 books, including *Investor Behavior—The Psychology of Financial Planning and Investing*, *Behavioral Finance—Investors, Corporations, and Markets*, *Portfolio Theory and Management*, *Survey Research in Corporate Finance*, and *Understanding Financial Management: A Practical Guide*. As one of the most prolific finance academics, he has published more than 160 peer-reviewed articles in such journals as the *Journal of Finance*, *Journal of Financial and Quantitative Analysis*, *Financial Management*, *Financial Analysts Journal*, and *Journal of Portfolio Management*. He has consulting and training experience with more than 100 organizations. Professor Baker holds a BSBA from Georgetown University; M.Ed., MBA, and DBA degrees from the University of Maryland; and an MA, MS, and two PhDs from American University.

Greg Filbeck, CFA, FRM, CAIA, CIPM, PRM holds the Samuel P. Black III Professor of Finance and Risk Management at Penn State Erie, the Behrend College, and serves as the Interim Director for the Black School of Business. He formerly served as Senior Vice-President of Kaplan Schweser and held academic appointments at Miami University and the University of Toledo, where he served as the Associate Director of the Center for Family Business. Professor Filbeck is an author or editor of seven books and has published more than 90 refereed academic journal articles in the *Financial Analysts Journal*, *Financial Review*, and *Journal of Business, Finance, and Accounting* among others. Professor Filbeck holds and conducts training worldwide for candidates for the CFA, FRM, and CAIA designations. Professor Filbeck holds a BS from Murray State University, an MS from Penn State University, and a DBA from the University of Kentucky.

Victor Ricciardi is Assistant Professor of Financial Management at Goucher College. He teaches courses in financial planning, investments, corporate finance, behavioral finance, and the psychology of money. He is a leading expert on the academic literature and emerging research issues in behavioral finance. He co-edited *Investor Behavior—The Psychology of Financial Planning and Investing*. Professor Ricciardi is the editor of several eJournals distributed by the Social Science Research Network (SSRN) at www.ssrn.com, including: behavioral finance, financial history, behavioral economics, and behavioral accounting. He received a BBA in accounting and management from Hofstra University and an MBA in finance and Advanced Professional Certificate (APC) at the graduate level in economics from St. John's University. He also holds a graduate certificate in personal family financial planning from Kansas State University. He can be found on Twitter@victorricciardi.

About the Contributors

Irene Aldridge is the Managing Director, Research and Development, AbleMarkets.com and ABLE Alpha Trading LTD, where she designs, implements, and deploys proprietary trading strategies. She is also President of AbleMarkets.com, a platform of predictive market microstructure analytics. Ms. Aldridge is the author of *High-Frequency Trading: A Practical Guide to Algorithmic Strategies and Trading Systems.* Before joining ABLE Alpha, she taught graduate quantitative finance courses at several U.S. universities. She has contributed to many government regulatory panels, including the U.K. Government Foresight Committee for Future of Computer Trading and the U.S. Commodity Futures Trading Commission's Subcommittee on High-Frequency Trading. Ms. Aldridge holds a BE in Electrical Engineering from Cooper Union, an MS in Financial Engineering from Columbia University, and an MBA from INSEAD. She has also studied in two PhD programs, including IEOR at Columbia University.

Michal Strahilevitz is a Visiting Associate Professor at The Center for Advanced Hindsight at Duke University. Previously, she was a faculty member at Golden Gate University, University of Arizona, University of Miami, and University of Illinois. She was also a visiting faculty member at the University of Michigan, and University of California at Berkeley. She has published in the *Journal of Consumer Research, Journal of Marketing Research, Journal of Consumer Psychology, Journal of Business Research,* and *Journal of Nonprofit & Public Sector Marketing.* Much of her published research focuses on how emotions affect decision making in areas related to investing, shopping, and donating to charity. She blogs for *Psychology Today* and consults for-profit and nonprofit companies. Professor Strahilevitz received an MBA from Tel Aviv University and a PhD from the University of California at Berkeley.

James E. Brewer Jr. is President of Envision Wealth Planning and Envision 401(k) Advisors. He works with individuals and small businesses to incorporate their values into their financial vision using a holistic, behavioral financial planning process. He is a Certified Financial Planner professional, Accredited Investment Fiduciary, Chartered Retirement Planning Consultant, and Professional Plan Consultant. Mr. Brewer was a Top 100 Social Media Financial Advisor in the United States from 2013 to 2015. His thought leadership has been featured or cited in *U.S. News and World Report, The Wall*

Street Journal, Voices: James Brewer, on Using ERISA 3(38) Investment Managers, and *Forbes*. He holds an M.S. from the Massachusetts Institute of Technology.

Peter Brooks is a Behavioral Finance Transformation Director with Barclays. He joined Barclays in March 2007 and works with a team of experts to develop and implement commercial applications drawing on behavioral portfolio theory, the psychology of judgment and decision making, and decision sciences. He has worked in London and Singapore, and his current position focuses on bringing the best of behavioral finance to self-directed investors through Internet channels. Dr. Brooks has published in the *Journal of Risk and Uncertainty, Theory and Decision*, and contributed to the *Wiley Encyclopedia of Operations Research and Management Science*. He has been a regular contributor to the leading print and television media on topics related to investing private wealth. He holds a PhD in behavioral and experimental economics from the University of Manchester. His doctoral thesis focused on experimental research into individual attitudes to monetary gains and losses.

Elissa Buie, CFP, is CEO of Yeske Buie, and holds an appointment as Distinguished Adjunct Professor in Golden Gate University's Ageno School of Business, where she teaches the capstone case course in the financial planning program. She is a past chair of both the Financial Planning Association and the Foundation for Financial Planning, the latter being the only nonprofit devoted solely to fostering and supporting the delivery of pro bono financial planning services to those in need. She is also a dean in the FPA's residency program. She has published in the *Journal of Financial Planning* and contributed chapters to the first and second editions of the CFP Board's *Financial Planning Competency Handbook* and *Investor Behavior: The Psychology of Financial Planning and Investing*. She holds a BS in commerce from the University of Virginia's McIntire School and an MBA from the University of Maryland.

Pattanaporn Chatjuthamard is an Associate Professor of Finance at Sasin Graduate Institute of Business Administration of Chulalongkorn University, Bangkok, Thailand. Before joining the faculty at Sasin, she was an assistant professor at Texas A&M International University in Laredo, Texas, between 2002 and 2006. She was also a visiting professor at Levin Graduate Institute, the University at Buffalo, in 2006. Her primary research interests include corporate finance, corporate governance, and international financial markets. She has published in leading scholarly and professional journals, including the *Journal of Financial Intermediation, Journal of Corporate Finance, Journal of Banking and Finance, Journal of Financial Research, Journal of Business Ethics*, and *International Review of Economics and Finance*. Professor Chatjuthamard received a PhD from the University of Wisconsin Milwaukee.

Marguerita M. Cheng is the Chief Executive Officer at Blue Ocean Global Wealth. Before co-founding Blue Ocean Global Wealth, she was a Financial Advisor at Ameriprise Financial and an analyst and editor at Towa Securities in Tokyo, Japan. Ms. Cheng is a spokesperson for the AARP Financial Freedom Campaign, a regular columnist for *Kiplinger*, and former Financial Planning Association (FPA) national board member. As a Certified Financial Planner Board of Standards (CFP Board) Ambassador, Ms. Cheng helps educate the public, policymakers, and media about the benefits of competent, ethical financial planning. She is a CFP professional, a Chartered

Retirement Planning Counselor, a Certified Divorce Financial Analyst, and Retirement Income Certified Professional.

C. W. Copeland is an Assistant Professor of Insurance for The American College of Financial Services. He has 18 years of college teaching experience and nearly 20 years as a financial services practitioner. He is a registered representative with Cape Securities and an Investment Advisor Representative with Cape Investment Advisors and maintains a Series 65, Series 7, Series 6, Series 63, Life and Health, Property and Casualty Insurance licenses in multiple states. He co-authored *Applications in Financial Planning II*, and edited *McGill's Life Insurance,* 10th Edition, *Essentials of Life Insurance Products,* 4th Edition, *Essentials of Disability Income Insurance,* 4th Edition, and *Financial Services Overview: FP99 Financial Services Practicum.* Professor Copeland holds a PhD in financial planning from the University of Georgia with a research focus on behavioral finance. He also holds the Retirement Income Certified Professional (RICP) designation, Chartered Financial Consultant (ChFC), and Chartered Life Underwriter professional designations.

Henrik Cronqvist is Professor of Finance at the University of Miami, where he conducts interdisciplinary research and teaches finance, entrepreneurship, and management. His research involves behavioral finance and corporate finance. His work has been published in top journals in economics, including the *American Economic Review* and *Journal of Political Economy,* as well as in finance, including the *Journal of Finance, Journal of Financial Economics,* and *Review of Financial Studies.* He is often invited to give seminars at academic conferences and to executives and public policymakers around the world. Several of his research papers have been recognized with best paper awards at international conferences, and have been sponsored by competitive research grants. His work has been featured in *BusinessWeek, The Economist, Financial Times, The Wall Street Journal,* and on CNBC and CNN. Professor Cronqvist received a PhD in finance from the University of Chicago.

Benjamin F. Cummings, CFP®, is an Associate Professor of Behavioral Finance at the American College of Financial Services. Before his current position, he was an Assistant Professor at Saint Joseph's University in Philadelphia, PA and a Scholar in Residence at CFP Board in Washington, DC. Professor Cummings also worked for FJY Financial, a fee-only financial planning firm in Reston, Virginia. He has completed award-winning research on the use and value of financial advice, and has worked on funded projects related to the regulation of professional financial advice. Professor Cummings received a PhD in personal financial planning from Texas Tech University.

Greg B. Davies recently founded Centapse, a firm dedicated to applying sophisticated behavioral insight to design, develop, and deploy solutions across industries to help people and organizations make better decisions. Over the last decade, as head of Behavioral-Quant Finance at Barclays, Dr. Davies built and led the world's first applied behavioral finance team, implementing behavioral design into the bank's tools, systems, propositions, products, and organizational processes. He is an Associate Fellow at Oxford University's Saïd Business School, and his first book, *Behavioral Investment Management,* was published in 2012. He has authored papers in multiple academic disciplines, and is a frequent media commentator on behavioral finance. Dr. Davies co-created the "reality opera" *Open Outcry*, which turns the behavior of a functioning trading floor into a musical performance, which received its première in London in November 2012. He holds an undergraduate degree from the University of Cape Town, and an MPhil in economics and PhD in behavioral decision theory, both from Cambridge University.

Erik Devos is the JP Morgan Chase Professor in Business Administration and Professor of Finance at the College of Business Administration of the University of Texas El Paso. He previously taught at Ohio University and Binghamton University (SUNY). He has published in finance and accounting journals such as *Review of Financial Studies, Journal of Accounting and Economics, Journal of Corporate Finance, Financial Management*, and *Journal of Banking and Finance*. He has also published in real estate journals such as *Real Estate Economics, Journal of Real Estate Economics and Finance*, and *Journal of Real Estate Research*. Professor Devos serves as an associate editor for the *Financial Review*. He received a master's degree in financial economics from Erasmus University in Rotterdam and a PhD in finance from Binghamton University (SUNY).

Paul Dolan is an internationally renowned expert on happiness, behavior, and public policy. He is currently Professor of Behavioural Science in the Department of Social Policy at the London School of Economics and Political Science, and Director of the new Executive MSc in Behavioural Science. In 2010, he co-authored the *Mindspace* report published by the U.K. Cabinet Office, advising local and national policymakers on how to effectively use behavioral insights in their policy setting. He received a PhD from the University of York.

Michael Dowling is an Associate Professor of Finance in ESC Rennes School of Business in France, where he primarily researches behavioral asset pricing, especially in energy markets. He has published in such journals as *Energy Economics and Energy Policy* and *Economics Letters*. Professor Dowling is currently the Co-Editor-in-Chief of the *Journal of Behavioral and Experimental Finance*, which concentrates on rigorously investigating the extent to which behavioral principles drive financial behavior. He received a PhD from Trinity College Dublin.

Harold Evensky is Chairman of Evensky & Katz/Foldes Financial, a 30-year-old wealth management firm, and Professor of Practice at Texas Tech University. He has served as chair of the CFP Board of Governors and the International CFP Council and he is the research columnist for the *Journal of Financial Planning*. Mr. Evensky has been named by *Investment Advisor* as one of the "25 most influential people in the financial planning industry," by *Financial Planning* as one of five "Movers, Shakers and Decision Makers, The Most Influential People in the Financial Planning Profession," and by *Investment News* as one of the "25 Power Elite" in the financial services industry. He co-authored *New Wealth Management, Wealth Management*, and co-edited *The Investment Think Tank: Theory, Strategy, and Practice for Advisors and Retirement Income Redesigned: A Master Plan for Distribution*. He received his BCE and MS degrees from Cornell University.

Steve Z. Fan is an Associate Professor of Finance at the College of Business and Economics, University of Wisconsin Whitewater. Before his career in finance, he worked as a research assistant professor at Marquette University. Professor Fan's research focuses on equity anomalies, corporate governance, and institutional investors. He has published in *Multinational Finance Journal, International Journal of Business and Finance Research,* and *Journal of Finance and Accountancy,* among others. Professor Fan received a BS in mechanical engineering from Zhangzhou University, China, a PhD in biomedical engineering from a joint program from University Tennessee and University of Memphis, and a PhD in finance from the University of Wisconsin Milwaukee.

Deborah W. Gregory is an Assistant Professor at Bentley University in Waltham, Massachusetts. As a certified Jungian psychoanalyst (IAAP, C.G. Jung Institute, Boston) and Chartered Financial Analyst (CFA). Professor Gregory's research focuses on the behavioral aspect of individuals' relation to money. She received a scholarly award from Bentley for her book *Unmasking Financial Psychopaths: Inside the Minds of Investors in the Twenty-First Century* (2014). She has published in the *Journal of Finance, Financial Analysts Journal, NYU Salomon Brothers Monograph Series, Journal of Business and Economic Studies, Journal of Financial Crime,* and *Journal of Behavioral Finance & Economics,* among others. Professor Gregory received a PhD in finance from the University of Florida.

John J. Guerin is the owner of Delta Psychological Associates, P.C. He has more than 30 years of experience in the practice of both clinical and organizational psychology. Experience with both group dynamics and family systems has allowed him to effectively coach individuals in organizations and to work with groups in corporate and family-based businesses. With more than 20 years of experience in mediation and forensic practice, he has demonstrated skills in forging consensus in challenging situations and helping organizations navigate difficult adversarial situations and cultural transitions. Dr. Guerin is an expert in organizational, team, and individual assessment, using high standards in scientific assessment methodology. He is active in emergent efforts to collaborate across professional boundaries and develop more effective tools for diagnosis and intervention. He is a Licensed Psychologist in independent practice in Pennsylvania and New Jersey, and collaborates with organizational consulting firms as an independent consultant. He received an M.A. degree from the University of Chicago and a PhD from Temple University in Philadelphia.

L. Paul Hood Jr. is the Director of Planned Giving at The University of Toledo Foundation. He previously served as Director of Gift Planning for The University of Montana Foundation. A self-styled "recovering tax lawyer," Mr. Hood practiced tax and estate planning law for 20 years in Louisiana. He is the author or co-author of five books on estate planning, charitable planning, buy-sell agreements, and business valuation and is a frequent speaker and writer on estate planning and business valuation. The father of two teenaged boys, he enjoys reading, but his passion is baseball. Mr. Hood served as President of the Toledo Area Partnership for Philanthropic Planning in 2014.

He obtained his undergraduate and law degrees from Louisiana State University and a LL.M. in taxation from Georgetown University Law Center.

Nancy Hubbard holds the Miriam Katowitz Chair in Management and Accounting at Goucher College, Maryland. She is also a member of the faculty of Moscow's School of Management, SKOLKOVO (Russia) and the University of Marseilles (France). She is a former lecturer at the Saïd Business School and Associate Fellow at Oxford University (Templeton College), as well as a management consultant with Spicer & Oppenheim (which is part of Booz, Allen & Hamilton) and KPMG. She has published in the *Human Resources Management Journal, Journal of Professional HRM,* and *European Retail Digest,* among others. She has published several books, including *Acquisition: Strategy and Implementation* and *Conquering Global Markets: Secrets from the World's Most Successful Acquirers.* She holds a BS in business from Georgetown University and a MS and PhD from Oxford University in management.

Danling Jiang is the Associate Professor of Finance at the College of Business, Stony Brook University. Her research involves studying investments, corporate finance, and financial decision-making from behavioral approaches. Her research integrates economics, psychology, political science, and sociology into finance. Professor Jiang's work has been published in leading journals spanning the fields of finance, management, accounting, and judgment and decision-making, including the *Review of Financial Studies, Management Science, Organizational Behavior and Human Decision Processes, Journal of Financial and Quantitative Analysis, Review of Finance,* and *Review of Accounting Studies,* among others. She has served as a reviewer for many journals in finance, economics, management, and psychology as well as various publishers and international funding agencies. She serves on the Advisory Council for the Financial Analysts Journal and in various roles for many conferences and associations. Professor Jiang received a PhD in finance from the Ohio State University.

Rebecca Li-Huang is a wealth advisor to high net work individuals. In addition to wealth management and investment advisory practices at Merrill Lynch, her professional experience includes capital markets, equity research, corporate finance, and project management at other financial services and technology firms. She is the author of *Green Apple Red Book: A Trial and Errors,* which was honorably mentioned in London, New York, San Francisco, and Paris Book Festivals. She has undergraduate study at the University of Science and Technology of China, a Master of Science in electrical engineering from Purdue University, and an MBA in finance and international economics from the University of Chicago Booth School of Business.

Brian Lucey is Professor of Finance in Trinity College Dublin. He has more than a 100 peer-reviewed publications across the spectrum of behavioral finance and beyond. Professor Lucey has published in such journals as the *Journal of Banking & Finance, Small Business Economics,* and *Quantitative Finance.* He is currently Editor-in-Chief of *International Review of Financial Analysis* and *Finance Research Letters,* and Associate Editor of the *Journal of Banking & Finance.* He received a PhD from the University of Stirling.

Duccio Martelli is an Assistant Professor of Finance at the University of Perugia (Italy) and summer school professor at Harvard University. He has also been a visiting professor of finance at the University of Applied Sciences in Augsburg, Germany. Professor Martelli teaches undergraduate and graduate courses in behavioral finance, corporate finance, private banking and financial markets. His main research interests include behavioral and neurofinance, financial education, real estate finance, and asset management. He has presented his research at national and international conferences and has published in *European Financial Management* and *Journal of Economics and Business*. He also serves as a referee on several peer-reviewed finance journals. Professor Martelli advises firms and not-for-profit organizations in the areas of financial education and asset management. He received a BA cum laude from Bocconi University and a PhD in banking and finance from University of Rome "Tor Vergata."

Nathan Mauck is an Assistant Professor of Finance at the Henry W. Bloch School of Management, University of Missouri-Kansas City. His research focuses on sovereign wealth funds, mergers and acquisitions, payout policy, corporate finance, and behavioral finance. He has published in *Journal of Banking & Finance, Journal of Behavioral Finance, Journal of Corporate Finance, Journal of Financial Intermediation, Journal of Financial Research,* and *Journal of International Business Studies,* among others. Professor Mauck is the recipient of the American Real Estate Society Best Paper in Real Estate Portfolio Management (2015) and multiple teaching awards, including the UMKC Chancellor's Early Career Award for Excellence in Teaching (2015) and Bloch Favorite Faculty Member of the Year (2014). He received a BS in finance from Kansas State University and a PhD in finance from Florida State University.

Peter J. May, CFP, is an independent wealth advisor. He created and manages "Art Solutions. . .Best in Practice," a LinkedIn discussion group with more than 4,300 members from professionally and geographically diverse backgrounds across the globe. Mr. May also developed "The Personal Wealth Spectrum," an integrated educational tool to assist clients in better understanding multi-generational risk mitigation. He has been a frequent speaker and contributor to articles on financial planning and art preservation techniques for individuals and families. Mr. May received a BS in accounting from St. Louis University, a JD from Capital University Law School, and an LLM in taxation from Villanova University School of Law. He passed the Uniform CPA Examination and the NASD Series 7.

Catherine McBreen is the Managing Director of Spectrem Group, a market research and consulting firm specializing in the affluent and retirement markets. Ms. McBreen is President and Editor of Spectrem Group's website, Millionaire Corner, which presents original research and reporting and feature stories to meet the informational needs of both new and seasoned investors. She is a member of the American Bar Association, Illinois Bar Association, and Chicago Bar Association. Ms. McBreen is a frequent speaker at industry conferences and has been widely quoted by the print and broadcast financial media, including *The Financial Times, The Wall Street Journal, CNBC Closing Bell, Neal Cavuto at Fox Business News,* and ABC and CBS radio. She coauthored *Get Rich, Stay Rich, Pass It On: The Wealth-Accumulation Secrets of America's Richest Families.*

She has a BS summa cum laude from Northwestern University and a JD from DePaul University School of Law.

Christopher Milliken, CFA, is an industry professional and Vice President of Hennion & Walsh Asset Management's Portfolio Management Program. Hennion & Walsh is a Registered Investment Advisory firm that uses ETFs to construct investment strategies. Mr. Milliken works under the chief investment officer, conducts research on capital markets and asset allocation strategy, and oversees the sales and trading desk. He received a BS in business administration with a focus in finance from Marist College.

James M. Moten Jr. is an Assistant Professor of Finance at East Central University. He has more than 10 years of college teaching experience. Professor Moten is a financial advisor, representative, and registered principal for PFS Investments and still maintains a Series 26, Series 65, Series 6, Series 63, Life and Health and Property and Casualty Insurance Licenses. BVT published his book, *Introductory Financial Management: Theory and Application*, second edition, in 2014. He received an MS in finance, MS in accounting, and MS in economics, all from Texas A&M University Commerce; an MBA from Cameron University; Graduate Certificate in Financial Planning from Kansas State University; an MS in acquisition and contract management from Florida Institute of Technology; and a PhD in business administration with a financial management concentration from Northcentral University. Professor Moten also holds the Certified Financial Planner (CFP), Chartered Financial Consultant (ChFC), Chartered Retirement Planning Counselor (CRPC), Chartered Mutual Fund Counselor (CMFC), and Retirement Income Certified Professional (RICP) professional designations.

Jeroen Nieboer is a behavioral economist specializing in financial decisions and decision-making under risk and is currently based at the London School of Economics and Political Science. His research originated using experimental methods to study financial risk taking in groups. He actively collaborates with financial advice charities such as StepChange and the Citizens Advice Bureau, and has acted as a consultant to many companies in the finance and insurance sectors. He obtained his PhD from the University of Nottingham.

Ehsan Nikbakht, CFA, FRM, is Professor of Finance in the Frank G. Zarb School of Business at Hofstra University and previously served as department chair and Associate Dean. He served on the Advisory Board of the International Association of Financial Engineers and Chair of Derivatives Committee of the New York Society of Security Analysts. Professor Nikbakht currently serves on the editorial board of *Global Finance Journal*. He authored *Finance* and *Foreign Loans and Economic Performance*. Professor Nikbakht received a BA from the Tehran School of Business, an MBA from the Iran Center for Management Studies, and a DBA in finance from the George Washington University.

John R. Nofsinger is the William H. Seward Endowed Chair in International Finance at the College of Business and Public Policy at the University of Alaska Anchorage. He is one of the world's leading experts on behavioral finance. He has authored/coauthored 10 finance trade books, textbooks, and scholarly books that have been translated into 11 languages. Professor Nofsinger is a prolific scholar who has published more than

50 articles in peer-reviewed journals, including prestigious scholarly journals such as the *Journal of Finance* and *Journal of Financial and Quantitative Analysis* and practitioner journals such as the *Financial Analysts Journal* and *Journal of Wealth Management.* He is often quoted in the financial media, including the *The Wall Street Journal, Financial Times, Fortune, Business Week, Smart Money, Money Magazine, Washington Post, Bloomberg, Nightly Business Report,* and CNBC, and other media from The Dolans to TheStreet.com. Professor Nofsinger received a PhD from Washington State University.

Alex Plastun is Associate Professor and the Chair of Accounting and Auditing at the Ukrainian Academy of Banking (UAB). Before joining the UAB, he was a trader and analyst in several investment companies, including Admiral Markets Ltd, ForexService Ltd., and SumyForexClub Ltd. He still trades in the different financial markets using his own trading strategies. Professor Plastun tries to reconcile his experience as a trader with the academic theory and is constantly searching for market inefficiencies. He has published in such outlets as the *Journal of Economics and Finance, Computational Economics,* and *Corporate Ownership and Control.* Professor Plastun holds a PhD in finance from the Ukrainian Academy of Banking.

Victor Ricciardi is an Assistant Professor of Financial Management at Goucher College. He teaches courses in financial planning, investments, corporate finance, behavioral finance, and the psychology of money. He is a leading expert on the academic literature and emerging research issues in behavioral finance. He co-edited *Investor Behavior—The Psychology of Financial Planning and Investing*. Professor Ricciardi is the editor of several eJournals distributed by the Social Science Research Network (SSRN) at www.ssrn.com including: behavioral finance, financial history, behavioral economics, and behavioral accounting. He received a BBA in accounting and management from Hofstra University and an MBA in finance and Advanced Professional Certificate (APC) at the graduate level in economics from St. John's University. He also holds a graduate certificate in personal family financial planning from Kansas State University. He can be found on Twitter@victorricciardi.

April Rudin, Founder of The Rudin Group, is an acclaimed financial services/wealth management marketing firm. Her expertise centers on wealth, millennials, and technology/fintech. The Rudin Group, founded in 2008, designs bespoke marketing campaigns for some of world's most important financial services firms. Ms. Rudin is a regularly featured source of expert commentary to international news/business outlets and trade publications. She has also created and maintains an extensive thought leadership domain featured on *Huffington Post, American Banker, CFA Enterprising Investor, Family Wealth Report,* Wealthmanagement.Com, and many other trade publications. Ms. Rudin is a judge for Family Wealth Report's Annual Wealth Management Industry awards, a member of the PAM (Private Asset Management) Advisory board, and serves on the Global Board of Directors for the Hedge Fund Association (HFA). She also heads the editorial board for NexChange, a global financial services' networking start-up.

Charles H. Self III, CFA, is Chief Operating Officer and Chief Investment Officer of iSectors, a provider of outsourced investment management services. He has experience in portfolio management and working with clients. He conducts interviews in various media, including *Fox Business News, Bloomberg Radio,* and *The Wall Street Journal.* Mr. Self has an MBA in statistics and finance from the University of Chicago.

Alexandre Skiba is an Assistant Professor at the Department of Finance and Economics at the University of Wyoming. He teaches international economics and business, macroeconomics, and econometrics. His research interests are in the areas of international trade and finance, institutional investors, and real estate finance. Specifically, his work deals with product quality of internationally traded goods and the effects of trade barriers on trade, as well as specializing and trading choices and performance of institutional trades. Professor Skiba has published in such journals as the *Journal of Political Economy, Journal of Development Economics,* and *Review of International Economics.* Professor Skiba received a PhD from Purdue University.

Hilla Skiba is an Assistant Professor at the Department of Finance and Real Estate at Colorado State University. She teaches courses in real estate, investments, and international finance with behavioral finance applications. Her research interests are mainly in the areas of international finance, institutional investor performance, and real estate finance. Specifically, her work deals with cultural influences on financial decision making, under-diversification and performance, and the behavior of real estate market participants. Professor Skiba has published in such journals as the *Journal of Financial Economics, Journal of Banking & Finance,* and *Journal of Corporate Finance.* Her research has earned several awards, including the best paper award at the Asian Finance Association meetings. Professor Skiba received a PhD in finance from the University of Kansas.

Sameer S. Somal is the Chief Financial Officer at Blue Ocean Global Wealth. Before co-founding Blue Ocean Global Wealth, he was a Senior Investment Analyst at The Bank of Nova Scotia and a Financial Advisor and Intermediary at Morgan Stanley and Merrill Lynch & Co. Mr. Somal serves on CFP Board's Council on Education and is a Women's Initiative (WIN) Advocate. He is an active member at CFA Institute, a Board Advisor at the iPlan Education Institute (New Delhi, India), and serves on the Board of Directors of the Philadelphia Tri-State Financial Planning Association (FPA). Mr. Somal is a CFA Charterholder, a CFP professional, and a Chartered Alternative Investment Analyst.

Andrew C. Spieler, CFA, FRM, CAIA, is a Professor of Finance in the Frank G. Zarb School of Business at Hofstra University. He has published in *Real Estate Economics, Journal of Real Estate Finance and Economics, Journal of Real Estate Portfolio Management, Journal of Applied Finance,* among others. He served as chair of the Derivatives Committee at the New York Society of Securities Analysts. Professor Spieler also serves as co-director of the annual real estate conference sponsored by the Wilbur F. Breslin Center for Real Estate Studies. He received undergraduate degrees in math and economics from Binghamton University (SUNY), an MS in finance from Indiana University, and an MBA and PhD from Binghamton University (SUNY).

Joseph M. Tenaglia, CFA, is an Emerging Markets Portfolio Specialist at Emerging Global Advisors, which is a boutique emerging and frontier markets asset management firm that offers core and thematic exchange-traded funds. Mr. Tenaglia is a member of the firm's Investment Strategy Team and is responsible for creating content around the emerging markets environment while also promoting the firm's research and strategies to institutional investors. He previously worked at Bank of New York Mellon Asset Management in several roles. Mr. Tenaglia graduated from Boston College with a BS in finance and marketing. He is a member of the New York Society of Security Analysts.

Ivo Vlaev joined Warwick Business School as a Professor of Behavioural Science in 2014. He previously worked at the University of Warwick, University College London, and Imperial College London. He studies decision making from the perspectives of psychology, neuroscience, and economics. In 2010, he co-authored the *Mindspace* report published by the U.K. Cabinet Office, advising local and national policymakers on how to effectively use behavioral insights in their policy setting. He received a DPhil in Experimental Psychology from St. John's College, Oxford.

Dave Yeske, CFP, is Managing Director at Yeske Buie and financial planning program director at Golden Gate University's Ageno School of Business, where he holds an appointment as Distinguished Adjunct Professor. He is a past chair of the Financial Planning Association, where he has also chaired the political action committee, Research Center Team, and Academic Advisory Council. He now serves as Practitioner Editor of FPA's *Journal of Financial Planning*. Professor Yeske has published in the *Journal of Financial Planning* and contributed chapters to the first and second editions of CFP Board's *Financial Planning Competency Handbook* and *Investor Behavior: The Psychology of Financial Planning and Investing*. He holds a BS in applied economics and MA in economics from the University of San Francisco, and a DBA from Golden Gate University.

Susan M. Young is an Associate Professor at the Gabelli School of Business, Fordham University. Before joining the faculty at Fordham University, Professor Young held academic positions at CUNY Baruch College and Emory University. Before her academic career, Professor Young held positions in public, private, and nonprofit accounting. She has published in the *Accounting Review, Journal of Business, Finance and Accounting, Accounting Horizons, Journal of Management Accounting Research, Review of Behavioral Finance,* and *Human Resource Management*. Professor Young earned a BS from California State University Stanislaus, an MBA from California State University Sacramento, and a PhD from the University of Southern California.

Linda Yu is a Professor of Finance at the College of Business and Economics, University of Wisconsin Whitewater. Before joining the University of Wisconsin, she worked as an assistant professor at the State University of New York Institute of Technology. Professor Yu's research focuses on fixed income, equity anomalies, corporate governance, and socially responsible investing. She has published in *Financial Management, Review of Quantitative Finance and Accounting, Journal of Fixed Income, International Review of Financial Analysis,* and *Multinational Finance Journal,* among others. Professor Yu received a BA in British literature from Jilin University China, an MBA from Pittsburg State University, and a PhD in Finance from the University of Memphis.

Part One

FINANCIAL BEHAVIOR AND PSYCHOLOGY

1

Financial Behavior

An Overview

H. KENT BAKER
University Professor of Finance
Kogod School of Business, American University

GREG FILBECK
Samuel P. Black III Professor of Finance and Risk Management
Penn State Erie, The Behrend College

VICTOR RICCIARDI
Assistant Professor of Financial Management
Goucher College

Introduction

Two major branches in finance are the well-established traditional finance, also called standard finance, and the more recent behavioral finance. *Traditional finance* is based on the premise of rational agents making unbiased judgments and maximizing their self-interests. In contrast, behavioral finance studies the psychological influences of the decision-making process for individuals, groups, organizations, and markets. Both schools of thought play important roles in understanding both investor and market behavior. Ackert (2014) provides a comparison of traditional and behavioral finance.

Traditional finance theory assumes normative principles to model how investors, markets, and others should act. In traditional finance theory, investors are supposed to act rationally. Additionally, this normative approach assumes that investors have access to perfect information, process that information without cognitive or emotional biases, act in a self-interested manner, and are risk-averse. According to Bloomfield (2010, p. 23), traditional finance

> sees financial settings populated not by the error-prone and emotional *Homo sapiens*, but by the awesome *Homo economicus*. The latter makes perfectly rational decisions, applies unlimited processing power to any available information, and holds preferences well-described by standard utility theory.

Traditional finance theory is based on classical decision making in which investors make economic decisions using utility theory by maximizing the benefit they receive from an action, subject to constraints. In utility theory, investors are assumed to make decisions consistently and independently of other choices. Utility theory serves as the foundation for standard finance theories based on modern portfolio theory and asset pricing models. A major tenet of traditional finance is fundamental analysis incorporating statistical measures of risk and return. A primary aspect of this macro-driven model is the study of investors within the financial markets, and the underlying assumption of investor *risk aversion* (i.e., investors must be compensated with higher returns in order to take on higher levels of risk). Notable examples in traditional finance include portfolio choice (Markowitz 1952, 1959), the capital asset pricing model (CAPM) (Sharpe 1964), and the efficient market hypothesis (EMH) (Fama 1970).

Modern portfolio theory (MPT) provides a mathematical framework for constructing a portfolio of assets such that the expected return is maximized for a given level of risk, as measured by variance or standard deviation. MPT emphasizes that risk is an inherent part of higher reward. An important insight provided by MPT is that investors should not assess an asset's risk and return in isolation, but by how it contributes to a portfolio's overall risk and return.

Further developments revealed that investors should not be compensated for risk that they can diversify away, which is called unsystematic or diversifiable risk. Instead, they should only be compensated for non-diversifiable risk, also called market or systematic risk. This insight led to the development of the CAPM. This model describes the relation between risk, as measured by market risk or beta, and expected return, and is used for the pricing of risky securities. Although a cornerstone of modern finance, the CAPM, as a single-factor model, cannot pick up other risk factors. Consequently, the CAPM does not perform well in explaining the cross-section of returns across stocks. Hence, others suggest that returns depend on other factors besides the market. For example, Fama and French (1996) identity two additional factors: firm size and the book-to-market ratio. Carhart (1997) extends the Fama–French three-factor model by including a momentum factor, which is the tendency for the stock price to continue rising if it is going up and to continue declining if it is going down.

The EMH states that asset prices fully reflect all available information. An implication of this dominant paradigm in traditional finance of the function of markets is that consistently beating the market on a risk-adjusted basis is impossible. Fama (1970) sets forth three versions of the EMH. According to *weak form efficiency*, prices on traded assets reflect all market information, such as past prices. The *semi-strong form* of the EMH asserts that prices reflect all publicly available information. The *strong form* of the EMH states that current asset prices reflect all information, both public and private (insider). Numerous research studies report anomalies, which are situations when a security or group of securities performs contrary to the notion of efficient markets. This stream of research was a driving force leading to the birth and growth of behavioral finance (Ackert 2014).

Although the traditional approach provides many useful insights, it offers an incomplete picture of actual, observed behavior. The normative assumptions of traditional finance do not apply to how most investors make decisions or allocate capital. Normative models often fail because people are irrational and the models are based on false assumptions.

By contrast, behavioral finance offers insights from other sciences and business disciples to explain individual behavior, market inefficiencies, stock market anomalies, and other research findings that contradict the assumptions of traditional finance. Behavioral finance examines the decision-making approach of individuals, including cognitive and emotional biases. Behavioral finance makes the premise that a wide range of objective and subjective issues influence the decision-making process. Various laboratory, survey, and market studies in behavioral finance show that individuals are not always rational and apply the descriptive model from the social sciences that documents how people in real life make judgments and decisions. A basis of the descriptive model is that investors are affected by their previous experiences, tastes, cognitive issues, emotional factors, the presentation of information, and the validity of the data. Individuals also make judgments based on bounded rationality. *Bounded rationality* is the premise that a person reduces the number of choices to a selection of smaller shortened steps, even when this oversimplifies the decision-making process. According to bounded rationality, an individual will select a satisfactory outcome rather than the optimal one.

In the 1960s and 1970s, the origin of behavioral finance and financial psychology was founded on seminal research from theorists in cognitive psychology, economics, and finance. During the 1980s, behavioral finance researchers began combining the research methods of psychology and behavioral economics with specific investment and financial subject matter. Since the mid-1990s, behavioral finance has been emerging as an important field in academia. For example, some notable developments in behavioral finance include work on prospect theory (Kahneman and Tversky 1979; Tversky and Kahneman 1974, 1981); framing effects, which are rooted in prospect theory; heuristics and biases (Kahneman, Slovic, and Tversky 1982; Gilovich, Griffin, and Kahneman 2002); and mental accounting (Thaler 1985). Baker and Nofsinger (2010) and Baker and Ricciardi (2014) provide a synthesis of the literature on behavioral finance and investor behavior.

In 2002, Daniel Kahneman and Vernon Smith, behavioral finance pioneers, received the Nobel Memorial Prize in Economics for their research in behavioral economics and psychology from the area of judgment and decision making. This prestigious award was a major turning point for the discipline because it provided wider acceptance within the financial community. Then, the financial crisis of 2007–2008 demonstrated the weakness of standard finance, with behavioral finance subsequently receiving even more attention and acknowledgment by academics and practitioners. In 2013, Robert J. Shiller, a noted behavioral economist, shared the 2013 Nobel Memorial Prize in Economic Sciences for empirical analysis of asset prices.

A Further Look at Behavioral Finance

Behavioral finance is an interdisciplinary subject based on the themes, theories, and research methods from a wide range of decision-making fields, such as psychology, behavioral accounting, economics, and neuroscience. In the early 1980s, researchers began to blend the research ideas and methodologies of psychology with specific investment and financial theories (Ricciardi 2006). Behavioral finance focuses on important cognitive factors and emotional influences during the judgment and decision-making process by individuals, groups, organizations, and markets. When individuals make judgments, they must develop, evaluate, and select among a series of choices or options, in which the final decision is based on a degree of risk and uncertainty (Ricciardi 2008a,

2010). In a rational setting, investors select the optimal choice. However, if qualitative and quantitative complexities are too intense, cognitive and emotional biases will influence the final outcome to a satisfactory choice. Another important premise of behavioral finance is that people are often irrational or quasi-rational (known as *bounded rationality*), and individuals make financial decisions based on past experience, values, mental mistakes, cognitive factors, and emotional impulses.

PROSPECT THEORY, LOSS AVERSION, AND THE DISPOSITION EFFECT

Kahneman and Tversky (1979) provide a unique behavioral theory about risk-taking behavior and uncertainty known as *prospect theory,* in which the stated probabilities and the diverse choices are provided. This theory posits the notion that people do not make decisions based on classical rationality; rather, they make judgments based on the premise of bounded rationality. A key tenet of prospect theory is that people assess choices on an individual basis and then use a reference point or anchor to make their choices, rather than decide within the context of an overall portfolio. Another principle underlying prospect theory is that individuals are *loss averse,* in which they place greater weight on losses than gains. That is, individuals apply more importance and mental effort to avoiding a loss than to achieving a gain.

Kahneman and Tversky (1979) asked subjects to review a pair of choices and to select one of the options:

> Consider a decision between these two choices:
> **Choice A:** A sure gain of $7,000 *or*
> **Choice B:** An 80 percent chance of earning $10,000 and a 20 percent chance of receiving $0.
> **Question:** Which choice would give you the best prospect to increase gains?

Their evidence shows that a solid majority of respondents select Choice A, which is the sure gain. These findings demonstrate that most individuals suffer from risk aversion when given the choice of a certain gain, and they find this outcome satisfactory. Although people tend to prefer Choice A because of the promise of a $7,000 gain, this should be the less favored option. If they select Choice B, their preference is to consider the optimal choice because an overall cumulative increase in wealth of $8,000 occurs. For a traditional finance portfolio, the answer is calculated as ($10,000 × 0.80) + (0 × 0.20) = $8,000. Most people dislike Choice B because of the 20 percent probability of earning nothing.

Another aspect of Kahneman and Tversky's (1979) study is to investigate the influence of losing, in which people assess the following two options:

> **Choice C:** A realized loss of $7,000 *or*
> **Choice D:** An 80 percent chance of losing $10,000 and a 20 percent chance of losing nothing.
> **Question:** Which option would provide you the best prospect to reduce losses?

Most subjects prefer Choice D. They prefer the 20 percent probability of not losing any money, even though this choice has more risk because within a portfolio framework the result would be an $8,000 loss. In other words, Choice C is the rational choice. In the behavioral finance domain, Oberlechner (2004) reports in a comparable study with traders in a foreign exchange setting showing that more than 70 percent select the risk-seeking option (or the equivalent of Choice D).

The results of these experiments demonstrate the concept known as *loss aversion,* in which people assign more importance to a loss than to an equivalent gain. The typical finding is that a gain on the upside of $2,000 is about twice as painful on the downside and feels like a $4,000 loss. This logic is contrary to the premise of traditional finance, which equates a $2,000 gain to a $2,000 loss within a diversified portfolio. For example, individuals tend to focus on downside risk when they own common stock. When people suffer an actual loss, they incur not only an objective loss in dollar terms but also a subjective loss in terms of an "emotional loss." This feeling can remain for a long time. Many investors who realize major losses during a market downturn subsequently avoid riskier asset classes such as stocks.

Another important aspect of loss aversion is that an "individual is less likely to sell an investment at a loss than to sell an investment that has increased in value even if expected returns are held constant" (Ricciardi 2008b, pp. 99–100), based on the disposition effect. The *disposition effect* refers to the tendency of selling securities that have appreciated in value over the original investment cost too early (or winners) and of holding on to losing securities too long (or losers). This bias is detrimental to the wealth of individuals because it can increase their capital gains taxes or can reduce investment returns even before taxes.

Olsen and Troughton (2000) examine the different meanings between uncertainty (ambiguity) and risk attributed to the work of Knight (1921). The study assesses several psychological factors, such as familiarity bias and loss aversion behavior. An expert group of more than 300 money managers completed a survey questionnaire about stocks. According to them, the two most important aspects of the assessment of risk are (1) downside or *catastrophic risk* (i.e., the probability of realizing a large loss); and (2) the role of *ambiguity* (i.e., the uncertainty about the actual distribution of potential returns in the future).

HEURISTICS

When individuals face complex judgments, information overload, or incomplete information, they often rely on conventional wisdom based on their personal experiences, known as *heuristics,* which reduce the decision to a simpler choice (Tversky and Kahneman 1974). Heuristics are straightforward, basic tools that people use to explain a certain category of choices under a high degree of risk and uncertainty. Heuristics are a "cognitive mechanism" for reducing the time commitment by simplifying the decision-making process for investors. Even though this type of cognitive approach sometimes results in satisfactory outcomes (also known as satisficing), heuristic judgments often result in inferior decisions. *Satisficing* is a decision-making strategy or cognitive heuristic that entails searching through the available alternatives until an acceptability threshold is met. Plous (1993, p. 109) states:

> For example, it is easier to estimate how likely an outcome is by using a heuristic than by tallying every past occurrence of the outcome and dividing by

> the total number of times the outcome could have occurred. In most cases, rough approximations are sufficient (just as people often satisfice rather than optimize).

Many stock brokers make fast purchase and sell decisions about equities by using heuristics because they are under strict time restrictions and have the objective of earning large short-term gains within the markets. Under such circumstances, these experts focus on a narrow amount of information and rely on previous experience to make final judgments. In many instances, these individuals are unaware they are employing these types of cognitive issues. Within an investment management setting, people use a tool known as the *1/N heuristic* when allocating retirement funds (Benartzi and Thaler 2001, 2007). For instance, an individual with five mutual funds will equally distribute 20 percent of the money invested into each fund for his monthly contribution to a 401k plan. This method is attractive to retirement savers because of its simplicity.

THE AVAILABILITY HEURISTIC

The *availability heuristic* reveals an inclination individuals have to be biased by information that is easy to recall, widely available, and highly publicized, which results in over-weighting or misinterpreting this information (Tversky and Kahneman 1973). As Schwartz (1998, p. 64) notes, "Biases may arise because the ease which specific instances can be recalled from memory affects judgments about the relative frequency and importance of data." According to Ricciardi (2008b), the main aspects of the availability heuristic that influence a person's judgments and decisions are (1) choices that induce affective reactions; (2) activities that are extremely dramatic; and (3) recent events, which have a tendency to be more readily available in an individual's memory. For example, investors overrate the importance of recent investment news and discount older information when evaluating a common stock. When a blue chip stock releases quarterly earnings above estimates and this information is reported online or on other financial news media, this may dramatically increase the company's short-term stock price. However, once the news fades from the memory of investors, the stock's volatility returns to its historical average.

OVERCONFIDENCE

Individuals are inclined to be overconfident about their skills, expertise, and intelligence. The subject matter of overconfidence is an important finding in behavioral finance because different categories of investors suffer from this bias. Overconfident investors believe they can influence the final outcome of a decision based on certain superior attributes when compared to the average investor. In the domain of finance, many people believe they are above average in their aptitude, overall decisions, and capability (Ricciardi 2008b). People are highly confident in their judgments formed under the application of heuristics and are inattentive to the actual method used to form their final judgments.

Barber and Odean (2001) explore the trading psychology between men and women for 35,000 accounts of individual investors over a six-year period. The study reveals that men are more overconfident than women about their financial skills and that men trade more within their investment accounts. Men are prone to sell common stock at an incorrect point in time and also to incur higher trading costs than women. Women are predisposed to trade less, employing a buy-and-hold approach that results in lower investment expenses. Men trade 45 percent more frequently than women, and single men trade 67 percent more frequently than single women. Trading costs reduce the net investment performance of men by 2.65 percentage points a year compared to only 1.72 percentage points for women. In other words, for the six-year period of the study, women earned 1 percentage point a year more than did men. This finding has even more dramatic consequences if the 1 percentage point yearly difference is applied over a 30 to 40-year time horizon because to the effects of compounding.

STATUS QUO BIAS

Individuals are inclined to experience *status quo bias,* in which they tend to default to the same choice or to accept the current decision. People find changing the behavior of procrastination or inertia entails strong incentives. This bias happens when individuals fail to revise their financial plans despite potential benefits from doing so. Retirement savers have the same behavior, such as holding onto an underperforming mutual fund instead of selling it. Employees delay contributing to their company retirement plan or procrastinate in seeking the advice of a financial planner to learn about different retirement options. After starting to contribute to a company retirement plan, many employees do not actively monitor their accounts.

For example, Agnew, Balduzzi, and Sunden (2003) evaluate 7,000 retirement accounts between April 1994 and August 1998. The authors report that most asset allocation choices are extreme or possess disproportionate diversification into risky securities (i.e., an individual who has multiple holdings in stocks or invests 100 percent of his assets in stocks) and retirement savers suffer from inertia or status quo bias regarding their asset allocation decisions. The study also finds exceptionally low portfolio turnover rates and asset rebalance transactions in these accounts, which further demonstrate status quo behavior.

About This Book

PURPOSE OF THE BOOK

This book provides a synthesis of the theoretical and empirical literature on the financial behavior of major stakeholders, financial services, investment products, and financial markets. Compared with traditional finance, the book offers a different way of looking at financial and emotional well-being and of the processing of beliefs, emotions, and behaviors related to money. It provides important insights about cognitive biases and emotional issues that influence various financial decision makers, services, products, and markets. This volume is a "contributed chapter" book in which noted academic researchers and practitioners provide chapters in their areas of expertise. Thus, readers can gain an in-depth understanding about this topic from experts from around the world.

In today's financial setting, the discipline of behavioral finance is an area that continues to evolve at a rapid pace. This book takes readers through not only the core topics and issues but also the latest trends, cutting-edge research developments, and real-world situations. Additionally, discussion of research on various cognitive and emotional issues is covered throughout the book. Thus, this volume covers a breadth of content from theoretical to practical, while attempting to offer a useful balance of detailed and user-friendly coverage. Those interested in a broad survey will benefit, as will those searching for more in-depth presentations of specific areas within this field of study. As the seventh book in the Financial Markets and Investment Series, *Financial Behavior: Players, Services, Products, and Markets* offers a fresh look at the fascinating area of financial behavior.

DISTINGUISHING FEATURES

Financial Behavior: Players, Services, Products, and Markets has several distinguishing features.

- The book examines highly relevant and timely aspects of financial behavior and blends the contributions of noted academics and practitioners who have varied backgrounds and differing perspectives. The book also reflects the latest trends and research from a unique perspective, as the content is organized by major players, financial services, investment products, and markets. By contrast, other books in behavioral finance and investor psychology often organize chapters by a specific subject matter or topic area, such as a cognitive issue, emotional bias, or theory.
- The results of empirical studies are presented in a user-friendly manner to make them understandable to readers with different backgrounds.
- The book provides discussion questions and answers to help to reinforce key concepts.

INTENDED AUDIENCE

The book's content and distinctive features should be of interest to a wide range of groups including academics, researchers, professionals, investors, students, and others interested in financial behavior. Academics can use this book not only as an integral part of their undergraduate and graduate finance courses but also as a way of understanding the various aspects of research emerging from this area. The book can help professionals navigate through the key areas in financial behavior. Individuals and financial planners can use the book to expand their knowledge base and can apply the concepts to managing the entire financial planning process. The book can serve as an introduction to students interested in these topics.

Structure of the Book

The 30 chapters in this book are grouped into seven parts. A brief summary of each part and chapter follows.

PART ONE: FINANCIAL BEHAVIOR AND PSYCHOLOGY

Chapter 1 Financial Behavior: An Overview (H. Kent Baker, Greg Filbeck, and Victor Ricciardi)

As you have seen, chapter 1 offers an enhanced discussion of behavioral finance and a description of this book.

Chapter 2 The Financial Psychology of Players, Services, and Products (Victor Ricciardi)

This chapter provides an overview of the emerging cognitive and emotional themes of behavioral finance that influence individual behavior. The behavioral finance perspective of risk incorporates both qualitative (subjective) and quantitative (objective) aspects of the decision-making process. An emerging subject of research interest and investigation in behavioral finance is an inverse (negative) relation between perceived risk and expected return (perceived return). This chapter highlights important topics such as representativeness, framing, anchoring, mental accounting, control issues, familiarity bias, trust, worry, and regret theory. It also examines the role of negative affective reactions on financial decisions. Financial worries and negative emotions influence all types of individuals including children, investors, and financial professionals. A host of biases that depend on specific aspects of the financial product or investment service influence the judgment and decision-making process of financial players.

PART TWO: THE FINANCIAL BEHAVIOR OF MAJOR PLAYERS

The second part has seven chapters involving the behavior of various players in the financial markets: individuals; institutional investors; corporate executives, directors, and boards; financial planners and advisors; financial analysts; portfolio managers; and financial psychopaths.

Chapter 3 Individual Investors (Henrik Cronqvist and Danling Jiang)

Traditional finance explains individual investors' behavior and financial decision-making based on economic incentives and rationality Modern finance, however, takes a holistic view and searches not only for economic but also for biological, psychological, and social factors that shape decision-making and investor behavior. In this new approach, genetics, life experiences, psychological traits, social norms, and peer influences, as well as beliefs, values, and culture in general, determine stock market decisions, share of equity holding, frequency of trading, extent of diversification, and preferences that make up the investment styles of individual investors. The collective preferences and actions of individual investors exert an impact on asset pricing and corporate decisions.

Chapter 4 Institutional Investors (Alexandre Skiba and Hilla Skiba)

A large body of behavioral finance literature focuses on the behavioral biases of individual investors in their trading choices. Research also shows that sophistication is related to the level at which behavioral biases influence investors' trading choices. This chapter reviews the literature on institutional investors' trading behavior and finds that, consistent with the level of investor sophistication, institutional investors are less subject to the common behavioral biases. However, some behavioral biases are present in institutional trading and more so among less sophisticated investor types. Evidence also shows that institutional investors engage in some trading choices, such as herding, momentum trading, and under-diversification, that could be symptoms of behavioral biases. Based on the reviewed research, these trading behaviors are not value reducing. Overall, the evidence indicates that institutional investors are less subject to behavioral biases, making markets more efficient.

Chapter 5 Corporate Executives, Directors, and Boards (John R. Nofsinger and Pattanaporn Chatjuthamard)

This chapter assesses the behavior of corporate managers and boards of directors within the framework of agency theory, stewardship theory, and psychological biases. In agency theory, a chief executive officer (CEO) is motivated to act in his own best interest rather than that of the shareholders. Stewardship theory posits that a CEO is a self-actualizing individual seeking to grow and reach a higher level of achievement through leading an organization. A CEO exhibits self-interested behavior in managing the firm. A CEO also exhibits optimism, overconfidence, and risk aversion behaviors that are not optimal for the firm. In the context of agency theory, the board of directors should enact incentive structures and monitoring to control these behaviors. However, directors also suffer from self-interests and cognitive biases. Specifically, boards may suffer from group dynamic problems such as social loafing, poor information sharing, and groupthink.

Chapter 6 Financial Planners and Advisors (Benjamin F. Cummings)

An increasing number of households use financial planners or advisors. This chapter seeks to provide insight into these professionals, their potential motivations, and their interactions with clients. The various regulatory regimes of financial planners and advisors are discussed, including the most common types of firms: registered investment advisors, broker-dealers, and insurance firms. Agency costs associated with employing a financial planner are also discussed, with emphasis on the potential conflicts of interest that can arise from various compensation structures that advisory firms typically use. Common areas of consumer confusion are highlighted. The chapter also discusses the empirical evidence on the use and value of financial advice. It concludes with some recommendations for consumers about selecting a financial planner or advisor.

Chapter 7 Financial Analysts (Susan M. Young)

Financial analysts are important players in the marketplace. Analysts' reports, which include forecasts of earnings and stock recommendations, move market prices. Investors, both large and small, rely on the information in reports when forming their investment decisions. Given the relevance of financial analysts' research, understanding whether their reports are biased is important because relying on them could harm investors using the information in these reports to inform their decisions. Despite an increase in market regulation, evidence suggests that analysts' reports are biased. The research also finds that analysts' bias increases when information uncertainty is high. Thus, investors should understand the possible dangers in blindly relying on research by financial analysts.

Chapter 8 Portfolio Managers (Erik Devos, Andrew C. Spieler, and Joseph M. Tenaglia)

In the oversight of most funds, the portfolio manager holds the key decision-making power. Often regarded as the foundation of the investment process, a few select managers can attract billions of dollars from investors, giving the managers increased prominence, credibility, and compensation. Despite their stature, portfolio managers are not immune to the same behavioral biases as other investors, which can distort the portfolio management process. This chapter offers an overview of portfolio management and compares characteristics of different fund types that portfolio managers oversee. It also reviews several important behavioral biases that portfolio managers display, as well as the consequences that each bias has on portfolio construction: overconfidence, herd mentality, risk-taking behavior, and the disposition effect. The chapter also contrasts the gender differences of portfolio managers and reviews the ramifications on their respective portfolios.

Chapter 9 Financial Psychopaths (Deborah W. Gregory)

The term *financial psychopath* emerged after the financial crisis of 2007–2008. Its media usage appears to have been intended as a term of derision for financial professionals, rather than an actual clinical profile. The expression succinctly conveys the post-2008 widespread public anger and resentment toward those in the finance profession, particularly on Wall Street, held responsible for damaging the world economy and destroying the personal wealth of many people. In the decades before the financial crisis, multiple factors had come together to change the operating structure of the financial landscape. This new environment was conducive to investment professionals' engaging in transactions bearing the hallmarks of psychopathic behavior, raising the critical questions: What defines a financial psychopath? Does it lie in the individual's personality traits, the behavioral edicts dictated by the environment within which he or she works, or both? This chapter attempts to answer these questions.

PART THREE: FINANCIAL AND INVESTOR PSYCHOLOGY OF SPECIFIC PLAYERS

The third part has five chapters on the financial and investor psychology of specialized players, including high net worth individuals, traders, women, and millennials.

Chapter 10 The Psychology of High Net Worth Individuals (Rebecca Li-Huang)

This chapter takes an economic view of the investment behavior of high net worth individuals (HNWIs), including the psychological aspects of private wealth and the practice of wealth management, current trends affecting the players and markets, and empirical findings on wealth creation and distribution that have fueled policy debates. Wealth concentrations and scarcity of skills have granted institutional advantages to HNWIs and the highly skilled, including higher returns on their physical and human capital investments. Besides achieving financial returns, HNWIs want to use their private wealth to have a social impact. Wealth managers respond to the attitude and behavior of HNWIs by shifting the focus from investment products and transactions to holistic investing and goal-based wealth management.

Chapter 11 The Psychology of Traders (Duccio Martelli)

In recent decades, trading has become very popular among retail investors, mainly due to the widespread use of technology and a reduction in transaction costs. However, the growing amount of information available to individuals and the higher complexity of financial markets have led these investors to make psychological mistakes more easily. The objective of this chapter is to describe the main types of behavioral bias that affect individual investors, especially retail traders who frequently churn their portfolios. The chapter compares momentum and contrarian trading strategies used by such traders. It also discusses the impact of new information on market sentiment and its effect on trader psychology. Finally, the chapter examines the main behaviors of novice traders, followed by a summary of various studies that analyze the conduct of novice investors in the course of investment challenges and trading simulations.

Chapter 12 A Closer Look at the Causes and Consequences of Frequent Stock Trading (Michal Strahilevitz)

This chapter examines the phenomenon of frequent stock trading. Specifically, it covers the ample research demonstrating the negative effects of frequent trading on investor returns, as well as several possible underlying causes for this irrational behavior. Among these possible causes of frequent trading are overconfidence, risk seeking, gambling addiction, frequency of negative emotions, and emotional instability. The chapter also examines gender differences. Although the vast body of research shows that frequent trading is bad for returns, many investors continue to trade too often for their own good. Therefore, besides discussing potential causes of frequent stock trading, this chapter also stresses the need for future research to identify effective methods of helping investors reduce this financially harmful behavior.

Chapter 13 The Psychology of Women Investors (Marguerita M. Cheng and Sameer S. Somal)

The role of financial decision maker in a household has evolved over time. Decades ago, women held traditional roles of caregiver, housekeeper, and wife. Today, more women are pursuing higher education, and female professionals and entrepreneurs are making great strides in business. Understanding what today's women value in all these roles helps to bridge the gap between financial literacy and its application. Training and mentoring women should be a priority for every financial institution, as women expect customized service and clear communication from financial experts. This chapter discusses the financial, psychological, and personal needs of women clients. It also explains how financial advisors should communicate with women to create a favorable client experience.

Chapter 14 The Psychology of Millennials (April Rudin and Catherine McBreen)

This chapter focuses on the financial mindset and behaviors of millennials, and how they interact with financial advisors. Millennials have surpassed baby boomers as the most productive generation and are projected to be the wealthiest. At 80 million strong, they are poised to leave their imprint on the financial services industry as well, which will have to adapt if it wants to engage a generation that communicates and invests differently from its predecessors. Millennials are often identified with unflattering and stereotypical portrayals, but financial advisors ignore this group at their peril. This generation is more apt to conduct its financial and investment affairs in nontraditional ways, laying the groundwork for their secure financial future.

PART FOUR: THE PSYCHOLOGY OF FINANCIAL SERVICES

The fourth part has five chapters on the psychological aspects of financial planning, financial advisory services, insurance and risk management, estate planning, and retirement planning and wealth management.

Chapter 15 Psychological Aspects of Financial Planning (Dave Yeske and Elissa Buie)

This chapter discusses personal financial planning, which is an interdisciplinary practice that employs a six-step process to develop integrated strategies for individuals and families hoping to mobilize their human and financial capital to achieve their life goals. Financial planning draws from various disciplines, including counseling, psychology, finance, economics, and law. It includes budgeting and cash flow planning, risk management, insurance planning, investment planning, retirement and employee benefits planning, tax planning, and estate planning. The strategic process involves developing integrated strategies that draw from all these fields in pursuit of client goals is the professional's unique domain. Heuristics and mental biases to which clients may be prone often overlay the entire financial planning process. Financial planners should understand and consider these issues in shaping recommendations uniquely suited to each client, maximizing the probability that the client will embrace and implement the recommended strategies.

Chapter 16 Financial Advisory Services (Jeroen Nieboer, Paul Dolan, and Ivo Vlaev)

Evidence from the behavioral sciences, notably economics and psychology, has profoundly changed the way policymakers and practitioners present expert advice to consumers. This chapter examines the evidence in regard to financial advice and explores its implications for the financial advisory profession. The authors explain how consumers of retail financial advice respond to certain aspects of the advice process in predictable ways, sometimes exhibiting behavioral biases or following certain conventions in their decision making. By recognizing and anticipating these responses, financial advisors can offer a more complete service, extending benefits beyond the strictly financial return to advice. But the behavioral needs of consumers may also provide advisors with incentives that are not strictly aligned with their clients' financial interests. Finally, the authors review the increasing role of technology and how it will play an important role in shaping the financial advisory services of the future.

Chapter 17 Insurance and Risk Management (James M. Moten Jr. and C. W. Copeland)

According to modern portfolio theory (MPT), rational market participants make most decisions and seek to be compensated for additional risk. However, behavioral finance shows how investors sometimes behave irrationally due to preconceived notions and biases based on past experiences. This chapter explores how individuals make decisions to buy different types of insurance even when faced with predicable outcomes involving the frequency and severity of the loss. That is, individuals appear to buy insurance only when the frequency of loss is low and the severity of loss is high; otherwise, they self-insure.

Chapter 18 Psychological Factors in Estate Planning (John J. Guerin and L. Paul Hood Jr.)

As an area of behavioral finance, estate planning is less concerned with systematic, cognitive errors than it is focused on a core, emotional ambivalence about mortality. The chapter explores the dynamics of the professional/client relationship in financial planning and estate planning, as well as the emotional conflicts concerning mortality in light of research about mortality salience and terror management theory. Additionally, including marital, family, and family business issues introduces inherent complications to efforts at estate planning, which may in turn affect succession planning, inheritance, heir preparation, and family dynamics. However, recent developments in assessing financial style/personality may enhance progress in estate planning. Tools for facilitating the process are discussed in this chapter, along with observations for further development in the field. Models in other areas of psychotherapy show the potential to inform this area of practice.

Chapter 19 Individual Biases in Retirement Planning and Wealth Management (James E. Brewer Jr. and Charles H. Self III)

Around the globe, the gradual move from defined benefit pensions to defined contribution pensions has increased the need for individual retirement planning. Examples of this need include U.S. savings rates being at historic lows, poor retirement prospects for citizens in various developed countries, and DALBAR analyses that disparage the gap between investor returns and market returns. Research indicates that individuals working with a financial advisor generally receive better results than those who do not. Working with a Certified Financial Planner (CFP) gives an added level of security, because a CFP takes an oath to keep the client's interests ahead of his or her own business interests. This chapter promotes use of nudges to help individuals close the savings, investing, and behavior gaps, thereby improving their total wealth and wealth transfer picture.

PART FIVE: THE BEHAVIORAL ASPECTS OF INVESTMENT PRODUCTS AND MARKETS

The fifth part has four chapters focusing on the behavioral aspects of traditional securities, pooled investment vehicles, international mergers and acquisitions, and the art and collectibles markets.

Chapter 20 Traditional Asset Allocation Securities: Stocks, Bonds, Real Estate, and Cash (Christopher Milliken, Ehsan Nikbakht, and Andrew Spieler)

Asset allocation models have evolved in complexity since the development of modern portfolio theory, but they continue to operate under the assumption of investor rationality, in addition to other assumptions that do not hold in the real world. For this reason, academics and industry professionals try to understand the behavioral biases of decision makers and the implications these biases have on asset allocation strategies. This chapter reviews the building blocks of asset allocation, which involve stocks, bonds, real estate, and cash. It also examines the history and theory behind two of the most popular portfolio management strategies: mean-variance optimization and the Black-Litterman model. Finally, the chapter examines five common behavioral biases that have direct implications on asset allocation: familiarity, status quo, framing, mental accounting, and overconfidence. Each behavioral bias discussion contains examples, warning signs, and steps to correct the emotional or cognitive errors in decision making.

Chapter 21 Behavioral Aspects of Portfolio Investments (Nathan Mauck)

Investors are inextricably linked to financial institutions, money managers, and the products they market. Mutual funds, exchange-traded funds (ETFs), hedge funds, and pension funds manage or hold roughly $55 trillion in combined wealth. This chapter examines these topics with a behavioral finance approach that focuses on two main themes. First, the chapter reviews the performance and rationality of each group; second, the chapter examines the behavioral biases that relate to individuals' selection of particular investments within each group. Research indicates actively managed mutual funds and hedge funds underperform passive investments. Pension funds generate alpha of roughly zero on a risk-adjusted basis. The fees involved in investing in such funds exacerbate the observed underperformance in mutual funds and hedge funds. Behavioral biases provide one perspective on sources of underperformance. Further, individuals exhibit a wide range of behavioral biases that may lead to suboptimal asset allocation, including the selection of mutual funds, ETFs, and hedge funds.

Chapter 22 Current Trends in Successful International M&As (Nancy Hubbard)

The worldwide landscape of merger and acquisition (M&A) activity has changed dramatically in the past decade. Acquirers, acquisition trends, and strategies behind those transactions now differ dramatically. Acquisition success rates also appear to be different, with recent research indicating that international acquisitions are more successful than they were previously. Successful acquisitions involve a complicated combination of melding systems and employees in an environment of cultural contrasts. Successful acquisitions on an international level also require financial rigor and discipline combined with an understanding of human behavior and motivation. This chapter examines both the changing trends and the key success factors for M&As in terms of financial inputs and behavioral elements so as to better understand the complex M&A process and identify indicators for future success.

Chapter 23 Art and Collectibles for Wealth Management (Peter J. May)

This chapter examines different psychological biases in the area of art and collectibles, which are part of every client's world to some degree. Wealth management has a tradition of management by silo with each silo guided by its own revenue stream. In a changing world guided by disrupting evolution due to the availability of big data, yesterday's knowledge and information are today's commodities. This evolution has escalated as information is now accessible globally by almost anyone with a mobile device. Wealth management must adjust its current client service model to leverage the informational commodity of art and to incorporate this commodity into its daily conversations. With the proliferation of social media and web-based resources, art and collectibles are now an asset class option.

PART SIX: MARKET EFFICIENCY ISSUES

Part six has four chapters that explore the behavioral finance market hypothesis, stock market anomalies, speculative behavior, and high-frequency trading.

Chapter 24 Behavioral Finance Market Hypotheses (Alex Plastun)

Although the efficient market hypothesis (EMH) is the leading theory describing the behavior of financial markets, researchers have increasingly questioned its efficacy since the 1980s because of its inconsistencies with empirical evidence. This challenge to the EMH has resulted in the development of new concepts and theories, and these new concepts rejecting the assumption of investor rationality. The most promising and convincing among these concepts are the adaptive markets hypothesis, overreaction hypothesis, underreaction hypothesis, noisy market hypothesis, functional fixation hypothesis, and fractal market hypothesis. This chapter provides a brief description of these theories and proposes using a behavioral perspective to analyze financial markets.

Chapter 25 Stock Market Anomalies (Steve Fan and Linda Yu)

Stock market anomalies representing the predictability of cross-sectional stock returns are one of most controversial topics in today's financial economic research. This chapter reviews several well-documented and pervasive anomalies in the literature, including investment-related anomalies, value anomalies, momentum and long-term reversal, size, and accruals. Although anomalies are widely accepted, much disagreement exists about the underlying reasons for their predictability. This chapter surveys two competing theories that attempt to explain the presence of stock market anomalies: rational and behavioral explanations. The rational explanation focuses on the improvement of existing asset pricing models and/or searching for additional risk factors to explain the existence of anomalies. By contrast, the behavioral explanation attributes the predictability to human behavioral biases in collecting and processing financial information, as well as in making investment decisions.

Chapter 26 The Psychology of Speculation in the Financial Markets (Victor Ricciardi)

This chapter discusses the role of speculation within financial markets that influences individual and group behavior in the form of bubbles and crashes. The chapter highlights behavioral finance issues associated with these bubbles, such as overconfidence, herding, group polarization, groupthink effect, representativeness bias, familiarity issues, grandiosity, excitement, and the overreaction and underreaction of prices in markets. The issues are important for understanding past financial mistakes because history often repeats itself. The chapter also examines the aftermath of the financial crisis of 2007–2008 on investor psychology, including the impact of a severe financial downturn, the anchoring effect, recency bias, worry, loss averse behavior, status quo bias, and trust. The aftermath of the financial crisis might have negative long-term effects on investor behavior in which some investors remain overly risk averse resulting in under-investment in stocks and over-investment in cash and bonds.

Chapter 27 Can Humans Dance with Machines? Institutional Investors, High-Frequency Trading, and Modern Markets Dynamics (Irene Aldridge)

This chapter examines high-frequency trading (HFT), including core groups of strategies and their resulting impacts. Using order-by-order market data analysis, the chapter shows that much of what is often construed to be useless noise of order cancellations actually represents meaningful order revisions, part of the real-time market bargaining. The chapter further shows that a small fraction of the order cancellations are a product of purely toxic liquidity. Market participants of different frequencies tend to react differently to such toxic orders, with higher-frequency traders largely ignoring them and lower-frequency investors interacting with toxic liquidity.

PART SEVEN: THE APPLICATION AND FUTURE OF BEHAVIORAL FINANCE

Part seven includes three chapters that explore applications of client behavior, implementing behavioral finance, and the future of behavioral finance.

Chapter 28 Applications of Client Behavior: A Practitioner's Perspective (Harold Evensky)

The purpose of this chapter is to discuss various behavioral concepts and strategies that can help clients avoid behavioral errors, with the result of increasing the probability of a successful plan design and implementation. The chapter discusses how the concepts introduced by research in behavioral finance have become integrated throughout Evensky & Katz/Foldes Financial's practice. The chapter begins with framing for new clients, which is part of the firm's approach to retirement planning called "anchoring on the efficient frontier." The "anchoring" refers to basing the client's return requirement at the intersection of a capital needs analysis and the client's risk tolerance. Framing is introduced as a powerful behavioral management tool for the practitioner. The chapter discusses how behavioral finance lessons are integrated into the risk tolerance and return discussions, as well as the reporting process.

Chapter 29 Practical Challenges of Implementing Behavioral Finance: Reflections from the Field (Greg B. Davies and Peter Brooks)

Behavioral finance is only useful if it can be applied to help people make better decisions. This chapter offers reflections on the good, the bad, and the ugly of a practical application of behavioral finance in a commercial banking setting. It explores the difficulties of non-experts who experiment with behavioral finance, and how effective applications require a unique mix of expert knowledge and an ability to effect change. Principles of good applications of behavioral finance are presented, along with information on how to start using behavioral finance within an organization. The chapter also discusses the importance of senior management's acknowledging that behavioral finance practitioners do not necessarily know the correct answers and that they will need to use randomized control trials to help discover them.

Chapter 30 The Future of Behavioral Finance (Michael Dowling and Brian Lucey)

Any positive future for behavioral finance necessitates that research areas of corporate finance and investor psychology develop richer models of financial decision-making. Behavioral corporate finance requires expanding the focus from chief executive officer to the entire top management team, and also involves greater understanding of organizational theory. There needs to be a clearer focus on cross-cultural factors and how these factors interact with behavioral influences. Investor psychology requires a more comprehensive theory of the drivers of investor behavior and better data. Investor sentiment research offers potential for advancing an understanding of the psychological influences on asset pricing. This chapter expands on these ideas and discuss the context for future philosophical development of behavioral finance, with its inevitable push for greater openness, replicability, and reliability in research.

Summary and Conclusions

Traditional finance assumes that investors make rational decisions. Behavioral finance acknowledges the contributions of traditional finance, but also recognizes cognitive and emotional biases that result in a decision-making process contradicting the assumptions of standard finance. Thus, behavioral finance examines the decision-making approach of individuals, including cognitive and emotional biases. *Financial Behavior: Players, Services, Products, and Markets* seeks to weave the contributions of both academics and practitioners into a single review of important but selective topics related to behavioral finance.

Behavioral finance affects the investment process on both micro and macro levels. The presence of investors who are influenced by behavioral biases can result in security and market pricing that deviates substantially from intrinsic values based on traditional finance. Such decision-making frameworks can also affect financial professionals and professional–client relationships. By better understanding financial behavior, readers can distinguish the contributions of investor psychology and the role investor behavior has on influencing the types of products and services offered, as well as judge the impact such behavior has on market efficiency.

REFERENCES

Ackert, Lucy F. 2014. "Traditional and Behavioral Finance." In H. Kent Baker and Victor Ricciardi (eds.), *Investor Behavior—The Psychology of Financial Planning and Investing*, 25–41. Hoboken, NJ: John Wiley & Sons, Inc.

Agnew, Julie, Pierluigi Balduzzi, and Annika Sunden. 2003. "Portfolio Choice and Trading in a Large 401(k) Plan." *American Economic Review* 93:1, 193–215.

Baker, H. Kent, and John R. Nofsinger (eds.). 2010. *Behavioral Finance—Investors, Corporations, and Markets.* Hoboken, NJ: John Wiley & Sons, Inc.

Baker, H. Kent, and Victor Ricciardi (eds.). 2014. *Investor Behavior—The Psychology of Financial Planning and Investing.* Hoboken, NJ: John Wiley & Sons, Inc.

Barber, Brad M., and Terrance Odean. 2001. "Boys Will Be Boys: Gender, Overconfidence, and Common Stock Investment." *Quarterly Journal of Economics* 116:1, 261–292.

Benartzi, Shlomo, and Richard H. Thaler. 2001. "Naıve Diversification Strategies in Defined Contribution Savings Plans." *American Economic Review* 91:1, 79–98.

Benartzi, Shlomo, and Richard H. Thaler. 2007. "Heuristics and Biases in Retirement Savings Behavior." *Journal of Economic Perspectives* 21:3, 81–104.

Bloomfield, Robert. 2010. "Traditional Versus Behavioral Finance." In H. Kent Baker and John R. Nofsinger (eds.), *Behavioral Finance—Investors, Corporations, and Markets,* 23–38. Hoboken, NJ: John Wiley & Sons, Inc.

Carhart, Mark M. 1997. "On Persistence in Mutual Fund Performance." *Journal of Finance* 52:1, 57–82.

Fama, Eugene F. 1970. "Efficient Capital Markets: A Review of Theory and Empirical Work." *Journal of Finance* 31:1, 383–417.

Fama, Eugene F., and Kenneth R. French. 1996. "Multifactor Explanations of Asset Pricing Anomalies." *Journal of Finance* 51:1, 55–84.

Gilovich, Thomas, Dale Griffin, and Daniel Kahneman (eds.). 2002. *Heuristics and Biases: The Psychology of Intuitive Judgment.* New York and Cambridge: Cambridge University Press.

Kahneman, Daniel, Paul Slovic, and Amos Tversky (eds.). 1982. *Judgment under Uncertainty: Heuristics and Biases.* New York and Cambridge: Cambridge University Press.

Kahneman, Daniel, and Amos Tversky. 1979. "Prospect Theory: An Analysis of Decisions under Risk." *Econometrica* 47:2, 263–291.

Knight, Frank. 1921. *Risk, Uncertainty, and Profit.* Chicago: University of Chicago Press.

Markowitz, Harry. 1952. "Portfolio Selection." *Journal of Finance* 7:1, 77–91.

Markowitz. Harry M. 1959. *Portfolio Selection: Efficient Diversification of Investments.* New Haven, CT: Yale University Press.

Oberlechner, Thomas. 2004. *The Psychology of the Foreign Exchange Market.* Chichester, UK: John Wiley & Sons, Ltd.

Olsen, Robert A., and George H. Troughton. 2000. "Are Risk Premium Anomalies Caused by Ambiguity?" *Financial Analysts Journal* 56:2, 24–31.

Plous, Scott. 1993. *The Psychology of Judgment and Decision Making.* New York: McGraw-Hill.

Ricciardi, Victor. 2006. "A Research Starting Point for the New Scholar: A Unique Perspective of Behavioral Finance." *ICFAI Journal of Behavioral Finance* 3:3, 6–23. Available at http://ssrn.com/abstract=928251.

Ricciardi, Victor. 2008a. "Risk: Traditional Finance versus Behavioral Finance." In Frank J. Fabozzi (ed.), *The Handbook of Finance, Volume 3: Valuation, Financial Modeling, and Quantitative Tools,* 11–38. Hoboken, NJ: John Wiley & Sons, Inc.

Ricciardi, Victor. 2008b. "The Psychology of Risk: The Behavioral Finance Perspective." In Frank J. Fabozzi (ed.), *The Handbook of Finance, Volume 2: Investment Management and Financial Management,* 85–111. Hoboken, NJ: John Wiley & Sons, Inc.

Ricciardi, Victor. 2010. "The Psychology of Risk." In H. Kent Baker and John R. Nofsinger (eds.), *Behavioral Finance: Investors, Corporations, and Markets,* 131–149. Hoboken, NJ: John Wiley & Sons, Inc.

Schwartz, Hugh H. 1998. *Rationality Gone Awry? Decision Making Inconsistent with Economic and Financial Theory.* Westport, CT: Greenwood Publishing Group, Inc.

Sharpe, William F. 1964. "Capital Asset Prices: A Theory of Market Equilibrium under Conditions of Risk." *Journal of Finance* 19:3, 425–442.

Thaler, Richard. 1985. "Mental Accounting and Consumer Choice." *Marketing Science* 4:3, 199–214.

Tversky, Amos, and Daniel Kahneman. 1973. "Availability: A Heuristic for Judging Frequency and Probability." *Cognitive Psychology* 5:2, 207–232.

Tversky, Amos, and Daniel Kahneman. 1974. "Judgment under Uncertainty: Heuristics and Biases." *Science,* 185:4157, 1124–1131.

Tversky, Amos, and Daniel Kahneman. 1981. "The Framing of Decisions and the Psychology of Choice." *Science* 211:4481, 453–458.

2

The Financial Psychology of Players, Services, and Products

VICTOR RICCIARDI
Assistant Professor in Financial Management
Goucher College

Introduction

Behavioral finance explains how cognitive and affective processes influence the decisions of individuals about financial issues. When people make financial choices, a collection of information, including both objective and subject factors, affects their final judgment. This chapter brings together themes within the behavioral finance literature that provide a strong foundation for understanding the issues influencing their decisions and client behavior. The following areas are fundamental topics and issues in behavioral finance:

- **Prospect theory**: Investors assess different options of losses and gains based on a subjective reference point (or anchor) in dollar terms based on the premise of loss averse behavior.
- **Loss aversion**: When assessing individual financial transactions, people assign more importance to a loss than to achieving an equivalent gain.
- **Disposition effect**: Investors sell securities with gains too quickly and hold investments with losses too long.
- **Heuristics**: Individuals use fundamental, realistic guidelines to assess information based on mental shortcuts because of information overload, time constraints, or other categories of pressures.
- **Availability heuristic**: Individuals have an inclination to favor information that is simple to recall and quickly accessible, a predisposition to information that is well known or recent and overemphasize this information.
- **Overconfidence**: Investors tend to overestimate their expertise, talent, and forecasts for investment performance.
- **Status quo bias**: Individuals suffer from inertia by defaulting to the same judgment or tolerating the present situation, and this involves robust reasons or inducements to modify these activities.

This chapter provides a discussion of the emerging cognitive and affective issues of behavioral finance that determine the decision-making process of individuals. The first section offers an overview of risk perception advocated by behavioral finance, including the inverse relation between perceived risk and return. Next, the chapter examines important biases such as representativeness, framing, anchoring bias, mental accounting, control issues, familiarity bias, and trust. The next section focuses on negative emotions, such as worry and regret theory, within the financial domain. The last section offers a summary and conclusions.

The Psychology of Risk

Risk is applicable across a wide variety of circumstances, events, and situation. This topic has a variety of definitions, dimensions, and descriptions by individuals and organizations. Experts have studied the risk-taking behavior of individuals and groups in great detail within the social sciences and business domains (Ricciardi 2006, 2008a, 2008b, 2010) and the fields of behavioral accounting, financial psychology, and behavioral economics (Ricciardi 2004). The academic literature shows that risk has different meanings, explanations, and measurements across many disciplines.

Risk perception is the subjective aspect of the decision-making process that individuals apply when evaluating risk and the amount of uncertainty. Perceived risk includes both objective and subjective factors that influence how people make judgments about all types of financial services and products. In terms of the objective aspects of risk, Ricciardi (2008a) reports more than 150 financial and accounting proxy variables from the risk perception literature as potential risk factors. Behavioral finance also incorporates a subjective aspect of risk and risk-taking (e.g., cognitive and emotional factors) that influences individual and group psychology in how people define, assess, and describe risk. Ricciardi (2004, 2008b) presents an extensive list of more than 100 behavioral risk factors from the behavioral finance literature and more than 10 behavioral risk attributes from the behavioral accounting literature.

The assessment of perceived risk is based on a descriptive model that explains how investors make actual choices and decisions. Risk perception is based on the tenets of bounded rationality, satisficing, loss aversion, and prospect theory (Ricciardi and Rice 2014). *Bounded rationality* is the idea that individuals reduce the number of choices to a smaller, abbreviated set based on past experiences, values, mental shortcuts, and emotions, even though this approach might oversimplify the final decision. Under the conditions of risk and uncertainty, individuals often select a satisfactory rather than the optimal choice, which is known as *satisficing*.

INVERSE RELATION BETWEEN RISK AND RETURN

A major tenet of traditional finance is the notion of a positive (linear) relation between historical risk and return. This association is mainly based on the assumption of risk aversion in which individuals only invest in higher-risk investments such as stocks if they expect to earn a higher return. However, this positive risk–return relation does not always exist. For example, Haugen and Heins (1975, p. 782) reveal "over the long run, stock portfolios with a lesser variance in monthly returns have experienced greater average returns than their riskier counterparts." Within behavioral finance, an emerging research topic is the exploration of the inverse (negative) relation between perceived risk and return (Ricciardi 2008a). The social sciences academic literature documents this inverse association in the form of perceived risk and perceived gain (benefit).

Although the notion of an inverse association has recently become more common in the behavioral finance academic literature, this relation has been an area of substantial interest in strategic management since the early 1980s. With accounting data from *Value Line*, Bowman (1980) reports a negative risk-return trade-off for 10 of 11 industries. Thus, Bowman's paradox indicates that corporate managers undertake higher risk despite expecting to earn lower returns. Bowman (1982) reveals that financially troubled companies take more risk during times of financial difficulty, resulting in higher risk-taking behavior and lower rates of return. The author attributes this negative association between risk and return to the principles of prospect theory.

Diacon and Ennew (2001) investigate the risk perceptions of U.K. consumers for various personal financial products. The authors administer a questionnaire to 123 respondents to measure their perceived risk for various financial items. For each of the 20 financial products, the questionnaire asked them whether they currently owned or previously owned any of the products to assess the potential investment ownership judgment. The 25 risk characteristics in the study are mainly behavioral in nature (e.g., issues of losses, knowledge, and time) with a few financial risk indicators. Diacon and Ennew use factor analysis to classify the 25 risk attributes into five main risk dimensions: (1) mistrust of the investment product or source (i.e., a salesperson), (2) dislike for adverse outcomes, (3) distaste to the volatility of a financial product, (4) inadequate knowledge of a financial item, and (5) the failure of regulation. These factors account for 59.5 percent of an individual's risk perception. Diacon and Ennew (2001, p. 405) also explore the notion of an inverse association between perceived risk and return and comment as follows:

> Although investors need to be compensated for some aspects of perceived risk (such as the possibility of adverse consequences and poor information) this does not apply to all dimensions of perceived risk. In particular there is little evidence that individual investors want compensation for volatility of returns.

Financial Biases Influencing Judgment and Decision Making

Individuals suffer from a wide range of documented biases that influence their financial judgments and decisions. This section focuses on some important psychological issues, including representativeness, framing, anchoring bias, mental accounting, control issues, and familiarity bias. These biases have a detrimental impact on how individuals perceive and process all types of information.

REPRESENTATIVENESS

The *representativeness bias* is a heuristic based on the idea that people have an automatic predisposition to advance a belief about a specific event and overrate how much this situation reminds them of other familiar circumstances. This bias is based on the notion that individuals are inclined to have a skewed belief about a financial event and then overestimate how much this situation is similar to other ones in the past. According to Busenitz (1999, p. 330), people are willing "to develop broad, and sometimes very detailed generalizations about a person or phenomenon based on only a few attributes of the person or phenomenon."

Representativeness results in investors' classifying a financial investment as good or bad based on its recent investment returns. For example, an individual may buy technology stocks after prices have risen, forecasting that these increases will continue into the near future and ignoring blue chip stocks when their prices are lower than their intrinsic valuations. As Ricciardi (2008b, p. 100) notes, another example of this bias is when "investors frequently predict the performance of an initial public offering by relating it to the previous investment's success (gain) or failure (loss)."

Shefrin (2001) offers an example of representativeness bias within the context of an inverse association between risk and return. Using a questionnaire, he conducts several studies over a five-year period with the same group to examine the risk–return relation among student or expert investment groups. Shefrin assumes that behavioral finance is based on the belief of a negative relation between expected return and perceived risk (beta). He suggests this notion of an inverse relation is based on the premise that investors depend on the representativeness heuristic to explain why individuals relate higher perceived returns from safe stocks (lower perceived risk for stocks). Shefrin describes safer stocks as good stocks/good companies in which individuals view higher-quality stocks based on such traits as the quality of the stock (e.g., financial soundness) and the perceived goodness of the firm (e.g., management reputation). Shefrin (2001, pp. 179–180) provides this perspective of the study:

> Why do characteristics like book-to-market equity provide additional information over and above the information conveyed by beta? I suggest that the answer to this question involves the representativeness-based heuristic "good stocks are stocks of good companies." Because good companies are associated with characteristics such as low book-to-market equity, representativeness will induce investors to expect higher returns from the stocks of good companies. In particular, representativeness will lead investors to associate higher long-run returns with low book-to-market equity. However, because the sign of the relationship between expected returns and each characteristic is opposite to that between realized returns and the characteristic, investors' perceptions are erroneous.

FRAMING

An individual exhibits a "framing effect" when an identical or equivalent description of an outcome results in a different final judgment or answer. As Kahneman and Tversky (1979) note, the framing process has two important components: (1) the setting or framework of the decision, and (2) the format in which the question is framed or phrased. For example, Weber (1991) illustrates the role of framing in the context of a new business venture by asking whether individuals prefer:

Option A: Would you invest all your money in a new business if you had a 50 percent chance of succeeding brilliantly?
Option B: Would you invest all your money in a new business if you had a 50 percent chance of failing miserably?

As Weber (1991, p. 96) notes, most individuals select the "success-frame in A makes it seem more appealing than the failure-framed B, although the probability of success versus failure is the same for both." The reason for selecting Option A is that the choice is a "positive frame," which people find more psychologically comforting and satisfying rather than Option B as the best option.

Roszkowski and Snelbecker (1990) investigate the role of framing within the context of gains and losses, using an investment case study with 200 financial planners. Although financial planners often suffer from similar framing effects, they are more conservative in their approach to managing their client's money than their own investments. Experts who chose the positive frame in the form of a gain demonstrate an inclination for risk avoidance, and other professionals who favor the negative frame in the form of a loss are predisposed to risk-seeking behavior.

ANCHORING

Anchoring is the tendency to apply a belief as a subjective reference point for making future judgments. People often base their financial assessments on the first information they receive (e.g., an original purchase price of a stock) and have difficulty adjusting their evaluation to new data. The process of anchoring is an example of when a certain piece of information influences an investor's heuristic judgments and this cognitive decision-making mechanism controls their final decision.

Even when aware of this anchoring bias, individuals have difficulty overcoming the anchoring effect (Ricciardi 2008b). Piatelli-Palmarini (1994, p. 127) makes the following comments about the anchoring process:

> Revising an intuitive, impulsive judgment will never be sufficient to undo the original judgment completely. Consciously or unconsciously, we always remain anchored to our original opinion, and we correct that view only starting from the same opinion.

Investors are sometimes inclined to focus on a specific piece of information, which then serves as a reference point that influences their decisions. For instance, many investors view a stock market decline as a negative reference point or anchor. They may remember the value of their portfolios at market highs, before the market declined, and become intent on getting back to the previous highest stock price of the past. When people anchor on a bad investment memory, they might suffer higher levels of risk and loss aversion, which results in higher levels of worry and leads to under-investing in stocks and over-weighting cash within their portfolios. For instance, Kaustia, Alho, and Puttonen (2008) examine the role of anchoring involving a sample of college students and investment professionals by evaluating stocks as an investment. The authors find a very large anchoring effect for the college students in which they base their long-term forecasts for stock performance on the original investment market value. Investment professionals also suffer from the anchoring bias, but to a smaller degree.

MENTAL ACCOUNTING

Mental accounting is a heuristic process in which people split their investments into different categories, groupings, or mental compartments. For instance, if an individual has a negative total return for the year on a corporate bond, he will use a cognitive judgment approach that focuses on the positive aspect of the financial security, such as a high current yield or the semi-annual coupon payment, by separating it into a pleasurable mental account. Behavioral finance academics view the mental accounting bias as a negative aspect of the decision-making process because the individual is not assessing their entire investment portfolio.

Shafir and Thaler (2006) evaluate how individuals allocate assets across different financial mental accounts. Their evidence reveals that an advanced purchase such as a bottle of wine is identified as an investment transaction rather than as a spending entry. If the buyer consumes and uses a product as anticipated, such as drinking wine at a meal, the buyer considers the item "on the house" (i.e., free or complimentary) or in certain instances labeled as a savings account. Shafir and Thaler (2006, p. 694) note:

> However, when it is not consumed as planned (a bottle is dropped and broken), then the relevant account, long dormant, is resuscitated and costs associated with the event are perceived as the cost of replacing the good, especially if replacement is actually likely.

In the financial-planning domain, financial practitioners consider mental accounting as having favorable characteristics for managing their clients. Yeske and Buie (2014) recommend labeling certain mental accounts, such as savings for a children's college education, as "buckets." According to Baker and Ricciardi (2015, p. 24), "If clients treat these accounts as long-term investments that should not be disturbed, they are more likely to reach their financial goals."

CONTROL ISSUES

Another bias that influences an individual's decision-making process is the issue of control. One major type is locus of control, which consists of external and internal controls (Rotter 1971). *Locus of control* describes the degree to which someone perceives the ability to exert control over his own behavior and personal outcomes of a specific decision. *External locus of control* provides a person with the idea that chance or outside factors affect one's judgment or final outcome of a decision event. *Internal locus of control* is the notion or belief that an individual controls his own fate in terms of the outcome of a decision or situation.

Langer (1983, p. 20) provides this viewpoint on psychology of control (perceived control) as the "active belief that one has a choice among responses that are differentially effective in achieving the desired outcome." Even in circumstances when control of an outcome is in short supply, an individual believes that he has control over the outcome of a decision is known as illusion of control (Langer 1975). *Illusion of control* is a prevalent bias within the behavioral finance academic literature. Individuals acknowledge a desire to control a specific circumstance, with the main purpose of influencing the results or outcomes in their favor. Strong (2006, pp. 273–274) presents this perspective of illusion of control within a gambling setting:

> Casinos are one of the great laboratories of human behavior. At the craps table, it is observable that when the dice shooter needs to throw a high number, he gives them a good, hard pitch to the end of the table. . . . We like to pretend we are influencing the outcome by our method of throwing the dice. If you force the issue, even a seasoned gambler will probably admit that the dice outcome is random.

The *hot hand fallacy* is the conviction or belief that an individual who had achievement or success with a chance past situation has a greater probability of additional success. For example, a basketball player believes he is more likely to make a basket based on the success of his previous shots or a hot streak (Gilovich, Vallone, and Tversky 1985). Many experts or professionals believe a "hot hand" influences an individual's assessment or perception of success. Traders make a connection of a "hot hand" based on the previous success of selecting winning stocks, and they develop the belief that they are more likely to select additional "winners" in the future.

Self-control bias is the propensity that causes individuals with an overwhelming impulse to focus on the short term. According to Shefrin (2005, p. 114), many investors suffer from "self-control problems that cause inadequate savings." In the short term, bad behavior, such as overeating that results in being overweight, influences individuals. In the investment domain, individuals focus on spending more money today at the cost of not saving money for the future. According to Baker and Ricciardi (2015, p. 125), "The high level of credit card debt and the generally inadequate level of retirement savings that many individuals face provide support for this self-control bias."

FAMILIARITY BIAS

Familiarity bias is prevalent when individuals have an overwhelming fondness for well-known financial securities regardless of the benefits based on portfolio diversification. Nofsinger (2002, p. 64) contends that in most circumstances, "people prefer things that are familiar to them. People root for the local sports teams. Employees like to own their company's stock." Investors prefer familiar local investments, which results in owning suboptimal portfolios. Investors perceive these securities as having an inverse relation between risk and return because they perceive highly familiar assets as possessing lower risk and higher return (Ricciardi 2008a). At the same time, they perceive unfamiliar assets as producing a higher risk and lower return.

Wang, Keller, and Siegrist (2011) evaluate the risk perception of more than 1,200 individuals from a German-language area of Switzerland about financial products. The study's major result is that respondents perceive less complicated (i.e., easier to understand) investments as having lower risk, which is consistent with familiarity bias. Participants also reveal a positive affective reaction to familiar financial securities. For financial advisors, Wang et al. (2011, p. 18) offer the following observation: "The clients might overestimate the risk of a certain investment due to their lack of knowledge or underestimate the risk due to their overconfidence of the self-perceived knowledge. To fill the knowledge gap is important for effective risk communication."

Financial Emotions that Influence Decisions

Emotional issues can also influence the financial judgment and decision-making process. Finucane, Peters, and Slovic (2003) provide this perspective about the differences among emotion, mood, and affect. An *emotion* is a state of consciousness related to the arousal of feelings. A *mood* or *feeling* is any subjective reactions, whether pleasurable or unlikable, that a person might experience from a specific circumstance or event. *Affect* is the emotional complex (i.e., positive or negative feelings) linked with an idea or thought. However, these terms are applied interchangeably within this chapter. Shefrin (2005, p. 10) provides the following perspective of affective (emotional) issues within finance:

> Most managers base their decisions on what feels right to them emotionally. Psychologists use the technical term *affect* to mean emotional feeling, and they use the term *affect heuristic* to describe behavior that places heavy reliance on intuition or "gut feeling." As with other heuristics, affect heuristic involves mental shortcuts that can predispose managers to bias.

Grable and Roszkowski (2008) use a mailed questionnaire to evaluate how an individual's mood influences financial risk tolerance. Their study examined two different perspectives: (1) the Mood Maintenance Hypothesis (MMH), which states if a person is in a positive (negative) mood, this deceases (increases) risk tolerance; and (2) the Affect Infusion Model (AIM), which is based on the premise that a positive (or negative) mood increases (decreases) an individual's risk tolerance. Based on the AIM premise, the authors find that individuals between 18 and 75 years old who are in a positive (or happy) mood exhibit a higher level of financial tolerance.

Rubaltelli, Pasini, Rumiati, Olsen, and Slovic (2010) investigate how individuals' affective reaction to different categories of mutual funds influences their judgment to sell this investment. After examining a socially responsible fund and a typical mutual fund, participants are asked to provide a response of what price they would be willing to sell the mutual fund. The authors report that selling prices influence how individuals feel about the funds, which reveals a subjective aspect to risk. Individuals with negative emotional responses about their funds (socially and non-socially responsible types) have the highest selling prices. This outcome demonstrates that only individuals initially having negative expectations toward a financial security are inclined to systematically counter the disposition effect. However, individuals having positive responses about the non-socially responsible fund anchor on their first impressions. Consequently, they cannot sell the losing investment as quickly as individuals with negative emotions.

Using a questionnaire involving more than 400 individual investors located in northern Europe, Aspara and Tikkanen (2011, p. 78) assess how emotional responses about a firm might increase motivation to invest a company's stock and find that

> most investors had affect-based, extra motivation to invest in stocks, over and beyond financial return expectations. The more positive an individual's attitude towards the company was, the stronger was his extra investment motivation.

The authors assign this strong positive connection to the firm's stock to a *self-affinity bias*, which asserts that the stronger a person's self-identification with a product or a company, the more likely this individual will buy the firm's product/service or invest in the company's stock.

Burns, Peters, and Slovic (2012) assess the impact of the financial crisis of 2007–2008 in order to examine the change in risk perception during the crisis period. The study uses seven questionnaires administered between September 2008 and October 2009. More than 600 individuals responded to each survey, and more than 400 participants completed all seven questionnaires. The findings reveal that a person's perceptions of risk declines mainly throughout the early stages of the crisis and then starts to become stable. The most significant factor attributing to increases in perceived risk among respondents is negative affect toward the crisis. The authors credit this result to the *risk as feelings effect* (i.e., the notion that people make quick, intuitive judgments about risky decisions attributed to their emotions).

TRUST

Trust between a financial professional and a client plays an important role in the financial-planning process. According to Howard and Yazdipour (2014), trust is a major component within the retirement-planning process and investment management. An important characteristic of the financial-planning process is developing a balance between trust and control issues within this client–advisor relationship (Baker and Ricciardi 2014a, 2014b, 2015). Clients who overly trust financial professionals or assign too much control about financial decisions might endure a bad outcome; Ponzi schemes are a major example of this result. Conversely, clients who reveal a lack of trust or who are excessively controlling may not listen to a financial planners' guidance. Experts should focus on fostering a balanced relationship of trust and control with their clients.

Within the risk domain, Olsen (2012) examines the connection among trust, individual risk perception, and cumulative market risk premiums. Based on survey responses from more than 600 members of the American Association of Individual Investors (AAII), the study discloses an inverse relation between trust and perceived risk in a financial environment. Olsen (2012, p. 311) also reports that on an economic countrywide basis, "ex-ante estimated common stock risk premiums and ex-post market interest rates vary inversely with national trust levels. In countries with greater interpersonal trust, risk premiums and interest rates are lower."

Negative Emotions Within Financial Decision Making

Negative feelings and money management have a long historical tradition and importance in the area of financial judgment and decision making. Emotional financial processes influence how people assess and make final decisions. This section provides a discussion of affective issues from different perspectives, such as money sickness, the role of different groups, the retirement domain, and neurofinance. This section also presents the negative emotions of worry, worry and perceived risk, and regret in behavioral finance.

MONEY SICKNESS

During the 1950s, William Kaufman, a psychosomaticist (i.e., an expert in medical science specializing in the interrelations of the mind and the body) coined the term "money sickness" in reference to the detrimental association between money and feelings (Anonymous 1954). Kaufman (1965) proposes a balanced emotional approach to money, recognizing a difference between the positive aspects described as "money health" versus the negative qualities known as "money sickness." Kaufman (1965, pp. 43–44) offers the following viewpoint:

> Inappropriate use of money becomes a serious emotional threat when the person is faced with the conflict between his desires and his conscience and with the consequences of his aberrant money behavior. Deep unconscious motivations may prevent him from spontaneously using money in constructive ways. Such people . . . often develop one of the most common psychosomatic illnesses of our time: *money-sickness.*

Even today many individuals are reluctant to admit they might have an emotional money disorder, which leads to negative feelings such as nervousness, worry, or stress.

Henderson (2006), an expert in stress management and mental health, conceptualizes the disorder known as the *money sickness syndrome.* For this type of syndrome, individuals exhibit symptoms of stress occurring from the worry and anxiety produced by feelings of not having control of their money or limited knowledge of their financial circumstance. AXA, an investment and insurance firm, sponsored Henderson's research survey of 1,022 U.K. adults over the age of 16. The study finds that 43 percent of the respondents exhibit the symptoms associated with money sickness syndrome. These results imply that the equivalent of 10.75 million of the U.K. population experience money worries and reveal the warning signs linked with this psychological condition (AXA 2006). For example, physical symptoms of the disorder include headaches, nausea, indigestion, palpitations, lack of appetite, and poor sleeping habits. Otherwise, the psychological indicators include mood changes, irritability, general anxiety, negative feelings, reduced concentration, poor memory, and inferior judgments. This condition is a noteworthy example of the emerging importance of the role of negative affect (emotion) and financial decision making. The behavioral finance literature reveals the evolving role of negative affect (emotion) within the judgment process in different areas, such as individual psychology, expertise of decision makers, retirement issues, and neurofinance (neuroeconomics).

INDIVIDUAL PSYCHOLOGY

This first grouping of research studies emphasizes the importance of negative feelings (e.g., financial worries) and individual psychology. For instance, Hira and Mugenda (1999, p. 78) investigate the role of perceived self-worth and worry, reporting the following results:

> Respondents with low self-worth compared with those with high self-worth exhibited concerns about their financial situation. A significantly larger proportion of respondents with low self-worth (63%) than those with high self-worth (29%) reported that they often worried about their finances often. On the other hand, three times as many respondents with high self-worth (23%) than those with low self-worth (7%) reported that they never worried about their finances.

Grable and Joo (2001) examine the financial worries (stressors) of 406 individuals by presenting them with a collection of "stressor event items" such as the potential decline in income, concern over declaring personal bankruptcy, and influence of experiencing an investment/business loss. The authors find an association between several factors in which individuals who reveal better financial behaviors and higher levels of financial confidence are more satisfied with their current financial circumstances. Those reporting less stressor events rank higher in terms of their level of self-esteem. Öhman, Grunewald, and Waldenström (2003) evaluate 200 pregnant women's worries in 16 areas and find that the major worry categories are the baby's health, birth and miscarriage troubles, and financial issues such as money and employment problems. In terms of the emotional aspects of decisions, Leahy (1992) uses a case study to describe the role of negative feelings and the narcissistic tendencies of his Wall Street clients.

EXPERT DECISION MAKERS

The following collection of research studies investigates the role of negative affect and financial judgments in terms of how these emotional issues influence the assessment of expert decision makers. Criddle (1993) suggests that within the financial and investment sectors, individuals experience a higher degree of stress connected to competitive tension, which results in episodes of anxiety and worry. Criddle (1993, p. 19) also comments about the role of a financial expert or investment professional as an "infinitely more dangerous 'emotional mine field' than the world of the amateur investor!" Garman and Sorhaindo (2005) examine the most important concepts of a "personal financial well-being construct" in the framework of a financial distress scale. An expert subject matter review panel unanimously identifies the two top-rated issues as worrying about the ability to meet monthly living costs and surviving on a paycheck-to-paycheck basis. Within a capital budgeting framework, Kida, Moreno, and Smith (2001) demonstrate that managers incorporate both affective (emotional) issues and financial statistics when assessing the utility of an investment option. Individuals evade financial choices connected with negative interpersonal responses. Moreno, Kida, and Smith (2002, p. 1331) report the following findings:

> Managers were generally risk avoiding for gains in the absence of affective reactions, as predicted by prospect theory. However, when affect was present, they tended to reject investment alternatives that elicited negative affect and accept alternatives that elicited positive affect, resulting in risk taking in gain contexts. The results also indicate that affective reactions can influence managers to choose alternatives with lower economic value.

Sawers (2005) conducts a capital budgeting study that examines the role of negative affect (emotions) related to the investment judgments of 120 executives. The study reports that managers presented with more complex decisions describe feeling more apprehensive, worried, and uncomfortable and reveal an increased need to delay making the judgment than members in the control group.

RETIREMENT ISSUES

Several studies examine the influence of worry (anxiety) and financial retirement issues. For example, Loewenstein, Prelec, and Weber (1999, p. 242), who evaluate the money anxiety involved in retirement issues, note:

> Before retirement, one has largely adapted to one's current income, and therefore its impact on well-being is slight. Moreover, one is not yet sure whether savings will be sufficient for retirement. All of this might increase overall money anxiety and, simultaneously, disconnect that anxiety from objective financial circumstances.

Cutler (2001) documents that individuals with incomes between $35,000 and $100,000 and the age categories of 35–43, 44–53, and 55–64 are more worried about squandering all their retirement wealth on long-term health care than about merely outlasting their savings and pension funds. Owen and Wu (2007) report households that acknowledge unfavorable financial pressures, worry more about the sufficiency (adequacy) of their financial situation in retirement, even after accounting for the influence of financial pressures (shocks) on overall wealth. Owen and Wu (2007, p. 515) comment: "we find supporting evidence that suggests that at least part of the increased worry about retirement is due to general pessimism rather than changes in an individual's own circumstances."

NEUROFINANCE

An emerging area of research within the behavioral finance literature involves negative affect (emotion) and neurofinance, also known as *neuroeconomics* (Glimcher 2004; Peterson 2007, 2014; Zweig 2007). Shiv, Loewenstein, Bechara, Damasio, and Damasio (2005) assess the financial judgments made by people who are incapable of feeling emotions as a result of brain lesions. The study reveals that individuals with specific types of brain damage generate more profits investing (i.e., produce higher gambling returns) than the normal and control groups. Evidence shows that because the brain-injured subjects cannot experience emotions such as worry, anxiety or fear, they are more inclined to accept risks with high rewards and are less likely to exhibit affective (emotional) reactions to prior gains or losses. Thus, these individuals are less likely to exhibit loss-averse behavior.

WORRY

For many investors, worrying is a regular occurrence. Worrying makes them feel as if they are reliving a past event or living out a future one, and individuals cannot stop these types of thoughts from happening (Ricciardi 2008b). Worry causes investors to reflect upon bad financial memories and produces mental pictures of futures that change short-term and long-term judgments regarding their finances. For instance, Ricciardi (2011) discloses that a large majority of investors identify the word *worry* with stocks (70 percent of the survey sample) compared to bonds (10 percent of the survey sample), based on the response of nearly 1,700 participants. A higher level of worry for a financial instrument such as common stocks increases its perceived risk, lowers the level of risk tolerance for investors, and increases the probability of not buying this asset.

Snelbecker, Roszkowski, and Cutler (1990) examine the factors that influence an investor's risk tolerance and return expectations so experts can provide better investment advice and clients can receive a more accurate risk-tolerance profile. The authors contend that financial planners base too much advice regarding risk tolerance and return expectations on the investment products and services, rather than on the client's personal characters such as feelings and attitudes about investment decisions. The authors conduct two studies that investigate risk tolerance and investment return prospects: one study involves 49 financial planners and the other involves 801 potential investors. On a group level, the financial planners demonstrate some uniformity about interpreting theoretical clients' statements. Yet, the study reveals significant differences in individual respondents' interpretations of the identical client statements.

In the second study, Snelbecker et al. (1990) conduct a telephone survey for a much larger sample of individual investors who receive a questionnaire with four sets of client statements of risk and return. The two client statements with the highest level of importance about the association between risk tolerance and return involve worry and a desire for an investment return above inflation. The survey measures the worry risk component using a question about whether a person is losing sleep worrying about his investments. The findings demonstrate how prevalent worrying is among individual investors. The authors conclude that financial professionals should consider such evidence when communicating and advising their clients.

WORRY AND RISK PERCEPTION

The study of worry and risk-taking behavior started in the social sciences and eventually appeared in the behavioral finance literature (Ricciardi 2008b). In the social science domain, the association between worry and perceived risk is an important area of investigation (Ricciardi 2004). Loewenstein, Hsee, Weber, and Welsh (2001) propose that judgments of risky behaviors and hazardous activities incorporate a component of negative emotions (feelings) such as dread, concern, worry, anxiety, depression, sadness, or fear. The foundation for the behavioral (psychological) factors of risk-perception studies in behavioral finance, accounting, and economics stem from the earlier endeavors on risky behaviors and hazardous activities in nonfinancial domains (Ricciardi 2004).

Decision Research, an organization founded by Paul Slovic, conducted groundbreaking research on risky and hazardous activities. This research documents specific behavioral risk factors that today are applied within a financial and investment decision-making context (Ricciardi 2010). The seminal work by Decision Research uses factor analysis to classify an extensive collection of risk indicators into two main risk constructs (dimensions) for nine standard behavioral risk characteristics and survey questions (Fischhoff, Slovic, Lichtenstein, Read and Comb 1978). The first factor is *dread risk*, measuring various risk-taking behaviors such as possessing catastrophic potential, severity of consequences, risk to future generations, and controllability of consequences. As Ricciardi (2008a) notes, this first factor documents an emotional response of worry or concern toward risk, which eventually became known as *dread* or *dreadness*, which affects an individual's perception of risk for a specific risky activity or hazardous behavior.

In a study from the behavioral accounting literature, Hodder, Koonce, and McAnally (2001) propose that dread risk might influence an individual's perception of risk for complex investment products such as derivative securities. Ultimately, negative affect (emotion) influences a person's risk perception during the financial and investment judgment process.

A study from the behavioral finance risk-perception domain by MacGregor, Slovic, Berry and Evensky (1999) examines the connection between the decision-making process and various aspects of investments/asset classes, especially expert's perceptions of returns, risk, and risk/return associations. The authors use completed surveys from 265 financial advisors involving their assessment of a series of 19 asset classes for 14 specific variables. Some of these 14 characteristics are behavioral in nature (i.e., attention, knowledge, and time horizon) while others are judgment related to perceived risk, perceived return, and likelihood of investing. The main finding reveals three significant factors—worry, volatility, and knowledge—as explaining 98 percent of the expert's risk perception. The study demonstrates that risk is a multi-factor decision-making process across a wide range of investment classes. Finucane (2002, p. 238) further comments on these findings as follows:

> Perceived risk was judged as greater to the extent that the advisor would worry about the investments that the investments had greater variance in market value over time, and how knowledgeable the advisor was about the investment option.

Since the 1970s, researchers have conducted hundreds of risk-perception studies in nonfinancial areas across a wide spectrum of disciplines (Ricciardi 2004, 2010). A noteworthy subject matter within the risk-perception literature concerns worry because this emotion might influence an individual's perception of risk. Ultimately, all types of individuals differ in their perceptions of worry and risk-taking behavior within the decision-making process. This perspective of behavioral finance is based on the assumption that the process of worry encompasses both cognitive and affective (emotional) issues. Negative emotions, especially worry, are an important risk indicator and this reaffirms the notion that risk is a multidimensional decision-making process across a range of accounting, financial, and investment settings (Ricciardi 2004, 2008a, 2008b).

REGRET THEORY

Regret aversion explains the emotion of regret encountered after making a decision that results in either an unfavorable or a second-rate choice. Individuals who are predisposed by projected regret are induced to take less risk because doing so reduces the prospect of bad outcomes. This regret bias helps explain why individuals possess a reluctance to sell "losing" investments because they do not want to admit a bad decision. Many individuals avoid selling securities that have declined in price to avoid feelings of regret and the distress of disclosing the loss.

For example, Strahilevitz, Odean, and Barber (2011) examine how individuals' past experiences with a stock influences their willingness to repurchase that the same investment. The study reveals that people are hesitant to buy back stocks previously sold for a realized loss and stocks that have increased in price subsequent to past sale transactions. Investors are dissatisfied when they sell stocks for a loss and experience regret for having purchased them originally. This negative affective reaction discourages them from later buying back stocks they sell for a loss. Because they sold such stocks, individuals are disenchanted if the stocks continue to increase in price and display regret for having sold them the first time. This negative affect prevents them from buying back stocks that increase in value after being sold. According to Stahilevitz et al. (p. S102), "investors engage in reinforcement learning by repurchasing stocks whose previous purchase resulted in positive emotions and avoiding stocks whose previous purchase resulted in negative emotions."

As evidence in this section shows, negative feelings play an important role within the realms of financial and investment judgments. In the domain of finance, negative emotions have real-world importance for many different aspects of investing. For example, the news media sometimes support the notion of worrying in the minds of stock market investors by focusing too much of their news coverage on market declines or bad financial news in a short period of time. This media coverage is communicated and overwhelms investors across various forms such as online new stories, print newspapers, and business segments of television news (Ricciardi, 2008b). Financial worries and negative feelings influence all types of individuals.

Summary and Conclusions

Behavioral finance attempts to describe and improve an individual's knowledge of the cognitive processes and affective reactions that shape financial outcomes. Risk perception involves the objective and subjective judgments that individuals apply to evaluate risk and the degree of uncertainty for all types of situations. The notion of an inverse (negative) connection between perceived risk and return is of growing importance. The chapter discusses a wide collection of biases that influence the judgment and decision-making processes of individuals, including representativeness bias, framing, anchoring affect, mental accounting, control factors, familiarity bias, trust, worry, and regret theory. The chapter also presents a detailed overview of the important influence of negative emotional issues within the financial judgments. Money worries and negative affect have detrimental impacts on the financial decisions of all types of people, including families, individual investors, and financial experts. These are important behavioral finance themes that financial professionals should use to better advise their clients. In effect, financial judgments are a situational, multidimensional decision-making process that depends on the specific traits of the financial product or service.

DISCUSSION QUESTIONS

1. List and explain some fundamental issues of behavioral finance.
2. Provide an overview of the behavioral finance perspectives of risk.
3. Define the heuristic biases of representativeness, anchoring, and mental accounting.
4. Define and describe the process of worrying within the finance domain.

REFERENCES

Anonymous. 1954. "Money, Money, Money." *Time*. January 11. Available at www.time.com/time/magazine/article/0,9171,819360,00.html.

Aspara, Jaakko, and Henrikki Tikkanen. 2011. "Individuals' Affect-Based Motivations to Invest in Stocks: Beyond Expected Financial Returns and Risks." *Journal of Behavioral Finance* 12:4, 78–89.

AXA. 2006. "Money Sickness Syndrome Could Affect Almost Half the UK Population." *Press Release*. Available at: www.axa.co.uk/newsroom/media-releases/2006/money-sickness-syndrome-could-affect-almost-half-the-uk-population/.

Baker, H. Kent, and Victor Ricciardi. 2014a. "How Biases Affect Investor Behaviour." *European Financial Review*, February-March, 7–10. Available at http://ssrn.com/abstract=2457425.

Baker, H. Kent, and Victor Ricciardi (eds.). 2014b. *Investor Behavior—The Psychology of Financial Planning and Investing*. Hoboken, NJ: John Wiley & Sons, Inc.

Baker, H. Kent, and Victor Ricciardi. 2015. "Understanding Behavioral Aspects of Financial Planning and Investing." *Journal of Financial Planning* 28:3, 22–26. Available at http://ssrn.com/abstract=2596202.

Bowman, Edward H. 1980. "A Risk/Return Paradox for Strategic Management." *Sloan Management Review* 21:3, 17–31.

Bowman, Edward H. 1982. "Risk Seeking by Troubled Firms." *Sloan Management Review* 23:4, 33–42.

Burns, William J., Ellen Peters, and Paul Slovic. 2012. "Risk Perception and the Economic Crisis: A Longitudinal Study of the Trajectory of Perceived Risk." *Risk Analysis: An International Journal* 32:4, 659–677.

Busenitz, Lowell W. 1999. "Entrepreneurial Risk and Strategic Decision Making: It's A Matter of Perspective." *Journal of Applied Behavioral Science* 35:3, 325–340.

Criddle, William D. 1993. "Teaching RET in the Financial and Investment Industry." *Journal of Rational-Emotive & Cognitive-Behavior Therapy* 11:1, 19–32.

Cutler, Neal E. 2001. "Who Uses a Financial Planner, and Why Not?" *Journal of Financial Service Professionals* 55:6, 33–36.

Diacon, Stephen, and Christine Ennew. 2001. "Consumer Perceptions of Financial Risk." *Geneva Papers in Risk & Insurance: Issues & Practice* 26:3, 389–409.

Finucane, Melissa L. 2002. "Mad Cows, Mad Corn, & Mad Money: Applying What We Know About the Perceived Risk of Technologies to the Perceived Risk of Securities." *Journal of Psychology and Financial Markets* 3:4, 236–243.

Finucane, Melissa L., Ellen Peters, and Paul Slovic. 2003. "Judgment and Decision Making: The Dance of Affect and Reason." In Sandra L. Schneider and James Shanteau (eds.), *Emerging Perspectives on Judgment and Decision Research*, 327–364. Cambridge: Cambridge University Press.

Fischhoff, Baruch, Paul Slovic, Sarah Lichtenstein, Stephen Read, and Barbara Combs. 1978. "How Safe Is Safe Enough? A Psychometric Study of Attitudes Toward Technological Risks and Benefits." *Policy Sciences* 9:2, 127–152.

Garman, E. Thomas, and Benoit Sorhaindo. 2005. "Delphi Study of Experts' Rankings of Personal Finance Concepts Important in the Development of the Incharge Financial Distress/Financial Well-Being Scale." *Consumer Interests Annual* 51, 184–194.

Gilovich, Thomas, Robert Vallone, and Amos Tversky. 1985. "The Hot Hand in Basketball: On the Misperception of Random Sequences." *Cognitive Psychology* 17:3, 295–314.

Glimcher, Paul. 2004. *Decisions, Uncertainty, and the Brain: The Science of Neuroeconomics*. Cambridge, MA: MIT Press.

Grable, John E., and So-Hyun Joo. 2001. "A Subsequent Study of the Relationships between Self-Worth and Financial Beliefs, Behavior and Satisfaction." *Journal of Family and Consumer Sciences* 93:5, 25–30.

Grable, John E., and Michael J. Roszkowski. 2008. "The Influence of Mood on the Willingness to Take Financial Risks." *Journal of Risk Research* 11:7, 905–923.

Haugen, Robert A., and A. James Heins. 1975. "Risk and the Rate of Return on Financial Assets: Some Old Wine in New Bottles." *Journal of Financial and Quantitative Analysis* 10:5, 775–784.

Henderson, Roger. 2006. "Money Sickness Syndrome: An Overview of the Problem and Strategies for Dealing with It." *AXA Press Release*. January 20.

Hira, Tahira K., and Olive M. Mugenda. 1999. "The Relationships between Self-Worth and Financial Beliefs, Behavior, and Satisfaction." *Journal of Family and Consumer* 91:4, 76–82.

Hodder, Leslie, D., Lisa Koonce, and Mary L. McAnally. 2001. "SEC Market Risk Disclosures: Implications for Judgment and Decision Making." *Accounting Horizons* 15:1, 49–70.

Howard, James, and Rassoul Yazdipour. 2014. "Retirement Planning: Contributions from the Field of Behavioral Finance and Economics." In H. Kent Baker and Victor Ricciardi (eds.), *Investor Behavior—The Psychology of Financial Planning and Investing*, 285–305. Hoboken, NJ: John Wiley & Sons, Inc.

Kahneman, Daniel, and Amos Tversky. 1979. "Prospect Theory: An Analysis of Decision under Risk." *Econometrics* 47:2, 263–291.

Kaufman, William. 1965. "Some Emotional Uses of Money." *Pastoral Psychology* 16:3, 43–56.

Kaustia, Markku, Eeva Alho, and Vesa Puttonen. 2008. "How Much Does Expertise Reduce Behavioral Biases? The Case of Anchoring Effects in Stock Return Estimates." *Financial Management* 37:3, 391–411.

Kida, Thomas E., Kimberly K. Moreno, and James F. Smith. 2001. "The Influence of Affect on Managers' Capital-Budgeting Decisions." *Contemporary Accounting Research* 18:3, 477–494.

Langer, Ellen, J. 1975. "The Illusion of Control." *Journal of Personality and Social Psychology* 32:2, 311–328.

Langer, Ellen, J. 1983. *The Psychology of Control*. Beverly Hills, CA: Sage Publications.

Leahy, Robert L. 1992. "Cognitive Therapy on Wall Street: Schemas and Scripts of Invulnerability." *Journal of Cognitive Psychotherapy* 6:4, 1–14.

Loewenstein, George F., Christopher K. Hsee, Elke U. Weber, and Ned Welsh. 2001. "Risk as Feelings." *Psychological Bulletin* 127:2, 267–286.

Loewenstein, George, Drazen Prelec, and Roberto Weber. 1999. "What Me Worry? A Psychological Perspective on Economic Aspects of Retirement." In Henry J. Aaron (ed.), *Behavioral Dimensions of Retirement Economics*, 215–246. Washington, DC: Brookings Institution Press.

MacGregor, Donald G., Paul Slovic, Michael Berry, and Harold R. Evensky. 1999. "Perception of Financial Risk: A Survey Study of Advisors and Planners." *Journal of Financial Planning* 12:8, 68–86.

Moreno, Kimberly, Thomas Kida, and James F. Smith. 2002. "The Impact of Affective Reactions on Risky Decision Making in Accounting Contexts." *Journal of Accounting Research* 40:5, 1331–1349.

Nofsinger, John. R. 2002. *The Psychology of Investing*. Upper Saddle River, NJ: Pearson Education, Inc.

Öhman, Susanne G., Charlotta Grunewald, and Ulla Waldenström 2003. "Women's Worries during Pregnancy: Testing the Cambridge Worry Scale on 200 Swedish Women." *Scandinavian Journal of Caring Sciences* 17:2, 148–152.

Olsen, Robert. 2012. "Trust: The Underappreciated Investment Risk Attribute." *Journal of Behavioral Finance* 13:4, 308–313.

Owen, Ann L., and Stephen Wu. 2007. "Financial Shocks and Worry about the Future." *Empirical Economics* 33:3, 515–530.

Peterson, Richard. L. 2007. *Inside the Investor's Brain: The Power of Mind over Money*. Hoboken, NJ: John Wiley & Sons, Inc.

Peterson, Richard, L. 2014. "Neurofinance." In H. Kent Baker and Victor Ricciardi (eds.), *Investor Behavior—The Psychology of Financial Planning and Investment*, 381–401. Hoboken, NJ: John Wiley & Sons, Inc.

Piatelli-Palmarini, Massimo. 1994. *Inevitable Illusions: How Mistakes of Reason Rule Our Minds*. New York: John Wiley.

Ricciardi, Victor. 2004. "A Risk Perception Primer: A Narrative Research Review of the Risk Perception Literature in Behavioral Accounting and Behavioral Finance." Working Paper, Goucher College. Available at http://ssrn.com/abstract=566802.

Ricciardi, Victor. 2006. "A Research Starting Point for the New Scholar: A Unique Perspective of Behavioral Finance." *ICFAI Journal of Behavioral Finance* 3:3, 6–23. Available at http://ssrn.com/abstract=928251.

Ricciardi, Victor. 2008a. "Risk: Traditional Finance versus Behavioral Finance." In Frank J. Fabozzi (ed.), *The Handbook of Finance, Volume 3: Valuation, Financial Modeling, and Quantitative Tools*, 11–38. Hoboken, NJ: John Wiley & Sons, Inc.

Ricciardi, Victor. 2008b. "The Psychology of Risk: The Behavioral Finance Perspective." In Frank J. Fabozzi (ed.), *The Handbook of Finance, Volume 2: Investment Management and Financial Management*, 85–111. Hoboken, NJ: John Wiley & Sons, Inc.

Ricciardi, Victor. 2010. "The Psychology of Risk." In H. Kent Baker and John R. Nofsinger (eds.), *Behavioral Finance: Investors, Corporations, and Markets*, 131–149. Hoboken, NJ: John Wiley & Sons, Inc.

Ricciardi, Victor. 2011. "The Financial Judgment and Decision-Making Process of Women: The Role of Negative Feelings." Third Annual Meeting of the Academy of Behavioral Finance and Economics, September. Available at https://ssrn.com/abstract=1936669.

Ricciardi, Victor, and Douglas Rice. 2014. "Risk Perception and Risk Tolerance." In H. Kent Baker and Victor Ricciardi (eds.), *Investor Behavior—The Psychology of Financial Planning and Investment*, 327–345. Hoboken, NJ: John Wiley & Sons, Inc.

Roszkowski, Michael J., and Glenn E. Snelbecker. 1990. "Effects of Framing on Measures of Risk Tolerance: Financial Planners Are Not Immune." *Journal of Behavioral Economics* 19:3, 237–246.

Rotter, Julian. B. 1971. "External Control and Internal Control." *Psychology Today* 5:1, 37–42, 58–59.

Rubaltelli, Enrico, Giacomo Pasini, Rino Rumiati, Robert Olsen, and Paul Slovic. 2010. "The Influence of Affective Reactions on Investment Decisions." *Journal of Behavioral Finance* 11:3, 168–176.

Sawers, Kimberly. M. 2005. "Evidence of Choice Avoidance in Capital Investment Judgments." *Contemporary Accounting Research* 22:4, 1063–1092.

Shafir, Eldar, and Richard H. Thaler. 2006. "Invest Now, Drink Later, Spend Never: On the Mental Accounting of Delayed Consumption." *Journal of Economic Psychology* 27:5, 694–712.

Shefrin, Hersh. 2001. "Do Investors Expect Higher Returns from Safer Stocks Than from Riskier Stocks?" *Journal of Psychology and Financial Markets* 2:4, 176–181.

Shefrin, Hersh. 2005. *Behavioral Corporate Finance: Decisions that Create Value.* New York: McGraw-Hill/Irwin.

Shiv, Baba, George Loewenstein, Antoine Bechara, Hanna Damasio, and Antonio R. Damasio. 2005. "Investment Behavior and the Negative Side of Emotion." *Psychological Science* 16:6, 435–439.

Snelbecker, Glenn E., Michael J. Roszkowski, and Neal E. Cutler. 1990. "Investors' Risk Tolerance and Return Aspirations, and Financial Advisors' Interpretations: A Conceptual Model and Exploratory Data." *Journal of Behavioral Economics* 19:4, 377–393.

Strahilevitz, Michal A., Terrance Odean, and Brad M Barber. 2011. "Once Burned, Twice Shy: How Naive Learning, Counterfactuals, and Regret Affect the Repurchase of Stocks Previously Sold." *Journal of Marketing Research* 48: Special Issue, S102–S120.

Strong, Robert. A. 2006. *Practical Investment Management*, 4th edition. Mason, OH: Thomson Higher Education.

Wang, Mei, Carmen Keller, and Michael Siegrist. 2011. "The Less You Know, the More You Are Afraid of a Survey on Risk Perceptions of Investment Products." *Journal of Behavioral Finance* 12:1, 9–19.

Weber, Ann, L. 1991. *Introduction to Psychology.* New York: HarperCollins.

Yeske, Dave, and Elissa Buie. 2014. "Policy-Based Financial Planning: Decision Rules for a Changing World." In H. Kent Baker and Victor Ricciardi (eds.), *Investor Behavior—The Psychology of Financial Planning and Investment*, 181–208. Hoboken, NJ: John Wiley & Sons, Inc.

Zweig, Jason. 2007. *Your Money and Your Brain: How The New Science of Neuroeconomics Can Help Make You Rich.* New York: Simon & Schuster.

Part Two

THE FINANCIAL BEHAVIOR OF MAJOR PLAYERS

3

Individual Investors

HENRIK CRONQVIST
Professor of Finance
School of Business Administration, University of Miami

DANLING JIANG
SunTrust Professor and Associate Professor of Finance
College of Business, Florida State University

Introduction

Over the past two decades, our understanding of individual investor behavior has changed dramatically. The traditional paradigm that focuses on economic incentives and rationality has been replaced by a new, more holistic paradigm that includes additional factors influencing investor behavior. These additional factors include investors' genetics, life experiences, nonstandard beliefs and preferences, societal norms and culture, and group identities. The holistic approach provides a more comprehensive perspective of what defines and shapes the decision-making process of individual investors, and whether their behaviors and decisions collectively matter for asset prices and corporate policies. This chapter examines recent advances in finance research along these dimensions that define individual investor behavior and have implications for asset pricing and corporate decisions. Owing to limited space, the chapter only reviews some representative work in each topic.

Innate and Learned Investor Behavior

The traditional paradigm in finance does not attempt to explain the origins of investors' preferences and beliefs. However, an emerging body of research attempts to do exactly that by tracing the heterogeneity in investor behavior back to genetic factors, cognitive ability, and various personal experiences.

GENETIC FACTORS AND NEURAL FOUNDATIONS

The longstanding debate in behavioral genetics and psychology about whether "nature" (i.e., genetic factors) or "nurture" (i.e., the environment) shapes individual traits has recently made its way into research on investor behavior. Barnea, Cronqvist, and Siegel

(2010) and Cesarini, Dawes, Johannesson, Lichtenstein, Sandewall, and Wallace (2010) combine data on identical and fraternal twins and data on portfolio allocations from tax registers, enabling them to decompose the cross-sectional variation in investor behavior into genetic and environmental components. They find that genetic factors explain about one-third of the variation in investment decisions. The authors interpret these results as evidence of innate differences in factors affecting stock market participation costs, as well as genetic variations in risk preferences. Experimental evidence in economics supports these studies (Cesarini, Dawes, Johannesson, Lichtenstein, and Wallace 2009; Zyphur, Narayanan, Arvey, and Alexander 2009).

Cronqvist and Siegel (2014) extend the notion that genetic factors may be responsible for heterogeneity in investment behavior by showing that several well-documented investment biases, such as the disposition effect, performance-chasing behavior, and a preference for skewness, are partly genetic. They interpret these results as implying behaviors that may result in investment mistakes may have been advantageous in evolutionary ancient times, in the sense that these behaviors resulted in greater "fitness" (i.e., reproductive success) and therefore became more common in the population.

A related string of research in neuroscience examines the neural foundations of investment behavior (Kuhnen and Knutson 2005). Evidence finds specific genes to be related to investor behavior. For example, the DRD4 gene explains financial risk preferences (Dreber, Rand, Fudenberg, and Nowak 2008), the monoamine oxidase A (MAOA) gene is related to risk-taking (Frydman, Camerer, Bossaerts, and Rangel 2011; Zhong, Israel, Xue, Ebstein, and Chew 2009), and two genes that regulate dopamine and serotonin neurotransmission (5-HTTLPR and DRD4) determine risk-taking in the investment domain (Kuhnen and Chiao 2009). The same brain areas involved in processing emotional states also process risk preferences and payoff beliefs (Kuhnen and Knutson 2011). Candidate gene studies and genome-wide association studies (GWAS) have both promises and potential pitfalls (Benjamin, Cesarini, Chabris, Glaeser, Laibson, Guonason, Harris, Launer, Purcell, and Smith 2012).

COGNITIVE ABILITY AND IQ

Several studies find that cognitive ability partly explains investor behavior. Using data from 11 European countries, Christelis, Jappelli, and Padula (2010) find that differences in individuals' cognitive ability partly explain the propensity to participate in the stock market. In a series of studies (2011, 2012, 2016), Grinblatt and his coauthors show that individuals with higher intelligence quotient (IQ) scores make better investment decisions. Higher IQ investors are more likely to participate in the stock market, diversify by holding mutual funds or a greater number of stocks, assume less risk, earn higher Sharpe ratios, display fewer investment biases, exhibit better timing and stock-picking skills, and avoid high management fees when selecting mutual funds (Grinblatt, Keloharju, and Linnainmaa 2011, 2012; Grinblatt, Ikaheimo, Keloharju, and Knupfer 2016).

Recent related research also pays close attention to the relations among aging, cognitive ability, and investor behavior, which are increasingly important with an aging population responsible for its own investments. Aging causes a well-documented decline in people's cognitive ability, but it also increases investment experience. The adverse effect of aging, however, empirically dominates any experience effect; older investors exhibit worse investment skills even though they are more experienced (Korniotis and Kumar

2011). In fact, financial mistakes appear to follow a U-shaped pattern, with the fewest mistakes made around age 53 (Agarwal, Driscoll, Gabaix, and Laibson 2009). Although aging decreases cognition and financial literacy, it is not associated with a drop in confidence in managing one's own finances (Gamble, Boyle, Yu, and Benett 2015).

PERSONAL LIFE EXPERIENCES

Life-course theory suggests that both early and late personal experiences in life may explain behavior later in life. As a result, an investor's behavior may be path dependent. In fact, one's first life experiences take place during the prenatal period, as an unborn fetus in the mother's womb. According to Cronqvist, Previtero, Siegel, and White, (2016), higher prenatal exposure to testosterone is associated with elevated risk-taking and trading in adulthood. Individuals with higher birth weight or a general measure of prenatal life experience are more likely to participate in the stock market. Additionally, investors with lower birth weight tend to prefer portfolios with higher volatility and skewness. Both pieces of evidence are consistent with compensatory behavior.

Later in life, individuals may be shaped by other personal life experiences, including macroeconomic experiences that influence many individuals simultaneously, such as the Great Depression of the 1930s or the financial crisis of 2007–2008. As Malmendier and Nagel (2011) show, individuals' long-term experiences with stock and bond markets determine their propensities to participate in those markets. They also show that macro experiences affect beliefs, rather than risk preferences, because experienced higher stock returns are associated with more optimistic beliefs about future stock returns. Weber, Weber, and Nosić (2013) and Guiso, Sapienza, and Zingales (2013), however, find that risk aversion increased substantially in the immediate aftermath of the financial crisis of 2007–2008, even among investors who did not suffer any losses. That is, negative macro experiences result in increased risk aversion or less optimistic beliefs about future stock returns.

As Knüpfer, Rantapuska, and Sarvimäki (2016) report, workers who experienced adverse labor market conditions during the Finnish Great Depression in the early 1990s are less likely to participate in the stock market later in life. Cronqvist, Siegel, and Yu (2015) find that individuals who experienced more adverse macroeconomic conditions are more likely to favor value stocks as opposed to growth stocks.

Individual experiences related to the stock market also explain subsequent investor behavior. For example, individual investors who experienced higher returns from subscriptions of initial public offerings (IPOs) are more likely to subscribe to future IPOs in Finland (Kaustia and Knüpfer 2008) and Taiwan (Chiang, Hirshleifer, Qian, and Sherman 2011). The evidence is consistent with naïve reinforcement learning, wherein individuals become overly optimistic after experiencing good returns. Consistent with the notion of "once burned, twice shy," Strahilevitz, Odean, and Barber (2011) find that investors are reluctant to repurchase stocks previously sold for a loss and that have risen in price subsequent to that sale. This behavior reflects investors' attempts to distance themselves from negative emotional experiences such as disappointment and regret. As Greenwood and Shleifer (2014) find in multiple surveys of individual investors, expected returns are all highly correlated with recent market returns, but are negatively related to the implied expected returns that are computed from aggregated data on dividends, consumption, and market valuation measures, as well as future market returns. A conclusion from these studies is that individuals appear to over-weight their personal experiences in the stock market with insufficient consideration of all available data.

Nonstandard Investor Preferences

The traditional paradigm summarizes investor preferences with respect to risk aversion and wealth. However, recent research introduces nonstandard preferences related to other factors—for example, prospect theory, mental accounting, realization utility of gains and losses, and preferences for skewness and familiarity.

THE DISPOSITION EFFECT, PROSPECT THEORY, MENTAL ACCOUNTING, AND REALIZATION UTILITY

Shefrin and Statman (1985) propose the *disposition effect*, which refers to the behavior of investors to sell winner stocks more readily than loser stocks. They suggest several explanations for this effect, including prospect theory (Kahneman and Tversky 1979) and the reluctance to close mental accounts with a loss (Thaler 1985).

Weber and Camerer (1998) offer evidence of the disposition effect using an experimental approach. Odean (1998a) tests the disposition effect by using brokerage account data and finds that individual investors on average realize about 15 percent of paper gains but less than 10 percent of paper losses. He focuses on the prospect theory explanation, which predicts that prior gains elicit risk aversion, whereas prior losses elicit risk seeking. In Taiwan stock markets where individual investors dominate, 84 percent of the investors sell winners faster than losers (Barber, Lee, Liu, and Odean 2007). The strength of the disposition effect varies across investors. More sophisticated investors, such as wealthy individuals with professional occupations or more trading experience and who execute more clustered trades, exhibit a weaker disposition effect (Dhar and Zhu 2006; Feng and Seasholes 2005; Kumar and Lim 2008).

However, Barberis and Xiong (2009) show theoretically that prospect theory cannot easily generate the disposition effect in a dynamic setting. Instead, Barberis and Xiong (2012) and Ingersoll and Jin (2013) suggest that investors receive utility by realizing paper gains and disutility by realizing paper losses—consistent with a mental accounting that involves a narrow framing of gains and losses. In a recent experimental study, Frydman, Barberis, Camerer, Bossaerts, and Rangel (2014) document the neural foundations of such realization utility. However, when investors can transfer a mental account from one stock to another by selling and buying on the same day, they exhibit no reluctance to sell the initial losers (Frydman, Hartzmark, and Solomon 2016).

Additionally, some propose *cognitive dissonance*, which is the psychology of feeling discomfort when one recognizes one's own mistakes or own incorrect beliefs as an explanation for the disposition effect. For example, individual day traders in Finland are unwilling to close their losing-day trades, and such unintended positions hurt their portfolio performance in subsequent months (Linnainmaa 2005). Although the disposition effect is present when trading individual stocks, it reverses when trading mutual funds for the same investor and at the same time, as investors can blame the managers in regard to the portfolio delegation (Chang, Solomon, and Westerfield 2016).

Whether the disposition effect is the determining factor in investors' selling decisions remains an active area of research. Evidence by Kaustia (2010) shows that selling propensity jumps at zero returns, but is insensitive to the magnitude of gains and losses. As Ben-David and Hirshleifer (2012) show, the probability of selling as a function of profit is V-shaped (i.e., at short holding periods, investors are more likely to sell bigger losers than smaller ones). Similarly, Hartzmark (2015) uncovers the rank effect in which investors are more likely to sell the extreme winning and losing stocks in their own portfolio. None of these findings can be easily reconciled with the disposition effect driven by prospect theory or the realization utility.

PREFERENCE FOR SKEWNESS

The idea that individuals prefer to gamble when making investment decisions emerged nearly 70 years ago, starting with Friedman and Savage (1948) and Markowitz (1952). Researchers propose several theoretical reasons for individuals exhibiting a skewness preference. Shefrin and Statman (2000) suggest that a preference for lotteries or lottery-type securities is a necessary consequence when investors aspire to move up in social status. Brunnermeier, Gollier, and Parker (2007) model the preference for skewness as an outcome of investors' being overly optimistic about the probability of good states of the world. Mitton and Vorkink (2007) model investors to have heterogeneous preferences for skewness. Barberis and Huang (2008) show that investors are willing to pay for skewness as they over-weight the probability of extremely rare events, a feature of the cumulative prospect theory (Tversky and Kahneman 1992).

A large body of empirical work supports conjectures that investors have a skewness preference. As Kumar (2009) shows, the portfolios of retail investors—but not those of institutional investors—over-weight lottery-type stocks, which are characterized by low price, high idiosyncratic volatility, and high idiosyncratic skewness. The demand for lottery-type stocks increases during economic downturns, and socioeconomic factors that induce greater expenditure on lotteries are also associated with greater investment in lottery-type stocks. As Doran, Jiang, and Peterson (2012) show, the Las Vegas gaming revenues and interstate lottery sales surge at the turn of the year, and simultaneously investors are bullish on lottery type stocks and options. Dorn, Dorn, and Sengmueller (2015) and Gao and Lin (2015) provide evidence consistent with investors' alternating between playing the lottery and gambling in financial markets. Kumar, Page, and Spalt (2011) use the ratio of the Catholic to Protestant adherents in a region in the United States to capture the gambling-tolerant culture; they show that in regions with higher Catholic to Protestant ratios, local investors exhibit a stronger propensity to hold lottery-type stocks.

PREFERENCE FOR FAMILIARITY

The mere-exposure effect in psychology implies that people have a strong preference for the familiar, even in the absence of information (Zajonc 1968). Indeed, the investment literature repeatedly documents a preference for the familiar. For example, Huberman (2001) shows that a regional Bell operating company's shareholders tend to live in the same region as the company serves. Massa and Simonov (2006) report that individual investors do not hedge but, rather, invest in stocks closely related to their nonfinancial income.

Individual investors tend to over-weight local stocks in their portfolios, where local stocks are of companies whose headquarters are located geographically close by. Ivković and Weisbenner (2005) find that individual investors earn higher average returns on local rather than nonlocal holdings, whereas Seasholes and Zhu (2010) find that local stocks purchased by individual investors generate future average returns inferior to local stocks sold by these investors, suggesting suboptimal decisions regarding trading local securities.

Stock in one's own company and in producers of consumer products are alternative sources of familiarity in the investment domain. Individuals have a strong preference for investment in their own company's stocks, although they do not have any information advantage (Benartzi 2001). Employees in standalone companies significantly over-weight their own company's stocks more than employees in conglomerate firms, which is consistent with loyalty-influencing portfolio choice (Cohen 2009). Furthermore, a company's long-term customers tend to be loyal investors in that company (Keloharju, Knüpfer, and Linnainmaa 2012).

Investor Psychology

Investor psychology plays a minimum role in the traditional paradigm that relies on rational optimization of expected utilities and Bayesian updating. However, the new paradigm, especially the development of behavioral finance, highlights the importance of heuristics and psychological traits in understanding individual behaviors. Several specific heuristics or rules of thumb have spurred considerable finance research.

OVERCONFIDENCE

Overconfidence refers to investors' tendency to overestimate their own signal precision or their personal ability to do well in trading. It is probably the most established psychological trait in theory and empirical tests of finance research. Earlier models (Daniel, Hirshleifer, and Subrahmanyam 1998, 2001; Odean 1998b; Scheinkman and Xiong 2003) establish the powerful insights of overconfidence to help understand excess trading, excess volatility, over- and underreactions, and event-based return predictability. Models of Daniel et al. (1998) and Gervais and Odean (2001) highlight the persistence of overconfidence when investors exhibit biased self-attribution.

In a series of empirical studies using individual trading records from a large U.S. brokerage house, Barber and Odean, together with their coauthors, uncover intriguing evidence that supports the theory of overconfident trading. Stocks sold by individual investors outperform stocks they purchase (Odean 1999). Investors who trade more have worse cost-adjusted trading performances (Barber and Odean 2000a). Males engage in more active trading than females, but suffer from worse returns (Barber and Odean 2001). In Finland, more overconfident investors, revealed by a standard psychological assessment upon induction into mandatory military service, tend to have higher portfolio turnover later in life (Grinblatt and Keloharju 2009).

In other words, active trading is the most important manifestation of overconfidence. However, it comes with considerable cost. In Taiwan, active trading by individual investors results in a loss of 3.8 percent in their aggregate portfolio, which is equivalent to 2.8 percent of their total personal income and above 2 percent of the country's gross domestic product (GDP) (Barber, Lee, Liu, and Odean 2009). Individual day traders account for 17 percent of the trading volume, but only 20 percent of them earn positive net returns in a given year and less than 1 percent do so in two consecutive years (Barber, Lee, Liu, and Odean 2014). French (2008) estimates that investors pay a net cost of 67 basis points of the aggregate market value a year as a result of attempting to beat the U.S. market.

Theories of overconfident trading and biased self-attribution lead to discoveries of market regularities. They include, for example, the positive correlation between turnover and lagged returns (Statman, Thorley, and Vorkink 2006), the existence of systematic mispricing that can be captured by firm external financing (Hirshleifer and Jiang 2010), the ability of the cross-sectional dispersion in firm valuation ratios to negatively forecast future aggregate returns (Jiang 2013), and the outperformance of stocks with upward continuing overreactions relative to stocks with downward continuing overreactions (Byun, Lim, and Yun 2016).

LIMITED ATTENTION

Individual investors have limited attention and limited processing power; thus, they can be attracted to, or distracted by the content, salience, and amount of news, as well as by activities outside the financial domain.

When selecting mutual funds, individual investors pay attention to the more salient front-end loads and recent fund performances, as opposed to the less salient operating expenses (Barber, Odean, and Zheng 2005). In establishing selection criteria, individual investors are net buyers of stocks that grab their attention, such as those with high abnormal trading volume or extreme one-day returns (Barber and Odean 2008). In China, stocks that hit their upper price limits are associated with high investor attention as measured by high volumes and more news coverage, but return reversals follow in the subsequent week (Seasholes and Wu 2007). On the day following a market-wide attention event, such as a record level for the Dow Jones Industrial Average (DJIA), individual investors sell more equity holdings (Yuan 2015).

This limited attention by individual investors leads to predictable returns and market reactions to news. Reactions to earnings announcements are weak, but subsequent drift is strong when earnings are announced on Fridays (DellaVigna and Pollet 2009), when many competing announcements occur in the same industry (Hirshleifer, Lim, and Teoh 2009), and when there is intensive industry-wide news (Jacobs and Weber 2016). Return shocks to large customer-product firms slowly diffuse to the stock prices of their supplier firms (Cohen and Frazzini 2008). Return shocks to straightforward (stand-alone) firms precede the return shocks to complicated (conglomerate) firms (Cohen and Lou 2012). Gradual, small changes in prices are accompanied by strong price momentum, whereas large, sudden changes are not (Da, Gurun, and Warachka 2014). When investors focus on earnings as opposed to cash flows, the firms with high net operating assets, which measure the cumulative differences between earnings and cash flows, on average earn low subsequent returns (Hirshleifer, Hou, Teoh, and Zhang 2004). Managers attract investor attention through advertisements to boost short-term stock prices; the timing of their advertisements coincides with insider trading (Lou 2014).

MOOD, EMOTION, AND SENTIMENT

Mood and emotion, which are the states of feelings at the time of decision making, may influence investor behavior (Loewenstein, Weber, Hsee, and Welch 2001). Positive emotions lead to investor optimism and increased willingness to take risk (Kuhnen and Knutson 2011). Numerous empirical findings support such a hypothesis. For example, Hirshleifer and Shumway (2003) report evidence consistent with "emotional misattribution," in the sense that weather conditions such as sunshine and cloud cover affect investor behavior. Edmans, Garcia, and Norli (2007) study changes in investor mood and behavior during sports events. Similar studies show that negative mood depresses stock markets, such as those involving aviation disasters (Kaplanski and Levy 2010). Investors do not exert any influence over these moderators of their moods, suggesting a causal interpretation.

Evidence also shows mood effects for reoccurring and predictable events. For example, Kamstra, Kramer, and Levi (2003) report that the number of hours of daylight drives investor behavior. Frieder and Subrahmanyam (2004); Białkowski, Etebari, and Wisniewski (2012); and Bergsma and Jiang (2016) study stock market behavior during cultural and religious holidays, and they conclude that festive mood is an explanation for some market movements.

Evidence by Karabulut (2013) shows that the Facebook's Gross National Happiness (GNH) index is a positive predictor of the next day's stock market returns. Da, Engelberg, and Gao (2015), who developed the Financial and Economic Attitudes Revealed by Search (FEARS) index as a proxy for negative mood state, show that higher returns today but lower returns the next day accompany increases in the FEARS index. Some evidence by Kaustia and Rantapuska (2016) shows that weather-based mood proxies, such as sunniness, temperature, and precipitation, are significantly related to the trading behavior of individual investors, who also exhibit seasonal behavior across days of the year and the week before holidays.

Related to mood is a large strand of literature on *investor sentiment*, which usually refers to collective, incorrect beliefs and preferences, and this can be thought of as a measure of investor affect state. Baker and Wurgler (2006) show that a sentiment index constructed from, for example, the closed-end fund discount, trading volume, initial public offering (IPO) first-day returns, and volume predicts the cross-sectional returns on hard-to-arbitrage stocks in the following year. Hwang (2011) finds that investor sentiment regarding a certain country causes changes in that country's closed-end fund discount. Both sentiment and mood measure the collective optimism versus the pessimism of investors toward market states and asset values. A possible difference between the two is, perhaps, that mood is tied to emotions that can vary frequently (daily or even hourly), whereas sentiment is tied to attitudes that are relatively slow moving.

More generally, firms that elicit positive affect receive a greater portfolio weight or a pricing premium, including those with euphonious (Alter and Oppenheimer 2006; Andersson and Rakow 2007) or patriotic (Morse and Shive 2011; Benos and Jochec 2013) names, and admired companies (Statman, Fisher, and Anginer 2008). In contrast, the market discounts stocks that elicit negative affect, such as those associated with tobacco, alcohol, gaming, firearms, military sales, and nuclear operations (Hong and Kacperczyk 2009; Statman and Glushkov 2009).

In turn, firms seem to exploit the investor affect. For example, dual-class companies strategically label their inferior voting shares as "Class A" but their superior voting shares as "Class B" and thus gain from IPOs (Ang, Chua, and Jiang 2010). The effect of investors' attitudes toward certain company characteristics can fade or even reverse when the macroeconomic environment changes. During the dot-com boom of the late 1990s, companies that changed to dot-com type names experienced positive market reactions (Cooper, Dimitrov, and Rau 2001). Yet, when the dot-com bubble burst in the early 2000s, the companies that switched to a conventional name experienced positive market reactions (Cooper, Khorana, Osobov, Patel, and Rau 2005).

Social Context

Individuals do not make investment decisions in isolation; rather, they make their decisions in the context of a variety of important social factors. Such factors include social interaction, social identity, social norms, and social capital, as well as more general culture effects.

SOCIAL INTERACTION AND PEER EFFECT

Individuals have social networks that include family, friends, co-workers, neighbors, and others. People in these networks may influence others' investment behaviors. The behavior of family is of the first order, understandably. Evidence by Li (2014) indicates that an investor's likelihood of entering the stock market within the next five years is 20 to 30 percent higher if the individual's parents or children have entered the stock market during the prior five years.

Importantly, social interaction effects extend beyond the family. Evidence shows that the behavior of peers—friends, neighbors, and co-workers—partly drives the decision to participate in the stock market (Hong, Kubik, and Stein 2004; Guiso and Jappelli 2005; Brown, Ivković, Smith, and Weisbenner 2008; Hvide and Östberg 2015). Shive (2010) applies a disease epidemic model and finds that the transmission rate of financial rumors through social contact predicts investor behavior.

However, the forces driving investor network effects such as simple imitation, herding, or biased information transfer remains unclear (Ozsoylev, Walden, Yavuz, and Bildik 2014). Evidence by Kaustia and Knüpfer (2012) shows that the investment performance of one's peers influences an individual's decision to enter the stock market. This social learning is truncated when a peer's returns fall below zero, which is consistent with the theoretical predictions by Han and Hirshleifer (2015), who model the self-enhancing transmission bias in social interactions leading to biased information sharing.

Group dynamics is a specific source of social interaction. Barber and Odean (2000b) find that investment clubs underperform the market even more than individuals. Furthermore, both clubs and individuals are more likely to invest in stocks that are associated with a good reason, such as a company on a most-admired companies list, but groups favor such stocks more than do individuals, despite the fact that such reasons do not improve performance (Barber, Heath, and Odean 2003).

SOCIAL IDENTITY AND SOCIAL NORMS

Evidence by Akerlof and Kranton (2000) and Bénabou and Tirole (2011) shows that an individual's social identity (i.e., personal sense of self) affects his or her investment behavior. Specific examples of social identity are civic engagement and political orientation. Politically active individuals, irrespective of their political affiliation, spend about 30 minutes more on acquiring news daily and are more likely to participate in the stock market (Bonaparte and Kumar 2013). According to Kaustia and Torstila (2011), moderate left voters are about 20 percent less likely to invest in stocks compared to moderate right voters, controlling for wealth and other individual characteristics. Their evidence is consistent with the notion that personal values affect investment decisions, in this case leading to "stock market aversion." Individual investors perceive stock markets as less risky and more undervalued when "their" party is in power (Bonaparte, Kumar, and Page 2012). Interestingly, a reverse effect of stock ownership exists in regard to political behavior. Plausibly exogenous demutualizations in certain regions in Finland resulted in an increase in the right-of-center vote share in those regions (Kaustia, Knüpfer, and Torstila 2015).

Social norms and values may also influence investors. For example, investors may have social preferences, implying that they internalize the utility of others in society. As Hong and Kostovetsky (2012) show, professional investors who donate primarily to the Democratic Party in political campaigns over-weight stocks of socially responsible firms, but avoid stocks in industries such as defense, gun manufacture, and tobacco. Some emerging evidence also shows that individual investors who exhibit prosocial behavior in experiments are more likely to invest in socially responsible mutual funds (Riedl and Smeets 2014). This research raises the question of whether social identity or norm-constrained investors underperform (i.e., pay a price for their behavior). Evidence by Hong and Kacperczyk (2009) shows that "sin" stocks earn higher than expected returns. Yet, other evidence suggests that the more socially responsible or employee-friendly firms deliver higher abnormal returns (Derwall, Guenster, Bauer, and Koedijk 2005; Edmans 2011).

SOCIAL CAPITAL AND TRUST

Trust refers to the confidence in receiving fair returns from economic transactions. As Guiso, Sapienza, and Zingales (2008) show, trusting individuals in the Netherlands are more likely to participate in stock markets and invest more in risky assets. Similar results are reported for the United States whereas more trusting individuals and households are better at managing investments (Balloch, Nicolae, and Philip 2015) and debts (Jiang and Lim 2016). Trust influences individual investment risk perceptions and equity premium (Olsen 2012), and it may also explain the specific securities that individuals select. Kelly (2014) finds that less trusting individuals have a preference for dividend-paying as opposed to non-dividend-paying stocks.

Some recent research shows that the behaviors of individual investors reflect changes in trust. As Giannetti and Wang (2016) show, stock market participation declines in a U.S. state after revelation of a prominent corporate fraud case in that state. Individuals decreased their holdings in non-fraudulent firms located in that state, even if they did not hold stocks in the fraudulent firms. Similarly, Gurun, Stoffman, and Yonker (2015) studied the effects of trust on investor behavior by exploiting the geographic dispersion of victims in the Bernie Madoff scandal. Their results show that investors in communities that were more exposed to the fraud withdrew their assets from their investment advisers and increased their cash deposits in banks.

Trust is an important component of social capital. In general, *social capital* refers to our connections with each other, and it can be measured by the general networks of those in a community that promotes social and political engagement (Putnam 2000). That is, sociability promotes investing. Guiso, Sapienza, and Zingales (2004) show that communities with higher social capital have better financial development, including more investments in stocks and less in cash. Georgarakos and Pasini (2011) and Changwony, Campbell, and Tabner (2015) also find that trust, and social engagement more generally, explains individuals' participation in stock markets.

CULTURE

Culture affects various economic outcomes (Guiso, Sapienza, and Zingales 2006). Cultural norms and proximity also affect behavior among individual investors. Evidence by Grinblatt and Keloharju (2001) shows that investors in Finland are more likely to trade stocks in companies that communicate in the investor's native tongue and that have a chief executive of the same cultural background. As Kumar, Niessen-Ruenzi, and Spalt (2015) show, financial managers with foreign-sounding names have 10 percent less annual fund flows, and for funds run by those managers, investors exhibit greater sensitivity to bad performance.

Cultural norms reflect values that change only very slowly over time, as they are transmitted from one generation to the next. Findings by D'Acunto, Prokopczuk, and Weber (2015) indicate that investors are less likely to participate in stock markets in counties of Germany where Jewish persecution was higher in the Middle Ages and the Nazi period. Their evidence is consistent with a persistent cultural norm of distrust in finance that varies regionally.

TECHNOLOGY

Technology can be considered an environmental factor that builds the venues and platforms for investing. In recent decades, technologic innovations have drastically changed how individual investors invest. Because technology has made investing more accessible and less costly, it has been beneficial. However, when technology interacts with behavioral biases, it can be detrimental.

Barber and Odean (2000a) show that the availability of online trading causes significant increases in trading volume, but investors who switch to online trading suffer from poor trading performance. Although Choi, Laibson, and Metrick (2002) find that web access by investors doubles the trading frequency, they find no evidence that online trading leads to higher returns.

With such technological innovations, information becomes more accessible, which enables measurement of investor attention and information acquisition more directly. Using the Google Search Volume Index (SVI) to capture individual investor attention, Da, Engelberg, and Gao (2011) show that this index predicts high subsequent returns within the next two weeks that are followed by a reversal. Leung, Agarwal, Konana, and Kumar (2016) use the search behaviors of individuals who visit the Yahoo!Finance website to identify return co-movement among stocks within the search clusters.

Summary and Conclusions

Within the last two decades, there has been a transformation from the traditional paradigm to a new approach that takes a broader view toward understanding individual investor behavior and financial decision making. This new paradigm attempts to understand the behavioral origin (genetics and neural roots), behavioral formation (personal life experiences), and behavioral motivation (psychology and preference), as well as the behavioral context (society, environment, and culture) of individual investors.

The growth of knowledge in this new paradigm recognizes the complexity of individual decision making and its collective influence on financial markets and company decisions. Hirshleifer (2015) refers to this new paradigm as "social finance," a more advanced form of behavioral finance. Moving forward, finance research is likely to continue expanding by integrating knowledge from other disciplines into the understanding of individual investors and their impacts on markets and companies.

DISCUSSION QUESTIONS

1. Discuss the main differences between the traditional and the modern finance paradigm in understanding the behavior of individual investors.
2. Explain the broad implications of studies of genetics, neural roots, and personal life experiences for understanding the behavior of individual investors.
3. Discuss the disposition effect and the proposed explanations for this effect.
4. Identify the social factors that influence individual investor decisions and discuss the importance of considering the social context when making investment decisions.

REFERENCES

Agarwal, Sumit, John C. Driscoll, Xavier Gabaix, and David Laibson. 2009. "The Age of Reason: Financial Decisions over the Life Cycle and Implications for Regulation." *Brookings Papers on Economic Activity*, Fall, 51–101.

Akerlof, George A., and Rachel E. Kranton. 2000. "Economics and Identity." *Quarterly Journal of Economics* 115:3, 715–753.

Alter, Adam L., and Daniel M. Oppenheimer. 2006. "Predicting Short-Term Stock Fluctuations by Using Processing Fluency." *Proceedings of the National Academy of Sciences* 103:24, 9369–9372.

Andersson, Patric, and Tim Rakow. 2007. "Now You See It Now You Don't: The Effectiveness of the Recognition Heuristic for Selecting Stocks." *Judgment and Decision Making* 2:1, 29–39.

Ang, James, Ansley Chua, and Danling Jiang. 2010. "Is A Better Than B? How Affect Influences the Marketing and Pricing of Financial Securities." *Financial Analysts Journal* 66:6, 40–54.

Baker, Malcom, and Jeffrey Wurgler. 2006. "Investor Sentiment and the Cross-Section of Stock Returns." *Journal of Finance* 61:4, 1645–1680.

Balloch, Adnan, Anamaria Nicolae, and Dennis Philip. 2015. "Stock Market Literacy, Trust, and Participation." *Review of Finance* 19:5, 1925–1963.

Barber, Brad M., Chip Heath, and Terrance Odean. 2003. "Good Reasons Sell: Reason-Based Choice among Group and Individual Investors in the Stock Market." *Management Science* 49:12, 1636–1652.

Barber, Brad M., and Terrance Odean. 2000a. "Trading Is Hazardous to Your Wealth: The Common Stock Investment Performance of Individual Investors." *Journal of Finance* 55:2, 773–806.

Barber, Brad M., and Terrance Odean. 2000b. "Too Many Cooks Spoil the Profits: Investment Club Performance." *Financial Analysts Journal* 56:1, 17–25.

Barber, Brad M., and Terrance Odean. 2001. "Boys Will Be Boys: Gender, Overconfidence, and Common Stock Investment." *Quarterly Journal of Economics* 116:1, 261–292.

Barber, Brad M., and Terrance Odean. 2008. "All That Glitters: The Effect of Attention and News on the Buying Behavior of Individual and Institutional Investors." *Review of Financial Studies* 21:2, 785–818.

Barber, Brad M., Terrance Odean, and Lu Zheng. 2005. "Out of Sight, out of Mind: The Effects of Expenses on Mutual Fund Flows." *Journal of Business* 78:6, 2095–2120.

Barber, Brad M., Yi-Tsung Lee, Yu-Jane Liu, and Terrance Odean. 2007. "Is the Aggregate Investor Reluctant to Realise Losses? Evidence from Taiwan." *European Financial Management* 13:3, 423–447.

Barber, Brad M., Yi-Tsung Lee, Yu-Jane Liu, and Terrance Odean. 2009. "Just How Much Do Individual Investors Lose by Trading?" *Review of Financial Studies* 22:2, 609–632.

Barber, Brad M., Yi-Tsung Lee, Yu-Jane Liu, and Terrance Odean. 2014. "The Cross-Section of Speculator Skill: Evidence from Day Trading." *Journal of Financial Markets* 18, 1–24.

Barberis, Nicholas, and Ming Huang. 2008. "Stocks as Lotteries: The Implications of Probability Weighting for Security Prices." *American Economic Review* 98:5, 2066–2100.

Barberis, Nicholas, and Wei Xiong. 2009. "What Drives the Disposition Effect? An Analysis of a Long-Standing Preference-Based Explanation." *Journal of Finance* 64:2, 751–784.

Barberis, Nicholas, and Wei Xiong. 2012. "Realization Utility." *Journal of Financial Economics* 104:2, 251–271.

Barnea, Amir, Henrik Cronqvist, and Stephan Siegel. 2010. "Nature or Nurture: What Determines Investor Behavior?" *Journal of Financial Economics* 98:3, 583–604.

Ben-David, Itzhak, and David Hirshleifer. 2012. "Are Investors Really Reluctant to Realize Their Losses? Trading Responses to Past Returns and the Disposition Effect." *Review of Financial Studies* 25:8, 2485–2532.

Bénabou, Roland, and Jean Tirole. 2011. "Identity, Morals, and Taboos: Beliefs as Assets." *Quarterly Journal of Economics* 126:2, 805–855.

Benartzi, Shlomo. 2001. "Excessive Extrapolation and the Allocation of 401(k) Accounts to Company Stock." *Journal of Finance* 56:5, 1747–1764.

Benjamin, Daniel J., David Cesarini, Christopher F. Chabris, Edward L. Glaeser, David I. Laibson, Vilmundur Guðnason, Tamara B. Harris, Lenore J. Launer, Shaun Purcell, Albert Vernon Smith, Magnus Johannesson, Patrik K.E. Magnusson, Jonathan P. Beauchamp, Nicholas A. Christakis, Craig S. Atwood, Benjamin Hebert, Jeremy Freese, Robert M. Hauser, Taissa S.

Hauser, Alexander Grankvist, Christina M. Hultman, and Paul Lichtenstein. 2012. "The Promises and Pitfalls of Genoeconomics." *Annual Review of Economics* 4, 627–662.

Benos, Evangelos, and Marek Jochec. 2013. "Patriotic Name Bias and Stock Returns." *Journal of Financial Markets* 16:3, 550–570.

Bergsma, Kelley, and Danling Jiang. 2016. "Cultural New Year Holidays and Stock Returns around the World." *Financial Management* 45:1, 3–35.

Białkowski, Jędrzej, Ahmad Etebari, and Tomasz Piotr Wisniewski. 2012. "Fast Profits: Investor Sentiment and Stock Returns During Ramadan." *Journal of Banking & Finance* 36:3, 835–845.

Bonaparte, Yosef, and Alok Kumar. 2013. "Political Activism, Information Costs, and Stock Market Participation." *Journal of Financial Economics* 107:3, 760–786.

Bonaparte, Yosef, Alok Kumar, and Jeremy K. Page. 2012. "Political Climate, Optimism, and Investment Decisions." American Finance Associaiton (AFA) 2012 Chicago Meetings Paper. Available at http://ssrn.com/abstract=1509168.

Brown, Jeffrey R., Zoran Ivković, Paul A. Smith, and Scott Weisbenner. 2008. "Neighbors Matter: Causal Community Effects and Stock Market Participation." *Journal of Finance* 63:3, 1509–1531.

Brunnermeier, Markus K., Christian Gollier, and Jonathan A. Parker. 2007. "Optimal Beliefs, Asset Prices, and the Preference for Skewed Returns." *American Economic Review* 97:2, 159–165.

Byun, Suk-Joon, Sonya S. Lim, and Sang Hyun Yun. 2016. "Continuing Overreaction and Stock Return Predictability." *Journal of Financial and Quantitative Analysis*. Forthcoming.

Cesarini, David, Christopher T. Dawes, Magnus Johannesson, Paul Lichtenstein, and Björn Wallace. 2009. "Genetic Variation in Preferences for Giving and Risk Taking." *Quarterly Journal of Economics* 124:2, 809–842.

Cesarini, David, Magnus Johannesson, Paul Lichtenstein, Örjan Sandewall, and Björn Wallace. 2010. "Genetic Variation in Financial Decision-Making." *Journal of Finance* 65:5, 1725–1754.

Chang, Tom, David H. Solomon, and Mark M. Westerfield. 2016. "Looking for Someone to Blame: Delegation, Cognitive Dissonance, and the Disposition Effect." *Journal of Finance* 71:1, 267–301.

Changwony, Frederick K., Kevin Campbell, and Isaac T. Tabner. 2015. "Social Engagement and Stock Market Participation." *Review of Finance* 19:1, 317–366.

Chiang, Yao-Min, David Hirshleifer, Yiming Qian, and Ann Sherman. 2011. "Do Investors Learn from Experience? Evidence from Frequent IPO Investors." *Review of Financial Studies* 24:5, 1560–1589.

Choi, James J., David Laibson, and Andrew Metrick. 2002. "How Does the Internet Affect Trading? Evidence from Investor Behavior in 401(k) Plans." *Journal of Financial Economics* 64:3, 397–421.

Christelis, Dimitris, Tullio Jappelli, and Mario Padula. 2010. "Cognitive Abilities and Portfolio Choice." *European Economic Review* 54:1, 18–38.

Cohen, Lauren. 2009. "Loyalty-Based Portfolio Choice." *Review of Financial Studies* 22:3, 1213–1245.

Cohen, Lauren, and Andrea Frazzini. 2008. "Economic Links and Predictable Returns." *Journal of Finance* 63:4, 1977–2011.

Cohen, Lauren, and Dong Lou. 2012. "Complicated Firms." *Journal of Financial Economics* 104, 383–400.

Cooper, Michael J., Orlin Dimitrov, and P. Raghavendra Rau. 2001. "A Rose.com by Any Other Name." *Journal of Finance* 56:6, 2371–2388.

Cooper, Michael J., Ajay Khorana, Igor Osobov, Ajay Patel, and P. Raghavendra Rau. 2005. "Managerial Actions in Response to a Market Downturn: Valuation Effects of Name Changes in the Dot.com Decline." *Journal of Corporate Finance* 11:1, 319–335.

Cronqvist, Henrik, and Stephan Siegel. 2014. "The Genetics of Investment Biases." *Journal of Financial Economics* 113:2, 215–234.

Cronqvist, Henrik, Stephan Siegel, and Frank Yu. 2015. "Value Versus Growth Investing: Why Do Different Investors Have Different Styles?" *Journal of Financial Economics* 117:2, 333–349.

Cronqvist, Henrik, Alessandro Previtero, Stephan Siegel, and Roderick E. White. 2016. "The Fetal Origins Hypothesis in Finance: Prenatal Environment, the Gender Gap, and Investor Behavior." *Review of Financial Studies* 29:3, 739–786.

D'Acunto, Francesco, Marcel Prokopczuk, and Michael Weber. 2015. "The Long Shadow of Jewish Persecution on Financial Decisions." Working Paper, University of California—Berkeley. Available at http://ssrn.com/abstract=2368073.

Da, Zhi, Joseph Engelberg, and Pengjie Gao. 2011. "In Search of Attention." *Journal of Finance* 66:5, 1461–1499.

Da, Zhi, Umit G. Gurun, and Mitch Warachka. 2014. "Frog in the Pan: Continuous Information and Momentum." *Review of Financial Studies* 27:7, 2171–2218.

Da, Zhi, Joseph Engelberg, and Pengjie Gao. 2015. "The Sum of All Fears Investor Sentiment and Asset Prices." *Review of Financial Studies* 28:1, 1–32.

Daniel, Kent D., David Hirshleifer, and Avanidhar Subrahmanyam. 1998. "Investor Psychology and Security Market Under and Overreactions." *Journal of Finance* 53:6, 1839–1885.

Daniel, Kent D., David Hirshleifer, and Avanidhar Subrahmanyam. 2001. "Overconfidence, Arbitrage, and Equilibrium Asset Pricing." *Journal of Finance* 56:3, 921–965.

DellaVigna, Stefano, and Joshua M. Pollet. 2009. "Investor Inattention and Friday Earnings Announcements." *Journal of Finance* 64:2, 709–749.

Derwall, Jeroen, Nadja Guenster, Rob Bauer, and Kees Koedijk. 2005. "The Eco-Efficiency Premium Puzzle." *Financial Analysts Journal* 61:2, 51–63.

Dhar, Ravi, and Ning Zhu. 2006. "Up Close and Personal: An Individual Level Analysis of the Disposition Effect." *Management Science* 52:5, 726–740.

Doran, James S., Danling Jiang, and David R. Peterson. 2012. "Gambling Preference and the New Year Effect of Assets with Lottery Features." *Review of Finance* 16:3, 685–731.

Dorn, Anne Jones, Daniel Dorn, and Paul Sengmueller. 2015. "Trading as Gambling." *Management Science* 61:10, 2376–2393.

Dreber, Anna, David G. Rand, Drew Fudenberg, and Martin A. Nowak. 2008. "Winners Don't Punish." *Nature* 452:7185, 348–351.

Edmans, Alex. 2011. "Does the Stock Market Fully Value Intangibles? Employee Satisfaction and Equity Prices." *Journal of Financial Economics* 101:3, 621–640.

Edmans, Alex, Diego Garcia, and Øyvind Norli. 2007. "Sports Sentiment and Stock Returns." *Journal of Finance* 62:4, 1967–1998.

Feng, Lei, and Mark S. Seasholes. 2005. "Do Investor Sophistication and Trading Experience Eliminate Behavioral Biases in Financial Markets?" *Review of Finance* 9:3, 305–351.

French, Kenneth R. 2008. "Presidential Address: The Cost of Active Investing." *Journal of Finance* 63:4, 1537–1573.

Frieder, Laura, and Avanidhar Subrahmanyam. 2004. "Nonsecular Regularities in Returns and Volume." *Financial Analysts Journal* 60:4, 29–34.

Friedman, Milton, and Leonard J. Savage. 1948. "The Utility Analysis of Choices Involving Risk." *Journal of Political Economy* 56:4, 279–304.

Frydman, Cary, Nickolas Barberis, Colin Camerer, Peter Bossaerts, and Antonio Rangel. 2014. "Using Neural Data to Test a Theory of Investor Behavior: An Application to Realization Utility." *Journal of Finance* 69:2, 907–946.

Frydman, Cary, Colin Camerer, Peter Bossaerts, and Antonio Rangel. 2011. "Maoa-L Carriers Are Better at Making Optimal Financial Decisions under Risk." *Proceedings of the Royal Society of London B: Biological Sciences* 278:1714, 2053–2059.

Frydman, Cary D., Samuel M. Hartzmark, and David H. Solomon. 2016. "Rolling Mental Accounts." *Review of Financial Studies*. Forthcoming.

Gamble, Kieth Jacks., Patricia A. Boyle, Lei Yu, and David A. Bennett. 2015. "Aging and Financial Decision Making." *Management Science* 61:11, 2603–2610.

Gao, Xiaohui, and Tse-Chun Lin. 2015. "Do Individual Investors Treat Trading as a Fun and Exciting Gambling Activity? Evidence from Repeated Natural Experiments." *Review of Financial Studies* 28:7, 2128–2166.

Georgarakos, Dimitris, and Giacomo Pasini. 2011. "Trust, Sociability, and Stock Market Participation." *Review of Finance* 15:4, 693–725.

Gervais, Simon, and Terrance Odean. 2001. "Learning to Be Overconfident." *Review of Financial Studies* 14:1, 1–27.

Giannetti, Mariassunta, and Tracy Yue Wang. 2016. "Corporate Scandals and Household Stock Market Participation." *Journal of Finance*. Forthcoming.

Greenwood, Robin, and Andrei Shleifer. 2014. "Expectations of Returns and Expected Returns." *Review of Financial Studies* 27:3, 714–746.

Grinblatt, Mark, and Matti Keloharju. 2001. "How Distance, Language, and Culture Influence Stockholdings and Trades." *Journal of Finance* 56:3 1053–1073.

Grinblatt, Mark, and Matti Keloharju. 2009. "Sensation Seeking, Overconfidence, and Trading Activity." *Journal of Finance* 64:2, 549–578.

Grinblatt, Mark, Matti Keloharju, and Juhani Linnainmaa. 2011. "IQ and Stock Market Participation." *Journal of Finance* 66:6, 2121–2164.

Grinblatt, Mark, Matti Keloharju, and Juhani T. Linnainmaa. 2012. "IQ, Trading Behavior, and Performance." *Journal of Financial Economics* 104:2, 339–362.

Grinblatt, Mark, Seppo Ikäheimo, Matti Keloharju, and Samuli Knüpfer. 2016. "IQ and Mutual Fund Choice." *Management Science* 62:4, 924–944.

Guiso, Luigi and Tullio Jappelli. 2005. "Awareness and Stock Market Participation." *Review of Finance* 9:4, 537–567.

Guiso, Luigi, Paola Sapienza, and Luigi Zingales. 2004. "The Role of Social Capital in Financial Development." *American Economic Review* 94:3, 526–556.

Guiso, Luigi, Paola Sapienza, and Luigi Zingales. 2006. "Does Culture Affect Economic Outcomes?" *Journal of Economic Perspectives* 20:2, 23–48.

Guiso, Luigi, Paola Sapienza, and Luigi Zingales. 2008. "Trusting the Stock Market." *Journal of Finance* 63:6, 2557–2600.

Guiso, Luigi, Paola Sapienza, and Luigi Zingales. 2013. "Time Varying Risk Aversion." *NBER Working Paper No. 19284*. Available at http://www.nber.org/papers/w19284.

Gurun, Umit G., Noah Stoffman, and Scott E. Yonker. 2015. "Trust Busting: The Effect of Fraud on Investor Behavior." Working Paper, University of Texas at Dallas. Available at http://ssrn.com/abstract=2664307.

Han, Bing, and David Hirshleifer. 2015. "Self-Enhancing Transmission Bias and Active Investing." Working Paper, University of Toronto. Available at http://ssrn.com/abstract=2032697.

Hartzmark, Samuel M. 2015. "The Worst, the Best, Ignoring All the Rest: The Rank Effect and Trading Behavior." *Review of Financial Studies* 28:4, 1024–1059.

Hirshleifer, David. 2015. "Behavioral Finance." *Annual Review of Financial Economics* 7, 133–159.

Hirshleifer, David and Tyler Shumway. 2003. "Good Day Sunshine: Stock Returns and the Weather." *Journal of Finance* 58:3, 1009–1032.

Hirshleifer, David and Danling Jiang. 2010. "A Financing-Based Misvaluation Factor and the Cross-Section of Expected Returns." *Review of Financial Studies* 23:9, 3401–3436.

Hirshleifer, David, Sonya Seongyeon Lim, and Siew Hong Teoh. 2009. "Driven to Distraction: Extraneous Events and Underreaction to Earnings News." *Journal of Finance* 64:5, 2289–2325.

Hirshleifer, David, Kewei Hou, Siew Hong Teoh, and Yinglei Zhang. 2004. "Do Investors Overvalue Firms with Bloated Balance Sheets?" *Journal of Accounting and Economics* 38, 297–331.

Hong, Harrison, and Marcin Kacperczyk. 2009. "The Price of Sin: The Effects of Social Norms on Markets." *Journal of Financial Economics* 93:1, 15–36.

Hong, Harrison, and Leonard Kostovetsky. 2012. "Red and Blue Investing: Values and Finance." *Journal of Financial Economics* 103:1, 1–19.

Hong, Harrison, Jeffrey D. Kubik, and Jeremy C. Stein. 2004. "Social Interaction and Stock-Market Participation." *Journal of Finance* 59:1, 137–163.

Huberman, Gur. 2001. "Familiarity Breeds Investment." *Review of Financial Studies* 14:3, 659–680.

Hvide, Hans K., and Per Östberg. 2015. "Social Interaction at Work." *Journal of Financial Economics* 117:3, 628–652.

Hwang, Byoung-Hyoun. 2011. "Country-Specific Sentiment and Security Prices." *Journal of Financial Economics* 100:2, 382–401.

Ingersoll, Jonathan E. Jr., and Lawrence J. Jin. 2013. "Realization Utility with Reference-Dependent Preferences." *Review of Financial Studies* 26:3, 723–767.

Ivković, Zoran, and Scott Weisbenner. 2005. "Local Does as Local Is: Information Content of the Geography of Individual Investors' Common Stock Investments." *Journal of Finance* 60:1, 267–306.

Jacobs, Heiko, and Martin Weber. 2016. "Losing Sight of the Trees for the Forest? Attention Allocation and Anomalies." *Quantitative Finance* 16:11, 1679–1693.

Jiang, Danling. 2013. "The Second Moment Matters! Cross Sectional Dispersion of Firm Valuations and Expected Returns." *Journal of Banking & Finance* 37:10, 3974–3992.

Jiang, Danling, and Sonya S. Lim. 2016. "Trust and Household Debt." *Review of Finance*. Forthcoming.

Kahneman, Daniel, and Amos Tversky. 1979. "Prospect Theory: An Analysis of Decision under Risk." *Econometrica* 47:2, 263–292.

Kamstra, Mark J., Lisa A. Kramer, and Maurice D. Levi. 2003. "Winter Blues: A Sad Stock Market Cycle." *American Economic Review* 93:1, 324–343.

Kaplanski, Guy, and Haim Levy. 2010. "Sentiment and Stock Prices: The Case of Aviation Disasters." *Journal of Financial Economics* 95:2, 174–201.

Karabulut, Yigitcan. 2013. "Can Facebook Predict Stock Market Activity?" Working Paper, Erasmus University. Available at http://ssrn.com/abstract=1919008.

Kaustia, Markku. 2010. "Prospect Theory and the Disposition Effect." *Journal of Financial and Quantitative Analysis* 45:3, 791–812.

Kaustia, Markku, and Samuli Knüpfer. 2008. "Do Investors Overweight Personal Experience? Evidence from IPO Subscriptions." *Journal of Finance* 63:6, 2679–2702.

Kaustia, Markku, and Samuli Knüpfer. 2012. "Peer Performance and Stock Market Entry." *Journal of Financial Economics* 104:2, 321–338.

Kaustia, Markku, and Elias Henrikki Rantapuska. 2016. "Does Mood Affect Trading Behavior?" *Journal of Financial Markets* 29:June, 1–26.

Kaustia, Markku, Samuli Knüpfer, and Sami Torstila. 2015. "Stock Ownership and Political Behavior: Evidence from Demutualizations." *Management Science* 62:4, 945–963.

Kaustia, Markku, and Sami Torstila. 2011. "Stock Market Aversion? Political Preferences and Stock Market Participation." *Journal of Financial Economics* 100:1, 98–112.

Kelly, Peter. 2014. "Dividends and Trust." Working Paper, University of Notre Dame. Available at http://ssrn.com/abstract=2311512.

Keloharju, Matti, Samuli Knüpfer, and Juhani Linnainmaa. 2012. "Do Investors Buy What They Know? Product Market Choices and Investment Decisions." *Review of Financial Studies* 25:10, 2921–2958.

Knüpfer, Samuli, Elias Henrikki Rantapuska, and Matti Sarvimäki. 2016. "Formative Experiences and Portfolio Choice: Evidence from the Finnish Great Depression." *Journal of Finance*. Forthcoming.

Korniotis, George M., and Alok Kumar. 2011. "Do Older Investors Make Better Investment Decisions?" *Review of Economics and Statistics* 93:1, 244–265.

Kuhnen, Camelia M., and Joan Y. Chiao. 2009. "Genetic Determinants of Financial Risk Taking." *PLOS ONE* 4:2, e4362.

Kuhnen, Camelia M., and Brian Knutson. 2005. "The Neural Basis of Financial Risk Taking." *Neuron* 47:5, 763–770.

Kuhnen, Camelia M., and Brian Knutson. 2011. "The Influence of Affect on Beliefs, Preferences, and Financial Decisions." *Journal of Financial and Quantitative Analysis* 46:03, 605–626.

Kumar, Alok. 2009. "Who Gambles in the Stock Market?" *Journal of Finance* 64:4, 1889–1933.

Kumar, Alok, and Sonya Seongyeon Lim. 2008. "How Do Decision Frames Influence the Stock Investment Choices of Individual Investors?" *Management Science* 54:6, 1052–1064.

Kumar, Alok, Jeremy K. Page, and Oliver G. Spalt. 2011. "Religious Beliefs, Gambling Attitudes, and Financial Market Outcomes." *Journal of Financial Economics* 102:3, 671–708.

Kumar, Alok, Alexandra Niessen-Ruenzi, and Oliver G. Spalt. 2015. "What's in a Name? Mutual Fund Flows When Managers Have Foreign-Sounding Names." *Review of Financial Studies* 28:8, 2281–2321.

Leung, Alvin, Ashish Agarwal, Prabhudev Konana, and Alok Kumar. 2016. "Network Analysis of Search Dynamics: The Case of Stock Habitats." *Management Science*. Forthcoming.

Li, Geng. 2014. "Information Sharing and Stock Market Participation: Evidence from Extended Families." *Review of Economics and Statistics* 96:1, 151–160.

Linnainmaa, Juhani. 2005. "The Individual Day Trader." Working Paper, University of Chicago. Available at http://faculty.chicagobooth.edu/juhani.linnainmaa/dtperformance.pdf.

Loewenstein, George F., Elke U. Weber, Christopher K. Hsee, and Ned Welch. 2001. "Risk as Feelings." *Psychological Bulletin* 127:2, 267–286.

Lou, Dong. 2014. "Attracting Investor Attention through Advertising." *Review of Financial Studies* 27:6, 1797–1829.

Malmendier, Ulrike, and Stefan Nagel. 2011. "Depression Babies: Do Macroeconomic Experiences Affect Risk Taking?" *Quarterly Journal of Economics* 126:1, 373–416.

Markowitz, Harry. 1952. "The Utility of Wealth." *Journal of Political Economy* 60:2, 151–158.

Massa, Massimo, and Andrei Simonov. 2006. "Hedging, Familiarity and Portfolio Choice." *Review of Financial Studies* 19:2, 633–685.

Mitton, Todd, and Keith Vorkink. 2007. "Equilibrium Underdiversification and the Preference for Skewness." *Review of Financial Studies* 20:4, 1255–1288.

Morse, Adair, and Sophie Shive. 2011. "Patriotism in Your Portfolio." *Journal of Financial Markets* 14:2, 411–440.

Odean, Terrance. 1998a. "Are Investors Reluctant to Realize Their Losses?" *Journal of Finance* 53:5, 1775–1798.

Odean, Terrance. 1998b. "Volume, Volatility, Price, and Profit When All Traders Are Above Average." *Journal of Finance* 53:6, 1887–1934.

Odean, Terrance. 1999. "Do Investors Trade Too Much?" *American Economic Review* 89:5, 1279–1298.

Olsen, Robert. 2012. "Trust: The Underappreciated Investment Risk Attribute." *Journal of Behavioral Finance* 13:4, 308–313.

Ozsoylev, Han N., Johan Walden, M. Deniz Yavuz, and Recep Bildik. 2014. "Investor Networks in the Stock Market." *Review of Financial Studies* 27:5, 1323–1366.

Putnam, Robert D. 2000. *Bowling Alone: The Collapse and Revival of American Community*. New Yori: Simon & Schuster.

Riedl, Arno, and Paul Smeets. 2014. "Social Preferences and Portfolio Choice." Working Paper, Maastricht University. Available at http://ssrn.com/abstract=2334641.

Scheinkman, Jose A., and Wei Xiong. 2003. "Overconfidence and Speculative Bubbles." *Journal of Political Economy* 111:6, 1183–1220.

Seasholes, Mark S., and Guojun Wu. 2007. "Predictable Behavior, Profits, and Attention." *Journal of Empirical Finance* 14:5, 590–610.

Seasholes, Mark S., and Ning Zhu. 2010. "Individual Investors and Local Bias." *Journal of Finance* 65:5, 1987–2010.

Shefrin, Hersh, and Meir Statman. 1985. "The Disposition to Sell Winners Too Early and Ride Losers Too Long: Theory and Evidence." *Journal of Finance* 40:3, 777–790.

Shefrin, Hersh, and Meir Statman. 2000. "Behavioral Portfolio Theory." *Journal of Financial and Quantitative Analysis* 35:02, 127–151.

Shive, Sophie. 2010. "An Epidemic Model of Investor Behavior." *Journal of Financial & Quantitative Analysis* 45:1, 169–198.

Statman, Meir, and Denys Glushkov. 2009. "The Wages of Social Responsibility." *Financial Analysts Journal* 65:4, 33–46.

Statman, Meir, Steven Thorley, and Keith Vorkink. 2006. "Investor Overconfidence and Trading Volume." *Review of Financial Studies* 19:4, 1531–1565.

Statman, Meir, Kenneth L. Fisher, and Deniz Anginer. 2008. "Affect in a Behavioral Asset Pricing Model." *Financial Analysts Journal* 64:2, 20–29.

Strahilevitz, Michal Ann, Terrance Odean, and Brad M Barber. 2011. "Once Burned, Twice Shy: How Naïve Learning, Counterfactuals, and Regret Affect the Repurchase of Stocks Previously Sold." *Journal of Marketing Research* 48:SPL, S102–S120.

Thaler, Richard. 1985. "Mental Accounting and Consumer Choice." *Marketing Science* 4:3, 199–214.

Tversky, Amos, and Daniel Kahneman. 1992. "Advances in Prospect Theory: Cumulative Representation of Uncertainty." *Journal of Risk and Uncertainty* 5:4, 297–323.

Weber, Martin, and Colin F. Camerer. 1998. "The Disposition Effect in Securities Trading: An Experimental Analysis." *Journal of Economic Behavior & Organization* 33:2, 167–184.

Weber, Martin, Elke U. Weber, and Alen Nosić. 2013. "Who Takes Risks When and Why: Determinants of Changes in Investor Risk Taking." *Review of Finance* 17:3, 847–883.

Yuan, Yu. 2015. "Market-Wide Attention, Trading, and Stock Returns." *Journal of Financial Economics* 116:3, 548–564.

Zajonc, Robert B. 1968. "Attitudinal Effects of Mere Exposure." *Journal of Personality and Social Psychology* 9:2, pt. 2, 1–27.

Zhong, Songfa, Salomon Israel, Hong Xue, Richard P. Ebstein, and Soo Hong Chew. 2009. "Monoamine Oxidase a Gene (Maoa) Associated with Attitude Towards Longshot Risks." *PLOS ONE* 4:12, e8516–e8516.

Zyphur, Michael J., Jayanth Narayanan, Richard D Arvey, and Gordon J. Alexander. 2009. "The Genetics of Economic Risk Preferences." *Journal of Behavioral Decision Making* 22:4, 367–377.

4

Institutional Investors

ALEXANDRE SKIBA
Assistant Professor of Economics
Department of Economics of Finance, University of Wyoming

HILLA SKIBA
Assistant Professor of Finance and Real Estate
Department of Finance and Real Estate, Colorado State University

Introduction

Behavioral biases in the financial markets are well documented. For example, evidence shows that investors are overconfident, prone to the disposition effect, exhibit loss aversion, demonstrate familiarity bias, and are driven by mood and sentiment. Although investors show tendencies toward cognitive and emotional biases, the literature also documents that the extent of the biases differs among investors. One of the most important differences is investor sophistication, so that less sophisticated investors make poorer choices with their investment decisions, which also leads to market underperformance, especially after considering trading costs. Less sophisticated investors are usually considered to be individual or retail investors, whereas more sophisticated investors are professional money managers and traders. The vast majority of behavioral studies focus on the behavioral biases of individual investors.

This chapter's purpose is to review the literature on behavioral biases. The chapter specifically examines how behavioral biases may influence more sophisticated investors (i.e., institutional investors). An *institutional investor* refers to a variety of professional investors, including banks, insurance companies, pension funds, endowment funds, mutual funds, and hedge funds, as well as investment professionals such as investment advisors and wealth managers. This chapter compares behavioral biases between institutional and individual investors. It also investigates whether differences exist among types of institutional investors, given the disparity between the objectives and the skill levels of such investors.

Although the literature on the behavioral biases of institutional investors is limited, it documents that institutional investors engage in trading behaviors that could be a symptom or a consequence of various behavioral biases. For example, institutional investors engage in *herding*, whereby their buying and selling behavior is correlated with other institutional investors' trades; they hold under-diversified, especially home-country biased, portfolios; and they use a momentum strategy in which they appear to buy past winners.

This chapter investigates the literature on these various trading behaviors and whether the behaviors are value reducing and/or whether they destabilize financial markets.

The evidence from the extant literature suggests that the behavior of institutional investors is rational compared to that of individual investors. Cognitive and emotional mistakes that individuals make are largely absent among institutional investors. Yet, some contrarian evidence exists. Mood seems to drive institutional investors. Also, cultural differences influence trading and portfolio allocation of institutions, but to a lesser extent relative to the individual investors. Although some behavioral biases are present among the professional money managers, overall the institutional investors truly are "smart."

Trading behaviors that could be a symptom of some behavioral bias are actually value generating for the institutions. For example, herd behavior seems to be information driven rather than based on fear and greed, or other behavioral factors. In fact, herding by institutional investors appears to be price stabilizing rather than price destabilizing. Similarly, recent empirical literature shows that portfolio under-diversification among institutional investors generates positive risk-adjusted returns.

The chapter has the following organization. The first section reviews the literature on behavioral biases of institutional investors. The next section investigates differences in behavioral biases across types of institutions, specifically based on the sophistication of the institutional managers. The following section reviews three trading behaviors of institutional investors that could be symptoms of behavioral biases: herding, momentum trading, and under-diversification. The chapter then reviews the literature on each of the documented trading behaviors, shows how institutional investors engage in these trading behaviors, and explains how the behavior affects institutional returns and market efficiency.

The chapter concludes by investigating whether institutional investors take advantage of individuals prone to behavioral biases. Institutions are becoming increasingly educated about behavioral finance, which is now included in university curriculums and textbooks worldwide. Behavioral finance is also a part of professional education, such as the Chartered Financial Analyst (CFA) curriculum. A growing body of literature documents that institutions are profiting from stock market anomalies and systemic changes in securities prices, caused by behavioral biases. For example, institutions appear to profit from post-earnings announcement drifts. Also, during extreme swings in the market, such as during market bubbles and consecutive market crashes, institutions, unlike individuals, appear to exit their positions from overvalued securities before the market turns.

Behavioral Biases of Institutional Investors

The literature documents that sentiment, fads, and emotions drive less experienced individual investors (Shiller, Fisher, and Friedman 1984; De Long, Shleifer, Summers, and Waldmann 1990). Because of poor decision making, individuals underperform the market both before and after fees (Barber and Odean 2001). Because professional investors are generally on the other side of these poor trades, they appear to trade rationally and profit at the expense of individual investors. The finance literature documents some compelling evidence to support this claim. For example, Barber, Lee, Liu, and Odean (2009) find that in the Taiwanese market, individual investors lose 3.8 percentage points annually and it is institutional investors who mainly harvest this loss. The following sections discuss the most commonly studied behavioral biases (overconfidence, disposition effect, and familiarity bias) and how the empirical evidence for these biases differs for institutions and individual investors.

OVERCONFIDENCE

Much of the seminal work on overconfidence in behavioral finance is based on samples of individual investors and is typically proxied by gender (Barber and Odean 2001; Gervais and Odean 2001). Evidence on the overconfidence of institutional investors is less available, perhaps because finding a suitable proxy is more difficult. Chuang and Susmel (2011) investigated overconfidence among traders in Taiwan, and show that Taiwanese individual investors are much more prone to overconfident trading behavior compared to the institutional investors. Chou and Wang (2011) also examine overconfidence among different types of investors in Taiwan. They find that overconfidence is present among both individual and institutional investors, but the level of overconfidence among institutional investors is much lower. However, institutional investors buy more aggressively after they have experienced gains, which is consistent with overconfidence hypothesis. Chen, Kim, Nofsinger, and Rui (2007) study overconfidence in a sample of Chinese trading accounts, which includes both individual and institutional investors. After splitting their sample into individual (less sophisticated) and institutional (more sophisticated) investors, they find that although overconfidence bias is present in both groups, the bias is stronger in the sample of less sophisticated, individual investors.

Gender Bias

Another stream of literature compares trading choices between male and female professional money managers. Although these studies are not always tests of the overconfidence of professional investors, the results are still consistent with the more direct overconfidence studies previously discussed. Barber and Odean (2001) were the first to document that male investors make poorer trading choices than female investors. They attribute this to overconfidence. Several other studies have investigated gender differences among professional money manager. Atkinson, Boyce, Frye, and Frey (2003) study how gender affects mutual fund management, and they find no real differences between the genders. They suggest that perhaps differences between the genders, documented among individual investors, change when factoring in experience and sophistication. Similarly, Bliss and Potter (2002) hypothesize that female mutual fund managers are less overconfident compared with their male counterparts; but contrary to their prediction, they find no difference in the turnover rates of female managers. Beckmann and Menkhoff (2008) also find in their sample of 649 fund managers from the United States, Germany, Italy, and Thailand, that overconfidence among female and male mutual fund managers is not statistically significantly different. Overall, gender differences in overconfident tendencies do not seem to exist among professional managers. This evidence may suggest that experience and investor sophistication eliminate, or at least lessen, common behavioral biases, a conclusion that is similar to other evidence discussed in this section.

DISPOSITION EFFECT

The *disposition effect* is an investor's tendency to sell winning securities too soon and to retain losing securities too long. Most studies document the disposition effect among individual investors, but some studies also use samples of either institutional investors or both types of investors. The results are similar to those in the overconfidence literature previously reviewed.

Chou and Wang (2011) study the disposition effect among both individual and institutional trades in Taiwan. Their evidence shows that the disposition effect holds true only among individual investors. Similarly, in a study of individual and professionally managed accounts in Israel, Shapira and Venezia (2001) find that the disposition effect is present among both types of investors, but is much stronger for individual investors than for professionally managed accounts. Feng and Seasholes (2005) study investors' sophistication, trading experience, and the disposition effect; the authors report strong evidence that investors' sophistication, combined with trading experience, eliminates the reluctance to sell losing stocks. Experience and sophistication also reduce the propensity to realize gains too soon. Although their sample consists only of individuals, this finding still supports the idea that more sophisticated institutional investors with long trading experience are less likely to suffer from the disposition effect.

O'Connell and Teo (2009) investigate institutional investors' disposition effect in U.S. markets and find little evidence that institutions are prone to the disposition effect. However, the authors find evidence that past performance affects investors so that they lower their risk-taking after losses and increase their risk-taking after gains, which is consistent with dynamic loss aversion and overconfidence. Statman, Thorley, and Vorkink (2006) study overconfidence and the disposition effect in U.S. markets and find evidence for both. Specifically, their evidence shows that stocks with large historical gains experience larger trading volume in subsequent time periods. Interestingly, the relation of past returns and volume is strongest in the earlier part of the sample and in smaller securities. This finding suggests that stocks dominated by individual rather than institutional investors show greater evidence of both behavioral biases. Similar to the U.S. result, Chen et al. (2007) find that in a Chinese sample of individual and institutional trading accounts, evidence exists for similar results regarding overconfidence and the disposition effect is present in both groups of traders. However, the bias is stronger in the sample of less sophisticated individual investors.

By contrast, Frazzini (2006), conducting a study of U.S. mutual fund holdings and the disposition effect, finds that U.S. mutual fund managers exhibit the disposition effect and that such behavior also negatively affects their returns. However, the evidence still aligns with findings that more sophisticated investors are less subject to behavioral biases. Specifically, Frazzini reports that successful mutual fund managers are more likely to sell their losers than are underperforming managers. Coval and Shumway (2005) finds that U.S. futures trades suffer from loss aversion, which refers to people's tendency to strongly prefer avoiding *losses* over acquiring gains. Also, Locke and Mann (2005) study professional U.S. commodities traders and find that professional traders hold onto their losers for longer than their winners, but the behavior does not seem to produce lower than average returns, contrary to the findings by Coval and Shumway (2005).

FAMILIARITY AND REPRESENTATIVENESS BIAS

In a large universe of securities, investors must narrow the set of available investment options. One way investors can to do this is by using mental shortcuts and heuristics, which can ultimately lead to mean-variance inefficient portfolios. Familiarity and representativeness biases are examples of such heuristics. *Familiarity bias* is the tendency of investors to invest in what they know or what is familiar to them. *Representativeness bias* is often linked to investors' tendency to extrapolate probabilities for future events from past or recent outcomes. Similar to overconfidence and the disposition effect, familiarity and representativeness bias studies often use samples of individual investors (Huberman 2001), but little empirical research is available on institutional investors.

In a direct comparison study of individual versus institutional investors, Barber and Odean (2008) find that individual investors are much more likely to be drawn to attention-grabbing stocks, such as stocks in the news or those with large price swings. Individual investors do not possess the same resources as large institutions. Because of their limited attention, individual investors need to narrow the set more than do institutions, and consequently they are much more likely to choose attention-grabbing securities. Limited attention and resources are also major reasons for a familiarity bias-based portfolio construction.

Similar to the evidence for overconfidence and the disposition effect, Chen et al. (2007) find that in the Chinese sample of individual and institutional trading accounts, representativeness bias is present in both groups of traders. However, the bias is stronger in the sample of less sophisticated individual investors.

Studies involving familiarity bias often examine investors' portfolio composition, because familiarity bias can result in under-diversified portfolios; for example, these are often home-biased portfolios, in which investors over-weight the familiar home market. (This chapter discusses equity home bias and its consequences for institutional investors in more detail in a later section.) The evidence shows that institutional investors also hold home-biased portfolios. Further, some research links home bias with familiarity bias. Ke, Ng, and Wang (2010) study investments in foreign markets made by mutual funds, and find that managers prefer to invest in firms in foreign markets that have a presence in their domestic markets. The authors rule out an information advantage as a possible explanation for this finding, concluding that familiarity bias is likely to be the driver. Chan, Covrig, and Ng (2005) find that home bias and foreign market underweighting by mutual funds are associated with economic development and familiarity variables. The authors proxy familiarity by a common language between the investors' home market and foreign markets, geographic distance, and bilateral trade flows.

Heterogeneity Among Types

As investor sophistication increases from individual investors to institutional investors, the existing research shows that behavioral biases decrease and even disappear. Large heterogeneity exists in the sophistication level among different institutional investors. For instance, hedge fund managers earn the highest compensation and attract the top talent, and thus are likely to be the most sophisticated investors, followed by managers of other actively managed, well-compensated institutions such as mutual funds, independent investment advisors, pension funds, and endowments. The less sophisticated managers are then in the more passive institutions, such as insurance companies and banks (Lerner, Schoar, and Wongsungwai 2007; French 2008; Choi, Fedeia, Skiba, and Sokolyk 2016). Based on this finding, studies that examine the trading behavior of different institutional types are likely to find fewer behavioral biases among hedge fund and mutual funds managers compared to the passive investor types.

The research in this area is limited. Barber, Lee, Liu, and Odean (2007) study the disposition effect in the Taiwanese stock market among different groups of investors. Their evidence shows that the disposition effect exhibits a strong presence in the market. Besides individual investors, corporate investors (private and government-owned firms) and dealers (financial firms) are subject to the disposition effect. By contrast, mutual funds and foreign investors (foreign banks, insurance companies, securities firms, and mutual funds) are not subject to the disposition effect.

Although research that directly investigates behavioral biases among institutional types is limited, several papers have examined how institutional investors' heterogeneity is reflected in the level of their sophistication and performance. Lerner et al. (2007) examine different institutional types including investment advisors, banks, pension funds, insurance companies, and endowments. They find that endowments earn the highest returns, specifically in their private equity investments. Similarly, Bennett, Sias, and Starks (2003) document a difference between raw returns among different types of institutional investors, so that mutual funds and advisors earn larger returns compared with managers at banks and in insurance. According to Choi et al. (2016), investor sophistication is related to information advantage and subsequent performance, thus, hedge funds, mutual funds, and advisors, followed by endowments and pensions and then by banks and insurance companies, earn the highest risk-adjusted returns on their global portfolios. The fact that the level of investor sophistication and returns is positively related, and that behavioral biases are more common among less sophisticated investors, suggests that behavioral biases might at least partially explain the observed differential in risk-adjusted returns between institutional types.

Institutional Trading Behavior

As previously discussed, the research on behavioral biases among institutional investors is limited but increasing. However, large streams of literature exist on the trading behaviors of institutional investors that could be symptoms of some underlying behavioral biases. The following sections provide a review of these well-documented trading behaviors and discuss the consequences of each to market efficiency and/or investors' risk-adjusted performance. The trading behaviors include the following: (1) momentum trading by institutions, which could be driven by representativeness bias, self-attribution, and/or overconfidence, and would have a destabilizing effect on the financial markets; (2) herding, which could be driven by behavioral motivations, such as fads, fear, or greed, or reputational concerns, and would have a destabilizing effect on the financial markets; and (3) portfolio under-diversification, which could be a symptom of overconfidence or familiarity bias, both which would most likely result in lower risk-adjusted returns to the investor.

MOMENTUM TRADING

Since Jegadeesh and Titman's (1993) seminal work, others have documented momentum in security prices across various asset classes and markets. Momentum in security prices is usually linked to market inefficiency, and the result is correlation in security returns from one period to another. Momentum can be present in two ways. Prices either are pushed away from their fundamental values because of fear and greed or are extrapolated from past returns to predict the future. Alternatively, markets fail to incorporate information into the prices efficiently but, rather, over extended periods of time. Institutional investors tend to be momentum traders on a large scale (Grinblatt, Titman, and Wermers 1995; Nofsinger and Sias 1999; Wermers 1999; Badrinath and Wahal 2002). Empirical evidence supports the following explanations about momentum: (1) institutions chase past winners and extrapolate past outcomes into the future; or (2) institutions take advantage of market inefficiency upon discovering that some fundamental information is slow to incorporate, and hence institutional trading helps push the security prices toward their fundamental values.

Evidence has documented momentum trading among all types of institutions. Nofsinger and Sias (1999) find that institutions are momentum traders when they examine the intra-period trades of individual securities. Momentum trading is also present in mutual funds (Grinblatt et al. 1995; Wermers 1999). Badrinath and Wahal (2002) investigate institutional investors' entry and exit decisions into and out of securities. They find that institutions trade on momentum when they initiate positions in securities. Yet, some variation in momentum trading exists across institutional investors. Evidence by Badrinath and Wahal shows that investment advisors are more likely to be momentum traders than are pension funds and banks. Lakonishok, Shleifer, and Vishny (1992) investigate pension funds' momentum trading and find little supporting evidence.

The evidence generally shows that the price impact of momentum trading by institutional investors is overall price stabilizing. This observation supports the notion that institutional investors do not trade on momentum because of greed, fear, overconfidence, or representativeness bias but, rather, because of fundamental reasons. For example, in a sample of institutional investors, Badrinath and Wahal (2002) find little evidence for price-destabilizing effects of institutional momentum trading.

Hvidkjaer (2006) conducts a trade-level study that provides support for institutional investors stabilizing momentum trading. Based on an analysis of large and small trades, the author finds that small traders' underreaction may be a reason for the observed momentum effect. In contrast, institutional investors do not underreact. Choe, Kho, and Stulz (1999) discover similar evidence in the Korean markets, while specifically examining trading behavior by foreigners and Korean institutional investors versus Korean individual investors. The authors find that institutions in Korean markets are largely momentum traders. Again, no evidence indicates that the traders would have a price-destabilizing effect on the Korean market.

HERDING BEHAVIOR

Much evidence shows that institutional investors tend to herd or to follow each other's trades (Lakonishok et al. 1992; Sias 2004). Herding in asset markets occurs within individual securities, within industries, and within entire markets. Herding, at least in the popular media, is often associated with some irrational behavior, where investors are chasing fads (Shiller et al. 1984) and are motivated by fear and greed or other behavioral reasons. Institutional investors may also have reputational concerns; consequently, they would rather be wrong within a group than on their own (Scharfstein and Stein 1990; Trueman 1994). If the reasons for herding are irrational or behavioral in nature, then herding should destabilize asset prices and push them away from their fundamental values. However, herding could be rational behavior if it results in more efficient markets and/or higher risk-adjusted returns for investors.

The empirical evidence shows a large propensity by institutions to herd in and out of securities and markets. The vast majority of evidence supports information-based reasons for such herding. These information-based, rational reasons for herding include cascading and investigative herding. In about half of the studies, the documented herding occurs because of informational cascades. *Informational cascades* occur when institutional investors intentionally follow each other from security to security, but only because they infer information from each other's trades. The other half of the studies find that herding behavior is investigative in nature. This is when institutional investors analyze the same underlying fundamental information and draw the same conclusions about the securities' fair values, and they trade similarly; yet, the observed movement in and out of securities is unintentional and based only on underlying information. The consequence of both information-based herding tendencies is that prices adjust faster to fundamental information. In other words, herding is information-based and thus increases market efficiency rather than destabilizes the markets.

Evidence documents herding by institutional investors across markets, asset classes, and different types of institutional investors. Sias (2004) finds that at the security level, institutional investors in the United States follow each other from security to security, or that their trades are correlated with their own and other institutions' lagged trades. He also finds that institutions are momentum traders. However, momentum trading only partially explains the herding. According to Sias, the most likely explanation for herding is that institutions follow each other's trades, but that herding is information-based and institutions infer information from others (cascading) rather than are just chasing fads.

Grinblatt et al. (1995) report widespread herding behavior among managers at U.S.-based mutual funds. In support of a rational explanation of herding, the authors find little evidence for herding that was intentionally following others. Kim and Nofsinger (2005) study the Japanese market and herding by its institutional investors. The authors also documented that institutions herd in Japan, but to a lesser extent than they do in U.S. markets. Herding in Japanese markets is more likely to be investigative, and the price impact of herding is generally positive, so that investors' herding speeds up the price adjustments, rather than destabilizes them.

Nofsinger and Sias (1999) report a positive relation between changes in institutional ownership and returns on securities. Thus, momentum in security returns also appears to be related to institutional herding. That is, a positive relation exists between institutional demand and contemporaneous security returns. The authors also report little evidence of mean reversion in the security returns after periods of positive demand and positive security returns. This finding suggests that institutional demand and momentum in securities incorporates information faster into the security prices, instead of irrational return chasing by institutions. In other words, institutions help to create faster price adjustment and greater market efficiency.

PORTFOLIO UNDER-DIVERSIFICATION AND EQUITY HOME BIAS

The finance literature documents the phenomenon of portfolio under-diversification. According to the traditional asset pricing theory stemming from the work of Markowitz (1952), investors should hold diversified portfolios. Evidence exists, however, that investors, including institutional investors, do not always do this. For example, studies document under-diversification with respect to investors' domestic and foreign holdings, so that investors have a tendency to over-weight their home market relative to its capitalization weight (i.e., investors have a home bias).

Equity home bias is widespread in international portfolio investment. For example, U.S. institutional investors hold about 86 percent of their assets in domestic equities, whereas the U.S. share of the world portfolio is only about 40 percent. This difference means that U.S. investors hold a 46 percentage point over-weight in their domestic market. Similar figures occur across the globe (Chen et al. 2007; Anderson, Fedenia, Hirschey, and Skiba 2011; Choi et al. 2016). Also, the small portion of the portfolio invested in foreign countries is usually allocated to countries that are the most similar and the most correlated with the investor's home market (Tesar and Werner 1995; Chan et al. 2005; Anderson et al. 2011).

Evidence documents equity home bias across all investor groups. Many reasons led to an equity home bias in the past that are no longer valid. Capital controls, new investment vehicles, and ease of trading over the Internet now make foreign equity markets accessible to all investors. Although the persistent equity bias presents a puzzle, various behavioral reasons provide possible explanations. In the behavioral finance literature, portfolio under-diversification is often a symptom of some behavioral bias. For example, evidence links overconfidence and familiarity to portfolio under-diversification.

French and Poterba (1991) were the first to document equity home bias. They offer several explanations for it, including over-optimism about the prospects of the domestic securities. Based on survey evidence, Strong and Xu (2003) find that institutional managers are more optimistic about domestic equities. This relative optimism implies a positive bias toward domestic equities and a negative bias toward foreign equities. In turn, these biases would lead to over-weighting domestic equities and under-weighting foreign equities. Based on survey evidence from institutional managers from the United States, United Kingdom, Japan, and continental Europe, Strong and Xu also find evidence of familiarity-based asset allocation by institutional investors.

To investigate whether the observed under-diversification is irrational behavior driven by familiarity bias, over-optimism, overconfidence, or a rational choice, researchers have investigated the performance consequences of under-diversification specific to institutional investors. First, several authors of theoretical papers contend that under-diversification can also be a rational strategy. The seminal papers in this area include Merton (1987), Gehrig (1993), Levy and Livingston (1995), and more recent work by Van Nieuwerburgh and Veldkamp (2009, 2010). If under-diversification is a rational strategy driven by information advantage, then it should not deteriorate performance.

Although individual investors with under-diversified position also underperform the market even before accounting for excessive trading and related fees, the same is not necessarily true for institutional investors. Choi et al. (2016) find that under-diversified positions relative to the optimal efficient world market portfolio earn higher risk-adjusted returns than do globally diversified portfolios. This evidence suggests that under-diversified portfolios can be value enhancing. The authors also report that more skilled investors are more likely to deviate from the optimal portfolios, providing further evidence that under-diversification can be optimal behavior if it derives from a rational, information-based process. Coval and Moskowitz (2001) find similar evidence in the United States. Studies have documented local bias in U.S. equities across investor classes and often have linked it to familiarity bias in investment choices. Thus, investors choose to irrationally invest in familiar securities (Huberman 2001). Coval and Moskowitz also find that institutional investors, especially mutual funds, actually outperform when they hold locally concentrated portfolios and outperform in nearby securities. This finding provides further evidence that under-diversification, if motivated by some information advantage, can be optimal.

Other Drivers of Institutions' Trading Behavior

This section reviews two emerging streams of literature in behavioral finance that deal with how mood and national culture influence investor behavior. Many of the papers in these streams use institutional investors as their subjects. Their results show that institutional investors are often moody traders and that the national culture of the investors' home markets influences their trading behavior.

MOOD

Investor mood is an important determinant of security returns and it affects stock markets around the world. For example, Hirschleifer and Shumway (2003) show that the amount of sunlight, associated with the positive mood of investors, has a corresponding positive effect on market returns. Kamstra, Kramer, and Levi (2003) find that seasonal affective disorder (SAD), which results from people's experiencing fewer hours of daylight during certain times of the year, is related to an increase in investor risk aversion and security returns. The impact is also stronger in higher latitudes, where the hours of daylight fluctuate more from season to season.

The evidence on behavioral biases consistently shows that more sophisticated investors are less susceptible to psychological influences. However, the evidence also shows that mood affects the trading behavior of institutional investors. Goetzmann and Zhu (2005) study weather patterns, comparing it to the stock market trading activity of individuals across different cities. Their findings show no relation between cloud coverage and trading activity. The authors suggest that, instead of traders, perhaps market makers and other professional agents located in the cities of the stock exchanges may be driving the effect. In a more direct study of institutions and mood, Goetzmann, Kim, Kumar, and Wang (2015) examine weather patterns and they show that relative overpricing of securities of the Dow Jones Industrial Average (DJIA) increases on cloudier days, as does the securities-selling propensities of institutional investors. The authors also construct a stock-level mood proxy from the institutional investors' holdings, and find that this mood proxy is positively related to a stock's returns, especially in more difficult-to-arbitrage securities.

CULTURE

Culture and finance have become a popular topic in recent finance literature. Studies of samples of both different investors and markets show that culture influences economic exchange, such as saving and investment decisions, market participation rates, and cross-border investment and trade (Guiso, Sapienza, and Zingales 2009). In many of these culture studies, institutional investors are the main subjects, with evidence showing that culture influences institutional investors.

In a study of investors' decision making in Finland, Grinblatt and Keloharju (2001) find that the proximity, language, and cultural similarity of investors and the chief executive officers (CEOs) of the companies are all significantly related to an investor's allocation decision. The authors' dataset contained both individual and institutional investors. The authors find that both groups behave this way, but the bias toward culturally similar firms is greater for individual investors. Furthermore, Grinblatt and Keloharju document the differences in institutional investors, in which the less savvy institutional investors, specifically nonprofits and governmental organizations, exhibit stronger preference for culturally similar firms compared to more financially savvy institutional investors.

Beracha, Fedenia, and Skiba (2014) show that institutions' trading frequency declines when shifting from home markets to culturally similar foreign countries, and on to culturally distant environments. The authors also find that institutional investors from cultures marked by lower levels of trust toward others, as well as higher levels of ambiguity aversion, generally trade with lower frequencies, perhaps because of their lower levels of faith in market-based finance generally.

As previously discussed, institutions hold home-biased portfolios and under-diversify their foreign holdings. Although many variables can explain these under-diversification patterns, one answer concerns national culture. For example, portfolio allocation studies by Anderson et al. (2011) on institutional investors and by Beugelsdijk and Frijns (2010) on mutual funds across the global markets find that national culture is significantly related to the heterogeneity in an institution's level of home bias. More specifically, these papers investigated the effect of Hofstede's (1980, 2001) uncertainty avoidance, masculinity, and individualism on home bias, and they find that uncertainty avoidance is positively related to the level of home bias. Moreover, evidence by Anderson et al. (2011) shows that a cultural similarity of the investor's home market to the asset's home market is positively related to the level of asset holdings. Cultural distance, as measured along Hofstede's primary dimensions of culture, decreases cross-border portfolio allocation, so that institutional investors prefer culturally similar markets.

Summary and Conclusions

This chapter provides a synthesis of the literature on institutional investors' trading behavior. The chapter initially investigated whether common behavioral biases—overconfidence, the disposition effect, familiarity, and representativeness biases—are present in the trades of financial institutions. As discussed, overall the literature provides little evidence that institutions make the same behavioral mistakes as do individual investors in their trades. The chapter also investigated how behavioral biases can explain institutions' trading behavior—herding, momentum trading, and under-diversification. As shown, the literature finds that institutional trading behavior is rational and mainly driven by information-based motivations. Institutional investors apparently benefit from their strategies and make markets more efficient. Thus, the literature suggests that sophisticated investors make rational decisions in their trading choices and are free of the common behavioral downfalls documented as befallen individual investors.

Institutional investors are becoming increasingly educated about behavioral finance and the inefficiencies that behavioral biases can create in the stock markets. Institutions are apparently aware enough of potential biases as to take advantage of them For example, Ke and Ramalingegodwa (2005) show that transient institutional investors (i.e., those investors with a shorter-term view and with active engagement) take advantage of the post-earnings announcement drift in their trades. Cohen, Gompers, and Vuolteenaho (2002) show that institutional investors are, on average, on the right side of trades when trading on market underreaction to cash-flow surprises, Furthermore, institutions seem to exploit such trading at the expense of individual investors.

The evidence also shows that institutional investors construct trading strategies based on mood. For example, Bollen, Mao, and Zeng (2011) find that mood in social media predicts DJIA returns; several hedge funds developed a strategy based on this research paper. Also, many hedge funds employ psychologists on their management teams, because sophisticated investors understand the importance of mood and sentiment to security prices.

Behavioral biases also affect institutional investors through the underlying investor base. A perfectly rational institutional manager with perfect ability to analyze securities' risk and return characteristics still needs to be aware of underlying investor tendencies for behavioral bias. Indeed, understanding the underlying investor base is an especially important topic in the field of wealth management. Different models of individual behavior help wealth managers understand the wide range of clients and how to best serve their individual needs. For example, Pompian (2012) has divided clients into four distinct groups: preservers, followers, independents, and accumulators; each group has its unique characteristics, as well as displays the most likely behavioral biases. Pompian's work has become a centerpiece of attention for the behavioral finance sections of the CFA program, taught to the future institutional managers.

DISCUSSION QUESTIONS

1. Discuss whether institutional investors are subject to behavioral biases to the same extent as individual investors.

2. Explain whether mood, not directly related to financial fundamentals, affects institutional investors.
3. Discuss whether evidence showing that institutions herd with their trades supports irrational (market destabilizing) or rational (market stabilizing) reasons for institutional herding.
4. Identify how institutions can exploit behavior biases of individual investors' in their trading choices.
5. Discuss how institutional agents can use behavioral finance to benefit their clients.

REFERENCES

Anderson, Christopher W., Mark Fedenia, Mark Hirschey, and Hilla Skiba. 2011. "Cultural Influences on Home Bias and International Diversification." *Journal of Banking and Finance* 35:4, 916–934.

Atkinson, Stanley M., Samantha Boyce, Baird Frye, and Melissa B. Frey. 2003. "Do Female Mutual Fund Managers Manage Differently?" *Journal of Financial Research* 26:1, 1–18.

Badrinath, S. G., and Sunil Wahal. 2002. "Momentum Trading by Institutions." *Journal of Finance* 57:6, 2449–2478.

Barber, Brad M., Yi-Tsung Lee, Yu-Jane Liu, and Terrance Odean. 2007. "Is the Aggregate Investor Reluctant to Realise Losses? Evidence from Taiwan." *European Financial Management* 13:3, 423–447.

Barber, Brad M., Yi-Tsung Lee, Yu-Jane Liu, and Terrance Odean. 2009. "Just How Much Do Individual Investors Lose by Trading?" *Review of Financial Studies* 22:2, 609–632.

Barber, Brad M., and Terrance Odean. 2001. "Boys Will Be Boys: Gender, Overconfidence, and Common Stock Investment." *Quarterly Journal of Economics* 116:1, 261–292.

Barber, Brad M., and Terrance Odean. 2008. "All That Glitters: The Effect of Attention and News on the Buying Behavior of Individual and Institutional Investors." *Review of Financial Studies* 21:2, 785–818.

Beckmann, Daniela, and Lukas Menkhoff. 2008. "Will Women Be Women? Analyzing the Gender Difference among Financial Experts." *Kyklos* 61:3, 364–384.

Bennett, James A., Richard W. Sias, and Laura T. Starks. 2003. "Greener Pastures and the Impact of Dynamic Institutional Preferences." *Review of Financial Studies* 16:4, 1203–1238.

Beracha, Eli, Mark Fedenia, and Hilla Skiba. 2014. "Culture's Impact on Institutional Investors' Trading Frequency." *International Review of Financial Analysis* 31:January, 34–47.

Beugelsdijk, Sjoerd, and Bart Frijns. 2010. "A Cultural Explanation of the Foreign Bias in International Asset Allocation." *Journal of Banking and Finance* 34:9, 2121–2131.

Bliss, Richard T., and Mark E. Potter. 2002. "Mutual Fund Managers: Does Gender Matter?" *Journal of Business & Economic Studies* 8:1, 1–91.

Bollen, Johan, Huina Mao, and Xiaojun Zeng. 2011. "Twitter Mood Predicts the Stock Market." *Journal of Computational Science* 2:1, 1–8.

Chan, Kalok, Vicentiu Covrig, and Lilian Ng. 2005. "What Determines the Domestic Bias and Foreign Bias? Evidence from Mutual Fund Equity Allocations Worldwide." *Journal of Finance* 60:3, 1495–1534.

Chen, Gongmeng, Kenneth A. Kim, John R. Nofsinger, and Oliver M. Rui. 2007. "Trading Performance, Disposition Effect, Overconfidence, Representativeness Bias, and Experience of Emerging Market Investors." *Journal of Behavioral Decision Making* 20:4, 425–451.

Choe, Hyuk, Bong-Chan Kho, and René M. Stulz. 1999. "Do Foreign Investors Destabilize Stock Markets? The Korean Experience in 1997." *Journal of Financial Economics* 54:2, 227–264.

Choi, Nicole, Mark Fedenia, Hilla Skiba, and Tatyana Sokolyk. 2016. "Portfolio Concentration and Performance of Institutional Investors Worldwide." *Journal of Financial Economics*. Forthcoming.

Chou, Robin K., and Yun-Yi Wang. 2011. "A Test of the Different Implications of the Overconfidence and Disposition Hypotheses." *Journal of Banking and Finance* 35:8, 2037–2046.

Chuang, Wen-I, and Rauli Susmel. 2011. "Who Is the More Overconfident Trader? Individual vs. Institutional Investors." *Journal of Banking and Finance* 35:7, 1626–1644.

Cohen, Randolph P., Paul A. Gompers, and Tuomo Vuolteenaho. 2002. "Who Underreacts to Cash Flow News? Evidence from Trading between Individuals and Institutions." *Journal of Financial Economics* 66:2–3, 409–462.

Coval, Joshua D., and Tobias J. Moskowitz. 2001. "The Geography of Investment: Informed Trading and Asset Prices." *Journal of Political Economy* 109:4, 811–841.

Coval, Joshua D., and Tyler Shumway. 2005. "Do Behavioral Biases Affect Prices?" *Journal of Finance* 60:1, 1–34.

De Long, J. Bradford, Andrei Shleifer, Lawrence H. Summers, and Robert J. Waldmann. 1990. "Noise Trader Risk in Financial Markets." *Journal of Political Economy* 98:4, 703–738.

Feng, Lei, and Mark S. Seasholes. 2005. "Do Investor Sophistication and Trading Experience Eliminate Behavioral Biases in Financial Markets?" *Review of Finance* 9:3, 305–351.

Frazzini, Andrea. 2006. "The Disposition Effect and Underreaction to News." *Journal of Finance* 61:4, 2017–2046.

French, Kenneth R. 2008. "Presidential Address: The Cost of Active Investing." *Journal of Finance* 63:4, 1537–1573.

French, Kenneth R., and James M. Poterba. 1991. "Investor Diversification and International Equity Markets." *American Economic Review* 81:2, 222–226.

Gehrig, Thomas. 1993. "An Information Based Explanation of the Domestic Bias in International Equity Investment." *Scandinavian Journal of Economics* 95:1, 97–109.

Gervais, Simon, and Terrance Odean. 2001. "Learning to Be Overconfident." *Review of Financial Studies* 14:1, 1–27.

Goetzmann, William N., Dasol Kim, Alok Kumar, and Qin Wang. 2015. "Weather-Induced Mood, Institutional Investors, and Stock Returns." *Review of Financial Studies* 28:1, 73–111.

Goetzmann, William N., and Ning Zhu. 2005. "Rain or Shine: Where Is the Weather Effect?" *European Financial Management* 11:5, 559–578.

Grinblatt, Mark, and Matti Keloharju. 2001. "How Distance, Language, and Culture Influence Stockholdings and Trades." *Journal of Finance* 56:3, 1053–1073.

Grinblatt, Mark, Sheridan Titman, and Russ Wermers. 1995. "Momentum, Investment Strategies, Portfolio Performance, and Herding: A Study of Mutual Fund Behavior." *American Economic Review* 85:5, 1088–1105.

Guiso, Luigi, Paola Sapienza, and Luigi Zingales. 2009. "Cultural Biases in Economic Exchange?" *Quarterly Journal of Economics* 124:3, 1095–1131.

Hirschleifer, David, and Tyler Shumway. 2003. "Good Day Sunshine: Stock Market and the Weather." *Journal of Finance* 58:3, 1009–1032.

Hofstede, Geert. 1980. *Culture's Consequences: International Differences in Work-Related Values*. Beverly Hills, CA: Sage.

Hofstede, Geert. 2001. *Culture's Consequences: Comparing Values, Behaviors, Institutions and Organizations across Nations*, 2nd Edition. Thousand Oaks, CA: Sage.

Huberman, Gur. 2001. "Familiarity Breeds investment." *Review of Financial Studies* 14:3, 659–680.

Hvidkjaer, Soeren. 2006. "A Trade-Based Analysis of Momentum." *Review of Financial Studies* 19:2, 457–491.

Jegadeesh, Narasimhan, and Sheridan Titman. 1993. "Returns to Buying Winners and Selling Losers: Implications for Stock Market Efficiency." *Journal of Finance* 48:1, 65–91.

Kamstra, Mark J., Lisa A. Kramer, and Maurice D. Levi. 2003. "Winter Blues: A SAD Stock Market Cycle." *American Economic Review* 93:1, 324–343.

Ke, Dongmin, Lilian Ng, and Qinghai Wang. 2010. "Home Bias in Foreign Investment Decisions." *Journal of International Business Studies* 41:6, 960–979.

Ke, Bin, and Santhosh Ramalingegodwa. 2005. "Do Institutional Investors Exploit the Post-Earnings Announcement Drift?" *Journal of Accounting and Economics* 39:1, 25–53.

Kim, Kenneth A., and John R. Nofsinger. 2005. "Institutional Herding, Business Groups, and Economic Regimes: Evidence from Japan." *Journal of Business* 78:1, 213–242.

Lakonishok, Josef, Andrei Shleifer, and Robert W. Vishny. 1992. "The Impact of Institutional Trading on Stock Prices." *Journal of Financial Economics* 32:1, 23–43.

Lerner, Josh, Antoinette Schoar, and Wan Wongsungwai. 2007. "Smart Institutions, Foolish Choices: The Limited Partner Performance Puzzle." *Journal of Finance* 62:2, 731–764.

Levy, Azriel, and Miles Livingston. 1995. "The Gains from Diversification Reconsidered: Transaction Costs and Superior Information." *Financial Markets, Institutions, and Instruments* 4:3, 1–60.

Locke, Peter R., and Steven C. Mann. 2005. "Professional Trader Discipline and Trade Disposition." *Journal of Financial Economics* 76:2, 401–444.

Markowitz, Harry. 1952. "Portfolio Selection." *Journal of Finance* 7:1, 77–91.

Merton, Robert C. 1987. "A Simple Model of Capital Market Equilibrium with Incomplete Information." *Journal of Finance* 42:3, 483–510.

Nofsinger, John, and Richard Sias. 1999. "Herding and Feedback Trading by Institutional and Individual Investors." *Journal of Finance* 54:6, 2263–2295.

O'Connell, Paul G. J., and Melvyn Teo. 2009. "Institutional Investors, Past Performance, and Dynamic Loss Aversion." *Journal of Financial and Quantitative Analysis* 44:1, 155–188.

Pompian, Michael. 2012. "Behavioral Finance and Investor Types." *Private Wealth Management* 2012:1, 1–3.

Scharfstein, David S., and Jeremy C. Stein. 1990. "Herd Behavior and Investment." *American Economic Review* 80:3, 465–479.

Shapira, Zur, and Itzhak Venezia. 2001. "Patterns of Behavior of Professionally Managed and Independent Investors." *Journal of Banking and Finance* 25:8, 1573–1587.

Shiller, Robert J., Stanley Fisher, and Benjamin M. Friedman. 1984. "Stock Prices and Social Dynamics." *Brookings Papers on Economic Activity* 2, 457–510.

Sias, Richard W. 2004. "Institutional Herding. *Review of Financial Studies* 17:1, 165–206.

Statman, Meir, Steven R. Thorley, and Keith Vorkink. 2006. "Investor Overconfidence and Trading Volume." *Review of Financial Studies* 19:4, 1531–1565.

Strong, Norman, and Xinzhong Xu. 2003. "Understanding the Equity Home Bias: Evidence from Survey Data." *Review of Economics and Statistics* 85:2, 307–312.

Tesar, Linda L., and Ingrid M. Werner. 1995. "Home Bias and High Turnover." *Journal of International Money and Finance* 14:4, 467–492.

Trueman, Brett. 1994. "Analyst Forecasts and Herding Behavior." *Review of Financial Studies* 7:1, 97–124.

Van Nieuwerburgh, Stijn, and Laura Veldkamp. 2009. "Information Immobility and the Home Bias Puzzle." *Journal of Finance* 64:3, 1187–1215.

Van Nieuwerburgh, Stijn, and Laura Veldkamp. 2010. "Information Acquisition and Under-Diversification." *Review of Economic Studies* 77:2, 779–805.

Wermers, Russ. 1999. "Mutual Fund Herding and the Impact on Stock Prices." *Journal of Finance* 54:2, 581–622.

5

Corporate Executives, Directors, and Boards

JOHN R. NOFSINGER
Professor and William H. Seward Endowed Chair in International Finance
University of Alaska Anchorage

PATTANAPORN CHATJUTHAMARD
Associate Professor of Finance
Chulalongkorn University

Introduction

This chapter examines the financial decision-making behavior of corporate managers and members of boards of directors. Traditionally, academics assumed that decision makers would be rational when making important financial decisions. Over the past few decades, scholars have discovered that decisions can better be framed as being normal. But what is normal versus irrational behavior? To some extent, whether the behavior of corporate leaders differs from the norm depends on the expectations of others. Therefore, this chapter begins by assessing the leadership behavior that is expected, based on two main theories of corporate management: agency theory and stewardship theory. *Agency theory* depicts the chief executive officer (CEO) as a self-interested agent who makes decisions that are personally beneficial. *Stewardship theory* describes a CEO as a benevolent shepherd seeking higher corporate achievement. These two management theories, which are described in more detail in the next section, put this topic into a framework that enables assessing corporate leadership behavior.

Besides viewing managerial behavior from agency and stewardship perspectives, the chapter also examines some psychological biases and traits of CEOs. For instance, managers exhibit optimism bias and overconfidence, and these biases can impact a manager's perception of the company's growth or a project's chances of success. Therefore, biased perceptions could lead to decisions that affect investment and capital structure. Similarly, managers can be risk averse, which might influence the company's investments and capital structure.

In the stewardship framework, a primary function of the board of directors is to enable the CEO by providing resources, direction, and advice as needed. However, in the agency framework, the directors act to control the CEO. Because the agency CEO acts in a self-interested manner and exhibits both behavioral biases and too much risk aversion, the board must provide incentives to overcome the agency problem, as well as the biases and risk aversion. The board must monitor the CEO's decisions and represent the shareholders' interests. In many instances, this duty suffers, because boards themselves exhibit biases and self-interested behavior. Specifically, boards may suffer from group dynamic problems, such as social loafing, poor information sharing, and groupthink.

The first section of this chapter describes the agency and stewardship theories, and identifies the key areas where they have different outcomes. Then the chapter describes the self-interested behavior, risk aversion, and psychological biases of top management. The behavior of the board of directors is illustrated next, including some individual and group dynamics. The final section offers a summary and conclusions.

Theories of Management

Many studies attempt to explain the relationships between ownership and management of a company. The classic framework of *agency theory* by Jensen and Meckling (1976) describes how individual self-interest utility motivates the conflict of interests between shareholders (principals) and management (agents), resulting in the potential problems of opportunism and the solutions of incentives and monitoring. This framework has been the dominate theory in the finance and economics literature. However, an alternative model of managerial motivation and behavior has also been popular in the management literature. It is known as *stewardship theory* (Donaldson and Davis 1991, 1993) and is derived from psychological and sociological factors.

AGENCY THEORY

During the 1960s and 1970s, economists explored risk-sharing among individuals or groups (Wilson 1968; Arrow 1971). This literature described the risk-sharing problem as one that arises when cooperating parties have different attitudes toward risk. Agency theory broadened this risk-sharing literature to include what is now called the *agency problem*, which occurs when cooperating parties have different goals and division of labor (Ross 1973; Jensen and Meckling 1976). Specifically, this theory is directed at the pervasive agency relationship in which one party delegates work to another agent, who performs that work. In describing this relationship using the metaphor of a contract, agency theory suggests that the firm can be viewed as a nexus of contracts (loosely defined) between the principal and the agent.

Agency theory attempts to deal with two specific problems: (1) aligning the goals of the agent so that they are not in conflict with the principal (agency problem); and (2) reconciling the principal and agent differences in risk tolerances. Further, it explores the ownership structure of the corporation, including how equity ownership by managers aligns managers' interests with those of owners. Fama (1980) discusses the role of efficient capital and labor markets as information mechanisms used to control the self-serving behavior of top executives. From an agency perspective, Fama and Jensen (1983) describe the role of the board of directors as an information system in which the stockholders in large corporations could implement to monitor the opportunism of top executives. When boards provide richer information, top executives are more likely to engage in behaviors that are consistent with stockholders' interests. Jensen (1984) and

Jensen and Ruback (1983) extend these ideas to controversial practices, such as golden parachutes and corporate raiding. A *golden parachute* is a large payment to a CEO as a result of the firm's being merged or acquired by another firm. *Corporate raiding* refers to a large block of shares purchased to pressure the firm to enact novel business measures that contrast with current management practices.

According to agency theory, an important component of the solution to the agency problem is to artificially bring management goals in line with shareholders goals. This goal is typically accomplished by structuring management incentives in such ways that they align management behavior with shareholder goals. For example, the shareholders could give the CEO shares or options of stock that vest over time, thus inducing long-term behavior and deterring short-run actions that harm future company value. When the interests of top management are brought in line with those of shareholders, agency theory argues that management will fulfill its duty to shareholders, not only because of any moral sense of duty to shareholders but also because of the incentives to maximize their own utility (Donaldson and Davis 1991).

Agency theory often uses the word *control*, meaning that the board of directors (as a proxy representation for the shareholders) must control top management. A major function of the board is to curtail such managerial "opportunistic behavior," including shirking and indulging in excessive perquisites at the expense of shareholder interests (Williamson 1985; Donaldson and Davis 1991). Although incentives are one solution to the agency problem, another solution is monitoring and oversight. The board conducts this oversight of management to further counter the agent's propensity to engage in opportunistic behavior. Besides providing monitoring of CEO actions on the behalf of shareholders, the board also offers inputs into decisions at the top management level. Thus, the behavior and decisions of the board affect the firm through the incentives created for management, the monitoring of management, and large corporate actions.

STEWARDSHIP THEORY

Although agency theory is built from an economics model, stewardship theory is derived from a psychology and sociology framework. Stewardship theory applies when managers choose the interests of shareholders over their own personal motivations or incentives. Generally, stewards are motivated by a need to achieve and excel in their work, and can distinguish between their work and the compensation for it. Further, stewards generally gain intrinsic satisfaction through successfully performing inherently challenging tasks. Stewards also often have a need to exercise responsibility and authority to gain recognition from peers and board members, or to obtain sufficient empowerment to get the job done properly. Therefore, an important aspect of stewardship theory occurs in the mind of the manager—a belief that a CEO steward is the owner of the company in proxy and fulfills his responsibility even when that responsibility conflicts with his personal interests.

The literature on stewardship focuses on enabling managers, rather than controlling them. Managers whose needs are based on achievement, growth, and self-actualization, and who are intrinsically motivated, will gain greater utility by accomplishing organizational rather than personal goals. Therefore, with this theory, the board of directors is a sounding board and resource for a steward CEO rather than a controlling body.

Stewardship theory also involves a high level of principal trust (Davis, Shoorman, and Donaldson 1997).

FACTORS DIFFERENTIATING AGENCY AND STEWARDSHIP THEORIES

Davis et al. (1997) explain various dimensions on which agency theory assumptions differ from those of stewardship theory. These dimensions are characterized as either the subordinate's psychological attributes or the organization's situational characteristics.

Psychological Factors

According to agency theory, top managers are viewed as rooted in economic rationality and individualistic self-serving behaviors. However, stewardship theory is motivated by the model of a person in top management as self-actualizing and someone who needs to grow beyond his or her current state to reach a higher level of achievement. The following assumptions reflect these differences.

- **Motivation.** Agency theory focuses on quantifiable extrinsic rewards or measurable market motivation. This reward system aims to reduce the agency conflicts by aligning interests. Additionally, some incentive rewards, such as medical insurance, savings, and retirement plans, are control mechanisms to reduce the likelihood of the CEO's leaving the firm. Alternatively, stewardship theory focuses on nonquantifiable intrinsic rewards, such as opportunities for growth and responsibility for doing the work. Achievement, affiliation, self-actualization, self-efficacy, and self-determination are important components. These intrinsic motivations relate to the importance of a shared organizational vision.
- **Identification.** In agency theory, managers may externalize organizational problems to avoid blame. By avoiding incriminating evidence, these self-serving managers may make organizational problems worse because they avoid accepting responsibility and avoid making decisions to rectify the problems (D'Aveni and MacMillan 1990). In stewardship theory, managers identifying with their organization will work toward the organization's goals, solve problems, and overcome barriers in order to help their organizations succeed (Mowday, Porter, and Steers 1982; Smith, Organ, and Near 1983; O'Reilly and Chatman 1986). These managers have high identification with and high value commitment to their organization.
- **Use of Power.** Gibson, Ivancevich, and Donnelly (1994) separate power into institutional and personal power. In agency theory, institutional power includes reward, legitimate, and coercive power (Adams, Almeida, and Ferreira 2005). Appropriate reward systems and the recognition of authority in the principal are pooled to create the required control level in the principal–agent relationship. Coercive power is used as a severe method of agent monitoring. Alternatively, in stewardship theory, personal power combines both expert and referent power. Top management is more likely to use personal power as a basis for influencing in a principal–steward relationship.

Situational Factors

Managing an organization includes many interactions among top leaders, middle management, and staff. These interactions can be structured with different levels of control, empowerment, and trust. The situational factors are often dependent on the prevailing culture.

- **Management philosophy**. Lawler (1986) categorizes management philosophy into control-oriented and involvement-oriented management approaches. Agency theory tends toward a control-oriented system, which is designed to avoid vulnerability and the need to trust. Management implements greater controls to reduce risk or uncertainty. Therefore, this system works best in a stable environment. Unlike agency theory, an involvement-oriented philosophy allows stewardship theory to build the relationships that help management deal with increased uncertainty and risk through more training, empowerment, and trust in workers.
- **Culture**. Cultures are often measured on an individualism–collectivism scale. Individualism culture emphasizes personal objectives over group goals and is generally common in Western culture. Individualism fosters agency theory. Collectivism culture defines self as a part of the group and prefers a long-term relationship. This culture enables stewardship theory. Another common measure of cultural dynamics is the distribution of power within a country or within its institutions and organizations. The term *power distance* describes this distribution. A high power distance culture indicates a more narrow distribution of power and is conductive to the development of principal–agent relationships because it supports and legitimizes the inherent inequality between shareholders and management. Conversely, a lower power distance culture is more conducive to the development of principal–steward relationships because all members emphasize a shared power system.

Summarizing the Theories

Sundaramurthy and Lewis (2003) show the underlying differences in assumed managerial and board behaviors between these two approaches. Agency theory assumptions include behavior that stems from individualism, opportunism, extrinsic motivation, conflict of interests, and distrust that lead to a control approach. By contrast, stewardship theory assumes behaviors that come from collectivism, cooperation, intrinsic motivation, goal alignment, and trust that lead to a collaborative approach. According to these assumptions, each approach suggests certain board roles and structures. A controlling board of directors acts as an ultimate internal monitor over management, whereas a collaborating board simply acts as an advisor and a supporter to management. In summary, although agency theory looks at top management as individualistic utility maximizers, stewardship theory perceives top management as collective self-actualizers caring about firm success. The next section examines managerial behavior with these two management theories in mind.

Corporate Executives and Their Financial Behavior

The CEO plays the most important role and bears the most significant responsibility, as well as has the greatest accountability and authority within a corporation. The CEO has the responsibility for the overall success of the organization and makes the financial decisions, but still reports to the corporation's board of directors. Given the leadership position of the CEO, much research has been dedicated to studying how CEOs make their decisions. These studies identify traits and psychological biases, and then have determined how those behaviors are related to compensation, financing choices, investing decisions, and firm performance.

MANAGERIAL TRAITS

Various studies identify specific managerial characteristics and attempt to explain which traits matter. Bertrand and Schoar (2003) study managers who move from one firm to another firm, and report evidence consistent with different managers having different styles, behavior, and performance. Bloom and Van Reenen (2007) find that various management practices are related to performance. Both Stulz and Rohan (2003) and Huang and Darren (2013) show that gender and religion have a strong influence on managers' mindsets, which is reflected in corporate decisions. They show that male managers exhibit overconfidence in important corporate decision-making relative to women. Additionally, Chatjuthamard, Lawatanatrakul, Pisalyaput, and Srivibha (2016) find that culturally based managerial mindsets affect firm risk. They show that practices consistent with the Sufficiency Economy Philosophy in Thailand, rooted in Buddhism, are less risky, but not less profitable. Furthermore, some studies attempt to identify the most important characteristics. Schoar and Zuo (2016) and Graham and Narasimham (2004), for example, find that CEO actions are related to measures of conservatism. According to Malmendier and Tate (2005, 2009), Ben-David, Graham, and Harvey (2013), and Graham, Harvey, and Puri (2013), CEO decisions and outcomes are related to measures of overconfidence, optimism, risk aversion, and time preference.

In corporate finance, the standard assumption is that managers are fully rational and make optimal decisions. Although behavioral finance assumes managers are normal, that may not always mean they are rational. According to behavioral finance, managers make decisions based on the notion of bounded rationality. *Bounded rationality* assumes that individuals are influenced by past decisions, values, cognitive biases, and emotions that result in people's making only satisfactory choices. Behavioral corporate finance criticizes the rationality hypothesis of managers and investors, and explores the effect of such criticisms on a company's decision making. Psychological biases may drive those decisions. For example, managers are not fully rational; instead, they may have too much confidence in their ability and judgment, a characteristic called *overconfidence*. Managers may also be too optimistic about future forecasts (Hackbarth 2008). Optimistic managers tend to overestimate the growth rate of earnings, a characteristic called *growth perception bias*, whereas overconfident managers tend to underestimate the riskiness of earnings, a characteristic known as *risk perception bias*.

Optimism

Contrary to the traditional corporate finance literature, managers do not always act rationally. They may present some optimism or overconfidence biases that influence company decisions. De Long, Scheifer, Summers, and Waldmann (1990) and Goel and Thakor (2000) describe the difference between optimism and overconfidence. According to them, *optimism* is an overvaluation of the likelihood of favorable future events. Specifically, CEOs may be optimistic about the success of their decisions. By contrast, *overconfidence* is an underestimate of the risk of future events. Sometimes overconfidence is also described as a better-than-average belief. Weinstein (1980) defines managers as optimistic when they overestimate the probability of good company performance and underestimate the probability of bad company performance. Heaton (2002) suggests that optimistic managers believe the capital market undervalues risky securities owned by the firm. Optimistic managers also overvalue their firm's investment opportunities, leading to investment in negative net present value (NPV) projects. This process occurs because managers overestimate the project's cash flows and underappreciate its risks. Graham et al. (2013) find that more optimistic managers use more short-term debt in their capital structure, because their optimism leads them to avoiding using more expensive long-term capital.

Managerial optimism can help explain the need for independent directors and a board chair who does not serve as the CEO for the monitoring purposes. According to Kahneman and Lovallo (1993), organizational optimism is best alleviated by introducing outsiders, because these outsiders can draw managerial attention to information that might indicate their perceptions are wrong. Additionally, Parades (2005) maintains that corporate governance should be reformulated in order to enlarge its scope to control the CEO's optimism. However, an optimal level of CEO optimism may maximize company value. Campbell, Gallmeyer, Johnson, Rutherford, and Stanley (2011) show that low levels of optimism lead to underinvestment, whereas high levels of optimism lead to overinvestment.

Overconfidence

Shefrin (2006, p. 6) describes the better-than-average aspect of overconfidence as "People make mistakes more frequently than they believe and view themselves as better than average." Bernardo and Welch (2001) incorporate this concept into managerial theory by building an informational cascades model and by suggesting that overconfident individuals act on their own information while ignoring the actions of others in the group. According to psychology and behavioral economics literature, a common source of overconfidence is *self-attribution bias*, in which managers over-credit their role in bringing about good outcomes and over-credit external factors or bad luck for bad outcomes. This leads to managers believing they are better than the average manager. Hirshleifer (2001) explains that self-attribution causes individuals to learn to be overconfident rather than converging to an accurate self-assessment. Thus, overconfidence persists over time. Other finance professionals also exhibit this bias. For example, Gervais and Odean (2001) suggest that self-attribution causes traders to become overconfident. Hilary and Menzly (2006) find evidence that self-attribution bias leads analysts with recent short-term success to become overconfident.

How do managers become overconfident? The source of the overconfidence has implications for corporate governance. The base case is that managers may be born overconfident. In this explanation, companies can avoid overconfident managers by not hiring them. Alternatively, managers develop overconfidence through experience as CEOs. In this explanation, companies might adjust their monitoring and incentives to guard against overconfidence developing (Parades 2005). Lastly, Gervais, Heaton, and Odean (2011) show how managerial overconfidence can result from the selection bias when hiring a manager. They explain that someone who is overconfident is more likely to be selected as a manager, because people who tend to apply for managerial posts are more likely to be very confidence about their own abilities. Goel and Thakor (2008) also find that overconfident managers are more likely to get promoted and outperform others.

Managerial Risk Aversion

Risk aversion is an important managerial trait. *Risk aversion* is the behavior that characterizes people seeking to reduce risk and uncertainty. Risk-averse CEOs are willing to accept the lower returns that accompany lower-risk projects. Many theoretical papers (Friedman and Savage 1948; Pratt 1964; Coase 1973; Kahneman and Tversky 1979; Caballero 1991; Sitkin and Pablo 1992; Parrino, Poteshman, and Weisbach 2005) explain the role of managerial risk aversion in corporate decision making. The different levels of risk aversion among managers can explain the differences in managers' reactions to decisions involving uncertainty. According to several recent studies, differences in managerial risk aversion affect corporate decision making and actions in general. For example, Graham et al. (2013) find that less risk-averse CEOs make more acquisitions. When firms try to control managerial risk-taking in an agency framework, Chava and Purnanandam (2010) find that providing risk-taking incentives leads to higher financial leverage and lower cash balances, while avoiding such incentives leads to lower leverage and higher cash balances. In contrast, Low (2009) reports that an increase in managerial risk aversion leads to lower company valuation, and thus firms may want to provide risk-taking incentives.

Top executives have different management styles with regard to investment, financing, and strategic decisions. This raises the question whether managerial attitudes and behavior might explain corporate decision making and actions. Many studies suggest that managerial characteristics indeed matter for corporate policies.

MANAGERIAL ATTRIBUTES AND COMPENSATION

In agency theory, the executive compensation package is designed to give managers a pattern of rewards so as to align their interests more closely with shareholders. This kind of incentive, usually in the form of stock options, is important to company performance (Fenn and Liang 2001; Hermalin and Wallace 2001). However, a limitation on this incentive is that managers tend to receive the incentive pay during a generally rising stock market (Bertrand and Mullainathan 2001). Paredes (2005) confirms this view and also shows that the incentive governance mechanism can lead to overconfidence bias, because managers get high rewards from a rising market and attribute those rewards to their ability and performance.

Are managerial traits related to compensation? Graham, Li, and Qiu (2012) find that more aggressive managers appear to be remunerated for taking additional risk. Evidence by Graham et al. (2013) shows that risk-taking CEOs are paid with a higher proportion of performance-based incentives and relatively lower cash salary. They also find that CEOs who are more impatient receive proportionately more in salary. Of course, determining if higher risk-taking managers will ask for more stock options or if CEOs given more performance sensitivity pay are induced to take more risk is difficult. Indeed, Smith and Stulz (1985) and Guay (1999) contend that the boards award equity-based compensation to managers to overcome managerial risk aversion and to induce optimal risk-taking behavior. Low (2009) supports their conjecture, and shows that companies that experience a decrease in risk are concentrated among firms with low managerial equity-based incentives.

CEO BEHAVIORAL BIASES AND FIRM CAPITAL STRUCTURE

Hackbarth (2008) suggests that growth and risk perception biases are important factors for corporate capital structure decisions. Managers with a growth perception bias are considered to be optimistic. Specifically, their optimism causes them to overestimate the company's future earnings growth rate, which leads them to perceive a larger cost for issuing equity than debt. Additionally, managers with risk perception bias are considered to be overconfident. They tend to underestimate the future earnings' risk and also favor issuing debt rather than equity. Recent articles support this view that managerial optimism and overconfidence lead to a greater debt financing. For example, Graham et al. (2013) show that more optimistic CEOs use more short-term debt, whereas Malmendier, Tate, and Yan (2011) find that overconfident managers view external financing to be costly and prefer to use cash.

CEO TRAITS AND CORPORATE INVESTMENT DECISIONS

According to Heaton (2002), managerial optimism is evidently bad, causing either over- or under-investment. Common distortions in corporate investment may be a result of manager biases. Building on Roll (1986) and Heaton (2002), Malmendier and Tate (2005) contend that one important link between investment levels and cash flow is the tension between beliefs about the company's value of the CEO versus the market. Empirically, Malmendier and Tate (2005, 2008) find that overconfident CEOs have higher investment cash flow sensitivities and are more likely to engage in value-destroying mergers. Moreover, Goel and Thakor (2008) show that a rational and risk-averse CEO under-invests in corporate projects and this under-investment reduces company value. Alternatively, they also present a model in which a moderately overconfident risk-averse CEO increases company value by reducing the under-investment problem. The reason for this is that the overconfident CEO overestimates the accuracy of private information and overreacts to it. Although a moderately overconfident CEO reduces under-investment and increases company value, a highly confident CEO generates over-investment and reduces company value. Campbell et al. (2011) complement Goel and Thakor's work by showing that a manager's optimism can beneficially offset the effect of the individual's aversion on the investment level chosen.

Roll's (1986) *hubris hypothesis*, which now seems to be labeled as overconfidence, suggests that managers engage in acquisitions with an overly optimistic opinion of their ability to create value. He suggests that overconfidence motivates many corporate takeovers. Furthermore, Doukas and Petmezas (2007) show that overconfidence is a fundamental component of corporate acquisitions. Recent studies confirm this view; for example, Liu and Taffler (2008) provide evidence that overconfident CEOs are more likely to conduct mergers and acquisitions (M&As) than are rational CEOs. Graham et al. (2013) report that more risk-tolerant CEOs make more acquisitions.

Billett and Qian (2008) explore managerial self-attribution bias in M&As by looking at the sequence of deals made by individual CEOs. They suggest that CEOs with self-attribution bias become overconfident. Their evidence shows that acquirers' first deals should have non-negative wealth effects. Acquirers who become overconfident from successful acquisition experience are then more likely to acquire again, and their future deals, driven by overconfidence, will result in poor wealth effects. Also, experienced acquirers who become overconfident are more likely to exhibit greater optimism about company prospects and exhibit such optimism when trading their companies' stocks. The evidence for this behavior is pervasive. For example, Li (2010) shows that a manager's self-attribution bias affects corporate policies. Gervais and Odean (2001), Barber and Odean (2002), Doukas and Petmezas (2007), and Billett and Qian (2008) all find that CEOs tend to become overconfident after successful acquisitions. As a result, these CEOs are more likely to follow those successful acquisitions with other acquisitions that negatively impact their company's stock price.

Bolton, Brunnermeier, and Veldkamp (2013) develop a theory of leadership that contrasts managerial resoluteness with communication and listening skills. *Resoluteness* is a form of overconfidence that arises when CEOs are unresponsive to outside information. More resolute and overconfident CEOs tend to perform better than CEOs who are better listeners and communicators in situations requiring greater coordination. This finding suggests a positive relation between resoluteness and overconfidence and company performance.

Directors, Boards, and Their Financial Behaviors

Boards of directors are an integral part of the governance of large organizations, including all corporate and many nonprofit organizations. The firm's stockholders elect the directors to govern the organization and guard the stockholders' interests. The board's main roles are to hire the CEO and to assess the overall direction and strategy of the business. Many finance and economics studies discuss whether the board of directors can help solve the problems associated with this separation of ownership and control. These studies examine all aspects of a board of directors and how its characteristics affect the company. However, this section focuses on a subset of this literature—specifically, how the behavior and characteristics of a board affect CEO behavior.

ROLES AND STRUCTURES

Boards of directors are an important topic of research in management studies, economics, finance, business strategy, and sociology as well as legal areas. Adam Smith (1776) was the first economist to address boards of directors in an agency context. The studies of Fama (1980) and Fama and Jensen (1983) suggest that boards of directors can alleviate the agency conflict of goals and interests between the owners and the managers. Generally, boards are composed of both insiders and outsiders. *Inside directors* are employees and therefore thought to be dependent on the CEO, whereas *outside directors* (sometimes called *independent directors*) are not employees and lack any business ties to the company. The roles of inside and independent directors are examined in the context of monitoring management.

EMPIRICAL EXAMINATIONS OF BOARDS OF DIRECTORS

Are boards effective at monitoring their managers and controlling their managers' behavioral biases? How can this effectiveness be determined? The primary mechanism for measuring the monitoring capability of a board is the proportion of outside to inside directors. The more directors who are independent of the CEO, the more likely they will be effective monitors. If they are successful at creating the right incentives and monitoring management, then the company should perform better. Thus, studies often examine whether more independent boards lead to greater company performance.

Board Independence and Company Performance

Different ways are available to measure company performance. Hermalin and Weisbach (1991), Mehran (1995), Klein (1998), and Bhagat and Black (2002) report an insignificant association between accounting performance measures, such as return on equity, and the proportion of outside directors on the board. Another measure of company performance is Tobin's Q, which is the market value of a company's assets (as measured by the market value of its outstanding stock and debt) divided by the replacement cost of the company's assets (book value). Morck, Shleifer, and Vishny (1988), Hermalin and Weisbach (1991), and Bhagat and Black (2002) all use Tobin's Q to reflect the value added by intangible factors, but they find no noticeable relationship between the proportion of outside directors and company performance. Bhagat and Black also examine the effect of board composition on long-term stock and accounting performance, but do not find any significant relation.

Does this mean that boards do not effectively control manager behavior? Possibly, but measurement errors could exist. Morck (2008) suggests that many directors classified as independent are actually associated with the firm's CEO. Specifically, the CEO recruits them through personal contacts or friendships. As more stringent definitions of independence are applied, though, a clearer relationship may emerge. Morck also suggests the possibility that behavioral constraints on board independence are high; if so, genuinely independent directors and board chairs may require institutional investors and public shareholders to nominate candidates for directorships. Such measures could entail corporate governance risks, in that they assume good governance is possible within institutional investors and shareholder rationality.

Boards, Their Monitoring Roles, and CEO Turnover

Other characteristics may affect a board's ability to control manager behavior. For example, do the attributes of the board, such as inside/outside composition, size, or compensation, directly influence the board's monitoring role? Besides examining board characteristics, various studies focus on board responsibility in choosing and monitoring a company's CEO. One way to assess a board's effectiveness is to analyze the quality of those decisions. Numerous studies illustrate a positive relation between CEO turnover and poor organization performance (Coughlan and Schmidt 1985; Warner, Watts, and Wruck 1988; Weisbach 1988; Barro and Barro 1990; Jensen and Murphy 1990; Kaplan 1994; Denis and Denis 1995; Huson, Parrino, and Starks 2001; Eldenburg, Hermalin, Weisbach, and Wosinska 2004). Namely, when company performance is poor, the board is more likely to find the current CEO unacceptable and make a change.

In particular, Weisbach (1988) shows that CEO turnover after poor performance is more likely in firms with more independent directors. Boards controlled by outside directors do a better job of monitoring the CEO than do boards controlled by inside directors. Rosenstein and Wyatt (1990) support the view that independent directors seem to affect at least some governance effectiveness, and they show that stock prices rise on news of outsiders joining boards.

Working in groups, such as boards of directors, can lead to the free rider problem, also known as *social loafing*. When more people are in a group, individuals in the group may believe that others will do the work required and thus they shirk their responsibilities. Although no studies of boards directly examine whether social loafing occurs, some studies use the size of the board as a proxy for the possibility of shirking. Smaller boards are purported to have less shirking, and thus be more effective in monitoring managers. Yermack (1996) and Wu (2000) examine CEO turnover and board size as it relates to firm performance. Both studies find that companies with smaller boards have a stronger likelihood of CEO turnover after poor performance. This finding is consistent with the view that smaller boards are more effective overseers of their CEOs than are larger boards.

Finally, Perry (2000) examines the relation between CEO turnover and company performance by showing whether the outside directors are paid using incentives. If incentive compensation is an effective tool in aligning CEO interests with the company's interests, then it might also work for the directors. Perry finds that outside directors who receive incentive pay tend to have a professional, rather than a personal, relationship with the CEO, and thus they are relatively more independent.

Boards and the Takeover Market

According to Harford (2003), understanding the reaction of boards to takeover bids requires a recognition of the incentives governing the directors. Harford's evidence shows that outside directors have strong financial incentives to resist a takeover bid. He also finds that, on average, the gain on the small amount of equity they hold in the company is too small to compensate them for their loss of directorship income. Therefore, at the margin, these personal financial considerations lead outside directors to resist possible acquisitions, even when those acquisitions are in the shareholders' interest.

Behavioral Biases of Boards of Directors

The board of directors is, by definition, a group setting. Scholarly research shows that groups often amplify the cognitive biases of individuals. To illustrate this point, consider a study conducted with both individuals and groups (Whyte 1993). When presented with a bad capital budgeting project for evaluation, 71 percent of the individual decision makers correctly terminated the project, as did a similar 74 percent of the groups. In the next round of experiments, Whyte adds an additional piece of information: a non-recoverable investment already spent on the project. Because people are averse to a sure loss, such as this sunk cost, they incorrectly include the sunk cost in their evaluation.

Thus, only 31 percent of the individual decision makers correctly reject the project, a result of loss-aversion bias. Did the groups do better? No, they did worse; only 24 percent of the groups correctly reject the project. In fact, the groups seem to be even more affected by the sure loss aversion.

Because meetings of the board of directors are private, few scholarly studies directly measure their interactions and biases (Forbes and Milliken 1999). However, many studies analyze group behavior in general. Hopefully, what is known from group behavior can be extrapolated to uncover potential problems in boards of directors.

So, why do group decisions often result in worse performance than individual decisions? Specifically, why are behavioral biases often magnified in groups? Three processes occur in group dynamics that are not factors for an individual: (1) social loafing, (2) poor information sharing, and (3) groupthink.

Social loafing, as mentioned earlier, is also known as the *free rider problem* (Jensen 1993), in which members of a group might not put in a high level of effort because they assume others will do the work. The motivation for this behavior is a person's feeling that he or she will not get much individual recognition for the success of the group (Linck, Netter, and Yang 2008). Instead, the social loafer puts more effort into other activities. Social loafing is more prevalent when responsibilities within the group are vague and diffused, and when the group's outcome is not linked well with individual efforts.

Boards of directors can be formed with members having different knowledge or skills. The hope is that each member shares with the rest any specialized knowledge. However, groups often display poor information sharing (Boivie 2016). Two factors can influence this information sharing: a feeling of power and an initial prevailing view. First, a feeling of power occurs when one person has information that others do not; sharing that information reduces that feeling of power. Second, if some members believe that other members favor a specific decision, they may withhold information that contradicts that view; this behavior is the group version of confirmation bias. *Confirmation bias* refers to selective thinking, whereby one searches for and interprets information that confirms prior beliefs while simultaneously ignoring or discounting relevant information that contradicts those beliefs.

When a group is formed to make a decision, it eventually needs to achieve a consensus. The drive to achieve that consensus can crowd out serious discussion of alternatives. This situation is another group form of confirmation bias, called *groupthink*. The group characteristics that foster groupthink are: (1) a strong or charismatic leader, (2) a friendly atmosphere, (3) no clear procedure for making the decision, (4) an overt desire for conformity, and (5) a stressful decision that has to be made. Boards of directors are likely to experience at least some of these characteristics, and thus be susceptible to groupthink (Zhu 2013).

Summary and Conclusions

Agency theory is the prevailing model of CEO behavior in the finance and economics literature. This theory describes CEOs as self-interested agents who make decisions based on what is best for them, even if it is not in the best interests of the shareholders.

By contrast, stewardship theory describes CEOs as benevolent shepherds of the company, seeking higher achievement by leading the firm. The expected behavior of management spans the two theories; therefore, each theory specifies different roles for the board of directors.

Evidence indicates that CEOs tend to be optimistic, overconfident, risk averse, and self-interested. Optimistic and overconfident CEOs overestimate future earnings growth and underestimate the earnings' risk, thereby perceiving a larger cost for issuing equity than debt. These biased CEOs are also more likely to engage in wealth-destroying investments, particularly M&As. Lastly, risk-averse CEOs may choose to use too little debt financing or under-invest, holding high cash balances. With these behaviors, boards should provide incentives to control these behavioral biases and increase risk-taking, as well as align their CEOs with shareholder interests.

Besides these rational roles of boards, directors have their own self-interests, and so boards can suffer from group dynamic biases. Specifically, boards may display social loafing, poor information sharing, and groupthink. These problems may make the boards less effective in controlling their top management. However, far more research is needed in this area; although many studies investigate these group biases, few focus on the board of directors.

DISCUSSION QUESTIONS

1. Identify and explain three psychological factors that differentiate CEOs in the agency and stewardship frameworks.
2. Discuss how CEO optimism might lead to poor capital investments.
3. Explain how a CEO might become overconfident.
4. Identify and explain group dynamic biases that might affect a board of directors.

REFERENCES

Adams, Renee B., Heitor Almeida, and Daniel Ferreira. 2005. "Powerful CEOs and Their Impact on Corporate Performance." *Review of Financial Studies* 18:4, 1403–1432.

Arrow, Kenneth J. 1971. *Essays in the Theory of Risk Bearing*. Chicago: Markham Publishing Company.

Barber, Brad M., and Terrance Odean. 2002. "Online Investors: Do the Slow Die First?" *Review of Financial Studies* 15:2, 455–488.

Barro, Jason R., and Robert J. Barro. 1990. "Pay, Performance, and Turnover of Bank CEOs." *Journal of Labor Economics* 8:4, 448–481.

Ben-David, Itzhak, John R. Graham, and Campbell R. Harvey. 2013. "Managerial Miscalibration." *Quarterly Journal of Economics* 128:4, 1547–1584.

Bernardo, Antonio E., and Ivo Welch. 2001. "On the Evolution of Overconfidence and Entrepreneurs." *Journal of Economics & Management Strategy* 10:3, 301–330.

Bertrand, Marianne, and Sendhil Mullainathan. 2001. "Are CEOs Rewarded for Luck? The Ones without Principals Are." *Quarterly Journal of Economics* 116:3, 901–932.

Bertrand, Marianne, and Antoinette Schoar. 2003. "Managing with Style: The Effect of Managers on Firm Policies." *Quarterly Journal of Economics* 118:4, 1169–1208.

Bhagat, Sanjai, and Bernard S. Black. 2002. "The Non-Correlation between Board Independence and Long-Term Firm Performance." *Journal of Corporation Law* 27:2, 231–273.

Billett, Matthew T., and Yiming Qian. 2008. "Evidence of Self-Attribution Bias from Frequent Acquirers." *Management Science* 54:6, 1037–1051.

Bloom, Nick, and John Van Reenen. 2007. "Measuring and Explaining Management Practices Across Firms and Countries." *Quarterly Journal of Economics* 122:4, 1351–1408.

Boivie, Steven. 2016. "Are Boards Designed to Fail? The Implausibility of Effective Board Monitoring." *The Academy of Management Annals* 10:1, 319–407.

Bolton, Patrick, Markus K. Brunnermeier, and Laura Veldkamp. 2013. "Leadership, Coordination and Corporate Culture." *Review of Economic Studies* 80:2, 512–537.

Caballero, Ricardo J. 1991. "On the Sign of the Investment-Uncertainty Relationship." *American Economic Review* 81:1, 279–288.

Campbell, T. Colin, Michael Gallmeyer, Shane A. Johnson, Jessica Rutherford, and Brooke W. Stanley. 2011. "CEO Optimism and Forced Turnover." *Journal of Financial Economics* 101:3, 695–712.

Chatjuthamard, Pattanaporn, Vacin Lawatanatrakul, Nick Pisalyaput, and Vasu Srivibha. 2016. "Sufficiency Economy Philosophy and Firm Risks." Working paper, Sasin Chulalongkorn University.

Chava, Sudheer, and Amiyatosh Purnanandam. 2010. "CEOs vs. CFOs: Incentives and Corporate Policies." *Journal of Financial Economics* 97:2, 263–278.

Coase, Ronald H., 1973. "Business Organization and the Accountant." In James M. Buchanan and George F. Thirlby (eds.), *L.S.E. Essays on Cost*, 95–132. London: Weidenfeld and Nicolson.

Coughlan, Anne T., and Ronald M. Schmidt. 1985. "Executive Compensation, Management Turnover, and Firm Performance: An Empirical Investigation." *Journal of Accounting and Economics* 7:1–3, 43–66.

D'Aveni, Richard A., and Ian C. MacMillan. 1990. "Crisis and the Content of Managerial Communications: A Study of the Focus of Attention of Top Managers in Surviving and Failing Firms." *Administrative Science Quarterly* 35:4, 634–657.

Davis, James H., David F. Schoorman, and Lex Donaldson. 1997. "Davis, Schoorman, and Donaldson Reply: The Distinctiveness of Agency Theory and Stewardship Theory." *Academy of Management Review* 22:3, 611–613.

De Long, J. Bradford, Andrei Shleifer, Lawrence H. Summers, and Robert J. Waldmann. 1990. "Noise Trader Risk in Financial Markets." *Journal of Political Economy* 98:4, 703–738.

Denis, David J., and Diane K. Denis. 1995. "Performance Changes Following Top-Management Dismissals." *Journal of Finance* 50:4, 1029–1057.

Donaldson, Lex, and James H. Davis. 1991. "Stewardship Theory or Agency Theory: CEO Governance and Shareholder Returns." *Australian Journal of Management* 16:1, 49–64.

Donaldson, Lex, and James H. Davis. 1993. "The Need for Theoretical Coherence and Intellectual Rigour in Corporate Governance Research: Reply to Critics of Donaldson and Davis." *Australian Journal of Management* 18:2, 213–225.

Doukas, John A., and Dimitris Petmezas. 2007. "Acquisitions, Overconfident Managers and Self-Attribution Bias." *European Financial Management* 13:3, 531–577.

Eldenburg, Leslie, Benjamin E. Hermalin, Michael S. Weisbach, and Marta Wosinska. 2004. "Hospital Governance, Performance Objectives, and Organizational Form." *Journal of Corporate Finance* 10:4, 527–548.

Fama, Eugene. 1980. "Agency Problems and the Theory of the Firm." *Journal of Political Economy* 88:2, 288–307.

Fama, Eugene F., and Michael C. Jensen. 1983. "Agency Problems and Residual Claims." *Journal of Law & Economics* 26:2, 327–350.

Fenn, George W., and Nellie Liang. 2001. "Corporate Payout Policy and Managerial Stock Incentives." *Journal of Financial Economics* 60:1, 45–72.

Forbes, Daniel P., and Frances J. Milliken. 1999. "Cognition and Corporate Governance: Understanding Boards of Directors as Strategic Decision-Making Groups." *Academy of Management Review* 24:3, 489–505.

Friedman, Milton, and L. J. Savage. 1948. "The Utility Analysis of Choices Involving Risk." *Journal of Political Economy* 56:4, 279–304.

Gervais, Simon, J. B. Heaton, and Terrance Odean. 2011. "Overconfidence, Compensation Contracts, and Capital Budgeting." *Journal of Finance* 66:5, 1735–1777.

Gervais, Simon, and Terrance Odean. 2001. "Learning to Be Overconfident." *Review of Financial Studies* 14:1, 1–27.

Gibson, James L., John M. Ivancevich, and James H. Donnelly 1994. *Organizations*, 8th edition. Burr Ridge, IL: Irwin.

Goel, Anand M., and Anjan V. Thakor. 2000. "Rationality, Overconfidence and Leadership." Working Paper, University of Michigan Business School Faculty. Available at https://www.researchgate.net/publication/249845188_Rationality_Overconfidence_and_Leadership.

Goel, Anand M., and Anjan V. Thakor. 2008. "Overconfidence, CEO Selection, and Corporate Governance." *Journal of Finance* 63:6, 2737–2784.

Graham, John R., and Krishnamoorthy Narasimhan. 2004. "Corporate Survival and Managerial Experiences during the Great Depression." Working Paper, Duke University. Available at https://papers.ssrn.com/sol3/papers.cfm?abstract_id=489694.

Graham, John R., Campbell R. Harvey, and Manju Puri. 2013. "Managerial Attitudes and Corporate Actions." *Journal of Financial Economics* 109:1, 103–121.

Graham, John R., Si Li, and Jiaping Qiu. 2012. "Managerial Attributes and Executive Compensation." *Review of Financial Studies* 25:1, 144–186.

Guay, Wayne R. 1999. "The Sensitivity of CEO Wealth to Equity Risk: An Analysis of the Magnitude and Determinants." *Journal of Financial Economics* 53:1, 43–71.

Hackbarth, Dirk. 2008. "Managerial Traits and Capital Structure Decisions." *Journal of Financial and Quantitative Analysis* 43:4, 843–882.

Harford, Jarrad. 2003. "Takeover Bids and Target Directors' Incentives: The Impact of a Bid on Directors' Wealth and Board Seats." *Journal of Financial Economics* 69:1, 51–83.

Heaton, J. B. 2002. "Managerial Optimism and Corporate Finance." *Financial Management* 31:2, 33–45.

Hermalin, Benjamin E., and Nancy E. Wallace. 2001. "Firm Performance and Executive Compensation in the Savings and Loan Industry." *Journal of Financial Economics* 61:1, 139–170.

Hermalin, Benjamin E., and Michael S. Weisbach. 1991. "The Effects of Board Composition and Direct Incentives on Firm Performance." *Financial Management* 20:4, 101–112.

Hilary, Gilles, and Lior Menzly. 2006. "Does Past Success Lead Analysts to Become Overconfident?" *Management Science* 52:4, 489–500.

Hirshleifer, David. 2001. "Investor Psychology and Asset Pricing." *Journal of Finance* 56:4, 1533–1597.

Huang, Jiekun, and Darren J. Kisgen. 2013. "Gender and Corporate Finance: Are Male Executives Overconfident Relative to Female Executives?" *Journal of Financial Economics* 108:3, 822–839.

Huson, Mark R., Robert Parrino, and Laura T. Starks. 2001 "Internal Monitoring Mechanisms and CEO Turnover: A Long-Term Perspective." *Journal of Finance* 56:6, 2265–2297.

Jensen, Michael C. 1984. "Takeovers: Folklore and Science." *Harvard Business Review* 62:6, 109–121.

Jensen, Michael C. 1993. "The Modern Industrial Revolution, Exit, and the Failure of Internal Control Systems." *Journal of Finance* 48:3, 831–880.

Jensen, Michael C., and William H. Meckling. 1976. "Theory of the Firm: Managerial Behavior, Agency Costs and Ownership Structure." *Journal of Financial Economics* 3:4, 305–360.

Jensen, Michael C., and Kevin J. Murphy. 1990. "Performance Pay and Top-Management Incentives." *Journal of Political Economy* 98:2, 225–264.

Jensen, Michael C., and Richard S. Ruback. 1983. "The Market for Corporate Control: The Scientific Evidence." *Journal of Financial Economics* 11:1–4, 5–50.

Kahneman, Daniel, and Dan Lovallo. 1993. "Timid Choices and Bold Forecasts: A Cognitive Perspective on Risk Taking." *Management Science* 39:1, 17–31.

Kahneman, Daniel, and Amos Tversky. 1979. "Prospect Theory: An Analysis of Decisions Under Risk." *Econometrica* 47:2, 263–292.

Kaplan, Steven N. 1994. "Top Executive Rewards and Firm Performance: A Comparison of Japan and the United States." *Journal of Political Economy* 102:3, 510–546.

Klein, April. 1998. "Firm Performance and Board Committee Structure." *Journal of Law and Economics* 41:1, 275–304.

Lawler, Edward E. 1986. *High Involvement Management.* San Francisco: Jossey-Bass.

Li, Feng. 2010. "Managers' Self-Serving Attribution Bias and Corporate Financial Policies." Working Paper, Stephen M. Ross School of Business, University of Michigan. Available at https://papers.ssrn.com/sol3/papers.cfm?abstract_id=1639005.

Linck, James S., Jeffry M. Netter, and Tina Yang. 2008. "The Determinants of Board Structure." *Journal of Financial Economics* 87:2, 308–328.

Liu, Yue, and Richard Taffler. 2008. "CEO Overconfidence in M&A Decision Making and Its Impact on Firm Performance." Working Paper, University of Edinburgh.

Low, Angie. 2009. "Managerial Risk-Taking Behavior and Equity-Based Compensation." *Journal of Financial Economics* 92:3, 470–490.

Malmendier, Ulrike, and Geoffrey A. Tate. 2005. "Overconfidence and Corporate Investment." *Journal of Finance* 60:6, 2661–2700.

Malmendier, Ulrike, and Geoffrey A. Tate. 2008. "Who Makes Acquisitions? CEO Overconfidence and the Market's Reaction." *Journal of Financial Economics* 89:1, 20–43.

Malmendier, Ulrike, and Geoffrey A. Tate. 2009. "Superstar CEOs." *Quarterly Journal of Economics* 124:4, 1593–1638.

Malmendier, Ulrike, Geoffrey Tate, and Jon Yan. 2011. "Overconfidence and Early-Life Experiences: The Effect of Managerial Traits on Corporate Financial Policies." *Journal of Finance* 66:5, 1687–1733.

Mehran, Hamid. 1995. "Executive Compensation Structure, Ownership, and Firm Performance." *Journal of Financial Economics* 38:2, 163–184.

Morck, Randall. 2008. "Behavioral Finance in Corporate Governance: Economics and Ethics of the Devil's Advocate." *Journal of Management and Governance* 12:2, 179–200.

Morck, Randall, Andrei Shleifer, and Robert W. Vishny. 1988. "Management Ownership and Market Valuation: An Empirical Analysis." *Journal of Financial Economics* 20:1–2, 293–315.

Mowday, Richard T., Lyman W. Porter, and Richard M. Steers. 1982. *Organization Linkages: The Psychology of Commitment, Absenteeism, and Turnover.* New York: Academic Press.

O'Reilly, Charles A., and Jennifer A. Chatman. 1986. "Organizational Commitment and Psychological Attachment: The Effects of Compliance, Identification and Internalization on Prosocial Behavior." *Journal of Applied Psychology* 71:3, 492–499.

Paredes, Troy A. 2005. "Too Much Pay, Too Much Deference: Behavioral Corporate Finance, CEOs, and Corporate Governance." *Florida State University Law Review* 32, 673–762.

Parrino, Robert, Allen M. Poteshman, and Michael S. Weisbach. 2005. "Measuring Investment Distortions When Risk-Averse Managers Decide Whether to Undertake Risky Projects." *Financial Management* 34:1, 21–60.

Perry, Tod. 2000. "Incentive Compensation for Outside Directors and CEO Turnover." Working Paper, Kelley School of Business, Indiana University. Available at https://papers.ssrn.com/sol3/papers.cfm?abstract_id=236033.

Pratt, John W. 1964. "Risk Aversion in the Small and in the Large." *Econometrica* 32:1–2, 122–136.

Roll, Richard. 1986. "The Hubris Hypothesis of Corporate Takeovers." *Journal of Business* 59:2, 197–216.

Rosenstein, Stuart, and Jeffrey G. Wyatt. 1990. "Outside Directors, Board Independence, and Shareholder Wealth." *Journal of Financial Economics* 26:2, 175–184.

Ross, Stephen A. 1973. "The Economic Theory of Agency: The Principal's Problem." *American Economic Review* 63:2, 134–139.

Schoar, Antoinette, and Luo Zuo. 2016. "Shaped by Booms and Busts: How the Economy Impacts CEO Careers and Management Styles." *Review of Financial Studies*. Forthcoming. Available at http://aschoar.scripts.mit.edu/aschoar2016/wp-content/uploads/2016/07/Schoar-and-Zuo-11062011.pdf.

Shefrin, Hersh. 2006. *Behavioral Corporate Finance.* New York: McGraw-Hill.

Sitkin, Sim B., and Amy L. Pablo. 1992. "Reconceptualizing the Determinants of Risk Behavior." *Academy of Management Review* 17:1, 9–38.

Smith, Adam. 1776. *An Inquiry into the Nature and Causes of the Wealth of Nations.* New York: Modern Library.

Smith, Clifford W., and René M. Stulz. 1985. "The Determinants of Firms' Hedging Policies." *Journal of Financial and Quantitative Analysis* 20:4, 391–405.

Smith, C. Ann, Dennis W. Organ, and Janet P. Near. 1983. "Organizational Citizenship Behavior: Its Nature and Antecedents." *Journal of Applied Psychology* 68:4, 653–663.

Stulz, René M., and Rohan Williamson. 2003. "Culture, Openness, and Finance." *Journal of Financial Economics* 70:3, 313–349.

Sundaramurthy, Chamu, and Marianne Lewis. 2003. "Control and Collaboration: Paradoxes of Government." *Academy of Management Review* 28:3, 397–416.

Warner, Jerold B., Ross L. Watts, and Karen H. Wruck. 1988. "Stock Prices and Top-Management Changes." *Journal of Financial Economics* 20:1–2, 461–492.

Weinstein, Neil D. 1980. "Unrealistic Optimism about Future Life Events." *Journal of Personality and Social Psychology* 39:5, 806–820.

Weisbach, Michael S. 1988. "Outside Directors and CEO Turnover." *Journal of Financial Economics* 20:1–2, 431–460.

Whyte, Glen. 1993. "Escalating Commitment in Individuals and Group Decision Making: A Prospect Theory Approach." *Organizational Behavior and Human Decision Processes* 54:3, 430–455.

Williamson, Oliver E. 1985. *The Economic Institutions of Capitalism.* New York: The Free Press.

Wilson, Robert. 1968. "The Theory of Syndicates." *Econometrica* 36:1, 119–132.

Wu, YiLin. 2000. "Honey, I Shrunk the Board." Working Paper, Graduate School of Business, University of Chicago.

Yermack, David. 1996. "Higher Market Valuation of Companies with a Small Board of Directors." *Journal of Financial Economics* 40:2, 185–212.

Zhu, David H. 2013. "Group Polarization on Corporate Boards: Theory and Evidence on Board Decisions about Acquisition Premiums." *Strategic Management Journal* 34:7, 800–822.

6

Financial Planners and Advisors

BENJAMIN F. CUMMINGS
Associate Professor of Behavioral Finance
The American College of Financial Services.

Introduction

A growing number of individuals use financial advisors to provide guidance in navigating an increasingly complex financial marketplace. Using data from the Survey of Consumer Finances, Hanna (2011) reports that 21 percent of households used a financial planner in 1998, which increased to 25 percent in 2007. More recently, the Certified Financial Planner Boards of Standards, Inc. (CFP Board) (2015) estimates that 28 percent of consumers used a financial advisor in 2010, increasing to 40 percent in 2015. The Society of Actuaries (SOA) (2013) estimates that 55 percent of retirees and 48 percent of pre-retirees use financial advisors to help them make financial decisions.

The increasing demand for professional financial advice is accompanied by an increasing demand for talent in financial planning, which can be an attractive career. In 2012, *CNN Money* (2012) ranked financial advisors as the sixth best job in America. More recently, *U.S. News and World Reports* (2016) ranked the job of a financial advisor as the fourth best business job. The College for Financial Planning (2014) finds that 90 percent of survey respondents are extremely satisfied with their choice to pursue a career in financial advice. Additionally, the number of financial advisors is projected to grow for the foreseeable future. The Bureau of Labor Statistics (BLS) (2015) estimates that the number of personal financial advisors will grow by 30 percent over the next decade, suggesting good prospects for individuals who are considering the financial advice profession.

This chapter seeks to provide insight about the role of financial planners and advisors in helping others manage their financial resources. Particular attention is given to the behavior of and incentives for various players within the financial advice profession, especially to areas where financial planners and advisors may present behavioral biases. *Bias* can be described as a partiality for or against someone or something, often as a result of varying influences, incentives, or constraints. The incentives for financial planners and advisors ought to be considered when analyzing their role in a client–planner relationship. For example, the incentives tied to compensation structures may bias financial professionals. These professionals may also be biased by regulatory constraints or incentives. How incentives may affect the behavior and recommendations of financial planners and advisors is a primary focus in this chapter.

The first section of this chapter reviews the regulation of financial advice and the types of firms that exist, with particular attention given to registered investment advisers, broker-dealers, and insurance firms. The next section discusses agency costs as they relate to financial advice and addresses potential conflicts of interest that arise in regard to various compensation structures. The third section covers a few issues within the financial advice profession that can confuse consumers. The fourth section considers the empirical evidence about the use and value of financial advice. The final section summarizes the chapter and its main points before concluding with advice for consumers about selecting a financial professional.

The Regulation of Financial Advice

Different firm structures exist within the financial advice industry. These firms vary considerably in terms of service, business models, regulatory requirements, and standards of care. Before describing the most common types of firms that provide financial advice, this section offers a discussion of financial advisors and financial planners so as to provide a context for examining the various firm structures.

REGULATION OF FINANCIAL PLANNERS

Although financial planners are not regulated as a distinct profession, the Government Accountability Office (GAO 2011) suggests that most activities a financial planner may perform are regulated. However, CFP Board has long advocated regulating financial planners distinct from any other existing regulatory regimes (CFP Board 2016). CFP Board (2016, Why Does Regulation Matter? section, para. 2) also states that

> fragmented regulation creates legal "loopholes" and conflicting standards of conduct for the different components of financial planning, allowing providers to choose the standard that is most financially advantageous to them, rather than what is best for the client.

The Financial Planning Coalition, consisting of CFP Board, the Financial Planning Association (FPA), and the National Association of Personal Financial Advisors (NAPFA), has also expressed concern about the lack of federal regulation of financial planners. In 2014, the Financial Planning Coalition released a white paper highlighting evidence that the lack of federal regulation of financial planners harms consumers (Financial Planning Coalition 2014). For example, many practitioners who identify themselves as a financial planner do not actually provide financial planning services. The Financial Planning Coalition (2014, p. 17) also cites data of from Cerulli Associates that "only 38 percent of the self-identified financial planners actually had financial planning focused practices."

REGISTERED INVESTMENT ADVISERS

Registered Investment Advisers (RIAs) are firms established primarily to provide investment advice. Although other financial professionals may focus on the transaction of financial products, RIAs concentrate on advice related to investment decisions. As such, they are compensated not for transacting financial products but for providing advice related to investment strategies, philosophies, and/or ongoing investment management. Advisors of RIAs are known as Investment Adviser Representatives (IARs).

Regulation of RIAs dates back to the Investment Advisers Act of 1940. Despite some exceptions, an *investment advisor* is defined as follows:

> any person who, for compensation, engages in the business of advising others, either directly or through publications or writings, as to the value of securities or as to the advisability of investing in, purchasing, or selling securities, or who, for compensation and as part of a regular business, issues or promulgates analyses or reports concerning securities. (Investment Advisers Act of 1940, Section 202(a) (11), p. 3)

The Securities and Exchange Commission (SEC) and state securities regulators oversee investment advisers throughout the country. Historically, the respective responsibilities of the SEC and state securities regulators were not completely clear. Congress clarified those responsibilities with the Investment Advisers Supervision Coordination Act, which was part of the National Securities Markets Improvement Act of 1996 (Macey 2002). To reduce redundancy in regulation, this act prohibited firms from registering with the SEC unless or until they had at least $25 million in assets under management (AUM), and firms had to register if they had at least $30 million of AUM. Then the Dodd-Frank Wall Street Reform and Consumer Protection Act of 2010 increased the AUM threshold so that, in general, firms with over $100 million of AUM register with the SEC, and firms must register if they have at least $110 million of AUM (Securities and Exchange Commission 2011c). Additionally, all investment advisers based in Wyoming also register with the SEC, because Wyoming does not regulate investment advisers (Macey 2002). The division of the SEC that is responsible for oversight of investment advisers is the Office of Compliance Inspections and Examinations (OCIE). According to the Securities and Exchange Commission (2014), as of March 2014 the OCIE oversees more than 10,000 firms that collectively manage over $18 trillion of AUM.

All RIAs are required to file a Form ADV as part of their registration with the SEC or state securities regulator (Securities and Exchange Commission 2011a). Form ADV consists of two parts, both of which are intended to provide regulators and consumers with relevant information about the firm. Part 1 of Form ADV includes specific information about the firm, such as its main address, ownership, number of employees and clients, types of clients the firm serves, and any disciplinary actions. Part 2 provides information relevant to clients and potential clients. It includes a brochure used to communicate the services offered, the fees charged, any conflicts of interest and disciplinary actions, and information about the management and key personnel of the firm (Securities and Exchange Commission 2011a). Once firms are registered, they must provide their clients and regulators with an annual update of any material changes in their Form ADV. Form ADV for any firm is publicly available through the Investment Adviser Public Disclosure (IAPD) database, whether the firm is registered with the SEC or with one or more state securities regulators (Securities and Exchange Commission 2016).

IARs must submit Form U4 (the Uniform Application for Securities Industry Registration or Transfer) as part of their registration with the SEC or with state securities regulators (Financial Industry Regulatory Authority 2009). IARs typically file these forms electronically with the Investment Adviser Registration Depository (IARD) (Securities and Exchange Commission 2011b). IARs are urged to amend or update any material changes in the information reported on the Form U4 in a timely manner.

BROKER-DEALERS

As in other industries, brokers serve consumers by connecting buyers and sellers of a particular product or products. In the financial services industry, brokers typically provide transactional support for buyers and sellers of financial securities. The Securities Exchange Act of 1934 (1934, Section 3(a)(4)(A), p. 4) states that "The term 'broker' means any person engaged in the business of effecting transactions in securities for the account of others." In contrast, dealers sell products from their inventory. The Securities Exchange Act (Section 3(a)(5)(A), p. 10) states that "The term 'dealer' means any person engaged in the business of buying and selling securities . . . for such person's own account through a broker or otherwise." Many firms involved in transacting financial products provide services as both broker and dealer, either by connecting a buyer with a potential seller of a financial security or by connecting a buyer with a financial security that the firm has within its own inventory. Because these firms often perform both types of services, today they are commonly known as broker-dealers.

Individuals who work for a broker-dealer are commonly known as *registered representatives* of a broker-dealer, or by the nickname, registered reps, or even more simply, stockbroker or broker. A registered representative may be either an employee of the broker-dealer or an independent contractor. Regardless of the employment arrangement, broker-dealers are required to supervise the activities of their representatives (Colby, Schwartz, and Zweihorn 2015). As with IARs, representatives of a broker-dealer must also file Form U4 electronically except they do so through the Central Registration Depository (CRD) as part of their registration process (Financial Industry Regulatory Authority 2009). Information recorded on Form U4 is publicly available online through FINRA's BrokerCheck website (Financial Industry Regulatory Authority 2016b).

A self-regulatory organization (SRO) oversees broker-dealers and their registered representatives. The Maloney Act of 1938 amended the Securities Exchange Act of 1934 to create the National Association of Securities Dealers (NASD) as an SRO to provide oversight to the brokerage industry. In 2007, the NASD merged with the regulatory division of the New York Stock Exchange (NYSE) to form the Financial Industry Regulatory Authority (FINRA) (Financial Industry Regulatory Authority 2007). FINRA now provides regulatory oversight of almost 4,000 securities firms and over 600,000 representatives (Financial Industry Regulatory Authority 2016a). Although FINRA operates as a self-regulatory organization, the SEC oversees FINRA with considerable cost. In a report released by the Boston Consulting Group (2011), the SEC employs an examiner to oversee about every 2.2 FINRA examiners.

INSURANCE FIRMS

Insurance products are often a component of a comprehensive financial plan. In addition, agents who sell personal lines of insurance frequently provide financial advice. Insurance agents typically focus on one or a few lines of insurance. For example, an insurance agent may focus on property and casualty insurance for individuals and families. These property and casualty insurance agents work to secure for individuals and families insurance policies that will protect them in case of a financially catastrophic loss, whether from loss of property or from liability claims for damages or injuries. For most households, these insurance products typically include automobile insurance and homeowner's insurance, and may also include umbrella insurance, which is extra liability insurance designed to help protect individuals from major claims and lawsuits. Depending on the type of property and the risks to which the household is exposed, other insurance policies may also be purchased, like insurance for watercraft or recreational vehicles.

Insurance agents may focus on other risks to which households may be exposed, such as a premature death or an unexpected disability. These agents, often called life insurance agents, provide advice about the appropriateness of life insurance and disability insurance policies. They may also offer guidance about health insurance, or an agent may focus specifically on health insurance, although these agents commonly focus their services on employers who provide access to health insurance for their employees. Other insurance agents may focus on risks specifically dealing with a particular profession or professional role, such as professional liability insurance, malpractice insurance, errors and omissions (E&O) insurance, and volunteer involvement, such as directors and officers (D&O) insurance.

Unlike other sources of financial advice, the regulation of insurance rests solely at the state level. States have regulated insurance since the 1850s, emphasized as a state right in 1869, in *Paul v. Virginia,* in which the Supreme Court ruled that insurance policies were not transactions of commerce and, therefore, not under the purview of Congress. In 1944, the Supreme Court reversed *Paul v. Virginia* in *United States v. South-Eastern Underwriters Association* by declaring that insurance is considered commerce and is subject to federal oversight. In response, Congress passed the McCarran-Ferguson Act of 1945 to legislatively allow states to regulate insurance and establish licensing requirements. As such, insurance is regulated by state insurance commissions. The need to support state insurance commissioners in fulfilling their responsibilities led to the creation of the National Association of Insurance Commissioners (NAIC) (2016). Individual insurance agents must also be licensed in any state in which they sell insurance products, and these licensing requirements may vary depending on the state.

OTHER SOURCES OF FINANCIAL ADVICE

Besides the firms and affiliated individuals previously discussed, other firms and individuals may provide financial advice. For example, many accountants offer tax preparation and tax planning, as well as broader financial advice. Certified Public Accountants (CPAs) can obtain the Personal Financial Specialist (PFS) designation from the American Institute of CPAs (AICPA) as a way to distinguish themselves as an accounting professional who provides financial advice. Attorneys may also offer financial advice, especially relating to legal matters such as estate planning.

Other professionals may focus on other aspects of personal and family finance. Financial counseling and credit counseling firms often help individuals seeking to avoid bankruptcy or desiring assistance with debt and cash-flow management concerns. Most reputable firms that offer credit counseling services are established as nonprofit organizations and are members of the National Foundation for Credit Counseling (NFCC) and/or the Financial Counseling Association of America (FCAA).

Other providers of advice may be housed within other financial institutions, such as a local bank or credit union. Although these types of advisors may be employees or independent contractors working with or for the banks or credit unions, they are often registered representatives of affiliated broker-dealers or IARs, or both. They may also be licensed life and disability insurance agents affiliated with a life insurance firm.

Another source of financial advice can come from a financial therapist, who most often falls under one of the previously mentioned providers of financial advice. The Financial Therapy Association (FTA) defines *financial therapy* as the "integration of cognitive, emotional, behavioral, relational, and economic aspects that influence financial well-being, and ultimately, quality of life" (Financial Therapy Association 2015, para. 1). In essence, financial therapists extend the perspective of the client–planner relationship beyond the financial decisions involved as they consider the broader behavior and psychological picture of the individual and family.

Agency Costs in Financial Advice

Because of the nature of the service, consumers may have difficulty determining the quality of the financial advice they receive from a financial professional. With search goods, consumers can make comparisons and research the products to determine quality before making a purchase (Nelson 1970). Even with experience goods, such as a haircut or a massage, consumers can at least determine the quality of the good or service after they have experienced it. However, with credence goods, such as medical procedures or vehicle repairs, consumers often have difficulty determining quality even after receiving the good or service (Darby and Karni 1973). Because credence goods largely rely on the specialized knowledge of an expert, the expert knows more about the quality of the good or service than do the consumers (Dulleck and Kerschbamer 2006). As such, unscrupulous professionals who provide low-quality goods or services can exploit consumers of credence goods. Financial products and recommendations could also be considered credence goods because consumers rely on the expert knowledge of a financial professional. Additionally, the results of financial recommendations are often not realized until years in the future.

In a principal–agent relationship, a principal delegates specific responsibilities or tasks to an agent. Often, the delegated responsibilities are tasks that the principal either does not want to perform, does not have time to perform, or does not have the knowledges, skills, abilities, or tools to perform. In the case of financial planning, the principal is a client who hires an agent who is a financial advisor to perform some array of duties related to the financial affairs of the principal.

As in other agency relationships, using a financial professional can create agency conflicts (Jensen and Meckling 1976). In other words, the interests of the advisor may not be the same as the interests of the client. In such cases, the advisor may act in self-interested ways to the detriment of the client. Three types of agency costs that arise in these types of relationships are monitoring costs, bonding costs, and residual losses.

Monitoring costs refer to the responsibility of the principal to monitor the efforts performed by the agent. That is, the principal needs to perform due diligence to ensure that the hired agent is competent and ethical. In situations in which the agent possesses specialized knowledge that the principal does not have, adequate monitoring can be challenging. This information imbalance often provides the justification for government regulation, thereby outsourcing at least some of the monitoring responsibilities to a governmental entity that can hire a competent regulator to perform some monitoring functions on behalf of all principals who employ a particular agent. The previous section provided a discussion of government regulators who offer monitoring services of financial planners and advisors. Most notably, the SEC, FINRA, state securities regulators, and state insurance commissions provide oversight of many professionals who provide financial advice.

Although regulators provide monitoring services, agents still have a responsibility to perform monitoring functions. For example, consumers can check the public records of advisors with whom they are considering trusting with their financial affairs. These records are available through the SEC's IAPD, FINRA's BrokerCheck, and certifying organizations, such as CFP Board.

Bonding costs is another form of agency cost, in which the interests of the agent are bonded in some way to become more closely aligned with the interests of the principal. Unlike monitoring costs, which are typically borne by the principal, the agent generally bears bonding costs, often in an effort to demonstrate to consumers that there is commitment to a higher moral principle. In financial planning, an example of a bonding cost is a certification. For example, financial planners may work to achieve the Certified Financial Planner (CFP) certification to signal to the public that they have acquired considerable knowledge related to financial planning, are committed to abiding by CFP Board's Code of Ethics, and are willing to suffer the consequences if they violate the code.

Another example of a bonding cost is the standard of care to which an advisor is held. For example, IARs are held to a *fiduciary* standard of care, in which they are obligated to act in the interest of their clients. Conversely, registered representatives of a broker-dealer are merely held to a *suitability* standard, which requires that a financial product is suitable for a particular client. Given that some financial recommendations may be suitable for a client but not in the interest of the client, these standards of care may yield different advice, depending on the regulatory regime of the advisor.

Lastly, despite the best efforts of the principal to incur adequate monitoring costs and to find an agent who has incurred bonding costs, the principal may still experience a loss. Jensen and Meckling (1976) call these losses *residual losses*. Unfortunately, unscrupulous advisors may exploit investors while maintaining a clean public record before someone discovers unethical concerns with their practices; as a result, consumers may lose considerable sums of money. Residual losses can also represent the losses experienced by consumers who rely on advice from advisors who have conflicts of interest.

In 2015, the White House (2015) released an analysis by the Council of Economic Advisers (CEA), which estimates that conflicted advice on retirement assets costs Americans roughly $17 billion each year.

COMPENSATION STRUCTURES AND AGENCY COSTS

As with any profession, providers of financial advice are compensated for the services they provide, although many advisors also provide pro bono advice for individuals and families who cannot afford it. However, the form of compensation can create a conflict of interest in which the interests of the principal (i.e., client) and the agent (i.e., advisor) may not be fully aligned. Although all forms of compensation can give rise to conflicts of interest, some forms of compensation may be more prone to conflicts than others. That said, honest, trustworthy financial advisors can operate under each of these compensation structures, and no compensation method is completely free of conflicts of interest.

Commissions

Broadly speaking, a *commission* is a fee paid to a firm, or an agent or employee of a firm, often as a form of compensation for providing or assisting in the transaction of a good or service. As related to financial decisions, commission-based compensation typically focuses on the transactions of financial products, but it can be arranged in various ways. Commissions in financial services are also known as *sales charges* or *loads*. They are often assessed when purchasing investments through broker-dealers and when purchasing insurance policies through insurance agents.

An example of one of the most common commission structures is a *front-end load* on an investment product. When an investor determines an amount of money to invest in a product that has a front-end load, the amount invested is reduced by the amount of the front-end load. For example, if someone invests $1,000 with a registered representative of a broker-dealer, and the mutual fund in which he or she wants to invest has a front-end load of 5 percent, then the amount actually invested is $950. The remaining $50 is a commission that goes to the brokerage firm, with a portion of it going to the registered representative as a form of compensation.

Other commission structures exist. Another example of a load is a *back-end load*, also known as a *deferred sales charge* or a *contingent deferred sales charge*. A deferred sales charge occurs when an investor pays a set percentage when the product is sold or surrendered. The size of the sales charge may decrease over time so that if the investor owns the product long enough he or she might be able to avoid the deferred sales charge. However, waiting until the sales charge ends does not mean that the investor pays no sales charge. These products also typically include a *level load*, in which they charge an ongoing fee separate from the front-end or back-end load. For example, *12b-1 fees* are a level load assessed by mutual fund companies and are used to compensate advisors for distributing shares of the mutual fund.

Not surprisingly, commission-based compensation includes conflicts of interest in which the interests of the client and the registered representative may not be aligned. Because commissions are based on transactions, advisors may be incentivized to encourage more transactions that may not be optimal for a client. Excessive trading in an effort to generate commissions is called *churning*. Not only do front-end loads have conflicts, other forms of commission also have conflicts. For example, because back-end loads discourage investors from selling the investment, an advisor may be incentivized to sell an investment that includes both an ongoing level load (e.g., a 12b-1 fee) and a back-end load (i.e., a deferred sales charge). Thus, investors are discouraged from selling the investment, even if it may be advantageous to do so, yet the advisor continues to receive the level load.

Commissions on other financial products can also generate conflicts of interest. For example, commissions on life insurance products may incentivize advisors to encourage individuals to purchase more insurance than is optimal for them. Similarly, they may promote insurance products that have higher commissions, even when those types of products may not be best for a particular client.

Commissions can also be quite opaque, which increases the potential for conflicts of interest. Consumers may not realize the size of the commissions they pay and may assume that the services they receive are free of charge. Inderst and Ottaviani (2012) created a model suggesting that when commissions are not disclosed, they tend to be higher than if consumers are told the amount of the commission. Other commissions come directly from firms, so consumers do not directly see the costs associated with the commissions, and likewise, they may assume they are not bearing the cost of compensating an advisor.

Assets under Management

Firms managing investments for clients on an ongoing basis may charge a fee based on the size of the managed portfolio. These fees may be structured as a percentage of AUM, a flat percentage, or tiered with lower rates charged per managed dollar for larger portfolios. For example, a consumer with $2 million of investable assets who works with a firm charging a flat 1 percent of AUM annually will pay $20,000 per year for the services performed by the firm. Alternatively, a firm with a tiered-rate schedule, which charges 1 percent of AUM on the first million dollars of AUM and 0.75 percent of AUM on the second million dollars, would charge that same consumer $17,500 per year. Most firms with an AUM-based fee bill quarterly, either directly to the client or by deducting the fees from the investment account. Because asset values tend to fluctuate throughout the year, individual firms specify the process of calculating each quarterly payment.

Although AUM-based compensation is most common among investment advisors, others, such as dually registered advisors, may charge based on AUM as part of a wrap account or a separately managed account. A *wrap account* allows investors to be charged a single fee for their managed account rather than paying commissions on each transaction. *Separately managed accounts* allow for personalized portfolio management and investment decisions that are separate from other investors.

At first glance, compensation based on AUM may appear to properly align incentives. A financial advisor is rewarded with a larger asset base to manage when the client's investment portfolio performs well, which is often a goal for clients. However, as with any form of compensation in a principal–agent relationship, conflicts of interest can arise from a compensation structure based on AUM. Because the fee scales with the size of the portfolio, AUM-based advisors are incentivized to maintain and even increase the amount of investable assets. Although such a goal may seem aligned with the client's interests, this may not always be the case. For example, a household may be averse to holding debt and may want to pay off a mortgage using assets from their investment portfolio, but an AUM-based advisor might discourage such a decision. Likewise, an AUM-based advisor might discourage a client from withdrawing money from his or her portfolio at a rate that could maximize lifetime utility for a household.

Further, even when other financial products may be optimal to greater ensure lifetime income (e.g., annuity products), AUM-based advisors may be discouraged from recommending such products unless those products could still be included as part of the managed investment portfolio. These advisors are also discouraged from spending much time managing a particular client's portfolio because their compensation is not largely tied to the amount of time they spend managing the assets. As such, they may be tempted to spend minimal time on a particular client's portfolio. AUM-based advisors often suggest that because they do not charge commissions, they can provide financial advice that is free of conflicts of interest. However, such advisors often forget about the conflicts that exist within their own compensation structure.

Hourly

Some financial advisors who provide comprehensive financial planning advice view their value proposition much more broadly than merely providing investment advice and services. As such, they may be concerned about tying their compensation to only one aspect of their services (e.g., transacting financial products or managing investment portfolios) when the value they provide their clients includes many other aspects of their clients' financial lives. Because of their concerns with commission-based and AUM-based compensation, some financial advisors instead choose to charge hourly. This arrangement typically involves assessing an hourly fee for time spent meeting with an advisor and time the advisor spends working on a client's financial plan. Many advisors who work with clients on an hourly basis do not manage assets. Instead, they often provide recommendations that clients can implement on their own.

Although many advisors contend that hourly compensation is free of conflicts of interest, this compensation structure can also have misaligned incentives. Charging on an hourly basis may motivate an advisor to take longer on a particular client's case than is actually needed. Charging on an hourly basis also increases the saliency of the cost of advice for clients. Thus, clients may be less inclined to rely on the services of their financial advisor because of concerns about the incremental cost incurred each time they contact their financial advisor. As a result, clients may seek less advice than may be appropriate for them because of their price sensitivity to the hourly rate.

Retainer

Some financial advisors recognize the conflicts inherent in commission-based and AUM-based compensation structures, so they may choose instead to charge a monthly, quarterly, or annual retainer. Retainer fees are also attractive because they can provide a steady stream of income for a firm that depends neither on the number of transactions incurred (as is a commission-based compensation) nor on the performance of investment markets (as is an AUM-based compensation). As with other forms of compensation, the retainer model may also have conflicts of interest. Because advisors receive the same compensation regardless of the amount of time they devote to a particular client, they may be tempted to shirk their responsibilities and spend as little time as possible focusing on each client.

Project-Based Fees

With a desire to align the services that an advisor provides with the fees that clients pay, some firms charge project-based fees. These fees are often associated with the creation of a financial plan or an extensive review of a particular aspect of a client's financial situation. Because of the temporary nature of this form of engagement, advisors may encourage clients to continue the engagement under a different compensation structure. For example, if a client pursues ongoing investment management after completing the initial project, the fee arrangement could include a discount. As with all other compensation structures, charging project-based fees can also give rise to conflicts of interest. An advisor may be tempted to overestimate the amount of resources a particular project will require or, conversely, intentionally complete the project using fewer resources than initially outlined, thereby charging the client more than they otherwise might charge.

CONFLICTS OF INTEREST IN FINANCIAL PLANNING

All compensation structures can create conflicts of interest; such is the nature of principal–agent relationships. However, the existence of a conflict of interest does not imply that no advisors will act in the interests of their clients. Many financial advisors provide fair and ethical financial planning services for clients regardless of the compensation structure and despite these conflicts. To deal with these inherent conflicts, advisors should disclose such conflicts to their clients.

CFP Board (2013) stresses the importance of disclosing conflicts of interest in writing and not just conflicts that arise owing to compensation structure. Conflicts may also arise owing to the nature of the planner–client relationship, and advisors may be swayed for personal interests and benefits. Conflicts may also occur between a client and the advisor's firm, not just between a client and the advisor. To properly mitigate any conflicts, CFP Board encourages financial planners to disclose any known conflicts at the beginning of the client–planner engagement and to promptly disclose any conflicts that arise during the engagement.

Consumer Confusion

With different regulatory regimes and multiple compensation structures, consumers can easily be confused about the advice they are receiving. A study sponsored by the SEC reports considerable consumer confusion resulting from the use of generic terms such as financial advisor (Hung, Clancy, Dominitz, Talley, Berrebi, and Suvankulov 2008). For example, consumers do not realize that important regulatory distinctions in the industry generate different standards of care. This section highlights some areas of consumer confusion related to using professional financial advice.

FINANCIAL PLANNERS AND FINANCIAL ADVISORS

Many individuals use the financial advisor and financial planner terms synonymously, without clearly distinguishing between them. Although the terms may represent financial professionals with slightly different concentrations, the use of this terminology is not consistent across all individuals.

Financial advisor describes a professional who provides guidance related to financial decisions. Many financial advisors have acquired considerable knowledge relevant to household financial decisions, with which they can provide their clients with specialized guidance for their unique situations. Because the term is unregulated, some individuals may use the term without having requisite knowledge. That is, they may use the term *financial advisor* as a marketing tool despite lacking any specialized financial knowledge.

Financial planner typically describes a specific subset of financial advisors who give particular attention to financial decisions across time in order to reach future financial goals. Under this distinction, most financial planners could also be considered financial advisors, but some financial advisors may not be financial planners. Further, some individuals who claim to be financial advisors or financial planners may actually be neither type of financial professional.

ADVISERS AND ADVISORS

Two different spellings of *advisor* are commonly used to describe providers of financial advice. *Adviser* with an "e" is the spelling used in the Investment Advisers Act of 1940 and is often associated with RIAs. *Advisor* with an "o" is often the spelling used in the more generic and unregulated term, *financial advisor*. Although this spelling distinction is commonly employed, consistency in this spelling distinction is difficult and rare. Even the SEC website includes both spellings, which are commonly used interchangeably.

MULTIPLE REGULATORY REGIMES

A confusing aspect of the financial advice industry is that a single advisor may operate under multiple auspices. In other words, a financial advisor may be a registered representative of a broker-dealer and an investment adviser representative. Advisors who are affiliated with a broker-dealer and with a RIA are often described as having a dual registration or as being dually registered. To further complicate matters, the same dually registered advisor may also be licensed to sell insurance products. As a result, consumers may understandably have difficulty identifying the regulatory regime of a financial professional.

The Use and Value of Financial Advice

Various studies examine the use and value of financial advice. Studies focusing on the use of financial advice often seek to identify the characteristics of individuals who employ the services of a financial planner or financial advisor. Other studies seek to identify factors that lead someone to begin using the services of a financial professional. Attempting to quantify the value of financial advice is another common research initiative, whereas identifying qualitative factors that contribute to the value of financial advice is also beneficial. This section discusses each of these aspects of the use and value of financial advice.

SURVEY QUESTIONS ABOUT FINANCIAL ADVICE

Although various nationally representative datasets include questions about the use of financial advice, these questions differ considerably in wording and purpose. As a result, the measurement of who uses of a financial advisor differs depending on the dataset. For example, the National Longitudinal Survey of Youth (NLSY) includes the following question that focuses on retirement preparation and the use of a financial planner: "People begin learning about and preparing for retirement at different ages and in different ways. Have you (or your spouse/partner) consulted a financial planner about how to plan your finances after retirement?" The Asset and Health Dynamics among the Oldest Old (AHEAD) once included a broader question in its survey: "Do you have a financial advisor who helps make decisions?" Yet, the AHEAD, now merged with the Health and Retirement Study (HRS), has not asked about using a financial advisor since the early 1990s. The Survey of Consumer Finances (SCF) asks about using various financial professionals in its triennial survey. The SCF asks two separate questions about sources of information in making financial decisions. The first question focuses on borrowing or credit decisions, and the second question deals with savings and investment decisions. The second question asks: "I am going to read you a list. Please tell me which sources of information do you (and your family) use to make decisions about saving and investments?" A *financial planner* is the twelfth item on the list.

THE USE OF FINANCIAL ADVICE

Using empirical data from the 1998 Retirement Confidence Survey, Joo and Grable (2001) find that among pre-retirees, women are more likely to seek professional retirement planning help than men. The authors also find that income, better financial behaviors, proactive retirement attitudes, and risk tolerance are positively related to seeking professional retirement planning help. In 2006, the Investment Company Institute sought to learn more about the use of investment advice among mutual fund shareholders (Leonard-Chambers and Bogdan 2007). The authors find that about two-thirds of mutual fund shareholders engage the ongoing services of a financial advisor. Using data from a German bank, Bluethgen, Gintschel, Hackethal, and Müller (2008) find that users of financial advice tend to have more diversified investment portfolios. Users of professional financial advice are generally more educated (Hanna 2011), have higher net worth (Chang 2005; Bluethgen et al. 2008; Hanna 2011), have higher income (Joo and Grable 2001), and are older (Bluethgen et al. 2008; Hanna 2011) than those who do not use professional financial advice.

SEEKING FINANCIAL ADVICE

An analysis of those who use a financial advisor is somewhat different from an analysis of those who are likely to seek financial advice, which can be further differentiated by analyzing those who seek professional financial advice. Using a random sample of clerical workers, Grable and Joo (1999) provide insights about *financial help-seeking behavior*, broadly defined as seeking help from different sources such as a financial planner, attorney, credit counselor, friend, relative, and co-worker. Not surprisingly, the authors find that recently experiencing more financial stressors influences seeking financial advice from others. Exhibiting fewer positive financial behaviors is also related to seeking financial advice. Additionally, younger individuals and renters are more likely to seek advice from others. Women also tend to be more likely to seek financial advice than are men (Joo and Grable 2001; Bluethgen et al. 2008).

Using data from the 1998 Survey of Consumer Finances, Chang (2005, p. 1469) finds that "social networks are by far the most frequently used source of saving and investment information; however they are used most often by those with the least wealth." Chang also reports that wealthier households are more likely to rely on multiple sources for financial guidance, including financial professionals and media. Hanna (2011) suggests that the likelihood of using a financial advisor peaks in the mid-forties. This finding suggests that many individuals may wait until retirement decisions appear more pressing before seeking professional financial advice. Experiencing major life changes, including losing a spouse (Leonard-Chambers and Bogdan 2007; Korb 2010; Cummings and James 2014), declining cognition (Cummings and James 2014), or having a sudden change in income or net worth (Leonard-Chambers and Bogdan 2007; Cummings and James 2014), can also induce someone to seek financial advice from a professional.

MEETING WITH A FINANCIAL ADVISOR

A growing area of research includes psychophysiological economics, which can provide insights about the psychological and physiological responses during a meeting with a financial professional (Grable 2013). In a clinical intervention pilot study of college students, Archuleta, Burr, Carlson, Ingram, Kruger, Grable, and Ford (2015) find that meeting with a financial counselor can not only improve psychological well-being and financial behavior but also decrease financial distress. Individuals meeting with a financial advisor also present considerable discrepancy between objective and subjective measures of financial stress, suggesting that few individuals can accurately assess the impact of their financial stress during a meeting with a financial advisor (Grable and Britt 2012). Grable, Heo, and Rabbani (2014) study the interaction of financial anxiety and physiological arousal; they find that individuals with low financial anxiety but moderate to high physiological arousal are most likely to seek professional financial advice. Those with high financial anxiety are less likely to seek professional financial help because the anxiety may cripple their ability to seek help.

THE VALUE OF FINANCIAL ADVICE

Analyses of the value of financial advice often focus on the quantitative, financial benefits of using a professional financial advisor. However, the value of financial advice extends beyond merely financial benefits. Hanna and Lindamood (2010) recognize the difficulty of quantifying many of the financial benefits of using a financial planner. The benefits of sound financial advice can also include qualitative considerations. For example, consumers often seek the services of various professionals, not in an attempt to save money but because they find value in the advice they receive, which can help them make decisions with greater confidence. The advice of knowledgeable professionals can also dispel fears and concerns about an unknown future. As related to financial advice, Leonard-Chambers and Bogdan (2007) report that using an advisor provides fund owners with greater peace of mind, and James (2013) finds evidence that individuals who rely on a certified financial professional are less likely to second guess the expertise of their advisor during periods of market underperformance.

Evidence is mixed when focusing solely on portfolio metrics as a benefit of using a financial advisor. In a study of German investors, individuals who use a financial advisor tend to have more diversified portfolios that also include more asset classes (Bluethgen et al. 2008) However, these same individuals tend to turn over their portfolios more often and subsequently pay more transaction fees. An analysis of Dutch investors also suggests greater diversification in portfolios of individuals who use financial advisors, but these portfolios do not have significantly superior risk-adjusted performance (Kramer 2012). However, using the NLSY, Grable and Chatterjee (2014) find that on average, individuals with financial planners have superior risk-adjusted performance. Other studies suggest that investors who use financial advisors experience lower portfolio returns (Hackethal, Haliassos, and Jappelli 2012; Karabulut 2013).

Differing agency costs inherent in financial planning relationships may create varying incentives to act in the interest of investors, hence the mixed results about the value of financial advice in portfolio management. Using trained auditors who met with financial advisors, Mullainathan, Noeth, and Schoar (2012) find that financial advisors tend to encourage investment behavior and options that favor the advisor's interests. These findings suggest the importance of properly aligned incentives when working with a financial professional.

Other studies focus on the benefits of financial advice where the value may be more difficult to quantify. For example, households using a financial planner are more likely to have adequate life insurance protection (Finke, Huston, and Waller 2009) and are more likely to use Roth Individual Retirement Arrangements (IRAs) (Smith, Finke, and Huston 2012; Cummings, Finke, and James 2013). These findings suggest that a financial planner can help households acquire and maintain helpful risk-management tools and tax-sheltered vehicles, but quantifying the value of adequate insurance protection and optimal tax sheltering is challenging. Winchester, Huston, and Finke (2011) show that investors who use a financial advisor during a recession are more likely to maintain a long-term focus, suggesting that advisors can help investors maintain focus on their financial goals. Among individuals in their forties, Finke (2013) reports that using a financial planner is positively related to net worth and accumulated retirement assets. Although the direct effect of this relation is unclear, the evidence could suggest that financial planners may play a role in helping investors determine and implement tax advantageous accumulation strategies.

Several studies attempt to quantify the overall value of financial advice. An advisor can provide substantial value to clients through a combination of benefits, such as using low-cost investments, appropriate asset allocation and location, and portfolio rebalancing (Kinniry, Jaconetti, DiJoseph, and Zilbering 2014). This value creation is captured in what the authors term Vanguard Advisor's Alpha, which when all components are implemented, the gain in net returns to clients is estimated to be about 3 percentage points (300 basis points). Perhaps one of the most notable contributions an advisor can make is behavioral coaching, which accounts for the value of an advisor in helping clients maintain their long-term investment objectives when markets are volatile. The authors estimate that behavioral coaching alone can provide about 150 basis points in net return.

Blanchett and Kaplan (2013) quantify the value of intelligent investment decisions, which they term *gamma*. Advisors can provide value for their clients by helping them implement intelligent investment decisions, such as optimal asset allocation, tax-efficiency considerations, and appropriate portfolio withdrawal strategies. These authors estimate that gamma can generate a superior retirement income strategy, essentially equivalent to increasing the annual return by 159 basis points. This gamma estimate is within the same range as the Vanguard Advisor's Alpha estimate.

Advisor Biases

As mentioned previously, financial planners and advisors may present behavioral biases in response to the incentives that exist for them. For example, financial advisors may receive kickbacks from portfolio managers, which allows for higher fees and lower net returns for investors (Stoughton, Wu, and Zechner 2011). Del Guercio, Reuter, and Tkac (2010) find evidence that suggests mutual fund families target either clients who value brokerage services or do-it-yourself investors, but rarely do fund families target both types of clients. Mutual fund investors of broker-sold funds tend to pay higher fees and have lower risk-adjusted returns than investors who purchase funds directly without a broker (Bergstresser, Chalmers, and Tufano 2009). Further, actively managed broker-sold funds tend to underperform index funds (Del Guercio and Reuter 2014), and clients with brokers tend to earn lower risk-adjusted returns than similarly matched target-date funds (Chalmers and Reuter 2012).

Because of the potential for conflicting interests, clients may be willing to compensate advisors whom they trust. Because of this trust, fees for financial advice are higher than costs, and managers tend to underperform the market after accounting for fees, yet investors often prefer to rely on a professional rather than invest on their own (Gennaioli, Schleifer, and Vishny 2015). Being somewhat financially literate increases trust, but higher levels of financial literacy also decrease trust (Lachance and Tang 2012). As mentioned previously, disclosure is a commonly proposed solution to combat conflicted advice, thereby requiring advisors to disclose potential conflicts, but evidence suggests that disclosures do not discourage clients with low financial literacy from acting on conflicted advice (Carmel, Carmel, Leiser, and Spivak 2015). Although unbiased advice may be beneficial, few investors take advantage of it when it is offered, and even fewer actually follow the advice (Bhattacharya, Hackethal, Kaesler, Loos, and Meyer 2012).

Summary and Conclusions

Financial planners and advisors provide financial advice in various business models, regulatory regimes, and compensation structures. RIAs, broker-dealers, and insurance firms tend to be the most common types of firms where households seek financial advice, but other providers also exist. Advisors often play multiple roles and fall under different regulatory regimes, which can be confusing for consumers. A simplified regulatory structure that provides similar protections for consumers under each regulatory regime is warranted to reduce this confusion.

Regardless of the business model, all compensation structures contain potential conflicts of interest, and advisors and consumers ought to be cognizant of these potential conflicts. Investors can find ethical advisors within each regulatory regime and compensation structure. To increase the likelihood of using an ethical advisor, consumers have a responsibility to perform their own due diligence, rather than relying solely on government regulators. Seeking advisors who have incurred bonding costs can reduce agency conflicts. Consumers ought to ask questions of potential advisors and check publicly available records about them. By working with a financial planner or advisor with properly aligned incentives, consumers are likely to benefit both financially and psychologically.

DISCUSSION QUESTIONS

1. Explain the various regulatory regimes that encompass financial planners and advisors, and identify when a particular advisor would fit under each regime.
2. Discuss the agency costs involved in receiving professional financial advice and how to mitigate those costs.
3. Describe the common compensation structures used by financial advisory firms, and identify potential conflicts of interest within each compensation structure.
4. Discuss the characteristics of individuals who typically employ the services of financial planners and advisors.
5. Discuss empirical evidence about the value of financial advice.

REFERENCES

Archuleta, Kristy L., Emily A. Burr, Mary Bell Carlson, Jurdene Ingram, Laura Irwin Kruger, John E. Grable, and Megan Ford. 2015. "Solution Focused Financial Therapy: A Brief Report of a Pilot Study." *Journal of Financial Therapy* 6:1, 1–16. Available at http://dx.doi.org/10.4148/1944-9771.1081.

Bergstresser, Daniel, John M. R. Chalmers, and Peter Tufano. 2009. "Assessing the Costs and Benefits of Brokers in the Mutual Fund Industry." *Review of Financial Studies* 22(10), 4129–4156. doi:10.1093/rfs/hhp022.

Bhattacharya, Utpal, Andreas Hackethal, Simon Kaesler, Benjamin Loos, and Steffen Meyer. 2012. "Is Unbiased Financial Advice to Retail Investors Sufficient? Answers from a Large Field Study." *Review of Financial Studies* 25:5, 975–1032.

Blanchett, David M., and Paul Kaplan. 2013. "Alpha, Beta, and Now ... Gamma." *Journal of Retirement* 1:2, 29–45. Available at http://corporate1.morningstar.com/uploadedFiles/US/AlphaBetaandNowGamma.pdf.

Bluethgen, Ralph, Andreas Gintschel, Andreas Hackethal, and Armin Müller. 2008. "Financial Advice and Individual Investors' Portfolios." Working Paper, EBS Business School, JPMorgan, and Goethe University Frankfurt. Available at http://ssrn.com/abstract=968197.

Boston Consulting Group. 2011. "Investment Adviser Oversight: Economic Analysis of Options." Available at http://www.cfp.net/docs/public-policy/bcg_investment_adviser_oversight_economic_analysis.pdf?sfvrsn=2.

Bureau of Labor Statistics (BLS). 2015. "Personal Financial Advisors." Available at http://www.bls.gov/ooh/business-and-financial/personal-financial-advisors.htm.

Carmel, Eyal, Dana Carmel, David Leiser, and Avia Spivak. 2015. "Facing a Biased Adviser While Choosing a Retirement Plan: The Impact of Financial Literacy and Fair Disclosure." *Journal of Consumer Affairs* 49:3, 576–595.

Certified Financial Planner Board of Standards, Inc. (CFP Board). 2013. "Conflicts of Interest between CFP® Professionals and Clients." Available at https://www.cfp.net/docs/for-cfp-pros---professional-standards-enforcement/cfpboard_advisoryopinion_conflicts_of_interest.pdf?sfvrsn=4.

Certified Financial Planner Board of Standards, Inc. (CFP Board). 2015. "Survey: Americans' Use of Financial Advisors, CFP® Professionals Rises; Agree Advice Should Be in Their Best Interest." Available at https://www.cfp.net/news-events/latest-news/2015/09/24/survey-americans-use-of-financial-advisors-cfp-professionals-rises-agree-advice-should-be-in-their-best-interest.

Certified Financial Planner Board of Standards, Inc. (CFP Board). 2016. "Regulation of Financial Planners." Available at http://www.cfp.net/public-policy/public-policy-issues/regulation-of-financial-planners.

Chalmers, John, and Jonathan Reuter. 2012. "Is Conflicted Investment Advice Better than No Advice." NBER Working Paper No. 18158. Available at http://www.nber.org/papers/w18158.

Chang, Mariko L. 2005. "With a Little Help from My Friends (And My Financial Planner)." *Social Forces* 83:4, 1469–1497.

CNN Money. 2012. "Best Jobs in America: 6. Financial Adviser." Available at http://money.cnn.com/pf/best-jobs/2012/snapshots/6.html.

Colby, Robert L. D., Lanny A. Schwartz, and Zachary J. Zweihorn. 2015. "What Is a Broker-Dealer?" In Clifford E. Kirsch (ed.), *Broker-Dealer Regulation,* Second Edition, Volume 1, 1–133. New York: Practicing Law Institute.

College for Financial Planning. 2014. "2014 Survey of Trends in the Financial Planning Industry." Available at http://www.cffpinfo.com/download/survey_of_trends/2014SOT.pdf.

Cummings, Benjamin F., and Russell N. James. 2014. "Factors Associated with Getting and Dropping Financial Advisors Among Older Adults: Evidence from Longitudinal Data." *Journal of Financial Counseling and Planning* 25:2, 129–147.

Cummings, Benjamin F., Michael S. Finke, and Russell N. James. 2013. "Bounded Rationality Strikes Again: The Impact of Cognitive Ability and Financial Planners on Roth IRA Adoption and Ownership." Working Paper, Saint Joseph's University and Texas Tech University. Available at SSRN: http://ssrn.com/abstract=1968984.

Darby, Michael R., and Edi Karni. 1973. "Free Competition and the Optimal Amount of Fraud." *Journal of Law and Economics* 16:1, 67–88.

Del Guercio, Diane, and Jonathan Reuter. 2014. "Mutual Fund Performance and the Incentive to Generate Alpha." *Journal of Finance* 69:4, 1673–1704.

Del Guercio, Diane, Jonathan Reuter, and Paula A. Tkac. 2010. "Broker Incentives and Mutual Fund Segmentation." NBER Working Paper No. 16312. Available at http://www.nber.org/papers/w16312.

Dulleck, Uwe, and Rudolf Kerschbamer. 2006. "On Doctors, Mechanics, and Computer Specialists: The Economics of Credence Goods." *Journal of Economic Literature* 44:1, 5–42.

Financial Industry Regulatory Authority (FINRA). 2007. "NASD and NYSE Member Regulation Combine to Form the Financial Industry Regulatory Authority—FINRA." Available at https://www.finra.org/newsroom/2007/nasd-and-nyse-member-regulation-combine-form-financial-industry-regulatory-authority.

Financial Industry Regulatory Authority (FINRA). 2009. "Form U4: Uniform Application for Securities Industry Registration or Transfer." Available at https://www.finra.org/sites/default/files/AppSupportDoc/p015111.pdf.

Financial Industry Regulatory Authority (FINRA). 2016a. "About FINRA." Available at https://www.finra.org/about.

Financial Industry Regulatory Authority (FINRA). 2016b. "BrokerCheck® by FINRA." Available at http://brokercheck.finra.org/.

Financial Planning Coalition. 2014. "Consumers Are Confused and Harmed: The Case for Regulation of Financial Planners." Available at http://financialplanningcoalition.com/wp-content/uploads/2014/06/Financial-Planning-Coalition-Regulatory-Standards-White-Paper-Final.pdf.

Financial Therapy Association (FTA). 2015. "What Is Financial Therapy?" Available at http://www.financialtherapyassociation.org/.

Finke, Michael S. 2013. "Financial Advice: Does It Make a Difference?" In Olivia S. Mitchell and Kent Smetters (eds.), *The Market for Retirement Financial Advice*, 229–248. Oxford: Oxford University Press.

Finke, Michael, Sandra Huston, and William Waller. 2009. "Do Contracts Influence Comprehensive Financial Advice?" *Financial Services Review* 18:2, 177–193.

Gennaioli, Nicola, Andrei Schleifer, and Robert Vishny. 2015. "Money Doctors." *Journal of Finance* 70:1, 91–114.

Government Accountability Office (GAO). 2011. "Consumer Finance: Regulatory Coverage Generally Exists for Financial Planners, but Consumer Protection Issues Remain." Available at http://www.gao.gov/new.items/d11235.pdf.

Grable, John E. 2013. "Psychophysiological Economics: Introducing an Emerging Field of Study." *Journal of Financial Service Professionals* 67:5, 16–18.

Grable, John E., and So-hyun Joo. 1999. "Financial Help-Seeking Behavior: Theory and Implications." *Financial Counseling and Planning* 10:1, 13–24.

Grable, John E., and Sonya L. Britt. 2012. "Assessing Client Stress and Why It Matters to Financial Advisors." *Journal of Financial Service Professionals* 66:2, 39–45.

Grable, John E., and Swarn Chatterjee. 2014. "Reducing Wealth Volatility: The Value of Financial Advice as Measured by Zeta." *Journal of Financial Planning* 27:8, 45–51.

Grable, John E., Wookjae Heo, and Abed Rabbani. 2014. "Financial Anxiety, Physiological Arousal, and Planning Intention." *Journal of Financial Therapy* 5:2, 1–18. Available at http://dx.doi.org/10.4148/1944-9771.1083.

Hackethal, Andreas, Michael Haliassos, and Tullio Jappelli. 2012. "Financial Advisors: A Case of Babysitters?" *Journal of Banking & Finance* 36:2, 509–524.

Hanna, Sherman D. 2011. "The Demand for Financial Planning Services." *Journal of Personal Finance* 10:1, 36–62.

Hanna, Sherman D., and Suzanne Lindamood. 2010. "Quantifying the Economic Benefits of Personal Financial Planning." *Financial Services Review* 19:2, 111–127.

Hung, Angela A., Noreen Clancy, Jeff Dominitz, Eric Talley, Claude Berrebi, and Farrukh Suvankulov. 2008. "Investor and Industry Perspectives on Investment Advisors and Broker-Dealers." RAND Institute for Civil Justice, sponsored by the U.S. Securities and Exchange Commission. Available at https://www.sec.gov/news/press/2008/2008-1_randiabdreport.pdf.

Inderst, Roman, and Marco Ottaviani. 2012. "Financial Advice." *Journal of Economic Literature* 50:2, 494–512.

Investment Advisers Act of 1940. 1940. Securities and Exchange Commission. Available at https://www.sec.gov/about/laws/iaa40.pdf.

James, Russell N. 2013. "Brain Activity Suggests Planning Designation Helps Calm Investors." *Journal of Financial Planning* 26:2, 52–59.

Jensen, Michael C., and William H. Meckling. 1976. "Theory of the Firm: Managerial Behavior, Agency Costs and Ownership Structure." *Journal of Financial Economics* 3:4, 305–360.

Joo, So-hyun, and John E. Grable. 2001. "Factors Associated with Seeking and Using Professional Retirement-Planning Help." *Family and Consumer Sciences Research Journal* 30:1, 37–63.

Karabulut, Yigitcan. 2013. "Financial Advice: An Improvement for Worse?" Working Paper. Available at http://ssrn.com/abstract=1710634.

Kinniry, Francis M., Colleen M. Jaconetti, Michael A. DiJoseph, and Yan Zilbering. 2014. "Putting a Value on Your Value: Quantifying Vanguard Advisor's Alpha." Vanguard. Available at http://www.vanguard.com/pdf/ISGQVAA.pdf.

Korb, Brian. 2010. "Financial Planners and Baby Boomer Widows: Building a Trusting Relationship." *Journal of Financial Planning* 23:1, 48–53.

Kramer, Marc M. 2012. "Financial Advice and Individual Investor Portfolio Performance." *Financial Management* 41:2, 395–428.

Lachance, Marie-Eve, and Ning Tang. 2012. "Financial Advice and Trust." *Financial Services Review* 21:3, 209–226.

Leonard-Chambers, Victorio, and Michael Bogdan. 2007. "Why Do Mutual Fund Investors Use Professional Financial Advisers?" *Research Fundamentals* 16:1. Investment Company Institute. Available at http://www.ici.org/pdf/fm-v16n1.pdf.

Macey, Jonathan R. 2002. "Regulation of Financial Planners." White Paper. Financial Planning Association.

Mullainathan, Sendhil, Markus Noeth, and Antoinette Schoar. 2012. "The Market for Financial Advice: An Audit Study." NBER Working Paper 17929. Available at http://www.nber.org/papers/w17929.

National Association of Insurance Commissioners (NAIC). 2016. "About the NAIC." Available at http://www.naic.org/index_about.htm.

Nelson, Phillip. 1970. "Information and Consumer Behavior." *Journal of Political Economy* 78:2, 311–329.

Securities and Exchange Commission (SEC). 2011a. "Form ADV." Available at https://www.sec.gov/answers/formadv.htm.

Securities and Exchange Commission (SEC). 2011b. "Form ADV: General Instructions." Available at https://www.sec.gov/about/forms/formadv-instructions.pdf.

Securities and Exchange Commission (SEC). 2011c. "Investor Bulletin: Transition of Mid-Sized Investment Advisers from Federal to State Registration." Available at https://www.sec.gov/investor/alerts/transition-of-mid-sized-investment-advisers.pdf.

Securities and Exchange Commission (SEC). 2014. "About Office of Compliance Inspections and Examinations." Available at https://www.sec.gov/ocie/Article/about.html.

Securities and Exchange Commission (SEC). 2016. "Investment Adviser Public Disclosure." Available at http://www.adviserinfo.sec.gov/.

Securities Exchange Act of 1934. 1934. Available at https://www.sec.gov/about/laws/sea34.pdf.

Smith, Hyrum, Michael Finke, and Sandra Huston. 2012. "The Influence of Financial Sophistication and Financial Planners on Roth IRA Ownership." *Journal of Financial Service Professionals* 66:6, 69–81.

Society of Actuaries (SOA). 2013. "Retirement Survey Report Key Findings and Issues: Understanding and Managing the Risks of Retirement." Available at https://www.soa.org/Files/Research/research-2014-retire-survey-findings.pdf.

Stoughton, Neal M., Youchang Wu, and Josef Zechner. 2011. "Intermediated Investment Management." *Journal of Finance* 66:3, 947–980.

U.S. News and World Reports. 2016. "Best Jobs: Financial Advisor." Available at http://money.usnews.com/careers/best-jobs/financial-adviser.

White House. 2015. "The Effects of Conflicted Investment Advice on Retirement Savings." Available at https://www.whitehouse.gov/sites/default/files/docs/cea_coi_report_final.pdf.

Winchester, Danielle D., Sandra J. Huston, and Michael S. Finke. 2011. "Investor Prudence and the Role of Financial Advice." *Journal of Financial Service Professionals* 65:4, 43–51.

7

Financial Analysts

SUSAN M. YOUNG
Associate Professor of Accounting
Gabelli School of Business, Fordham University

Introduction

A wealth of academic research examines financial analyst behavior during the past 30 years. These studies use many different approaches to determine how analysts make decisions. For example, a recent survey investigates the "black box" of equity analysts (Brown, Call, Clement, and Sharp 2015). Various experiments also examine analyst behavior (Young 2009). More commonly, researchers use data now widely available through the Thomson Reuters I/B/E/S database to examine analysts' decision processes (Clement 1999). This database allows researchers to measure many individual characteristics of the analysts who are included in the database. These characteristics are associated with the accuracy and bias in analysts' forecasts and recommendations. Examples of these analyst characteristics include past forecast accuracy and bias, brokerage house size, and forecasting experience.

Financial analysts, similar to other decision makers, are subject to many of the same biased judgments. For example, they are limited in their capacity, ability, and resources during their forecasting tasks. However, given their expertise in analyzing firms, they could be less biased or more accurate than the average decision maker. Early studies in analyst expertise have established that analysts are more accurate than basic random-walk models and become more accurate as their experience in forecasting increases. For example, Brown, Griffin, Hagerman, and Zmijewski (1987) compare the accuracy of analysts' forecasts to basic time-series models based on historical earnings data. They find analysts' forecasts to be more accurate and attribute this finding to both the informational and the timing advantage of analysts above and beyond a simple mapping of historical earnings. Mikhail, Walther, and Willis (1997) find that analysts become more accurate in their forecasts of earnings per share (EPS) as they build experience in the forecasting task. Evidence also shows that analysts are optimistic in both their forecasts and their recommendations (Francis and Philbrick 1993; Lim 2001).

Studies typically measure forecast bias as the observed, signed difference between the analyst's forecast and the observed actual EPS of the firm. Accuracy in forecasts is measured as the absolute difference between an analyst's forecast and the ex-post realization of the firm's EPS. Biases in recommendations are measured by forming trading portfolios based on analysts' recommendations. Ex-post returns, both short and long term, are then measured to determine whether excess positive or negative returns are realized from relying on analysts' reports. Interestingly, one analyst can produce both more accurate and more biased forecasts than another analyst. For example, if Analyst A issues two forecasts that are both two cents more than the actual EPS, and Analyst B issues one forecast that is three cents more and one forecast that is three cents less than the actual EPS, Analyst A is considered more accurate, but also more optimistically biased. This chapter focuses on the bias in analysts' reports, with occasional mention of how this relates to analyst accuracy.

Prior research provides evidence that analysts "add value" or are informative to the market as information intermediaries. Studies find that analysts' forecasts and recommendations move stock prices, measured as the stock price reaction and changes in trading volume in response to changes in analyst outputs, such as earnings forecasts, recommendations, target price forecasts, and cash-flow forecasts. For example, Cheng (2005) finds that analysts' forecasts explain 22 percent of the variation in market-to-book ratios not captured by other information variables. However, research also finds that analysts may produce biased reports in certain situations, which may be predictable, and certain types of analysts may be more likely to be biased in their reports.

Analysts have competing incentives in their jobs. They benefit from having accurate reports, which can increase their reputation and lower job turnover. However, analysts also want to please management with optimistic long-term forecasts, price targets, and recommendations. As a result, they curry favor with managers to obtain access to better information and encourage more trading and banking deals, which lead to higher analyst compensation. Given the context of the analyst's work environment, disentangling analyst bias from economic incentives (rational or purposeful bias) versus behavioral bias (nonrational or unintentional bias) due to environmental factors is difficult.

Research on whether the market understands and incorporates these biases is mixed. The following sections examine the research related to these topics. The first section presents a discussion of the role of equity analysts in the market. This section also reviews some regulations enacted in the early 2000s relating to the conflicts of interest among financial analysts, brokerage house structure, and the managers of publicly traded firms. The second section discusses the psychological theories that explain bias in decision making. The third section explores the relation between information uncertainty in a forecasting task and analyst bias. The fourth section examines whether certain analyst characteristics can moderate analyst bias. The penultimate section discusses whether decision makers can de-bias their judgments. The chapter then concludes with a summary.

Role of Financial Analysts and Market Regulation

As information intermediaries, sell-side financial analysts play a critical role in analyzing, interpreting, and distributing information to market participants about the prospects of publicly traded firms. The main outputs of their analyses include quarterly and annual EPS forecasts and recommendations on the firms they follow: buy recommendations for those firms they believe are undervalued, hold recommendations for those they believe are appropriately valued, and sell recommendations for those they believe are overvalued. Analysts also provide a monitoring role, which positively influences market efficiency by reducing agency costs (Chung and Jo 1996). The empirical literature provides evidence that changes in analysts' trading recommendations and EPS estimates affect financial market valuations (Ramnath, Rock, and Shane 2008).

In response to large market failures such as Enron and WorldCom beginning in 2000, market participants, including the U.S. Congress, called for regulation that would increase analyst objectivity and reduce bias in analysts' reports by reducing or eliminating analyst conflicts of interest. In late 2000, the Securities and Exchange Commission (SEC) issued Regulation Fair Disclosure (Reg FD) to address some of these concerns. Reg FD barred management from selectively disclosing material nonpublic information to select analysts, thereby reducing the incentive for analysts to bias reports in order to gain access to privileged information. Following the release of Reg FD, the National Association of Securities Dealers (NASD) and the SEC enacted further rules to mitigate what they considered a significant optimistic bias in analysts' reports.

During 2002 and 2003, the SEC approved a series of rules to address possible conflicts of interest for equity analysts. These rules included a strict separation of investment banking from equity research activities. The rules also required changes in analysts' compensation arrangements, as well as more informative disclosure by analysts who own shares in the companies they follow. Also in 2003, the New York Stock Exchange (NYSE), the SEC, NASD, and the attorney general of New York announced that 10 of the top brokerage houses in the nation had settled an enforcement action relating to conflicts of interest between research and investment banking, referred to as the Global Settlement. The brokerage firms paid fines and penalties in excess of $1.3 billion. Although the Global Settlement enforcement issues only applied to the 10 investment firms, it virtually established new precedents for the limits to conflicts between banking and research in full-service brokerage firms. The SEC accepted NASD Rule 2711, NYSE Rule 472, in addition to the Global Settlement in late 2002 and early 2003. These regulations further addressed analysts' conflicts of interest and limited information transmission between analysts and brokerage house investment banking branches. In summary, the banks agreed to implement a series of reforms to address the pervasive concerns related to conflicts of interest and optimistic analyst research.

Subsequently, in July 2007, Financial Industry Regulatory Authority (FINRA) was created by consolidating the NASD and the NYSE. FINRA is responsible for rule writing, firm examination, enforcement, arbitration, and mediation functions, along with all functions previously overseen solely by the NASD.

OPTIMISM IN EARNINGS FORECASTS

Much of the empirical research finds that before these regulations, analysts were excessively optimistic in both their earnings forecasts and their stock recommendations. For example, Lim (2001) asserts that management prefers optimistic forecasts because these forecasts increase market valuations and therefore management compensation. Lim proposes that analysts may be willing to bias their forecasts upward in order to receive preferred treatment from management and therefore obtain better nonpublic information about the firm. Lim's results show that firms exhibiting higher uncertainty, which is proxied by the standard deviation of weekly excess stock returns, are associated with more optimistic analyst earnings forecasts. Das, Levine, and Sivaramakrishnan

(1998) suggest that analysts are more likely to require nonpublic information to develop an accurate forecast of EPS for firms with low earnings predictability and this higher demand for information causes analysts to be more optimistic to please firm management. Their assumption is that analyst optimism will assist with access to management's nonpublic information. Therefore, analysts should optimally provide optimistic forecasts to improve the amount, timing, and type of information they receive from management. The authors' results show a consistent negative relation between earnings predictability and forecast optimism, which confirms their management relations hypothesis.

OPTIMISM IN STOCK RECOMMENDATIONS

In addition to the literature that provides evidence of optimism in analysts' forecasts, the evidence also shows optimism in analysts' recommendations. For example, Womack (1996) finds that analysts are seven times more likely to issue a new buy recommendation than a new sell recommendation. Mikhail, Walther, and Willis (2004) find that sell recommendations constitute only 6 percent of their sample of recommendations, whereas buy and hold recommendations make up the remaining 94 percent. Several rational, economic factors may influence analysts' incentives and cause them to avoid sell recommendations. For instance, analysts' desire to maintain access to important management-provided information may cause them to take actions to curry favor with management, making them reluctant to issue sell recommendations. Sell recommendations may also jeopardize the investment banking business of the analysts' employers (Lin and McNichols 1998), or they may adversely affect commissions generated from customer trading transactions (Michaely and Womack 1999). An optimistic bias in recommendations may also improve an analyst's chances of being promoted by his employer (Hong and Kubik 2003).

Francis and Philbrick (1993) find that analysts' earnings forecasts are more optimistically biased for sell and hold recommendations than for buy recommendations. They conclude that this pattern is consistent with analyst incentives to improve management relations and is inconsistent with the economic incentives of trade boosting. *Trade boosting* assumes that equity analysts are driven by the economic incentive to increase trading in the stocks they cover and therefore to increase their compensation. In contrast to these findings, Eames, Glover, and Kennedy (2002) show that analyst earnings forecasts are optimistic for buy recommendations and pessimistic for sell recommendations. These results support the presence of both a trade boosting incentive and a behavioral explanation: analysts unintentionally bias their output of forecasts stock recommendations to achieve consistency between the two.

BEHAVIOR OF ANALYSTS ACROSS THE PRE- AND POST-REGULATION PERIODS

Given that the goal of the increased regulation was to reduce analyst conflicts of interest, many studies examine the behavior of analysts across the pre- and post-regulation periods in an attempt to determine whether the regulatory goals were achieved. To the extent that optimism in analysts' reports is due to conflicts of interest that regulation reduced, the expectation would be to see analyst optimism also reduced or eliminated. However, if analyst optimism is due to behavioral reasons (as discussed in the next two sections), the regulation may not have achieved these goals. The following is a brief survey of the post-regulation research.

Gintschel and Markov (2004) study whether Reg FD reduced the informativeness of analysts' forecasts and recommendations, which implies that Reg FD was effective in reducing or curtailing selective disclosure to certain analysts. Their findings support this conjecture. They find that in the post-Reg FD period, the absolute price impact of analyst information was 28 percent lower than the pre-regulation level. The authors also report that the drop in price impact varied systematically with brokerage house and stock characteristics. For example, the difference in price impact between optimistic analysts and non-optimistic analysts in the post-Reg FD period is 50 percent lower compared to its pre-regulation levels.

Ertimur, Sunder, and Sunder (2007) also compare analyst recommendations issued before and after Reg FD and they find that the integrity of "buy" and "hold" recommendations improved post-regulation; the change is more pronounced for analysts they expected to be more conflicted. The authors measure the intensity of conflicts of interest by classifying analysts into three groups: (1) firms with no investment banking business (nonconflicted firms), (2) firms with a relatively low reputation in the investment banking business (medium conflicted), and (3) firms with a high reputation in the investment banking business (highly conflicted). They find that regulation increased the relation between earnings forecast accuracy and recommendations of profitability for buy recommendations with regard to those analysts expected to be the most conflicted. Additionally, Ertimur et al. find that treating hold recommendations as sells results in significantly negative mean abnormal returns after regulation. This finding is in contrast to the positive returns earned from such a recommendation strategy before Reg FD, indicating that post-regulation, analysts reduced the optimism in their recommendations.

Kadan, Madureira, Wang, Zach, and Bathala (2009) find that conflicts of interest, defined as the past presence of an underwriting relationship between the brokerage house and the firm the analyst is following, is a key determinant of stock recommendations before regulation. After regulation, however, the distribution of analysts' reports became more balanced and less optimistic. They report that conflicted analysts are no longer more likely to issue optimistic recommendations than unaffiliated analysts, but are still less likely to issue pessimistic recommendations.

Chih-Ying and Chen (2009) also examined the impact of regulation on analyst behavior. They find a significantly stronger relation between recommendations and analysts' earnings forecasts relative to stock prices after the regulation came into effect. Their evidence also shows a weaker relation between stock recommendations and proxies for analyst conflicts of interest (net external financing and amount of underwriting business) after implementation of the regulation. Further, they find that stock recommendations issued by analysts with greater potential conflicts experience a larger decrease in bias after this regulation.

Barniv, Hope, Myring, and Thomas (2009) show that regulations have strengthened the relation between residual income valuations of firm equity and analyst recommendations. They also find evidence of increased usefulness of analysts' earnings forecasts for investors. Additionally, their evidence shows that residual income valuations have an increasingly positive association with future returns after the adoption of Reg FD and additional regulations (NASD Rule 2711, NYSE Rule 472, and Global Settlement). Lach, Highfield, and Treanor (2012) examine the long-run performance of analyst ratings of initial public offerings (IPOs) following regulation to assess changes in bias during this period. They find a reduction in the amount of positive bias contained in analysts' reports after regulation.

Lee, Strong, and Zhu (2014) also hypothesize that the series of regulations occurring between 2000 and 2003 strengthened the information environment of U.S. capital markets. Their findings show that these regulations reduced mispricing and increased market efficiency. These results are more pronounced among higher information uncertainty firms. The authors use several proxies for firm information uncertainty, including accruals quality, firm size, firm age, analyst coverage, analyst forecast dispersion, and cash flow and stock return volatility. Lee et al. find forecast accuracy also improved in these firms and conclude that this is consistent with an improved information environment after the regulations took effect.

Some research, however, continues to find evidence of remaining conflicts of interest among analysts. For example, Brown et al. (2015) administered a survey and conducted interviews with more than 350 analysts. They note that management relationships and the underwriting business continue to be very important to analysts' compensation. Brown et al. (p. 4) state:

> In spite of regulators' efforts, 44 percent of our respondents say their success in generating underwriting business or trading commissions is very important to their compensation, suggesting conflicts of interest remain a persistent concern for users of sell-side research.

Additional studies report that a majority of recommendations continue to be biased upward toward buy recommendations (Agrawal and Chen 2008) and that analysts continue to rarely issue sell recommendations (Shon and Young 2015). Groysberg, Healy, and Maber (2011) find that the buy recommendations of sell-side analysts underperform the buy recommendations from buy-side analysts by 5.8 percent. Buy-side analysts usually work for a pension fund or mutual fund, whereas sell-side analysts typically work with a brokerage house. According to Chen and Matsumoto (2006), access to manager-provided information is important even in the post-Reg-FD era.

In summary, much of the empirical research shows that the regulations reduced, but did not eliminate, the amount of bias in analyst recommendations following regulation. However, additional research continues to find evidence of bias related to analysts' conflicts of interest. The following two sections discuss the behavioral theories that hypothesize the explanation for the observed optimism in analysts' reports.

Psychological Theories About Analyst Bias

The cognitive psychology literature suggests that individuals generally tend to be over-optimistic (Armor and Taylor 2002). For example, as Helweg-Larsen and

Shepperd (2001) note, individuals believe that they are less likely to be victims of auto accidents, crime, and earthquakes and that they are less likely than others to suffer from illness, depression, unwanted pregnancies, or a host of other negative health events (Weinstein 1980). The psychology literature further suggests that uncertainty in a task affects the decision maker's level of judgment and may exacerbate this optimistic bias.

HEURISTICS

Based on a series of experiments, Tversky and Kahneman (1974) report that people rely on heuristic principles, or short-cuts, to reduce complex and uncertain tasks of predicting values to simpler judgments. These heuristics may lead to severe and systematic errors. Uncertainty in forecasting may result from a low perceived reliability in the task (i.e., the information provided for the task is inconsistent) or a low perceived validity in the task (i.e., the information may not properly reflect true values) (Ganzach 1994). Studies report that decision makers become more optimistic as a task becomes more uncertain, and that this is robust across a number of tasks (Kahneman and Tversky 1973; Markus and Zajonc 1985; Ganzach and Krantz 1991).

Both financial analysis and forecasts of a company's earnings and future performance are complex, unstructured tasks that vary across industries and across firms within industries. As such, forecasting tasks naturally vary across firms on both the perceived reliability (e.g., high variance in past earnings) and the perceived validity (e.g., presence of earnings management) of the information used. For example, consider an evaluation of two companies based on two equally important variables, such as last year's earnings and management's forecast of this year's earnings. The two companies have the same mean across the two variables, but one has two moderate numbers whereas the other has one high number and one low number. The results of this research suggest that the more inconsistent company would receive a higher, or more optimistic, forecast or recommendation from a financial analyst.

One explanation in the psychology literature for this optimism under uncertainty is the *leniency heuristic,* whereby people have a tendency to give the benefit of the doubt when predicting performance (Kahneman and Tversky 1973). In other words, when cues are inconsistent, a decision maker will under-weight negative information and over-weight positive information, thereby leading to an optimistic judgment. In accordance with these cognitive models, Kahneman and Tversky find the optimism bias is an increasing function of task uncertainty.

Durand, Limkriangkrai, and Fung (2014) find related results when examining the herding behavior of financial analysts. The authors examined analysts who lag behind their analyst cohort in forecasting for individual firms (laggards). Their evidence shows that as the forecasting task becomes more difficult to analyze, the laggards are more likely to move away from the consensus forecast (anti-herding). Durand et al. also find that as the laggards become more confident (measured as the analyst's forecast frequency), they are also less likely to anti-herd. The authors conclude that these results indicate that laggard analysts have lower meta-cognitive skills.

CONFIRMATION BIAS

A complementary theory for optimism under uncertainty suggests that an individual's preferences can influence the manner in which a person processes information and forms beliefs (Kahneman and Tversky 1979). This preference is known as *confirmation bias,* which suggests that people over-weight information that confirms their prior beliefs and under-weight information that runs counter to their prior beliefs. This preference applies to both analysts and investors. A similar theory is *motivated reasoning,* which suggests that investors are more likely to arrive at conclusions that they prefer and that this preference encourages using strategies that are most likely to yield the desired results (Kunda 1990).

Tests of these optimism theories include observing analyst forecasts and recommendations. Studies such as Odean (1998) report that investors over-weight information that confirms their prior beliefs and under-weight information that is contrary to their prior beliefs. In his survey of investor psychology as a determinant of asset pricing literature, Hirshleifer (2001, p. 1549) states, "People tend to interpret ambiguous evidence in a fashion consistent with their own beliefs. They give careful scrutiny to inconsistent facts and explain them as due to luck or faulty data gathering." Similarly, Hales (2007, p. 613) states "when people are presented with information that is counter to their directional preferences, they are motivated to interpret it skeptically." An experiment conducted by Hales shows that investor subjects automatically agree with information that suggests they will make money and disagree with information that suggests they will lose money, which is consistent with confirmation bias. The theory of confirmation bias is also consistent with Eames et al. (2002), who find that analyst forecasts are significantly optimistic for buy recommendations and pessimistic for sell recommendations.

To summarize, based on these theories, analysts are likely to exhibit optimistic bias in their reports even after Reg FD and the Global Settlement. Given that research confirms that these behavioral biases are intrinsic to the analysts' tasks of forecasting earnings and issuing recommendations, optimism should be even more likely in situations that are more ambiguous or uncertain.

Information Uncertainty and Analyst Bias

Much of the literature conducted before Reg FD finds that as uncertainty in a firm's information environment increases, optimism increases in equity analysts' earnings forecasts. Das et al. (1998) and Groysberg et al. (2011) both suggest that the observed optimism in analysts' reports is primarily due to the economic incentives of the analysts (i.e., analyst compensation is based to a large extent on trading volume and investment banking business). The post-regulation research provides some evidence that this optimism is reduced, because some conflicts of interest have been removed from the analysts' environment. As previously discussed, the effectiveness of regulation in reducing analyst bias depends on the origin of the bias. To the extent that analysts' optimism for high uncertainty firms stems from cognitive biases in their decision making, the effects of regulation such as those enacted will not completely eliminate the optimism in analysts' reports.

To isolate the cause of the observed bias in analysts' reports, Young (2009) used an experimental setting to remove economic incentives from the analyst's decision process. The results of her experiment show that an increase in the analyst's perceived uncertainty of the forecasting task results in significantly lower relative optimism in the analyst's earnings forecasts. This finding indicates that regulation to remove conflicts of interest may have the ability to reduce optimism in analysts' forecasts. Her evidence also shows that relative forecast optimism bias is positively related to the level of the analysts' recommendations. This finding is consistent with behavioral theories that analysts process information in a manner that supports their goals. Regulation would not resolve this behavior.

Research on analyst decision making under uncertainty uses many proxies for information uncertainty, including poor credit quality, high accounting accruals, and dispersion in analyst forecasts. Grinblatt, Jostova, and Philipov (2016) use poor credit quality as a proxy for information uncertainty. The authors acknowledge that analyst recommendations and forecasts move market prices; therefore, they examine whether these price movements are justified by analysts' superior information (the efficient market perspective) or are unmerited and based on investors' blindly following expert opinions (the behavioral perspective). Their results show significantly higher optimism in analysts' earnings forecasts for low-credit-quality firms and no significant relation between analysts' forecast bias and stock returns for higher-credit-quality firms, supporting the behavioral perspective. Their evidence also shows that firms with more optimistic consensus in analyst forecasts subsequently earn lower risk-adjusted returns, also consistent with the behavioral perspective.

Bradshaw, Richardson, and Sloan (2001) find that an over-optimistic analyst forecast is greater for firms with high accruals. The authors interpret this finding as analysts' not fully incorporating the predictable earnings reversals of the accruals.

Zhang (2006) used dispersion in analysts' forecasts as a proxy for information uncertainty. The author finds that greater information uncertainty leads to more positive (or negative) forecast errors and subsequent forecast revisions following good (or bad) news. These results imply that information uncertainty appears to delay the absorption of uncertain information into the analysts' forecasts. Zhang also discovers that these effects are much stronger following bad news than following good news. In general, analysts underreact to new information and underreact more when information uncertainty is greater.

Additional studies examine the motives behind analysts' overly optimistic reports. A sample of these motives include investment banking relationships (Chan, Karceski, and Lakonishok 2007; Ljungqvist, Marston, Starks, Wei, and Yan 2007; Agrawal and Chen 2012), career or reputation concerns (Hong and Kubik 2003; Ertimur, Muslu, and Zhang 2011), better access to management's private information (Ke and Yu 2006; Westphal and Clement 2008), and other behavioral reasons (Willis 2001; Hales 2007). In general, these studies report higher levels of optimism when these motives are present.

In summary, the research finds evidence of optimistic bias in analysts' reports across many situations and that the level of optimism increases in situations of high information uncertainty. The next section provides a discussion of the research that examines whether certain analyst characteristics, such as experience, can reduce optimism.

Analyst Characteristics as Moderators of Optimism

Cognitive psychology research reports that increased experience and ability can lead to decreased optimism in forecasts and estimates. This research suggests that performance feedback and experience with the task moderate the tendency toward optimism. Therefore, analysts with more experience are likely to develop superior private information about a company's economics the longer they follow the firm. This is supported by the findings of Mikhail et al. (1997). Ertimur et al. (2007) and Bowen, Chen, and Cheng (2008) who also find that analysts' ability increases with experience. Further, evidence presented by Ke and Yu (2006) shows that analysts improve their effectiveness in translating earnings forecasts into recommendations as their experience increases.

Additional research identifies analyst-specific factors that have the potential to reduce the bias in analysts' reports. Drake and Myers (2011) examine whether analyst characteristics may reduce the relation between optimism in analyst forecasts and firms with high accounting accruals. Their evidence shows that analysts with more general experience and analysts following fewer firms have lower accrual-related overoptimism. Stickel (1992) finds that *Institutional Investor* magazine's all-star analysts supply forecasts more often than other analysts. More frequent forecasts can be more advantageous for the generation of recommendations because they can incorporate the latest earnings-relevant information and will be less optimistic. Results obtained by Lim (2001) show that less experienced analysts produce more optimistic forecasts in order to build access to management.

Cao and Kohlbeck (2011) examine whether analyst characteristics are associated with analysts' effectiveness in processing public information and in avoiding optimistic bias. The authors hypothesize that high quality analysts can more easily attract new banking business owing to their high reputations, and they are therefore more likely to reflect bad news in their reports on a timely basis, whereas low quality analysts have incentives to remain optimistic to please management, even in the face of bad news. Using a sample of large price changes, the authors find an asymmetric reaction in the analyst response to large positive and large negative information shocks. Cao and Kohlbeck also find that their proxy for analyst quality is inversely associated with the probability of recommendation downgrades after large negative price shocks, indicating a reduction in asymmetry as analyst quality improves. They conclude that their findings are consistent with the asymmetry being associated with a general information processing bias among lower-quality analysts. Such a bias affects superior analysts less often, owing at least in part to their effectiveness in translating earnings forecasts into recommendations. These findings are consistent with studies that find more expert analysts issue more profitable stock recommendations than do less expert analysts (Stickel 1995; Mikhail et al. 2004).

However, a few early studies do not find a difference between experience levels and bias in analyst forecasts. For example, Mikhail et al. (1997) report an increase in accuracy but no change in forecast bias as experience increased. In summary, the majority of the literature consistently finds that some analyst characteristics, such as experience, may help reduce analyst bias.

Analyst Bias and the Impact on Market Reactions

The literature provides mixed results on the effect of analyst bias on investors. Although some studies report that analyst conflicts of interest do not have a systematic impact on investors (Mehran and Stulz 2007; Agrawal and Chen 2008), other studies find that analysts' biased reports adversely affect investors.

Several studies establish bias in analysts' reports. For example, evidence presented by Barber, Lehavy, and Trueman (2007) shows that buy recommendations from independent research firms outperform those from investment banks by roughly 8 percent. However, investment banks' hold and sell recommendations outperform those from independent firms by approximately 4.5 percent. This finding is consistent with recommendations from investment banks being positively biased, resulting in sell recommendations containing more information.

Additional studies differentiate the effects of this bias on institutional and retail investors. These studies tend to find that individuals are less aware of bias than are institutional investors and they are more susceptible to it. For example, Michaely and Womack (1999) present evidence that the market does not fully account for analyst bias. For instance, stocks that underwriter analysts recommend perform more poorly than buy recommendations made by unaffiliated brokers. The authors estimate the mean excess return for IPOs recommended by underwriter analysts is −18 percent after two years, compared with +45 percent for recommendations made by unaffiliated brokers.

Further, Malmendier and Shanthikumar (2007) find that large traders (a proxy for institutional investors) adjust their trading response downward to analysts' reports, but small traders (a proxy for retail investors) do not, suggesting that individuals may be unaware of analyst bias. The authors show that an investment strategy of strictly following analyst recommendations produces negative abnormal returns for a buy-and-hold strategy, which may harm small investors.

Baker and Dumont (2014) also analyzed the performance of buy-and-hold ratings and surveyed retail investors about their reliance on analyst recommendations. Although the authors find that buy ratings of firm equity significantly underperform hold ratings, retail investors report that they rely on these recommendations when making investment decisions.

Mikhail, Walther, and Willis (2007), who use trade size to distinguish between large (sophisticated) and small (unsophisticated) investors, find that large investors respond more to the information contained in recommendation revisions, whereas small investors respond more to the occurrence of a recommendation and trade more in response to upgrades and buys. As a result, the authors find that in the five days after recommendation revisions, large traders earn an average raw return of 5.1 percent, whereas small traders earn −1.8 percent. De Franco, Lu, and Vasvari (2007) examine 50 events in which analysts issued misleading reports. According to the authors, small investors are differentially affected. Small traders lost $2.2 billion—two-and-a-half times as much as large traders.

Cheng, Liu, and Qian (2006) present evidence suggesting that institutional investors are more likely to rely on buy-side analysts than on potentially conflicted sell-side analysts. In summary, substantial evidence indicates that analyst bias may harm small and unsophisticated investors.

De-Biasing the Bias

Can financial analysts improve their judgment and decision making by reducing the bias in their reports? Analysts should be motivated to reduce their optimistic bias if this bias reduces their reputation and therefore reduces their compensation. However, they would not be motivated if the optimistic bias helps with management relations and therefore increases their compensation. Research shows that analysts have incentives to build and maintain a reputation for objectivity throughout their career (Ljungqvist, Marston, and Wilhelm 2006; Hugon and Muslu 2010). Research also provides evidence that analysts who have been identified as superior performers are more likely to experience favorable career outcomes, such as moving up to a high-status brokerage house (Hong, Kubik, and Solomon 2000; Hong and Kubik 2003). If a reduction in optimism ties into a higher reputation, cognitive psychology suggests several remedies.

According to cognitive psychology research, repetition, feedback, and experience tend to mitigate judgmental biases (Einhorn and Hogarth 1978; Kagel and Levin 1986; Rose and Windschitl 2008). For example, Kagel and Levin find that subjects who overbid in early rounds of an auction become less optimistic in their bids as they gain experience. Outcomes that indicate a large discrepancy between forecasted and actual performance are expected to motivate the decision maker to increase effort, adjust performance expectations, or both. Ericsson, Krampe, and Tesch-Romer (1993) and Radhakrishnan, Arrow, and Sniezak (1996) confirm that these corrections should improve the accuracy and reduce the optimism of future evaluations. Therefore, introducing new information or knowledge, which is used in future judgments and decisions, reduces optimism (Shepperd, Oullette, and Fernandez 1996). This reduction in optimism would occur for analysts as they receive feedback that is accurate and timely (i.e., actual quarterly and annual reported EPS), adjust their performance, and learn from general experience with the task.

Analyst studies find that several different variables can mitigate optimism, including reputation concerns (Fang and Yasuda 2009; Bradley, Clarke, and Cooney 2012), competition (Hong and Kacperczyk 2010; Sette 2011), the presence of independent analysts (Gu and Xue 2008), or the presence of institutional investor-owners (Ljungqvist et al. 2007; Gu, Li, and Yang 2013). Ability may also be a mitigating factor. Evidence by Cao and Kohlbeck (2011) shows that analysts of particularly high skill and reputation are less likely to issue overly optimistic recommendations or to overreact to news. In general, analysts can reduce their optimistic bias, and they do so in many situations.

Summary and Conclusions

The bias in financial analysts' reports has been a concern of investors and regulators for several decades. Some have alleged that analysts' reports lack independence and objectivity, due to the conflicts of interest between the equity analyst function in the brokerage house and the banking side. Investors have complained that managers of publicly traded firms are providing select material information to a chosen group of analysts, who in turn, disclose this to their preferred clients. The results of this behavior harmed investors by excluding them from these inner circles. To address these conflicts, several pieces of regulation were put into place in the early 2000s. The object of these regulations was to eliminate this selective disclosure of information and thereby level the playing field across investor categories.

Although the market environment changed with Reg FD and the additional regulations, several studies find that a relation with management still appears to be important for today's analysts. Evidence shows that the bias in analysts' reports, despite being somewhat reduced, still remains. Further, this bias may hurt small or unsophisticated investors. In light of these findings, regulators should consider the sources of analyst bias when evaluating what regulations would help to eliminate this bias and achieve regulatory goals. Investors should also consider both the source of analyst bias and the analyst characteristics, which may help them to select less optimistic analysts' reports.

DISCUSSION QUESTIONS

1. Discuss whether regulation solves the problem of bias in analysts' reports.
2. Identify two incentives or environmental factors that increase analyst bias.
3. Identify analyst characteristics that reduce analyst bias.
4. Discuss whether the market recognizes and adjusts for the bias in analysts' reports.

REFERENCES

Agrawal, Anup, and Mark A. Chen. 2008. "Do Analyst Conflicts Matter? Evidence from Stock Recommendations." *Journal of Law & Economics* 51:3, 503–537.

Agrawal, Anup, and Mark A. Chen. 2012. "Analyst Conflicts and Research Quality." *Quarterly Journal of Finance* 2:2, 1–40.

Armor, David A., and Shelley E. Taylor. 2002. "When Predictions Fail: The Dilemma of Unrealistic Optimism." In Thomas Gilovich, Dale Griffin, and Daniel Kahneman (eds.), *Heuristics and Biases: The Psychology of Intuitive Judgment*, 334–347. New York: Cambridge University Press.

Baker, William, and Gregory Dumont. 2014. "Equity Analyst Recommendations: A Case for Affirmative Disclosure?" *Journal of Consumer Affairs* 48:1, 96–123.

Barber, Brad M., Reuven Lehavy, and Brett Trueman. 2007. "Comparing the Stock Recommendation Performance of Investment Banks and Independent Research Firms." *Journal of Financial Economics* 85:2, 490–517.

Barniv, Ran, Ole-Kristian Hope, Mark J. Myring, and Wayne B. Thomas. 2009. "Do Analysts Practice What They Preach and Should Investors Listen? Effects of Recent Regulations." *Accounting Review* 84:4, 1015–1039.

Bowen, Robert M., Xia Chen, and Qiang Cheng. 2008, "Analyst Coverage and the Cost of Raising Equity Capital: Evidence from Underpricing of Seasoned Equity Offerings." *Contemporary Accounting Research* 25:3, 657–700.

Bradley, Daniel, Jonathan Clarke, and John Cooney Jr. 2012. "The Impact of Reputation on Analysts' Conflicts of Interest: Hot Versus Cold Markets." *Journal of Banking and Finance* 36:8, 2190–2202.

Bradshaw, Mark, Scott Richardson, and Richard Sloan. 2001. "Do Analysts and Auditors Use Information in Accruals?" *Journal of Accounting Research* 39:1, 45–74.

Brown, Lawrence D., Paul Griffin, Robert Hagerman, and Mark Zmijewski. 1987. "An Evaluation of Alternative Proxies for Market's Assessment of Unexpected Earnings." *Journal of Accounting and Economics* 9:2, 159–193.

Brown, Lawrence D., Andrew C. Call, Michael B. Clement, and Nathan Y. Sharp. 2015. "Inside the 'Black Box' of Sell-Side Financial Analysts." *Journal of Accounting Research* 53:1, 1–47.

Cao, Jian, and Mark Kohlbeck. 2011. "Analyst Quality, Optimistic Bias, and Reactions to Major News." *Journal of Accounting, Auditing & Finance* 26:3, 502–526.

Chan, Louis K. C., Jason Karceski, and Joseph Lakonishok. 2007. "Analysts' Conflicts of Interest and Biases in Earnings Forecasts." *Journal of Financial & Quantitative Analysis* 42:4, 893–913.

Chen, Shuping, and Dawn A. Matsumoto. 2006. "Favorable versus Unfavorable Recommendations: The Impact on Analyst Access to Management-Provided Information." *Journal of Accounting Research* 44:4, 657–689.

Cheng, Qiang. 2005. "The Role of Analysts' Forecasts in Accounting-based Valuation: A Critical Evaluation." *Review of Accounting Studies* 10:1, 5–31.

Cheng, Yingmei, Mark H. Liu, and Jun Qian. 2006. "Buy-side Analysts, Sell-side Analysts, and Investment Decisions of Money Managers." *Journal of Financial and Quantitative Analysis* 41:1, 51–83.

Chih-Ying, Chen, and P. F. Chen. 2009. "NASD Rule 2711 and Changes in Analysts' Independence in Making Stock Recommendations." *Accounting Review* 84:4, 1041–1071.

Chung, Kee H., and Hoje Jo. 1996. "The Impact of Security Analysts' Monitoring and Marketing Functions on the Market Value of Firms." *Journal of Financial and Quantitative Analysis* 31:4, 493–512.

Clement, Michael. B. 1999. "Analyst Forecast Accuracy: Do Ability, Resources, and Portfolio Complexity Matter?" *Journal of Accounting and Economics* 27:3, 285–303.

Das, Somnath, Carolyn Levine, and K. Sivaramakrishnan. 1998. "Earnings Predictability and Bias in Analysts' Earnings Forecasts." *Accounting Review* 73:2, 277–294.

De Franco, Gus, Hai Lu, and Florin P. Vasvari. 2007. "Wealth Transfer Effects of Analysts' Misleading Behavior." *Journal of Accounting Research* 45:1, 71–110.

Drake, Michael, and Linda Myers. 2011. "Analysts' Accrual Over-optimism: Do Analyst Characteristics Play a Role?" *Review of Accounting Studies* 16:4, 59–88.

Durand, Robert B., Manapon Limkriangkrai, and Lucia Fung. 2014. "The Behavioral Basis of Sell-Side Analysts' Herding." *Journal of Contemporary Accounting and Economics* 10:3, 176 190.

Eames, Michael, Steven M. Glover, and Jane Kennedy. 2002. "The Association between Trading Recommendations and Broker-analysts' Earnings Forecasts." *Journal of Accounting Research* 40:1, 85–104.

Einhorn, Hillel J., and Robin M. Hogarth. 1978. "Confidence in Judgment: Persistence of the Illusion of Validity." *Psychological Review* 85:5, 395–416.

Ericsson, K. Anders, Ralf T. Krampe, and Clemens Tesch-Romer. 1993. "The Role of Deliberate Practice in the Acquisition of Expert Performance." *Psychological Review* 100:3, 363–406.

Ertimur, Yonca, Volkan Muslu, and Frank Zhang. 2011. "Why Are Recommendations Optimistic? Evidence from Analysts' Coverage Initiations." *Review of Accounting Studies* 16:4, 679–718.

Ertimur, Yonca, Jayanthi Sunder, and Shyam V. Sunder. 2007. "Measure for Measure: The Relation between Forecast Accuracy and Recommendation Profitability of Analysts." *Journal of Accounting Research* 45:3, 567–606.

Fang, Lily, and Ayako Yasuda. 2009. "The Effectiveness of Reputation as a Disciplinary Mechanism in Sell-Side Research." *Review of Financial Studies* 22:9, 3735–3777.

Francis, Jennifer, and Donna R. Philbrick. 1993. "Analysts' Decisions as Products of a Multi-Task Environment." *Journal of* Accounting *Research* 31:3, 216–230.

Ganzach Yoav. 1994. "Inconsistency and Uncertainty in Multi-attribute Judgment of Human Performance." *Journal of Behavioral Decision Making* 7:3, 193–211.

Ganzach, Yoav, and David Krantz. 1991. "The Psychology of Moderate Prediction: Leniency and Uncertainty." *Organizational Behavior and Human Decision Processes* 48:2, 169–193.

Gintschel, Andreas, and Stanimir Markov. 2004. "The Effectiveness of Regulation FD." *Journal of Accounting and Economics* 37:3, 293–314.

Grinblatt, Mark, Gergana Jostova, and Alexander Philipov. 2016. "Analysts' Forecast Bias and Mispricing." Working Paper, UCLA Anderson School of Management. http://dx.doi.org/10.2139/ssrn.2653666.

Groysberg, Boris, Paul M. Healy, and David A. Maber. 2011. "What Drives Sell-Side Analyst Compensation at High-Status Investment Banks?" *Journal of Accounting Research* 49:4, 969–1000.

Gu, Zhaoyang, Zengquan Li, and Yong George Yang. 2013. "Monitors or Predators: The Influence of Institutional Investors on Sell-Side Analysts." *Accounting Review* 88:1, 137–169.

Gu, Zhaoyang, and Jian Xue. 2008. "The Superiority and Disciplining Role of Independent Analysts." *Journal of Accounting & Economics* 45:2/3, 289–316.

Hales, Jeffrey. 2007. "Directional Preferences, Information Processing, and Investors' Forecasts of Earnings." *Journal of Accounting Research* 45:3, 607–628.

Helweg-Larsen, Marie, and James A. Shepperd. 2001. "Do Moderators of the Optimistic Bias Affect Personal or Target Risk Estimates? A Review of the Literature." *Personality and Social Psychology Review* 5:1, 74–95.

Hirshleifer, David. 2001. "Investor Psychology and Asset Pricing." *Journal of Finance* 56:4, 1533–1597.

Hong, Harrison, and Marcin Kacperczyk. 2010. "Competition and Bias." *Quarterly Journal of Economics* 125:4, 1683–1725.

Hong, Harrison, and Jeffrey D. Kubik. 2003. "Analyzing the Analysts: Career Concerns and Biased Earnings Forecasts." *Journal of Finance* 58:1, 313–351.

Hong, Harrison, Jeffrey D. Kubik, and Amit Solomon. 2000. "Security Analysts' Career Concerns and Herding of Earnings Forecasts." *RAND Journal of Economics* 31:1, 121–144.

Hugon, Artur, and Volkan Muslu. 2010. "Market Demand for Conservative Analysts." *Journal of Accounting and Economics* 50:1, 42–57.

Kadan, Ohad, Leonardo Madureira, Rong Wang, Tzachi Zach, and Chenchuramaiah T. Bathala. 2009. "Conflicts of Interest and Stock Recommendations: The Effects of the Global Settlement and Related Regulations." *Review of Financial Studies* 22:10, 4189–4217.

Kagel, John, and Dan Levin. 1986. "The Winner's Curse and Public Information in Common Values Auctions." *American Economic Review* 76:5, 894–920.

Kahneman, Daniel, and Amos Tversky. 1973. "On the Psychology of Prediction." *Psychological Review* 80:4, 237–251.

Kahneman, Daniel, and Amos Tversky. 1979. "Prospect Theory: An Analysis of Decision Under Risk?" *Econometrica* 47:2, 263–291.

Ke, Bin, and Yong Yu. 2006. "The Effect of Issuing Biased Earnings Forecasts on Analysts' Access to Management and Survival." *Journal of Accounting Research* 44:5, 965–999.

Kunda, Ziva. 1990. "The Case for Motivated Reasoning." *Psychological Bulletin* 108:3, 480–498.

Lach, Patrick A., Michael J. Highfield, and Stephen D. Treanor. 2012. "The Quiet Period Has Something to Say." *Applied Financial Economics* 22:1, 71–86.

Lee, Edward, Norman Strong, and Zhenmei Zhu. 2014. "Did Regulation Fair Disclosure, SOX, and Other Analyst Regulations Reduce Security Mispricing?" *Journal of Accounting Research* 52:3, 733–774.

Lim, Terrence. 2001. "Rationality and Analysts' Forecast Bias." *Journal of Finance* 56:1, 369–385.

Lin, Hsiou-wei, and Maureen McNichols. 1998. "Underwriting Relationships, Analysts' Earnings Forecasts, and Investment Recommendations." *Journal of Accounting and Economics* 25:1, 101–127.

Ljungqvist, Alexander, Felicia Marston, Laura T. Starks, Kelsey D. Wei, and Hong Yan. 2007. "Conflicts of Interest in Sell-Side Research and the Moderating Role of Institutional Investors." *Journal of Financial Economics* 85:2, 420–456.

Ljungqvist, Alexander, Felicia Marston, and William J. Wilhelm, Jr. 2006. "Competing for Securities Underwriting Mandates: Banking Relationships and Analyst Recommendations." *Journal of Finance* 61:1, 301–340.

Malmendier, Ulrike, and Devin Shanthikumar. 2007. "Are Small Investors Naive about Incentives?" *Journal of Financial Economics* 85:2, 457–489.

Markus, Hazel, and Robert B. Zajonc. 1985. "The Cognitive Perspective in Social Psychology." In Gardner Lindzey and Elliot Aronson (eds.), *The Handbook of Social Psychology* 3, 137–230. New York: Random House.

Mehran, Hamid, and René M. Stulz. 2007. "The Economics of Conflicts of Interest in Financial Institutions." *Journal of Financial Economics* 85:2, 267–296.

Michaely, Roni, and Kent L. Womack. 1999. "Conflict of Interest and the Credibility of Underwriter Analyst Recommendations." *Review of Financial Studies* 12:4, 653–686.

Mikhail, Mikhail B., Beverly R. Walther, and Richard H. Willis. 1997. "Do Security Analysts Improve Their Performance With Experience?" *Journal of Accounting Research* 35:1, 131–166.

Mikhail, Mikhail B., Beverly R. Walther, and Richard H. Willis. 2004. "Do Security Analysts Exhibit Persistent Differences in Stock Picking Ability?" *Journal of Financial Economics* 74:1, 67–91.

Mikhail, Mikhail B., Beverly R. Walther, and Richard H. Willis. 2007. "When Security Analysts Talk, Who Listens?" *Accounting Review* 82:5, 1227–1253.

Odean, Terrence. 1998. "Are Investors Reluctant to Realize Their Losses?" *Journal of Finance* 53:5, 1775–1798.

Radhakrishnan, Phanikiran, Holly Arrow, and Janet A. Sniezek. 1996. "Hoping, Performing, Learning and Predicting: Changes in the Accuracy of Self-Evaluations of Performance." *Human Performance* 9:1, 23–49.

Ramnath, Sundaresh, Steve Rock, and Phillip Shane. 2008. "A Review of Research Related to Financial Analysts' Forecasts and Stock Recommendations." *International Journal of Forecasting* 24:1, 34–75.

Rose, Jason P., and Paul D. Windschitl. 2008. "How Egocentrism and Optimism Change in Response to Feedback in Repeated Competitions." *Organizational Behavior and Human Decision Processes* 105:2, 201–220.

Sette, Enrico. 2011. "Competition and Optimistic Advice of Financial Analysts: Evidence from IPOs." *Journal of Financial Intermediation* 20:3, 441–457.

Shepperd, James A., Ouellette, Judith A., and Julie K. Fernandez. 1996. "Abandoning Unrealistic Optimism: Performance Estimates and the Temporal Proximity of Self-Relevant Feedback." *Journal of Personality and Social Psychology* 70:4, 844–855.

Shon, John, and Susan M. Young. 2015. "Do Sell Recommendations Increase or Decrease an Analyst's Credibility? The Role of Confirmation Bias and Market Sentiment." Working Paper, Fordham University.

Stickel, Scott E. 1992. "Reputation and Performance Among Security Analysts." *Journal of Finance* 47:5, 1811–1836.

Stickel, Scott E. 1995. "The Anatomy of the Performance of Buy and Sell Recommendations." *Financial Analysts Journal* 51:5, 25–39.

Tversky, Amos, and Daniel Kahneman. 1974. "Judgment under Uncertainty: Heuristics and Biases." *Science* 185:4157, 1124–1131.

Weinstein, Neil D. 1980. "Unrealistic Optimism about Future Life Events." *Journal of Personality and Social Psychology* 39:5, 806–820.

Westphal, James D., and Michael B. Clement. 2008. "Sociopolitical Dynamics in Relations Between Top Managers and Security Analysts: Favor Rendering, Reciprocity, and Analyst Stock Recommendations." *Academy of Management Journal* 51:5, 873–897.

Willis, Richard H. 2001. "Mutual Fund Manager Forecasting Behavior." *Journal of Accounting Research* 39:3, 707–725.

Womack, Kent L. 1996. "Do Brokerage Analysts' Recommendations Have Investment Value?" *Journal of Finance* 51:1, 137–167.

Young, Susan M. 2009. "The Effect of Perceived Uncertainty on Analysts' Recommendations and Earnings Forecasts." *Review of Behavioral Finance* 1:1, 62–82.

Zhang, X. Frank, 2006. "Information Uncertainty and Analyst Forecast Behavior." *Contemporary Accounting Research* 23:2, 565–590.

8

Portfolio Managers

ERIK DEVOS
JP Morgan Chase Professor in Business Administration and Professor of Finance
College of Business Administration, University of Texas - El Paso

ANDREW C. SPIELER
Professor of Finance
Frank G. Zarb School of Business, Hofstra University

JOSEPH M. TENAGLIA
Emerging Markets Portfolio Specialist
Emerging Global Advisors

Introduction

Portfolio managers are professional investors who oversee and control discretionary pools of capital known as funds, which are available for investment to a larger base of investors. Portfolio managers often employ a team of analysts and junior portfolio managers who report to them. The analysts help provide ideas to managers and perform research on possible investments for the fund. Ultimately, however, the final decision-making power typically lies solely with portfolio managers. A single fund could potentially have millions of investors, with each of them counting on the portfolio manager to achieve a specific goal, such as income or growth. With so many stakeholders involved, the portfolio manager needs to develop and adhere to a plan when managing the fund.

The portfolio management process may vary depending of the type of fund, but generally follows the same basic steps: (1) setting the investment objective, (2) developing and implementing the portfolio strategy, and (3) monitoring and adjusting the portfolio (Maginn, Tuttle, McLeavey, and Pinto 2007). In the first step, the portfolio manager selects a benchmark to which he compares the fund, both in composition and in performance. If the manager seeks a targeted level of outperformance relative to that benchmark, that goal is set during this step. Any constraints to which the fund must comply are also established here. The constraints can range from restrictions on the fund's risk, such as that no allocation can exceed 5 percent of the fund, to its composition, such as that only invest in companies with minority chief executive officers (CEOs).

In the second step, the portfolio manager details a plan as to how he manages the fund to achieve the pre-established goals. For example, this could be a "top-down" investment allocation, in which the manager identifies macro trends and broadly allocates the fund among asset classes. This approach contrasts with a "bottom up" security selection, in which the research and picking of individual securities drive the investment process. At this stage, the manager selects and invests in securities to create the desired portfolio.

Lastly, the manager constantly monitors the fund and makes necessary adjustments. For example, if one of the securities in the portfolio has increased in value to the point where the manager believes it no longer has sufficient upside potential, the manager may elect to sell and replace the security. This stage of the portfolio management process is continuous. That is, the portfolio manager must continuously monitor many factors and analyze the impact on every security in the fund. The magnitude of this daunting task and the sustained success of so few in being able to do it well help explain why portfolio managers can sometimes be referred to as the "rock stars of the financial world" (Myers 2008). This chapter explores the behavioral tendencies of portfolio managers at asset management firms, as well as those responsible for institutional portfolios.

Asset management is a service in which an investment management company uses capital provided from investors to implement an investment strategy, and offers a product in which the investors own a participation stake (Concannon 2015). Often referred to as the *buy side,* asset managers purchase securities on behalf of their clients in order to assemble an investable portfolio. The flip side is the *sell side,* in which firms perform research on securities in order to sell their work to asset managers or use it to generate business for their brokerage arm (Maginn et al. 2007). The portfolio manager of the fund that is created by the asset manager then taps into the global capital markets and allocates the investors' capital into securities that the manager finds attractive.

Asset managers cater to two investor types: individuals and institutions. Individual investors are often referred to as retail investors, and they include private families or individuals who are looking to reach their retirement and financial goals. Institutional investors can represent entities such as the ongoing support fund of a university or the pool of all retirement funds of a government's employees. Both individual and institutional investors provide the asset manager with capital, and in turn, the portfolio managers at these firms seek to generate a return on the capital. For this service, asset managers receive a fee for their efforts, with the implication that the portfolio manager is creating value that the investor otherwise cannot create. Within asset management, firms generally fall into one of two categories: traditional and alternative. Differentiating between the two types is important because the structure of each firm plays a large role in the financial behavior of the respective portfolio manager.

Traditional asset management firms offer investment products and earn fees based on a percentage of the total assets under management (AUM). These firms offer products such as mutual funds or exchange-traded funds (ETFs), which typically take long-only positions in conventional securities such as stocks and bonds. A longtime staple of retirement plans and brokerage accounts, mutual funds totaled more than $15.8 trillion in assets at the end of 2014 (Investment Company Institute 2015). The appeal of mutual funds is that they provide exposure to financial markets via a diversified portfolio, where the decision to buy and sell securities is delegated to a professional money manager. Additionally, the pooling of investors' capital in mutual funds enables the fund to achieve economies of scale, helping reduce its total costs, as opposed to owning each of the individual underlying securities outright (Baker, Filbeck, and Kiymaz 2015). These products are regulated under the Investment Company Act of 1940 and are required to register with the Securities and Exchange Commission (SEC). The purpose of the registration is to minimize conflicts of interest and to disclose information about the fund and its objectives to the investing public. The act requires the fund to provide its financial condition and investment policies to its investors on a regular basis (Securities and Exchange Commission 2016a). As a result of the SEC regulation, portfolio managers of mutual funds are relatively restricted in the types of securities in which they can invest, the size and nature of their positions, and how they advertise to the public. With scrutiny from regulators, coupled with the overall simplicity of most strategies, traditional asset management firms typically are more tailored to the demands of the retail investor audience.

Alternative asset managers, similar to traditional asset managers, also earn fees based on a percentage of their AUM. Many of these funds include hedge funds and private equity funds. One important distinction, however, is that alternative managers also receive a portion of the profits (i.e., incentive) of the strategies they manage (Concannon 2015). Although incentive fees have been compressed in recent years, hedge funds have historically charged an annual management fee of 2 percent of the fund's assets managed, as well as 20 percent of the fund's profits over its high water mark (HWM), which is a continuous running tally of the fund's maximum AUM level. The fees levied by hedge funds are substantially higher than those charged by most mutual funds, which had an average expense ratio of 0.70 percent in 2014 (Investment Company Institute 2015). Performance incentives provide portfolio managers at alternative firms with additional motivation to generate returns and outperform their benchmarks; the better the portfolios perform, the more money the portfolio managers make.

Besides fees, the portfolios managed by alternative firms sharply differ from those by their traditional counterparts in other ways. First, hedge funds are subject to considerably less regulation than mutual funds. Hedge funds are not required to register with the SEC, so the financial condition and investment policies followed are less transparent to investors than those of mutual funds.

Next, perhaps related to the lack of regulation, the investment strategies of alternative funds tend to be more complex in nature than traditional funds. Although many different substyles of hedge funds are available, most have the ability to invest in publicly and privately traded securities in all global financial markets, such as derivatives, as well as engaging in the short-selling of securities. *Short-selling* is the sale of a security that is not owned by the seller, or that the seller has borrowed. Short-selling is motivated by the belief that a security's price will decline, enabling the seller to buy it back at a lower price to make a profit. Some hedge funds take a small number of sizable positions in their portfolios, which can pay off when the gambles taken by the portfolio manager succeed.

Lastly, to ensure that the only investors in alternative funds such as hedge funds can bear the economic risk of investing in unregistered products, certain funds are only available to "accredited investors." The SEC defines *accredited investors* as certain types of firms and their directors (e.g., banks, savings and loan associations, investment advisers, and insurance companies) and individuals whose net worth (or combined with their spouse) exceeds $1 million (Securities and Exchange Commission 2016b). Whereas individuals can invest in some mutual funds for as little as $100, hedge funds investors are required to reach a minimum level of annual income or net worth in order to invest, limiting their availability to sophisticated and wealthy investors. For purposes of this chapter, however, the major difference between traditional and alternative firms relates to the performance fee at alternative firms, as it drives much of the financial behavior of its portfolio managers.

Outside of asset management firms, portfolio managers may also directly oversee pools of money for institutional entities, such as pensions. A *pension fund* is a pool of money managed on behalf of the employees of a corporation or government that provides employees with payments upon their retirement. Also known as *defined benefit (DB) plans,* pension funds promise to pay a specific dollar amount to each beneficiary on an ongoing basis after they retire. *Defined contribution (DC) plans* are also available whereby the beneficiary makes the investment decisions and hence bears the risk. This chapter primarily focuses on DB plans.

Employees in civil service positions, such as firefighters, policemen, and teachers, rely primarily on their pensions as their source of retirement funding. The pension payment to the beneficiary depends on an actuarial formula that includes inputs such as the number of years the beneficiary worked at the employer and salary in the final year of employment. In anticipation of the future payments that the fund must distribute, the employer makes regular contributions to the pension fund. The employer needs these contributions to sufficiently grow to satisfy the fund's future obligations, which is why the pension fund manager is paramount in the process.

Using assumptions and future projections of the formula's inputs, the pension fund manager establishes a target rate of return that it must achieve. The portfolio manager has two goals: to grow the contributions so that all obligations to current and future beneficiaries are satisfied, and to maintain enough liquidity to make payments to current beneficiaries. Although the mandatory growth of the contributions allows the fund's portfolio manager to have a long-term investment horizon, the annual distribution requirement forces the manager to balance the portfolio with a short-term mindset. Many public and private pension plans have operated for decades, and beneficially invest billions and sometimes trillions of dollars under management. As supervisors of the retirement funds of potentially thousands of individuals, pension fund portfolio managers may find themselves as some of the most influential investors in the world.

Another type of institutional entity that relies on a portfolio manager to oversee its investments is an endowment. An *endowment* is a gift of money or income-producing property to a public organization such as a hospital or university for a specific purpose, such as research or scholarships. The endowed asset is usually kept intact and only the income generated by it is consumed. Endowments represent the permanent funds of an organization and are responsible for providing money to support the operations of the institution in perpetuity (Swensen 1994). Similar to a pension fund manager, the endowment manager's goals are twofold: preserve the purchasing power of the assets in the endowment over time, and provide resources to the institution to help fund operations in the present.

Because their existence is assumed perpetual, the structure of an endowment allows the portfolio manager to invest in riskier and less liquid securities with higher return profiles, mindful that the endowment can recoup most large capital losses over time. The manager must also balance the risk-taking portion of the portfolio with enough short-term liquidity to make payments to support the institution. The impact of the performance of the portfolio manager has ramifications beyond the financial universe. For example, if the endowment fund of a hospital cannot make the full payments it requires, and the hospital's operations are not fully funded as a result, the consequences could be catastrophic. Thus, the investment manager in charge of an endowment portfolio plays an incredibly pivotal role in the organization's viability.

Behavioral Biases in Portfolio Management

Contrasting the types of portfolios in the previous section is necessary because each contains particular nuances that act as catalysts for the financial behavior of the portfolio managers. Particular behavioral biases are inherent in nearly all portfolio managers to some degree, but the nature of the fund being managed can also provide a clear delineation in behavior. Many factors can drive the behavior of a portfolio manager outside those typically thought to drive the assumed rational investment decision-making process.

OVERCONFIDENCE

Overconfidence bias is an unwarranted faith in one's intuitive reasoning, judgments, and cognitive abilities. In short, overconfidence bias deduces that investors think they are smarter than they truly are and have better information than they actually do (Pompian 2006). Psychologically, people in general tend to overestimate their own abilities. Specific to portfolio managers, overconfidence can impact decision making because portfolio managers are professional investors who are in their respective positions because of their perceived skills in managing money. In fact, professionals who are overconfident in their own skills are hardly limited to the field of portfolio management. Psychologists, doctors, engineers, entrepreneurs, lawyers, and other professionals have all consistently displayed overconfidence in their judgments and abilities (Odean 1998). For any population, by definition, half the constituents must be below average. Not surprising, professionals are more likely to consider themselves to be above average at their job than below average. Ironically, the adept abilities that helped professional portfolio managers earn their positions could also be the sources of the bias for which they are much more susceptible than the average investor.

Investing has two main types of overconfidence: prediction overconfidence and certainty overconfidence. *Prediction overconfidence* occurs when an investor assigns too narrow a confidence interval to his investment forecasts. That is, an investor believes that his prediction of the future value of a security must lie within a tight band because he is confident in the accuracy of his prediction. This phenomenon leads investors to be surprised when outcomes vary greatly from predictions. As a result, they often underestimate the downside risks. As related to portfolio managers, prediction overconfidence may cause them to build portfolios that are unprepared for large losses. If a manager expects a security's performance to fall within a narrow band and the actual performance of the security falls short of the manager's predicted worst-case scenario, the portfolio may be substantially more risky than the manager anticipated.

Certainty overconfidence occurs when investors assign too high a probability to their prediction and have too much confidence in the accuracy of their own judgments. The effects of certainty overconfidence can appear in several forms during the portfolio management process. Odean (1998, p. 1888) contends that increased trading activity is the "most robust effect of overconfidence." Investors who are overconfident in the precision of their forecasted values of securities are likely to trade more often. Believing they have better information than other investors, overconfident investors place a greater weight on their own opinion and think that they can beat the market by increasing the number of trades that they place. Increased trading activity drives up transaction costs, creates the opportunity for taxable events, and can reduce the total return of a portfolio. Odean focuses on individual investors, but studies show that the phenomenon of overconfidence leading to increased trading activity and poor performance also holds true for professional portfolio managers. For example, Chuang and Susmel (2011) report that institutional traders in Taiwan exhibit overconfidence, albeit less than individual traders. In the context of mutual funds, Carhart (1997, p. 67), who finds that a portfolio's turnover is significantly negatively correlated to its performance, states that "the turnover estimate implies transactions costs of 95 basis points per round-trip transaction." Further, Bogle (2006) reports that mutual funds in the top quartile of their universe in portfolio turnover between 1996 and 2006 underperformed the funds in the bottom quartile of turnover by 1.7 percentage points on an annual basis. Additionally, the funds in the top quartile of turnover are 27.1 percent more volatile than the bottom quartile funds. These findings are consistent with the notion that the portfolio managers who are most confident in their abilities to beat the market are among the worst at doing so on both an absolute and a risk-adjusted basis.

Another consequence of overconfidence bias by portfolio managers in the portfolio construction process is concentration. If portfolio managers are very confident in assessing a security's forecasted value, they may allocate a greater weight to that security within a portfolio. Fund managers who are willing to make large bets on a small number of securities increase the risk of under-diversifying the portfolio. Concentrated positions in only a few securities reduce the diversification benefits inherent in the structure of a portfolio and can increase the fund's overall volatility. If the reason behind a portfolio's concentration is the portfolio manager's overconfidence, the manager may be associated with poorer risk-adjusted performance (Baks, Busse, and Green 2006). However, evidence suggests that portfolios with a degree of concentration tend to outperform their benchmarks on both an absolute and a risk-adjusted basis (Yeung, Pellizzari, Bird, and Abidin 2012). Studies also suggest that managers who manage concentrated portfolios display some skill in correctly picking stocks (Baks et al. 2006). Although most mutual fund managers fail to outperform their respective benchmarks over the long term (Soe 2015), the confident ones managing concentrated portfolios may stand the best chance of outperformance.

HERDING BEHAVIOR

Herding refers to disregarding one's opinion or analysis in order to follow the crowd. Individuals may be unwilling to take a stance against a popular opinion for fear of being incorrect and facing reputational harm as a result (or worse). As Keynes (1936, p. 158) notes, "Worldly wisdom teaches that it is better for reputation to fail conventionally than to succeed unconventionally." Herd behavior is a behavioral phenomenon present in a many social situations, but is particularly prevalent in financial markets. Studies report that investors typically do not fire the portfolio managers of funds who are merely mediocre relative to their peers. Rather, a manager must significantly underperform both his benchmark and his peers before the fund experiences substantial outflows (Sirri and Tufano 1998). This phenomenon may be a major derivation of herding behavior because it provides the portfolio manager with a strong incentive to follow the herd or be left behind and face the consequences.

A key repercussion of herding behavior by portfolio managers is the creation of financial bubbles and crashes. When a new financial innovation or "disruption" occurs in an industry, such as the rise of Internet companies or the advent of securitization, investors try to profit from it. Often, the potential growth of these assets may not yet be fully understood by investors, and thus cannot be accurately measured, providing seemingly unlimited growth potential. Initially, the gains in the prices of these assets can be gradual and the valuations they achieve may be justified. As prices continue to rise when more investors attempt to capitalize on its momentum, portfolio managers may observe their peers investing in these assets and be incentivized to invest in them as well. Recall that portfolio managers with average performance do not tend to see redemptions from investors. However, as investors continue to chase trends by purchasing an investment, the asset's market value can wildly exceed its fundamental value and its lofty valuations can no longer be supported. At this point a bubble has formed.

Investors often fail to realize that a bubble exists until it is too late (Brunnermeier and Oehmke 2013). Some type of event eventually triggers the bursting of the bubble. Whatever the catalyst may be, investors realize that the asset is overvalued and decide to sell their stake in it, driving down its price. Seeing the decline in price, portfolio managers want to salvage the maximum value possible for their ownership and sell the asset as soon as they can, exacerbating the fall. A crash is now under way. Few investors may be willing to buy the asset, and the lack of demand further reduces its market value. Frequently, a spillover effect into other related and even unrelated assets can occur. This contagion effect may affect a large portion of the overall marketplace. Regardless, portfolio managers who are left holding the asset at the end of a crash are likely to suffer severe losses and create unhappy investors as a result.

Portfolio managers face a conundrum pertaining to herd behavior. If they do not follow the herd, they risk trailing behind their peers. However, if they follow the herd, they may get caught on the wrong side of an artificially attractive trade opportunity. Consider the case of two hedge fund managers during the technology bubble of the late 1990s. One manager refused to invest in technology stocks during their rise, believing them to be overvalued. Despite a successful track record for almost two decades beforehand, the manager had to dissolve the fund in 2000 because it did not keep up with the high returns from technology companies and the competing funds that invested in them. Conversely, a different hedge fund manager heavily invested in technology stocks during their boom. As the dot-com bubble popped and technology stocks fell precipitously, the fund faced massive losses. Even though the portfolio manager had strong performance for 12 years before the crash, he resigned from the fund in 2000 (Pompian, McLean, and Byrne 2011). Portfolio managers must carefully weigh their options when facing a herd-driven environment.

Aside from the competitive pressures, herd behavior can also arise from emulation. Many social and financial situations may enable and encourage a person to "follow the leader" when presented with an opportunity to do so. In the portfolio management universe, if a portfolio manager sees that one of his peers is performing exceptionally well, he may be incentivized to copy what the successful manager is doing. In this fashion, either the "copycat" fund performs in line with the best funds in the universe, or it is not alone should its performance falters. Indeed, several studies show that copycat behavior is pervasive among mutual fund managers (Phillips, Pukthuanthong, and Rau 2014; Lesmond and Stein 2015). Interestingly, the top-performing mutual funds most frequently mimicked typically end up underperforming in subsequent periods. Additionally, portfolio managers who run copycat funds also lag the average mutual fund.

Although following the leader has not benefited mutual fund portfolio managers, managers of endowments are currently experiencing a wave of successful imitations, albeit in a much different fashion. Rather than mimicking stock picks from the top managers, endowment managers are electing to hire away the personnel from the top funds. David Swensen, Chief Investment Officer of the Yale University endowment, was among the first endowment managers to embrace alternative funds and stray outside of the securities typically associated with traditional asset allocation, such as equities and fixed income. In what became known as the "Yale Model," Swensen used the structure of an endowment fund to his advantage by investing in less liquid and instruments with lower correlations, such as private equity, real estate, and timberland. The fund was the top-performing endowment of all colleges and universities from 2004 to 2014 (Yale 2014). Given such successful results, other colleges and universities hired many of the analysts who worked under Swensen to manage their endowments. In 2015, Yale's endowment, along with each of the endowments managed by five of Swensen's former protégés, outperformed the average university endowment benchmark by at least 3.0 percentage points (McDonald and Lorin 2015). Perhaps mutual fund managers would be more successful if they were to hire their peers rather than try to copy them.

Herd behavior varies by the type of fund managed. In particular, the previous example of herd behavior by hedge fund managers during the technology bubble had negative consequences. Wermers (1999) finds that among mutual funds, those managing growth-focused stock mutual funds are most likely to engage in herding, particularly in smaller stocks. In fact, Wermers concludes that mutual fund portfolio managers who herd have a better chance of being profitable than those who do not. Conversely, managers of pension funds do not display herding behavior in stocks (Lakonishok, Shleifer, and Vishny 1992). This lack of herding is perhaps attributed to the structure of the pension fund. Because pension funds have a longer-term investment horizon, managers have more leeway in that they are unlikely to face a backlash or outflows from investors if their funds underperform over a short time frame. As endowments only have a singular investor, they also do not face the short-term pressures that normally drive herd behavior. Nevertheless, portfolio managers of all types constantly face an evolving market with opportunities to seize new trends. How exactly they manage their portfolios when a herd opportunity presents itself can dictate a portion of their overall success.

RISK-TAKING BEHAVIOR

The concept of moral hazard is one of frequent debate, particularly in the years following the financial crisis of 2007–2008. *Moral hazard* stems from the principal–agent conflict and is a situation in which one party (the agent) is responsible for the interests of another party (the principal). The interests of both parties are unlikely to be completely aligned, and the agent may be incentivized to place his own interests before those of the principal. If the agent knows that the majority of the total costs lie with the principal, the agent may be incentivized to take excessive risks while performing the task at hand. Because the agent has limited personal downside risks, this situation creates a convex payoff structure for the agent and encourages risky behavior. In the end, either the agent succeeds and is compensated for that accomplishment, or the agent fails, with the principal disproportionately bearing the consequences. This situation is summarized with the euphemistic coin flip: "Heads, I win; tails, you lose" (Dowd 2009).

Much recent discussion about moral hazard is based on the actions of financial institutions leading up to the financial crisis of 2007–2008. The question at hand is whether top bank executives knowingly took excessive risks with their capital and lending requirements. That is, because lenders believed that if their loans were to go bad and their assets lost value, the Federal Reserve, and ultimately American taxpayers, would bail out their banks. Although this belief presents a common explanation, predatory borrowers who secured loans they were unable or unsure they could repay also share the blame. Yet, moral hazard clearly extends beyond banking to portfolio managers.

As previously discussed, traditional asset management firms earn fees based on a percentage of AUM. As a result, these traditional firms have an incentive to maximize the total amount of assets managed. Portfolio managers can increase the size of their portfolio either by investing the fund's assets in securities that grow or by earning additional inflows from investors into the fund. As discussed shortly, portfolio managers who are adept at the former typically benefit from the latter. However, the stated objective of a mutual fund may not necessarily be to seek maximum growth. For example, consider a short-term government bond fund whose goal is to outpace inflation. The fund's portfolio manager would likely be violating the mandate by investing in the stocks of small-cap companies, even if the stocks generate higher total returns than the short-term bonds. Even though portfolio managers want the highest possible positive return, risk is a crucial component. Consumers generally invest in a mutual fund because they trust the portfolio manager's judgment in maximizing the fund's risk-adjusted returns, not just the total returns (Chevalier and Ellison 1995). This incongruent objective between the portfolio manager and investor creates a situation in which the portfolio manager may be incentivized to increase the fund's risk profile beyond its typical standards.

Interestingly, situations may also arise in which portfolio managers are incentivized to reduce the risk levels of their funds. Chevalier and Ellison (1995) examine the relation between mutual fund performance and flows by analyzing the behavioral tendencies of mutual fund investors. The authors find that a mutual fund's year-end performance heavily influences investors, owing to the availability of year-end information and other factors. A strong relation exists between a fund's excess return against its benchmark in a given year and the fund's flows in the following year. Of the funds that outperform their benchmarks, a sharp increase tends to occur in inflows for those funds that have an excess return greater than 15 percent. Although funds that slightly trail their benchmarks do not see disastrous outflows, evidence of an acceleration of outflows occurs from the funds that trail by more than 15 percent. This finding is consistent with the conclusions from Sirri and Tufano (1998).

Assume a portfolio manager is conscious of how his fund compares to its benchmark during a given year, and he is aware that flows in the following year are related to performance. As the year-end approaches, will the fund's performance relative to its benchmark affect the way the manager adjusts the portfolio before year-end? According to Chevalier and Ellison (1995), portfolio managers of mutual funds adjust the riskiness of their portfolios from October through December, depending on their relative positions at the end of September. Managers who substantially outperform their benchmarks for the year-to-date period through September tend to de-risk their portfolios at year-end. This defensive measure will track the index and "lock in" the fund's excess return, which would enable the manager to reap the benefits of strong inflows in the next year. Conversely, managers whose portfolios lag their benchmarks by a sizable margin through September tend to increase their portfolio's systematic risk, hoping to close the gap below its benchmark before the end of the year and avoid potential outflows in the upcoming year. As a result, the end of the year in the mutual fund industry tends to have a divide between portfolio managers who avoid risk and those who actively seek it. According to Baker (1998), the choice of benchmark is not the only factor that matters in determining a fund manager's attitudes to risk. A series of interviews with fund managers shows that managers also state that the timing of performance evaluation affects fund managers' attitudes toward risk and that quarterly performance evaluations lead to a short-term attitude and approach to fund management.

Given their restrictions relative to alternative asset management firms, the fact that portfolio managers at traditional asset management firms engage in risk-seeking behavior to raise their AUM, and subsequently their fees, or to attract inflows from investors may surprise some. However, due to the fee structure at alternative asset management firms such as hedge funds, the possibility of the portfolio manager's taking excessive risks should be more obvious. Recall that the fee structure at alternative firms is two-pronged: a management fee on a fund's AUM and a performance fee for profits above the fund's HWM. Similar to mutual fund portfolio managers, hedge fund managers have an inherent incentive to maximize the amount of assets managed. The way in which they attempt to accomplish this goal differs. Hedge fund managers are generally not constrained by a mandate in the types of securities in which they can invest and how they invest in them. Therefore, the previous example of a portfolio manager adjusting a fund's risk profile by adding small-cap stocks to a short-term government bond fund may not be interpreted as irregular. Also, hedge funds may contain a "lockup" provision that restricts investors from withdrawing their capital for a specific period of time. As a result, the average investor's holding period of hedge funds tends to be much longer than that of the average mutual fund. This relation implies that the flow-seeking behavior displayed by mutual fund portfolio managers at year-end is less prevalent in hedge funds. A strong relation still exists between past performance and flows, but the flows are more highly correlated with performance persistence over several years rather than the performance in the most recent calendar year (Agarwal, Daniel, and Naik 2004).

Prior performance also affects the choice of risk level. For example, fund managers who recently completed a successful year for their portfolio tend to take on more risk in the following calendar year. To be specific, they increase volatility, beta, and tracking error, and they assign a higher proportion of their portfolio to value stocks, small firms, and momentum stocks. Poor-performing fund managers switch to passive strategies (Ammann and Verhofen 2007). However, evidence also suggests that declining performance does not necessarily lead the fund manager to raise the volatility of the fund's return (Chen and Pennacchi 2009). The researchers report a tendency for mutual funds to increase the standard deviation of tracking errors, but not the standard deviation of returns, as their performance declines. They also find that this risk-shifting behavior is more common for managers with longer tenure.

Ultimately, the management fee aligns the interests of the manager and the investors, as the manager is a de facto equity investor in the fund (Lan, Wang, and Yang 2011). Instead, the most important cause of risk-taking behavior by a hedge fund manager comes from the performance fee. On its face, a performance fee with a HWM provision appeals to both the hedge fund manager and the investors. Investors find comfort in the fact that unless their investment makes a profit, the manager will not receive a bonus (i.e., a performance fee), and must fully recover previous losses before being eligible to receive the bonus (Goetzmann, Ingersoll, and Ross 1997). For the manager, the attraction is simple: perform well and be compensated handsomely. However, the AUM and performance combined fee structure essentially acts as a series of call options for the portfolio manager, with a floor on the downside risk (i.e., the management fee), with unlimited upside potential (Lan et al. 2011). This asymmetrical payoff feature clearly encourages the hedge fund manager to increase portfolio risk.

Consider a hedge fund that has recorded several consecutive years of negative returns. As the fund falls further away from its HWM, receiving a bonus for performance becomes less likely for the manager. In this situation, little downside exists for the manager to engage in risk-seeking behavior. If the fund's added risk pays off and the manager succeeds, he may regain the opportunity to earn a hefty performance bonus. If the manager fails, he still receives an AUM fee. In the worst-case scenario, if the fund's added risk causes it to fall further, and the manager completely loses hope of reaching the HWM, he can elect to simply close the fund and start a new fund with a more realistic and attainable HWM. In baseball terms, trailing the HWM gives the manager a chance to swing for the fences: the manager either hits a home run or goes down swinging. Therefore, the presence of a performance fee creates an incentive for an alternative investment portfolio manager to increase a portfolio's riskiness particularly when the fund is below its HWM.

A similar question to whether portfolio managers exhibit specific risk-taking behavior is how portfolio managers perceive risk. Whether this perception of risk differs from theoretical models of risk and return and/or other investors is unclear. A substantial literature investigates this issue. In the 1970s, McDonald and Stehle (1975) analyze responses from financial analysts and portfolio managers about their risk perceptions. Despite anecdotal evidence suggesting the contrary, the study finds that historical risk measures, such as historical beta and non-market risk, are highly correlated to the perceived risk as described by institutional investors. In a different survey of portfolio managers, Gooding (1978) reports that risk expectations based on company risk, beta, and standard deviation of returns are all important components of analysts' risk analysis. In a more recent survey of sophisticated investors including portfolio managers, Olsen (1997) reports that the principal risk attributes appear to be the potential for a below-target return, the potential for a large loss, the investor's feeling of control, and the level of knowledge about an investment.

In a related survey, Olsen and Troughton (2000) document that finance professionals are ambiguity averse. This aversion is important because traditional asset pricing models, such as the capital asset pricing model (CAPM) do not incorporate this type of ambiguity. This failure to incorporate ambiguity aversion may account for the relatively large discounts in initial public offers (IPOs) and the observation that required returns on large, non-routine, capital expenditures are set relatively high. Similar in spirit are the findings by Worzala, Sirmans, and Zietz (2000), who report that when portfolio managers are asked to rank investment alternatives by risk and return, these managers tend to not rank these alternatives (e.g., large cap, small cap, and bonds) consistent with the idea that risk and return are positively correlated. The authors suggest that this oversight may explain why actual investment portfolios are inconsistent with theoretically suggested portfolios. Finally, Muradoglu (2002) investigated portfolio managers' forecasts of risk and return using business students and finance professionals in an experimental setting, and found differences between finance professionals and students. The latter group tends to be more optimistic, but hedges its optimism better.

A related question is how finance professionals form their opinions of ex-ante risk. Mear and Firth (1988) find that accounting reports are an important source of information that professionals use to infer ex-ante risk. In another experiment, Cooley (1977) finds that portfolio managers seem to care about both the first-order moment of returns and the second-order moment (i.e., concern with downside risk) involving perceived risk.

DISPOSITION EFFECT

On the opposite side of the spectrum from risk-seeking behavior, *risk avoidance* is when investors actively seek to remove the potential for losses in their portfolios. Whereas risk-averse investors take additional risk as long as they are compensated with sufficient return, investors engaging in risk avoidance try to avoid risk, regardless of the potential returns being offered. Occasionally, the divide between risk-seeking and risk-avoiding behavior can blur. In fact, a portfolio manager may exhibit both of these behaviors in monitoring a single security in a portfolio.

Kahneman and Tversky (1979) find that investors treat the gains and losses in their portfolio differently. *Prospect theory*, which is a more popular term for the disposition effect, posits that investors weigh all gains and losses against a particular reference point, and their behavior depends on which side of the point their position lies. Because investors feel more strongly about losses than they do about gains, the pain experienced in a losing investment far outstrips the utility of an equal-sized profit. Thus, the investor's utility function takes an asymmetrical S-shape, with gains in a concave shape above the reference point and losses forming a steep convex shape below. Given that investors do not want to realize a loss, they may hold onto an investment that has dropped substantially in value, hoping to recover their investment. Alternatively, investors overly focus on avoiding losses, so they often lock in any gains and sell positive positions. The result is that the investor engages in risk-seeking behavior when experiencing losses and risk-avoidance behavior when experiencing gains (Pompian 2006). This is known as the *disposition effect*, which is the desire to sell winners too early and ride losers too long (Shefrin and Statman 1985).

Although mutual fund managers are less likely to exhibit disposition-driven behavior than individual investors, studies report strong evidence for the disposition effect among such managers (Ammann, Ising, and Kessler 2011). Unlike the other biases discussed in this chapter, the consequences on the portfolio management process are not necessarily negative. Mutual funds run by managers who have a higher disposition effect tend to have less systematic risk than their peers (Cici 2010). Little evidence suggests a negative impact occurs on the fund's performance (Ammann et al. 2011). Evidence also shows that hedge fund managers show the disposition effect, particularly when they engage in short-selling (von Beschwitz and Massa 2015) or after they personally experience a marriage or divorce (Lu, Ray, and Teo 2015). Unlike the performance of mutual fund managers, the performance of hedge fund managers falters as a result of this bias.

The disposition effect is not limited to equity markets. Researchers identify the disposition effect within a real estate investment trust (REIT), which is a professionally managed sector of the real estate market. Specifically, a REIT is an investment vehicle that aggregates properties into an investable portfolio. Similar to a mutual fund, a REIT is a pooled fund with shareholders who participate in the fund's gains and losses and a manager who decides which properties to buy and sell. In the case of a REIT, the portfolio manager is typically the company's CEO. Changes in the values of the underlying properties dictate a REIT's value. Crane and Hartzell (2010) find evidence of the disposition effect among REIT managers, particularly those who manage smaller properties. By holding onto properties that continue to lose value and selling winning properties at lower prices than other relative properties, the manager's behavior has negative implications on both the REIT and its investor base. In summary, although each portfolio manager type displays evidence of the disposition effect, the impact of the performance differs.

GENDER DIFFERENCES

Women now play a larger investing role in U.S. households. In fact, they are the primary provider in more than 40 percent of American households, a startling increase from 11 percent in 1960 (Wang, Parker, and Taylor 2013). Within American households, the percentage of couples where women are the primary decision maker of long-term retirement plans has more than doubled, from 9 percent in 2011 to 19 percent in 2013 (Fidelity Investments 2013). However, this trend has hit a ceiling and does not appear at the professional portfolio manager role. Among the entire universe of U.S.-listed mutual funds, women represent only 9 percent of fund portfolio managers. Further, only 2.5 percent of all mutual funds exclusively have women portfolio managers, and the funds that they do manage represent less than 2 percent of all mutual fund assets (Lutton 2015). Based on these findings, the potential exists for more female managers to enter this market and capture more AUM.

Within mutual funds, Lutton (2015) finds that funds managed by female portfolio managers perform in line with those managed by men. Interestingly, funds with mixed-gender teams of portfolio managers fared the best. In the hedge fund universe, empirical evidence indicates that female portfolio managers perform better than average. From 2007 to 2015, the average women-led hedge fund generated a return of 59.4 percent, trouncing the industry average return of 36.7 percent (KPMG 2015).

Why does this performance disparity exist between male and female portfolio managers? Jones (2015) posits several reasons for female portfolio managers performing better than males. The recurring theme is that women are less likely to suffer overconfidence bias than men. By gender, evidence shows that both males and females display overconfidence in their abilities (Lundeberg, Fox, and LeCount 1994). However, although both genders are guilty of this bias to a degree, men are consistently more overconfident than women in their predictions, particularly when related to financial decisions (Barber and Odean 2001). Additionally, in the absence of certainty, Lenney (1977) finds that women have lower opinions of their abilities than men. Following this logic, Barber and Odean note that women display less confidence in their abilities in investing in the market than men.

Earlier, this chapter reviewed the negative consequences of overconfidence bias in the portfolio management process. Overconfidence leads to increased trading activity, concentrated positions, and a decreased emphasis on the downside protection of a portfolio. Jones (2015) contends that male portfolio managers participate in each of these activities more than females, potentially explaining why only a few can match the performance of their female counterparts. As related to overconfidence bias, Lundeberg et al. (1994) find a difference in the confidence of predictions of men and women involving when their respective predictions are incorrect. In contrast to men, women are more self-aware of their potentially incorrect predictions than are men, and are less confident in their forecasts as a result. In contrast, when their predictions are incorrect, men show inappropriately excessive confidence in their answers. The ramifications of this behavior on portfolio management relate to a fund's downside protection. That is, female managers are more likely than men to admit mistakes. A female portfolio manager is less afraid of capping her losses and exiting a position from an investment that did not meet expectations. This enhances the drawdown protection in female-led funds and may help explain why they outperform male-led funds.

Besides overconfidence bias, Jones (2015) also suggests that one possible reason female-led funds have return patterns that are superior to the general fund universe is that female managers are less likely to display herd behavior. Because female managers represent such a minority portion of the portfolio manager population, they may be less vulnerable to the pitfalls of groupthink than are their more homogenized male peers.

As the investing public further recognizes the superior track records of female portfolio managers, more opportunities may materialize for women in the future. As the sample size of female portfolio managers expands, the behavioral differences relative to male managers are likely to manifest themselves more prominently. A related question is whether risk-taking behavior crosses over into other activities. For example, do portfolio managers who like to take risks in other activities, such as skydiving or flying airplanes, also exhibit more risk in picking portfolios? Although theoretical arguments exist in either direction, experimental evidence suggests that risk taking does not appear to cross activities (Belcher 2010).

Summary and Conclusions

In the asset management world, portfolio managers occupy highly important and visible positions. Consequently, both investors and outside stakeholders can feel shockwaves from their work. They must constantly keep track of many moving parts and quickly make adjustments. Failing to properly do so can severely damage their performance record, reputation, and level of compensation. To fully understand the actions of portfolio managers requires considering the behavioral biases that provide motives for their behavior.

The overconfidence bias displayed by portfolio managers has both negative (increased trading activity) and positive (concentrated portfolios) effects. Herd mentality can trace its roots to social behavior and can lead in extreme cases to creating financial bubbles and crashes. Risk-taking behavior is most prevalent in alternative asset managers, who are incentivized to seek the highest return possible because of performance fees. The disposition effect is prevalent among mutual fund, hedge fund, and real estate portfolio managers, but it has differing effects on their respective performance. Lastly, female portfolio managers are less likely to fall victim to both overconfidence bias and herd behavior, an assertion supported by their superior performance records.

Owing to the structure of certain funds, completely removing particular biases from the mindset of a portfolio manager is difficult. However, as long as the manager is cognizant of the presence of a specific bias at hand, reducing the impact of the bias on the portfolio is possible.

DISCUSSION QUESTIONS

1. Describe the primary steps of the portfolio management process.
2. Compare the structure of traditional and alternative asset management firms and identify biases that may arise as a result of their differences.
3. Describe the disposition effect and how it affects portfolios based on an investor's utility.
4. Contrast the different biases displayed by male and female portfolio managers and the consequences of each on their respective portfolios.

REFERENCES

Agarwal, Vikas, Naveen D. Daniel, and Narayan Y. Naik. 2004. "Flows, Performance, and Managerial Incentives in Hedge Funds." Working Paper, Centre for Financial Research, University of Cologne. Available at http://www.fep.up.pt/investigacao/cempre/actividades/sem_fin/sem_fin_01/PAPERS_PDF/paper_sem_fin_31mai04.pdf

Ammann, Manuel, Alexander Ising, and Stephan Kessler. 2011. "Disposition Effect and Mutual Fund Performance." Working Paper, University of St. Gallen. Available at https://papers.ssrn.com/sol3/papers.cfm?abstract_id=1858930 and http://poseidon01.ssrn.com/delivery.php?ID=071026118068008000017118123091085007002025021011043039068075070028100091086024083117099118061101105098112122005119092104068126010078017061000094080101076093013124052065049115020066017001067122000092030067080074004105006109067115009127100089108126031&EXT=pdt

Ammann, Manuel, and Michael Verhofen. 2007. "Prior Performance and Risk-Taking of Mutual Fund Managers: A Dynamic Bayesian Network Approach." *Journal of Behavioral Finance* 8:1, 20–34.

Baker, H. Kent, Greg Filbeck, and Halil Kiymaz (eds.). 2015. *Mutual Funds and Exchange-Traded Funds: Building Blocks to Wealth*. New York: Oxford University Press.

Baker, Mae. 1998. "Fund Managers' Attitudes to Risk and Time Horizons: The Effect of Performance Benchmarking." *European Journal of Finance* 4:3, 257–278.

Baks, Klaas P., Jeffrey A. Busse, and T. Clifton Green. 2006. "Fund Managers Who Take Big Bets: Skilled or Overconfident." Working Paper, Emory University. Available at https://papers.ssrn.com/sol3/papers.cfm?abstract_id=891727 and http://poseidon01.ssrn.com/delivery.php?ID=9230940920200250861150011040040300811130000250390220620 22074076 12200810900900309907505305203300001104511406406700712311409205002106805403909300106509406712 302004106400912209409 309610500912403010 51200720 860 0009901600712310703108012210011 0086000&EXT=pdf

Barber, Brad M., and Terrance Odean. 2001. "Boys Will Be Boys: Gender, Overconfidence, and Common Stock Investment." *Quarterly Journal of Economics* 116:1, 261–292.

Belcher, Lawrence J. 2010. "Prior Perceptions, Personality Characteristics and Portfolio Preferences among Fund Managers: An Experimental Analysis." *Journal of Behavioral Finance* 11:4, 239–248.

Bogle, John. 2006. "Mutual Funds and Taxes." *The Bogle eBlog*. Available at http://johncbogle.com/wordpress/2006/04/12/mutual-funds-and-taxes/#more-62.

Brunnermeier, Markus K., and Martin Oehmke. 2013. "Bubbles, Financial Crises, and Systemic Risk." In *The Handbook of the Economics of Finance*, Volume 2, Part B, 1221–1288. Amsterdam: Elsevier.

Carhart, Mark M. 1997. "On Persistence in Mutual Fund Performance." *Journal of Finance* 52:1, 57–82.

Chen, Hsiu-lang, and George G. Pennacchi. 2009. "Does Prior Performance Affect a Mutual Fund's Choice of Risk? Theory and Further Empirical Evidence." *Journal of Financial and Quantitative Analysis* 44:4, 745–775.

Chevalier, Judith A., and Glenn D. Ellison. 1995. "Risk Taking by Mutual Funds as a Response to Incentives." *Journal of Political Economy* 105:6, 1167–1200.

Chuang, Wen-I, and Rauli Susmel. 2011. "Who Is the More Overconfident Trader? Individual vs. Institutional Investors." *Journal of Banking and Finance* 35:7, 1626–1644.

Cici, Gjergji. 2010. "The Relation of the Disposition Effect to Mutual Fund Trades and Performance." Working Paper No. 11-05, Centre for Financial Research, University of Cologne. Available at https://papers.ssrn.com/sol3/papers.cfm?abstract_id=645841 and http://poseidon01.ssrn.com/delivery.php?ID=52408608907400809110200000008708810902700804204300103310302700609 51271260310240011030130390020371111250480681010031021121060850520470880340540960040060241250890310400170860860800060860240830010921140021200091160060680 850880261021140900650 93030073069&EXT=pdf

Concannon, Owen. 2015. *CFA Institute Industry Guides: The Asset Management Industry*. Charlottesville, VA: CFA Institute.

Cooley, Philip L. 1977. "A Multidimensional Analysis of Institutional Investor Perception of Risk." *Journal of Finance* 32:1, 67–78.

Crane, Alan D., and Jay C. Hartzell. 2010. "Is There a Disposition Effect in Corporate Investment Decisions? Evidence from Real Estate Investment Trusts." Working Paper, McCombs School of Business, University of Texas at Austin. Available at https://papers.ssrn.com/Sol3/papers.cfm?abstract_id=1031010 and http://poseidon01.ssrn.com/delivery.php?ID=77711908109011311812600712707107202911704602506800401006611710402800610210410211211902903505500900804400510710012612402501312010607106002301411807110606711108907706601105410011207012710203010501910006808609811510009509601802809207 0072084001094084020&EXT=pdf

Dowd, Kevin. 2009. "Moral Hazard and the Financial Crisis." *Cato Journal* 29:1, 141–166.

Fidelity Investments. 2013. "2013 Couples Retirement Study Executive Summary: Disconnect between Couples; Women Less Engaged." Available at https://www.fidelity.com/static/dcle/welcome/documents/CouplesRetirementStudy.pdf.

Goetzmann, William N., Jonathan Ingersoll Jr., and Stephen A. Ross. 1997. "High Water Marks." Working Paper, Yale School of Management, Yale University. Available at http://viking.som.yale.edu/will/research.papers/Hwm.pdf.

Gooding, Arthur E. 1978. "Perceived Risk and Capital Asset Pricing." *Journal of Finance* 33:5, 1401–1424.

Investment Company Institute. 2015. *2015 Investment Company Fact* Book. 55th Edition. Available at https://www.ici.org/pdf/2015_factbook.pdf.

Jones, Meredith A. 2015. *Women of the Street: Why Female Money Managers Generate Higher Returns (and How You Can Too)*. New York: Palgrave Macmillan.

Kahneman, Daniel, and Amos Tversky. 1979. "Prospect Theory: An Analysis of Decision under Risk." *Econometrica* 47:2, 263–291.

Keynes, John Maynard. 1936. *The General Theory of Employment, Interest, and Money*. London: Macmillan Cambridge University Press.

KPMG. 2015. "Breaking Away: The Path Forward for Women in Alternatives." Available at https://www.kpmg.com/BM/en/IssuesAndInsights/ArticlesPublications/Documents/Investments/2015-documents/Women-Alternative-Investments.pdf.

Lakonishok, Josef, Andrei Shleifer, and Robert W. Vishny. 1992. "The Impact of Institutional Trading on Stock Prices." *Journal of Financial Economics* 32:1, 23–44.

Lan, Yingcong, Neng Wang, and Jinqiang Yang. 2011. "The Economics of Hedge Funds: Alpha, Fees, Leverage, and Valuation." *Journal of Financial Economics* 110:2, 300–323.

Lenney, Ellen. 1977. "Women's Self-Confidence in Achievement Settings." *Psychological Bulletin* 84:1, 1–13.

Lesmond, David, and Roberto Stein. 2015. "Imitation Is the Sincerest Form of Flattery: Fund Manager Stock Picking Skill and the Skill of Copycat Managers to Pick Good Stock Pickers." *CHEST* 108:5, 1185–1229.

Lu, Yan, Sugata Ray, and Melvyn Teo. 2015. "Limited Attention, Marital Events and Hedge Funds." Working Paper, Warrington College of Business, University of Florida, and Lee Kong Chian School of Business, Singapore Management University. Available at http://www1.villanova.edu/content/dam/villanova/VSB/assets/marc/marc2015/MARC%202015%20-%20113%20-%20Sugata%20Ray%20Paper%20%231.pdf.

Lundeberg, Mary A., Paul W. Fox, and Judith LeCount. 1994. "Highly Confident but Wrong: Gender Differences and Similarities in Confidence Judgments." *Journal of Educational Psychology* 86:1, 114–121.

Lutton, Laura Pavlenko. 2015. "Women Are Scarce Among Fund Managers." *Morningstar Advisor*. Available at http://www.morningstar.com/advisor/t/105995619/women-are-scarce-among-fund-managers.htm.

Maginn, John L., Donald L. Tuttle, Dennis W. McLeavey, and Herald E. Pinto. 2007. *Managing Investment Portfolios: A Dynamic Process*. Third Edition. Hoboken, NJ: John Wiley & Sons, Inc.

McDonald, Michael, and Janet Lorin. 2015. "Yale Endowment Model Thrives as Swensen, Proteges Post Top Gains." *Bloomberg Business*. Available at http://www.bloomberg.com/news/articles/2015-10-06/yale-endowment-model-thrives-as-swensen-proteges-post-top-gains.

McDonald, John G., and Richard E. Stehle. 1975. "How Do Institutional Investors Perceive Risk?" *Journal of Portfolio Management* 2:1, 11–16.

Mear, Ross, and Michael Firth. 1988. "Risk Perceptions of Financial Analysts and the Use of Market and Accounting Data." *Accounting and Business Research* 18:72, 335–339.

Muradoglu, Gülnur. 2002. "Portfolio Managers' and Novices' Forecasts of Risk and Return: Are There Predictable Forecast Errors?" *Journal of Forecasting* 21:6, 395–416.

Myers, Daniel. 2008. "Top 5 All-Time Best Mutual Fund Managers." *Investopedia*. Available at http://www.investopedia.com/articles/mutualfund/08/top-mutual-fund-managers.asp/.

Odean, Terrance. 1998. "Volume Volatility, Price, and Profit When All Traders Are Above Average." *Journal of Finance* 53:6, 1887–1934.

Olsen, Robert A. 1997. "Investment Risk: The Experts' Perspective." *Financial Analysts Journal* 53:2, 62–66.

Olsen, Robert A., and George H. Troughton. 2000. "Are Risk Premium Anomalies Caused by Ambiguity?" *Financial Analysts Journal* 56:2, 24–31.

Phillips, Blake, Kuntara Pukthuanthong, and P. Raghavendra Rau. 2014. "Detecting Superior Mutual Fund Managers: Evidence from Copycats." *Review of Asset Pricing Studies* 4:2, 286–321.

Pompian, Michael M. 2006. *Behavioral Finance and Wealth Management: How to Build Optimal Portfolios That Account for Investor Biases*. Hoboken, NJ: John Wiley & Sons, Inc.

Pompian, Michael M., Colin McLean, and Alistair Byrne. 2011. "Behavioral Finance and Investment Processes." In *Behavioral Finance, Individual Investors, and Institutional Investors—CFA® Program Curriculum. 2015, Level III*. Volume 2, 44–77. Hoboken, NJ: John Wiley & Sons, Inc.

Securities and Exchange Commission. 2016a. "Investor Bulletin: An Introduction to the U.S. Securities and Exchange Commission—Rulemaking and Laws." Available at https://www.investor.gov/news-alerts/investor-bulletins/investor-bulletin-introduction-us-securities-exchange-commission-rule.

Securities and Exchange Commission. 2016b. "Regulation D—Rules Governing the Limited Offer and Sale of Securities Without Registration Under the Securities Act of 1933." §230.501. Available at http://www.ecfr.gov/cgi-bin/retrieveECFR?gp=&SID=8edfd12967d69c02448 5029d968ee737&r=SECTION&n=17y3.0.1.1.12.0.46.176.

Shefrin, Hersh, and Meir Statman. 1985. "The Disposition to Sell Winners Too Early and Ride Losers Too Long: Theory and Evidence." *Journal of Finance* 40:3, 777–790.

Sirri, Erik R., and Peter Tufano. 1998. "Costly Search and Mutual Fund Flows." *Journal of Finance* 53:5, 1589–1622.

Soe, Aye M. 2015. "SPIVA® U.S. Scorecard." S&P Dow Jones Indexes, McGraw Hill Financial. Available at https://us.spindices.com/documents/spiva/spiva-us-yearend-2015.pdf.

Swensen, David F. 1994. "Endowment Management." *AIMR Conference Proceedings* 1994:8, 30–40.

von Beschwitz, Bastian, and Massimo Massa. 2015. "Biased Shorts: Short Sellers' Disposition Effect and Limits to Arbitrage." International Finance Discussion Papers 1147. Available at https://www.federalreserve.gov/econresdata/ifdp/2015/files/ifdp1147.pdf.

Wang, Wendy, Kim Parker, and Paul Taylor. 2013. "Breadwinner Moms: Mothers Are the Sole or Primary Provider in Four-in-Ten Households with Children; Public Conflicted about the Growing Trend." Pew Research Center. Available at www.pewsocialtrends.org/2013/05/29/breadwinner-moms/.

Wermers, Russ. 1999. "Mutual Fund Herding and the Impact on Stock Prices." *Journal of Finance* 54:2, 581–622.

Worzala, Elaine, G. Stacy Sirmans, and Emily N. Zietz. 2000. "Risk and Return Perceptions of Institutional Investors." *Journal of Real Estate Portfolio Management* 6:2, 153–166.

Yale Investments Office. 2014. "Yale Endowment Update." Available at http://investments.yale.edu/index.php/reports/endowment-update.

Yeung, Danny, Paolo Pellizzari, Ron Bird, and Sazali Abidin. 2012. "Diversification versus Concentration . . . And the Winner Is?" Working Paper Series 18, The Paul Woolley Centre for the Study of Capital Market Dysfunctionality, University of Technology Sydney. Available at https://www.uts.edu.au/sites/default/files/wp18.pdf.

9

Financial Psychopaths

DEBORAH W. GREGORY
Assistant Professor
Bentley University

Introduction

Mention financial psychopaths and for many people, two pop-culture characters immortalized by Hollywood spring to mind: Patrick Bateman, the iconic Wall Street investment banker who stars in the 1980s novel adaptation, *American Psycho* (2000); and more recently Jordan Belfort, the so-called and self-named "Wolf of Wall Street"' (Belfort 2008), in the film of the same name (*The Wolf of Wall Street* 2013). Bateman's character in the first film is purely fictional. He is a man borne of the Wall Street culture during the 1980s, who differs from his colleagues in his proclivity for literally killing people. The latter film, adapted from Belfort's memoir, depicts his lifestyle on Wall Street from the late 1980s through the mid-2000s. It is replete with details of illegal financial deals involving corruption and fraud, drug usage, and his extreme fluency in foul language, sexual promiscuity, and violence. Belfort's self-depiction as a self-aggrandizing person apathetic to the negative consequences of his actions on others is not fiction—rather, it is a close rendering of his actual life and character.

Does either or both of these characters qualify as financial psychopaths? Both work on Wall Street and engage in excessive drinking, drugs, general debauchery, and deceptive practices to achieve financial gain. Moreover, neither Bateman nor Belfort cares about the effects of their actions on the people with whom they interact. That Bateman's character additionally enjoys manslaughter might mark him as a traditional psychopath, but that alone does not answer the question: Is Bateman better described as a financial psychopath? Similarly, is Belfort really a financial psychopath, or is he a psychopath who works in the financial sector? Another possibility might be that Belfort is not a psychopath at all but, rather, a clinically diagnosable sociopath. Although the shared behavioral characteristics of both men would suggest they are likely deserving of a clinical diagnosis of some form of antisocial personality disorder (APD), determining whether either might be considered a financial psychopath requires a deeper examination of what precisely differentiates a financial psychopath from all other forms of antisocial behavioral patterns.

Away from the silver screen, other real-life former financial professionals, such as Nick Leeson of Barings Bank and Turney Duff of Galleon Group, Argus Group, and J. L. Berkowitz, have written exposés of their own time while embedded in the Wall Street environment (Leeson 1996; Duff 2013). Belfort, Leeson, and Duff all worked during the last part of the twentieth century, with Duff and Belfort's tenures extending into the beginning of the twenty-first century as well, a time when financiers were the envy of many outside the profession owing to their ability to generate massive incomes for themselves, seemingly with ease. Leeson and Duff's tales weave together many of the same threads as Belfort's—excessive and regular drug use, promiscuous sex, and fraudulent and illicit financial dealings. Only Belfort has been called to task publicly for engaging in "psychopathic behaviors" by the adult child of his former business associate, Tom Prousalis (McDowell 2013). The strongest acknowledgment of Leeson's fraudulent dealings and his hand in the demise of Barings, a venerated, centuries-old investment bank, has been his placement on the lists of "top" or "worst" rogue traders by multiple news organizations such as *The Guardian* (Hawkes and Wearden 2011) and CNN (Thompson 2011). Duff's behavior warrants even less public interest. His recent online publicity stresses how he strayed while working under the influence of Wall Street, reassuring the public that he is no longer held in its thrall by having returned to a life of normalcy (Duff 2015).

Placing aside provocative publicity purposefully designed to elicit greater book and DVD sales, a commonality exists among all three men's experiences working in the modern financial trading/investment sector. These shared qualities suggest that the Wall Street environment has been accepting of and even condoning behaviors viewed by the general public as psychopathic in nature. Given this, clearly defining what constitutes a financial psychopath becomes necessary to understand these men's behaviors and their resultant impact on the wider financial industry and society. Once determined, the possibility exists to investigate whether the environment of finance attracts such individuals and/or if the environment itself encourages and shapes financially oriented psychopathic behaviors in those who remain inculcated.

Defining Financial Psychopaths

Those working in the financial sector on Wall Street and its environs have come under extensive public and governmental scrutiny since the financial crisis of 2007–2008. That the clinical term of "psychopath" has been appropriated to apply to financial professionals in the aftermath of the crisis speaks volumes about the depth of the global damage on all strata of societies caused by those in the financial industry. Until recently, psychopaths were usually identified as being like Patrick Bateman—someone who acts violently by killing and physically harming victims without any remorse for his or her actions. At no other time in history—including the dramatic stock market crash of 1929—have financial professionals been labeled with such a term as one usually reserves for the most violent of criminals with no moral capacity. By first outlining the clinical indicators for classical psychopaths, it then becomes possible to establish a baseline that leads to an explicit definition of observed behaviors constituting appropriate labeling of an individual as a financial psychopath.

The primary source for guidelines when making a psychiatric diagnosis and developing a treatment plan is the classic *Diagnostic and Statistical Manual of Mental Disorders*, which is now in its fifth edition (American Psychiatric Association 2013), referred to as *DSM-5*. The *DSM-5* classifies hundreds of mental disorders in a system that corresponds with that used by the World Health Organization and insurance companies. By providing behaviors and symptoms associated with a particular disorder, clinicians are guided in formulating the most appropriate diagnosis for an individual.

Before delving into this diagnostic checklist, noting a description of psychopaths written in plain English is worthwhile because it helps to understand the core personality of people so diagnosed. Robert I. Simon, a forensic psychiatrist, describes psychopaths as:

> people who have severe antisocial impulses. They act on them without regard for the inevitable and devastating consequences. . . . [T]hey are the predators among us, chronic parasites and exploiters of the people around them. . . . [They] are unable to put themselves in other people's shoes, any more than a snake can feel empathy for its prey. (Simon 2008, p. 34)

In other words, psychopaths have total disregard for other people and focus solely on themselves. Although people are naturally concerned about themselves, some have personality structures that require constant feedback from others about how great they are in order to feel good about themselves. Psychopaths are narcissistic to such a degree that they are harmful to those within their reach.

This pathological excessive emphasis on oneself is also a feature of narcissistic personality disorder, as well as a component of Asperger's syndrome (now subsumed under autism in the *DSM-5*), so care must be taken to ensure making a correct diagnosis. What would constitute a suitable treatment plan or strategy for managing interactions with a person displaying pathological narcissistic symptoms would be vastly different for psychopaths than for narcissistic personalities or autistic-inclined individuals, given the wide variances in the expected outcomes for each diagnosed personality type.

ROLE OF SUBSTANCE ABUSE

An important external factor that also needs to be considered when making any clinical diagnosis is the use of drugs and alcohol by an individual. The presence of any mind-altering substance can obfuscate an accurate assessment of a person's underlying personality attributes. Addiction of any kind must be ruled out before making a diagnosis of psychopathy. Smith and Newman's (1990) study of incarcerated men shows 92.9 percent of psychopaths are addicted to alcohol and 73.5 percent are addicted to drugs, which is significantly higher than for the control group. A co-morbidity study of psychopathy and addiction by Regier, Farmer, Rae, Locke, Keith, Judd, and Goodwin (1990) estimates 75 percent of psychopaths are addicted to alcohol and 50 percent abuse other drugs. Different schools of psychological thought attribute this high level of co-morbidity to different factors. At the core of the issue is the psychopathic need for constant stimulation, which can be met by self-medicating with alcohol and drugs.

Although little academic literature exists about drug use in the finance industry, anecdotal evidence suggests that it is prevalent and has been for decades (Dealbook 2007; Schuster 2009; *Inside Job* 2011). Belfort, Leeson, and Duff became heavily involved with drugs, particularly cocaine, while working in the investment/trading arena. Both Leeson and Duff did not intend to start using drugs, but found stopping difficult once they started participating at parties with colleagues and clients. This tolerant attitude toward drug use serves to reinforce and could even exacerbate impulsive behavior, one of the hallmarks of psychopathy. In his memoir, Duff (2013) discusses at length the impact his drug misuse had on his personal and professional life.

Some research studies examine the impact on the brain physiology of both cocaine and money. Interestingly, functional magnetic resonance imaging (fMRI) shows that cocaine use lights up the same pleasure centers of the brain as money (Goldstein and Volkow 2002). Further study reveals that cocaine addicts register activity in the pleasure centers of the brain from smaller amounts of monetary rewards than non-cocaine addicts (Goldstein et al. 2003). In other words, non-cocaine addicts do not receive the same type of pleasurable experience for smaller amounts of monetary rewards as those who are addicted. The consequence of intensive cocaine abuse, even after periods of abstinence, includes "more marked deficits in . . . executive control, visuospatial abilities, psychomotor speed and manual dexterity" (Rogers and Robbins 2001, p. 252). For those working on Wall Street, these actions portend a future with diminished cognitive capacity, impairing a person's ability to make sound deals.

Additional studies that compare the brain physiology of psychopaths to the areas of the brain affected by drug use show a similar dysfunction occurring in two identical regions of the brain. Those two affected areas are related to the ability to be socialized and to "frustration-based aggression" (Blair 2005, p. 885). This finding again underscores the need to be circumspect when making a psychopathic diagnosis, as the addict may still have moral and empathic abilities intact—traits that will be lacking in the psychopathic individual.

PSYCHOPATHY

Contrary to what most non-clinicians might expect, the *DSM-5* does not include a separate entry for psychopaths. Instead, the diagnosis is grouped under the classification of APD, which is a broad category that also encompasses sociopathy and psychopathy. To diagnose APD requires a pervasive life-long pattern of problematic behaviors originating before the age of 15 and relates to the person's disregard for other people and other sentient beings. The primary features—of which only three must be met to diagnose—include deceitfulness, impulsivity, irritability and aggressiveness, reckless disregard for the safety of self or others, consistent irresponsibility, and lack of remorse (American Psychiatric Association 2013).

An often-overlooked feature of psychopathy is the charming nature of those with the diagnosis; such behaviors are known to catch otherwise well-informed clinical practitioners and others off-guard. The response to uncovering a heinous deed performed by a previously known-to-be charming individual is often disbelief: "No way! He [or she] is such a great person." The atrocity of the deed is subsequently discounted because of the dissonance between the outer behavior of the "charming" person and the observed result of his or her heinous action. This discord between perception and reality frequently enables psychopathic individuals to continue behaving with impunity until they are literally caught in the act. Even then, psychopaths might avoid major repercussions for their actions owing to the dissonance between their charming public persona and the severity of their actions.

Robert D. Hare, a Canadian psychologist, developed the Hare Psychopathy Checklist (PCL) in the late 1970s based on his work with violent criminals and later revised it in the 1990s. Both long and short versions are available. Professionals use the PCL to ascertain whether a person is psychopathic rather than simply antisocial. Hare and Paul Babiak, his co-researcher on corporate psychopathic behavior and a management-oriented psychologist, estimate that approximately 1 percent of the general population is psychopathic (Babiak and Hare 2006). This statistic compares with 3 percent given by the *DSM-5* for the incidence of antisocial personality disordered individuals occurring in the general population. According to Babiak and Hare (p. 19), those who lie on the sociopathic spectrum can be differentiated from psychopaths by the sociopaths' "sense of right and wrong based on the norms and expectations of their subculture or group."

The distinction between these two types within the APD classification emphasizes the awareness of group cultural norms by a sociopath, but not so for psychopaths. Those individuals who are following group norms in the financial sector cannot thus be deemed psychopathic purely for adhering to practices that their firm and/or colleagues condone. Because most financial employees are aware of group cultural norms, the possibility arises that some people in the financial sector could be sociopathic, provided they meet the other criteria for APD. Certain behaviors might not be considered aberrant within the subculture of finance, whereas those same behaviors might be deemed antisocial by society at large. Excessive or extreme drug use can serve as an example: Within the general society, such behaviors would be considered deeply antisocial with the potential for great harm. In the Wall Street culture of the last two decades of the twentieth century, such behavior might not have been considered aberrant, provided a person's financial performance was unaffected.

The *DSM-5* emphasizes that "criminal behavior undertaken for gain that is not accompanied by the personality features characteristic of this disorder [psychopathy]" (American Psychiatric Association 2013, p. 663) does not provide sufficient grounds for making a psychopathic diagnosis. The mental health professionals who developed the *DSM-5* are aware that behavior resulting in criminal charges does not necessarily signify the presence of severe psychopathology. Rather, what the *DSM-5* does stress is that the observed psychopathic personality traits be, "inflexible, maladaptive, persistent and cause significant functional impairment or subjective distress" (American Psychiatric Association 2013, p. 663). For example, when considering whether a financial professional could be considered a financial psychopath owing to his manipulating financial markets in such a way that it results in enormous monetary gains for himself or his firm, such a behavior alone is an insufficient basis for a psychopathic diagnosis based on *DSM-5* criteria. Instead, the underlying personality structure of the individual is the key to the psychopathic portion of the diagnosis, not the financial venue.

Technological advances in both brain imaging and genetics have enabled further identification of psychopathic individuals based on physiological and DNA characteristics, rather than relying on behavioral characteristics alone. Results from studies using functional MRIs to scan brain physiology indicate the regions of the brain responsible for indicating the presence or absence of specific behaviors associated with psychopathy. For example, the center in the brain responsible for empathy does not light up in the brains of psychopaths (Kiehl, Smith, Hare, Mendrek, Forster, Brink, and Liddle 2001). A more recent study by Motzkin, Newman, Kiehl, and Koenigs (2011) confirms that the ventromedial prefrontal cortex, which controls emotions such as empathy and guilt, does not communicate properly with the amygdala, which is responsible for fear and anxiety, in psychopaths. Finally, Glenn, Raine, Schug, Young, and Hauser (2009) find that increased activity in the prefrontal cortex, which is the region of the brain that provides cognitive control to offset emotional responses to moral dilemmas, increases in psychopaths when making emotional moral decisions. This activity is positively associated to the "impulsive lifestyle" and "antisocial" factors of psychopathy. Glenn et al. (p. 910) note a possible implication of their findings is "a failure to link moral judgment to behavior with appropriately motiving emotions."

The genetic component for psychopathy is currently recognized as being somewhere between a third and a half, with the remaining proportion attributable to environmental or other causes. Epigenetics, the study of genetics and environment, shows that genes contain coded information and also a switch or "promoter," cues in the cell itself, as well as the outer environment, activating the promoter and hence the information in the gene. Thus, if someone has a high genetic propensity toward psychopathy, whether it becomes prominent depends on internal and external environmental cues (Roessler 2012). Because cues are not one-time switches, an affected individual could theoretically become psychopathically "activated" when placed in an appropriate environment that elicits and rewards psychopathic behavior.

These new tools enable identifying psychopaths in settings other than where violent crimes have occurred or in prisons. Physiological tests are confirming earlier behaviorally based assertions that psychopaths can be more frequently found among those who are well educated and held in high regard by society, such as doctors, lawyers, and businesspeople (Smith 1978; Hare 1993; Stout 2005; Babiak and Hare 2006). Boddy (2010) focuses on the incidence of psychopathy among Australian managers and discovers more in financial service companies and the civil service. Both Hare and Simon individually suggest that Wall Street is a prime location for finding nontraditional psychopaths. Simon (2008, p. 44) states "if one wants to study psychopaths, one should go to Wall Street. Sometimes it is hard to tell the successful person from the psychopath." In fact, Hare states that the stock exchange itself would be his preferred location to study psychopaths outside the prison environment (Dutton 2012, p. 112).

DIAGNOSING IN THE BUSINESS ENVIRONMENT

Together, Babiak and Hare (2006) developed a more specific diagnostic tool that focuses on identifying noncriminal psychopaths in the general corporate sector. Their Business-Scan 360 (B-scan 360) is not in either clinical or commercial use at the time of this publication, but is being employed in research studies with businesses to test its validity. From their research, Babiak and Hare identified three distinct subsets of corporate psychopaths: (1) corporate manipulators or cons (more passive), (2) bullies (more aggressive), and (3) puppet masters who display both manipulative and bullying behaviors. The latter category is likened to the dangerous violent criminal psychopath known through the *DSM-5*. Manipulators and bullies both display the same traits as their corresponding criminal psychopathic counterparts.

Using results from administering Hare's PCL short version to 200 high-potential executives, Babiak and Hare (2006) report that seven, or 3.5 percent, of the executives fit the psychopathic profile using the short version of the PCL. Contrasting this with the general incidence of psychopathy in the population at large of 1 percent, this group of executives exhibits a higher rate of psychopathy. Babiak and Hare also note that only two of the 200 executives fell in the bully category and none in the puppet master category. This finding suggests that the proportion of violent, psychopathic individuals who are employed in the corporate sector is on par with the national proportion. The majority of psychopathic corporate executives are known as "passive" psychopaths. Earlier research (Cleckley 1988/1941; Babiak and Hare 2006; Simon 2008; Brown 2010) shows that this type of psychopath is less likely to be involved in legal conflicts resulting from their manipulative behavioral patterns and if they are prosecuted, receive little or no punishment for their offenses.

According to Hare (1993), what renders white-collar crime so appealing to psychopathic personalities is the array of high-payoff opportunities coupled with historically limited punishments if they are caught. Instead of a possible maximum of 20 years for his role in defrauding banks of $23.5 million, the authorities eventually sentenced John Grambling Jr. in 1987 to six months of jail time. Hare (1993, p. 104) identifies Grambling as a psychopathic individual and comments that this case:

> is a model for using education and social connections to separate people and institutions from their money without using violence. . . . [T]he deceit and manipulation of these individuals are not confined to simply making money; these qualities pervade their dealing with everyone . . . including family, friends, and the justice system.

The financial damage inflicted by Grambling was extensive, but the punishment meted out was light. Not much has changed since Grambling's time. As reflected in the clean-up phase of the financial crisis of 2007–2008, the authorities sentenced very few financial executives to time in prison for their role in defrauding the public. Apuzzo and Protess (2015) report on a September 9, 2015, memo issued by the Department of Justice changing their approach to dealing with financial malfeasance. According to Apuzzo and Protess (p. 1), the new rules confirm what the public had already observed, namely that "the Justice Department often targets companies themselves and turns its eyes toward individuals only after negotiating a corporate settlement. In many cases, that means the offending employees go unpunished."

A job or occupation that provides a high-payoff opportunity is insufficient for a psychopathic individual to be successful. The position also needs to make the best use of psychopathic behavior traits. For example, a person who likes to bully others and kill people may do well in a setting that includes warfare. In such a setting, the person's behavior would be lauded and not condemned. Hare (1993, p. 109) notes that occupations most likely to attract psychopathic personalities are those in which, "requisite skills are easy to fake, the jargon is easy to learn, and the credentials are unlikely to be thoroughly checked"; additionally, "the profession also places a high premium on the ability to persuade or manipulate others." These criteria fit positions available on Wall Street and other financial sector work environments. Lewis (1989) describes young male traders working in investment banks during the heydays of the late 1980s in language that conveys many accepted behavioral characteristics. Lewis (p. 9) first allows that they are "masters of the quick killing," a phrase that brings psychopaths to mind. Lewis (p. 61) then attributes the young traders' ability to make great quantities of money quickly, despite their lack of experience, to being "less a matter of skill and more a matter of intangibles—flair, persistence, and luck" when talking with potential buyers on the telephone.

Successful traders possess certain attributes, many of which match psychopathic traits. For example, the psychopathic trait of impulsivity may display in a successful trader as a willingness to take high degrees of risk in a situation when others think it would be foolish, such as when the market has taken an unexpected plunge. However, the non-psychopathic trader may in fact be well prepared and waiting for such an opportunity to present itself. In actuality, he is not acting impulsively, but from the outside perspective it may appear so. Differentiating between the two is not as simple as watching their outer behaviors.

Trading skills evolve over time and an outer personality develops to present to the world at large. The purpose of this outer personality or persona is to enable a person to engage in the world, and may or may not accurately reflect the trader's true inner personality. The trader in this case may not want people to know what he is actually intending and may present with charming banter that is totally unrelated to the trading opportunity closest to his heart. Thus, this fictitious trader displays two more psychopathic traits: deception and a charming persona. Based on the guidelines given in the *DSM-5* earlier, these characteristics are all in service of obtaining financial gain and are not life-long, inflexible traits. The trader is not pathologically psychopathic.

GENDER BIAS

Thus far, the discussion of psychopathy has focused solely on men. This bias exists in the literature because women are underrepresented in both the disorder and the financial sector, so very little has been written about them in this regard. Researchers are finding that psychopathy displays differently in women (Kreis and Cooke 2011; Wynn, Høiseth, and Patterson 2012), which may account for the lower percentage present in the general population. Kreis and Cooke (p. 644) describe a "prototype" female psychopath as "manipulative, deceitful, self-justifying, self-centered, domineering, detached, uncaring, antagonistic, insincere, and self-aggrandizing." Many of their descriptors reflect the traditional psychopath checklist developed with male subjects. Like her male counterpart, she also lacks empathy. Yet, as Kreis and Cook (p. 614) note, the prototype female psychopath also could be "more manipulative, emotionally unstable, and have a more unstable self-concept." Women, however, show a distinct preference for using relationally oriented techniques, such as flirting, to abuse their victims (Forouzan and Cooke 2005). Given no obvious physical abuse is generally associated with sexual promiscuity or flirting, pinpointing the more aggressive psychopathic behavioral trait in women is more difficult than for men.

Financial Psychopaths

A possible shape and face can now be formulated for a potential financial psychopath. Although many perceive psychopaths as charming individuals, they display a variety of pervasive, life-long anti-social traits, such as deceitfulness, narcissistic orientation, consistent irresponsibility, and a lack of remorse. A subset within the general psychopathic designation is the corporate psychopath. Most corporate psychopaths are primarily passive types who do not display obvious violent behaviors, as would be found in the general psychopathic population. They tend to exploit and manipulate others for their own gain, and in so doing, they behave in such a way as to avoid becoming entangled with the legal system. Because finance is part of the business environment, a financial psychopath may be considered a subgroup of corporate psychopaths.

First, a financial psychopath is far more likely to be male. This observation is due partly to the presence of fewer women who are currently in positions to control finances owing to prevailing sociocultural biases, and also owing to the lower incidence of women diagnosed as psychopaths overall. Psychopathic women tend to use their sexuality to manipulate people. As a result, they would be far less likely to be caught holding the "smoking gun" of financial manipulation and instead be censured for their sexual behaviors.

Second, violence is not a normal or primary attribute of the corporate psychopath. However, it cannot be ruled out completely. Babiak and Hare's (2006) research indicates that a very small minority of bully and puppeteer corporate psychopaths use physical violence when manipulating others.

Differentiating between the corporate and financial psychopath narrows the focus to the resources over which each has control. The primary responsibility of corporate executives is the strategic management of a company, not the handling of money belonging to other people on a short- or long-term basis. The exception to this is the chief financial officer (CFO), who can be considered eligible for the financial psychopath diagnosis. However, McKinsey & Company notes (Agrawal, Goldie, and Huyett 2013) that not all CFOs have backgrounds in finance. Accounting and general MBA backgrounds are more prevalent, but a change has occurred since 2009. Approximately one-third of CFOs hired to "grow" a company have had Wall Street careers in investment banking and related sectors. Thus, the proportion of CFO financial psychopaths may very well be much smaller than for corporate executives in general, with the potential for an increasing trend in certain segments.

Trust has been placed in financiers of all types to honor their implied or explicit fiduciary duty to manage that money wisely. When others perceive financial professionals as violating that trust by not acting prudently on behalf of clients, and instead taking care of their own financial needs first, this should sound an alarm. Furthermore, if investment professionals are unremorseful and callous about financial outcomes from their dealings, particularly if the outcomes are negative, then a key psychopathic feature has become apparent.

Thus, distinct and separate from the corporate psychopath, a *financial psychopath* is a predator who ruins the lives of others through activities involving financial transactions; this person is emotionally detached, narcissistic, and shows no remorse, perhaps even taking pleasure in the destruction of the lives of others. His or her outer demeanor may be charming. To be considered a financial psychopath also requires meeting the basic criterion from the *DSM-5*—doing harm to others must be a pervasive, life-long pattern, not isolated to when adulthood is attained and having access to financial resources. Recognizing that in early childhood money is not an easily controllable instrument for a child, infliction of physical or emotional pain to others without accompanying remorse would need to be present. Incorporating the findings from epigenetics that environmental cues may trigger underlying psychopathic tendencies, DNA testing may be necessary for confirmation if no early pattern of inflicting harm to others is otherwise evident.

Instead of using guns and other weapons of destruction to kill, financial psychopaths use the tools of their trade—computers and financial transactions—to purposefully harm others. Financial psychopaths are not limited by geography because they do not need to operate locally. In fact, financial psychopaths have the ability to inflict more harm to a greater proportion of the population globally, without resorting to physical violence, because they require no personal relationship with intended victims and can carry out damage anonymously. Moreover, no blood needs to be spilled—any damage can be inflicted from arm's length. As with other passive types of psychopaths, financial psychopaths are less likely to become entangled with the law and might escape discovery and punishment for their crimes.

IDENTIFYING FINANCIAL PSYCHOPATHS

Based on the preceding discussion, Bateman's character in *American Psycho* can be classified as a traditional psychopath. Although he happens to work in the financial industry, according to this working definition he is not a financial psychopath. Belfort, by contrast, does not present as a classic psychopath. Whether his personality is best described as a financial psychopath or as a person who works in the financial sector and displays sociopathic tendencies needs further clarification.

To find other financial practitioners who have exhibited behaviors that might indicate they are financial psychopaths requires in-depth investigation into their lives and actions. The media have highlighted many financial professionals since 2007 for fraud and mismanagement of money. Few have been prosecuted. One high-profile case was Bernie Madoff, accused of running a Ponzi scheme that defrauded investors of billions of dollars over decades. Diane Henriques spent hours interviewing Madoff in prison and concluded he was psychopathic. She found him to be charming and not the least remorseful for what he had done. Without formal clinical training, Henriques (2012) had followed the guidelines in the *DSM-5* and formulated a diagnosis.

Madoff's case illustrates the ease with which someone in the right situation with the appropriate connections and tools can take money from others. Another person inadvertently caught in the fallout from the mortgage securitization debacle is Lee B. Farkus, former chairman and owner of Taylor, Bean & Whitaker Mortgage Corporation (TBW), a mortgage-processing firm based in Ocala, Florida. Farkus also used financial transactions and took advantage of low-grade computer technology to make enormous sums of money while defrauding banks, government agencies, and homeowners. When his firm was shut down in 2009, TBW's books showed a portfolio valued by the Federal Home Loan Mortgage Corporation, known as Freddie Mac, at more than $51.2 billion, but no real assets backed up the paper. The failure of TBW badly damaged the economy of Ocala, Florida, as TBW had been a major employer that paid relatively well. Gregory (2014) details Farkus's background and subsequent behaviors using financial instruments and transactions to perpetrate his crimes.

Farkus's profile more closely corresponds to the description of a financial psychopath outlined in this chapter than does Madoff. However, both men were culpable of wreaking havoc on the lives of people they knew—as well as countless others with whom they had no relationship—simply by using financial transactions, enabled by low-grade computer technology.

Emergence of Psychopathy in the Financial Environment

In the aftermath of the financial crisis of 2007–2008, the general public worldwide became informed through media stories about the activities of financiers in the period leading up to the crisis. Most people did not understand the financial instruments or strategies that financial practitioners used to leverage returns, but the general public did comprehend that average people were now suffering. They attributed the cause of their pain to the actions taken by those affiliated with Wall Street and its environs. Forgotten were the immediately preceding years of record increases in 401(k)s and other retirement plans, as well as the meteoric rise in housing prices that increased household wealth and homeownership rates.

Financial practitioners suddenly became pariahs. Across the globe, they had devoured people's dreams of stability and future financial security through their greed. What caused even more outrage was the perception by the general public that financial professionals did not appear to be suffering to the same extent. In fact, many practitioners seemed to be benefiting from the crisis and making money and taking care of themselves, which is a narcissistic quality of psychopaths. The majority of observers outside Wall Street perceived the attitude of these professionals toward the damage they had incurred to be callous and uncaring, which are both psychopathic qualities. As Gapper (2012, p. 13) notes, "the culture of the trading floor is remarkably immune to shame." The response of many in the financial sector to allegations of imprudent behavior was evasive of accepting responsibility for causing global harm. Consistent irresponsibility is yet another psychopathic trait. These incongruent perceptions of the behaviors engaged in by financial professionals are indicative of a lack of agreement over what constitutes acceptable and expected behavior when involved with professional money management.

The general public expects those in the financial sector who are tasked with managing money on behalf of others to do so in a prudent and responsible manner. In short, they are expected to act as fiduciaries. Many other individuals engaged in the financial sector do not act in a fiduciary capacity, and as such, do not have the same responsibility to the average person. From the viewpoint of the general public, all these financial practitioners fall under the same umbrella. Differentiating one from the other is difficult as an outsider. Given the hostility and resulting lack of trust that emanated from the fallout of the financial crisis, the term "financial psychopath" was coined in an effort to capture the despicability of the actions of certain financiers whose actions bore the hallmarks of psychopathy.

Until 2008, the media portrayed investment practitioners who had been caught manipulating financial markets as "rogue traders." Jérôme Kerviel of BNP Paribas and Nick Leeson of Barings Bank serve as prime examples of this classification. From the outside, their actions could be construed as simply not following the written protocol of their respective banks. The resulting financial turmoil from their actions was restricted to losses among large and well-funded banks, although Kerviel's actions had the possibility of inflicting severe damage to the general financial system, given the size of his original position (Matlack 2008). The average person, however, saw no direct effect on his or her 401k or bank statement.

Conversely, smaller scale financial scams have been in existence since recorded history, with cautionary tales to warn people to be careful about where and with whom they trust their life savings. Con artists and swindlers are commonly applied terms within the financial sectors to denote people who are untrustworthy in handling others' money. No term so pejorative or personally pathological as "financial psychopath" existed until 2008. The expression itself suggests no possible redemption. It infers that these particular financial professionals should be removed from society for the safety of all, as is the case for traditional psychopaths. Yet, for centuries, swindlers of all sorts have been involved with financial scams. What is different about this time that provoked the emergence of a new label? Was it the size of the meltdown? Was it the attitude of those who were accused of causing the problem? Was it fear of financial annihilation and lack of control over future resources on the part of the average citizen?

IDENTIFYING KEY CHANGES IN THE FINANCIAL ENVIRONMENT

Many facets of the financial environment have changed since the 1980s. Most of these changes are not brought to public awareness unless a negative event occurs that is broadcast in the general media, such as the Flash Crash of 2010. The flash crash occurred during the afternoon of May 6. U.S. share and futures indices went into a seemingly inexplicable tailspin and fell 10 percent in a matter of minutes. Stock indexes, such as the S&P 500, Dow Jones Industrial Average, and Nasdaq 100, collapsed and rebounded very rapidly. The short-lived plunge raised questions about whether trading rules had failed to keep up with markets that now handle orders in milliseconds.

The biggest factors from the past 40 years that have influenced the investment/trading sectors of finance are advances in technology and computing ability. The ripple effects of these rapid advancements reach far into the regulatory arena and how the markets function, as well as the type of person employed in the financial industry. The impact in each of these areas has incurred consequences, some of which could not have been easily predicted. Taken together, a new financial environment evolved that has allowed for a change regarding who is operating in the sector, resulting in psychopathic-like behaviors being condoned in a desire to maximize return on investment using faster technology.

Overarching the impact from technological advances has been the shift in the approach to the economic environment within which financial practitioners operate. According to Chandler (1994), "industrial capitalism" defines the period from 1945 to 1980, a time during which the Northern Hemisphere was rebuilding from the ravages of World War II. Financial markets were instrumental in helping to reallocate capital from investors to companies that were establishing themselves in peacetime. Relational skills between financial professionals and individuals at the helm of corporations were paramount to solidifying deals. Physical assets underlay much of the financing required. The financial markets were physical locations where traders and brokers met face-to-face to make deals and discover information—again, relational skills were critical to being successful. Because people met regularly and worked together in close physical proximity, those who were psychopathically inclined could not sustain a façade that would enable them to maintain "normal" everyday interactions with the same people. Less opportunity was thus available for a financial psychopath to be successful over the long term, as behaviors were more closely monitored by peers.

During this time period, a new, modern theory of finance was also introduced that would have resounding implications for decades to come. Modern portfolio theory (MPT) and the efficient markets hypothesis (EMH) both originated during this era, as did the concept that the goal of the financial manager is to maximize shareholder wealth by maximizing the value of the firm. Another major contribution to financial theory during this period was the capital asset pricing model (CAPM). One of its basic assumptions, as with many economic models of the time, was that all participants act in an economically rational manner. Taken together, these theories helped to shape not only how people approached markets but also the type of person who would succeed financially. Logical, analytical people who could spot inefficiencies and take advantage of them before they were no longer available did well. The processing speed of computers was slow enough and markets were not as electronically connected. Enough time was available to discover mispriced assets and make profitable trades before other market participants would notice the mispricing and arbitrage it away, returning markets to an efficient state.

By 1980, the pace of the markets had quickened with the advent of faster technologies, along with a loosening of regulations that governed the markets. Neal (1993) describes this time period as the start of "financial capitalism," which lasted until 2008. Financial firms began to focus more on how they could profit from these changes rather than on providing capital where it was needed. The most sought after employees became those with superior mathematical and computer skills, who could effectively write trading programs to take advantage of the rapid computer speeds now available. Technology-driven platforms provided new venues for trading, circumventing the old, more relationally based exchanges with higher fees and slower processing times. Financial markets of all kinds across the globe became more intertwined in this fast-paced electronic network.

During this phase, U.S. workers became responsible for their own retirement accounts with the introduction of defined contribution retirement plans. Whether they manage the money themselves or rely on a financial professional, the ability for almost all workers to fund their retirement now depends on their personal ability to invest in the financial markets. Before this time period, average individuals did not directly interact with Wall Street unless they chose to participate in the market for investment or speculative reasons. Investment professionals managed company-sponsored pension plans, known as defined benefit plans. Employees would be told how much they would be receiving when they retired. Most workers did not understand where or how a financial professional would invest money earmarked for retirement funds; they simply knew how much they could expect to receive when they retired. Vesting periods became increasingly important. A *vesting period* is the length of time someone has to stay with a company before being eligible to receive pension benefits. With the change to defined contribution plans, average citizens became far more aware of how much their personal financial life was inextricably linked with activities on Wall Street. Later, they would understand that the financial markets were the provinces of financial professionals who may or may not be working in the best interests of all people.

The financial theories that had been developed during the period of industrial capitalism continued to be refined during the next 30 years. For example, Lo (2005, p. 39) furthered the EMH with his adaptive markets hypothesis, based on the assumption that "individuals act in their own self-interest," as well as rationality. Simply because people act rationally and in their own best interest does not imply they make decisions that are not damaging to the greater society. To the contrary, the outcome of Lo's evolutionary-based model that the richest survive, lends support to the contention that individuals in the financial sector who embrace the tenets of this model may be narcissistic and predatory in nature.

Risk management became more prominent with further development of the option pricing theory (OPT) made possible by the advances in computing technology. Investment and speculation in derivative instruments became widespread, relieving the need for tangible, physical assets as proof of ownership. Many financial instruments became disconnected from the physical form they had assumed for millennia, thus enabling the less scrupulous and more psychopathically inclined individuals to thrive in this new environment.

Summary and Conclusions

This brief synopsis of key changes indicates that the professional financial environment has been transformed from the more relational, personally connected milieu that existed for many centuries. The enhanced speed with which information is delivered globally and ingested into trading strategies that are carried out in nanoseconds has shifted the ages-old objective of maximizing returns into a pure numbers game. Individuals seeking to maximize returns for themselves or their firm, regardless of what happens to other participants, can inflict more damage (whether intentional or not) to a wider swath of global economies, in a shorter time than previously. This environment offers abundant opportunities for financial psychopaths to be successful. Additionally, the possibility exists of hiding a disruptive internal psyche structure behind a façade of polished respectability and social decorum, which makes exposing and prosecuting financial psychopaths more difficult. The power that accompanies control of large sums of money further exacerbates this problem.

The two potential financial psychopaths identified earlier, Madoff and Farkus, differ greatly from the Hollywood depictions of Bateman and Belfort, both of whom have been held up as Wall Street psychopaths. Both Madoff and Farkus escaped public detection and prosecution for years. The impact of their financial misdoings affected a much wider range of people in all walks of life. Only through chance coincidences was either discovered. Had they been able to continue, the damage would have been even greater.

Despite now being able to clearly differentiate a financial psychopath, the problem remains that any type of passive psychopath functions in society in such a way as to avoid prosecution. Rarely are the more insidious psychopaths caught and prosecuted. Instead, less powerful and influential individuals in the financial sector, many of whom are not psychopathic and are not personally responsible for the most egregious financial crimes, bear the brunt of any investigation and face prosecution.

DISCUSSION QUESTIONS

1. Identify the distinguishing characteristics of a traditional psychopath.
2. Explain how traditional and financial psychopaths differ.
3. Discuss the key changes in the economic and financial environment that facilitated an increase in the psychopathic-like behavior exhibited by financial professionals.
4. Explain why correctly identifying financial psychopaths is important.

REFERENCES

Agrawal, Ankur, John Goldie, and Bill Huyett. 2013. "Today's CFO: Which Profile Best Suits Your Company?" McKinsey & Company, *Insights and Publications*, January. Available at http://www.mckinsey.com/insights/corporate_finance/todays_cfo_which_profile_best_suits_your_company.

American Psychiatric Association. 2013. *Diagnostic and Statistical Manual of Mental Disorders*. Fifth Edition. Arlington, VA: American Psychiatric Association.

American Psycho. 2000. Mary Harron (Director). Lionsgate, [DVD].

Apuzzo, Matt, and Ben Protess. 2015. "Justice Department Sets Sights on Wall Street Executives." *New York Times*, September 10, 1.

Babiak, Paul, and Robert D. Hare. 2006. *Snakes in Suits: When Psychopaths Go to Work*. New York: ReganBooks.

Belfort, Jordan. 2008. *The Wolf of Wall Street*. New York: Bantam.

Blair, R. J. R. 2005. "Applying a Cognitive Neuroscience Perspective to the Disorder of Psychopathy." *Development and Psychopathy* 17:3, 865–891.

Boddy, Clive R. P. 2010. "Corporate Psychopaths and Organizational Type." *Journal of Public Affairs* 10:4, 300–312.

Brown, Pat. 2010. *The Profiler: My Life Hunting Serial Killers and Psychopaths*. New York: Voice.

Chandler Jr., Alfred D. 1994. *Scale and Scope: The Dynamics of Industrial Capitalism*. Cambridge, MA: Belknap Press.

Cleckley, Hervey M. 1988/1941. *The Mask of Sanity*. Augusta, GA: Emily S. Cleckley.

Dealbook. 2007. "Drugs and Today's Wall Street." Available at http://dealbook.nytimes.com/2007/12/21/drugs-and-todays-wall-street/?_r=0.

Duff, Turney. 2013. *The Buy Side: A Wall Street Trader's Tale of Spectacular Excess*. New York: Crown Business.

Duff, Turney. 2015. "Bio" [web blog]. Available at http://turneyduff.com/bio/.

Dutton, Kevin. 2012. *The Wisdom of Psychopaths: Lessons in Life from Saints, Spies and Serial Killers*. London: William Heinemann.

Forouzan, Elham, and David J. Cooke. 2005. "Figuring Out La Femme Fatale: Conceptual and Assessment Issues Concerning Psychopathy in Females." *Behavioral Sciences and the Law* 23:6, 765–778.

Gapper, John. 2012. "Trading Floor Culture No Longer Acceptable." *Financial Times*, July 5, 13.

Glenn, Andrea, Adrian Raine, Robert A. Schug, Liane Young, and Marc Hauser. 2009. "Increased DLPFC Activity during Moral Decision-Marking in Psychopathy." *Molecular Psychiatry* 14:10, 909–911.

Goldstein, Rita Z., and Nora D. Volkow. 2002. "Drug Addiction and Its Underlying Neurobiological Basis: Neuroimaging Evidence for the Involvement of the Frontal Cortex." *American Journal of Psychiatry* 159:10, 1642–1652.

Goldstein, R. Z., S. A. Berry, A. C. Leskovjan, E. C. Caparelli, D. Tomasi, L. Chang, F. Telang, N. D. Volkow, N. K. Squires, and T. Ernst. 2003. "Money Activates Reward Circuits in Cocaine Addiction: A Functional MRI Study at 4 T." *Proceedings of the International Society of Magnetic Resonance Medicine* 11, 1918.

Gregory, Deborah W. 2014. *Unmasking Financial Psychopaths: Inside the Minds of Investors in the Twenty-First Century.* New York: Palgrave Macmillan.

Hare, Robert D. 1993. *Without Conscious: The Disturbing World of the Psychopaths among Us.* New York: Pocket Books.

Hawkes, Alex, and Graeme Wearden. 2011. "Who Are the Worst Rogue Traders in History?" *The Guardian*, September 15. Available at http://www.theguardian.com/business/2011/sep/15/who-are-worst-rogue-traders.

Henriques, Diane. 2012. Speech, University of New England, April 12.

Inside Job. 2011. Charles Ferguson (Director). Sony Pictures Home Entertainment, [DVD].

Kiehl, Kent A., Andra M. Smith, Robert D. Hare, Adrianna Mendrek, Bruce B. Forster, Johann Brink, and Peter F. Liddle. 2001. "Limbic Abnormalities in Affective Processing by Criminal Psychopaths as Revealed by Functional Magnetic Resonance Imaging." *Biological Psychiatry* 50:9, 677–684.

Kreis, Mette K. F., and David J. Cooke. 2011. "Capturing the Psychopathic Female: A Prototypical Analysis of the Comprehensive Assessment of Psychopathic Personalities (CAPP) across Gender." *Behavioral Sciences and the Law* 29:5, 634–648.

Leeson, Nick. 1996. *Rogue Trader.* Boston: Little, Brown.

Lewis, Michael. 1989. *Liar's Poker.* New York: W.W. Norton.

Lo, Andrew. 2005. "Reconciling Efficient Markets with Behavioral Finance: The Adaptive Markets Hypothesis." *Journal of Investment Consulting* 7:2, 21–44.

Matlack, Carol. 2008. "Jérôme Kerviel in His Own Words." *Businessweek Online* 14, January 30. Available at http://www.bloomberg.com/bw/stories/2008-01-30/jerome-kerviel-in-his-own-wordsbusinessweek-business-news-stock-market-and-financial-advice.

McDowell, Christina. 2013. "An Open Letter to the Makers of *The Wolf of Wall Street* and the Wolf Himself." *LA Weekly,* December 26. Available at http://www.laweekly.com/news/an-open-letter-to-the-makers-of-the-wolf-of-wall-street-and-the-wolf-himself-4255219.

Motzkin, Julian C., Joseph P. Newman, Kent A. Kiehl, and Michael Koenigs. 2011. "Reduced Prefrontal Connectivity in Psychopathy." *Journal of Neuroscience* 30:48, 17348–17357.

Neal, Larry. 1993. *The Rise of Financial Capitalism: International Capital Markets in the Age of Reason.* New York: Cambridge University Press.

Regier, Darrel A., Mary E. Farmer, Donald S. Rae, Ben Z. Locke, Samuel J. Keith, L. J. Judd, and F. K. Goodwin. 1990. "Comorbidity of Mental Disorders with Alcohol and Other Drug Abuse: Results from the Epidemiologic Catchment Area Study." *Journal of the American Medical Association* 264:19, 2511–2518.

Roessler, Christian. 2012. "Are Archetypes Transmitted More by Culture Than by Biology? Questions Arising from Conceptualizations of the Archetype." *Journal of Analytical Psychology* 57:2, 223–246.

Rogers, Robert D., and Trevor W. Robbins. 2001. "Investigating the Neurocognitive Deficits Associated with Chronic Drug Misuse." *Current Opinion in Neurobiology* 11:2, 250–257.

Schuster, Mike. 2009. "Wall Street's Long and Sordid History with Cocaine." *Minyanville.com,* Business News, 27 October. Available at http://minyanville.com/businessmarkets/articles/wall-street-cocaine-bernie-madoff-fridays/10/27/2009/id/25132.

Simon, Robert I. 2008. *Bad Men Do What Good Men Dream: A Forensic Psychiatrist Illuminates the Darker Side of Human Behavior.* Washington, DC: American Psychiatric Publishing.
Smith, Robert J. 1978. *The Psychopath in Society.* New York: Academic Press.
Smith, Stevens S., and Joseph P. Newman. 1990. "Alcohol and Drug Abuse-Dependence Disorders in Psychopathic and Nonpsychopathic Criminal Offenders." *Journal of Abnormal Psychology* 99:4, 430–439.
Stout, Martha. 2005. *The Sociopath Next Door.* New York: Three Rivers Press.
Thompson, Nick. 2011. "The World's Biggest Rogue Traders in Recent History." *CNN,* September 15. Available at http://edition.cnn.com/2011/BUSINESS/09/15/unauthorized.trades/.
Wolf of Wall Street. 2013. Martin Scorsese (Director). Paramount Pictures, [DVD].
Wynn, Rolf, Marita H. Høiseth, and Gunn Patterson. 2012. "Psychopathy in Women: Theoretical and Clinical Perspectives." *International Journal of Women's Health* 4, 257–263.

Part Three

FINANCIAL AND INVESTOR PSYCHOLOGY OF SPECIFIC PLAYERS

10

The Psychology of High Net Worth Individuals

REBECCA LI-HUANG
Wealth Advisor

Introduction

This chapter explores the economic and psychological aspects of private wealth and the practice of wealth management from a holistic perspective. It focuses on the investor psychology and investment behavior of individuals or households with more than $1 million in investable assets, commonly known as *high net worth individuals* (HNWIs). HNWIs, or simply the wealthy, constitute 0.7 percent of the world's adult population, but they own 45.2 percent of global wealth, as of 2015. The wealthy also control most of the world's power. According to Piketty (2014, p. 277), the top percentile of wealth holders occupies a very prominent place in any society and "structures the economic and political landscape." Deaton (2013, p. 212) observes that "the rapid growth in top incomes can become self-reinforcing through the political process that money can bring." Stiglitz (2015, p. 91) describes the political landscape in the United States as "wealth begets power, which begets more wealth." Regardless of ideological persuasions and political motivations, observers and stakeholders agree that the current economic system favors the top income earners and wealth holders.

This chapter highlights the classical economic frameworks of wealth creation. It also examines recent studies and empirical findings on wealth accumulation and distribution that have increased the policy debate. The distribution of income and wealth is widely discussed globally and has increasingly become politically charged and partisan in policy debate in the United States, where average wealth has increased but not equally over the past 50 years. A statement such as "the top 1 percent of Americans own 40 percent of the nation's wealth" is in stark contrast to "the bottom 80 percent own only 7 percent" and the phrase "the disappearing middle class." The global trend is similar in that the share of income and wealth going to those at the very top has risen sharply over the last generation, marking a return to a pattern that prevailed before World War I. The world's top 1 percent of wealth holders now owns half of all household wealth (Credit Suisse 2015).

HNWIs have varied psychological and behavioral responses to the inequity debate and anti-rich rhetoric among populists. In the United States, HNWIs increasingly direct their investment according to their personal beliefs or family values, and they play a large role in public life through philanthropy and politics. At 1.4 percent of gross domestic product (GDP), "tax breaks with a social purpose" are the largest in the United States where private spending on social welfare is four times the average in advanced economies (Organization for Economic Cooperation and Development 2014). At the pinnacle of the wealth pyramid, billionaires Bill Gates, Warren Buffett, and Mark Zuckerberg pledge the majority of their wealth to tax-advantaged charitable entities founded, funded, and directed by themselves or their representatives. They urge their cohorts to invest their wealth in public good in their own visions, such as "advancing human potential and promoting equality" advocated by Zuckerberg, not that of the governments. At the other end of ideological spectrum, self-claimed billionaire and political outsider Donald Trump runs the most powerful government. Ironically, Trump's promise to use his own private wealth to acquire political power has become part of the populist appeal to his economically disadvantaged supporters. Despite the debate that philanthropy and political activism both serve to return yet more power to the super-wealthy, driving social impact holds broad appeal for a cross-section of HNWIs globally, who are increasingly focused on leaving a legacy by giving back to society, as well as generating a financial return on investment. The holistic returns on cultural, environmental, social, and political causes are gaining importance in wealth management. The trend toward helping HNWIs address their personal aspirations and social-impact needs is part of a broader wealth management industry transition toward giving holistic wealth advice.

HNWIs are prone to behavioral biases and judgment errors in decision-making processes. Their behaviors and attitudes toward the future cannot be encapsulated in a single, inexorable psychological parameter. The luck of inherited wealth (for some) aside, HNWIs have not all won the evolutionary lottery in possessing the genetic traits of the perfectly rational, utility-maximizing, unemotional *Homo economicus*, which is the economic behavioral role model for *Homo sapiens*. Even though case studies and legends abound for entrepreneurs and investors who become self-made millionaires or billionaires by exploiting their fellow human's "irrationalities" and market inefficiencies, HNWIs are humans with biases, not a homogenous group of rational agents as prescribed by traditional economic model. Research in behavioral finance has uncovered a lengthy list of psychological biases, but offers few tools for investors to correct the persistent errors in their investment decision-making process. An age-old strategy to overcome cognitive illusions and biases is to avoid the groupthink. Wealth managers add value by bringing objective but goal-based inputs to the decision-making process.

HNWIs are inundated with choices in every decision they make, from consumption and investment of private and public wealth as stakeholders and policy makers, to family life and social impact as private and global citizens. Their decision choices for any given goal, in the pursuit of wealth, health, and happiness, depend on personal motivations and satisfactions, family expectations and limitations, peer influences, and the social, cultural, and institutional environment. Financial investment is but one component in the "well-lived life" portfolios and its importance varies depending on the life stages of HNWIs. Investment in publicly traded securities as consumer of financial products is not the primary contributor of initial wealth accumulation for most HNWIs. Stanley (2001) reveals that only about one in eight millionaires indicated that "investing in the equities of public corporations" was a very important factor in explaining their economic success. Many HNWIs are successful in their own fields of expertise, but few can distinguish luck from skills in investing in public financial markets. Chhabra (2015) finds that concentration and leverage are often the building blocks of substantial private wealth. Nevertheless, investment in diversified markets and tax-efficient strategies are essential for HNWIs to preserve and generate income from wealth. Since these investors experienced the brunt of the financial crisis of 2007–2008 and other market "failures," HNWIs' needs for a full spectrum of wealth management services have grown.

Wealth managers increasingly focus on HNWI behaviors, and they translate the significance of current events in terms of clients' needs and goals. With a behavioral focus, wealth management practice is transitioning from portfolios and markets to individuals and objectives, and from products and transactions to advice and relationships. With competition from technology-based new entrants, not only transactions but also basic asset allocation and investment services are becoming increasingly commoditized. Wealth managers adapt to the new landscape by focusing on the human aspect of the advisory relationship and reorienting their role toward delivering goals-based financial planning and addressing HNWIs' holistic investing needs.

Many anecdotes and much literature are available with examples of spectacular financial ruin as the result of poor investments or conspicuous consumptions on an individual level. Yet, on a collective and long-term basis, HNWIs are the most successful in both preserving and growing their numbers and total wealth in absolute and relative terms, especially in the countries and regions with the highest economic growth in recent decades. As Piketty (2014) shows, the rate of return of capital has outpaced the rate of economic growth, and the rate of return is persistently higher for the HNWIs than that for the less wealthy. He credits the concentration of wealth and the service of private wealth managers as the primary sources of the outperformance for HNWI.

Economic policies continue to shape the global wealth landscape. Asset allocation and human capital investment are the most important long-term factors determining overall investment returns and wealth accumulations. Led by the United States and now China, global trade and economic growth have been the main forces in creating, and to some extent reshuffling, the wealthy class in the twenty-first century. In the United States, monetary policy set by the Federal Reserve and the tax code by Congress directly affect financial asset prices and real incomes, especially those of HNWIs and corporations, and they implicitly project the outlook for economic output, rate of return on investment, and income and wealth distribution. To the extent that the wealth of HNWIs and corporate profits are intertwined, and the size of wealth correlates with the power to influence policy, the collective investment behavior of HNWIs resembles that of corporations and institutional investors more than that of retail investors.

As a case in point, HNWIs with institutional-size wealth are "activist" investors whose investment decisions move the price and affect the return of publicly traded securities (Cohan 2013). The investor psychology of an activist investor who has "skin in the game" and faces known risks is by institutional design more forward-looking, calculating, and profit-maximizing than that of a price-taking individual investor who faces uncertainties. The beneficial tax treatment and legal structure of limited liability corporations further insulate HNWIs from individual behavioral biases such as risk aversion. HNWIs sometimes exhibit investment behavior that is more rational than that of corporations or organizations managed by agents with distorted incentives. Examples are Warren Buffett's "vote of confidence" investment in Goldman Sachs and HNW private investors' cash buying of bank-owned properties amid the widespread foreclosures between 2008 and 2010.

The first section of this chapter defines HNWI and introduces the players and markets of the private wealth management industry. Drawing on the industry's HNWI and wealth manager surveys, as well as empirical research, the next section identifies the trends related to HNWI attitudes and investment behaviors, shifting demographics of private wealth, and evolving expectations and needs of HNWIs. The next section then highlights relevant behavioral finance research and applications to lay a foundation for the holistic investing and goal-based wealth management practice trend. With the third section, the chapter takes an economic view of behavior and wealth by presenting the macro factors that affect HNW investor behavior on a long-term and aggregated basis. The fourth section presents the theoretical framework and empirical findings of economic researchers of different historical times and ideological persuasions, and the final section summarizes and concludes the chapter.

The World of HNWI and Wealth Management

Wealth has varied connotations and subtexts in social, economic, political, and historical contexts. As a source of finance for future consumption, wealth is one of the key components of the economic system. The wealth management industry is primarily concerned with the financial assets of wealthy individuals and households.

WEALTH AND HNWI DEFINED

Although wealth has various definitions, one involves net worth. As defined in the World Wealth Report (Gapgemini Consulting and RBC Wealth Management 2015), *net worth* is synonymous with *investable assets* excluding one's primary residence, collectibles, consumables, and consumer durables. *High net worth* (HNW) refers to an individual or household with more than $1 million in investable assets. However, some private banks use a higher net worth threshold to denote HNWIs. Also, depending on the market segmentation of a wealth manager or surveyor, the *ultra-high net worth* (UHNW) designation usually refers to net worth above $30 million. When accounting for illiquid and nonmarketable assets such as real estate and land, physical commodities, art and collectibles, business ownerships and partnership interests, a HNWI's total wealth is often higher than net worth.

On a global basis, having $1 million net worth puts an individual in the top 1 percent, as HNWIs account for 0.7 percent of world's adult population. In the United States, being in the top 1 percent club takes $380,000 annual income (Dewan and Gebeloff 2012) or $8.4 million net worth (Gebeloff and Dewan 2012) to qualify, according to a 2012 demographic profile of the top earners and wealth holders by the *New York Times*. Income and wealth are different measures, but they often go hand in hand. The U.S. tax code is more favorable for investment income than for wages, especially for those already at or near the top at either category. Although the top earners (based on census data) and top wealth holders (based on Federal Reserve data) are not exactly the same group of people, Dewan and Gebeloff report that the two measures overlap by half, and "most 1 percenters were born with socioeconomic advantages."

In contrast to the top 1 percent, those with a net worth between $1 and $5 million are considered entry-level HNWIs in the United States and are often referred as the "millionaires next door." With data spanning 20 years from the 1970s, Stanley and Danko (1996) contend that wealth accumulation is more often the result of a lifestyle of planning, perseverance, discipline, and hard work, instead of consumption, inheritance, advanced degrees, or even high intelligence. Wealth earned through entrepreneurship and hard work, not through inheritance or aristocracy, is at the core of the American ideal of dynamic capitalism. Paradoxically, China's HNWIs today, a group almost entirely self-made, fit the characteristics describing their American counterparts two decades earlier. Although the commonsensical rule of wealth accumulation does not change fundamentally in the "new economy," social media algorithms exacerbate human cognitive biases from the self-selection of "likes" and the like-minded to the systemic overexposure of outliers.

WEALTH MANAGEMENT: PLAYERS AND MARKETS

Wealth management is a relationship between an advisor and an individual or household. A financial advisor is the general title for the profession, whereas a wealth manager or private banker is often someone who works exclusively with HNWIs or UHNWIs. Wealth managers are also broadly defined as financial institutions serving HNWIs with banking, investment, lending, and other financial services.

In Western Europe, wealth managers are commonly known as private banks and take the form of onshore boutiques, onshore universal banks, or offshore banks. Private banks generally observe multi-jurisdictional fiscal rules. Historically dominated by Swiss banks, offshore banks offer secrecy, low-tax jurisdiction, and protection against political instabilities. Two prominent jurisdictions for offshore banking are Switzerland and the Cayman Islands. Starting in 2007, Switzerland lost its "tax haven" and secrecy appeal to wealthy U.S. taxpayers as a result of the enforcement of the Internal Revenue Service (IRS) rules for offshore assets of U.S. citizens held at Swiss banks. Paradoxically, a few states in the United States are becoming offshore jurisdictions for the private wealth of non-U.S. residents who seek secrecy and political stability (Drucker 2016).

In Asia, private wealth management is extremely fragmented, combining offshore private banking hubs in Hong Kong and Singapore with different sizes of onshore markets. Asian HNWIs have a relatively strong risk appetite for alternative and offshore assets, as shown by the surge in cross-border real-estate investments made by wealthy Chinese. In response to the upswing in new wealth particularly from China and India, the ex-Japan Asia market is growing rapidly, while the new Chinese onshore market alone is expected to account for more than half of all growth in ex-Japan Asia. With high saving rates, wealth management in China is still largely a product-driven market spurred by the proliferation of bank wealth management products offered by large state-controlled banks. Myriad shadow banks are filling the wealth management demand gap and becoming a source of private lending and unregulated investment vehicles in China.

In the United States, wealth managers are well regulated and have a variety of business models including full-service broker-dealers (wirehouses), independent broker-dealers

(IBDs), independent Registered Investment Advisers (RIAs), private banking, and multi-family offices (MFOs). Broker-dealers cover the broadest client base and are regulated by Financial Industry Regulatory Authority (FINRA). The largest national broker-dealers are integrated with an investment bank or commercial bank or both, and offer a large variety of services, such as research, investment advice, order execution, retirement planning, and lending. Financial advisors employed by or affiliated with broker-dealers serve the mass-market affluent (i.e., those with investable assets between $250,000 and $1 million) to HNW clients. They are compensated on a fee basis (by a percentage of client assets under management, or AUM) or commission basis (by transactions). Financial advisors are often licensed with relevant state regulators to sell insurance products such as viable life and annuities, and long-term care insurance.

RIAs offer investment advice on a fee-only basis and are regulated by the Securities and Exchange Commission (SEC) or relevant states. In the RIA model, client assets are "held away" with a third-party custodian that often offers its own discount brokerage and investment services to do-it-yourself clients. Although many independent financial advisors focus on insurance products with investment components such as variable life and annuities, and provide financial planning to less affluent clients, some investment advisors specialize in managing portfolios of securities for HNWIs and institutional clients. Since the financial crisis of 2007–2008, RIAs have gained market share in both the number of practitioners and client AUM.

Private banks in the United States usually operate as the private wealth management subsidiaries of integrated universal banks, as independent trust companies, or as MFOs. Private banks typically offer a full range of services, including investment, family office, wealth structuring, and trust and philanthropy services to HNWIs with investable assets of more than $5 million. By contrast, some boutiques cater exclusively to private foundations or UHNWIs with investable assets of more than $30 million. The private bank model emphasizes personalized long-term relationships between the relationship manager (i.e., the private banker or client advisor) and the client. Client investment portfolios are generally managed on a discretionary basis based on client-specific investment policies developed by a team of specialists, including portfolio managers and trust officers. Private banking relationships often last for decades and cover several generations.

A *multi-family office* (MFO) is a commercial enterprise that typically caters to UHNWIs with a net worth above $50 million. MFOs provide various family office services, including investment, tax, trust, estate planning, and foundation management. Some MFOs offer lifestyle and personal services such as concierge and household staff management. In the United States, MFOs can operate as RIAs, trust companies, accounting or law firms, or other combinations depending on their niches.

GLOBAL HNWI AND WEALTH TREND

Since 2005, substantial growth has occurred in the number of HNWIs and total wealth. Gapgemini Consulting and RBC Wealth Management (2015) provide the following statistics about HNWIs and total wealth. Global HNWI wealth is forecast to cross $70 trillion by 2017, growing at an annualized rate of 7.7 percent from the end of 2014 through 2017. Wealth is concentrated in a similar pattern at the top among

HNWIs: UHNWIs—those with more than $30 million of investable assets—make up only 1 percent of all HNWIs, but account for roughly 35 percent of HNWI wealth. UHNWIs are also major drivers of global wealth growth, as wealth has been growing at higher rates with higher concentration. Geographically, Asia-Pacific and North America drive the majority of growth. In 2015, Asia-Pacific overtook North America to become the region with the largest HNWI population at 4.69 million, compared to North America's 4.68 million. The top four HNWI markets—the United States, Japan, Germany, and China—account for the majority (60.3 percent) of global HNWI population and also generate the majority (67 percent) of growth in 2014, with the greatest increase occurring in China (17 percent) and the United States (9 percent). Together, the United States and China drive more than half the global HNWI population growth. The two most populous countries with high economic growth rates, China and India, are expected to be the biggest engines to drive global HNWI growth during the next few years.

CHANGING NEEDS OF HNWIs

HNWIs have complex financial needs and they do not all want to be involved in the daily management of their investments. Instead of an investment product, a new generation of HNWIs today wants a higher level of advisory experience and a relationship with their wealth managers that focuses on their concerns, goals, and dreams. The advice required by HNWIs today is more comprehensive than the transactional and product-centric relationship that was prevalent decades ago, when financial advisors were synonymous with stock brokers.

CHANGING LANDSCAPE OF WEALTH MANAGEMENT

Many forces are changing the wealth management landscape. These include more diverse clients with more complex needs, new technology-based advisory service entrants, increasing regulations, and evolving global markets; and these are just the tip of the iceberg. As basic asset allocation, investment advisory, and risk-profiling services become commoditized, the value proposition of wealth managers is transitioning from security selection and investment management to goals-based financial planning and a holistic wealth management model characterized by personal relationships and customized advice. HNWIs are offered integrated financial planning and wealth management advice and solutions encompassing investment, lending, tax and estate planning, insurance, philanthropy, and succession planning, both for businesses and for personal wealth.

Goals-based wealth management with holistic investing has now become an industry standard, particularly among younger HNWIs. Goals-based wealth management differs from traditional wealth management by taking into account the short, intermediate, and long-term personal theme of HNWIs and helping them prioritize their goals holistically. Success is measured by how clients are progressing toward their personalized goals against the broad range of needs and concerns versus the traditional approach of measuring performance based on relative returns against benchmark market indices.

CHANGING ATTITUDES AND INVESTMENT BEHAVIORS OF HNWIS

One important theme of holistic investing is philanthropy. Although tax and estate incentives are integral to philanthropic planning, the majority of HNWIs express the desire to drive social impact and give back to society as part of a holistic life goal. According to Gapgemini Consulting and RBC Wealth Management (2015), 92 percent of HNWIs identify some level of importance to driving *social impact*, which refers to making a positive impact on society by way of thoughtful investments of time, money, or expertise. HNWIs are looking to their wealth managers for support and advice, such as setting goals and defining their personal role in their areas of interest, identifying and structuring investments, and measuring the outcomes of their social impact efforts. Wealth managers respond to these needs by providing access to a team of experts such as tax and philanthropy specialists, and educating their clients with seminars and discussions, which in turn drive marketing and prospecting opportunities for the sponsoring wealth managers.

Cash and credit are two major themes related to HNWI asset allocation behavior (Gapgemini Consulting and RBC Wealth Management 2015). Regional and demographic differences in risk attitudes aside, overall HNWIs keep larger amounts of cash in their investment portfolios than what are optimal for their lifestyle needs and risk profiles. Yet, HNWIs are more inclined than the less wealthy investors to use credit or leverage. Nearly one-fifth of HNWIs globally use leverage, and 60 percent consider it a key criterion in choosing a wealth manager. Younger, wealthier, and emerging markets HNWIs—the demographic groups with the highest growth rate—often have the greatest interest in using leverage.

VALUE OF WEALTH MANAGEMENT ADVICE

An open question is whether and to what extent financial advisors add value. Researchers have produced mixed findings on the retail side that cover smaller investors. A study by Foerster, Linnainmaa, Melzer, and Previtero (2014) of 800,000 Canadian retail investors finds that financial advisors tend to encourage retail investors to accept more risk, which in turn increases investors' earning expectations. Although this increase in risk may raise yield, the extra yield tends to be offset by the 2.5 percent in fees that clients pay to their advisors. Beyond risk, the study finds that advisors' stock picking and market timing have no impact on returns. Nevertheless, as Foerster et al. (p. 5) note, "households display a strong revealed preference for using financial advisors, which suggests that many expect the benefits to outweigh the costs." The authors posit that financial advisors add value by mitigating psychological costs, such as reducing anxiety rather than improving investment performance, and clients benefit from their relationship with the advisor, specifically through financial planning and advice on savings and asset allocation.

On a higher wealth level, the majority of HNWIs are satisfied with their financial advisors. According to Gapgemini Consulting and RBC Wealth Management (2015), HNWIs are mostly satisfied with the service they receive from their wealth managers, giving them a satisfaction rating of 72.5 percent globally. Not surprisingly, HNWIs who have been with their primary wealth managers for the longest time period (at least 21 years) are the most satisfied, registering a satisfaction rating of 84.3 percent. Regionally, HNWIs in North America are the most satisfied (82.1 percent), followed by those in Latin America (75.6 percent) and Asia-Pacific excluding Japan (72.7 percent). Among HNWIs who place high importance on their wealth needs, the average satisfaction level with the ability of wealth managers to fulfill these needs is 86.4 percent. To earn their HNW clients' satisfaction, wealth managers must understand HNWI concerns and risk tolerance, deliver strong investment performance, and provide fee transparency.

A U.S. survey of HNWIs reveals overall satisfaction consistent with that found by Gapgemini Consulting and RBC Wealth Management (2015). The Spectrem Group (2015) reports the level of satisfaction varies by occupation: 86 percent of senior corporate executives and 74 percent of business owners are satisfied with their advisors. Regarding fees, 55 percent of HNWIs are comfortable with the fees they are paying to their advisors. In fact, 33 percent of HNWIs are unconcerned about the fees they are paying as long as their assets are growing.

Why are HNW investors more satisfied with their wealth managers than retail or the less wealthy investors are with their financial advisors? The size of the wealth explains most, if not all of the difference. First, HNWIs pay lower fees as a percentage of AUM because of management-fee break points. Other than alternative investments such as hedge funds or private equity, a $1 million or higher managed account is rarely charged a fee of 2.5 percent by regulated wealth managers in the United States, thanks to the prevailing competition. Except for the hourly fee–based financial planners, the vast majority of wealth managers are not directly compensated for hours worked; larger accounts are generally more profitable for the same amount of routine work. Second, HNWIs receive higher-quality service because fee-based compensation ties wealth managers' incentives with that of their clients—to grow assets. Wealth concentration in fewer accounts creates economies of scale that improve the overall productivity of wealth managers, whose higher service output—measured qualitatively—is reflected in the higher satisfaction rate from their HNWI clients.

Are wealthy investors more satisfied because they get higher returns? Surprisingly, investment performance is not the top priority, but is rated third in HNWI overall satisfaction ratings (Gapgemini Consulting and RBC Wealth Management 2015). Does wealth concentration increase the rate of return on wealth? Financial market participants contest any definitive answer to this question. Piketty (2014) finds that wealthier investors obtain higher average returns on their capital than less wealthy investors, despite conventional economic models that assume the return on capital is the same for all owners, regardless of the size of the wealth. Ideological debate notwithstanding, the primary reason behind the long-term higher return is that the wealthy have greater means to employ wealth management consultants and financial advisors, not because they take more risks. Evidence by Piketty shows the first explanation "more important in practice" than the second.

Wealth managers hardly expect an unsolicited endorsement from an economist, much less a proponent of global tax on wealth. Yet, many HNW clients do expect tax and estate planning advice if Piketty's findings prompt government interventions through progressive taxation and other wealth distributional measures. As Piketty

(2014, p. 294) notes, "Europe in 1914–1945 witnessed the suicide of rentier society, but nothing of the sort occurred in the United States."

Rentiers are those who live off income from property rather than labor. They do not get good press in continental Europe, where the members of a "rentier society" are regarded disapprovingly as property owners who "do nothing" to create value for society to earn their profits—rent, in economic terms. In the United States, however, to live off one's own saving and wealth—regardless of the solvency of a government sponsored social safety net—is exactly what retirement planning is all about. Not only is private property ownership revered but earnings from investments are generally taxed at lower effective rates than wages. The complexity of tax code further advantages those who employ professional services to plan and prepare their tax returns. Specifically, Scheiber and Cohen (2015) find that the wealthiest Americans "pay millions" for such services to devise sophisticated tax strategies to "save billions." Unless mandated by clients, wealth managers do not discriminate against wealth by ideology. Based on Piketty's (2014) observations, wealth managers have done well by their HNW clients, especially in the United States. Benjamin Franklin's famous two certainties in life—death and taxes— substantially affect private wealth and are professionally managed for many HNWIs through tax and estate planning.

Behavioral Themes

Behavioral economics has gained relevance as a field seeking to explain and predict investment and consumption behavior. Behavioral economists observe that humans, when left to their natural devices, are not good at making optimal decisions as prescribed by traditional economic models. This section covers representative themes of HNWI investment behavior.

TRADITIONAL VS. BEHAVIORAL FINANCE

The traditional finance model, drastically simplified, is based on the existence of a perfect market for capital, in which each owner of capital receives a return equal on the highest marginal productivity available in the economy. On investor psychology and behavior, the standard rational-choice model assumes that investors are completely rational, emotionless, self-interest maximizers of expected utility with stable preferences. Furthermore, it assumes that investors are a homogenous group with identical information sets and expectations.

In contrast, behavioral finance recognizes real human behaviors and focuses on cognitive biases and heuristics. In a behavioral model, real-world investors make decisions based on a rationality bounded by personal values and preferences. They also select satisfactory options rather than optimal ones, and they have emotions. Behavioral finance combines psychology with financial theory to understand the interplay between markets and human emotions, personality and reason.

Complete coverage of the cognitive biases and heuristics recognized by behavioral finance requires more than a book. However, this subsection selectively describes the most relevant features for HNWI investment behavior and the wealth management advisory relationship.

THE EMOTIONAL INVESTORS

Investors are affected by psychological biases and are subject to conscious emotions in their decision making. Psychologists observe physiological and psychological symptoms that point to varying levels of stress during the decision-making process. Mann, Janis, and Chaplin (1969) observe marked increases in stress, as indicated by a sharp increase in heart rate when a decision maker is required to choose between alternatives, both of which are known to have some unpleasant consequences. Janis and Mann (1977) find that the intensity of that stress depends upon the perceived magnitude of loss the decision maker anticipates. The stress is a pathological factor for a human being's *loss aversion*—the tendency to weigh potential loss more heavily than potential gain—as diagnosed by behavioral economists.

Financial markets are vastly more complex than a controlled experiment. Investors' decisions under any market conditions are seldom limited to two alternatives with known risks. Investors often deviate from long-term objectives and from making optimal investment decisions when they encounter fluctuations along the investment journey, especially during periods of market exuberance or turmoil. They leave large portions of wealth in "safe" instruments such as cash during a bear market, are overconfident and overactive during a bull market, and inevitably capitulate to a strong psychological tendency to buy high and sell low. Although many investors can recite the basic rules of investing, among which "to be fearful when others are greedy and greedy only when others are fearful" (Buffett 2005), few could implement this advice if left to their own devices. Buffett captured the phenomenon amid the market turmoil in 2008: "So wild things happen in the markets. And the markets have not gotten more rational over the years. They've become more *followed*. But when people panic, when fears take over, or when greed takes over, people react just as irrationally as they have in the past."

The irrationality results because human beings, programmed as they are with emotions and unconscious motives, as well as limited cognitive abilities, seldom can approximate a state of emotional detachment when making investment decisions. Much anxiety arises from emotional responses independent of risk. Investment decision making has emotional costs that standard investment risk-return analysis does not take into account. The empirical evidence suggests that investors' need for emotional comfort costs the average investor around 3 percentage point a year in lost investment return (Barclays 2015) and two-thirds of total return in comparison with a market index for the 30-year period between 1984 and 2013 (Chhabra 2015).

The additional cost of stress is a loss of time, productivity, and life quality. Recent research in behavior finance challenges the traditional assumption that investors want the best risk-adjusted returns. According to those findings, what investors really want is the best returns they can achieve for the level of stress they have to experience. Barclays (2015) finds that actual investor returns are improved by focusing on achieving the best *anxiety-adjusted returns*, which are the best possible returns relative to the anxiety, discomfort, and stress they have to endure during the volatile investment journey.

Unlike the emotionless *Homo economicus*, investors—especially HNWIs—practice "emotional inoculation" by outsourcing the part of the investment decision-making process that induces stress. This explains why some successful wealth management advisors characterize their value to their HNW clients as modeled after psychologists and therapists, and this is also why the low-fee emotionless technology-driven robo-advisors have not replaced (and unlikely will fully replace) human advisors.

HUMAN VS. ROBO-ADVISORS

Among the major disruptors of the wealth management industry are automated advisory services, commonly referred as *virtual advisors* or *robo-advisors*, which eschew personalized advice in favor of algorithm-based asset allocation and basic investments in low-fee index and exchange-traded funds (ETFs). Robo-advisors tap into the growing prominence of digital and self-service tools, which are of particular interest to younger or less wealthy individuals who are attracted to the convenience and low cost.

Human advisors are skeptical of their virtual competitors, noting that robo-advisors forgo the personal relationships that enable wealth managers to build trust and deliver tailored advice and solutions. Although the value of robo-advisors has yet to be tested in a full market cycle, automated advisory services do not appear to be a passing trend and HNWI interest in them has been underestimated. Globally, 48.6 percent of HNWIs say they would consider using them, compared to only 20 percent of wealth managers who think HNWIs would consider using them. The HNWI propensity to use an automated service is particularly high in Asia-Pacific (excluding Japan) and Latin America, whereas interest is lowest in North America (Spectrem Group 2015).

Why does this difference occur? In the United States, online investment services are not yet built to address the depth and variety of financial planning needs and concerns of investors who have a fair understanding of the relative value of human vs. robo-advisors. Among the 6 percent of investors of the abovementioned 20 percent who do use robo-advisors, only 47 percent say they are satisfied overall with these virtual advisors. In contrast, the 90 percent of investors who use a human advisor report an 85 percent satisfaction rate (Spectrem Group 2015).

TRUST HEURISTIC

Heuristics are decision-making shortcuts that save time and money in a world of uncertainty. Investors employ the *trust* heuristic in their investment decision-making process. For example, they assume that portfolio managers are relatively better informed in a world of complex and often misleading information. Emotional and intuitive variables affect the trust heuristic (Altman 2014). According to the Spectrem Group (2015) survey of U.S. HNWI and wealth managers, HNWIs put higher trust than the less wealthy retail investors in their financial advisors. Instead of past investment performance or standard professional credentials, honesty and trustworthiness are the primary factors that HNWIs consider when selecting new financial advisors. This does not suggest that professional credentials and competence do not matter in these investors' minds. In fact, the performance, capabilities, and reputations of the wealth management firms and those of the individual financial advisors are the necessary but not sufficient parameters in the initial advisory relationship selection process. Constrained by limited time and resources for due diligence, investors employ the trust heuristic, assuming that the category leaders are among the fittest in a highly regulated and competitive market, and that the advisors referred by family members or friends and *acquaintances* are among the best available to them. Indeed, referral is by far the most common source of new relationships in the wealth management industry. Aside from standard quantitative performance measures, trust is the main qualitative measure in a wealth management relationship that can survive the setbacks in investment performance or market downturns.

HNWIs use proxies for trustworthiness, defining trust as a financial advisor's looking out for clients' best interests, being proactive in contacting clients to inform important developments, charging reasonable fees that reflect the value of the services provided, making no mistakes in the work they perform, and admitting when they are wrong. The HNWI's trust in a financial advisor tends to increase with age. Although the size of the wealth is not a major factor in how HNWI investors define trust as it relates to working with a financial advisor, there are marked differences by occupation. Business owners are the most likely to define trust as mistake-free work, whereas corporate executives are most likely to define it as an advisor's looking out for their best interests (Spectrem Group 2015).

INVESTOR PSYCHOLOGY: NUDGE OR PREDICT?

Investor psychology is an emerging field that uses the psychology field to understand how investors make decisions. Devotees of the rational ideology of traditional finance criticize investor psychology for merely exploring abnormality and biases, but failing to deliver robust tools or "cures" to improve investment decision making en masse. Psychologists find that the assumptions about human behavior, including perfect rationality and homogeneity, are false. In essence, the conflict between behavioral and traditional finance is misplaced. Each has a different approach and has different accomplishments in studying human behavior: behavioral finance proponents use an evidence-based approach to observe and "nudge," whereas traditional finance advocates apply normative models to predict.

Reality emerges from the interactions of many different agents and forces, including blind luck, often producing large and unpredictable outcomes (Tetlock 2006). Like weather forecasts during a Northeast U.S. winter, normative finance models are not always accurate but are relied on for guidance; for example, they help an Uber driver decide whether to work, or a hardware store manager how many snow shovels to stock. In contrast, the behavioral analysis can help a ski resort price its season tickets regardless of snowfall outcome, and it explains why neither the Uber driver nor the hardware store should raise prices during a storm based simply on the fundamental supply-and-demand principle (Thaler 2015).

All investment decisions are forward-looking. The idea that the future is unpredictable is undermined every day by the ease with which the past is seemingly explained. The illusion that people understand the past fosters an overconfidence in their ability to predict the future (Taleb 2010). As Kahneman (2011, pp. 224–225) concludes, "to maximize predictive accuracy, final decisions should be left to formulas," because complexity more often than not reduces validity and "humans are incorrigibly inconsistent in making summary judgments of complex information." The simplified and unrealistic assumption about individual rational behavior has provided the analytical power to enable classical finance to predict aggregated human investment behavior in systematic ways. Imperfect as the existing models and algorithms are, they are the best available and are the most useful for investment decision making involving the future.

The Economic Way of Looking at Behaviors

The behavioral basis described here is central to modern economics. Economic theories and models explain how the market works, how wealth is created and distributed, and how people allocate resources that are scarce and have many alternative uses. According to Sowell (2014, p. 4), "economics studies the consequence of decisions that are made about the use of land, labor, capital, and other resource." Economics has evolved as an intellectual genus and is anything but a settled body of thought. In a holistic sense, economics embraces many principles. Yet, an analytical framework entailing mathematics is firmly embodied in modern economic analysis.

To an economist, mathematical tools are just the means to study human behavior, which remains too complex to perfectly fit any computational models developed by humans. Intuitive assumptions about behavior are only the starting point of systematic analysis.

THE WEALTH OF NATIONS IN THE EIGHTEENTH CENTURY

Many regard Adam Smith as the father of modern economics. Smith established the behavioral basis for economic analysis in *The Wealth of Nations,* initially published in 1776. According to Smith (1976, p. 449), political economy is "a branch of the science of a statesman or legislator." He postulated that the division of labor allows the greatest production, and that economic activity, income, and wealth are morally beneficial to human. The fundamental explanation of human behavior, in Smith's view, is found in the rational, persistent pursuit of self-interest. In the preface to the 1976 bicentennial edition of *The Wealth of Nations,* Stigler (1976, p. xi) notes that modern economists label the drive of self-interest as "utility-maximizing behavior."

HUMAN CAPITAL IN THE TWENTIETH CENTURY

Becker (1964) "humanized" economic analysis by challenging the assumption that the prospect of selfish and material gain was the sole motivation for individuals. Instead, Becker asserts that a much richer set of values and preferences drives behavior, including altruism, loyalty, and spite. He assumes that individuals try as best they can to anticipate the uncertain consequences of their actions. Forward-looking behavior may still be rooted in the past, though, because the past can exert a long shadow on one's attitudes and values. Actions are constrained by time, income, cognitive capacities, and opportunity costs determined by the actions of other individuals and organizations. Different constraints are decisive for different situations, but the most fundamental constraint is limited time. "So while goods and services have expanded enormously in rich countries," Becker (1996, p. 3) argues that "the total time available to consume has not. Thus wants remain unsatisfied in rich countries as well as in poor ones." Becker's forward-looking statement has predictive accuracy on consumer behavior toward "unanticipated" new products, such as the Apple watch that came to market after his time; that is, gadgets-rich consumers remain unsatisfied.

Becker (1964) pioneered human capital analysis on investments in education, skills, and knowledge. His economic approach interprets marriage, divorce, fertility, and relations through the lens of utility-maximizing, forward-looking behavior. Human capital analysis starts with the assumption that individuals decide on their education, training, medical care, and other investments in knowledge and health by weighing the benefits and costs of each. Benefits include cultural and other nonmonetary gains along with improvement in earnings and occupations, whereas costs depend mainly on the forgone value of the time spent on these investments.

Even though Becker's analysis incorporates the rising value of time owing to economic growth, tuition and medical care costs were not nearly as important factors in the original benefit versus cost analysis. To approach schooling as an investment rather than as a cultural experience was considered "unfeeling and extremely narrow" before Becker developed the human capital analysis, which was considered controversial when he presented it in the 1960s.

One of the conclusions of the human capital analysis was not intuitive at the time, but has become axiomatic: families gain from financing all investments in the education and skills of children that will yield a higher rate of return in aggregate than the return on savings. That is, both parents and children are better off when parents make investments in their children, as that yields a higher return than savings invested for bequests.

CAPITAL IN THE TWENTY-FIRST CENTURY

A half century after Becker's introduction of human capital theory, Murphy, Piketty, and Durlauf (2015) explain different causes and solutions to inequality in a panel discussion that was brought together by the Becker Friedman Institute and held on the University of Chicago campus.

Murphy focused his analysis on human capital, which "you take home with you when you go home at night. It affects your skill at raising children, at maintaining your own health, at running your financial life" (Murphy et al. 2015). Returns on human capital go up when demand for skills grows faster than supply. People respond to the incentives when demand outgrows supply, invest more in their human capital, and are rewarded with even higher wages. This effect is especially important in an intergenerational context, where the skills and resources of high-income families beget greater human capital investment in their offspring.

For HNW families, resources allocated for human capital investments are higher than the less endowed in both absolute and relative terms. Besides more financial resources, their higher investment allocation in human capital includes better input and more involvement in education, access to superior schools, interactions with comparably advantaged peers, and other institutional advantages, such as the controversial legacy admissions at elite institutions that perpetuate intergenerational human capital accumulation. The human capital investment premium is empirically evident in the United States, where highly skilled individuals enjoy rapid and sustained income growth, whereas the unskilled have stagnated since the mid-1970s. The incentive of advantaged investors to acquire even more human capital has driven up the price of higher education sharply. According to Bloomberg (2012), college tuition and fees have surged 1,120 percent since such recordkeeping began in 1978, four times faster than the increase in the consumer price index (CPI).

Evidence by Murphy and Topel (2014) shows that human capital investment responds to an increase in the "price" of skills. They observe that skill-biased technical change or other shifts in economic fundamentals, such as a decline in the price of physical capital, drive the steadily rising demand for skills. Greater incentives to invest in human capital, owing to a higher price of skills, also raise the returns for using human capital intensively, which in turn increases the returns on investment. That is, the "able" investors benefit disproportionately from an increase in the relative scarcity of skilled labor because they are well positioned to exploit the resulting higher returns on human capital investment and utilization. Increased skill utilization causes yet a higher rate of return for the most skilled. This human capital concentration effect is similar to that of wealth concentration. Murphy concludes that market fundamentals favoring more skilled workers are the driving force behind rising inequality, to which he proposes policies that encourage or enable the acquisition of skills as a solution (Murphy et al. 2015).

Focusing on physical capital for causes, Piketty's analysis of inequality does not take full account of human capital. Piketty (2014) posits that the global rate of return on capital depends on many technological, psychological, social, and cultural factors, which result in a return of roughly 4 to 5 percent, which is distinctly and persistently greater than the economic growth rate of 1 percent. Piketty takes this observation to be a historical fact, not a logical necessity by existing rational economics models which would predict the increased competition on capital accumulation to cause global return on capital to fall until equilibrium emerges. He believes that the difference between the rate of return on capital and economic growth can explain the logic of wealth accumulation that accounts for a very high concentration of wealth. Piketty, a French economist, contends that the inequality has nothing to do with market imperfections, and will not disappear as markets become freer and more competitive. He concludes that wealth concentration, instead of the scarcity of skilled labor, is the cause of inequality, and he proposes a global tax on wealth.

The difference in the analyses and policy recommendations between French economist Piketty and his American counterparts is telling: different sets of data and different ways are available to interpret the same data, even among the economists who use the same set of mathematical tools and hold the same basic assumptions about human behavior. Economists speak different languages, literarily and figuratively, to interpret the past and attempt to predict the future. As Yogi Berra is reputed to have said, "It's difficult to make predictions, especially about the future." The most likely future will be in the vision of those who can "predict" the past convincingly.

Summary and Conclusions

HNWI attitudes toward the future and their investment decisions not only determine their individual life goals on a micro level but also disproportionally affect the economy and the collective investment return on a market level. Economists' past predictions imbedded in investment decisions and their policy "prescriptions," right or wrong, intended or not, have shaped the present wealth and power landscape. Sound economic analyses of the past continue to influence investors' attitudes toward the future.

Wealth concentrations and the scarcity of skilled labor have contributed to the institutional advantages of HNWIs, including higher returns on physical and human capital investments. Although not immune to heuristics and cognitive biases on the individual level, the investment behavior of HNWIs resembles that of corporations and institutional investors more than that of retail "consumer" investors. HNWIs are collectively successful in both growing their numbers and growing total wealth. Empirical studies show that the rate of return on capital has outpaced the rate of economic growth, and the rate of return is persistently higher for HNWIs. Some credit the service of wealth managers for this collective and long-term success.

Wealth has increased disproportionally at the very top during the past 50 years. Additionally, inequality has driven global policy debate. HNWIs are increasingly focused on driving social impact, as well as on generating a financial return on investment. The holistic returns on health, culture, environment, as well as their social and political causes, are gaining importance in wealth management.

The wealth management industry increasingly focuses on investor psychology and behavior of HNWIs. As basic transaction and asset allocation has become commoditized, the value proposition of wealth managers is transitioning from products and markets to goals-based financial planning and a holistic wealth management model characterized by personal relationship, frequent human interaction, and customized advice.

DISCUSSION QUESTIONS

1. Define HNWIs and discuss the demographic trend.
2. Identify the key players in the wealth management industry in the United States.
3. Discuss the different assumptions and approaches of behavioral vs. traditional finance.
4. Describe goal-based wealth management and holistic investing.

REFERENCES

Altman, Morris. 2014. "Behavioral Economics, Thinking Processes, Decision Making, and Investment Behavior." In H. Kent Baker and Victor Ricciardi (eds.), *Investor Behavior: The Psychology of Financial Planning and Investing*, 43–61. Hoboken, NJ: John Wiley & Sons, Inc.

Barclays. 2015. "Anxiety-Adjusted Return." Behavioral Finance White Paper. Available at https://wealth.barclays.com/en_gb/home/research/research-centre/white-papers/Behavioural-Finance/Anxiety-adjusted-returns.html.

Becker, Gary S. 1964. *Human Capital: A Theoretical and Empirical Analysis*. Chicago: University of Chicago Press.

Becker, Gary S. 1996, "The Economic Way of Looking at Behavior: The Nobel Lecture." Hoover Institution, Stanford University, CA. Available at http://www.hoover.org/research/economic-way-looking-behavior-nobel-lecture.

Bloomberg. 2012. "Cost of College Degree in U.S. Soars 12 Fold: Chart of the Day." *Bloomberg*, August 15. Available at http://www.bloomberg.com/news/articles/2012-08-15/cost-of-college-degree-in-u-s-soars-12-fold-chart-of-the-day.

Buffett, Warren. 2005. "Berkshire Hathaway Chairman's Letter." Berkshire Hathaway. Available at http://www.berkshirehathaway.com/letters/2004ltr.pdf.

Chhabra, Ashvin B. 2015. *The Aspirational Investor: Taming the Markets to Achieve Your Life's Goals.* New York: HarperCollins.

Cohan, William. 2013. "The Big Short War." *Vanity Fair,* March 31. Available at http://www.vanityfair.com/news/2013/04/bill-ackman-dan-loeb-herbalife.

Credit Suisse. 2015. *Global Wealth Databook 2015.* Available at https://publications.credit-suisse.com/.

Deaton, Angus. 2013. *The Great Escape: Health, Wealth, and the Origins of Inequality.* Princeton, NJ: Princeton University Press.

Dewan, Shaila, and Robert Gebeloff. 2012. "Among the Wealthiest 1 Percent, Many Variations." *New York Times,* January 14. Available at http://www.nytimes.com/2012/01/15/business/the-1-percent-paint-a-more-nuanced-portrait-of-the-rich.html.

Drucker, Jesse. 2016. "The World's Favorite New Tax Haven Is the United States." *Bloomberg,* January 27. Available at http://www.bloomberg.com/news/articles/2016-01-27/the-world-s-favorite-new-tax-haven-is-the-united-states.

Foerster, Stephen, Juhani Linnainmaa, Brian Melzer, and Alessandro Previtero. 2014. "The Costs and Benefits of Financial Advice." Working Paper, University of Chicago Booth School of Business. Available at http://www.aleprevitero.com/wp-content/uploads/2014/05/foerster_al_WP_201404.pdf.

Gapgemini Consulting and RBC Wealth Management. 2015. "World Worth Report 2015." Available at https://www.worldwealthreport.com.

Gebeloff, Robert, and Shaila Dewan. 2012. "Measuring the Top 1% by Wealth, Not Income." *New York Times,* January 17. Available at http://economix.blogs.nytimes.com/2012/01/17/measuring-the-top-1-by-wealth-not-income/.

Janis, Irving L., and Leon Mann. 1977. *Decision Making: A Psychological Analysis of Conflict, Choice, and Commitment.* New York: Free Press.

Kahneman, Daniel. 2011. *Thinking, Fast and Slow.* New York: Farrar, Straus and Giroux.

Mann, Leon, Irving L Janis, and Ruth Chaplin, 1969, "Effects of Anticipation of Forthcoming Information on Predecisional Processes." *Journal of Personality and Social Psychology* 11:1, 10–16.

Murphy, Kevin, Thomas Piketty, and Steven Durlauf. 2015. "Understanding Inequality and What to Do About It." Media, Becker Friedman Institute at the University of Chicago, November 6. Available at http://bfi.uchicago.edu/events/understanding-inequality-and-what-do-about-it.

Murphy, Kevin M., and Robert H. Topel. 2014. "Human Capital Investment, Inequality and Growth." Working Paper No. 253, The University of Chicago. Available at http://econ.ohio-state.edu/seminar/papers/150402_Murphy.pdf.

Organization for Economic Cooperation and Development. 2014. "Social Expenditure Update." Available at http://www.oecd.org/els/soc/OECD2014-Social-Expenditure-Update-Nov2014-8pages.pdf.

Piketty, Thomas. 2014. *Capital in the Twenty-First Century.* Translated by Arthur Goldhammer. Cambridge, MA: Belknap Press of Harvard University Press.

Scheiber, Noam, and Patricia Cohen. 2015. "For the Wealthiest, a Private Tax System That Saves Them Billions" *New York Times,* December 29. Available at http://www.nytimes.com/2015/12/30/business/economy/for-the-wealthiest-private-tax-system-saves-them-billions.html.

Smith, Adam. 1976. *The Wealth of Nations.* Chicago: University of Chicago Press.

Sowell, Thomas. 2014. *Basic Economics: A Common Sense Guide to the Economy.* New York: Basic Books.

Spectrem Group. 2015. "Advisor Relationships and Changing Advice Requirements." Available at http://spectrem.com/.

Stanley, Thomas J. 2001. *The Millionaire Mind.* Kansas City, MO: Andrews McMeel Publishing.

Stanley, Thomas J., and William D. Danko. 1996. *The Millionaire Next Door: The Surprising Secrets of America's Wealthy.* New York: Rosetta Books.

Stigler, George J. 1976. Preface to *The Wealth of Nations.* Chicago: University of Chicago Press.

Stiglitz, Joseph E. 2015. *The Great Divide, Unequal Societies and What We Can Do About Them.* New York: W. W. Norton & Company, Inc.

Taleb, Nassim Nicholas. 2010. *The Black Swan: The Impact of the Highly Improbable.* Second Edition. New York: Random House.

Tetlock, Philip E. 2006. *Expert Political Judgment: How Good Is It? How Can We Know?* Princeton, NJ: Princeton University Press.

Thaler, Richard H. 2015. *Misbehaving: The Making of Behavioral Economics.* New York: W. W. Norton & Company, Inc.

11

The Psychology of Traders

DUCCIO MARTELLI
Assistant Professor of Finance
University of Perugia

Introduction

Professional traders differ from retail traders. Professional traders often possess privileged information and knowledge, which allows them to take advantage of market imperfections. In contrast, retail traders (i.e., individual investors who buy and sell securities for their personal accounts) are usually noise traders who lack the means and skills to exploit market anomalies. According to the efficient markets hypothesis (EMH), the price of each asset essentially moves in a random pattern as prices rapidly incorporate new information (Fama 1970). Thus, professional traders can use arbitrage strategies to realign current market prices to the real value of securities. Such profitable behavior for professionals is at the expense of retail traders, who eventually leave the market because of recorded losses or become sophisticated investors by learning from their past mistakes.

Many studies relating to behavioral finance show that markets are not completely efficient and that information asymmetries exist. Traders, even retail investors, can generate profits by exploiting an information advantage derived from such sources as the availability of more accurate information about the value of the underlying, more reliable models of asset value measurement and a better understanding of the behavior of market actors. Nevertheless, distinguishing between new market information and noise is difficult. Traders who perform better than the market average over time can use this ability to their advantage.

A trader's basic task is to make decisions under conditions of uncertainty. These types of choices are difficult, given the complexity and the amount of information needed, the limited amount of time and resources available to make those choices, and the consequences of the decisions. Thus, successful traders are generally people who have the necessary intellectual abilities and personal characteristics to allow them to survive and be profitable (Fenton-O'Creevy, Nicholson, Soane, and Willman 2007). Yet, cognitive and motivational factors affect their operations. The automatic nature of their decisions represents a danger to traders.

According to Kahneman (2012), this way of thinking involves two systems. The first system is fast, automatic, and always active, based on unconscious and emotional aspects, and it requires a limited effort. The second system is slow, laborious, and activated when needed, based on personal experience, and it requires much concentration. People use the first system when performing automatic tasks and the second system when there is a need to focus on something specific or perform a challenging task. Given the general aversion to making decisions, people are inclined to use the first system, even in making complex decisions, because that system requires limited effort and generates a decision more quickly than does the second.

Traders need to gain new knowledge and skills and to develop the analytical capabilities to understand market dynamics. Traders must also be able to handle emotional stress during both the initial phase and in managing a new position. A portfolio's fluctuating performance often leads to much emotional upheaval. Although being a trader may appear to be a solitary career, this is not the case. Peers play a particularly important role by facilitating an exchange of opinions on the state of the markets and by confirming a trader's views. New technologies have increased the importance of these relationships among traders. Traders face substantial change because future market developments and shifts in their peers' strategies. Therefore, becoming a trader means acquiring new knowledge to apply to the market and adapting knowledge from past events and personal experience to anticipate likely future developments.

Algorithmic trading has completely changed the daily business of traders. *Algorithmic trading* is the process of using computers that have been programmed to follow a defined set of instructions for placing a trade so as to generate profits at a speed and frequency that is impossible for a human trader to accomplish. Only those traders who have managed to adapt and be flexible are likely to be profitable. Traders who remain firm in their decisions and who follow an outdated line of reasoning are likely to suffer losses and ultimately to leave the market.

Biases Affecting a Trader's Decision-Making Process

According to the neoclassical theory of financial decision making, individuals behave rationally to reach the optimal solution (Von Neumann and Morgenstern 1944; Markowitz 1952). However, since the late 1970s, considerable evidence contradicts this theory. For example, individuals tend to acquire and process information using approximate rules, resulting in satisficing rather than optimizing behavior. Simon (1956) used the term *satisficing* (satisfactory/sufficing) to explain the behavior of decision makers under circumstances in which they lack the necessary cognitive resources to reach an optimal decision. Given that people rarely know the exact probability distribution of events, they have difficulty in accurately evaluating all possible outcomes. People's memories are also weak and unreliable. They tend to settle on a suitable solution, rather than seek the best alternative. Thus, people rely on mental shortcuts and use general rules or heuristics to reduce both the perceived complexity of a problem and the time involved in making a decision.

As Tversky and Kahneman (1974) note, such behavior can result in errors. In particular, the mistakes that individuals tend to make in their financial decisions may result from internal conditioning or external factors. The former are errors associated with the psychology of the subject, consisting of cognitive and emotional biases. *Cognitive bias*

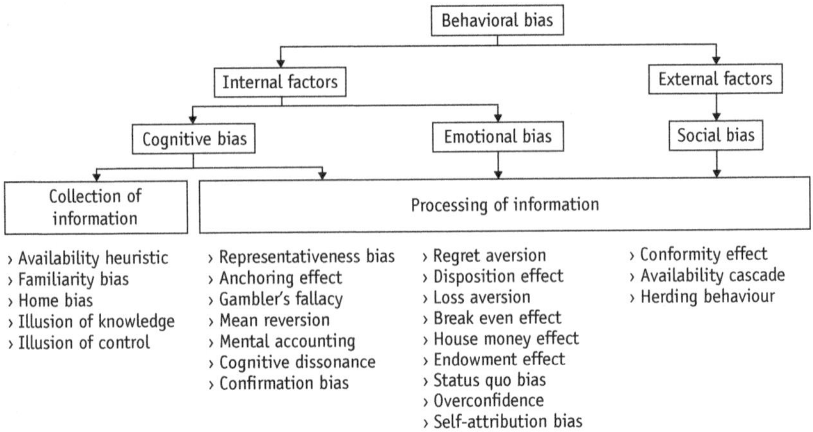

Figure 11.1 Main Types of Bias Affecting Traders' Investment Decisions. The figure shows several types of bias affecting traders' investment decisions. Source: Adapted from Alemanni, Brighetti, and Lucarelli (2012).

results from a limited way of thinking and manifests itself in both collecting and processing data. By contrast, *emotional bias* typically occurs during the processing of the data collected. External bias is primarily due to *social conditioning*, in that it induces individuals to behave according to the judgment they expect to receive from their community. This conditioning, similar to emotional bias, influences the information-processing phase, thus affecting the individual's final decision. Figure 11.1 shows the main types of bias that affect traders' investment decisions.

Errors in the Information Collection Phase

As mentioned, cognitive bias refers to behavioral mistakes in the information collection phase. This type of error arises from an individual's mental structure taking intellectual or heuristic shortcuts to compensate for one's cognitive limits (Simon 1955; Tversky and Kahneman 1974; Gabaix and Laibson 2000). In other words, *heuristics* are approximate modes of reasoning that allow the individual to collect and process information in a short time and with limited processing effort.

A typical error that traders commit in the information gathering phase is the *availability heuristic* (Kahneman and Tversky 1973). The ease with which individuals can recall information from memory can influence their behavior. Consequently, individuals tend to consider frequent events that they can easily remember. Events that individuals remember more easily, as well as those that occur more often, tend to arouse the strongest emotions, as well. In particular, the familiarity of investors with one or more events and the belief that they have a more thorough understanding of certain events are common features among traders. *Familiarity bias* induces investors to concentrate their investments in companies they consider less risky. *Home bias* refers to the tendency to concentrate investments in specific geographic areas, such as in domestic rather than foreign stocks (Kilka and Weber 2000; Huberman 2001). Investors choose nearby investments owing to an excessive sense of confidence with and security about the available information for these investments. They consider such information as more reliable than for "distant" investments in foreign companies (Lewis 1999).

Cognitive limits can also lead traders to commit various errors involving illusions. The *illusion of knowledge* refers to the amount of information available. Counter-intuitively, collecting a considerable amount of information does not guarantee either the quality or the correct use of this information in arriving at an optimal decision. In the presence of too much information, investors tend to prefer and take account of the information they understand better, thus arriving at suboptimal decisions (Barber and Odean 2001). Using the Internet to collect information and having the availability of financial databases amplify the tendency of investors to focus on readily understandable information. Unfortunately, recent changes in the financial markets such as algorithmic-trading techniques do not necessarily provide the most relevant information. Algorithmic means, or algo-trading, encompasses trading systems that heavily rely on complex mathematical formulas and high-speed computer programs to determine trading strategies. Using easily understood information can create the perception that individuals can influence events that are actually beyond their control (Langer 1975). This illusion confirms, especially among novice and small traders, their ability to determine their success in the markets, thus they neglect the importance of random factors; this is termed *illusion of control*.

Errors in the Information Processing Phase

Figure 11.1 shows that traders often commit cognitive or emotional errors during the information-processing phase. Cognitive errors are usually the result of investors' making decisions based on stereotypes (termed *representativeness heuristic*) or they fail to alter their initial decisions, even when new information reaches the market (termed *anchoring heuristic*). The representativeness heuristic leads investors to draw conclusions based on limited information. Indeed, this heuristic is the basis of two common mistakes among traders: applying base rate neglect, and following the law of small numbers.

Base rate neglect results from the inability of individuals to estimate the probability of an event. When attempting to estimate probability, they neglect important information and depend on beliefs developed from personal experience and social stereotypes. Tversky and Kahneman (1974) present a sample of individuals in a case format to illustrate these points. For example, Linda, a single woman aged 31 with a philosophy degree, who as a student participated in demonstrations against nuclear power, was deeply concerned with issues of discrimination and social justice. The researchers asked respondents to choose which alternative is more likely in their opinion: (1) Linda is a bank teller; and (2) Linda is a bank teller and is active in the feminist movement. Although the second option is incompatible with Bayes's theorem, which describes how the probability of two joint events is always less than the probability of the individual events, the majority of respondents chose option 2. Linda's behavior at the university led the sample to pay limited attention to the basic information—namely, that Linda working in a bank is present in both alternatives.

The law of small numbers refers to an inability to take into account the size of a sample and applying rules to small groups that are only apparent in much larger sample sizes (Rabin 2002). One example of this is the *gambler's fallacy*, in which people believe that a random event is more likely to occur simply because it has not occurred for a certain period, such as the eventual selection of a certain number in a lottery. Another example is *mean reversion*, which is the tendency of individuals to ignore that extreme events usually tend to return to their average value. Such biases mean that traders tend to overestimate or underestimate the performance of stocks that have achieved results either above or below the market average in the recent past. However, as De Bondt and Thaler (1985) show, stocks that have performed better or worse than the market during the prior three years tend to record results that are worse or better, respectively, than the average in the following three years.

With the high number of transactions carried out over a certain period by an individual trader, another typical error is their subdivision into mental accounts. *Mental accounting* consists of classifying operations separately according to their result (profit or loss) or the desired objectives, such as protecting invested capital and generating income (Thaler 1985). The separate management of investments in multiple mental accounts often creates the impression that the trader's activities are profitable most of the time, as the profitable trades are over-weighted from a psychological perspective. This attitude remains unchanged, even after several years and especially when unsuccessful traders keep alive their memories of the few operations that generated substantial profits. They tend to forget or understate the weight of the many operations that closed with substantial losses.

The *anchoring effect* refers to the habit of traders to take past information, usually the carrying value of securities in the portfolio, as a reference point for the future. Although the securities may have dropped in price, the anchoring effect helps traders maintain their initial conviction, despite the availability of new information. The difference between the trader's initial decision and the contrasting market performance creates an unpleasant feeling for the trader when faced with evidence that the original belief was wrong. This uneasy feeling is *cognitive dissonance*, or the discomfort that emerges when beliefs and actions conflict with market behavior. Although the more rational way to reduce an uncomfortable feeling is to align one's convictions with the market scenario, traders may act irrationally. For instance, traders may avoid new information that is inconsistent with their original ideas or they may develop fanciful arguments to justify their old opinions. Such behavior is termed *confirmation bias* (McFadden 1999).

Besides the errors resulting from cognitive bias, mistakes arising from emotional bias also play an important role in a trader's decision-making process. Among the many emotions that a trader feels when buying or selling a financial instrument, regret is one of the strongest involving investment decisions. Although regret is a feeling that occurs after a decision is made, fear of making the wrong choice, which might lead to regret, can be strong enough to halt the trader and prevent him or her from making the most appropriate decision.

The *aversion to regret* is the basis of a classic error known as the *disposition effect*, in which traders tend to sell winners too early and hold on to losers too long (Shefrin and Statman 1985). The disposition effect results from other biases discussed earlier. For example, assume a trader bought a stock whose price declines immediately after purchase. In the trader's mind, the purchase price continues to represent an anchor of reference, leading him to ignore information suggesting the immediate sale of the security. The trader continues to hold the stock, hoping its price will return to levels close to the purchase price. Often, however, the price continues to drop. In these situations, cognitive dissonance comes into play, generated by the incongruity between the investor's initial expectations and the market's actual behavior.

To ease an uncomfortable feeling, the trader sees the drop in stock price as a profit opportunity to reduce the book value of his portfolio. By buying new securities at lower prices, the trader reduces the average carrying price of the individual assets, but simultaneously increases the concentration and hence the portfolio's risk. Such behavior usually recurs whenever the trader can invest new resources in this position. This irrational behavior occurs because the theoretical gain achieved by the trader represents an anchor of reference. Less profit generates a level of emotional stress much greater than the regret the trader would feel for having closed a position that might increase future performance (Kahneman, Slovic, and Tversky 1982).

The weighing of costs and benefits of closing the position at a profit or leaving the way open for further gains, but also possible losses, causes the trader to opt for the former option. To limit such irrational behavior as allowing losses to accumulate and closing profitable positions early, most expert traders have learned to use stop-loss orders. A *stop-loss order* sets a price at which to sell (or buy) a security so as to limit any loss should the security decline (or increase) in price. The most advanced traders use stop-loss orders to avoid allowing their emotion to overcome their reason. Thus, a stop-loss order represents a trader's implicit admission of the possibility of committing an error when buying a stock. By instituting a stop-loss order, the trader is admitting the possibility of psychological discomfort similar to cognitive dissonance.

Determining which cognitive or emotional biases have the greatest influence on a trader's decision-making process is difficult. An inappropriate use of stop-loss orders reflects a particularly strong emotional bias called loss aversion. *Loss aversion* is the behavior of avoiding regret; that is, a loss is experienced as greater than a gain, hence is best avoided.

A particularly interesting aspect of trader behavior occurs when investors experience negative performance. One might expect that the degree of risk aversion would rise after incurring losses. In practice, however, past losses, particularly if substantial, can encourage further risk-taking behavior in an attempt to recover the loss and restore the initial level of wealth. This behavior is termed the *break-even effect* (Thaler and Johnson 1990).

Two other phenomena closely linked to loss aversion are the house-money effect and the endowment effect. Individuals experiencing the *house-money effect* are more likely to risk money that has resulted from a win or investment returns than money earned through work. Thus, individuals perceive the funds as other people's money rather than their own. The *endowment effect* is the tendency of individuals to give greater value to their own possessions than to those of others. This shows up as a possible delay in liquidating existing positions because the current market price does not reflect the perceived value of those assets. The endowment effect can also influence traders who do not have open positions in the market. An *open position* is any trade that an investor has entered but has not yet closed with an opposing trade. Such traders are inclined to wait for a drop in stock prices because they assign a value that is usually lower than the market price, as they do not own these stocks.

Another psychological attitude that characterizes how traders operate is a general reluctance to alter positions taken in the past. This behavior, known as *status quo bias*, is closely related to regret that comes from realizing that a prior change in position has not generated the expected results, and that maintaining the original position would have offered better performance (Samuelson and Zeckhauser 1988). Overconfidence is the main limitation that characterizes most traders, especially retail traders (Chuang and Susmel 2011). This attitude stems at least partially from combining the illusion of knowledge and the illusion of control.

Overconfidence induces investors to overestimate their knowledge and their capability to influence events. Overconfident investors presume they have superior skills compared to other market participants (the *better-than-average effect*) and underestimate both the risks of the investments in their portfolios and the real distribution of the probability of events (termed *miscalibration*). One way to demonstrate this latter phenomenon is by asking investors to define a range they are strongly convinced contains the correct answer to a question. In most cases, the correct answer lies outside the interval selected, because overconfidence makes the investor too certain and thus he or she opts for a too narrow range.

Investors are most overconfident when they perceive that they can influence the outcome of events. One example is a coin toss. Individuals tend to bet larger amounts of money if the coin has yet to be tossed. If the coin been already tossed but the result remains unknown, they tend to bet lower amounts because they perceive they can no longer influence the results (Langer 1975). In the trading world, the phenomenon of overconfidence is a common feature among investors, leading them to believe that their investment decisions are correct in most cases and thus produce a return superior to others.

Barber and Odean (2000) demonstrate how the portfolios of overconfident individuals have a higher level of risk owing to a greater concentration of investments in a limited number of stocks. These traders strongly believe that the securities included in their portfolios will register a better performance than those they chose not to purchase. Hence, they perceive that portfolio diversification is a waste of resources, given that it encourages some investment in underperforming securities. Barber and Odean also highlight how overconfident investors engage in more trading. Although the gross performance is higher for overconfident traders, the net performance when transaction costs are considered is generally higher for traders who are not overly self-confident.

Barber and Odean (2001) find that men are generally more overconfident than are women, leading male investors to trade more frequently. Online trading systems have amplified the phenomena related to overconfidence, including loss aversion and the break-even effect. Such systems have a greater speed of execution and lower transaction costs. This change has caused a large increase in transactions carried out by individual traders and, ultimately, a reduction in net performance (Barber and Odean 2002).

Herding and Contrarian Behaviors

In addition to internal biases (cognitive and emotional errors), there are *social biases*, which are forms of conditioning originating in the fear of judgment by others or the desire to obtain social approval. The influence of the decisions and opinions of others in one's group affect individual behavior, especially in situations marked by a high degree of uncertainty (Ghosh and Ray 1997). This is one reason individuals may manifest the *conformity effect*, which is the tendency to fall in line with the "average" judgments and behaviors of other individuals in one's group (Bond and Smith 1996). Shiller (1999) confirms that investors tend to pay more attention to ideas or facts when supported by conversations, habits, or symbols (known as *availability cascades*).

The main type of social bias is *herding*, which refers to behavior that induces investors to abandon their own convictions so as to go along with those of a group, even when the group's beliefs seem erroneous (Christie and Huang 1995; De Bondt and Forbes 1999). The phenomenon of herding is due in part to *self-attribution bias*, which is the inclination to look for an external cause to which to attribute responsibility for wrong choices, while profitable decisions remain attributable solely to the individual trader's merit. In fact, the tendency to go along with the behavior of the group not only reduces dissatisfaction and recriminations that might arise from having made wrong decisions independently, but it also generates less psychological and reputational damage than the prejudice caused by the individual's error. As the saying goes, a trouble shared is a trouble halved (Caparrelli, D'arcangelis, and Cassuto 2004).

Herding originally described the foolish behavior of masses. Recently, though, scholars have clarified that herding is not necessarily irrational if individuals prefer to follow the decisions of those whom they believe are best informed or who are endowed with superior decisional capacities (Chang, Cheng, and Khorana 2000; Demirer and Kutan 2006).

Jegadeesh and Titman (2001) document how trading rules based on momentum-type strategies (i.e., those linked to purchasing high-performing stocks and simultaneously selling less stellar ones) show positive performance, and they demonstrate that the profitability of such rules has persisted over time. From a behavioral point of view, the profitability of momentum strategies is linked to *expectation extrapolation* (De Long, Shleifer, Summers, and Waldmann 1990) and *conservatism in expectations* (Barberis, Shleifer, and Vishny 1998). In general, traders who want to exploit momentum strategies look for major movements affecting markets (Menkhoff and Schmidt 2005). As Nofsinger and Sias (1999) note, profitable momentum strategies challenge the efficient market hypothesis.

Understanding the causes of profitable strategies by analyzing the various types of operational approaches that institutional investors and retail traders can employ is meaningful. Those following momentum strategies may be able to take advantage of temporary strong-trending market situations in which quotations differ substantially from base stock values. However, retail traders tend to buy toward market peaks, owing to optimism and excessive confidence in their own abilities. They also tend to close their position during market bottoms with heavy losses because of behavioral biases, such as the disposition effect. The loss then makes the trader delay opening buyer positions in the future, when the markets are once again positive.

This frame of mind is due to the *snakebite effect*, a psychological state strongly conditioned by a prior negative experience, such as a financial loss. The effect usually has the most impact on those who feel regret and have less financial education. Such traders tend to delay opening long positions in rising market situations because they are still smarting from losses suffered as a result of a recent market collapse. In fact, the disposition effect hinders retail traders from closing unprofitable positions at the opportune moment, leaving them exposed to even greater losses. Not until such traders feel a sense of frustration and a desire to abandon the world of investing do they close those positions. Yet, stocks are most likely to bounce back at this moment.

Recent disgust and frustration impede the trader from reacting by opening positions consistent with new market scenarios. Analogous behaviors, but with opposite effects to those just described, are seen when traders have long positions open in markets that have reached their peak and are most likely to correct themselves in the near future. In these situations, the disposition effect, in conjunction with an anchoring effect, leads the trader to hold positions open even when they are showing negative performance, in the trader's hope they will achieve the heights reached in the past. The consequence of such behaviors is that only a small percentage of investors in the market make money.

A few studies suggest that, on average, only between 15 and 30 percent of investors make money through their investments (Barber, Lee, Liu, and Odean 2009, 2014). This means that even though momentum strategies perform well under certain conditions, traders should consider using investment strategies that run contrary to those followed by the majority of investors who incur losses. That is, investors should consider contrarian strategies. Employing a contrarian strategy does not mean moving in the opposite direction to the majority in all market conditions. *Contrarian strategies* largely characterize markets; operating contrarily to the majority of investors would mean systematically incurring negative performance. Traders who want to use a contrarian strategy profitably must be capable of identifying areas of inversion in which behavioral errors might lead most investors to make the wrong choices.

According to Neill (2003), when people think the same way, they are likely to be wrong. Adopting a contrarian strategy requires understanding human behavior and markets, experience, patience, and the ability to manage one's own emotions. These latter two characteristics are fundamental, because no market situations are exactly alike, despite history and investor behavior sometimes repeating themselves. This fact is true particularly when strong variations occur in a stock's market price compared to its fundamental value (i.e., speculative bubbles). Objectively recognizing a difference in value is a relatively simple task. The problem is identifying the exact moment when the bubble is about to burst. Especially in periods of very bullish markets, investors tend to exhibit gregarious behaviors, prompted by the financial success of other members of the group. In these situations, thinking differently from the majority is difficult. Yet, as Neill suggests, the basis of a contrarian strategy is mentally training oneself to think independently and to move in the opposite direction from the group, taking into due consideration factors that may alter the current trend.

Investors can use this way of thinking in both bull and bear markets. For example, assume that all investors are bullish. The lack of selling investors serving as counterparts to buyers would result in no new sales. A stock's price cannot continue to rise and eventually will fall. The opposite situation occurs during strong downward market phases. In those situations, once all the sellers have liquidated their positions, the stock market prices will increase.

The difficulty in correctly applying contrarian strategies is not in understanding the methodology but in managing the emotions a trader feels throughout the decision process. In fact, traders will find themselves alone when they believe a point of inversion is imminent. In bullish phases, traders will be the only ones hypothesizing bearish scenarios. An analogous case occurs when a contrarian trader expects an inversion of a bearish trend. As noted earlier, investors typically do not like living in solitude; most people prefer to reduce their psychological risks by imitating the behavior of others.

Some contrarian strategy skeptics see the method's popularity as a potential limit to its profitability. If all investors adopted a contrarian view, the methodology would no longer be profitable. Citing Neill (2003), one of the founding fathers of this strategy, Pring (1995, p. 133) states "the theory of contrary opinion will never become so popular that it destroys its own usefulness. Anything that you have to work hard at and to think hard about, to make it workable, is never going to become common practice." Yet, contrarian strategies have become popular owing partly to the development of technology that allows for keener and timelier analysis of the beliefs and behaviors of the majority of investors, or what is termed *market sentiment*.

Investor Sentiment and the Role of the Media

Many traders believe that a combination of factors leads to market movements. Investors often refer to "market psychology," confirming the fact that markets have their own way of thinking. This psychological state of the market or market sentiment allows traders to anticipate its bullish or bearish movements. *Market sentiment* is a summary of how investors perceive the market. These feelings are clear as new market tops or bottoms are imminent, and most investors are strongly optimistic or pessimism reigns. Investor sentiment is more complex in intermediate situations, when markets do not show a defined trend.

Sentiment indicators usually fall into two broad groups: the opinion style and the action style. *Opinion-style indicators* reflect the expression of surveys of opinions of one or more categories of investors, such as advisors, consumers, and companies. *Action-style indicators* summarize the behaviors that investors have taken in the markets, such as open interest and cash flows.

Some of these indicators represent leading indicators of market psychology. Perhaps the best-known sentiment index is the Commitments of Traders (COT). The COT reports show the positioning of traders with opposite purposes (speculative or commercial) in different futures markets. The U.S. Commodity Futures Trading Commission (CFTC) issues weekly reports, and investors can freely download the documents from the CFTC's website. Traders use three items in the reports to decide their own trading strategies: (1) open interest, (2) net speculative positions and (3) net commercial positioning. *Open interest* is the total amount of all futures contracts that investors have entered not offset by a transaction, delivery, or exercise. *Net speculative positions* show whether investors have bullish or bearish expectations in the markets, depending on the predominance of purchases or short sales within their portfolios. Traders analyze potential differences between the positioning of commercial traders such as farmers and multinational corporations, the latter which use derivatives for hedging purposes, and the positioning of noncommercial investors such as large individual traders and hedge funds, who by contrast use futures purely for speculative aims. These two basic groups of futures traders usually have opposite investment styles, which helps retail traders better understand the market phase in which they are operating. Speculators are more trend-followers, whereas commercial traders appear to adopt a contrarian strategy, holding the largest long or short positions in proximity to market bottom or top turns.

Besides the COT, retail traders use several other indicators depending on their investment style. For example, the CBOE Volatility Index (VIX) measures the 30-day implied volatility priced into S&P 500 index options. Many traders consider the VIX as one of the most important measures of sentiment in the stock markets, because it serves as a proxy for investors' risk appetite as market volatility increases or decreases.

Although action-style indicators are perhaps the most used in practice, traders also adopt some opinion-style measures as inputs to their trading strategies. For instance, market participants use indices of consumer or business confidence to estimate market sentiment. For example, the University of Michigan Consumer Sentiment Index surveys consumers to gather their expectations about the overall economy. The Purchasing Managers' Index (PMI), which is provided by the Institute for Supply Management, results from several hundred interviews conducted among purchasing managers in major companies operating at a national level.

Over the years, traders have learned to shift their focus from classic market data to the media. Cover stories still provide one of the best indicators of the psychology of the general population by identifying trend reversal points in the market. Publication on the front page of a newspaper signals that the publisher considers that story particularly important to investors and the public. As already discussed, extreme emotions expressed by general public are usually associated with market turns. Newspapers often publish strong positive front-page news as markets reach their top. By contrast, strong negative news is usually associated with the approach of a market bottom. This principle usually applies regardless of the type of market or the instrument considered by traders, because the investors' way of reasoning follows similar patterns. Therefore, traders can exploit different investment strategies, depending on whether they consider the market to be in an intermediate phase or close to a turn-around. In the first situation, both good news and bad news are not particularly meaningful; they become relevant in the second situation, when markets are near making a turn. In this case, financial news stories are more frequent and have a more incisive tone, whether positive or negative. Considering the influence on prices of news stories in the traditional media only (i.e., television, radio, and print media) would prove to be not only limiting but also counter-productive.

The majority of both retail and institutional investors devote increasing attention to the analysis of comments and opinions posted on newsgroups or in specialized chatrooms, as well as on social media platforms such as Twitter, Facebook, and LinkedIn. Social media have a double role. On the one hand, by reading messages left by other investors, traders can get an idea of market sentiment. On the other hand, as each investor can post his own opinions about future economic and financial scenarios, traders can directly influence market psychology. The social media enable investors to reach a much larger number of peers than do traditional media, with an information transmission speed unimaginable only a few decades ago. Therefore, understanding how to measure the market sentiment in a proper way represents a challenge that all traders have to face today. For this reason, more researchers are focusing their studies on issues closely related to market sentiment. Their aim is to identify advanced methodologies for estimating market sentiment and to verify whether the market psychology, as determined by analyzing messages posted on different social media platforms, directly influences financial market performance.

Regarding the latter aspect, Bollen, Mao, and Zen (2011) found a high correlation between the tone of messages left on Twitter and short-term equity market returns. An increasing number of traders believe that considering market sentiment as part of their trading strategies is an essential strategy to remain profitable in the market. Not surprisingly, specialized companies have created proprietary methodologies to estimate and disclose to their clients the levels of sentiment as they relate to specific markets, countries, and securities. One company in this sector is MarketPsych, which launched with Thomson Reuters a series of indices (Thomson Reuters MarketPsych Indices) in 2012 based on an analysis of news and social media messages. The purpose was to provide investors with information specific to certain countries, securities, or economic sectors. Zhang (2014) discusses how to use market sentiment in trading strategies and summarizes some quantitative methodologies to correctly measure and profitably apply investor sentiment to trading strategies.

Over time, more traders will have adopted sentiment indicators, purchased from external providers or created internally, for their investment decisions. The use of technology aims to increase the capacity and speed of analysis of relevant high-frequency data and is likely to have a greater influence on trading profitability. The effective application in the financial sector of methodologies related to Big Data, combined with an increasing use of high-frequency investment algorithms (high-frequency trading), is now the most important challenge that retail traders face.

The Role of Simulations and the Behavior of Novice Traders

Successful high-earning traders have above-average knowledge, aptitude, and skills. Because each trader's personal history and experiences seem to be indispensable elements for success in the markets, authors have increasingly sought to verify whether simulated trading activities can help investors in their professional careers.

A *simulation* is a method based on probable situations. Compared to traditional learning methodologies, simulations bridge the gap between theoretical concepts and real-life decision making (Kumar and Lightner 2007), and they help participants learn from the empirical results of different strategies (Tiwari, Nafees, and Krishman 2014). The use of simulations in the field of finance is an effective financial education teaching method (Alonzi, Lange, and Simkins 2000). Although use of simulations has grown substantially, the results of laboratory experiments remain inconclusive and are often contradictory. According to Alonzi et al., students participating in a simulation involving the use of derivatives obtain benefits in terms of learning. Camerer and Hogarth (1999) counter that the learning process can only occur in the long term; further, such learning is insufficient to eliminate individual behavioral biases.

Several studies continue to fuel the debate. For example, Ascioglu and Kugele (2005) assert that experience and time can help investors to curb nonrational behaviors. Yet, Duggal and Meyer (2008) find no significant empirical relation between the use of a trading simulation based on bond buying and selling and students' level of understanding, even though the game helped participants to grasp the theoretical concepts studied in class.

Nevertheless, experience is a critical factor in successful trading operations (Gervais and Odean 2001; Nicolosi, Peng, and Zhu 2009). This evidence does not imply that subjects behave in a rational manner simply because they have become more experienced. Indeed, the majority still has some biases that affect performance.

Martelli (2013) attempts to verify whether using simulation with students could help novice traders overcome or limit the cognitive errors, especially overconfidence, to which they may have been subject in the early phases of competition. He based his research on analyzing data from trading games played with real money, in which 44 teams from different universities participated during a six-month period. The behavior of simulation participants shows no signs of reducing overconfidence, which would have led to improvement in the teams' performance during the course of the game. In fact, most teams seem to demonstrate increasingly speculative or, rather, opportunistic behaviors as the simulation drew nearer to conclusion. Martelli asserts that the cause of such opportunistic behaviors is mainly an asymmetry in the distribution of final performance results. Although the teams benefited from any capital gains realized at the end of the simulation, the process allocated any capital losses entirely to the initiative's sponsor. This sort of a lack of penalty in the case of negative results directly influenced the poorly performing teams, leading them to increase speculative/opportunistic behavior.

These conclusions may apply to other simulations carried out in the financial markets, which present asymmetry in the final phase of a remuneration of the various participants. However, this does not mean that these types of simulations and trading games are useless or non-educational because of the participants' opportunistic behaviors. Moffit, Stull, and McKinney (2010) compared participants' scores before and after an online trading stock market simulation and they show a significant improvement in students' learning. The authors conclude that stock market simulations are an effective tool for increasing students' financial knowledge, but the topic requires further study. Although some participants may fail to show improved performance during simulation periods, their progress is measurable once the game has ended. Such improvements are due both to a new awareness gained and to participants' analysis of their own past errors.

Martelli (2013) suggests several possible solutions that limit participants' behavioral anomalies. For example, one solution is the sharing of participant profits/losses with the subject promoting the trading game. These proposed remedies seem to show initial positive effects and reduce participants' speculative behaviors.

Dal Santo and Martelli (2015) examine a competition in which participants could neither see the other competitors' performance nor calculate the distance between them. The preliminary results show that such a solution can be more useful in educating that year's novice traders than those participating in past editions of the same competition in which these new rules were not present. The authors stress that not all students exploit the benefits of a simulation. A few participants, especially lower-ranked ones, may feel a sense of growing frustration that leads to irrational behaviors. At the same time, such students' motivation tends to decrease. As Gentner, Lowenstein, and Thompson (2003) demonstrate, individuals, regardless of their experience, have difficulty extrapolating and applying learning from past contexts to new situations. The resulting risk is that prior inappropriate behaviors may continue over time, even among expert traders. This finding confirms that experience alone is insufficient to make individual investors into successful traders. To become successful, traders require continuous learning and the flexibility to handle changing market situations.

Summary and Conclusions

The trading profession has dramatically changed during the last decade. For example, technology has undergone profound innovations. Traders can now analyze huge amounts of data and clearly identify investor sentiment. Only those traders who can adapt their investment strategies to new market scenarios will likely be profitable, whereas the others will ultimately leave the market. Although gaining some experience by participating in trading simulations before investing in real markets is useful, investment challenges do not usually take into account possible opportunistic behaviors that participants can use to win the competitions.

DISCUSSION QUESTIONS

1. Define overconfidence and give some examples of how overconfidence affects trading strategy.
2. Describe the main differences between gregarious and contrarian investment strategies.
3. Explain the meaning of investor sentiment and provide some examples.
4. Define possible solutions to mitigate opportunistic behavior in trading simulations.

REFERENCES

Alemanni, Barbara, Gianni Brighetti, and Caterina Lucarelli. 2012. *Decisioni di investimento, assicurative e previdenziali. Tra finanza e psicologia*. Bologna: Il Mulino.

Alonzi, Peter, David R. Lange, and Betty J. Simkins. 2000. "An Innovative Approach in Teaching Futures: A Participatory Futures Trading Simulation." *Financial Practice and Education* 10:1, 228–238.

Ascioglu, Asli, and Lynn P. Kugele. 2005. "Using Trading Simulations to Teach Microstructure Concepts." *Journal of Financial Education* 31:2, 69–81.

Barber, Brad M., Yi-Tsung Lee, Yu-Jane Liu, and Terrance Odean. 2009. "Just How Much Do Individual Investors Lose by Trading?" *Review of Financial Studies* 22:2, 609–632.

Barber, Brad M., Yi-Tsung Lee, Yu-Jane Liu, and Terrance Odean. 2014. "The Cross-section of Speculator Skill: Evidence from Taiwan." *Journal of Financial Markets* 18:3, 1–24.

Barber, Brad M., and Terrance Odean. 2000. "Trading Is Hazardous to Your Wealth: The Common Stock Investment Performance of Individual Investors." *Journal of Finance* 55:2, 773–806.

Barber, Brad M., and Terrance Odean. 2001. "Boys Will Be Boys: Gender, Overconfidence, and Common Stock Investment." *Quarterly Journal of Economics* 116:1, 261–292.

Barber, Brad M., and Terrance Odean. 2002. "Online Investors: Do the Slow Die First?" *Review of Financial Studies* 15:2, 455–487.

Barberis, Nicholas, Andrei Shleifer, and Robert Vishny. 1998. "A Model of Investor Sentiment." *Journal of Financial Economics* 49:2, 307–343.

Bollen, Johan, Huina Mao, and Xiao-Jun Zeng. 2011. "Twitter Mood Predicts the Stock Market." *Journal of Computational Science* 2:1, 1–8.

Bond, Michael H., and Peter B. Smith. 1996. "Cross-cultural Social and Organizational Psychology." *Annual Reviews of Psychology* 47:1, 205–235.

Camerer, Colin F., and Robin M. Hogarth. 1999. "The Effects of Financial Incentives in Experiments: A Review and Capital-labor-production Framework." *Journal of Risk and Uncertainty* 19:1, 7–42.

Caparrelli, Franco, Anna M. D'arcangelis, and Alexander Cassuto. 2004. "Herding in the Italian Stock Market: A Case of Behavioral Finance." *Journal of Behavioral Finance* 5:4 222–230.

Chang, Eric C., Joseph W. Cheng, and Ajay Khorana. 2000. "An Examination of Herd Behavior in Equity Markets: An International Perspective." *Journal of Banking & Finance* 24:10, 1651–1679.

Christie, William G., and Roger D. Huang. 1995. "Following the Pied Piper: Do Individual Returns Herd around the Market?" *Financial Analysts Journal* 51:4, 31–37.

Chuang, Wen-I, and Rauli Susmel. 2011. "Who Is the More Overconfident Trader? Individual vs. Institutional Investors." *Journal of Banking and Finance* 35:7, 1626–1644.

Dal Santo, Andreas, and Duccio Martelli. 2015. "Increasing Financial Literacy through Simulations: The Case of the CFA Society Italy Fund Management Challenge." *Journal of Financial Management Markets and Institutions* 3:1, 69–100.

De Bondt, Werner F. M., and William P. Forbes. 1999. "Herding in Analyst Earnings Forecasts: Evidence from the United Kingdom." *European Financial Management* 5:2, 143–163.

De Bondt, Werner F. M., and Richard Thaler. 1985. "Does the Stock Market Overreact?" *Journal of Finance* 40:3, 793–805.

De Long, Bradford J., Andrei Shleifer, Lawrence H. Summers, and Robert J. Waldmann. 1990. "Positive Feedback Investment Strategies and Destabilizing Rational Speculation." *Journal of Finance* 45:2, 379–395.

Demirer, Riza, and Ali M. Kutan 2006. "Does Herding Behavior Exist in Chinese Stock Markets?" *Journal of International Financial Markets, Institutions & Money* 16:2, 123–142.

Duggal, Rakesh, and Thomas Meyer. 2008. "Does a Trading Simulation Exercise Enhance Financial Learning?" *Journal of Business Case Studies* 4:5, 7–12.

Fama, Eugene F. 1970. "Efficient Capital Markets: A Review of Theory and Empirical Work." *Journal of Finance* 25:2, 383–428.

Fenton-O'Creevy, Mark, Nigel Nicholson, Emma Soane, and Paul Willman. 2007. *Traders: Risks, Decisions, and Management in Financial Markets*. Oxford: Oxford University Press.

Gabaix, Xavier, and David Laibson. 2000. "A Boundedly Rational Decision Algorithm." *American Economic Review* 90:2, 433–438.

Gentner, Dedre, Jeffrey Lowenstein, and Leigh Thompson. 2003. "Learning and Transfer: A General Role for Analogical Encoding." *Journal of Educational Psychology* 95:2, 393–408.

Gervais, Simon, and Terrance Odean. 2001. "Learning to Be Overconfident." *Review of Financial Studies* 14:1, 1–27.

Ghosh, Dipankar, and Manash Ray. 1997. "Risk, Ambiguity and Decision Choice: Some Additional Evidence." *Decision Science* 28:1, 81–103.

Huberman, Gur. 2001. "Familiarity Breeds Investment." *Review of Financial Studies* 14:3 659–680.

Jegadeesh, Narasimhan, and Sheridan Titman. 2001. "Profitability of Momentum Strategies: An Evaluation of Alternative Explanations." *Journal of Finance* 56:2, 699–720.

Kahneman, Daniel. 2012. *Thinking, Fast and Slow*. New York: Penguin.

Kahneman, Daniel, Paul Slovic, and Amos Tversky (eds.). 1982. *Judgment under Uncertainty: Heuristics and Biases*. Cambridge: Cambridge University Press.

Kahneman, Daniel, and Amos Tversky. 1973. "On the Psychology of Prediction." *Psychological Review* 80:4, 237–251.

Kilka, Michael, and Martin Weber. 2000. "Home Bias in International Stock Return Expectations." *Journal of Psychology and Financial Markets* 1:3–4, 176–193.

Kumar, Rita, and Robin Lightner. 2007. "Games as an Interactive Classroom Technique: Perceptions of Corporate Trainers, College Instructors and Students." *International Journal of Teaching and Learning in Higher Education* 19:1, 53–63.

Langer, Ellen J. 1975. "The Illusion of Control." *Journal of Personality and Social Psychology* 32:2, 311–328.

Lewis, Karen K. 1999. "Trying to Explain Home Bias in Equities and Consumption." *Journal of Economic Literature* 37:2, 571–608.

Markowitz, Harry. 1952. "Portfolio Selection." *Journal of Finance* 7:1, 77–91.

Martelli, Duccio. 2013. "Learning from Experience or Learning for Convenience?" *Qualitative Research in Financial Markets* 5:3, 244–255.

McFadden, Daniel. 1999. "Rationality for Economists?" *Journal of Risk and Uncertainty* 19:1, 73–105.

Menkhoff, Lukas, and Ulrich Schmidt. 2005. "The Use of Trading Strategies by Fund Managers: Some First Survey Evidence." *Applied Economics* 37:15, 1719–1730.

Moffit, Timothy, Charles Stull, and Hannah McKinney. 2010. "Learning Through Equity Trading Simulation." *American Journal of Business Education* 3:2, 65–73.

Neill, Humphrey B. 2003. *The Art of Contrary Thinking, 12th Edition*. Caldwell: Caxton Printers.

Nicolosi, Gina, Liang Peng, and Ning Zhu. 2009. "Do Individual Investors Learn from Their Trading Experience?" *Journal of Financial Markets* 12:2, 317–336.

Nofsinger, John R., and Richard W. Sias. 1999. "Herding and Feedback Trading by Institutional and Individual Investors." *Journal of Finance* 54:6, 2263–2295.

Pring, Martin J. 1995. *Investment Psychology Explained: Classic Strategies to Beat the Markets*. New York: John Wiley & Sons, Inc.

Rabin, Matthew. 2002. "Inference by Believers in the Law of Small Numbers" *Quarterly Journal of Economics* 117:3, 775–816.

Samuelson, William, and Richard Zeckhauser. 1988. "Status Quo Bias in Decision Making." *Journal of Risk and Uncertainty* 1:1, 7–59.

Shefrin, Hersh M., and Meir Statman. 1985. "The Disposition to Sell Winners Too Early and Ride Losers Too Long." *Journal of Finance* 40:3, 777–790.

Shiller, Robert J. 1999. "Human Behavior and the Efficiency of the Financial System. In John B. Taylor and Michael Woodford (eds.), *Handbook of Macroeconomics*, 1305–1340. Amsterdam: Elsevier.

Simon, Herbert A. 1955. "A Behavioral Model of Rational Choice." *Quarterly Journal of Economics* 69:1, 99–118.

Simon, Herbert A. 1956. "Rational Choice and the Structure of the Environment." *Psychological Review* 63:2, 129–138.

Thaler, Richard H. 1985. "Mental Accounting and Consumer Choice." *Marketing Science* 4:3, 199–214.

Thaler, Richard H., and Eric J. Johnson. 1990. "Gambling with the House Money and Trying to Break Even: The Effects of Prior Outcomes on Risky Choice." *Management Science* 36:6, 643–660.

Tiwari, Shalini R., Lubna Nafees, and Omkumar Krishnan. 2014. "Simulation as a Pedagogical Tool: Measurement of Impact on Perceived Effective Learning." *International Journal of Management Education* 12:3, 260–270.

Tversky, Amos, and Daniel Kahneman. 1974. "Judgment under Uncertainty: Heuristics and Biases." *Science* 185:4157, 1124–1131.

Von Neumann, John, and Oskar Morgenstern. 1944. *The Theory of Games and Economic Behavior*. Princeton, NJ: Princeton University Press.

Zhang, Ying. 2014. *Stock Message Boards. A Quantitative Approach to Measuring Investor Sentiment*. New York: Palgrave Macmillan.

12

A Closer Look at the Causes and Consequences of Frequent Stock Trading

MICHAL STRAHILEVITZ
Visiting Associate Professor
The Center for Advanced Hindsight, Duke University

Introduction

A wide body of research clearly indicates that frequent stock trading negatively affects investor returns. For example, Barber and Odean (2000) investigate portfolios held between 1991 and 1996 and find that frequent traders pay a huge financial penalty, earning an average of 7.1 percent less than infrequent traders. The authors attribute this loss of return primarily to the high commissions associated with intensive trading. More recent research also finds that individual investors lose by trading (Barber, Lee, Liu, and Odean 2009).

After accounting for trading costs, individual Taiwanese investors who trade frequently generally underperform relevant benchmarks such as the TAIEX, a value weighted index of all listed securities on the Taiwan Stock Exchange. After controlling for all other variables, the more often investors trade, the more money they lose. Despite the level of knowledge and experience of investors, little chance exists that frequent trading is more profitable than following a buy-and-hold strategy (Schlomer 1997; Talpsepp 2011; Hoffmann, Post, and Pennings 2013).

Meanwhile, investor overtrading is an epidemic. For their sample of clients of a discount brokerage in the United States, Barber and Odean (2000) report an average annual turnover of 75 percent. Perhaps even more alarming, the quintile of most active traders exhibits an average annual portfolio turnover rate of more than 250 percent. More recently, the turnover on the New York Stock Exchange (NYSE) reached over 150 percent in 2015 (World Bank 2016).

Researchers demonstrate that rational reasons, such as portfolio risk-rebalancing needs, tax considerations, and liquidity reasons do not explain even half of the turnover (Barber and Odean 2002; Dorn and Sengmueller 2009). In short, agreement exists among top researchers in finance that frequent trading is both pervasive and irrational. Such trading is both bad for individual investors who engage in it and the stock market as a whole. Still, there is little agreement on why investors engage in frequent trading.

The purpose of this chapter is to review research that is relevant to understanding both the causes and consequences of frequent stock trading. The chapter starts with reviewing several published articles that examine frequent trading both in terms of the financial costs and psychological causes. The next section discusses unpublished research that looks more closely at the emotional side of frequent trading, going beyond the financial costs to consider the psychological consequences as well. The chapter ends by suggesting directions for future research that may help identify ways frequent traders can stop engaging in this irrational and potentially quite harmful pattern of investing.

Does Investor Overconfidence Lead to Frequent Trading?

Barber and Odean (2001a) propose that an irrational sense of overconfidence is the main driver of frequent trading. They contend that investors' beliefs that their abilities are better than average make them think they can outperform the market indexes. Overconfidence means that these investors believe their trades are smarter than the trades of most other investors (De Bondt and Thaler 1995; Odean 1999; Gervais and Odean 2001). Yet, Markiewicz and Weber (2013) maintain that overconfidence is unlikely to be the main reason some people trade far more often than they should. They offer an alternative explanation.

Specifically, Markiewicz and Weber (2013) note that Barber and Odean's (2001a) explanation for frequent trading is inconsistent with many empirical findings (Glaser and Weber 2003, 2007; Biais, Hilton, Mazurier, and Pouget 2005). Glaser and Weber (2003) used a questionnaire to elicit nine proxies for overconfidence in a sample of 200 German discount brokerage customers, and then related those overconfidence proxies to actual portfolio turnover. None of the proxies accounted for the average monthly portfolio turnover. Additionally, in trading experiments with students, Biais et al. report little or no relation between proxies for overconfidence and observed trading activity. Markiewicz and Weber suggest that Barber and Odean (2000) did a relatively poor job of supporting their argument that frequent trading is about overconfidence. They note that Barber and Odean talked about overconfidence without actually measuring overconfidence. Instead, Odean and Barber use whether the investor is male or female as a proxy for overconfidence, contending that men are more confident than women when investing. A problem with this view is that gender is correlated with many other variables as well, including risk-seeking tendencies (Charness and Gneezy 2010, 2012).

Studies by other researchers that have tried to directly assess the degree of investor overconfidence show an inconsistent relation between investor overconfidence and trading volume. Although some studies have found an association between overconfidence and high trading frequency (Dorn and Huberman 2005; Graham, Harvey, and Huang 2009), others fail to find such a relation (Dorn and Sengmueller 2009). Glaser and Weber (2007) are only able to observe a correlation between overconfidence and frequent trading if they exclude the most active of the frequent traders from their analyses. Their evidence suggests that something other than overconfidence drives the frequent traders who trade the most often. One possibility is that the extremely frequent traders see selling a stock after buying it as "undoing" a mistake. They are in effect second-guessing themselves, which is more indicative of low confidence than of high confidence. Another possibility is that because trading frequency hurts performance, these ultra-frequent traders perform so badly that it affects their confidence in their ability to trade wisely.

Another challenge with the overconfidence explanation is that multiple methods are available to measure overconfidence (Moore 2007; Markiewicz and Weber 2013). Not all the same methods of measuring overconfidence yield the same results. In other words, someone could be rated as highly overconfident using one measure of overconfidence, but not particularly confident using another measure. To illustrate, Moore and Healy (2008) find significant gender differences in overconfidence when they defined overconfidence as a better-than-average effect, but not when they define overconfidence as miscalibration, which is the inability to assess one's own performance accurately (Grinblatt and Keloharju 2009). When overconfidence is defined as miscalibration, little support exists for Barber and Odean's (2001a) proposition that overconfidence drives frequent trading.

As Glaser and Weber (2007) report, overconfidence using the miscalibration approach has no influence on investors' trading volume for the most active investors in their study. Similarly, Biais et al. (2005) find that miscalibration reduces financial performance, but does not affect trading volume. Other studies also find no relation between overconfidence and trading frequency (Dorn and Huberman 2002; Oberlechner and Osler 2008). As Markiewicz and Weber (2013) note, overconfidence may play a role in some excessive trading, but it is unlikely to be the primary reason so many investors trade more often than they should.

Are Risk-Seekers More Likely to Be Frequent Traders?

Several authors report an association between frequent trading and higher levels of risk-taking. For example, Grinblatt and Keloharju (2009) find a correlation between the number of recent speeding tickets male Finnish investors received and their stock trading volume. Speeding involves risk, because it increases both the chance of receiving a traffic ticket and of being in an accident. This finding thus suggests that people who are most comfortable with danger—both financially and in terms of safety—may be most likely to trade more often. Some researchers suggest that substitutes may be available for satisfying the thrill some investors derive from frequent trading. Specifically, Barber, Lee, Liu, and Odean (2009) suggest that the introduction of a national lottery in Taiwan may have contributed to a sizable drop in the turnover volume on the Taiwanese Stock Exchange at the same time. They propose that some investors may view investing and gambling as substitutes, so the introduction of the chance to win a lottery may have reduced the desire to trade so often. In other words, similar to speeding or gambling, frequent trading may be a way for those who love to take risks to satisfy their desires for risk.

Similar conclusions can be drawn from research by Dorn and Sengmueller (2009), which shows that investors who enjoy gambling turn over their portfolios at twice the rate of their peers. The authors suggest at least three possible motives for frequent trading: (1) the *recreation/leisure* motive, which treats active investing as a source of fun; (2) the *aspiration for riches* motive, which treats investing like a lottery that provides a very small chance for a possibly huge payoff; and (3) the *sensation-seeking* motive, which uses trading with its uncertainties as providing the stimulation and novelty some people may require to feel that their life is not boring.

According to Dorn and Sengmueller (2009), two categories of investors—hobby investors and sensation seekers—trade for emotional reasons. This view suggests that the motives for investing and trading often may vary among investors, with some making rational calculations and others trading for emotional reasons. Their work implies that motives for trading may influence how often individual investors trade. Hence, Dorn and Sengmueller offer that some investors may trade simply because they find it entertaining.

Building on Dorn and Sengmueller (2009), Markiewicz and Weber (2013) contend that risk-seeking behavior drives frequent trading. They build on the notion that some association exists between personality and risk-taking (Zaleskiewicz 2001) and stress that risk-seeking has multiple dimensions. Dorn and Sengmueller (2009) agree with other researchers who note that risk involves several domains that should be considered, such as financial, social, and safety (Weber, Blais, and Betz 2002; Figner and Weber 2011). Markiewicz and Weber (2013) also reiterate Dorn and Sengmueller's (2009) emphasis on understanding different motives. Specifically, they maintain that a sensation or stimulation-seeking motive exists whereby the driver of the action is the thrill of taking a risk. This might be considered a hot motive with fast thinking (Figner and Weber 2011; Kahneman 2013). Markiewicz and Weber (2013) explain that the stimulation motive is distinct from the instrumental motive, the latter which is considered cold and slow (Figner and Weber 2011; Kahneman 2013). Cognition and deliberation drive cold and slow decisions, whereas emotions drive hot and fast decisions. With the instrumental motive, the primary driver is the possible achievement of material returns. Markiewicz and Weber (2013) find that only emotion-driven risk-taking predicts trading frequency. In other words, those who are taking risks for profit may be wise enough to realize that their profits will not improve from trading more often.

Markiewicz and Weber's (2013) research suggests that investors who focus more on excitement and less on the possible financial rewards may be most likely to become frequent traders, or even day traders. This group pays greater transaction fees, spends more time on investing, and still manages to underperform compared to their less frequent trading counterparts. For this group of traders, gambling risk propensity (i.e., the hot need for stimulation) is significantly related to the extent of their day-trading activity. This finding is in line with prior work suggesting that some traders simply find trading to be fun (Glaser and Weber 2007; Anderson 2008; Dorn and Sengmueller 2009; Kumar 2009). Although day trading may seem a time-consuming, costly, and financially risky way to be entertained, recent research supports the notion that frequent traders find trading to be more exciting than buying and holding (Strahilevitz, Harvey, and Ariely 2015).

Is Frequent Trading Motivated by Emotions or Rational Thinking?

According to several researchers who have examined risk-seeking and trading frequency, a desire for stimulation may drive frequent trading. Researchers in the areas of psychology and decision making have made similar suggestions about risky behavior (Belsky and Gilovich 2000). In their acclaimed work on risk as feelings, Loewenstein, Weber, Hsee, and Welch (2001) note that emotion often drives much risk-taking behavior. They point out that the basis of prior theories used to explain risk-taking was the assumption that rational thinking underlies decisions. Loewenstein et al., however, maintain that an expectation-based calculus is not what drives all risk-seeking behavior. They propose a new theoretical framework, which they call the *risk-as-feelings* hypothesis. Drawing on research from clinical, physiological, and other subfields of psychology, they show that emotional reactions to risky situations often diverge from cognitive assessments of those risks. When such divergence occurs, emotional reactions often drive behavior. They present evidence showing that the risk-as-feelings hypothesis explains a wide range of phenomena that have resisted interpretation in cognitive consequentialist terms. Although Loewenstein et al. (2001) do not discuss stock trading, based on their theoretical framework, emotions could logically drive frequent trading as much, if not more than, rational calculations.

Additionally, Loewenstein et al. (2001) propose that the emotions experienced at the moment of decision making have an enormous influence on that decision. Others have noted that emotions drive much of compulsive behavior (Faber and O'Gunin 1989, 1992; Faber and Vohs 2011). Applying the risk-as-feelings hypotheses to frequent trading, the risk of making yet another trade may involve some sort of thrill, and for some investors, that emotional thrill may influence their behavior even more than thinking about expected outcomes.

Strahilevitz, Odean, and Barber (2011), who also address the emotion-based argument for financial decisions, find that traders generally buy stocks on which they previously made a profit, whereas they avoid buying stocks on which they previously lost money. This behavior is not for rational reasons, because it does not improve returns. Avoiding past losers and buying past winners is really about avoiding previous bad feelings and repeating previous good feelings. Strahilevitz et al. (2015) contend that emotional responses, not rational thinking, condition this pattern. Although this pattern was pervasive, it did not improve the traders' performance. This research also found that investors deliberately attempt to reduce regret, even when the actions they take do not improve their returns.

How Do Day Traders Behave?

Although day traders are an extreme form of frequent traders, few researchers have examined the drivers of day trading. Day traders pay higher transaction fees overall, but did not get higher profits than others in a study conducted by Barber et al. (2005). To understand drivers of this behavior, using a student population with trading simulations, Markiewicz and Weber (2013) find that a gambling risk propensity predicts a day-trading propensity.

Markiewicz and Weber (2013) also looked at financial risk-taking propensity regarding two motives: gambling and investing. They defined these two motives as follows: (1) *gambling* is a stimulation or sensation-seeking motive that has the process of taking a risk as its goal; and (2) *investing* is an instrumental risk-taking motive that focuses on the potential financial outcome of the risky choice (i.e., the achievement of material returns) as its goal. They find that these two measures are not significantly correlated and that only gambling risk-taking propensity predicts trading volume. In other words, in their sample, a desire for stimulation drove the day traders more than a desire to make money. They conclude that day traders are thrill-seekers more than profit-seekers.

According to Markiewicz and Weber (2013), compared to other investors, day traders spend more money, in the form of transaction fees, and more time, in the form of hours spent trading. Nevertheless, as with previous analyses (Barber et al. 2005), day traders show lower profits for their efforts than do those who are not day traders. This finding is consistent with research in general on frequent trading. The more frequently investors trade, the more time they spend, the greater their transaction fees, and the lower their profits. Financially, day trading is clearly a losing proposition.

Does Frequent Trading Involve Gender Differences?

Gender is not a cause of frequent trading. However, research suggests that men and women behave differently as investors, including how often they trade. Thus, a review of literature that looks at gender differences can illuminate the world of frequent trading.

According to Barber and Odean (2001a), men are more confident than women especially in the financial domain, and therefore men trade more frequently than their female counterparts. The authors suggest that more frequent trading among males stems from overconfidence. The problem with this explanation is that overconfidence is not the only relevant gender difference. Specifically, men are more impulsive and have greater risk-seeking tendencies (Charness and Gneezy 2010, 2012).

Evidence shows that all these factors influence trading frequency, and they are not just stereotypes. In fact, some research suggests that hormones could affect investing behavior. Coates and Herbert (2008) find a positive relationship between the testosterone levels of male stock traders and their financial returns. Similarly, Coates, Gurnell, and Rustichini (2009) find that the presence of another masculine hormone, prenatal androgen, increases the risk preferences of high-frequency stock traders.

In short, although women trade less often than men, the reasons for this are not totally clear. What is clear is that frequent trading is more common among men, but it is potentially financially harmful to both genders. Thus, any insights to help frequent traders to trade less often are likely to help both men and women.

Frequent Trading and Gambling

Given that Barber et al. (2009) view trading as another form of gambling, examining the nature of the gambling disorder as well as who is most likely to suffer from it is worthwhile. Gambling disorder is currently recognized as a psychiatric condition and is part of the fifth edition of the American Psychiatric Association's Diagnostic and Statistical Manual of Mental Disorders, DSM-5 (American Psychiatric Association 2013; Reilly and Smith 2013). Below are the official diagnostic criteria from the *Diagnostic and Statistical Manual of Mental* Disorders (DSM-5):

Gambling Disorder: Diagnostic Criteria 312.31 (F63.0)

A. Persistent and recurrent problematic gambling behavior leading to clinically significant impairment or distress, as indicated by the individual exhibiting four (or more) of the following in a 12-month period:
   1. Needs to gamble with increasing amounts of money in order to achieve the desired excitement.
   2. Is restless or irritable when attempting to cut down or stop gambling.
   3. Has made repeated unsuccessful efforts to control, cut back, or stop gambling.
   4. Is often preoccupied with gambling (e.g., having persistent thoughts of reliving past gambling experiences, handicapping or planning the next venture, thinking of ways to get money with which to gamble).
   5. Often gambles when feeling distressed (e.g., helpless, guilty, anxious, depressed).
   6. After losing money gambling, often returns another day to get even ("chasing" one's losses).
   7. Lies to conceal the extent of involvement with gambling.
   8. Has jeopardized or lost a significant relationship, job, or educational or career opportunity because of gambling.
   9. Relies on others to provide money to relieve desperate financial situations caused by gambling.

B. The gambling behavior is not better explained by a manic episode.

According to the DSM-5 manual, in many cultures, individuals gamble on games and events, and they do this generally without severe negative consequences. However, some individuals develop substantial impairment related to their gambling activities. The manual stresses that the essential feature of gambling disorder is persistent and recurrent maladaptive gambling behavior that disrupts personal, family, and/or vocational pursuits (Criterion A). A *gambling disorder* is defined as a cluster of four or more of the symptoms listed in Criterion A, occurring at any time in the same 12-month period. The manual also notes that although some behavioral conditions that do not involve ingestion of substances have similarities to substance-related disorders, only one disorder—gambling disorder—has sufficient data to be included in the non-substance-related disorders section of DSM-5.

The manual also states that overconfidence can be present in individuals who have a gambling disorder, and that those with a gambling disorder can be impulsive, competitive, energetic, restless, and easily bored. The manual notes that those suffering from disordered gambling may be overly concerned with the opinions of others. They can also be depressed and lonely, and they may gamble when feeling helpless, guilty, or depressed. This evidence is consistent with the findings of research on eating disorders, which shows that binge eating often occurs when one is depressed (Kemp, Bui, and Grier 2011).

Gender differences have also been found in the context of disordered gambling. Specifically, in line with Odean and Barber's research on gender differences, males are more likely than females to suffer from gambling disorder (Martin, Usdan, Cremeens, and Vail-Smith 2014). According to the *DSM-5* (American Psychiatric Association 2013), males start gambling at a younger age and tend to develop gambling disorder earlier in life than females, who are more likely to begin gambling at an older age and to develop gambling disorder in a shorter timeframe. Among those with gambling disorders, females seek treatment sooner than men (American Psychiatric Association 2013).

Although multiple researchers have suggested that the thrill of gambling motivates some frequent traders (Dorn and Sengmueller 2009; Jadlow and Mowen 2010; Markiewicz and Weber 2013), and that others view frequent trading as a substitute for gambling (Barber et al. 2009), no published work has addressed the possible addictive disordered dimension of frequent trading. However, new unpublished research (Strahilevitz et al. 2015) has investigated whether frequent trading might also have an addictive component. Specifically, Strahilevitz et al. (2015) have identified strong connections between trading frequency and both emotional vulnerability and a sense of feeling addicted to trading. They also find that frequent trading is correlated with both considering oneself to be an adrenaline junkie and viewing trading as stimulating and exciting. Furthermore, Strahilevitz et al. (2015) also find trading frequency to be correlated with impulsivity, risk-seeking in multiple domains and the frequency of experiencing a wide range of negative emotions. They also find frequent traders have a higher levels of confidence in their skill as investors.

The findings linking adrenaline, stimulation, and excitement to frequent trading reinforce the risk-as-feelings argument (Loewenstein et al. 2001). This suggests that emotion rather than rational decision making drives many of the risk-seeking behaviors seen across domains. In ongoing research, Strahilevitz et al. (2015) are adapting much of the *DSM-5*'s diagnostic criteria to further explore the similarities between frequent trading and gambling disorder.

THE CONNECTION BETWEEN GAMBLING, IMPULSIVITY, AND NEGATIVE EMOTIONS

Given that researchers including Barber et al. (2009) and Markiewicz and Weber (2013) note that frequent trading is sometimes just another form of gambling, some understanding of frequent trading can be achieved by closely reviewing the literature on compulsive gambling. Results of various studies on gambling suggest that impulsivity, as well as several emotional variables, may play a role in problem gambling (Williams, Grisham, Erskine, and Cassedy 2012; von Ranson, Wallace, Holub, and Hodgins 2013; Andrade and Petry 2014; Grant and Chamberlain 2014; Canale, Vieno, Griffiths, Rubaltelli, and Santinello 2015). These studies all stress that impulsivity is a core issue underlying many addictive behaviors, including problem gambling. In terms of emotions, and examining different populations, Barrault and Verescon (2013); Holdsworth, Nuske, and Breen (2013); and Martin et al. (2014) find that problem gambling is linked to depression. Similarly, Dowling et al. (2016) provide a meta-analysis of research showing a connection between problem gambling and clinical anger. Self-esteem may also be an issue related to gambling addiction. According to Rockloff, Greer, Fay, and Evans (2011), individuals who think negatively about themselves are more likely to gamble more intensively.

Ferentzy, Skinner, and Antze (2006) note that sponsorship organizations such as Gamblers Anonymous give people a safe place to express and handle their emotions, without resorting to compulsive gambling. This suggests that although casual gambling can be fun, compulsive gambling is a painful disorder (Blume 1986; Rachlin 1990). In describing the addictive nature of gambling, Rantala and Sulkenen (2012, p. 8) explain: "players do get hooked. The feelings of competence go away, Lady Luck turns her back, and excitement and joy disappear."

NEGATIVE EMOTIONS AND FREQUENT TRADING

Although research demonstrates that frequent trading is bad for one's wealth, Strahilevitz et al. (2015) suggest that it may also affect one's well-being. Besides the self-identified addiction and impulsivity components found commonly among frequent traders in their sample, the authors also see differences in emotions. Specifically, when compared to infrequent traders, frequent traders report that their performance in the stock market has strong effects on their self-esteem, relationships with others, and overall happiness. Frequent trading is also positively correlated with negative emotions including feeling depressed, being sad, feeling stupid, experiencing regret, being angry with oneself, and feeling angrier about things in general. Finally, a positive correlation also exists between frequent trading and feelings of social isolation. Further evidence connecting trading behavior to emotional distress comes from Coates and Herbert (2008), who find a positive correlation between levels of the stress hormone cortisol in stock traders and their financial uncertainty, the latter measured by the difference between economic return and expected market variance. Surprisingly, Kandasamy et al. (2014) find that when traders experience high levels of cortisol, they become more risk-averse.

According to Strahilevitz et al. (2015), research on self-regulation and self-control (Vohs and Faber 2007; Hedgcock, Vohs, and Rao 2012; Hofmann, Baumeister, Förster, and Vohs 2012; Hofmann, Luhmann, Fisher, Vohs, and Baumeister 2014; Greenaway, Storrs, Philipp, Louis, Hornsey, and Vohs 2015; Hofmann et al.2015), and particularly work on the self-regulation of emotion (Koole, van Dillen, and Sheppes 2010; Faber and Vohs 2011), may offer promising suggestions for ways to help frequent traders trade less often. Vohs, Mead, and Goode (2006); Vohs and Baumeister (2011); Vohs, Baumeister, and Schmeichel (2012); and Vohs (2015) also suggest a connection between time spent thinking about money and both unhappiness and competitiveness. Because trading involves thinking about making and losing money, this may explain why Strahilevitz et al. (2015) find frequent traders to be less happy and more competitive than infrequent traders.

The results of Strahilevitz et al.'s (2015) work suggest that solving the problem of frequent trading may require more than simply informing investors that frequent trading is bad for their financial well-being. Indeed, if an emotionally charged addictive component is present in frequent trading, interventions may need to go beyond merely educating investors about the financial downside of frequent trading. Indeed, such interventions may need to be similar to those used for treating compulsive gambling and other addictions.

THE TRADING IMPLICATIONS OF MOBILE TECHNOLOGY

Mobile technology is rapidly changing the world. With global smartphone usage now in the billions, most investors are likely to own a smartphone. Tablet usage is also very high. This increase is accompanied by a rise in mobile applications that provide access to market information, detailed research, and trading platforms. Despite considerable research on frequent stock trading and problem gambling, little research is available on the effect of new mobile technologies. What has been the emotional and behavioral effect of the huge increase in the use of mobile technology?

La Plante, Nelson, and Gray (2014) and Gainsbury, Russell, Wood, Hing, and Blaszczynsi (2015) find higher rates of disordered gambling among Internet gamblers than among land-based gamblers. Similarly, Phillips, Ogeil, Chow, and Blaszczynsi (2013) show that with the evolution of the Internet and mobile devices, problem gamblers have gained access to new forms of gambling. Thus, the ubiquity of mobile devices is likely to increase the tendency that some investors have to indulge in overtrading. Basically, the more opportunities to gamble, the more likely someone is to engage in disordered gambling (Lester 1994; Campbell and Lester 1999; Breen and Zimmerman 2002). Barber and Odean (2001b) note that Internet trading has greatly increased trading volume; however, mobile trading platforms are even more recent. Although some research suggests that mobile usage can increase trading frequency (Strahilevitz et al. 2015), and others are proposing to do additional research in this area (Zhang and Teo 2014), much remains to be learned about the effect of mobile devices on trading frequency.

Summary and Conclusions

Researchers tend to agree that frequent trading is financially unwise, given both the time and the transaction costs involved. An implication is that those engaging in trading stocks regularly should modify their behavior. The evidence shows that a far better path for achieving financial success in the stock market is to buy and hold a highly diversified portfolio that is composed of low-fee index-tracking funds. The balance of stock-related investments to other assets should reflect an investor's financial and emotional risk tolerance. Frequent trading is like playing with fire; it may seem exciting, but the possibility of getting burned is high.

Although researchers agree that frequent trading is both irrational and common, they fail to agree on why so many investors still engage in this practice. One possibility is that investors may view themselves as smarter than they actually are. Other explanations are that some investors hunger for risk, have impulsivity issues, enjoy gambling, or suffer some sort of addiction. Regardless of the underlying reason, frequent trading is an issue that is worthy of future research. Research examining a potential addictive component of the phenomenon of frequent trading, which falls in line with the psychiatric condition of gambling disorder, may be particularly promising (Strahilevitz et al. 2015). Given the complexity of the problem of frequent trading, future research should focus not only on understanding what drives frequent traders but also on how researchers in this area can best help frequent traders stop this irrational way of investing.

DISCUSSION QUESTIONS

1. Explain why frequent stock trading is bad for investor returns.
2. Identify the major factors that might drive frequent trading.
3. Differentiate among recreational, aspirational, and sensation-seeking motives for investing, and explain which of these motives lead to the greatest trading frequency.
4. Identify and explain the gender differences that exist in investing and gambling behavior.
5. Discuss how mobile technology is likely to affect frequent trading.
6. Discuss the prevalence of frequent stock trading.

REFERENCES

American Psychiatric Association. 2013. "Gambling Disorder." In *Diagnostic and Statistical Manual of Mental Disorders, 5th Edition*, 585–589. Arlington, VA: American Psychiatric Association.

Anderson, Anders. 2008. "Is Online Trading Gambling with Peanuts?" Research Report, Swedish Institute for Financial Research. Available at http://sifr.org/wp-content/uploads/research/sifr-wp62.pdf.

Andrade, Leonardo F., and Nancy M. Petry. 2014. "White Problem Gamblers Discount Delayed Rewards Less Steeply Than Their African American and Hispanic Counterparts." *Psychology of Addictive Behaviors* 28:2, 599–606.

Barber, Brad M., Yi-Tsung Lee, Yu-Jane Liu, and Terrance Odean. 2005. "Do Individual Day Traders Make Money? Evidence from Taiwan." Available at http://www.econ.yale.edu/~shiller/behfin/2004-04-10/barber-lee-liu-odean.pdf

Barber, Brad M., Yi-Tsung Lee, Yu-Jane Liu, and Terrance Odean. 2009. "Just How Much Do Individual Investors Lose by Trading?" *Review of Financial Studies* 22:2, 609–632.

Barber, Brad M., and Terrance Odean. 2000. "Trading is Hazardous to Your Wealth: The Common Stock Investment Performance of Individual Investors." *Journal of Finance* 4:2, 773–806.

Barber, Brad M., and Terrance Odean. 2001a. "Boys Will Be Boys: Gender, Overconfidence, and Common Stock Investment." *Quarterly Journal of Economics* 116:1, 261–292.

Barber, Brad M., and Terrance Odean. 2001b. "The Internet and the Investor." *Journal of Economic Perspectives* 15:1, 41–54.

Barber, Brad M., and Terrance Odean. 2002. "Online Investors: Do the Slow Die First?" *Review of Financial Studies* 15:2, 455–488.

Barrault, Servane, and Isabelle Verescon. 2013. "Cognitive Distortions, Anxiety and Depression Among Regular and Pathological Gambling Online Poker Players." *Cyberpsychology, Behavior and Social Networking* 16:3, 183–188.

Belsky, Gary, and Thomas Gilovich. 2000. *Why Smart People Make Big Money Mistakes and How to Correct Them: Lessons from the New Science of Behavioral Economics.* New York: Simon and Schuster.

Biais, Bruno, Denis Hilton, Karine Mazurier, and Sebastien Pouget. 2005. "Judgmental Overconfidence, Self-Monitoring, and Trading Performance in an Experimental Financial Market." *Review of Economic Studies* 72:2, 287–312.

Blume, Sheila B. 1986. "Treatment for the Addictions: Alcoholism, Drug Dependence and Compulsive Gambling in a Psychiatric Setting." *Journal of Substance Abuse Treatment* 3:2, 131–133.

Breen, Robert B., and Mark Zimmerman. 2002. "Rapid Onset of Pathological Gambling in Machine Gamblers." *Journal of Gambling Studies* 18:1, 31–43.

Campbell, Frank, and David Lester. 1999. "The Impact of Gambling Opportunities on Compulsive Gambling." *Journal of Social Psychology* 139:1, 126–127.

Canale, Natale, Alessio Vieno, Mark Griffiths, Enrico Rubaltelli, and Massimo Santinello. 2015. "How Impulsivity Traits Influence Problem Gambling Motives. The Role of Perceived Gambling Risk/Benefits." *Psychology of Addictive Behaviors* 29:3, 813–823.

Charness, Gary, and Uri Gneezy. 2010. "Portfolio Choice and Risk Attitudes: An Experiment." *Economic Inquiry* 48:1, 122–146.

Charness, Gary, and Uri Gneezy. 2012. "Strong Evidence for Gender Differences in Risk Taking." *Journal of Economic Behavior & Organization* 83:1, 50–58.

Coates, John M., Mark Gurnell, and Aldo Rustichini. 2009. "Second-to-fourth Digit Ratio Predicts Success among High-frequency Financial Traders." *Proceedings of the National Academy of Sciences* 106:2, 623–628.

Coates, John M., and Joseph Herbert. 2008. "Endogenous Steroids and Financial Risk-taking on a London Trading Floor." *Proceedings of the National Academy of Sciences* 105:16, 6167–6172.

De Bondt, Werner F. M., and Richard H. Thaler. 1995. "Financial Decision-Making in Markets and Firms: A Behavioral Perspective." In Robert Jarrow, Vojislav Maksimovic, and William T. Ziemba (eds.), *Handbooks in Operations Research and Management Science, Vol. 9, Finance*, 385–410. North Holland: Elsevier B.V.

Dorn, Daniel, and Gur Huberman. 2002. "Who Trades?" *EFA 2003 Annual Conference Paper No. 645*. Available at http://papers.ssrn.com/sol3/papers.cfm?abstract_id=423995.

Dorn, Daniel, and Gur Huberman. 2005. "Talk and Action: What Individual Investors Say and What They Do." *Review of Finance* 9:4, 437–481.

Dorn, Daniel, and Paul Sengmueller. 2009. "Trading as Entertainment?" *Management Science* 55:4, 591–603.

Dowling, Nicki, Aino Suomi, Alun Jackson, Tiffany Lavis, Janet Patford, Suzanne Cockman, Shane Thomas, Maria Bellringer, Jane Kozial-Mclean, Malcolm Battersby, Peter Harvey, and Max Abbott. 2016. "Problem Gambling and Intimate Partner Violence: A Systematic Review and Meta-Analysis." *Trauma, Violence & Abuse* 17:1, 43–61.

Faber, Ronald J., and Thomas C. O'Guinn. 1989. "Classifying Compulsive Consumers: Advances in the Development of a Diagnostic Tool." *Advances in Consumer Research* 16:1, 738–744.

Faber, Ronald J., and Thomas C. O'Guinn. 1992. "A Clinical Screener for Compulsive Buying." *Journal of Consumer Research* 19:3, 459–469.

Faber, Ronald J., and Kathleen D. Vohs. 2011. "A Model of Self Regulation: Insights for Impulsive and Compulsive Problems with Eating and Buying." In David Glen Mick, Simone Pettigrew, Cornelia Pechmann and Julie L. Ozanne (eds.), *Transformative Consumer Research For Personal and Collective Well-Being*, 467–484. London: Taylor and Francis.

Ferentzy, Peter, Wayne Skinner, and Paul Antze. 2006. "Recovery in Gamblers Anonymous." *Journal of Gambling Issues* 17: 6–14.

Figner, Bernd, and Elke U. Weber. 2011. "Determinants of Risk Taking: Who Takes Risks, When, and Why?" *Current Direction in Psychological Science* 20:4, 211–216.

Gainsbury, Sally M., Alex Russell, Robert Wood, Nerilee Hing, and Alex Blaszczynski. 2015. "How Risky Is Internet Gambling? A Comparison of Subgroups of Internet Gamblers based on Problem Gambling Status." *New Media and Society* 17:6, 861–879.

Gervais, Simon, and Terrance Odean. 2001. "Learning to be Overconfident." *Review of Financial Studies* 14:1, 1–27.

Glaser, Markus, and Martin Weber. 2003. "Overconfidence and Trading Volume." *AFA 2004 San Diego Meetings*. Available at http://link.springer.com/article/10.1007/s10713-007-0003-3#/page-1.

Glaser, Markus, and Martin Weber. 2007. "Overconfidence and Trading Volume." *GENEVA Risk and Insurance Review* 32:1, 1–36.

Graham, John R., Campbell R. Harvey, and Hai Huang. 2009. "Investor Competence, Trading Frequency, and Home Bias." *Management Science* 55:7, 1094–1106.

Grant, Jon E., and Samuel R. Chamberlain. 2014. "Impulsive Action and Impulsive Choice across Substance and Behavioral Addictions: Cause or Consequence?" *Addictive Behaviors* 39:11, 1632–1639.

Greenaway, Katharine H., Katherine R. Storrs, Michael C. Philipp, Winnifred R. Louis, Matthew J. Hornsey, and Kathleen D. Vohs. 2015. "Loss of Control Stimulates Approach Motivation." *Journal of Experimental Social Psychology* 56:1, 235–241.

Grinblatt, Mark, and Matti Keloharju. 2009. "Sensation Seeking, Overconfidence, and Trading Activity." *Journal of Finance* 64:2, 549–578.

Hedgcock, William M., Kathleen D. Vohs, and Akshay R. Rao. 2012. "Reducing Self-Control Depletion Effects through Enhanced Sensitivity to Implementation: Evidence from fMRI and Behavioral Studies." *Journal of Consumer Psychology* 22:4, 486–495.

Hoffmann, Arvid O. I., Thomas Post, and Joost M. E. Pennings. 2013. "Individual Investor Perceptions and Behavior during the Financial Crisis." *Journal of Banking & Finance* 37:1, 60–74.

Hofmann, Wilhelm, Roy F. Baumeister, Georg Förster, and Kathleen D. Vohs. 2012. "Everyday Temptations: An Experience Sampling Study of Desire, Conflict, and Self-Control." *Journal of Personality and Social Psychology* 102:6, 1318–1335.

Hofmann, Wilhelm, Hiroki P. Kotabe, Kathleen D. Vohs, and Roy F. Baumeister. 2015. "Desire and Desire Regulation." In Wilhelm Hofmann and Loran F. Nordgren (eds.), *The Psychology of Desire*, 61–81. New York: Guilford Press.

Hofmann, Wilhelm, Maike Luhmann, Rachel R. Fisher, Kathleen D. Vohs, and Roy F. Baumeister. 2014. "Yes, But Are They Happy? Effects of Trait Self-Control on Affective Well-Being and Life Satisfaction." *Journal of Personality* 82:4, 265–277.

Holdsworth, Louise, Elaine Nuske, and Helen Breen. 2013. "All Mixed Up Together: Women's Experiences of Problem Gambling, Comorbidity and Co-occurring Complex Needs." *International Journal of Mental Health Addiction* 11:1, 315–328.

Jadlow, Janice W., and John C. Mowen. 2010. "Comparing the Traits of Stock Market Investors and Gamblers." *Journal of Behavioral Finance* 11:2, 67–81.

Kahneman, Daniel. 2013. *Thinking, Fast and Slow*. New York: Farrar, Straus, and Giroux.

Kandasamy Narayanan, Ben Hardy, Lionel Page, Markus Schaffner, Johann Graggaber, Andrew S. Powlson, Paul C. Fletcher, Mark Gurnell, and John Coates. 2014, "Cortisol Shifts Financial Risk Preferences." *Proceedings of the National Academy of Sciences of the United States of America (PNAS)* 111:9, 3608–3613.

Kemp, Elyria, My Bui, and Sonya Grier. 2011. "Eating Their Feelings: Examining Emotional Eating in At-Risk Groups in the United States." *Journal of Consumer Policy* 34:2, 211–229.

Koole, Sander L., Lotte F. van Dillen, and Gal Sheppes. 2010. "The Self Regulation of Emotion." In Kathleen D. Vohs and Roy F. Baumeister (eds.), *Handbook of Self-Regulation Volume 2*, 22–40. New York: Guilford Press.

Kumar, Alok. 2009. "Who Gambles in the Stock Market?" *Journal of Finance* 64:4, 1889–1933.

La Plante, Debi A., Sarah E. Nelson, and Heather M. Gray. 2014. "Breadth and Depth Involvement: Understanding Internet Gambling Involvement and Its Relationship to Gambling Problems." *Psychology of Addictive Behaviors* 28:2, 396–403.

Lester, David. 1994. "Access to Gambling Opportunities and Compulsive Gambling." *International Journal of the Addictions* 29:12, 1611–1616.

Loewenstein, George F., Elke U. Weber, Christopher K. Hsee, and Ned Welch. 2001. "Risk as Feelings." *Psychological Bulletin* 127:2, 267–286.

Markiewicz, Lukasz, and Elke U. Weber. 2013. "DOSPERT's Gambling Risk-Taking Propensity Scale Predicts Excessive Stock Trading." *Journal of Behavioral Finance* 14:1, 65–78.

Martin, Ryan J., Stuart Usdan, Jennifer Cremeens, and Karen Vail-Smith. 2014. "Disordered Gambling and Co-morbidity of Psychiatric Disorders among College Students: An Examination of Problem Drinking, Anxiety and Depression." *Journal of Gambling Studies* 30:2, 321–333.

Moore, Don A. 2007. "Not So Above Average After All: When People Believe They Are Worse Than Average and Its Implications for Theories of Bias in Social Comparison." *Organizational Behavior and Human Decision Processes* 102:1, 42–58.

Moore, Don A., and Paul J. Healy. 2008. "The Trouble with Overconfidence." *Psychological Review* 115:2, 502–517.

Oberlechner, Thomas, and Carol Osler. 2008. "Overconfidence in Currency Markets." Available at http://people.brandeis.edu/~cosler/documents/Overconfidence.pdf.

Odean, Terrance. 1999. "Do Investors Trade Too Much?" *American Economic Review* 89:5, 1279–1298.

Phillips, James G., Rowan Ogeil, Yang-Wai Chow, and Alex Blaszczynski. 2013. "Gambling Involvement and Increased Risk of Gambling Problems." *Gambling Studies* 29:4, 601–611.

Rachlin, Howard. 1990. "Why Do People Gamble and Keep Gambling Despite Heavy Losses?" *Psychological Science* 1:5, 294–297.

Rantala, Varpu, and Pekka Salkunen. 2012. "Is Pathological Gambling Just a Big Problem or Also an Addiction?" *Addiction Research and Theory* 20:1, 1–10.

Reilly, Christine M., and Nathan Smith. 2013. "The Evolving Definition of Pathological Gambling in the DSM-5." Beverly, MA: National Center for Responsible Gaming.

Rockloff, Matthew J., Nancy Greer, Carly Fay, and Lionel J. Evans. 2011. "Gambling on Electronic Gaming Machines Is an Escape from Negative Self Reflection." *Journal of Gambling Studies* 27:1, 63–72.

Schlomer, Erika M. 1997. "The Role of Managerial Risk Perception and Risk Propensity in the Selection of Countertrade Form." PhD Dissertation in Business Administration, Washington State University.

Strahilevitz, Michal, Joseph Harvey, and Dan Ariely. 2015. "How Frequent Stock Trading Is Related to Overconfidence, Negative Emotions, Impulsivity and Feeling Addicted." Presented at the October 2015 Conference of the Association of Consumer Research, New Orleans, Louisiana.

Strahilevitz, Michal, Terrance Odean, and Brad Barber. 2011. "Once Burned, Twice Shy: How Naive Learning, Counterfactuals, and Regret Affect the Repurchase of Stocks Previously Sold." *Journal of Marketing Research* 48:SPL, 102–120.

Talpsepp, Tõnn. 2011. "Reverse Disposition Effect of Foreign Investors." *Journal of Behavioral Finance* 12:4, 183–200.

Vohs, Kathleen D. 2015. "Money Priming Can Change People's Thoughts, Feelings, Motivations, and Behaviors: An Update on 10 Years of Experiments." *Journal of Experimental Psychology: General* 144:4, 86–93.

Vohs, Kathleen D., and Roy F. Baumeister. 2011. "What's the Use of Happiness? It Can't Buy You Money." *Journal of Consumer Psychology* 21:2, 139–141.

Vohs, Kathleen D., Roy F. Baumeister, and Brandon J. Schmeichel. 2012. "Erratum to Motivation, Personal Beliefs, and Limited Resources All Contribute to Self-Control." *Journal of Experimental Social Psychology* 48:4, 943–947.

Vohs, Kathleen D., and Ronald J. Faber. 2007. "Spent Resources: Self-Regulatory Resource Availability Affects Impulse Buying." *Journal of Consumer Research* 33:4, 537–547.

Vohs, Kathleen D., Nicole L. Mead, and Miranda R. Goode. 2006. "The Psychological Consequences of Money." *Science* 314:5802, 1154–1156.

von Ranson, Kristin M., Laurel M. Wallace, Alice Holub, and David C. Hodgins. 2013. "Eating Disorders, Substance Use Disorders, and Impulsiveness among Disordered Gamblers in a Community Sample." *European Eating Disorders Review* 21:2, 148–154.

Weber, Elke U., Ann-Renée Blais, and Nancy E. Betz. 2002. "A Domain-Specific Risk-Attitude Scale: Measuring Risk Perceptions and Risk Behaviors." *Journal of Behavioral Decision Making* 15:4, 263–290.

Williams, Alishia D., Jessica R. Grisham, Alisha Erskine, and Eva Cassedy. 2012. "Deficits in Emotion Regulation Associated With Pathological Gambling." *British Journal of Clinical Psychology* 51:2, 223–238.

World Federation of Exchanges Database. 2016. "Stocks Traded Turnover Ration of Domestic Shares (%), 1975–2015." Distributed by Washington D.C., World Bank. Available at http://data.worldbank.org/indicator/CM.MKT.TRNR?end=2015&locations=US&start=1975.

Zaleskiewicz, Tomasz. 2001. "Beyond Risk Seeking and Risk Aversion: Personality and the Dual Nature of Economic Risk Taking." *European Journal of Personality* 15:1, 105–122.

Zhang, Zhensheng, and Hock Hai Teo. 2014. "The Impact of Mobile Trading Technology on Individual Investors' Trading Behaviors: The "Two-Edged Sword" Effect." *Proceedings of the Twenty Second European Conference on Information Systems*, 1–10.

13

The Psychology of Women Investors

MARGAUERITA M. CHENG
Chief Executive Officer
Blue Ocean Global Wealth

SAMEER S. SOMAL
Chief Financial Officer
Blue Ocean Global Wealth

Introduction

Women are integral members of corporate America and the global business landscape. Their emergence as leaders, entrepreneurs, and innovators has made them an indispensable part of the economic environment and the future of global enterprise. Women are assuming greater professional and leadership responsibilities while still managing their personal and family finances. The increasing availability of education to women is not only changing their lives but also reshaping public attitudes toward gender differences and equality. Traditional gender roles no longer retain much currency in contemporary households. The women's colleges that opened starting in the late 1800s trained for careers that were acceptable for women to enter at the time, such as nursing and teaching. Today these institutions and many others offer degrees in business, law, medicine, psychology, and other professions, once thought of as work for men only. This demographic and societal evolution, particularly rapid in the last several decades, has produced a new set of gender-based competitive advantages, enabling women to emerge as influential leaders in fields such as business and finance. Women are now an essential and integrated part of the global economy. By leveraging their strengths and expounding upon their skills and experience, women will continue to realize success and create value.

The Emerging Influence and Affluence of Women

According to a survey of investors across various earning categories (Fidelity Investments 2015b), the demographics of the emerging affluent look very different from those of previous generations of upper-middle-income individuals. More than two-thirds are female and one-fourth are nonwhite. Women have surpassed men and now control more than half of all wealth in the United States (Gorman 2015). Women own nearly one-third of all private enterprises, employing an estimated 7.8 million Americans. The influence of women in the business arena is expected to grow in the future.

This rise of female entrepreneurs and executives coincides with an increase in the number of women pursuing higher education. Presently, women outnumber men in American colleges and universities. Differences in educational attainment by gender have changed over the preceding decades, with female attainment rates higher than those of males.

The reason for these differences in educational attainment stems from needs or motivations (Gage and Brijesh 2012). A motivational model cites four basic components: (1) needs (motivations), (2) behaviors (activities), (3) goals (satisfaction), and (4) feedback. Motivations are factors that trigger a person to carry out an action. Money is a major motivational factor and need in society; few things occupy as central a place in people's lives as money. Money plays a special role in personal and social lives, exerting more power over human lives than any other commodity (Oleson 2004). Increasingly, women are motivated to enter careers requiring higher levels of education, such as the medical and business management fields. Women strive to earn more money and attain a sense of personal achievement, just as their male counterparts always have.

The educational attainment of women between the ages of 25 and 64 in the labor force has increased substantially since the 1970s. In 2011, 37 percent of these women held college degrees, compared with 11 percent in 1970. About 7 percent of women had less than a high school diploma in 2011, down from 34 percent in 1970 (Bureau of Labor Statistics 2013).

Improved educational opportunities for young women have contributed to increased influence and affluence. Women are acquiring individual wealth through corporate employment, as well as entrepreneurial pursuits. In terms of earning power, women are now the primary breadwinners in 17.4 million U.S. families, more than double the number from 30 years ago. Families with two working parents have become the standard. In 1979, women working full time earned 62 percent of what men did; today, women's earnings are only 22 percent less than full-time male employees. The wage gap is smaller for younger workers than for older workers, but clearly opportunity for improvement still exists (Bureau of Labor Statistics 2008). According to Wang, Parker, and Taylor (2013, p. 1), "Four in 10 American households with children under age 18 now include a mother who is either the sole or primary earner for her family. This share, the highest on record, has quadrupled since 1960."

Two-thirds (66 percent) of young women between the ages of 18 and 34 rate professional success as "very important" or "one of the most important things" in their lives. Conversely, only 59 percent of their male counterparts cite professional success as a life priority. When the Pew Research Center issued this survey, more than half (56 percent) of young women cited career success as a top priority (Patten and Parker 2012). The fact that this reorganization of life priorities has occurred within a single generation is remarkable.

THE LEADERSHIP OF WOMEN

The continued struggle of women for success in professional settings is well documented. However, with today's greater exposure to the workplace and more opportunities for career advancement, female professionals and entrepreneurs are securing positions in previously male-dominated industries.

Women are obtaining executive and board positions in Fortune 500 companies and being appointed to top government posts. A record number of women (104) were sworn in to the 114th U.S. Congress. Canadian Prime Minister Justin Trudeau assembled the first cabinet with an equal number of male and female representatives. In the legal and medical professions, women are achieving parity with their male colleagues. Women now hold 52.2 percent of all managerial and professional positions compared with 30.6 percent in 1968 (Pew Research Center 2015).

Currently, women manage $14 trillion in personal wealth, and that number could reach $22 trillion by the end of the decade. By the year 2030, women are expected to control approximately two-thirds of the national wealth. This projection is a product of both organic growth rates and impending transfer of wealth between spouses and family members (BMO Wealth Institute 2015).

WOMEN ENTREPRENEURS

Female entrepreneurs are establishing new businesses at more than twice the rate of men. The number of women-owned businesses with more than $10 million in revenue has increased by 40 percent since 1997. Small and mid-size companies led by women employ more workers than all Fortune 500 enterprises combined. Women entrepreneurs also have more success in growing their primary businesses, with an average $9.1 million in annual sales, compared to $8.4 million for male entrepreneurs (Grace 2014).

Women are well positioned to become the new economic leaders. They are likely to create half of the nearly 10 million small-business jobs by 2018. A bright spot during the past several years has been the job growth spurred by women-owned firms, especially in the retail marketplace. Since 2007, private companies owned by women have added an estimated 340,000 jobs. Firms owned by women now account for nearly one-third of all enterprises and are only expected to continue their upward ascent (American Express Open 2015).

In terms of innovation or introducing products that are new to some or all consumers, women entrepreneurs outperform their male counterparts. This trend is not limited to the United States and Europe, because various emerging markets and underdeveloped countries also exhibit this trend (BMO Wealth Institute 2015).

Although the United States is ranked as the most favorable environment for female entrepreneurs, followed closely by Canada, Australia, and Sweden, the private sector is still a work in progress. The most common concern for women is securing financing for their fledgling enterprise. Nearly three-fourths of women cite financial capital as a critical challenge to launching their firms (Robb, Coleman, and Stangler 2014). In 2013, a Senate committee found that women lack sufficient access to loans and venture capital (Powell 2014). In fact, male entrepreneurs are more than three times as likely to secure equity financing through an angel investor or venture capitalist than women (14.4 percent compared to 3.6 percent). Men also have more success utilizing networks of close friends and business associates. For most female entrepreneurs (55.4 percent), bank financing is their sole source of capital. Robb and Coleman (2009) find that men start with almost twice as much capital as women entrepreneurs. This disadvantage affects both the growth trajectory and the employment potential of women-owned firms. President Susan Sobbott of American Express Open warned that enterprises between one-fourth and half a million dollars in revenues are at a turning point in their development (American Express Open 2015). Until this sizable gap in financing is resolved, women entrepreneurs will fall short of maximizing their full economic potential.

TRANSFER OF WEALTH

Besides personal income, women of the baby boomer generation are expected to inherit wealth from two other sources: their parents and their spouses. Baby boomers are poised to inherit as much as $15 trillion over the next 20 years (Nielsen 2012). Of married American women, 7 out of 10 will eventually become widows and at the relatively early age of 59. Though life expectancy has risen for both men and women due to childhood immunization, improved health infrastructure, better living conditions, and other factors, a long-lasting discrepancy in life expectancy still exists between men and women. Statistically, women outlive men by an average of 5 to 10 years. Among those age 100 or older, 85 percent are women. In 2010, 40 percent of women over age 65 were widows, compared to just 13 percent of men. Nearly 50 percent of women age 75 or older lived alone. With women surviving their partners, much of this accrued wealth will fall under their control (Blue 2008).

According to AARP, individuals over the age of 50 possess 79 percent of all financial assets, 80 percent of money in savings accounts, and 66 percent of all money invested in the stock market. The looming transfer of wealth, in size and scope, has no precedent in contemporary American history (Brennan 2009).

Contrary to wealth transfers in past generations, today's beneficiaries are unlikely to reside in the same community as their parents and family members. This is likely to result in much reshuffling for small and mid-size financial companies, as children can no longer be counted on to remain with the same advisors and financial institutions as their parents. This outcome is especially true of women, who in surveys have expressed dissatisfaction with the financial industry as a whole. Despite their rising affluence, the financial service professionals, the majority of whom are men, often overlook women. According to State Farm Insurance (2008), only one in three women trusts financial services professionals, and three in four women are skeptical when initially meeting with a financial professional. A study by the Boston Consulting Group (2010) find that men are 1.7 times as likely as women to be approached by a financial advisor. Financial professionals should view the expanding influence of women as a business opportunity for increasing their client base and assets under management (AUM).

The Psychology of Women Investors

Every investor has unique wants and needs. Research shows that women value personal relationships and big picture thinking more than men. Studies also show that men tend to be more competitive than women in deal making. According to Larimer and Hannagan (2010, p. 43), "Women prefer altruistic, reciprocal relationships and men prefer competition and struggle." Women investors value financial advisors who recognize their needs as part of a whole, as opposed to framing discussions in purely monetary terms.

Women often grew up assuming that men handle financial responsibilities. As a result of their limited opportunity set, they did not develop a financial knowledge framework. That knowledge gap has tended to lessen women's confidence in money matters. Because of a lack of financial literacy, women have often refrained from discussing finances and have deferred questions to the male in the family (Fidelity Investments 2015a).

Women think and behave differently from men in terms of the evaluation and decision-making processes. Compared to men, women consider more factors, raise more questions, and consult with more people, such as online groups, friends, and colleagues, before making an educated decision. Their methods diverge when measuring results, as well. Men focus more on symbols of power and success, whereas women need to understand how power and success affects the financial position of their families and themselves.

Women want to understand how their decisions influence other areas of their lives. They do not focus on performance numbers because they are on their continued progress toward achieving their life goals. This observation lends credence to the fundamental divergence between men and women in terms of their competitive nature.

Moreover, women communicate differently from men. Researchers at the University of Texas, Austin, conclude that both genders speak about the same number of words each day—women at 16,215 words and men at 15,669. The research also notes that women talk more about other people, whereas men discuss objects in their environment (Newman, Groom, Handelman, and Pennebaker 2008).

Women are typically drawn to advisors who can hold an engaging conversation and cultivate an environment that invites broader discussion of their work and family life. They need financial professionals who can empathize with their needs and respect their points of view. Clear and straightforward language is preferable to jargon-heavy dialogue. Financial decision making is a multifaceted and emotion-invoking process. People sense the likely interactions of others and act based on that assessment. In that regard, women often prominently display nonverbal responses. They are more attuned to eye contact, facial expressions, and hand gestures, using these cues as a means to decipher both mood and meaning.

For women, listening skills require consistent eye contact and nonverbal feedback. For example, when a couple is buying a house, if the real estate agent is inattentive and has poor eye contact, the wife may feel uncomfortable about buying from this person—a lack of eye contact and attention could jeopardize the sale. Conversely, men do not consider eye contact and feedback as measures of effective listening. Numbers and facts speak louder than facial expressions. Accordingly, men are more comfortable talking side by side, whereas women strongly prefer direct, face-to-face contact (Newman et al. 2008).

Although various stereotypes exist about gender and emotions, many factual differences exist in the ways males and females function emotionally. These differences include the extent to which each recognizes emotions in others and expresses individual emotions through facial and vocal expressions, words, physiological arousal, and behaviors such as aggression. These gender differences vary according to the particular situation involved and the cultural background of the participants (Levinson, Ponzetti, and Jorgensen 1999).

Women have a natural affinity for details, and their "checklists" often result in a more comprehensive decision-making process. However, they may place less emphasis on details such as numbers, facts, and figures, and prefer to focus on articulating their vision for life after retirement and how their portfolio needs to be oriented toward achieve this lifestyle. "Women continue to pursue a diverse range of long-term financial goals. According to the Pew Research Center (2015, p. 1), "they want to save enough money to maintain their lifestyle through retirement, cover health care expenses and avoid becoming a financial burden to loved ones." For these women, the importance of financial independence even after retirement is the driving force. Rather than prestige, this ability of not having to rely on others motivates the investment planning.

Women want to understand how their decisions influence other areas of their lives. Men are used to thinking that mutual funds or stocks are either green with life (when they are up) or red with death (when they are down). Women typically are not as focused on performance numbers as they are on their continued progress toward their life goals. This observation lends credence to the fundamental divergence between men and women in terms of their competitive natures. Women prioritize long-term goal achievement rather than current performance numbers. Conversely, women prefer consistency and measured progress toward achieving their financial objectives or goal. Women tend to value the progress they are making toward their life goals and the context of investment returns.

CUSTOMER LOYALTY

Customer loyalty has been the object of interest for businesses, and it is situated at the heart of customer relationship management (CRM). Women exhibit mixed loyalty toward individual service providers and corporations. The difference in cognitive processes and behavior of male and female consumers is reflected in the widespread use of gender as a segmentation variable in marketing practices.

According to Durukan and Bozac (2011), customers reflect three types in terms of customer loyalty: (1) those who are not loyal, (2) those who are forced to be loyal because of some factors such as switching costs, and (3) those who are fiercely loyal with no intentions of changing brands, services, or firms. The third type is the ultimate goal for any business, because such customers have no negative feelings and obtain information by word of mouth. People are loyal to products that offer high satisfaction rates, as well as competitive prices and positive company image. Customers want to be remembered and have products that meet their needs.

However, research reveals that women are not necessarily more loyal clients than men. It is important to provide some clarity on the context of loyalty. Although women tend to be more loyal to individual services providers, they are less loyal than men to grouplike entities, such as a particular company or institution (Melnyk, Van Osselaer, and Bijmolt 2009).

This observation is encouraging news for financial advisors who work closely with women clients on a one-on-one basis. Actually, women tend to refer an advisor more often to their families and friends, especially if they feel genuinely engaged and connected to the advisor's communication style and performance.

Women share their experiences with others, meaning that they tell many—family, friends, colleagues, and even strangers—about their financial advisor experience. The word-of-mouth marketing or referral marketing benefits financial advisors by improving client satisfaction and retention. This first-hand testimony creates loyalty to a brand by sharing these personal, relatable experiences. The concept of loyalty presents a compelling opportunity for financial professionals to make their female client engagements memorable, because these clients will then communicate their excitement with ease. If done thoughtfully, referrals can come with enhanced velocity and purpose. According to Blaney (2010, p. 18), "Women rarely try to compete with the advisor, or think they know better. A women trusts her advisor, she can be a powerful source of referrals. Men by contrast, often like to keep a great advisor for themselves." This statement shows the fundamental difference in the thought processes of women and men. Women want to share their success, whereas men tend to fear that sharing the information will cost them in some way. Women's lower risk preference makes them a natural fit to focus on managing risk and capital preservation as part of their written financial plan. By extension, a lower risk tolerance leads to a more diversified portfolio preference to mitigate loss potential for women, rather than the more risky preference for men in general.

Women are generally relationship driven, whereas men are typically results driven. Consequently, women prioritize the client experience over pure results. They value the experience of being heard, respected, and valued. A survey by Prudential Financial (2015) concluded that women face challenges in trying to meet their long-term financial goals. The research shows that women are confident in their knowledge of day-to-day financial matters. In fact, the study reports that 33 percent of women evaluate themselves highest on their knowledge of managing debt and 7 percent rank themselves lowest on their knowledge of investing. In terms of knowledge of managing money or debt, women grade themselves as a B or B minus. The survey also found that 27 percent of married women are relatively confident in their knowledge of key financial decisions, such as securing financing for a home and purchasing life insurance. Although the study indicated that women feel confident to handle financial planning and decision making on their own and feeling more financially secure, only 31 percent are now using a financial professional. The study suggests that companies can meet their needs by fine-tuning, rather than reinventing, their approach to serving women clients.

THE INVISIBLE PARTNER

A lack of confidence about their personal finance decisions has long been a source of frustration for women, hindering their ability to take greater control of family finances. As young women and girls, they often hear the message that money is a man's responsibility. That idea paved the way for women not to worry as much about what would happen if they needed to take on multiple caregiver roles and/or be financially independent.

Women are becoming financially and psychologically independent from their husbands at an increasing rate, while also gaining greater confidence in personal finance and wealth management. Yet, in many cases, women are neglected in their conversations with an advisor when their husbands are present. Because of this disadvantaged position, women generally need more time to gather information, especially from top influencers such as their husbands, parents, and close friends. In today's digital age, women are using the Internet to familiarize themselves with financial terminology and products. According to a study by Prudential Financial (2015, p. 10), "a third of women count financial company websites (31 percent) and financial news websites (29 percent) as tools for researching and learning about financial products." In terms of social media, women consumers use Facebook over other social media platforms.

A thoughtful financial professional needs to respect a woman's time and give her the space to make an informed decision. Advisors should clearly articulate their messages and not offer solutions until their clients fully understand their options. Offering more information to a female client than just facts and figures will give them a greater comfort and confidence in their decision-making abilities and their ability to plan. A positive trait of women clients is that they tend to have a better and more comprehensive picture of their family's financial position than do men because women often assume the dual roles of caregiver of family members and manager of household expenses. Thus, consulting the female head of household before beginning a financial planning engagement makes sense. For this reason, an advisor should not dismiss or ignore the needs and opinions of the wife, even when the husband is present.

DIFFERENCES BETWEEN THE MALE AND FEMALE BRAIN

Women process and receive information differently from men. Through advances in neuroscience, researchers now understand that women depend more heavily on certain regions of the brain. Female brains are generally connected across the right and left hemispheres, whereas male brains forge a stronger connection between the front and back lobes. Women tend to use both sides of the brain, whereas men primarily employ the left side—the lobe that controls logic and reason—when making decisions or performing tasks (Ingalhalikar et al. 2014).

The most striking difference between the male and female brain is the corpus callosum, a stretch of tissue connecting the right and left hemispheres of the brain. The right hemisphere is the nexus of emotion and creativity. The left hemisphere processes data in a more linear and mathematical fashion (Ingalhalikar et al. 2014). Although both men and women possess right and left hemispheres, women can shuttle information between the two sides more effectively than can men, as a result of being graced with a larger corpus callosum. For this reason, women can draw connections between words and emotions more easily and intuitively than men (Niu 2014).

Additionally, women tend to be more comfortable multitasking than men. Women are more sensitive to sound and language and have an easier time expressing their emotions verbally. Although a larger inferior-parietal lobule helps men excel in mathematics, women have a more complex limbic system, making them better attuned to their own feelings and the emotions of those around them. Because of this difference, women adopt a more holistic and inclusive approach to decision making. Men struggle to understand emotions when not clearly stated; their decision-making process is narrower, focusing on precise issues and dismissing information they deem superfluous to the matter at hand.

Finally, men are more amenable to risk than are women. Their brains receive a greater rush of endorphins when presented with a risk or challenge. This knowledge is absolutely critical to understanding the psychology of women investors and will be discussed further in the next section.

RISK TOLERANCE

Wealth holds a different meaning for men and women. A study by Fidelity Investments (2015b) finds that the majority of women (54 percent) connect wealth with security. Conversely, men generally associate the term with status or power. This distinction shapes the way men and women approach and think about investing. Men often have a short-term perspective, whereas women value relationships and long-term goal setting.

However, the notion that women are more risk-averse than men has been somewhat overstated. For example, Nelson (2012) performs a statistical review of existing studies on gender and risk tolerance. He finds that the difference in risk-aversion is considerably weaker than previously thought. In fact, Nelson reports that some studies show no difference.

Rather than consider women as risk-averse, financial professionals would be better served to think of them as "risk-aware." Women need a firm understanding of the risk before proceeding. When making a major investment decision, they desire some clarity on the potential trade-offs. Additionally, women require more time when making an investment decision. They are collaborative decision makers and prefer to consult close friends, wealth experts, and other financial resources. Perhaps a more accurate term to describe men is "risk-enthusiasts." In a survey conducted by Prudential Financial (2012), 70 percent of men expressed a willingness to assume some risk in exchange for greater financial reward. Also, 40 percent of men said that they enjoy the "sport of investing," compared to just 22 percent of women.

Hormones, specifically testosterone, may play a role in the willingness of men to assume additional risk. Neuroscientist John Coates conducted an experiment with 17 high-volume traders from the London financial district. Twice a day, they reported their gains and losses and provided Coates with a sample of saliva. His results show that above-average gains correlate with higher testosterone levels, whereas market volatility affects cortisol levels. As Coates and Herbert (2007, pp. 4–5) note,

> Cortisol is likely, therefore, to rise in a market crash and, by increasing risk aversion, to exaggerate the market's downward movement. Testosterone, on the other hand, is likely to rise in a bubble and, by increasing risk-taking, to exaggerate the market's upward movement. These steroid feedback loops may help to explain why people caught up in bubbles and crashes often find it difficult to make rational choices.

The fact that women have substantially less testosterone than men may explain their diligent and measured approach to risk-taking. Rational thought influences their investment decisions more than chemical processes. Women are, therefore, less likely to succumb to market panic or "irrational exuberance." This difference may be one reason a lower percentage of women dumped equities during the Great Recession, which officially lasted from December 2007 to June 2009. This "look before you leap" approach to investing can be both a blessing and a curse for the female investor. Although women may take more time to review the information before making a decision, their decisions are less haste and more long term. Once they decide on a course of action, they prefer to see it through.

WOMEN AND FINANCIAL LITERACY

Basic financial knowledge helps women make financial decisions with greater confidence. Whether men actually have a more complete understanding of financial product or women suffer the effects of low self-esteem from generations of social conditioning is unclear. In either case, with the increasing number of single-mother households, women must feel confident in their financial literacy. This development has both a short- and long-term effect on their lives and households. By increasing women's financial literacy, the change can become permanent and also can be passed on to future generations.

This change to social conditioning is likely to occur over time. However, today's financial advisors can drive such change by providing guidance toward supporting the understanding of finance. Guidance includes encouraging clients to read books about people who have overcome financial obstacles. Also, offering several workshops for various financial literacy levels—beginners, intermediate, and expert—can help.

Financial literacy is the ability to comprehend basic features of personal finance, such as credit, debt, and consumer protections. This includes the capacity to make informed decisions about saving, budgeting, investing, and managing money. Evidence shows that a large portion of the population possesses low financial literacy skills, which makes building and protecting personal wealth challenging. Despite the prevalence of financial education classes, the average American is still critically deficient in his or her basic financial knowledge. According to a Harris Poll (2014), only 39 percent of U.S. adults keep close track of their spending and 32 percent do not place any portion of their income into a retirement savings account.

Poor financial literacy can be especially costly for women, who endure more pronounced economic challenges than men, such as greater longevity and its attendant healthcare costs. Caregiving and familial responsibilities can also impede their ability to conserve and grow their wealth. Because of childbirth and responsibilities associated with parenting, women are more likely than men to have transitioned out of the workforce at some point in their lives. By the age of 62, 90 percent of men have at least 35 years of earning history versus 30 percent of women at that age. For this reason, women must make a concerted effort to remain financially "fit." To achieve this, women must understand their financial position, investment opportunities and risks, and how much they need to save to ensure a comfortable retirement.

For some women, money remains an uncomfortable topic of conversation. According to Fidelity Investments (2015b), 80 percent of women report refraining from discussing finances with those close to them. Less than half of the women surveyed indicate they would feel confident discussing money with a qualified professional. Yet, 77 percent indicate they would feel confident discussing medical issues with a doctor. In certain cases, their reluctance to discuss money with close friends and financial professionals prevents them from gathering important financial information. This underscores the need for increased financial literacy for women. Although their lack of comfort talking to financial professionals may be a result of social conditioning, it can be overcome through increased understanding of the goals and decision-making process for women.

Women under the age of 35 are dealing with unexpected hardships. The Great Recession and the rising cost of education have made advancement especially difficult for them. They have the highest unemployment rate of any age group and the lowest rate of financial product ownership. According to Prudential Financial (2012), 22 percent of women under 35 lack a checking or savings account. Additionally, 67 percent of those surveyed depend on family or friends for financial support. Although this demographic is also the most eager for financial information, financial professionals must to a better job educating younger women in order to prevent them from accruing debt and ruining their credit. This group of women more than their predecessors sees the value and need for financial literacy and stability. However, reaching them must be done on their terms. As previously stated, this demographic relies heavily on the word of friends, family, and social media sources such as Facebook. The ability to gather information from these sources is paramount to them.

DEFINING SUCCESS AND FAILURE

As men and women define success differently, they also have contrasting views of failure. Although both male and female business owners state that hard work is the key factor in recovering from a business failure, men are much more likely than women to ascribe the recovery to self-confidence (33.3 percent versus 17.5 percent) (Robb et al. 2014). When a man fails, he points to factors like "didn't study enough" or "not interested in the subject matter." When a woman fails, she is more likely to believe that failure results from an inherent lack of ability. In situations in which a man and a woman each receive negative feedback, the women's self-confidence and self-esteem drop by a much greater degree. The internalization of failure and the insecurity it breeds hurt future performance, so this pattern has serious long-term consequences (Sandberg 2013). This difference means that men recover from failure and are quickly ready to move forward and even take risks again. Yet, women tend to feel the failure and need a longer period of time before moving forward. This characteristic can also result in decreased risk tolerance for women. During this post-failure period it is imperative for women to have more support to overcome these effects on their self-esteem and self-confidence.

Men possess a more positive opinion of their capabilities as entrepreneurs. Despite similar levels of education and experience, less than half of women (47.7 percent) express confidence in their ability to start a business, compared with nearly two-thirds (62.1 percent) of men. In Japan, where women assume a secondary role to men, only 5 percent of women surveyed believe they have the requisite skills to launch a business (Clifford 2013). However, this social engineering and conditioning can be overcome.

Supporting women entrepreneurs during the early stages of a business venture is critical to their success. Talented women should be encouraged to return to entrepreneurship-related activities after initial setbacks and develop new opportunities for future success. Helping women understand the cause of the setback by providing practical education can help them return to entrepreneurship. This period of growth can also be a catalyst for their future achievement, because they will carry this information forward and help inform future decisions.

GENDER INEQUALITY IN FINANCE

In the financial industry, women continue to be severely underrepresented. Although finance organizations now recognize the need for greater diversity in the workplace, progress has moved at a very slow pace. As Chandler (2015) reports, women constitute just 9 percent and 6 percent of senior management in venture capital and private equity firms, respectively. Women occupy just 3 percent of senior positions in hedge funds. Although the figures have improved from a decade ago, they have not kept pace with other industries. To rectify this imbalance, financial companies must identify talent early and implement plans to prepare female professionals for future leadership positions. A study by Bardon, Devillard, and Hazelwood (2015) reveals that gender diversity was a top 10 strategic priority for just 28 percent of companies. One-third of companies surveyed had no plans for improving gender diversity within their structures or culture.

According to the Bureau of Labor Statistics (2015), financial planning is expected to be one of the fastest-growing fields in the United States, yet the number of women joining practices has stagnated. Only 23 percent of Certified Financial Planners (CFPs) are women, even as the number of CFPs has increased (Certified Financial Planner Board of Standards, Inc. 2015). A report by the Certified Financial Planner Board of Standards, Inc. (2014) shows that 42 percent of CFP® professionals believe that more women would be drawn to the profession if firms used a salary-based pay model instead of commissions or pay based on AUM. According to Kingsbury (2015, p. 4),

> It is a myth that women are not interested in their financial lives. They're interested, but they want a female-friendly advisor who will coach and educate them about how to best navigate the twists and turns of their financial lives. Not one that just sells products.

Women are especially well suited for careers in financial planning. They tend to be good listeners, forward looking, and holistic in their approach to planning. Although married and single women rarely express a gender preference, one in four women who are widowed or divorced strongly prefer a female advisor (Ettinger and O'Connor 2011). For this demographic, the driving forces in the decision on choosing an advisor are comfort and relatability. To remain competitive, senior partners must do a better job advocating for gender balance in the workplace.

Gender equality in finance will be realized only when public and private institutions make a commitment to foster a more inclusive corporate culture. Even after decades of progress, many companies still lack gender diversity. Consequently, balancing the scales involving gender diversity and equality is likely to take time.

FINANCIAL CONCERNS FOR WOMEN

The thought of running out of money in their later years is a concern shared by many successful women. Even those with considerable financial knowledge often fear they may not have enough money set aside to support their families after retirement.

The pressures of caregiving can compound these worries. Many women assume full responsibility for caretaking needs, which takes both an emotional and a financial toll. Adults over the age of 50 who look after their parents lose roughly $3 trillion in wages, Social Security, and pensions. The financial cost is higher for women, who exhaust an estimated $324,044 as a result of caregiving—$40,328 more than men in caregiving roles. Rising healthcare costs threaten to only exacerbate the problem. Additionally, women are more likely than men to sacrifice career ambitions to care for others: 16 percent of women take less demanding jobs (compared to 6 percent of men) and 12 percent give up work entirely (3 percent of men). A total of 70 percent of working caregivers report difficulties at work because of their responsibilities at home (Family Caregiver Alliance 2012).

Between caregiving and increased life expectancies, the financial concerns of women are justified. These uncertainties force women to be more cautious and pragmatic when planning for retirement. Men approaching retirement age tend to focus narrowly on the needs of their partners, whereas women consider all members of their extended family: grown children, grandchildren, parents, siblings, and other relatives.

Although women still save less for retirement than their male counterparts, their attitudes toward saving and planning are changing. In a survey by Fidelity Investments (2015b), 74 percent of female respondents said that they are proactive about saving for the future. Additionally, 81percent said that they have become more involved in their long-term financial planning over the past five years, and 83 percent want to become more involved within the coming year.

Closing the Gender Gap in Financial Wellness

Studies on financial wellness demonstrate tangible results. For example, an annual survey by Financial Finesse (2015) reports a 4.2 percent increase between 2012 and 2014 in the number of women who consider themselves on track for retirement. For men, this figure dropped 1.5 percent over the same time span (Hannon 2015), Women professionals are taking greater control of their personal finances and reaping the rewards.

The number of women who have placed money in an emergency fund has also increased. Though women are doing a better job preparing for the future, they still trail behind their male colleagues in money management and investment practices. Men tend to be more confident in their investment strategy. Only 34 percent of women feel confident that their investments are properly allocated compared to 48 percent of men. Similarly, 55 percent of men say they have taken a risk-tolerance assessment; just 40 percent of women offer the same response (Financial Finesse 2015).

According to the U.S. Census Bureau (2015), women are losing an average of $10,672 in annual income due to gender-based wage discrimination. A more aggressive and diversified investment strategy could help counterbalance this income disparity. Yet, the cautiousness of women investors often keeps them from committing to more proactive investment plans.

Summary and Conclusions

Women often unintentionally neglect their personal finances because of other responsibilities. An increasing number of women find themselves in the "sandwich generation," simultaneously responsible for raising their own children and caring for their elderly parents. In many cases, women have to coordinate care for the whole family, such as for both an 8-year-old daughter and an 80-year-old father. Some women are struggling to balance their careers with their family responsibilities. As a result of feeling overwhelmed, overextended, and overworked, many women pay less attention to financial planning. Often this causes women to set aside their jobs to fulfill these responsibilities. Consequently, this leads to a loss in future financial planning opportunities.

A pressing need exists to educate financial professionals on the psychology of women investors. Firms should instruct professionals on how to ask better questions, listen more attentively, and read verbal cues and body language. Professional communication courses should become a prerequisite for advisors. This will ensure a level of service that opens the door to long-term relationships and enhanced client satisfaction. Moreover, the precise skills that strengthen relationships with female investors—such as patience and empathetic listening—will facilitate improved communication and understanding.

Financial professionals who continue to ignore the individual values, motivations, and needs of women investors can expect to see their businesses gradually decline. Instead, increasing the number of women clients should be considered a business opportunity to expand the client base and Assets Under Management (AUM). As women assume a larger role in the global economy, firms should consider adapting their client service and/or business model. The one-size-fits-all approach is no longer an appropriate solution. Women expect customized service and clear communication from financial experts. Women who have experienced major life events, such as divorce or death of a spouse, will undoubtedly have unique needs and preferences. Firms committed to building strong, personal ties with their female clients will enjoy improved client retention and acquisition.

Training and mentoring talented women should be a priority for every financial institution. A diverse workplace is a more adaptable, marketable, and profitable one. Women add value to companies through their intuitive and collaborative approach to client relationships. With women inheriting a greater share of wealth, the demand for female financial advisors and wealth professionals will only grow.

To bridge the confidence gap, financial professionals must improve how they engage women with low financial literacy before providing them with the necessary tools to manage their money with greater ease. They need to remember that women clients often want more time to consider their decision. By making a commitment to better serve women clients, financial professionals will help their clients safeguard their money and gain confidence at any stage of their lives.

DISCUSSION QUESTIONS

1. Explain how men and women view investing differently and why advisors should know this.

2. Explain why women often lack confidence about financial matters and how this may affect their financial decisions.
3. Identify several important financial concerns of women.
4. Discuss how the caregiver role affects investing.
5. Discuss how advisors should treat women.

REFERENCES

American Express Open. 2015. "The 2015 State of Women-Owned Businesses Report." May. Available at http://www.womenable.com/content/userfiles/Amex_OPEN_State_of_WOBs_2015_Executive_Report_finalsm.pdf.

Barton, Dominic, Sandrine Devillard, and Judith Hazelwood. 2015. "Gender Equality: Taking Stock of Where We Are." *McKinsey & Company,* September. Available at http://www.mckinsey.com/insights/organization/gender_equality_taking_stock_of_where_we_are.

Blaney, Eleanor. 2010. *Women's Worth: Finding Your Financial Confidence.* McLean, VA: Direction$ LLC.

Blue, Laura. 2008. "Why Do Women Live Longer Than Men"? *Time,* August 6.Available at http://content.time.com/time/health/article/0,8599,1827162,00.html.

BMO Wealth Institute. 2015. "Financial Concerns of Women." March 1. Available at https://www.bmo.com/privatebank/pdf/Q1-2015-Wealth-Institute-Report-Financial-Concerns-of-Women.pdf.

Boston Consulting Group. 2010. "Leveling the Playing Field; Upgrading Wealth Management Experience for Women." July 1. Available at https://www.bcg.com/documents/file56704.pdf.

Brennan, Bridget. 2009. *Why She Buys: The New Strategy for Reaching the World's Most Powerful Consumers.* New York: Crown Business.

Bureau of Labor Statistics. U.S. Department of Labor. 2008. "The Economics Daily, Women's Earnings as a Percentage of Men's." October 14. Available at http://www.bls.gov/opub/ted/2009/ted_20091014.htm.

Bureau of Labor Statistics. U.S. Department of Labor. 2013. "Women in the Labor Force: A Databook." February 2013. Available at http://www.bls.gov/cps/wlf-databook-2012.pdf.

Bureau of Labor Statistics. U.S. Department of Labor. 2015. "Personal Financial Advisors." December 17. Available at http://www.bls.gov/ooh/business-and-financial/personal-financial-advisors.htm.

Certified Financial Planner Board of Standards. 2014. *Making More Room for Women in the Financial Planning Profession: Recommendations to Increase the Number of Women CFP from CFP Board's Women's Initiative.* Washington, DC: Certified Financial Planner Board of Standards.

Certified Financial Planner Board of Standards. 2015. *CFP® Professional Demographics.* December 31. Available at http://www.cfp.net/news-events/research-facts-figures/cfp-professional-demographics.

Chandler, Sarah. 2015. "Why Are So Few Women in Finance? It's Complicated." *Investopedia.com,* September 23. Available at http://www.investopedia.com/articles/investing/092315/why-are-so-few-women-finance-its-complicated.asp.

Clifford, Catherine. 2013. "Lack of Confidence, Fear of Failure Hold Women Back From Being Entrepreneurs." *Entrepreneur.com.* July 31. Available at http://www.entrepreneur.com/article/227631.

Coates, J. M., and J. Herbert. 2007. *Endogenous Steroids and Financial Risk Taking on a London Trading Floor.* Proceedings of the National Academy of Sciences of the United States of America, New York. Available at http://www.pnas.org/content/105/16/6167.full.pdf.

Durukan, Tulin, and Ibrahim Bozaci. 2011. "The Role of Individual Characteristics on Customer Loyalty." *International Journal of Business and Social Science* 2:23, 213–218.

Ettinger, Heather R., and Eileen M. O'Connor. 2011. "Why Does the Financial Services Industry Still Not Hear Them?" *Women of Wealth*. Family Weath Advisors Council. Available at http://familywealthadvisorscouncil.com/wp-content/uploads/pdf/FWAC_WomenOfWealth_12pp.pdf.

Family Caregiver Alliance. 2012. "Selected Caregiver Statistics." December 31. Available at https://www.caregiver.org/selected-caregiver-statistics.

Fidelity Investments. 2015a. "Fidelity Investments Are Today's Emerging Affluent Investors Millionaires in the Making." *Fidelity.com*. Available at https://www.fidelity.com/about-fidelity/institutional-investment-management/emerging-affluent-investors.

Fidelity Investments. 2015b. "Money Fit Women Study: Executive Summary." Available at. https://www.fidelity.com/bin-public/060_www_fidelity_com/documents/women-fit-money-study.pdf.

Financial Finesse. 2015. "2015 Gender Gap in Financial Wellness." September 14.

Gage, III, Richard L., and Thapa Brijesh. 2012. "Volunteer Motivations and Constraints among College Students: Analysis of the Volunteer Function Inventory and Leisure Constraints Models." *Nonprofit and Volunteer Sector Quarterly* 41:3, 405–430.

Gorman, Ryan. 2015. "Women Now Control More Than Half of US Personal Wealth, Which 'Will Only Increase in Years to Come.'" *BusinessInsider.com*, April 7. Available at http://www.businessinsider.com/women-now-control-more-than-half-of-us-personal-wealth-2015-4.

Grace, Willie. 2014. "Women Build Bigger Businesses." *Houston Style Magazine*, November 6. Available at http://stylemagazine.com/news/2014/nov/06/women-build-bigger-businesses/.

Hannon, Kerry. 2015. "The Unexpected News about Women, Men and Retirement." *Forbes*, September 17. Available at http://www.forbes.com/sites/nextavenue/2015/09/17/the-unexpected-news-about-women-men-and-retirement/#210637d7ffd9.

Harris Poll. 2014. *The 2014 Consumer Financial Literacy Survey*. The National Foundation for Credit Counseling. Available at https://www.nfcc.org/NewsRoom/FinancialLiteracy/files2013/NFCC_2014FinancialLiteracySurvey_datasheet_and_key_findings_031314%20FINAL.pdf.

Ingalhalikar, Madhura, Alex Smith, Drew Parker, Theodore D. Satterthwaite, Mark A. Elliott, Kosha Ruparel, Hankon Hankonarson, Raquel C, Gur, Ruben C. Gur, and Ragini Verma, R. 2014. "Sex Differences in the Structural Connectome of the Human Brain." *Proceedings of the National Academy of Sciences* 111:2, 823–828.

Kingsbury, Kathleen Burns. 2015. "Wealth Institute Report Financial Concerns of Women." *BMO.com*, March. Available at https://www.bmo.com/privatebank/pdf/Q1-2015-Wealth-Institute-Report-Financial-Concerns-of-Women.pdf.

Larimer, Christopher, and Rebecca Hannagan. 2010. "Gender Differences in Follower Behavior: An Experimental Study of Reactions to Ambitious Decision Makers." *Politics and the Life Sciences* 29:3, 40–54.

Levinson, David, James Ponzetti, and Peter Jorgensen. 1999. *Encyclopedia of Human Emotions*. New York: Macmillan Reference.

Melnyk, Valentina, Stijn M. J. Van Osselaer, and Tammo H. A. Bijmolt. 2009. "Are Women More Loyal Customers Than Men? Gender Differences in Loyalty to Firms and Individual Service Providers." *Journal of Marketing* 73:4, 82–96.

Nelson, Julie A. 2012. "Are Women Really More Risk-Averse Than Men?" Working Paper No. 12-05, Global Development and Environment Institute. Available at http://www.ase.tufts.edu/gdae/Pubs/wp/12-05NelsonRiskAverse.pdf.

Newman, Matthew L., Carla J. Groom, Lori D. Handelman, and James W. Pennebaker. 2008. "Gender Differences in Language Use: An Analysis of 14,000 Text Samples." *Discourse Processes* 45:3, 211–236.

Nielsen. 2012. "Don't Ignore Boomers—*The Most Valuable Generation.*" August 6. Available at http://www.nielsen.com/us/en/insights/news/2012/dont-ignore-boomers-the-most-valuable-generation.html.

Niu, Ariel. 2014. "Gender & the Brain: Differences between Women & Men." *Fitbrains.com*, February 18. Available at http://www.fitbrains.com/blog/women-men-brains/.

Oleson, Mark. 2004. "Exploring the Relationship between Money Attitudes and Maslow's Heirarchy of Needs." *International Journal of Consumer Studies* 28:1, 83–92. Available at https://www.deepdyve.com/lp/wiley/exploring-the-relationship-between-money-attitudes-and-maslow-s-BNREIMQYm3.

Patten, Eileen, and Kim Parker. 2012. "A Gender Reversal On Career Aspirations." *PewSocialTrends.org*, April 19. Available at http://www.pewsocialtrends.org/2012/04/19/a-gender-reversal-on-career-aspirations/.

Pew Research Center. 2015. "Women in Leadership Positions." *PewSocialTrends.org*, January 14. Available at http://www.pewsocialtrends.org/2015/01/14/chapter-1-women-in-leadership/.

Powell, Farran. 2014. "Black Women Struggle to Fund Startups." *CNN Money*, November 10. Available at http://money.cnn.com/2014/11/10/smallbusiness/minority-women-entrepreneurs/index.html.

Prudential Financial. 2012. "Financial Experience and Behaviors Among Women: 2010-2011 Prudential Research Study." Available at http://www.prudential.com/media/managed/Womens_Study_Final.pdf.

Prudential Financial. 2015. "Financial Experience and Behaviors Among Women: 2014-2015 PrudentialResearch Study." Available at http://www.prudential.com/media/managed/wm/media/Pru_Women_Study_2014.pdf?src=Newsroom&pg=WomenStudy2014.

Robb, Alicia M., and Susan Coleman. 2009. "Characteristics of New Firms: A Comparison by Gender." Kaufman Foundation. January. Available at http://www.kauffman.org/~/media/kauffman_org/research%20reports%20and%20covers/2009/02/kfs_gender_020209.pdf.

Robb, Alicia M., Susan Coleman, and Dane Stangler. 2014. "Sources of Economic Hope: Women's Entrepreneurship." Kaufman Foundation. Available at http://www.kauffman.org/what-we-do/research/2014/11/sources-of-economic-hope-womens-entrepreneurship.

Sandberg, Sheryl. 2013. *Lean In: Women, Work and the Will to Lead.* New York: Knopf Doubleday.

State Farm Insurance. 2008. "Many Women Would Rather See the Dentist Than Talk Money with Their Spouse." December 16. Available at http://www.thefreelibrary.com/Many+Women+Would+Rather+See+the+Dentist+Than+Talk+Money+With+Their... -a0190682200.

U.S. Census Bureau. 2015. "Income, Poverty and Health Insurance Coverage in the United States: 2014." *Census.gov*, September 16. Available at http://www.census.gov/newsroom/press-releases/2015/cb15-157.html.

Wang, Wendy, Kim Parker, and Paul Taylor. 2013. "Breadwinner Moms." *PewSocialTrends.org*, May 29. Available at http://www.pewsocialtrends.org/2013/05/29/breadwinner-moms/.

14

The Psychology of Millennials

APRIL RUDIN
Founder and President
Rubin Group

CATHERINE MCBREEN
Managing Director
Spectrem Group

Introduction

The premiere episode of the 41st season of *Saturday Night Live* in October 2015 featured a parody of a commercial for a new TV workplace drama called "The Millennials." Crammed into this short sketch was perhaps every stereotype attached to a generation deemed to be self-absorbed, entitled, and irritating. For instance, one character demands a promotion after having worked at the company for three days. Others engage in obsessively texting on their phones, oblivious to all around them. A third character needs "perspective" and tells her boss she will no longer come to work, but that she is not quitting. The boss, who has spent 25 years working and sacrificing to "claw his way to the top" of this company, sums up his disdain for this new generation of workers: "I hate these kids." The show has never done similar generational parodies about baby boomers or Gen Xers. But millennials seem to be a major target, especially by their elders.

In his *Time* magazine story profiling the demographic of young adults born between 1980 and 2000, Stein (2013) reflects on what he calls the "Me Me Me Generation." This barbed portrait casts millennials in the worst light as coddled, lazy, and above all, narcissistic. Yet, regarding how millennials will shape the financial services industry and the future of advisor–client relationships, maybe the attention is all about them—if not today, then certainly tomorrow and for decades to come. To paraphrase Bob Dylan, the times are changing once again.

Currently, baby boomers dominate the ownership of investment assets. They also represent the largest percentage of investors to currently reply on financial advisors. Millennials, at 80 million strong, have surpassed baby boomers as the largest generation. In 2015, millennials represented more than one-fourth of the U.S. population (Census Bureau 2015) and represented more than one in three American workers (Fry 2015a). By 2020, millennials will constitute about 46 percent of all U.S. workers (Brack and Kelly 2012). This group also has the potential to become the wealthiest generation so far.

This chapter discusses qualitative and quantitative age and wealth-segment research of millennials by the Spectrem Group and the investment attitudes and behaviors of millennials by the Rudin Group. It specifically examines how the financial crisis of 2007–2008 helped shape their attitudes toward personal financial situations, the overall financial services industry, and financial advisors. This research indicates that millennials, as were the boomers before them, are poised to leave their imprint on the financial services industry, changing business as usual in the way they interact with advisors, whether human or robo, and whether they use twenty-first-century tools and resources to shape their financial futures.

Millennials and Boomers—Two Different Worlds

The rules of engagement by which financial advisors conduct business with their baby boomer clients is unlikely to be as effective with the millennials, who grew up during financially unstable times. According to Facebook IQ (2016), a little over half, or 53 percent of millennials feel they have no one they can trust for financial guidance, and in fact only 8 percent trust financial institutions for such advice. The Facebook study reports that millennials drive 40 percent of the financial conversations on the social network, generating 6.5 million posts, comments, likes, and shares. Baby boomers are the TV generation, but millennials are not bound by one screen; they are "cutting the cord" and viewing the media on their own terms and schedules. More tech-savvy than baby boomers, millennials are also more responsive to the latest gadgets and are quicker to integrate them into their daily lives. Similarly, they are not utilizing the traditional communication platforms; for example, two-thirds of millennials do not have landlines.

But millennials do share their elders' concept of the American dream as envisioned by Pulitzer Prize-winner James Truslow Adams, who coined the term in 1931. He saw America as a land of equal opportunity that would allow people to attain to the fullest stature of which they are innately capable, regardless of the circumstances of birth or position (Adams 1931). Similarly, 6 in 10 millennials define the America dream as "equal opportunity for all people." The second highest percentage of millennials (56 percent) believe that the American dream translates to educational opportunities, whereas 44 percent see it as owning one's own home (Spectrem Group 2015a).

For many financially beleaguered millennials, however, this goal is a dream deferred. Among non-millionaire millennials, ownership of a principal residence is down considerably from 2014—from 62 percent to 50 percent. Nearly half (46 percent) see the American dream as having sufficient retirement assets. This finding indicates that despite financial challenges, millennials view the American dream as aspirational. Figure 14.1 shows the generational divide on how millennials view the American dream as compared to their older counterparts.

MILLENNIALS AND FINANCIAL LITERACY

Several studies provide information about the financial literacy of American millennials. For example, Tang, Baker, and Peter (2015) find that when presented with three basic questions about stocks, interest rates, and inflation, only one-fourth of respondents could answer all three correctly. Furthermore, only 2 percent of respondents show consistently

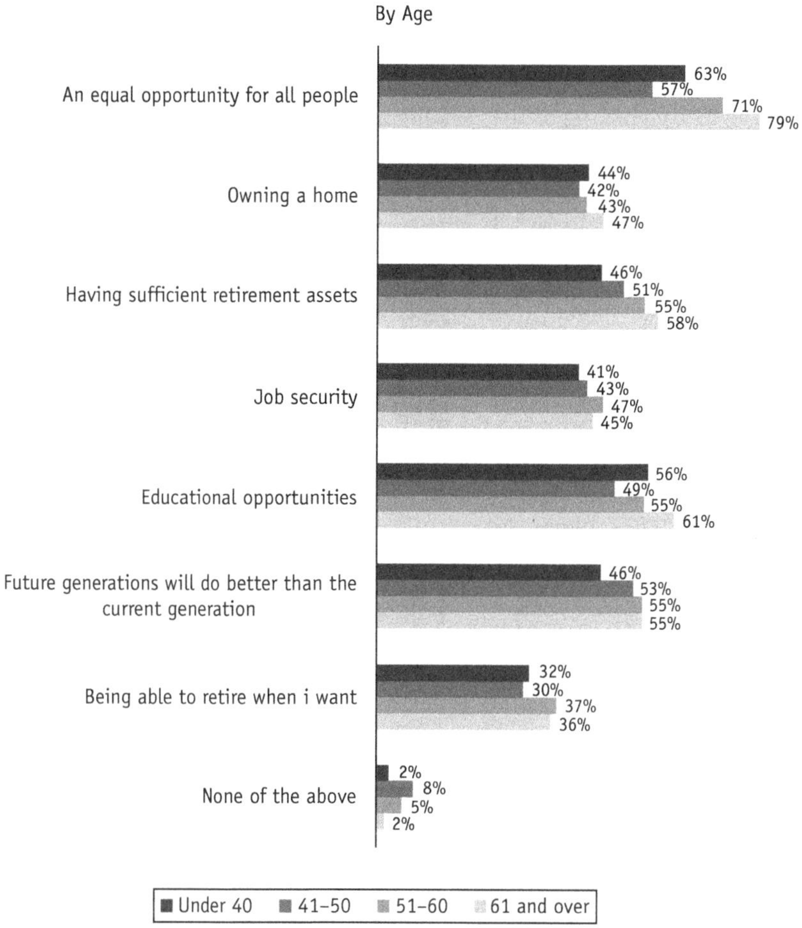

Figure 14.1 Views of the American Dream, by Age Group. This figure shows survey-based data on what the American Dream means to millennials compared to previous generations. Source: Spectrem Group (2015a).

responsible money management behavior in three categories: paying off debts in a timely manner, setting and sticking to a budget, and saving toward retirement; the average survey respondent exhibited responsible behavior in only one of these categories. The study also showed a disconnect between financial knowledge and money management behavior, in that millennials make poor financial choices even though they may know better.

A study by T. Rowe Price (2015) finds a generation that is practicing good financial habits, especially compared with baby boomers. The study also reports that millennials are saving nearly as much for retirement as did baby boomers, but that more millennials have increased their 401(k) savings. The study also found that 75 percent of millennials carefully track their expenses, compared with 64 percent of baby boomers. According to the study, nearly 9 in 10 millennials indicate they are "pretty good" at living within their means, while roughly three-fourths profess being more comfortable saving and investing their extra money than spending it. According to a Wells Fargo

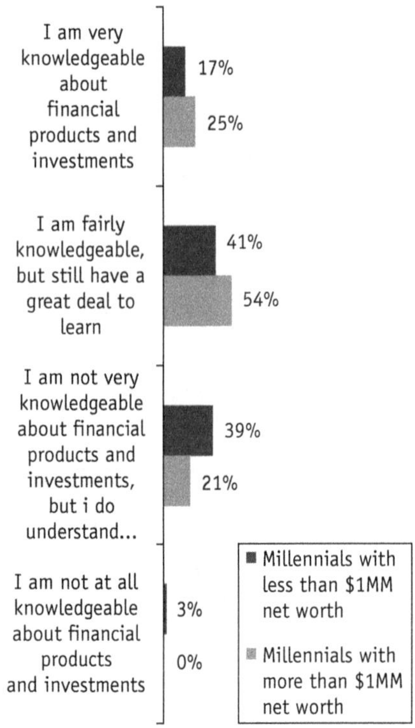

Figure 14.2 Knowledge Level for Investors, by Age Group and Income. This figure shows survey-based data on how non-millionaire and millionaire millennials perceive their financial literacy regarding financial products and investments. Source: Spectrem Group (2015i).

(2014) study, 8 out of 10 millennials report that the Great Recession taught them to save "now" to prepare in case of future economic problems.

According to a study by Bank of America/USA TODAY (2015), nearly 7 in 10 millennials (68 percent) learned about money from their parents. Although 60 percent feel their parents did a good job teaching them about finances, almost half (47 percent) wish they had started talking to them about money sooner.

Contrary to the common stereotype, millennials have few illusions about their financial literacy. Among non-millionaire and millionaire millennials, the highest percentages consider themselves only fairly knowledgeable, with still much to learn about financial products and investments (Spectrem Group 2015i), but millionaires are more likely than non-millionaires to describe their financial knowledge this way than non-millionaires (54 percent vs. 41 percent). Figure 14.2 shows the confidence levels of non-millionaire and millionaire millennials regarding their financial knowledge.

THE MILLENNIAL MINDSET

Millennials came of age during the financial crisis of 2007–2008, the worst economic crisis since the Great Depression. During this period, many of the largest and most recognized financial institutions folded, including Lehman Brothers, Bear Stearns, and Countrywide. Younger millennials witnessed the devastation that the financial crisis inflicted on their parents' financial situations, while older millennials entering the workforce found the job market rife with layoffs and unemployment.

The financial crisis was a profound reality check for millennials. Seven in 10 Americans believe that a college education is very important (Newport and Busteed 2013); interestingly, in 1978, when Gallup first asked this question in a survey, only 36 percent considered a college education to be very important. According to the Council of Economic Advisors (2014), though, millennials are the most educated generation, with almost half (47 percent) having earned some postsecondary degree, compared to nearly one-third of baby boomers who reached that same milestone. Millennials with a net worth of at least $1 million are more apt to credit their education, rather than hard work, as their primary wealth-creation factor, compared to Gen Xers, baby boomers, and seniors, who rank their education as second behind hard work (Spectrem Group 2013).

According to an analysis of government data, half of today's college graduates are either unemployed or underemployed in jobs for which they are either overqualified or not in their field of study (Yen 2012). The national unemployment rate for young adults ages 18 to 34 years old reached a recession height of 12.4 percent in 2010, but by the first half of 2015 this rate had dropped to 7.7 percent, yet it was still well above the national average of roughly 5.5 percent for the same period (Fry 2015b).

According to Patten and Fry (2015), millennial men are not only less likely than their Gen X counterparts to be employed but also less likely to be employed compared with baby boomers and seniors when they were the same age (primarily in the 1970s and 1980s). Millennial women are also less likely to be employed compared with Gen Xers, but they are in a better position employment-wise than their baby boomer and so-called silent generation forebears (women of previous generations who more commonly stayed home and raised a family). Many millennials are compelled to delay important long-term life decisions, such as starting a family and buying a house, because of the financial challenge of unprecedented student debt, which is reported at more than $1 trillion (Kantrowitz 2016).

This pattern has earned millennials the sobriquet of "boomerang children"—young adults waiting out a constrained job market or otherwise unable to afford a place of their own, and having returned home to live with their parents. In 2015, 15.1 percent of 25- to 34-year-olds were living at home (Matthews 2015), which is the fourth straight annual increase for this group.

In fact, U.S. Census Bureau data show that 36.4 percent of millennial women ages 18 to 34 lived with their families in 2014, the highest percentage since 1940. These young women are more likely to be college educated and unmarried than earlier generations of American women in this age group, as they struggle with economic issues such as student debt, high cost of living, prolonged economic downturn, and a challenging job market. As for millennial men, the data show that 42.8 percent lived with their parents or relatives in 2014, but this was below the 47.5 percent recorded for men in 1940 (Fry 2015c).

Besides getting room and board, 35 percent of millennials report receiving parental financial assistance (Bank of America/USA TODAY 2015). At least 20 percent get financial help to pay their cellphone bills, groceries, and unexpected expenses. Further,

80 percent of those who receive help from the "bank of mom and dad" report that they know many friends their age receiving similar assistance.

A ROSIER LONG VIEW

Despite their difficult circumstances, millennials are relatively optimistic about their short- and long-term financial futures. Rather than living only for today, as exemplified in some of the harsher media portrayals, many are proactively planning for their retirement. A generation that has never known a day without the Internet is using mobile devices to manage their finances, as well as to increase their financial literacy.

Three-fourths of non-millionaire millennials with a net worth of at least $100,000, excluding a primary residence, report that their financial situation is currently better than it was one year ago (Spectrem Group 2015c). This observation is on a par with Gen Xers and well above the 60 percent of those surveyed who ages 45 and up. Eight in 10 of non-millionaire millennials and their Gen X cohorts are equally confident that their financial situation will be stronger one year from now than at present.

Millionaire millennials with a net worth between $1 million and $5 million, excluding a primary residence, offer a more cautious view of their present and future financial situations, with 6 in 10 indicating that they are better off now than one year ago, and three-fourths expecting to be in a stronger position financially one year from now (Spectrem Group 2015h). This same trend exists for their ultra-high net worth (UHNW) counterparts, or those with a net worth between $5 million and $25 million. Six in 10 of them report they were better off financially in 2015 than in the previous year, whereas about 7 in 10 expect to be better off in the next 12 months (Spectrem Group 2015k).

Of the non-millionaire millennials, 71 percent indicate that they fully expect to have sufficient income to live comfortably during retirement. They are not alone in their guardedly optimistic forecasts. Of non-millionaire Gen Xers, 64 percent feel similarly, along with 62 percent of baby boomers and a more confident 78 percent of the seniors. Millionaire millennials are less confident than previous generations that they will have sufficient income to live comfortably during retirement (Spectrem Group 2015i). Figure 14.3 shows how non-millionaire and millionaire millennials gauge their retirement security.

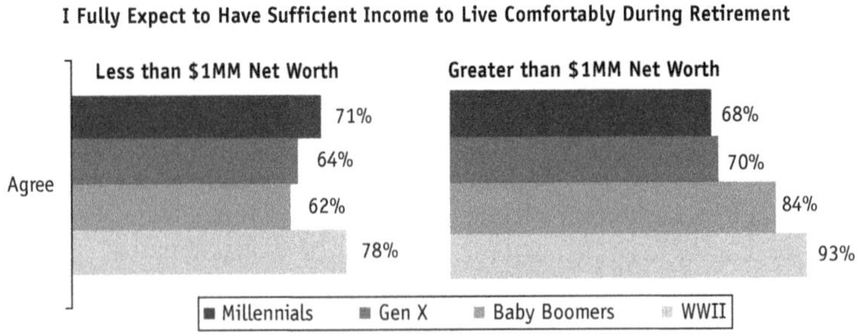

Figure 14.3 Survey Responses to Question about Retirement Planning. This figure shows survey-based data about how millennials view their retirement security compared to previous generations. Source: Spectrem Group (2015i).

A majority of young adults are confident they will be able to live comfortably in retirement on their income. This situation represents an opportunity for financial advisors to engage them on financial planning. As millennials embark on their careers, a primary concern is seeking adequate help that will allow them to reach their financial goals.

NATIONAL AND PERSONAL CONCERNS

Financial advisors seeking to engage millennials should know what national and personal issues weigh most on their minds. On the national front, young adults with a net worth of less than $1 million are most concerned about tax increases, followed closely by the fractious political environment. At least two-thirds rank the federal deficit as the national issue most on their minds. Additionally, 6 in 10 identify low interest rates on savings, inflation, and stock market performance as concerns. On the personal front, non-millionaire millennials are most concerned about two of the most pressing financial matters they will face in their lifetimes: financing their children's education, and being able to retire when they want to. These concerns even take precedence over maintaining their current financial situation (Spectrem Group 2015i).

Millennials recognize that health concerns could have a direct impact on their retirement savings. A majority of them express concern about taking responsibility for their aging parents, a percentage on a par with the Gen Xers and baby boomers. Roughly 4 in 10 non-millionaire millennials cite their own health, the health of their spouse, a family health catastrophe, and spending their final years in a healthcare facility as their primary personal concerns (Spectrem Group 2015c).

On two financial issues, non-millionaire millennials express even greater concern than their older counterparts. The first involves using their wealth to help others, while the second is about business revenues for an entity they own. The latter speaks to another generational difference. Unlike previous generations, whose careers followed the traditional 9-to-5 route at a company, millennials want to start their own businesses. Nearly one-third (32 percent) of millennials who are self-employed are running their own start-ups, compared to just 9 percent of their baby boomer cohorts (TD Ameritrade 2015).

Millennials and the Use of Financial Advisors

Millennials represent a strong growth opportunity for financial advisors. As Figure 14.4 shows, young adults with a net worth of less than $1 million are more likely than older investors to identify themselves as self-directed, meaning they make all their financial and investment decisions without the guidance of a professional advisor. Increasing age is generally associated with greater wealth and more instances in which investors seek a financial advisor. Figure 14.4 shows how millennials engage financial advisors compared to older households.

Figure 14.4 shows that millennials eschew using a financial advisor primarily as a matter of frugality and a perception that financial advisors would not deem them worthwhile clients. Almost half (46 percent) of non-millionaire millennial households believe they cannot afford a financial advisor, and at the same time they consider their assets

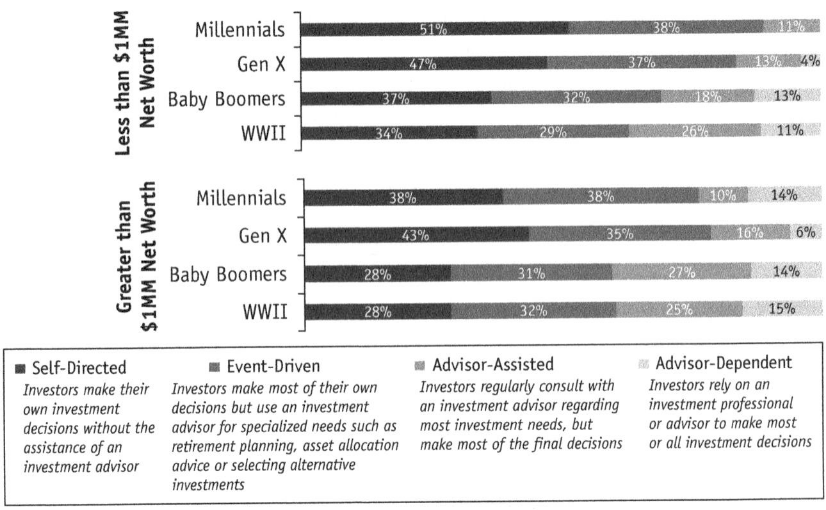

Figure 14.4 Degree of Advisor Use, by Age Group and Income. This figure shows how Millennials engage financial advisors compared with older households. Source: Spectrem Group (2015i).

insufficient to justify using one. Tellingly, their wealthier counterparts in millionaire and UHNW households indicate they do not use financial advisors primarily because they feel they can do a better job (Spectrem Group 2015b, 2015f, 2015j).

According to Bond (2015), millennials do not trust financial planners, for several reasons. One is the negative reputation of the financial industry as a result of the financial crisis of 2008. Additionally, reasons include the income inequality debate, confusing jargon, high fees, cultural differences, and Internet or media access to free financial planning information such as on Yahoo! Finance, *CNN Money*, and *MSN Money*.

And if many millennials are not seeking the advice of a financial advisor, the feeling seems to be mutual. Only 30 percent of financial advisors are actively looking for clients in this age demographic. The belief is that younger individuals have lower income and less wealth. And generally speaking, older households have more assets and most advisors get paid on a percentage of those assets. Older baby boomers own 22 times more in assets than households under age 35, so financial advisors understandably want to focus their attention on this older demographic (Steverman 2015).

However, according to Andree (2015), millennials possess some valuable qualities. For example, they have an entrepreneurial spirit and want to leave their mark on the world. Additionally, millennials are well informed and tech-savvy. They also want to build community and often seek information, especially online.

THE IMPETUS FOR SEEKING FINANCIAL ADVICE

What would compel millennials to consider using an advisor? Regardless of their wealth level, a majority cite three scenarios: (1) receiving a windfall of money with which they would need help investing; (2) a specific financial situation for which they would seek professional advice, such as creating a financial plan; and (3) a situation in which they could receive a financial advisor's services for what they perceive to be a fair price (Spectrem Group 2015b, 2015f, 2015j).

Non-millionaire millennials are much more likely than their older counterparts to consult a financial advisor in these situations. Nearly 4 in 10 (38 percent) would consider using an advisor following a change in their household status, such as marriage or a new baby, compared with 8 percent of Gen Xers, 16 percent of those ages 45 to 54, and 9 percent of baby boomers. They are also at least twice as likely as older households to consider using an advisor should they tire of managing their investments (Spectrem Group 2015b). Under these circumstances, millionaire millennials would be more likely than their older cohorts to consider engaging a financial advisor. As their wealth increases, the percentage of millennials who might consider using a financial advisor also increases if they no longer want to manage their investments.

HOW MILLENNIALS VIEW A FINANCIAL ADVISOR

Despite the popularity of technology, this age demographic finds advisors through referrals, which older generations also use. According to Johnson and Larson (2009, p. 66), consumers generally "use word-of-mouth referrals [because] they trust the people they are asking to give them a good recommendation, and consumers trust friends, relatives, and experts they know in a related field." Regardless of their wealth level, millennials are most likely to be referred to an advisor by a family member or friend (Spectrem Group 2015b, 2015f, 2015j).

Millennials seek specific characteristics from their advisors and place the highest premium on perceived honesty and trustworthiness. This first generation of digital natives, whose homes likely contain at least one computer and who post and tweet about their personal lives on Facebook, Twitter, and other social media, lives by transparency and expects similar openness from a financial advisor. Indeed, millennials place less emphasis on fees or commissions charged, or whether the advisor's firm is well known, than on the advisor's investment track record or the quality of referrals.

When they use them, millennials enter into a working relationship with a financial advisor armed with preferences and prejudices. First and foremost, they expect their advisors to respond promptly to inquiries and questions. They also prefer to work with one advisor who handles all facets of their wealth. That their advisor has professional registrations and licenses is less important than it is for older households, but millennials place more importance on their advisor's regularly outperforming the market. Nearly 6 in 10 non-millionaire millennials rate their advisors on whether they regularly outperforms the market, compared with 53 percent of millionaires and 42 percent of UHNW households (Spectrem Group 2015b, 2015f, 2015j).

Are financial advisors biased toward certain investment groups or products? A majority of millennials think so. To a lesser extent, they also feel that advisors are more concerned with selling products than with helping their clients. According to a study by the Pew Research Center (2014), this skepticism is perhaps endemic to millennials. The study reports that only 19 percent of millennials believe that most people can be trusted, compared with 31 percent of Gen Xers, 37 percent of seniors, and 40 percent of baby boomers.

TRUST ISSUES FOR MILLENNIALS

Among affluent investors, trust in one's financial advisor increases with age. This is not surprising. On a scale of from 0 to 100, with 100 equaling "great trust," non-millionaire millennials rate their trust of financial advisors at only 69, compared to 75 for Gen Xers, 79 for those ages 45 to 54, 82 for baby boomers, and 83 for seniors. Although the scores are relatively higher for millionaire and UHNW millennials, they nonetheless express less trust in financial advisors than do their older counterparts (Spectrem Group 2015b).

How do millennials define trust as it pertains to a financial advisor? The highest percentage consider trust to mean that the financial advisor is looking out for the client's best interests, followed by an advisor's admission if he is wrong. Also, millennials are much more likely to express these views than would their older cohorts. They are also most likely to see the advisor–client relationship as one in which the advisor can be counted on to make no mistakes (Spectrem Group 2015b, 2015f, 2015j).

Millennials are less likely than older investors to insist that the advisor contact them regularly. They are also generally less likely to expect the advisor to relay important information pertaining to their investments. That is, financial advisors find that millennials are engaged investors who may be less inclined to be actively involved in the day-to-day management of their investments, but who enjoy investing and would not want to give it up. Non-millionaire and millionaire millennials prefer advisors to contact them on a quarterly or at least a semi-annually basis (Spectrem Group 2015b, 2015f).

RISK TOLERANCE AND INVESTMENT PREFERENCES

As might be expected, millennial investors have a higher tolerance for risk than do older investors. Somewhat more than half (54 percent) of non-millionaire millennials indicate that they are willing to take substantial investment risk on a portion of their investments so as to earn a high return, compared with 44 percent of investors ages 45 to 54, 37 percent of baby boomers, and 27 percent of seniors ages 65 and up (Spectrem Group 2015c). This evidence does not suggest that millennials invest without regard to risk, however. Regardless of their wealth level, millennials consider the risk associated with an investment as the most important factor in investment selection, followed by an investment's tax implications and the diversity of the investment (Spectrem Group 2015b, 2015f, 2015j).

According a separate study, non-millionaire millennials are more likely to consider an investment's track record as an investment selection factor (79 percent) than are their millionaire (53 percent) and UHNW (54 percent) counterparts. They are also more impressed by the reputation of the firm making their investments. Three-fourths of non-millionaire millennials consider the firm's reputation when selecting an investment, compared with 62 percent of millionaire and 65 percent of UHNW millennials investors (Spectrem Group 2015c, 2015h, 2015k).

As Figure 14.5 shows, the social responsibility of an investment tends to have a higher priority among younger investors than among older households. More so than other generations, millennials are inclined to choose companies that are not only "performing well" but that also are "doing good." But across all wealth segments and all age

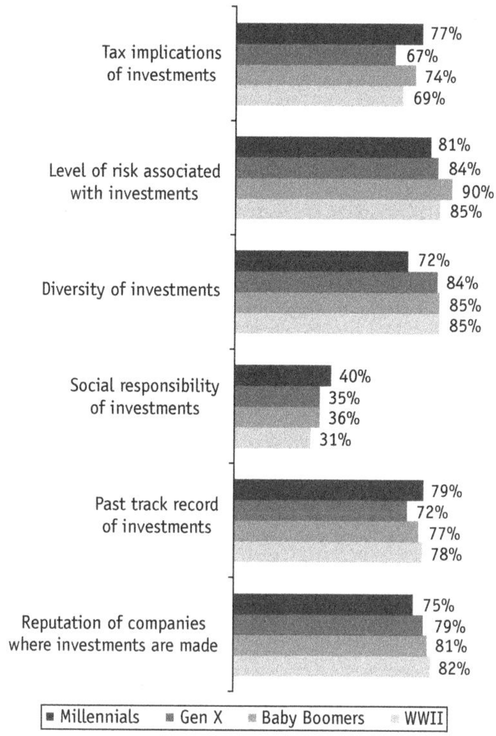

Figure 14.5 Generational Criteria for Making Investment Decisions. This figure shows survey-based data indicating the factors millennials consider to be the most important in selecting an investment, compared with previous generations. Source: Spectrem Group (2015i).

groups, less than 50 percent cite social responsibility as a primary investment selection factor. Millennials are no different than older generations; the highest percentage of them consider their investment objectives to be purely financial.

HOUSEHOLD MONEY MANAGEMENT

In terms of financial planning, there are several ways for financial advisors to engage millennials. One major category of millennials' concern is debt. Across all wealth segments, millennials make up the highest percentage of respondents who indicated concern about the amount of debt their households currently carry.

Debt is a real and growing concern. Whether the debt involves student loans, home mortgages, or car payments, two-thirds of millennials of ages 23 to 35 in 2012 reported having at least one source of outstanding long-term debt. Thirty percent indicated more than one loan, and 81 percent of college graduates mentioned having at least one source of long-term debt. One-third of millennials with annual household income above $75,000 doubt they will be able to repay their student loans. And besides student loans, or long-term debt, millennials carry short-term debt, mostly credit card balances. More than half of millennials who used credit cards in 2015 reported carrying a balance in the previous 12 months—a balance for which they were charged interest (Scheresberg and Lusardi 2015).

How are millennials handling their household finances? As have their elders, millennials are most likely to pool finances as a household (Spectrem Group 2015c, 2015h, 2015k). However, the number of millennial households that make their financial decisions jointly decreases with an increase in wealth. Seven in 10 non-millionaire millennial households make their decisions jointly, compared with 61 percent of millionaire households and just 35 percent of UHNW households. That is, the number of millennial households in which the husband makes most of the financial decisions increases with wealth, from just 15 percent of non-millionaires to 35 percent of millionaire and 59 percent of UHNW millennials. Accordingly, the rate of spousal agreement about finances is higher among non-millionaire millennials than it is for their wealthier counterparts. But between spouses and financial advisors, the latter are credited with being more helpful in making financial decisions as a household's net worth increases. Non-millionaire millennials scored financial advisors at 61 on a scale of 0 to 100, on which 100 equaled "very helpful." In comparison, they scored their spouses at 69. Millionaires gave their financial advisors a score of 60 and their spouses a 56 on the helpfulness scale, whereas UHNW millennials gave their financial advisors a 61 versus a 60 for their spouses.

The degree of wealth is a factor in how millennials engage financial advisors. Non-millionaire millennials report that they control 73 percent of their assets without any professional help, compared with millionaires, who control 53 percent of their assets and UHNW Millennials, who report controlling 52 percent. Across all wealth segments, older investors tend to cede more control of their assets to an advisor. Millionaire millennials have financial advisors controlling over the highest percentage of their assets—20 percent versus 9 percent among non-millionaires and 13 percent among UHNWs. The latter consult with a financial advisor, but make the final investment decisions themselves for over 35 percent of their assets, compared with 27 percent for millionaires and 18 percent for non-millionaires. Non-millionaire millennials are most likely to turn to a discount broker or independent financial planner, whereas their wealthier counterparts are more likely to engage the services of a full-service broker (Spectrem Group 2015b, 2015f, 2015j).

The Role for a Financial Advisor

What advice does an financial advisor most likely provide to millennials? Among non-millionaires, the likelihood of receiving advice about creating a financial plan increases with age. Millennials are twice as likely as earlier generations to receive this advice from someone other than a primary financial advisor. This means they are turning to lawyers, accountants, or even the Internet for this type of advice. Millionaire and UHNW millennials are also more likely than older generations to have received this advice from someone other than their primary advisor (Spectrem Group 2015b, 2015f, 2015j).

What do these affluent young adults think is most important to include in their financial plan? For non-millionaire and millionaire millennials, the most important items are the investment rate of return needed to meet their financial goals, as well as how to calculate their present net worth. Besides these factors, UHNW millennials think their financial plan should include tax-planning advice and guidelines (Spectrem Group 2015b, 2015f, 2015j).

Additionally, non-millionaires and millionaires in this age group are more likely than their older counterparts to indicate a willingness to seek advice in the future about a wider range of issues. These issues include diversifying their assets; selecting individual stocks, bonds, and mutual funds; implementing tax-advantage financial strategies; seeking alternative investments such as hedge funds; using credit effectively; and establishing retirement income streams. Currently, these millennials are the most likely to indicate they are already receiving advice about these issues from someone other than a primary advisor. Generally this means they are turning to family members or friends for advice, as well as researching topics on their own on the Internet (Spectrem Group 2015b, 2015f, 2015j).

As non-millionaire millennials are more likely than wealthier households to identify themselves as self-directed investors, they make up the highest percentage of millennials who would be "likely" (54 percent) to use an advisor in the future. In comparison, 25 percent of millionaire and UHNW millennials indicate they would "likely" use an advisor in the future (Spectrem Group 2015b, 2015f, 2015j).

ADVISOR SATISFACTION

Are millennials harder to please than older investors? Regardless of their wealth level, roughly half of all millennials report that overall they are satisfied with their advisors. The percentages increase with age.

Specifically, among surveyed non-millionaires, millennials are less likely than their older counterparts to express satisfaction with their advisor's knowledge and expertise (57 percent), responsiveness to requests (54 percent), and performance (45 percent). Millionaire and UHNW millennials are the least satisfied with their advisor's performance in comparison to older households (Spectrem Group 2015b, 2015f, 2015j).

The greatest concern of the millennial investors who work with a financial advisor is a failure to communicate. Yet, this is just one of the reasons millennials would switch advisors, in contrast with older generations. Among non-millionaire millennial investors who do use an advisor, nearly 7 in 10 indicate they would fire their advisor if their phone calls were not returned in a timely manner (e.g., by at least the next day). Only 50 percent of non-millionaires ages 36 to 44 feel likewise, as do 54 percent of those ages 45 to 54, with roughly two-thirds of baby boomers and seniors agreeing with that sentiment. Similarly, non-millionaire millennials are slightly more likely than older generations to indicate they would switch if their advisors did not return e-mails in a timely manner (Spectrem Group 2015b).

Non-millionaire millennials would also be more likely than older generations to change their financial advisors after losses accrued over the span of one, two, or five years, and if the advisor is underperforming compared to the overall stock market. Older investors express a willingness to change advisors because of a lack of proactive contact, as well as if their advisors talked to them only about investments and seemed not concerned about their overall financial situation.

Regarding fees, non-millionaire and millionaire millennials are more likely than older generations to consider the services of a professional advisor to be expensive; UHNW millennials feel less so in this regard. Especially, non-millionaire millennials do not adopt the mindset of being unconcerned about the fees they pay as long as their assets are growing. In fact, roughly one-fourth express being unconcerned about the fees they pay as long as their assets are growing, compared with 32 percent of Gen Xers, roughly 30 percent of baby boomers, and one-third of seniors. Among all surveyed non-millionaire and millionaire investors, millennials constitute the highest number who prefer to pay fixed fees for financial and investment advice (Spectrem Group, 2015b, 2015f, 2015j).

In fact, millennials consider fee-only planners more likely to possess the trustworthiness, honesty, and thoroughness they seek in an advisor (Johnson and Larson, 2009). The highest percentage of UHNW millennials prefer that the cost of financial advice be tied to product performance. Yet across all wealth segments, millennials' comfort level with the fees they pay is on a par with their older counterparts.

The actions that financial advisors take with their millionaire millennial clients seem to be working, because 42 percent of those millennials state they are more satisfied with their advisor today than they have been in the past, compared with 29 percent of Gen Xers, 31 percent of those ages 36 to 44, 37 percent of baby boomers, and 36 percent of seniors ages 65 and up. Non-millionaires and UHNW millennials are the least likely across all age groups to report they are currently more satisfied today than in the past with their advisor. Additionally, millionaire millennials are more likely than their older counterparts to believe their financial advisors are very professional or knowledgeable; UHNW millennials are the least likely to express this opinion (Spectrem Group 2015b, 2015f, 2015j).

What do millennials expect from their financial advisors? Regardless of wealth level, millennials put the highest premium on an advisor who offers products from different companies, has professional registrations and licenses, and responds promptly to their inquiries and questions. Although having their advisor call them regularly is less a priority across all wealth segments, this service is more important to millionaire millennials (42 percent) than it is for their non-millionaire (24 percent) and UHNW counterparts (33 percent) (Spectrem Group 2015b, 2015f, 2015j).

Millionaire millennials indicate they are most in agreement with their advisors. For example, 84 percent feel their advisor understands their appetite for risk, compared with 68 percent of non-millionaires and 71 percent of UHNW households. How does this translate to a referral? On a scale of 0 to 10, with 10 equaling "highly likely," the highest percentage of millennials who scored between 0 and 6 on whether they would recommend their primary advisor to a friend or colleague were non-millionaire and UHNW households. Millionaire millennials are more likely than older investors to score between 7 and 8 (Spectrem Group 2015f).

Not surprisingly, millionaire millennials express more loyalty to their financial advisors than do non-millionaires or UHNW households. When asked what they would do if their advisor left the firm for another, 58 percent of millionaires said they would move with their advisor. In comparison, 41 percent of non-millionaires and 46 percent of UHNW responded similarly. With the exception of Gen X millionaires, non-millionaire and UHNW millennials indicate they would be most likely across the generations to stay with the firm, indicating that changing would be too much of a hassle (Spectrem Group 2015f).

TECHNOLOGY AND FINANCIAL INFORMATION

Complicating the financial advisor–client dynamic, but representing yet another opportunity to engage young adults, is the Internet and mobile technology that put storehouses of news and information just a click away. According to the Council of Economic Advisers (2014), millennials are more connected to technology than older generations, and one-fourth of millennials believe that relationship to technology is what makes their generation unique. According to the Council of Economic Advisers (p. 7), "While all generations have experienced technological advances, the sheer amount of computational power and access to information that Millennials have had at their fingertips since grade-school is unparalleled."

Not surprisingly, millennials more than older age segments consider traditional news channels and platforms such as the telephone, newspapers, and television to be outdated, and are more apt to rely on social media to communicate and to obtain their information. Millennials, more than previous generations, indicate a greater likelihood of using their smartphones for activities such as corresponding with their financial advisors and obtaining market updates (Spectrem Group 2015d, 2015g, 2015l). But the pervasiveness of social media and mobile technology has not yet translated into widespread use of technology for financial activities beyond checking account balances, making purchases, and paying bills. Table 14.1 provides a sampling of current social media usage conducted by non-millionaire households for a variety of financial activities.

Young adults express the most interest in the prospect of reading financial blogs posted by financial or investment firms, preferably on the websites of major financial media outlets. They are also interested in reading blogs that pertain to financial topics (Spectrem Group 2015d, 2015g, 2015l).

Tech-savvy young adults would be considerably more interested than older affluent households if their financial service firms provided information via social media and through apps. They would also be more inclined to use a financial product or service they saw advertised or discussed on a social media platform. Tech-savvy young adults are more than twice as likely as older households to consider choosing a new financial advisor or provider based in part on how much that advisor communicates using social media (Spectrem Group 2015d, 2015g, 2015l).

Just as millennials have come of age accustomed to watching what they want, when they want, and on the portable screen they want, they are most open to watching videos on financial websites. Four in 10 non-millionaire millenials report having done so, compared with 35 percent of Gen Xers and fewer than 3 in 10 of baby boomers and seniors. The most commonly watched videos on the financial websites are financial information videos, followed by videos on current financial events and stock tips, as well as videos featuring financial commentators (Spectrem Group 2015d).

In gathering financial information, millennials share some of their older counterparts' old-school preferences for talking to someone in person and in reading an article. Yet, pertaining to communication with a financial advisor, millennials are the most likely age demographic to prefer email over the telephone or in person contact. Again,

Table 14.1 **Social Media Most Likely to Be Used for Specified Activities**

	Facebook %	*LinkedIn %*	*Twitter %*	*YouTube %*	*None or Not Applicable %*
Researching investment information	1	3	1	4	91
Finding a financial or investment advisor	2	7	0	1	90
Obtaining market updates	3	2	2	2	91
Reading articles about financial topics	8	7	1	2	81
Watching videos about financial topics	7	3	1	21	67

Note: This table shows survey-based data on the overall usage of social networks by non-millionaire investors for conducting their financial activities.

Source: Spectrem Group (2015d).

the percentages are small (less than one-fourth), but millennials have taken the lead in communicating with their financial advisors via Facebook, LinkedIn, Twitter, and Snapchat. Among all age segments, millennials are most likely to consider using a smartphone or e-reader to have a video chat with or meeting with a financial advisor. Nearly all millennials surveyed report having a smartphone, and almost three-fourths use a tablet (Spectrem Group 2015d, 2015g, 2015l).

Although older individuals are more likely to follow the news via their devices, millennials are the most likely to indicate they use such devices to research information on financial products and services (Spectrem Group 2015d, 2015g, 2015l). The highest percentages of millennial Twitter users follow family or friends, followed by movie stars, but they are more likely also to follow financial and/or investment commentators on Twitter than are older generations. Additionally, they are more frequent daily and weekly online buyers and sellers of stocks.

With this technology at their disposal, how tempted will millennials be to bypass human advisors and opt for a virtual or robo-advisor? Spectrem Group (2015b, 2015f, 2015j) indicates that, for now, human advisors can rest easy. For a wide range of services, including establishing a financial plan, obtaining insurance to meet personal needs, adjusting investments in conjunction with status changes, selecting investments for a retirement plan, and picking stocks that align with their risk tolerance, the highest percentage of investors regardless of age think a personal advisor would do a better job.

Financial advisors should consider that among the comparatively fewer who think a robo-advisor would do a better job, the highest percentage are millennials. According

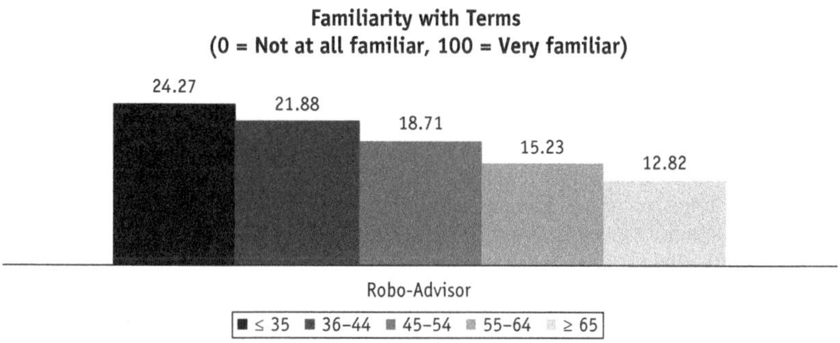

Figure 14.6 Client Familiarity with Investment Terms. This figure shows survey-based data about the familiarity of affluent millennial investors with the term "robo-advisor." Source: Spectrem Group (2015i).

to Observer (2015), robo-advisors are a possible "gateway to millennials." The *Journal of Financial Planning* article quotes a CNBC piece in which Adam Nash, founder of Wealthfront, a robo-advisor wealth management firm, observes that the financial advice industry has large ignored young people because servicing them is not economical. Technology changes that debate because helping young people with their money can now be economical. Figure 14.6 shows that familiarity with the term "robo-adviser" is low overall but highest among millennials.

Millennials embarking on that long road to a secure financial future are more inclined to seek advice and counsel from a professional in the future. Yet, the hurdles they face now—debt, a volatile market, an uncertain economy and job market, and "sandwich generation" responsibilities caring for their fledgling households and their aging parents—represent strong arguments for employing a financial advisor, whether human or technology-based. Figure 14.7 illustrates that millennials are more likely than previous generations to consider using a service that is either 100 percent technology-based or uses platforms such as Skype or FaceTime.

MILLENNIAL INVESTOR PROFILES

As with any generation, advisors should avoid painting millennials with one broad brushstroke. No "typical" millennial household exists; one-size-fits-all financial planning models are outmoded for this age segment. Nevertheless, some generalizations can be made. Based on interviews and surveys, Spectrem Group (2015e) has identified five millennial investor profiles that vary on demographics, wealth status, and investment mindset: The Climber, On My Own, No Worries, Family Matters, and the Worrier.

- *The Climber* is the most aggressive investor among his peers. Climbers tend to hold high-profile, high-income jobs such as attorneys, consultants, or information technology professionals and are the most advisor engaged.
- *On My Own* is the least wealthy millennial investor, but this type has a strong work ethic and conscientiously saves its money. Two-thirds are women. They are the most likely to prioritize getting advice to reach their financial goals. Nearly 7 in 10 of these

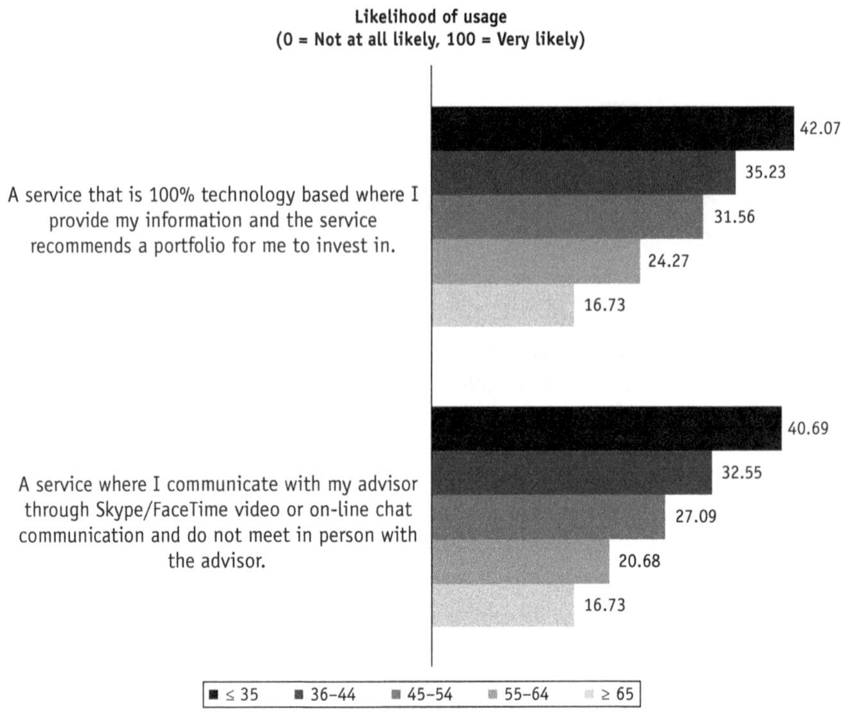

Figure 14.7 Likelihood of Client Use of Financial Services via Technology. This figure shows survey-based data involving a generation gap in interest about using a virtual advisor or communicating with an advisor via technology. Source: Spectrem Group (2015i).

investors consider themselves fairly or very knowledgeable about financial products and investments, and so they identify themselves as moderate to aggressive investors.

- *No Worries* are the wealthiest of the millennial investor personas with half crediting their wealth to receiving an inheritance and 67 percent to being in the right place at the right time. This group tends to be ethnically diverse and has the highest percentage of two-income households. They prefer regular financial advisor contact and are big users of technology in their dealings with them. In terms of investing, they are more likely than their peers to invest in pharmaceuticals and construction, and have the largest portion of their investible assets in equities.
- *Family Matters* are older millennials who have a "married with kids" mindset that influences their financial decisions. Concerns about retirement and health issues make frugality an important theme. With a moderate to aggressive risk tolerance, 21 percent of their investible assets are in fixed income and almost half (48 percent) are in equities. Less than half (44 percent) have an advisor. The primary reasons they give for not using an advisor are that they do not know whom to use, they get help from friends or family, and concerns that an advisor will not look out for their best interests.

- *The Worrier,* not surprisingly, is more likely than his or her peers to self-report being either "fairly" or "not very" knowledgeable about financial products and investments. Eight in 10 identify their risk tolerance as moderate. Although they tend to be well educated, they have the second lowest net worth of all millennial personas, just above the On My Own millennial. Paradoxically, more than half indicate they enjoy investing. Just over half (54 percent) have an advisor. Others who do not have an advisor believe they cannot afford one or that they do not have enough assets to warrant using an advisor.

Summary and Conclusions

How will the millennials impact the financial services industry? Given the financially volatile times in which they grew up, millennials can be cautious about its practitioners. They have witnessed the bursts of the dot-com and housing bubbles, the Enron and Bernie Madoff scandals, and the financial crisis of 2007–2008, its subsequent recession, and its prolonged economic recovery.

Non-millionaire and millionaire millennials profess to have a more moderate to aggressive risk tolerance than older investors. The largest percentage of their investable assets is in equities, but the next largest percentage is in cash and liquid assets.

As for the industry and its practitioners, millennials cannot be taken for granted. The Millennial Disruption Index (2015), a three-year survey by Scratch, an in-house unit of Viacom that identifies the industries "most likely to be transformed by Millennials," reports that banking is at the highest risk of disruption. Nearly 7 in 10 millennial respondents predict that in five years the means by which they access money and pay for things will be completely different.

The title of a *Time* magazine story by Kadlec (2014) indicates the generation gap in thinking about financial institutions. "Why Millennials Would Choose a Root Canal Over Listening to a Banker" reports the perception that banks do not address millennials' unique financial challenges "in a relevant way. . . . This generation is loaded with student debt that's difficult to refinance; grossly underemployed without access to capital to start a business . . . and hungry for financial guidance that isn't self-serving. Millennials also want to conduct their affairs on a smartphone, not go to a bank branch—ever." According to the Millennial Disruption Index (2015), nearly half of millennials are counting on tech start-ups to overhaul the way banks operate, and nearly three-fourths of them indicate they would be more excited about a new financial services offering from Google, Amazon, Apple, PayPal, or Square than from their own banks. One-third of this group does not think they will need a bank.

To engage this wary and independent-minded generation, financial advisors will need to prove their worth. Advisors must recognize how millennials differ from their older counterparts in regard to financial professionals. Communication is important to millennials, whether they use traditional channels such as the telephone or the increasingly digital landscape. Financial advisors will need to more widely use social media and the Internet for communicating with investors. They have the responsibility for engaging these younger clients with the communication platforms they are most comfortable using.

Even the less advisor-assisted millennials can be encouraged to turn to advisors to answer the questions they cannot find on Google or via a computer algorithm. A robo-advisor cannot fully project how financial decisions will affect their lives. Instead, millennials will turn to advisors who have reached out to them and have established their trust. Although millennials tend to do their own research on potential investments, they are seeking advice. According to LinkedIn (2015), about 34 percent of affluent millennials say that financial advisors are a "must-have," compared to 27 percent of affluent Gen Xers. Financial advisors who look beyond the millennial stereotypes will be better positioned to nurture enduring relationships and help put millennials in the most advantageous position for the success to which their popular culture indicates they feel entitled.

Discussion Questions

1. Explain why millennials are distrustful of the financial services industry.
2. Explain how millennials differ from baby boomers other than age.
3. Discuss how financial advisors can engage millennials.
4. Explain how the money habits of millennials disprove the stereotype that they are a lazy and an entitled generation.

References

Adams, James Truslow. 1931. *The Epic of America*. Boston: Little Brown.

Andree, Kristen. 2015. "Why Financial Advisers Shouldn't Ignore Millennials." *Investment News*, September 11. Available at http://www.investmentnews.com/article/20150911/FREE/150919979/why-financial-advisers-shouldnt-ignore-millennials.

Bank of America/USA TODAY. 2015. "Better Money Habits Millennial Report." April 21. Available at https://www.bettermoneyhabits.com/assets/images/v.2.0/tiles/infographics/pdf/fall-2015-millennial-report.pdf.

Bond, Casey. 2015. "5 Reasons Millennials Don't Trust Their Financial Planners." *Huffington Post*, June 9. Available at http://www.huffingtonpost.com/casey-bond/5-reasons-millennials-don_b_7548040.html.

Brack, Jessica, and Kip Kelly. 2012. "Maximizing Millennials in the Workplace." UNC Kenan-Flagler Business School, Executive Development, 1–15. Available at http://www.kenan-flagler.unc.edu/executive-development/custom-programs/~/media/DF1C11C056874DDA8097271A1ED48662.ashx/.

Census Bureau. 2015. "Millennials Outnumber Baby Boomers and Are Far More Diverse, Census Bureau Reports." June 25. Release Number: CB15-11.

Council of Economic Advisers. 2014. "15 Economic Facts about Millennials." October. Available at https://www.whitehouse.gov/sites/default/files/docs/millennials_report.pdf.

Facebook IQ. 2016. "Millennials and Money: The Unfiltered Journey." January 25. Available at https://fbinsights.files.wordpress.com/2016/01/facebookiq_millennials_money_january2016.pdf.

Fry, Richard. 2015a. "Millennials Surpass Gen Xers as the Largest Generation in U.S. labor force." Pew Research Center. Available at http://www.pewresearch.org/fact- tank/2015/05/11/millennials-surpass-gen-xers-as-the-largest-generation-in-u-s-labor-force/.

Fry Richard, 2015b. "More Millennials Living with Family Despite Improved Job Market." Pew Research Center. Available at http://www.pewsocialtrends.org/2015/07/29/more-millennials- living-with-family-despite-improved-job-market/.

Fry, Richard. 2015c. "Record Share of Young Women Are Living with Their Parents, Relatives." Pew Research Center, November 11. Available at http://www.pewresearch.org/fact-tank/2015/11/11/record-share-of-young-women-are-living-with-their-parents-relatives/.

Johnson, Scott D., and Stephen J. Larson. 2009. "Millennials: Strategies for Financial Planning with a New Generation." *Journal of Financial Planning* 22:5, 65–71.

Kadlec, Dan. 2014. "Why Millennials Would Choose a Root Canal Over Listening to a Banker." *Time,* March 28. Available at http://time.com/40909/why-millennials-would-choose-a-root-canal-over-listening-to-a-banker/.

Kantrowitz, Mark. 2016. "Why the Student Loan Crisis Is Even Worse Than People Think." *Time,* January. 11. Available at http://time.com/money/4168510/why-student-loan-crisis-is-worse-than-people-think/.

LinkedIn. 2015. "Winning Affluent Millennials: How This New Power Persona Is Reshaping the Finance Industry." Available at https://business.linkedin.com/content/dam/business/marketing-solutions/global/en_US/campaigns/pdfs/affluent-millennial-research-whitepaper-eng-us.pdf.

Matthews, Steve. 2015. "Here's Evidence That Millennials Are Still Living with Their Parents." *BloombergBusiness,* September 18. Available at http://www.bloomberg.com/news/articles/2015-09-18/here-s-evidence-that-millennials-are-still-living-with-their-parents.

Millennial Disruption Index. 2015. Available at http://www.millennialdisruptionindex.com.

Newport, Frank, and Brandon Busteed. 2013. "Americans Still See College Education as Very Important." Gallup. Available at http://www.gallup.com/poll/166490/americans-college-education-important.aspx.

Observer. 2015. "Robo-Advisers: The Gateway to Millennials." *Journal of Financial Planning* 28:9, 12–13.

Patten, Eileen, and Richard Fry. 2015, "How Millennials Today Compare with Their Grandparents 50 Years Ago." Pew Research Center. Available at http://www.pewresearch.org/fact-tank/2015/03/19/how-millennials-compare-with-their-grandparents/.

Pew Research Center, 2014. "Millennials in Adulthood." March 7. Available at http://www.pewsocialtrends.org/2014/03/07/millennials-in-adulthood/.

Scheresberg, Carlo de Bassa, and Annamaria Lusardi. 2015. "Gen Y Personal Finances: A Crisis of Confidence and Capability." Available at http://gflec.org/wp-content/uploads/2015/01/a738b9_b453bb8368e248f1bc546bb257ad0d2e.pdf.

Spectrem Group. 2013. "HNW Millennials." Spectrem Group Perspective. May. Available at http://spectrem.com/Content_Product/HNW.aspx.

Spectrem Group. 2015a. "Investor Pulse." September. Available at http://spectrem.com/Content_Whitepaper/Investor-pulse-september-2015.aspx.

Spectrem Group. 2015b. "Mass Affluent Investor 2015: Advisor Relationships and Changing Advice Requirements." Wealth Segmentation Series. Available at http://spectrem.com/Content_Product/advisor-relationships-2015-mass-affluent.aspx.

Spectrem Group. 2015c. "Mass Affluent Investor 2015: Financial Behaviors and the Investor's Mindset." Wealth Segmentation Series. Available at http://spectrem.com/Content_Product/2015-mass-affluent-q1.aspx.

Spectrem Group. 2015d. "Mass Affluent Investor 2015: Using Social Media and Mobile Technology in Financial Decisions." Wealth Segmentation Series. Available at http://spectrem.com/Content_Product/2015-mass-affluent-q2.aspx.

Spectrem Group. 2015e. "Millennial Investment Personas." Spectrem Group Perspective. Available at http://spectrem.com/Content_Product/Millennial-Personas.aspx.

Spectrem Group. 2015f. "Millionaire Investor 2015: Advisor Relationships and Changing Advice Requirements." Wealth Segmentation Series. Available at http://spectrem.com/Content_Product/Advisor-relationships-2015-millionaire-q3.aspx.

Spectrem Group. 2015g. "Millionaire Investor 2015: Using Social Media and Mobile Technology in Financial Decisions." Wealth Segmentation Series. Available at http://spectrem.com/Content_Product/2015-millionaire-q2.aspx.

Spectrem Group. 2015h. "Millionaire Investor 2015: Financial Behaviors and the Investor's Mindset." Wealth Segmentation Series. Available at http://spectrem.com/Content_Product/2015-millionaire-q1.aspx.

Spectrem Group. 2015i. "The Investing Habits of Millennials." Spectrem Group Perspective. Available at http://spectrem.com/Content_Product/investing-habits-millennials.aspx.

Spectrem Group. 2015j. "UHNW Investor 2015: Advisor Relationships and Changing Advice Requirements." Wealth Segmentation Series. Available at http://spectrem.com/Content_Product/2015-uhnw-advisor-relationships-and-advice-requirements.aspx.

Spectrem Group. 2015k. "UHNW Investor 2015: Financial Behaviors and the Investor's Mindset." Wealth Segmentation Series. Available at http://spectrem.com/Content_Product/2015-uhnw-q1.aspx.

Spectrem Group. 2015l. "UHNW Investor 2015: Using Social Media and Mobile Technology in Financial Decisions." Wealth Segmentation Series. Available at http://spectrem.com/Content_Product/2015-uhnw-q2.aspx.

Stein, Joel. 2013. "Millennials: The Me Me Me Generation." *Time*, May 20. Available at http://www.prjohnsonenglish.org/uploads/5/3/8/5/5385246/millennials_themememegeneration.pdf.

Steverman, Ben. 2015. "Financial Advisers Don't Care about Millennials, and the Feeling Is Mutual." *BloombergBusiness*, May 11. Available at http://www.bloomberg.com/news/articles/2015-05-11/financial-advisers-don-t-care-about-millennials-and-the-feeling-is-mutual.

T. Rowe Price. 2015. "Millennial, Gen X, and Baby Boomer Workers and Retirees: Retirement Savings & Spending Study." June 22. Available at http://rps.troweprice.com/mc/sites/RetirementForAll/articles/MillennialStudyIn-DepthFindings.pdf.

Tang, Ning, Andrew Baker, and Paula C. Peter. 2015. "Investigating the Disconnect between Financial Knowledge and Behavior: The Role of Parental Influence and Psychological Characteristics in Responsible Financial Behaviors among Young Adults." *Journal of Consumer Affairs* 49:2, 376–406.

TD Ameritrade. 2015. "2016 Self-Employed Survey." December 9. Available at http://s1.q4cdn.com/156458933/files/doc_downloads/research/AMTD-Self-Employed-Study-Research-Report-November-2015.pdf.

Wells Fargo. 2014. "2014 Wells Fargo Millennial Study." June. Available at https://www08.wellsfargomedia.com/downloads/pdf/press/2q14pr-millennials-save-survey.pdf.

Yen, Holly. 2012. "1 in 2 New Graduates Are Jobless or Unemployed." Associated Press, April 21. Available at http://news.yahoo.com/1-2-graduates-jobless-underemployed-140300522.html.

Part Four

THE PSYCHOLOGY OF FINANCIAL SERVICES

15

Psychological Aspects of Financial Planning

DAVE YESKE, CFP®
Managing Director, Yeske Buie
Distinguished Adjunct Professor, Golden Gate University

ELISSA BUIE, CFP®
CEO, Yeske Buie
Distinguished Adjunct Professor, Golden Gate University

Introduction

Personal financial planning is a process for uncovering client goals and values, and for developing integrated strategies to best utilize all a client's human and material resources in pursuit of those goals in a way that is consistent with that client's personal values and preferences. Change is a conceptual lens through which to view financial planning. Specifically, financial planners help their clients adapt to environmental changes, including death, disability, divorce, and inheritance, or to affect volitional changes, including retirement and financing children's education. Change can be challenging.

According to the World Health Organization (WHO), depression is the leading cause of disability worldwide (Moussav, Chatterji, Verdes, Tandon, Patel, and Ustun 2007). The WHO also notes that one of the biggest sources of clinical depression is an inability to adapt to unexpected change, or even, in many cases, "important and normal" life transitions. Other studies show that the incidences of ulcers, headaches, and depression are three to five times higher for those individuals under financial stress (Choi 2009). To the degree that it can help facilitate life transitions and mitigate financial stress, the financial planning process carries the potential to improve a person's mental and physical health.

Far fewer people will face a debilitating disease or legal crisis than will experience a bad financial outcome during their lifetimes. Therefore, financial planning holds more promise to deliver individual and societal benefits than many of the traditional professions, such as medicine and law. This chapter describes the nature of the financial planning process, discusses the challenges associated with effecting positive financial change in the lives of individuals and families, examines the nature of the underlying relationship between planner and client, and analyzes the behavioral challenges that financial planners must overcome when developing financial planning strategies to help their clients achieve their life goals.

The History and Development of Personal Financial Planning

On December 12, 1969, Loren Dutton laid the foundations upon which financial planning would emerge as a distinct professional practice, when he convened a gathering of 13 financial services industry leaders at a hotel near O'Hare Airport in Chicago. As a result of this meeting, the Society for Financial Counselling came to serve as the umbrella for a membership organization, the International Association for Financial Planning (IAFP), and an educational arm, the College for Financial Planning (Brandon and Welch 2009). The first graduating class of the college, in turn, formed the Institute of Certified Financial Planners (ICFP) in 1973. Before then, personal financial planning had existed largely in university home economics departments, where the focus was on teaching individuals how to use and protect their personal financial resources. Although a growing number of individuals engaged in the sale of financial products had already begun to cross traditional boundaries, cross-licensing in both insurance and securities, the IAFP, the ICFP, and College for Financial Planning created a focal point around which the financial planning profession would begin to coalesce (Brandon and Welch 2009).

In 1971, the College for Financial Planning developed a curriculum intended to prepare individuals to give financial advice to the public. It also created a credential, the Certified Financial Planner (CFP) designation, which would identify those individuals who had completed a series of five courses. The study guide for the first course, "Counseling the Individual—Basic Financial Planning," was divided into six sections: (1) Fundamentals of Financial Counseling, (2) Money Management and Personal Financial Reports, (3) Reviewing Financial Media, (4) The Investment Model, (5) Considerations in Effective Financial Planning, and (6) Counseling and Consumer Behavior.

Lesson 2 of this original curriculum enumerated the services of the financial planner as follows: collecting and evaluating financial and personal information, counseling on financial objectives and alternations, installing the financial program, coordinating the elements of the financial plan that involve others, and keeping the long-range financial plan current in light of internal and/or external changes (Brandon and Welch 2009). This foundation would later become the six-step financial planning process.

In 1985, the rights to the CFP trademarks became part of the newly formed nonprofit International Board for Standards and Practices for Certified Financial Planners (IBCFP), later renamed CFP Board of Standards (CFP Board), as part of transitioning control of the CFP trademarks to a new, nonprofit standards-setting body. Any institution of higher learning can now register a financial planning education program with CFP Board and qualify its graduates to take the CFP exam. What had been a series of six three-hour exams became a 10-hour exam administered over two days. In 2014, CFP Board moved to a six-hour exam administered electronically via testing centers and designed to be psychometrically comparable to the former 10-hour exam. The number of colleges and universities with educational programs registered with CFP Board grew from 20 in 1987 to 225 in 2014. These registered institutions offer certificate, bachelor's, master's, and doctoral degree programs. In the meantime, the College for Financial Planning became one of many among the various registered programs. In 1992, the college created the National Endowment for Financial Education (NEFE), which eventually became the parent entity for the college; and in 1997, NEFE sold the College for Financial Planning to the Apollo Group. Thereafter, NEFE became solely devoted to providing financial education to consumers.

In 1990, Australia became the first member of the International CFP Council and in 2004, CFP Board transferred the rights to the Certified Financial Planner and CFP trademarks outside the United States to the Financial Planning Standards Board (FPSB). As of 2015, the FPSB had 26 nonprofit organizations as members offering the CFP trademark in their respective territories.

The Financial Planning Process

Both standard-setting bodies for Certified Financial Planners—CFP Board in the United States and Financial Planning Standards Board in all other countries—define the financial planning process as the following six steps (Certified Financial Planner Board of Standards 2015):

1. Establishing and defining the client-planner relationship.
2. Gathering client data including goals.
3. Analyzing and evaluating the client's current financial status.
4. Developing and presenting recommendations and/or alternatives.
5. Implementing the recommendations.
6. Monitoring the recommendations.

Financial planners draw from the following six primary subject areas or knowledge domains when advising clients:

1. Financial statement preparation and analysis including cash flow analysis/planning and budgeting.
2. Risk management and insurance planning.
3. Investment planning.
4. Income tax planning.
5. Retirement planning.
6. Estate planning.

CFP Board and FPSB member organizations both employ a certification process for financial plans that revolves around what the organizations refer to as the "Four Es." These consist of the following:

- **Education.** A specified course of study covering topic areas and competencies specified by CFP Board and FPSB. Educational institutions must register their programs for them to satisfy this requirement. Candidates for certification must also hold a bachelor's degree.

- **Examination.** Candidates must pass an extensive certification exam designed to test applied knowledge.
- **Experience.** Candidates must have three years of relevant professional experience to become certified.
- **Ethics.** Both candidates and CFP professionals must agree to abide by an extensive code of ethics and professional conduct. Failure to do so may result in public or private censure, suspension of the right to use the marks, and permanent revocation.

The Strategic Dimension of Financial Planning

As might be expected in a practice-oriented profession, the financial planning literature has generally been dominated by material that is topical in nature and contingent on the current state of applicable laws and regulations, as well as on prevailing economic conditions. Certain themes can be seen to emerge from the more conceptual offerings, especially related to the financial planner's role as strategist.

QUANTITATIVE TECHNIQUES BORROWED FROM FINANCE AND ECONOMICS

Many of the more enduring insights that emerged from the early planning literature came from the application of traditional finance tools in new ways to better plan for individuals. Warschauer (1981), for example, offers a uniform risk-liquidity balance sheet approach to accounting for obtaining a client's true financial position. This framework went well beyond the traditional balance sheet for individuals by reflecting the embedded taxes in appreciated capital assets and the net present value (NPV) of employment-related benefits like pensions and Social Security. Rudd and Siegel (2013) later expanded on this concept with their "lifetime balance sheet." This extension explicitly included not just the present value of Social Security on the asset side of the ledger but also measures of "human capital," including the NPV of future earnings and bonuses. In this framework, the liability side of the statement includes the NPV of future goals including retirement spending and college funding. This process allows calculating *net resources* (i.e., the difference between total resources and total goals), and a *margin of safety* (i.e., net resources expressed as a percentage of total resources). Such an approach also allows for a more complete risk analysis of a family's total portfolio of assets and liabilities. For example, one's fixed income portfolio will consist not just of bonds, certificates of deposit (CDs), and money market funds (MMFs) but also mortgages, deferred taxes, and Social Security. The financial planner can then analyze the sensitivity of this rather exotic but more accurate fixed-income portfolio to various risks using traditional analytical tools such as *duration analysis,* which is the average life of a financial instrument such a bond.

As would be expected, such quantitative approaches to analyzing client needs and circumstances have only grown in number and sophistication. These tools most often represent the application of techniques from other fields to the realm of the individual. For example, Hopewell (1997) introduces stochastic modeling, especially Monte Carlo analysis. Hopewell observes that most of the analyses performed by financial planners, from calculating life insurance needs to estimating the cost of financing retirement or a child's education, involve uncertainty. These uncertainties can include future rates of return, inflation rates, and the timing and duration of future needs, among other things. Simple deterministic approaches can provide a point estimate or, at best, a series of point estimates allowing one to illustrate best and worst-case scenarios. However, as Hopewell (1997, p. 85) notes "such analyses show what is *possible*, but not what is *probable*." The author observes that although Bayesian probability analysis, decision trees, and Monte Carlo simulations have appeared in the business literature for 40 years, none of these techniques had previously made an appearance in the financial planning literature.

Following Hopewell (1997), stochastic modeling became a regular topic in the literature, including further forays by Kautt and Hopewell (2000) and Kautt and Wieland (2001). The shortcomings of the technique also drew scrutiny, as when Nawrocki (2001) observed the dangers of assuming that variables are normally distributed and uncorrelated when using Monte Carlo analysis. He suggests an alternative "exploratory simulation" technique that involves fewer assumptions.

Meanwhile, Daryanani (2002) offers "sensitivity simulations" as a faster alternative to Monte Carlo, and Brayman (2007) proposes an algorithmic approach to creating a "reliability forecast." Besides requiring less iteration to produce a result, this latter approach is useful in generating a matrix illustrating multiple "success factors" as opposed to the single success factor generated by the Monte Carlo technique.

Another quantitative technique that has emerged and grown in popularity is scenario planning. Ellis, Feinstein, and Stearns (2000) introduced this technique, originally developed by Royal Dutch Shell, to financial planners and it rapidly gained wide acceptance. Scenario planning involves identifying bundles of events that are likely to occur together and creating stylized "scenarios" from these bundles. The planner then analyzes these scenarios in terms of the appropriate strategic response that each would require (Stearns 2006). Other similar techniques include sensitivity simulations (Daryanani 2002) and discrete event simulation (Houle 2004). Other tools and perspectives borrowed from the fields of finance and economics have included life-cycle finance (Bodie 2002; Basu 2005) and real options (Kautt 2003).

DECISION RULES AND POLICY-BASED FINANCIAL PLANNING

Another thread running through the financial planning literature involves process-oriented techniques. These techniques often take the form of decision rules (Kautt 2002) that are meant to provide a framework for rapid decision making in the face of changing external circumstances. Financial planners have adopted tools and techniques developed in other fields, including the use of investment policies (Boone and Lubitz 2004). An extension of the investment policy concept is policy-based financial planning, a concept first proposed by Hallman and Rosenbloom (1987) and later developed by Yeske and Buie (2006, 2014).

Policy-based financial planning involves the development of statements (policies) that capture what clients intend to do and how they intend to do it in terms not limited to the present circumstances. Among the characteristics that mark a good financial planning policy are that it must be both broad enough to encompass changing external circumstances and time-specific enough to provide a clear answer. Policies are intended to be enduring touchstones that keep clients anchored to an appropriate course of action, especially when buffeted by turbulent environments. To be effective, policies must reflect to a large degree not only a client's explicit financial goals and the financial planning principles related to those goals but also a client's belief system and preference structure.

One can think of the sequence within which policies arise as follows: client beliefs or values give rise to goals and objectives, which are then formulated as policies that embody the relevant financial planning best practices, and the policies in turn dictate specific actions in the face of a particular set of external circumstances. If and when the external circumstances change—and assuming the client's underlying beliefs and goals have not changed—the policies will return new answers without repeating the entire analysis. Of course, if clients do not see their beliefs and values reflected in their policies, they are less willing to be guided by them. For this reason, the initial "data gathering" done by the financial planner must be expanded into an extensive "discovery" process. This extended discovery process is aimed at uncovering the personal history, beliefs, and values that ultimately give rise to a client's stated goals.

Another branch of this process-oriented work has developed around the concept of safe withdrawal rates. A *safe withdrawal rate* refers to the maximum rate at which individuals can spend from the investments earmarked for retirement to minimize the risk of prematurely consuming the entire principal. Bengen (1994, 1997, 2001) was the first to address this question in a rigorous manner, building upon theoretical foundations previously developed by pension actuaries. Recent developments have brought this area more fully into the policy-driven realm by incorporating active decision rules that can be used to support higher initial withdrawal rates (Guyton 2004; Guyton and Klinger 2006; Klinger 2007). As with policy-based financial planning, and unlike circumstances involving static withdrawal rates, the decision rules developed by Guyton and Klinger are most efficacious with the active understanding and participation of clients.

INTERIOR DIMENSION AND FINANCIAL LIFE PLANNING

As previously noted, more financial planning techniques require both a deeper understanding of clients' underlying motivations and their active engagement in the process itself. Fortunately, a growing body of work addressing this issue has evolved, almost entirely since 2000. Some refer to this area as interior finance, financial life planning, and life planning, with the last phrase garnering the greatest number of citations. The beginning of this body of work can be traced to a conference presentation given by Dick Wagner and George Kinder at the Institute of Certified Financial Planners (ICFP) 1994 Retreat at Cheyenne Mountain in Colorado. Titled "Money and the Meaning of Life," Wagner and Kinder's presentation offered more questions than answers. The standing-room-only attendance on all three days that the session was offered attested to the fact that the two presenters were not alone in thinking the time was right to address the interior (i.e., subjective and humanistic) dimension of money.

As a direct consequence of this now-famous gathering, an informal think tank called the Nazrudin Project (named for a Sufi mystic) emerged. Many of the original members of "Naz" went on to develop techniques and conceptual frameworks for dealing with the interior dimension of the financial planning process. These works include Wagner (2002) in the area of interior finance, which is a term he coined, Kinder's (2000) *The Seven Stages of Money Maturity*, Kinder and Galvan's (2005) EVOKE system, and Kahler's (2005) financial integration framework. Carol Anderson and Mitch Anthony coined the term "financial life planning" and much work has been done under that label (Diliberto and Anthony 2003; Anthony 2006; Diliberto 2006).

Wagner's work was notable for the novel way it used the integral framework of Wilbur (2001) to position the financial planning process. Wilbur's integralism is built around the concept of the holon, which is intended to represent the individual perspective of a human being. A *holon* is a process which is both a whole and a part.

Figure 15.1 shows that the holon is divided into quadrants with the two on the left representing the interior dimension and the two on the right representing the exterior dimension. The two top quadrants encompass the individual dimension and the two lower quadrants represent the collective dimension. When viewing a financial planning client from this perspective, the upper-left or individual-interior quadrant represents a client's values, beliefs, goals, and objectives, whereas the upper-right or individual-exterior quadrant encompasses all those objective facts about a client, including education, occupation, income, expenses, assets, and liabilities. The lower-left, or collective-interior, quadrant shows the beliefs and values that are collective, derived from family or society. Finally, the lower-right, or collective-exterior, quadrant indicates all the objective facts about the world, including tax rates, inflation rates, stat of the economy, and the financial markets.

For most of its history, financial planning has emphasized the two exterior quadrants, focusing primarily on powerful quantitative tools often applied to solve highly stylized goals and without much reference to a client's preference structure. The growing awareness that has led the planning profession to begin exploring the interior dimension with

Individual Interior Personal beliefs and attitudes.	**Individual Exterior** Objective facts about the individual such as education, occupation, assets, liabilities, income, and expenses.
Collective Interior Societal, family or other group norms and belief systems.	**Collective Exterior** Objective facts about the world such as tax laws, state of the economy, inflation rates, and financial market behavior.

Figure 15.1 The Holon in Financial Planning. This figure indicates the four lenses through which humans view and evaluate the world. Source: Wilbur (2001) and Wagner (2002).

such vigor is that simply finding financial solutions that are technically feasible is insufficient. For maximum success, the planner must choose from the many alternatives those strategies that are best matched to a client's personality, belief system, and personal history. These strategies have the highest probability of success, in part because they enlist a client's "bureaucracy of habits" (Heller and Surrenda 1995) in achieving the desired change.

Besides offering new perspectives, another notable aspect about the work being done on the interior dimension is that it generates specific tools and techniques for improving the discovery process and other elements of the financial planning process (Kinder and Galvan 2005). Although financial planners have previously addressed the interior dimension in their work with clients, what is undeniably new is the development of systematic approaches that can be applied successfully by planners of varying abilities and experience. Kinder's (2000) *The Seven Stages of Money Maturity* spawned two-day, week-long, and multi-week workshops that provide planners with new tools for exploring interior issues with clients. Besides worksheets of various types, these tools include questions designed to progressively strip away clients' preconceptions about the role of money in their lives and to allow a deeper understanding by the planner of the client's preference structure. With this deeper understanding, planners can do a better job of developing meaningful alternatives for clients. Others have developed formal systems for improved discovery, including Carol Anderson ("Money Quotient"), Mitch Anthony (Financial Life Planning), Lucerne and Colman Knight (Imagination Made Real), Diliberto (Financial Life Planning), and Klontz and Kahler (Insite).

CONNECTING THE INTERIOR AND EXTERIOR

Yeske (2010) suggests that, when viewed as a whole, the more conceptual portion of the financial planning literature naturally falls into the following three categories: (1) quantitative tools, (2) process-orientation, and (3) interior dimension. From this observation, Yeske proposes the Financial Planning Strategy Modes (FPSM) model as a way of organizing the skills, tools, and techniques used by financial planners around these three themes and in terms of the degree of relative involvement by planner and client in the planning process. It posits five modes of strategy making along this degree of involvement spectrum, beginning with the planner-driven mode and progressing through data-driven (quantitative tools), policy-driven (process orientation), relationship-driven (interior dimension), and client-driven mode at the other extreme. In empirical testing, Yeske finds that the policy-driven mode is most highly correlated with measures of client trust and relationship commitment, constructs that are discussed at greater length in the next section.

Client Trust and Commitment

Client trust and commitment have emerged in the financial planning research literature as two important predictors of a successful financial planning engagement. A client's trust in the financial planner and commitment to the financial planning relationship can lead directly to several positive outcomes, including high acquiescence, a low propensity to leave, a high degree of cooperation, and *functional conflict*, which is the ability to maintain a highly functional relationship even when conflicts arise (Morgan and Hunt 1994). These qualities in turn tend to lead to long-lasting relationships for which financial planners have both a process motive and a profit motive.

The process motive arises from the nature of personal financial planning itself, which involves multiple, integrated steps that must unfold over time, often requiring a period of years to successfully formulate, communicate, and implement (Christiansen and DeVaney 1998). Higher levels of commitment and trust are associated with client retention, client satisfaction, increased client openness in disclosing personal and financial information, and a greater propensity to implement financial planning recommendations (Anderson and Sharpe 2008).

According to Christiansen and DeVaney (1998), the profit motive arises from the fact that retaining existing clients costs much less than attracting new ones, which makes long-lasting relationships more profitable than those of shorter duration. Relationships exhibiting high trust and commitment are also associated with a greater client propensity to make referrals (Anderson and Sharpe 2008). Thus, financial planners should know what they can do to foster client trust and commitment, and thus reap these many benefits.

Answering this question is difficult because financial planning, similar to other professional services, has high credence properties, meaning consumers have difficulty judging the quality of the service even after it has been rendered (Sharma and Patterson 1999). One need only consider that financial planners are routinely asked to recommend strategies for attaining goals that are years or even decades in the future to see how this concept applies.

Notwithstanding the consumer's difficulty in directly assessing the value of high-credence services, many antecedents to trust and commitment in the context of professional services are available. These include switching costs, relationship benefits, shared values, communication, opportunistic behavior (Morgan and Hunt 1994; Christiansen and DeVaney 1998), client perception of technical and functional quality (Sharma and Patterson 1999), client satisfaction (Sharma and Patterson 2000), and communication tasks, skills, and topics (Anderson and Sharpe 2008). These antecedents are not unique to financial planning, but are present in almost any professional service relationship.

FACTORS INFLUENCING THE TRUST AND COMMITMENT RELATIONSHIP

The concept of client trust and commitment as key mediating variables first arose in the relationship marketing literature, notably in the work of Morgan and Hunt (1994). In the Morgan and Hunt model, illustrated in Figure 15.2, anything that leads to increased client trust and commitment is associated with positive outcomes such as high acquiescence, low propensity to leave, high cooperation, high functional conflict, and low uncertainty. Among their proposed antecedents to trust and commitment are relationship termination costs (i.e., switching costs), relationship benefits, shared values, communication, and opportunistic behavior.

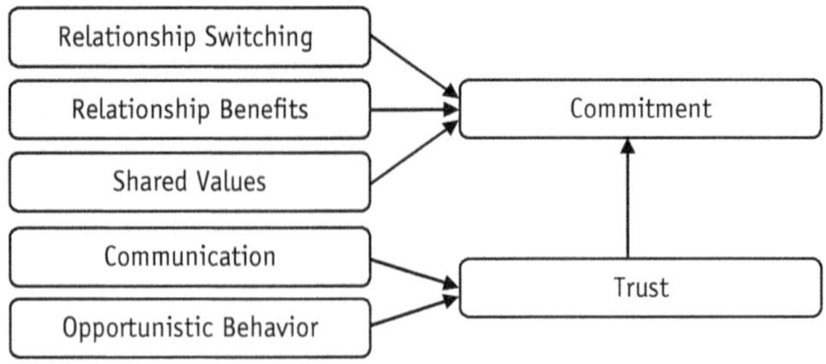

Figure 15.2 Components of Trust and Commitment. This figure shows the major factors that most influence client trust and commitment to the relationship during the financial planning process. Source: Morgan and Hunt (1994).

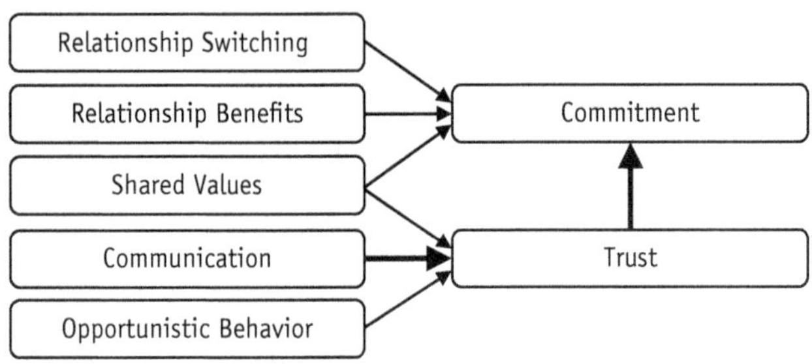

Figure 15.3 Major Factors for Building the Trust and Commitment Relationship. This figure shows that communication most influences client trust, which in turn drives the commitment to the relationship between the client and the financial planner. Source: Christiansen and DeVaney (1998).

Morgan and Hunt (1994) test this model with independent tire dealers and their suppliers and validated all the proposed linkages except the hypothesized link between relationship benefits and relationship commitment. Path analysis shows that relationship termination costs, relationship benefits, and shared values act directly on relationship commitment, whereas communication and opportunistic behavior act on trust, which in turn influences relationship commitment. Morgan and Hunt also tested an alternative, non-parsimonious model in which no indirect relationships were allowed and they found far fewer significant relationships than their "key mediating variable" or KMV model. Their data demonstrate that trust and commitment are the key mediating variables, not just two among many independent variables.

Christiansen and DeVaney (1998) apply this same model to financial planners, drawing data from members of three professional planning groups in the United States. They employed path analysis using the CALIS (Covariance Analysis of Linear Structural equations) procedures in the SAS statistical software. Figure 15.3 shows their findings that relationship termination costs, relationship benefits, and shared values are all antecedents of commitment, whereas shared values, communication, and opportunistic

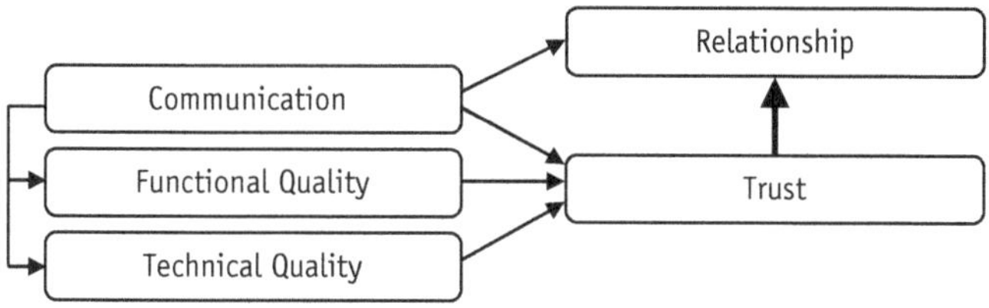

Figure 15.4 Technical Quality, Functional Quality, and Communication Effectiveness. This figure shows that communication affects trust and commitment both directly and indirectly through its impact on client perceptions of the technical and functional quality of the financial planner's services. Source: Sharma and Patterson (1999).

behavior are all antecedents of trust, which itself is an antecedent of commitment. These results match those of Morgan and Hunt (1994).

Interestingly, as an antecedent to commitment, trust has twice the explanatory power of any other variable. Shared values have a low significance as an antecedent to trust, and opportunistic behavior is not statistically significant. Communication has three times more explanatory power than shared values as an antecedent to trust and is highly significant. Christiansen and DeVaney conclude that communication is the single most powerful antecedent to trust and commitment, acting directly on trust and through trust on commitment.

Sharma and Patterson (1999, 2000) also addressed the question of which antecedents most influences client trust and commitment. As noted previously, they observed that financial planning is a "high credence" service that unfolds over time, leaving clients hard pressed to judge the quality of the advice in the present moment. As Sharma and Patterson (1999, p. 151) observed, "After all, if clients have trouble evaluating outcomes, then it seems reasonable that interactions ("how" the service is delivered) and all forms of communications will take on added significance as clients seek to minimize dissonance and uncertainty about the adviser they have chosen."

Sharma and Patterson (1999, 2000) also explored the links between perceptions of technical quality, functional quality, and communication effectiveness, on the one hand, and relationship commitment, on the other. Figure 15.4 illustrates their model. *Technical quality* refers to "what" is being delivered, and *functional quality* refers to "how" it is delivered. Sharma and Patterson included trust as an "endogenous mediating construct." They report that a client's perception of the technical and functional quality of the planner's advice is positively correlated with the client's level of trust in the planner. Higher levels of trust, in turn, are associated with higher levels of commitment to the relationship. Communication effectiveness acts both directly on trust and commitment and indirectly through its effect on perceived technical quality and functional quality. Although communication effectiveness has the smallest direct effect on commitment, it has the greatest total impact when including its indirect effects.

THE ROLE OF SATISFACTION

Sharma and Patterson (2000) later returned to analyzing the antecedents of relationship commitment, examining the role of trust and a new variable: satisfaction.

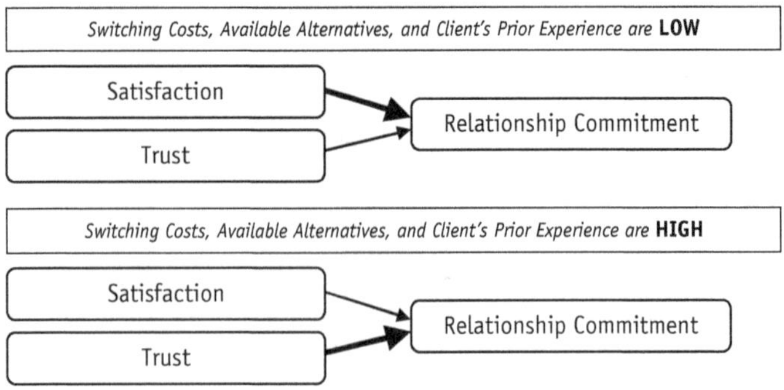

Figure 15.5 Satisfaction and Trust as Antecedents to Commitment. This figure shows that satisfaction drives client commitment when switching costs are perceived to be low, whereas trust drives commitment when switching costs are perceived to be high. Source: Sharma and Patterson (2000).

They tested the impact of trust and satisfaction on commitment in light of three contingencies: switching costs, availability of attractive alternatives, and prior experience. As Figure 15.5 illustrates, trust has the greatest impact on commitment when switching costs are high, available alternatives are low, and/or prior experience is low. In situations where switching costs are low, available alternatives are high, and/or prior experience is high, satisfaction is the dominant antecedent to commitment. The fact that financial services companies routinely try to raise switching costs by imposing surrender charges and deferred sales charges (back-end loads) on many of their financial products suggests that clients understand the role of this contingency.

THE COMMUNICATION DIMENSION

Anderson and Sharpe (2008) extend the work of Christiansen and DeVaney (1998) and Sharma and Patterson (1999, 2000) by focusing solely on the communication dimension. If communication is the single most significant antecedent to trust and commitment, what particular types of communication would have the greatest impact? They derived the communication elements to be examined from the life planning literature and organized them into three dimensions: (1) communication tasks, (2) communication skills, and (3) communication topics. According to Anderson and Sharpe, the following tasks, skills, and topics are most highly correlated with higher levels of trust and commitment among financial planning clients:

- **Communication tasks.** Systematic process to clarify goals and values; explaining how advice reflects goals and values.
- **Communication skills.** Eye contact, body language, verbal pacing, and facilitating difficult conversations about money.
- **Communication topics.** Client values and quality of life and initiating conversations about life changes.

Anderson and Sharpe (2008, p. 77) correlate these activities with relevant CFP Board practice standards related to uncovering clients' goals and communicating planning recommendations, noting that "our findings give strong support for the value of the specific financial planning communication tasks identified in these standards." Although the original development of practice standards resulted from capturing and codifying "established norms of practice," Anderson and Sharpe provide an empirically derived foundation for at least some of them.

Knowledge and Evidence-Based Financial Planning

Researchers have not revalidated many theoretical and practical approaches adapted from other fields. Moreover, many of the profession's "best practices" result from trial and error and accepted norms that possess intuitive appeal but lack empirical foundation. According to Buie and Yeske (2011, p. 39),

> Financial planning best practices also arise from both deductive and inductive reasoning. Some have developed from "self-evident" propositions and their natural implications, while others have arisen from a slow accumulation of observations that ultimately seem to form a pattern. That our best practices arise in ways that mirror the deductive/inductive methods of science shouldn't be a surprise; humans have evolved to think that way. As Albert Einstein put it, "the whole of science is nothing more than a refinement of everyday thinking." Of course, that word "refinement" is critical. Our trouble as a profession is that most of our best practices stop at the formation of a belief (the case study presented below, for example, involves a best practice that existed for decades before eventually being empirically-tested). And we're quite comfortable stopping there because our personal experience and the experience of colleagues will often seem to confirm and reinforce those beliefs (the field of behavioral finance calls this "confirmation bias"). However, such informal "evidence" is properly termed anecdotal and cannot be the foundation of a truly learned profession's best practices. Instead, we must take the next step: we must form our beliefs into hypotheses, then gather appropriate data and formally test those hypotheses. Only then can we say with confidence that our "best" practices are founded upon the "best" evidence:

A recent development in this area is the partnership between the Financial Planning Association (FPA) (US) and the Academy of Financial Services (AFS), the latter being a professional association founded in 1982 to serve the needs of professional academics teaching and researching in the area of financial planning. The purpose of the new partnership is to facilitate a deeper connection between practitioners and academics. The practical manifestations of this partnership include the following:

- A forum—The Theory into Practice Knowledge Circle—that serves as a clearinghouse for practitioners to share with academics topics or questions for research that

would substantially affect their work with clients and for academics to seek feedback and data from practitioners for financial planning research initiatives.
- A joint research track at the FPA's annual conference for presenting juried research papers by members of AFS, including prizes in the areas of theoretical and applied research.
- Joint publication of FPA's practice-oriented *Journal of Financial Planning* and AFS's *Financial Services Review*, with the latter being made available to FPA's members.

In another development, CFP Board of Standards, the standard-setting body for CFPs in the United States, has launched a series of programs also aimed at deepening the profession's academic roots. These efforts include the following initiatives:

- **Center for Financial Planning.** CFP Board is exploring the creation of a center that would serve as a credible source of research that advances the financial planning professional in these core areas:
  - Influencing and supporting academic research that is dedicated to helping financial planners better serve the public;
  - Supporting diversity within the profession so that it better mirrors the American public; and
  - Building capacity for the next generation of competent and ethical financial planners to meet public demand.
- **New Academic Financial Planning Journal.** John Wiley & Sons and CFP Board are collaborating on a peer-reviewed academic journal focused exclusively on financial planning. With this journal, the CFP Board will be creating an academic home for those faculty members who are teaching and conducting research in financial planning. The journal will be available free of charge to all CFP professionals (Iacurci 2015).

The Behavioral Dimension of Financial Planning

As previously noted, a major role of financial planners is to help clients adapt to change, whether environmental (imposed from without) or volitional (motivated from within). Among the many challenges that planners face in this role is the reality that financial planning clients are as subject to behavioral biases and heuristics as anyone else. *Heuristics* are mental shortcuts or rules of thumb individuals utilize to process information. These biases and heuristics often lead them to make suboptimal choices or to ignore financial planning recommendations altogether. In their work with clients, financial planners encounter most of the mental or cognitive biases identified by researchers in behavioral finance, such as mental accounting, representativeness, anchoring, overconfidence, loss aversion, and availability.

MENTAL ACCOUNTING

Mental accounting refers to the tendency for people to separate their money into separate accounts based on different subjective criteria, such as the source of the money and the intent for each account (Kahneman and Tversky 1979). Mental accounting may cause financial planning clients to spend differently, based on the size of the account or "bucket" from which the funds are supplied. For example, clients might spend more when using a debit card linked to a large brokerage account than when using a debit card linked to a much smaller checking account. Financial planners often discourage clients from choosing brokerage debit cards in lieu of automatic systems for moving budgeted funds electronically from brokerage to checking, where the smaller balances at any given time have a higher propensity to keep spending better aligned with budgets.

REPRESENTATIVENESS HEURISTIC

The *representativeness* heuristic refers to a propensity to see patterns, even where they do not exist (Tversky and Kahneman 1974). This tendency can cause financial planning clients to trade excessively in employer shares because they believe they have observed a pattern of regular reversal points in the company's stock price movements. As a result of this bias, individuals often ignore important information that should be included in the decision-making process. However, the new data or information are disregarded.

OVERCONFIDENCE, ANCHORING, AND LOSS AVERSION

Overconfidence, anchoring, and loss aversion can combine in ways that lead to a series of bad decisions (Fischoff, Slovic, and Lichtenstein 1977; Kahneman and Tversky 1984). *Overconfidence* is highly prevalent among investors, in which individuals overestimate their own abilities and predictions for success. For instance, overconfidence can lead employees to hold too much in employer shares, believing they have insider insights that are superior to market signals. *Anchoring* is the process by which individuals hold on to a belief and then apply this viewpoint to a specific reference point in time for making future judgments. *Loss aversion* is when clients apply greater weight to a loss than to an equivalent gain. Anchoring and loss aversion can cause these clients to continue to hold employer shares even when a reversal in the company's fortunes or those of its industry causes its stock price to fall (Shefrin and Statman 1986).

AVAILABILITY HEURISTIC

Availability bias refers to the propensity to be influenced by information that is easier to recall (Ricciardi 2008), such as highly impactful or more recent memories. A client's willingness to buy long-term care insurance frequently depends on whether he personally knew someone who had received home healthcare assistance or lodging at a skilled nursing facility. Personal experience of long- or short-lived relatives may influence the willingness to plan for a long retirement.

STRATEGIES FOR OVERCOMING BIASES IN FINANCIAL PLANNING

Although engaging in the financial planning process and being in a professional relationship with a financial planner can positively affect client behaviors, researchers and practitioners continue to develop extensions of the traditional six-step process in an attempt to better overcome the forgoing biases and heuristics. Among the suggested extensions are the EVOKE (Exploration, Vision, Obstacles, Knowledge, and Execution) model (Kinder and Galvin 2005). This framework proposes a greater focus on uncovering deeper goals, objectives, and values, as well as a more explicit examination of potential obstacles to implementation. Yeske and Buie (2014) propose using Policy-Based Financial Planning as a form of "decision architecture," along the lines of Thaler and Sunstein's (2008) concept of "choice architecture."

Financial planning policies represent compact decision rules that embody both a distillation of financial planning best practices in a given planning realm and the client's goals and values. To the degree that the planner can craft policies in which the clients can see their goals and values clearly reflected, they are more likely to embrace those policies as their own and be guided by them. This is consistent with the findings of Anderson and Sharpe (2008), who find that client trust and relationship commitment are higher when clients receive financial planning recommendations that are clearly connected to their values and goals.

Jacobson and Stearns (2013) propose appreciative inquiry as a way of dealing with behavioral finance issues, including in combination with the following "power tools" for overcoming the well-documented negativity bias (Kanouse 1984). Jacobson and Stearns (2013, pp. 25–29) provide the following explanations:

Possibility mindset

> People with a possibility mindset believe that positive outcomes are achievable, tune their radar to detect and highlight positive possibilities, potentials, and opportunities in new information and circumstances, and mobilize proven strengths, resources, and successes, as well as the potential in people and organizations. They don't dwell on mistakes, unskillful acts, and unfavorable outcomes. While they accurately detect downsides, their mindset allows them to lead with the positives to create upward spirals of effective thinking, productive conversation, and collaborative teamwork.

Realistic optimism

> A planner practicing realistic optimism collects and assimilates all relevant information, identifies and weighs its implications, and rather than planning for the lowest-risk, most-likely, or most favorable outcome, selects and plans for the best plausible outcome—the outcome that has both a significant probability of occurring and a significant payoff.

Positive conversational skills

> Positive conversational skills include:
>
> - acknowledging others' concerns, fears, and anxieties without prematurely citing factual grounds for optimism.

- asking positive questions and guiding conversations to identify and mobilize positive forces (such as strengths, resources, lessons learned, and wisdom gained from mastering previous challenges) to craft workable action strategies and plans.

Emotional self-management

> Emotional self-management (ESM) ... has two principal domains.... ESM related to one's inner experience includes awareness of one's moment-to-moment emotions and the events that trigger them (such as market gyrations, clients' responses to ST information, and one's own thoughts); and managing these emotions appropriately and effectively, neither denying them, suppressing them, nor giving them unfettered expression.... ESM in the interpersonal realm includes detecting others' emotions in response to ST information and remaining steady in the presence of these emotions, neither avoiding nor ignoring them nor attempting to combat them with facts.

Empathy and compassion

> Empathy entails accurately perceiving others' emotional reactions, internally experiencing something akin to their emotions (albeit a less intense version), and as appropriate, conveying one's understanding, non-verbally and/or verbally.
>
> The financial planner's inevitable role as a change agent means that the search for new perspectives, tools, and techniques to help mediate the impact of clients' mental biases and heuristics is a never-ending enterprise.

Summary and Conclusions

As a professional practice, financial planning arose about 1970 as a process for helping clients most efficiently use all of their human and financial resources in achieving personal goals and objectives. Financial planning is a six-step process that draws upon diverse knowledge domains to offer clients integrated strategies accounting for all the interlocking elements of their financial lives. In developing and implementing these strategies, financial planners must work to overcome clients' natural biases and heuristics that can derail or stall effective action and positive change. Because the financial planning process is both systematic and incremental in nature, it can be effective in helping clients understand the financial forces in their lives and the path toward achieving goals. In many cases, however, financial planners must use additional techniques as part of the process. These techniques could include appreciative inquiry, coaching, and policy-based financial planning, among others. A growing thread in the financial planning literature is devoted to helping clients effect positive change and how planners might help to overcome mental and emotional obstacles to that change. Considering the centrality of the financial planner's role as change agent, this trend is likely to continue to grow in the future.

DISCUSSION QUESTIONS

1. List the six steps of the financial planning process as defined by CFP Board of Standards and Financial Planning Standards Board.
2. Explain why financial planning clients tend to rely on secondary markers of quality when judging the advice they receive from their advisors.
3. Discuss how the availability heuristic can affect a financial planning client's perception of financial planning recommendations and/or propensity to act on them.
4. Describe how the mental biases of overconfidence, anchoring, and loss aversion can interact to cause financial planning clients to make suboptimal decisions.

REFERENCES

Anderson, Carol, and Deanna Sharpe. 2008. "The Efficacy of Life Planning Communication Tasks in Developing Successful lanner-Client Relationships." *Journal of Financial Planning* 21:6, 66–77.

Anthony, Mitch. 2006. *Your Clients for Life: The Definitive Guide to Becoming a Successful Financial Life Planner.* Second Edition. Chicago. Kaplan Business.

Basu, Somnath. 2005. "Age Banding Model for Retirement Planning." *Journal of Financial Counseling and Planning* 16:1, 29–36.

Bengen, William P. 1994. "Determining Withdrawal Rates Using Historical Data." *Journal of Financial Planning* 7:4. 171–180.

Bengen, William P. 1997. "Conserving Client Portfolios During Retirement Part III." *Journal of Financial Planning* 10:6, 84–87.

Bengen, William P. 2001. "Conserving Client Portfolios During Retirement Part IV." *Journal of Financial Planning* 14:5, 110–119.

Bodie, Zvi. 2002. "Life Cycle Finance in Theory and Practice." Boston University School of Management Working Paper #2002-02.

Boone, Norman M., and Linda S. Lubitz, L. 2004. *Creating an Investment Policy Statement.* Denver, CO: FPA Press.

Brandon, E. Denby Jr., and H. Oliver Welch. 2009. *A History of the Financial Planning Movement: The Transformation of Financial Services.* Hoboken, NJ: John Wiley & Sons, Inc.

Brayman, Shawn. 2007. "Beyond Monte Carlo Analysis: A Replacement for a Poor Practice." *Journal of Financial Planning* 20:12, 56–65.

Buie, Elissa, and Dave Yeske. 2011. "Evidence Based Financial Planning: To Learn . . . Like a CFP." *Journal of Financial Planning* 24:11, 38–43.

Certified Financial Planner Board of Standards. 2015. *Financial Planning Competency Handbook.* Second Edition. Hoboken, NJ: John Wiley & Sons, Inc.

Christiansen, Tim, and Sharon A. DeVaney. 1998. "Antecedents of Trust and Commitment in the Financial Planner-client Relationship." *Financial Counseling and Planning* 9:2, 1–10.

Choi, Laura. 2009. "Financial Stress and Its Physical Effects on Individuals and Communities." *Community Development Investment Review,* Federal Reserve Bank of San Francisco 5:3, 120–122.

Daryanani, Gobind. 2002. "Sensitivity Simulations: A Faster Alternative to Monte Carlo." *Journal of Financial Planning* 15:9,104–115.

Diliberto, Roy. 2006. "Uncovering and Understanding Your Clients' History, Values, and Transitions." *Journal of Financial Planning* 19:12, 52–59.

Diliberto, Roy, and Mitch Anthony. 2003. "Financial Life Planning: Navigating Life Transitions." *Journal of Financial Planning* 16:10, 26–29.

Ellis, Jeff, Steve Feinstein, and Dennis Stearns. 2000. "Scenario Learning: A Powerful Tool for the 21st Century Planner." *Journal of Financial Planning* 13:4, 82–90.

Fischhoff, Baruch, Paul Slovic, and Sarah Lichtenstein. 1977. "Knowing with Certainty the Appropriateness of Extreme Confidence." *Journal of Experimental Psychology: Human Perception and Performance* 3:4, 552–564.

Guyton, Jonathan. 2004. "Decision Rules and Portfolio Management for Retirees: Is the 'Safe' Initial Withdrawal Rate Too Safe?" *Journal of Financial Planning* 17:10, 54–63.

Guyton, Jonathan, and William Klinger. 2006. "Decision Rules and Maximum Initial Withdrawal Rates." *Journal of Financial Planning* 19:3, 50–58.

Hallman, Victor G., and Jerry S. Rosenbloom 1987. *Personal Financial Planning*. Fourth Edition. New York: McGraw-Hill.

Heller, Stuart, and David Sheppard Surrenda. 1995. *Retooling on the Run: Real Change for Leaders with No Time*. Berkeley, CA: North Atlantic Books.

Hopewell, Lynn. 1997. "Decision Making Under Conditions of Uncertainty: A Wakeup Call for the Financial Planning Profession." *Journal of Financial Planning*10:5, 84–91.

Houle, Gary R. 2004. "Application of Discrete Event Simulation to Financial Planning." *Journal of Financial Planning* 17:12, 52–60.

Iacurci, Greg. 2015. "CFP Board, with TD Ameritrade's Backing, Launches Center for Financial Planning." *Investment News*, November 18. Available at http://www.investmentnews.com/article/20151118/FREE/151119917/cfp-board-with-td-ameritrades-backing-launches-center-for-financial.

Jacobson, Edward A., and Dennis Stearns. 2013. "Power Tools for Handling Behavioral Finance Issues." *Journal of Financial Planning* 26:5, 24–30.

Kahler, Richard S. 2005. "Financial Integration: Connecting the Client's Past, Present, and Future." *Journal of Financial Planning* 18:5, 62–71.

Kahneman, Daniel, and Amos Tversky. 1979. "Prospect Theory: An Analysis of Decisions under Risk." *Econometrica*. 47:2, 263–292.

Kahneman, Daniel, and Amos Tversky. 1984. "Choices, Values, and Frames." *American Psychologist* 39:4, 341–350.

Kanouse, David E. 1984. "Explaining Negativity Biases in Evaluation and Choice Behavior: Theory and Research." In Thomas C. Kinnear (ed.), *NA—Advances in Consumer Research*, Volume 11, 703–708. Provo, UT: Association for Consumer Research.

Kautt, Glenn. 2002. "The Financial Planner as Decision Maker." *Journal of Financial Planning*. 15:10, 96–107.

Kautt, Glenn. 2003. "Real Options Analysis: The Profession's Next Cutting-Edge Tool." *Journal of Financial Planning* 16:2, 72–82.

Kautt, Glenn, and Lynn Hopewell. 2000. "Modeling the Future." *Journal of Financial Planning* 13:10, 90–100.

Kautt, Glenn, and Fred Wieland. 2001. "Modeling the Future: The Full Monte, the Latin Hypercube and Other Curiosities." *Journal of Financial Planning* 14:12, 78–89.

Kinder, George. 2000. *The Seven Stages of Money Maturity: Understanding the Spirit and Value of Money in Your Life*. New York: Dell Publishing.

Kinder, George, and Susan Galvan. 2005. "EVOKE: A Life Planning Methodology for the Coming Revolution in Client Relationships." *Journal of Financial Planning*. 16:4, 46–55.

Klinger, William J. 2007. "Using Decision Rules to Create Retirement Withdrawal Profiles." *Journal of Financial Planning* 20:8, 60–72.

Morgan, Robert M., and Shelby D. Hunt. 1994. "The Commitment-Trust Theory of Relationship Marketing." *Journal of Marketing* 58:3, 20–38.

Moussavi, Saba, Somnath Chatterji, Emese Verdes, Ajay Tandon, Vikram Patel, and Bederihan Ustun. 2007. "Depression, Chronic Diseases, and Decrements in Health: Results from the World Health Surveys." *Lancet* 370:9590, 851–858.

Nawrocki, David, 2001. "The Problems with Monte Carlo Simulation." *Journal of Financial Planning* 14:11, 92–106.

Ricciardi, Victor. 2008. "The Psychology of Risk: The Behavioral Finance Perspective." In Frank J. Fabozzi (ed.), *The Handbook of Finance, Volume 2: Investment Management and Financial Management*, 85–111. Hoboken, NJ: John Wiley & Sons, Inc.

Rudd, Andrew, and Laurence Siegel. 2013. "Using an Economic Balance Sheet for Financial Planning." *Journal of Wealth Management* 16:2, 15–23.

Sharma, Neeru, and Paul G. Patterson. 1999. "The Impact of Communication Effectiveness and Service Quality on Relationship Commitment in Consumer, Professional Services." *Journal of Services Marketing* 13:2, 151–170.

Sharma, Neeru, and Paul G. Patterson. 2000. "Switching Costs, Alternative Attractiveness and Experience as Moderators of Relationship Commitment in Professional, Consumer Services." *International Journal of Service Industry Management* 11:5, 470–490.

Shefrin, Hersh M., and Meir Statman. 1986. "How Not to Make Money in the Stock Market." *Psychology Today* 20:2, 52–54.

Stearns, Dennis. 2006. "From Doom and Gloom to Shangri-La: Scenario Learning Revisited." *Journal of Financial Planning* 19:5, 52–58.

Thaler, Richard H., and Cass R. Sunstein. 2008. *Nudge: Improving Decisions About Health, Wealth, and Happiness.* New York: Penguin Group.

Tversky, Amos, and Daniel Kahneman. 1974. "Judgment Under Uncertainty: Heuristics and Biases," *Science* 185:4157, 1124–1131.

Wagner, Dick. 2002. "Integral Finance: A Framework for a 21st Century Profession." *Journal of Financial Planning* 15:7, 62–71.

Warschauer, Thomas. 1981. "A Risk-Liquidity Uniform Balance Sheet Format for Financial Planners." *Journal of Institute of Certified Financial Planners* Spring, 175–182.

Wilbur, Ken. 2001. *A Theory of Everything: An Integral Vision for Business, Politics, Science and Spirituality*. Boston, MA: Shambala Publications.

Yeske, David B. 2010. "Finding the Planning in Financial Planning." *Journal of Financial Planning.* 23:9, 40–51.

Yeske, David B., and Elissa Buie. 2006. "Policy-Based Financial Planning Provides Touchstone in a Turbulent World." *Journal of Financial Planning* 19:7, 50–62.

Yeske, David B., and Elissa Buie. 2014. "Policy-Based Financial Planning as Decision Architecture." *Journal of Financial Planning* 27:12, 38–45.

16

Financial Advisory Services

JEROEN NIEBOER
Research Fellow in Behavioural Science,
London School of Economics and Political Science

PAUL DOLAN
Professor in Behavioural Science
London School of Economics and Political Science

IVO VLAEV
Professor in Behavioural Science
University of Warwick

Introduction

Making well-informed financial decisions is difficult. Consumers face an overwhelming choice of financial products, each with its own benefits, quirks, and conditions offered by a variety of product providers. On top of tackling the complexity of the retail financial landscape itself, consumers have to predict their own wants and needs in the distant future, make trade-offs over time, and consider various types of uncertainty. Perhaps unsurprisingly, a substantial market for financial advice has developed, served in most countries by a legion of educated finance professionals. The financial advice market is highly competitive, yet persuading consumers to part with their money in this industry requires not only knowledge of financial products but also a keen understanding of people's psychology involving money. This chapter presents empirical evidence on the role of financial advisors, not just as knowledge providers but also as decision-making experts and persuaders.

The chapter pays special attention to behavioral science research, which documents how psychological factors influence people's choices in ways that may seem irrelevant from a strictly financial perspective. The behavioral sciences are disciplines that test hypotheses about human behavior by systematically observing people in different settings, producing evidence that allows replacing some of the more implausible assumptions in the dominant theories of decision making with behaviorally informed ones. The behavioral science literature on giving and receiving advice has expanded considerably in recent years, most of it in the fields of behavioral finance, economics, and social psychology. The contributions surveyed in this chapter range from controlled laboratory experiments to field studies based on surveys or audit exercises, reflecting the richness and diversity of this interdisciplinary science.

Behavioral science research reveals countless ways in which an individual's financial choices systematically diverge from models of rational decision making. People are greatly influenced by details in the decision-making context that have no impact on the financial outcomes of their choices. They also frequently make decisions through *heuristics*, which are general rules that are thought to have evolved to allow the human brain to cope with complex choice environments (Gigerenzer and Todd 1999). Although heuristics and other decision-making shortcuts save the brain from computational overload, they can also lead to predictable mistakes, called *biases* (Kahneman and Tversky 2000; Kahneman 2003), particularly in the domain of financial decisions (Kahneman and Riepe 1998). Furthermore, consumers are often unaware of these influences. By mitigating the effects of context, heuristics, and biases whenever such influences are costly to consumers, financial advisors can provide a valuable service. But advisors have their own incentives, and as will be discussed later, the jury is still out on whether financial advisory services act as bias mitigating.

The presence of behavioral influences on decision making also means that well-intended products and policies aiming to improve choices solely by providing extra information to the decision maker often fail to deliver (Webb and Sheeran 2006). Rather than assuming that the consumer makes the best use of the information provided, a more realistic approach to product and policy design would be to put this assumption to the test. Based on existing evidence, people do not always pay sufficient attention to important messages such as the disclosure of conflicts of interest between the advisor and client (Inderst, Huck, and Chater 2010). On the positive side, timely reminder messages carefully designed to combat consumer inertia seem to hold promise (Karlan, McConnell, Mullainathan, and Zinman 2010; Financial Conduct Authority 2013). More generally, behaviorally informed approaches to financial decision making can claim some notable successes. These approaches include increasing participation and contributions in retirement plans (Madrian and Shea 2001; Thaler and Benartzi 2004), reducing the use of expensive credit products (Bertrand, Karlan, Mullaninathan, Shafir, and Zinman 2010; Bertrand and Morse 2011), and improving timely payment of taxes (Coleman 1996; Hallsworth, List, Metcalfe, and Vlaev 2014). Similar opportunities may exist for behaviorally informed financial advisory services, with technology playing a key role.

Although the focus of this chapter is on retail advice services, many of the insights from the behavioral science literature also apply to wholesale financial advice. The extent to which professional decision makers are subject to the same behavioral biases as the general public is still largely an open, empirical question, although evidence from experimental studies suggests that professionals are certainly not immune to bias.

This chapter starts with a summary of the evidence on the supply of financial advice. The next section discusses the characteristics of financial advice consumers, and is followed by a section on how these consumers respond to "behavioral" aspects of the advice process. Then, an exploration of how financial advisors may respond to the behavior of their clients is presented considering not only the opportunities for advisors to improve their clients' decisions but also the incentives created by different types of client behavior. The concluding section reflects on how a better understanding of the psychology of money affects both the nature of financial advice services and the traditional distinction between products and services.

Financial Advice—The Supply Side

This section introduces the supply side of financial advice: the professionals who offer these services, a brief description of the services offered, and some perspectives on the purpose served by financial advice in the retail market. A discussion of evidence on the financial return on using financial advice follows.

WHO OFFERS FINANCIAL ADVICE?

Various types of professionals offer financial advice. First, there is the *financial advisor,* who may also use the title *financial planner.* However, in most countries, the latter title is reserved for those who have earned a certification from a professional standards body affiliated with the Financial Planning Standards Board or a comparable body. Other certificates and titles may be available, depending on the country. In many countries, these qualifications are a legal requirement for opening a financial advice practice. Besides being qualified to give financial advice, individuals may also have earned a license to sell or recommend certain financial products requiring specialist knowledge, such as insurance products. Some individuals acting as financial advisors have accorded themselves titles such as *wealth manager* or *investment advisor,* but these titles are often not acknowledged by a professional body or are even unregulated.

Historically, financial advisors have operated independently of banks and fund providers, as is still largely the case. This means that, unlike brokers, financial advisors typically do not represent the firms whose products they recommend and sell. Furthermore, and again unlike brokers, most countries require by law that financial advisors put their clients' interests ahead of their own, which is referred to as their *fiduciary duty.*

Despite this duty, financial advisors may still receive commissions based on sales of certain financial products. Another common arrangement is *vertical integration* or a *tie-up* between advisors and fund providers, which means that the advisor is restricted to recommending products from the provider. Although the law stipulates that clients be made aware of such financial arrangements, this practice blurs the line between financial advisors and brokers. To resolve this ambiguity, the chapter defines *brokers* (or salespeople) as those whose variable earnings are entirely made up of commissions for sales and trades. By contrast, financial advisors may also receive income from charging for advice and contracting services, or receive fees based on assets under management or portfolio returns.

WHAT IS THE PURPOSE OF FINANCIAL ADVICE?

Financial advice given to consumers can cover any aspect of the client's finances. Most advice concerns investment, income security, and retirement planning, although some advisors also offer ad hoc advice on credit and mortgages.

At the start of the advice process, the advisor may help clients articulate their goals by asking a series of questions about their current finances and their plans for the future. As part of this process, the advisor also gauges how comfortable the client is with different levels of investment risk. Based on the information received from the client, the advisor then gives the client advice on saving, credit, taxation, the choice of financial products from different providers, investment opportunities, and various wealth and income risks. Key considerations are the suitability and costs of the different options. Regarding investment and savings, the stated objective is helping clients construct a well-diversified portfolio that reflects their appetite for risk, in line with modern portfolio theory (Markowitz 1952).

So, what purpose does this process of financial advice serve? The traditional economic explanation of markets for expertise, such as financial advisors, focuses on the returns on the information search (Stigler 1961). The consumer benefits from delegating the search for information to an advisor, who specializes and thus spreads the cost of acquiring such information across all clients. Because financial advice often concerns one-off decisions with high stakes, clear gains arise from specialization. This explanation, in its most basic form, assumes that consumers know how to evaluate the information they receive from advisors. Moreover, for the market to deliver good outcomes to consumers, those consumers need to understand the value proposition of different advisors. Whether these assumptions are warranted depends crucially on the consumer's sophistication, such as the individual's financial literacy and awareness of advisor incentives. Advisors may thus not have clear incentives to continue their information search until the client's marginal benefit equals marginal cost. In other words, the advisor may offer a suboptimal off-the-shelf solution without the client noticing. This situation is reminiscent of other markets for experts, such as doctors, lawyers, and car mechanics.

A related perspective is that consumers use financial advisors to protect themselves against their own cognitive biases, as argued by Bluethgen, Gintschel, Hackethal, and Mueller (2008). Financial advisors can identify and correct some cognitive biases, thus adding value by reducing costly mistakes. The authors cite the *disposition effect* (Shefrin and Statman 1985), or the tendency to sell winning stocks too soon and hold on to losers for too long, as a prominent example of the type of bias that advisors can correct. Conversely, advisors may guard against myopia by mitigating their clients' tendency to withdraw from the stock investment in a bear market. These examples show how an advisor may not only act as a purveyor of information but also provide guidance based on experience and by virtue of not being as emotionally involved as the client. The advisor can also act as a teacher, correcting mistakes to enable clients to make better choices for themselves. For example, McKenzie and Liersch (2011) show that the majority of participants in a laboratory study expect savings to grow linearly, rather than exponentially, through interest compounding. Highlighting the exponential nature of capital growth to these participants increases their motivation to save for retirement.

THE ADDED VALUE OF FINANCIAL ADVICE

Computing the added value of advisory services is challenging. The essential question is: Knowing the full, long-term costs and benefits of financial advice to a particular investor, is it in the investor's best interested to use an advisor? One approach to answering this question is to focus strictly on the financial benefits and to compare the portfolios of advised and non-advised investors. Chalmers and Reuter (2012), using data on U.S. university employees, and Hackethal, Haliassos, and Jappelli (2012), using data on customers of a German retail bank, both found that advised retirement portfolios carry more risk than self-directed portfolios and also underperform self-directed portfolios. By contrast, Kramer (2012) and Kramer and Lensink (2012) find that the advised retirement portfolios of Dutch entrepreneurs were better diversified and achieved better risk-adjusted returns. These studies controlled for the endogenous choice of using an advisor, thus ruling out selection effects (i.e., certain types of investors are more likely to receive advice).

In an attempt to reconcile these contradictory results, we need to highlight two differences between the former and the latter studies. First, all clients in the samples used by Kramer and Lensink (2012) had previous exposure to financial advice, potentially making them more sophisticated consumers of advice. Second, the financial advisors in the Kramer and Lensink study received a fixed wage, whereas those in the Chalmers and Reuter (2012) and Hackethal, Haliassos, and Jappelli (2012) studies received fees and commissions.

In an audit study, Mullainathan, Noeth, and Schoar (2012) provide controlled evidence on financial advisors' actual advice strategies. They randomly assigned professional auditors to unwitting financial advisors to ask for advice on a pre-designed investment portfolio. Instead of endowing all the auditors with well-diversified, low-cost portfolios, the authors purposely designed some of the fictional portfolios of their auditors to mimic common investment biases. They report that the recommendations of their studied financial advisors were in line with some of the predictions of portfolio theory, such as advising married clients to hold less liquidity and advising against holding employer stocks. They also note that the financial advisors were most supportive of those clients with a low-cost, well-diversified existing portfolio. But they also report that financial advisors often recommended actively managed funds with higher fees and that many financial advisors told clients to make changes even if they have low-cost, efficient portfolios. The latter result could reflect overzealous advice giving, but it does suggest that not all advice is strictly financially beneficial.

The Consumer of Financial Advice

This section examines the role of the consumer as the financial advice client, starting with an overview of the evidence on the relationship between individual characteristics and the demand for financial advice, followed by a discussion of the role of trust.

WHO LOOKS FOR FINANCIAL ADVICE?

Many studies find that women are more likely to seek financial advice than men (Joo and Grable 2001; Loibl and Hira 2011). This pattern may be due to women's preference for personal service rather than anonymous advice. Consistent with this explanation, Loibl and Hira report that women spend less time looking for financial information online or through other media.

An important factor is people's financial literacy, which is typically strongly positively correlated with experience and wealth. Using a large representative sample of the U.S. population, Lee and Cho (2005) report that financial advice clients are typically richer, older, better-educated, and more experienced investors. Using a large survey of German retail bank customers, Hackethal et al. (2012) also report that richer, older investors are more likely to have a financial advisor. Using survey data on customers from an Italian retail bank, Calcagno and Monticone (2015) find that wealthy and high financially literate individuals are more likely to consult advisors, whereas low financial literacy individuals are more likely to delegate the management of their portfolio or manage their own portfolio without advice. They also report that high financially literate individuals are more likely to invest in risky assets, such as stocks.

People's demand for advice is also affected by their psychology and emotional state. Meier and Sprenger (2013) report that individuals assigning greater value to the future are more likely to use financial advice. Gino, Brooks, and Schweitzer (2012) found that people who experience anxiety are more likely to seek out and rely on advice. They also report that anxious individuals are less able to discriminate between good and bad advice, a result that underlines the responsibility financial advisors have toward anxious clients. However, some anxiety about the future might be good for people's financial decisions. For example, Dolan and Metcalfe (2012) found that people with a negative attitude are more likely to open a savings account. Along similar lines, Hershfield, Goldstein, Sharpe, Fox, Yeykelis, Carstensen, and Bailenson (2011) find that presenting individuals with a computer-aged image of their future selves increases their pension contributions.

THE ROLE OF TRUST

What role does trust play in the advice process? In a large, pan-European survey, Georgarakos and Inderst (2014) included a measure of general trust in judging the advice given by financial institutions. They report that trust is positively related with holdings of risky assets for households with lower levels of education and self-reported financial literacy. Yet, for more educated households, trust in advice is less important, especially relative to their trust in the country's legal institutions. Calcagno and Monticone (2015) used a survey of customers of a large Italian bank. They measured the level of trust in the bank's financial advisor, which yielded both intuitive and surprising results. As might be expected, greater trust in the advisor increases the likelihood of delegating management of one's portfolio and decreases the likelihood of going it alone, but no significant relationship exists between trust and the likelihood of consulting an advisor. The survey respondents approached the bank's advisor regardless of their level of trust—this situation may have been due to the preexisting exclusive relationship with the advisor. When advice was instead offered "out of the blue," as in a field study on a random sample of customers of a German brokerage firm reported by Bhattarchaya, Hackethal, Kaesler, Loos, and Meyer (2012), customers will be wary of the quality of the advice. Only 5 percent of customers in the field study accepted the offer of advice provided by email and over the telephone.

The level of trust in an advisor also changes during the interaction between advisor and prospective client. Little evidence exists from the field, but experimental research on advisor–advisee interaction provides some clues. First, people are more likely to follow more experienced advisors (Harvey and Fischer 1997). Second, advisor–advisee similarity matters; Gino, Shang, and Croson (2009) report that individuals in a telephone survey experiment were more likely to follow advice from advisors that are similar to them in terms of gender, education, age, region, and political affiliation. The financial advisor's interest may therefore be served by highlighting such similarities before giving advice. Morris, Nadler, Kurtzberg, and Thompson (2002) report that business transactions are more likely to succeed when the initiating party highlights things that the two parties have in common before any negotiation occurs.

Trust is also a function of how the advisor communicates. Joiner and Leveson (2006) find that clients give higher ratings to financial advisors who use less technical language and investment jargon. Furthermore, more confident advisors do not always have a bigger impact. Although some evidence suggests that people are more likely to follow advisors with extreme and confident judgments (Price and Stone 2004; Van Swol and Sniezek 2005), this bias tends to disappear when information on advisors' accuracy is available (Tenney, Spellman, and MacCoun 2008). Moreover, Karmarkar and Tormala (2010) present experimental evidence that experts are actually perceived as more persuasive if they admit some uncertainty about their recommendations.

Yet, there may be a dark side to trustworthiness. Laboratory experiments on conflict-of-interest scenarios suggest that simply disclosing a conflict of interest does not make it go away. Paradoxically, advisors who disclose a conflict of interest to clients thereby build so much trust that their clients follow biased advice that is in their advisor's best interest but not their own (Loewenstein, Cain, and Sah 2011). Further experiments show that this social conflict is somewhat mitigated if the disclosure is done by a third party, or when the client is given time and privacy to make the advised decision (Sah, Loewenstein, and Cain 2013).

Behavioral Aspects of the Advice Process

The preceding section introduced some aspects of consumer psychology that determine consumers' demand and their perceptions of advisor trustworthiness. In this section, the advice process itself is unpacked, highlighting evidence on contextual factors and details that are not considered in typical models of financial advice, but which may substantially alter consumers' response to advice.

CHOOSING THE CHANNEL

Ciccotello and Wood (2001) experimentally simulated the process of procuring advice on investment scenarios through different communication channels, in this case using either live advisors (student participants) or online sources. They report that the variance in recommendations from both sources of advice is similar, but note that live advisors are better at taking the particularities of wealthy clients into account. However, the authors do not present any results on how clients perceive the advice. Evidence that people consider face-to-face advice more appropriate comes from a study on health advice by Labarère, Torres, Fourny, Argento, Gensburger, and Menthonnex (2003). The authors report that people prefer face-to-face contact because it allows them to better explain the particularities of their situation.

Riegelsberger, Sasse, and McCarthy (2005) present laboratory participants with financial advice that was provided through different channels: video, audio, virtual chat, text only, and text accompanied by a photo of the advisor. They find that participants prefer audio and video advice, but that their financial risk-taking is sensitive to any form of advice provided. Obviously, the latter result may not arise in real-world settings where investors have access to more than one type of advice and typically choose their own preferred channel.

Another prominent channel is on-line advice. Sillence and Briggs (2007) report survey evidence that consumers' evaluations of online advice are highly sensitive to indicators of trustworthiness. These indicators include known financial brands or personal recommendations, website design in line with the rest of the financial sector, and parallels with the off-line advice process (tailored information, personal involvement in the advice process, and identifiability of the people behind the website). Pi, Liao, and Chen (2012) find that perceptions of transaction security, reputation, design quality, and ease of navigation influence consumers' level of trust in advice websites.

ADVICE PACKAGING, FRAMING, AND PRIMING

How financial advisors "package" their advice is another key factor. These effects can be very subtle. For example, Brown, Kling, Mullainathan, and Wrobel (2008) show that the majority of individuals prefer a savings account to a life annuity when the choice is framed as an investment decision, but this pattern reverses when the choice is framed as a future consumption decision. Differences in presentation also affect the willingness to invest in riskier assets, such as stocks, that would give them greater returns on their investment. Recent laboratory and field studies suggest that the extent to which this happens depends on how portfolio risk is presented. Anagol and Gamble (2013) report that people select riskier portfolios when asset portfolio data are presented as aggregates instead of as a list of individual assets. Bateman, Eckert, Geweke, Louviere, Satchell, and Thorp (2014) report that individuals choose riskier portfolios when the risk is presented in a graph rather than when expressed as text percentages. The authors also report that people with lower financial literacy are more susceptible to presentation effects. Furthermore, Kaufmann, Weber, and Haisley (2013) show that letting people "experience" risk by having them draw sample returns from a historical returns distribution leads them to choose riskier portfolios, without increasing regret or anxiety afterwards.

People's financial decisions are also greatly sensitive to what is presented to them as the default option. According to Madrian and Shea (2001), 71 percent of savers in a U.S. retirement plan choose the default fund. Data from pension system reforms in Sweden presented by Engström and Westerberg (2003) tell a similar story. Despite the presence of many alternatives, aggressive advertising by fund providers, and a nationwide information campaign, 33 percent of Swedes stick to the default investment option provided by the government. Defaults are not just effective because they signal endorsement; they also capitalize on an individual's inertia (also known as status quo bias). An example of using inertia "for good," in combination with the basic human tendency to discount future cash flows, is the Save More Tomorrow program by Thaler and Benartzi (2004). In this program, people pre-commit to contributing higher percentages of future wages to a pension scheme whenever they receive a wage increase. Thaler and Benartzi report an increase in the contribution rate from 3.5 percent to 11.6 percent over a 28-month period.

Another subtle influence on decisions is what is termed peer effects: people often mimic their peers. Duflo and Saez (2003) show that individuals are more likely to enroll in a university pension plan when their co-workers attend retirement benefits information fairs. As Bursztyn, Ederer, Ferman, and Yuchtman (2014) show, investors are more likely to invest in a new investment vehicle offered by their brokers when others have done so or have simply indicated a desire to do so. However, providing information on peer choices does not always move people toward the planned or socially desirable outcome. Beshears, Choi, Laibson, Madrian, and Milkman (2015) find that informing employees of a U.S. manufacturing firm of their co-workers' savings rates actually lowers the chance that these employees will subsequently enroll in their employer's pension plan. The authors attribute this surprising result to the demotivating effect of upward social comparisons.

PAYING FOR ADVICE

A final aspect of financial advice that can be presented and packaged in different ways is its price. The most common model of paying for advice is indirect, through sales commissions paid by product providers to advisors. Inderst, Huck, and Chater (2010) provide evidence from a large pan-European survey that consumers often underestimate the potential conflicts of interest generated by a commission-based compensation model. Owing to policymakers' concerns about these conflicts of interest, some jurisdictions have now moved to a fee-based advice model. According to Hoffman, Franken, and Broekhuizen (2012), this solution may exclude some individuals from the benefits of financial advice because people are reluctant to pay for advice before they see the benefits. But over time, consumers may become accustomed to paying for advice up front. Evidence from experiments suggests that people may even attribute a specific value to paid-for advice: they are more likely to follow advice they paid for than follow free advice (Sniezek, Schrah, and Dalal 2004; Patt, Bowles, and Cash 2006).

Godek and Murray (2008) report results from a laboratory experiment showing that people pay more for advice when they are primed to think about future investment decisions than when they are primed to think about past decisions. Although speculative, this pattern of behavior may extend to the more general question of framing cost over time. That is, people are more likely to pay a fee when it is framed as a cost of expected benefits than for benefits already realized.

Behaviorally Informed Financial Advice

This section returns to the supply side of the market. The approach here can be summed up in the following question: Assuming that advisors are aware of the consumer characteristics and behaviors presented in the preceding two sections, how might advisors position themselves in the market? It will be insightful to compare some of the possible outcomes described here to the current situation in markets, or to the theoretical perspectives on financial advice presented in the first section. One outcome that seems consistent with at least a casual observation of markets is the *intangible value of advice*—the idea that many people value financial advice for more than just its expected financial return.

TOOLS FOR TAKING RISK

Much of the academic literature on investments highlights the fact that stocks have historically outperformed other asset classes. However, prospective investors will have to be comfortable with the greater level of risk associated with investing in stocks. One important role that financial advisors can play in this process is making their clients feel more comfortable with this risk, thus unlocking higher returns. The preceding section on consumer behavior has highlighted various tools that the advisor can use for this purpose, such as different ways of presenting investment risk and experiential simulation. Advisors may also feel that setting defaults and using "social proof" and "peer effect" type strategies will help to convince their clients to invest in stocks. As effective as these strategies may turn out to be, advisors should continue to educate their clients on the risk associated with these investments. Using persuasion strategies that prompt the client to engage with risk is much more (legally) defensible than strategies that tempt the client to blindly follow others.

SCREENING FOR UNSOPHISTICATES

Much of the survey evidence shows that the likelihood of having a financial advisor is positively related to financial literacy, itself positively correlated with education and wealth. Calcagno and Monticone (2015) present an explanation for this pattern, starting from the premise that advisors will find that providing high-quality advice is only worthwhile to well-informed and wealthy investors. If consumers anticipate they will be screened on this basis, advice will only serve a purpose for better-informed and relatively wealthy consumers. Consumers with lower levels of financial sophistication and wealth can still use financial intermediaries for portfolio management, but the relationship will not be based on the transmission of information or knowledge. The evidence reviewed here suggests that less sophisticated consumers are more likely to select their advisor on trust. In this segment of the market, a problem of asymmetric information may occur because the less sophisticated investor may be unable to verify whether advice is trustworthy. Inderst and Ottaviani (2012) show that investors who lack awareness of advisor commissions face similar challenges.

A related issue is that people value a personalized service, tailored to their needs and taking the peculiarities of their situation into account. For the wealthier investor, providing personalized service may be worth the advisor's time if the advisor can recoup his or her costs in fees. But for investors with less wealth, the extra time spent on personalization may have to be recouped some other way. If the client is loath to pay fees, then the only alternative for the advisor may be to recommend products with higher commissions.

THE INTANGIBLE VALUE OF ADVICE

Evidence shows that financial advisory services do not only have financial value but also provide clients with some intangible psychological benefits. Del Guercio and Reuters (2011) pursue this line of argument in their discussion of the U.S. mutual funds market. They contend that two types of retail investors exist: those who only care for fund returns, and those who derive intangible benefits of making advised investments. Del Guercio and Reuters present data that support the notion that mutual funds target these two consumer segments separately. Providing evidence from market outcomes, Bergstresser, Chalmers, and Tufano (2009) report that broker-sold funds deliver significantly lower risk-adjusted returns than do direct-sold funds. The authors point out that this difference may be due to the intangible benefits of broker services. However, they do not exclude the possibility that brokers' sales commissions play a role in generating the difference.

A clever observation by Canner, Mankiw, and Weil (1997) highlights another way in which advisors' recommendations may be tailored to provide intangible benefits. They note that one of the key implications of the influential capital asset pricing model (CAPM) is that investors can diversify their portfolio for a given risk appetite by changing the allocation of cash and a "market portfolio" comprising stocks and bonds. But a survey of advisors' advertised portfolio recommendations for investors with different risk profiles shows that the recommended portfolio ratio of stocks to bonds goes up as investor risk appetite increases. These results suggest that financial advisors consider factors other than the historical return data necessary for recommending portfolios on the efficient frontier. These factors may be intangible and "behavioral" in nature, such as clients' need to be convinced that the suggested portfolio matches their risk appetite. Further support for this notion comes from survey research of financial advisors themselves. A study by MacGregor, Slovic, Berry, and Evensky (1999) finds that the variance in financial advisors' perceptions of the risk of certain asset classes is 98 percent explained by three factors: volatility, knowledge, and worry.

Some experimental evidence indicates that the intangible benefits of advice can actually be measured in the brain. Engelmann, Capra, Noussair, and Berns (2009) conducted a neuroscience experiment and find that financial decisions are less taxing for individuals who receive advice. These findings raise questions especially concerning the outcomes of consumers who have a particularly strong preference for advised decision making. Clients who are anxious and/or value peace of mind particularly highly, for example, may be less sensitive to the costs of financial advisory services. If so, financial advisors may market specific products and services to these clients. *Portfolio churning*, or the excessive (and expensive) rebalancing of client portfolios by financial advisors, may be one such "service."

THE PRICE POINT

Although this chapter has highlighted various aspects of pricing financial advice, it is worth considering two final aspects of pricing. First, some fees may be more visible to consumers than others. Using the pricing of printers and printer cartridges as an example, Gabaix and Laibson (2006) show that people pay more attention to visible up-front costs than hidden expenses that occur later. In pricing financial advisory services, advisors may have an incentive to keep the fee of the initial advice relatively low, instead increasing less prominent fees such as ongoing management and administration fees. Another type of fee that may be left out of consumers' calculations is the exit charge for certain investment funds. Although these charges typically decrease over time, consumers may still overestimate the time they will hold a particular fund.

To reduce consumers' focus on a single cost or return figure, financial advisors may thus want to operate several different charges. Note that it is not just a question of whether costs are incurred immediately or later, or whether one-off larger expenditures are more likely to attract the consumer's attention. As the experimental findings of Godek and Murray (2008) illustrate, an incentive may also exist to frame ongoing charges as related to future investment gains instead of to current planning activity. Clients' evaluation of advice fees may be influenced by framing that suggests the fees belong in a certain "mental account" (Thaler 1985).

Summary and Conclusions

Advising people on their financial decisions requires a high level of detailed knowledge and skill. This chapter reviewed extensive evidence that this skill set comprises more than just financial expertise and that giving advice to clients goes beyond a review of their options, personal situation, and stated objectives. Contextual factors, decision-making frames, and perception of risk are just some of the behavioral aspects that feed into clients' overall assessment of the value of advice. The financial advisor seeking use the wealth of behavioral insights will be spoiled for choice. A useful starting point would be a more specific behavior-change framework as a checklist to explore the options available. Examples of such frameworks are Nudge (Thaler and Sunstein 2008) and Mindspace (Dolan, Elliott, Metcalfe, and Vlaev 2012).

The picture that emerges from this chapter is that of a sector of experts who do not serve simply as purveyors of information to those who need it. Certainly, a substantial segment of sophisticated consumers are willing to pay for advisory services and appear to benefit financially from receiving advice. For less sophisticated advisors, whether advice always delivers financial benefits is less clear. Especially in markets where commission payments from product providers are relatively large, consumers may be worse off with an advised portfolio. When financial advisors also offer education and planning services that compensate for common investment mistakes and consumer inertia, the balance may again tip in favor of advised portfolios. Evidence suggests that advisors actively help consumers eliminate common mistakes, helping them to lower expenses and create more diversified investment portfolios. Conversely, incentives exist for advisors to leverage some of the trust earned for generating profits through higher ongoing fees and more frequent transactions.

An important change in the sector is the increase in technologically driven financial advice. *Robo-advisors*, or online investment platforms that provide consumers with an online equivalent of a financial advice consultation, is a rapidly growing global phenomenon. They often provide a combination of financial advice and products because many of the funds they offer to clients are managed in-house. Because robo-advisors have a low marginal cost per extra client consulted, their business model allows them to reach out to consumers who might not have the means to access a traditional financial advisor. Some have raised the concern that such platforms will be unable to educate consumers sufficiently in the process. Some of these platforms do, however, offer educational content to appeal to more financially literate consumers, or offer private banking services beyond their automated advice. In fact, some robo-advisors are actively trying to establish a reputation for mitigating investor biases by building in features that protect against bias-driven behaviors. This is an interesting development, where the scale advantages of technology might bring behaviorally informed investing to consumers in ways that traditional financial advice would be unable to do. Although most advised clients will, for the foreseeable future, prefer to have a person in charge of their finances, dismissing online financial advice as a low-quality mass-market commodity is premature. Additionally, many hybrid forms of technological and personal advice may develop. A key question is whether robo-advisors will simply shift profits from the intermediary to the fund provider, or whether they will deliver suitable advice at a lower cost to consumers.

To advance the field, note three particular topics that would benefit from more investigation. First, there is a need for more detailed evidence on how advice reduces common investors' biases, not only at the point of portfolio composition but also throughout the advisor–investor interaction. Second, consumers' willingness to pay for advice services is underexplored—there is a lack of empirical evidence on how consumers respond to different pricing models. Third, many of the topics covered in this chapter might well have to be reevaluated in the context of the growing role of technology in financial decision making, which is slowly turning financial services into products across much of the sector. Understanding the impact of this process on firms, policymakers, and consumers is perhaps the greatest and most relevant challenge.

DISCUSSION QUESTIONS

1. Explain the difference between financial advisors and brokers.
2. Discuss the purpose of financial advice to consumers.
3. Describe the types of consumers who are more likely to look for financial advice.
4. Explain why high-quality financial advice may not reach those who would benefit the most from it.
5. Describe characteristics of financial advisors that affect the degree to which consumers follow their advice.

REFERENCES

Anagol, Santosh, and Keith J. Gamble. 2013. "Does Presenting Investment Results Asset by Asset Lower Risk Taking?" *Journal of Behavioral Finance* 14:4, 276–300.

Bateman, Hazel, Christine Eckert, John Geweke, Jordan Louviere, Stephen Satchell, and Susan Thorp. 2014. "Financial Competence, Risk Presentation and Retirement Portfolio Preferences." *Journal of Pension Economics and Finance* 13:1, 27–61.

Bergstresser, Daniel, John M. R. Chalmers, and Peter Tufano. 2009. "Assessing the Costs and Benefits of Brokers in the Mutual Fund Industry." *Review of Financial Studies* 22:10, 4129–4156.

Bertrand, Marianne, and Adair Morse. 2011. "Information Disclosure, Cognitive Biases, and Payday Borrowing." *Journal of Finance* 66:6, 1865–1893.

Bertrand, Marianne, Dean Karlan, Sendhil Mullainathan, Eldar Shafir, and Jonathan Zinman. 2010. "What's Advertising Content Worth? Evidence from a Consumer Credit Marketing Field Experiment." *Quarterly Journal of Economics* 125:1, 263–305.

Beshears, John, James J. Choi, David Laibson, Brigitte C. Madrian, and Katherine L. Milkman, 2015. "The Effect of Providing Peer Information on Retirement Savings Decisions." *Journal of Finance* 70:3, 1161–1201.

Bhattacharya, Utpal, Andreas Hackethal, Simon Kaesler, Benjamin Loos, and Steffen Meyer. 2012. "Is Unbiased Financial Advice to Retail Investors Sufficient? Answers from a Large Field Study." *Review of Financial Studies* 25:4, 975–1032.

Bluethgen, Ralph, Andreas Gintschel, Andreas Hackethal, and Armin Mueller. 2008. "Financial Advice and Individual Investors' Portfolios." Working Paper, European Business School. Available at http://papers.ssrn.com/sol3/papers.cfm?abstract_id=968197.

Brown, Jeffrey R., Jeffrey R. Kling, Sendhil Mullainathan and Marian V. Wrobel. 2008. "Why Don't People Insure Late Life Consumption: A Framing Explanation of the Under-annuitization Puzzle." NBER Working Paper, No. 13748.

Bursztyn, Leonardo, Florian Ederer, Bruno Ferman, and Noam Yuchtman. 2014. "Understanding Mechanisms Underlying Peer Effects: Evidence from a Field Experiment on Financial Decisions." *Econometrica* 82:4, 1237–1301.

Calcagno, Riccardo, and Chiara Monticone. 2015. "Financial Literacy and the Demand for Financial Advice." *Journal of Banking & Finance* 50:1, 363–380.

Canner, Niko, N. Gregory Mankiw, and David N. Weil. 1997. "An Asset Allocation Puzzle." *American Economic Review* 87:1, 181–191.

Chalmers, John, and Jonathan Reuter. 2012. "What Is the Impact of Financial Advisors on Retirement Portfolio Choices and Outcomes?" NBER Working Paper, w18158.

Ciccotello, S. Conrad, and Russell E. Wood. 2001. "An Investigation of the Consistency of Financial Advice Offered by Web-based Sources." *Financial Services Review* 10:1, 5–18.

Coleman, Stephen, 1996. "The Minnesota Income Tax Compliance Experiment: State Tax Results. MPRA Munich Working Paper, No. 4827.

Del Guercio, Diane, and Jonathan Reuter. 2011. "Mutual Fund Performance and the Incentive to Invest in Active Management." NBER Working Paper No. 17491.

Dolan, Paul, Antony Elliott, Robert Metcalfe, and Ivo Vlaev. 2012. "Influencing Financial Behavior: From Changing Minds to Changing Contexts." *Journal of Behavioral Finance* 13:1, 127–143.

Dolan, Paul, and Robert Metcalfe. 2012. "Feelings and Finances: The Role of Affect in Behavior Related to an Online Financial Health Check." Money Advice Service Working Paper No. 2392.

Duflo, Esther, and Emmanuel Saez. 2003. "The Role of Information and Social Interactions in Retirement Plan Decisions: Evidence from a Randomized Experiment." *Quarterly Journal of Economics* 118:3, 815–842.

Engelmann, Jan B., C. Monica Capra, Charles Noussair, and Gregory S. Berns, 2009. "Expert Financial Advice Neurobiologically "Offloads" Financial Decision-making under Risk." PLoS one 4:3, e4957. Available at: http://journals.plos.org/plosone/article?id=10.1371/journal.pone.0004957.

Engström, Stefan, and Anna Westerberg. 2003. "Which Individuals Make Active Investment Decisions in the New Swedish Pension System?" *Journal of Pension Economics and Finance* 2:3, 225–245.

Financial Conduct Authority. 2013. "Encouraging Consumers to Claim Redress: Evidence from a Field Trial." FCA Occasional Paper No 2. London, UK.

Gabaix, Xavier, and David Laibson, 2006. "Shrouded Attributes, Consumer Myopia, and Information Suppression in Competitive Markets." *Quarterly Journal of Economics* 121:2, 505–540.

Georgarakos, Dimitris, and Roman Inderst. 2014. "Financial Advice and Stock Market Participation." Working Paper, University of Frankfurt. Available at: http://papers.ssrn.com/sol3/papers.cfm?abstract_id=1641302.

Gigerenzer, Gerd, and Peter M. Todd. 1999. *Simple Heuristics that Make Us Smart*. Oxford: Oxford University Press.

Gino, Francesca, Alison Wood Brooks, and Maurice E. Schweitzer. 2012. "Anxiety, Advice, and the Ability to Discern: Feeling Anxious Motivates Individuals to Seek and Use Advice." *Journal of Personality and Social Psychology* 102:3, 497–504.

Gino, Francesca, Jen Shang, and Rachel Croson. 2009. "The Impact of Information from Similar or Different Advisors on Judgment." *Organizational Behavior and Human Decision Processes* 108:2, 287–302.

Godek, John, and Kyle B. Murray. 2008. "Willingness to Pay for Advice: The Role of Rational and Experiential Processing." *Organizational Behavior and Human Decision Processes* 106:1, 77–87.

Hackethal, Andreas, Michael Haliassos, and Tullio Jappelli. 2012. "Financial Advisors: A Case of Babysitters?" *Journal of Banking & Finance* 36:2, 509–524.

Hallsworth, Michael, John A. List, Robert D. Metcalfe, and Ivo Vlaev. 2014. "The Behavioralist as Tax Collector: Using Natural Field Experiments to Enhance Tax Compliance." NBER Working Paper No. 20007.

Harvey, Nigel, and Ilan Fischer. 1997. "Taking Advice: Accepting Help, Improving Judgment, and Sharing Responsibility." *Organizational Behavior and Human Decision Processes* 70:4, 117–133.

Hershfield, Hal E., Daniel G. Goldstein, William F. Sharpe, Jesse Fox, Leo Yeykelis, Laura L. Carstensen, Jeremy N. Bailenson. 2011. "Increasing Saving Behavior through Age-Progressed Renderings of the Future Self." *Journal of Marketing Research* 48:2, S23–S37.

Hoffman, Arvid O. I., Heiner Franken, and Thijs L. J. Broekhuizen. 2012. "Customer Intention to Adopt a Fee-based Advisory Model: An Empirical Study in Retail Banking." *International Journal of Bank Marketing* 30:2, 102–127.

Inderst, Roman, Steffen Huck, and Nick Chater, 2010. "Consumer Decision-making in Retail Investment Services: A Behavioural Economics Perspective." Final Report to the European Commission, No. 22.

Inderst, Roman, and Marco Ottaviani. 2012. "Financial Advice." *Journal of Economic Literature* 50:2, 494–512.

Joiner, Therese A., and Lynne Leveson. 2006. "Financial Planner Credibility: The Importance of Being Understood." *International Journal of Financial Services Management* 1:4, 438–449.

Joo, So-Hyun, and John E. Grable. 2001. "Factors Associated with Seeking and Using Professional Retirement-Planning Help." *Family and Consumer Sciences Research Journal* 30:1, 37–63.

Kahneman, Daniel. 2003. "Maps of Bounded Rationality: Psychology for Behavioral Economics." *American Economic Review* 93:3, 1449–1475.

Kahneman, Daniel, and Mark W. Riepe. 1998. "Aspects of Investor Psychology." *Journal of Portfolio Management* 24:4, 52–65.

Kahneman, Daniel, and Amos Tversky. 2000. *Choices, Values and Frames*. New York: Cambridge University Press and the Russell Sage Foundation.

Karlan, Dean, Margaret McConnell, Sendhil Mullainathan, and Jonathan Zinman. 2010. "Getting to the Top of Mind: How Reminders Increase Saving." NBER Working Paper No. w16205.

Karmarkar, Uma R., and Zakary L. Tormala. 2010. "Believe Me, I Have No Idea What I'm Talking About: The Effects of Source Certainty on Consumer Involvement and Persuasion." *Journal of Consumer Research* 36:6, 1033–1049.

Kaufmann, Christine, Martin Weber, and Emily Haisley. 2013. "The Role of Experience Sampling and Graphical Displays on One's Investment Risk Appetite." *Management Science* 59:2, 323–340.

Kramer, Marc M. 2012. "Financial Advice and Individual Investor Portfolio Performance." *Financial Management* 41:2, 395–428.

Kramer, Marc, and Robert Lensink. 2012. "The Impact of Financial Advisors on the Stock Portfolios of Retail Investors." Midwest Finance Association 2013 Annual Meeting.

Labarère, José, Jean-Pierre Torres, Patrice Francois, Magali Fourny, Philippe Argento, Xavier Gensburger, and Philippe Menthonnex. 2003. "Patient Compliance with Medical Advice given by Telephone." *American Journal of Emergency Medicine* 21:2, 288–292.

Lee, Jinkook, and Jinsook Cho. 2005. "Consumers' Use of Information Intermediaries and the Impact on Their Information Search Behavior in the Financial Market." *Journal of Consumer Affairs* 39:1, 95–120.

Loewenstein, George, Daylian M. Cain, and Sunita Sah. 2011. "The Limits of Transparency: Pitfalls and Potential of Disclosing Conflicts of Interest." *American Economic Review* 101:3, 423–428.

Loibl, Cäzilia, and Tahira K. Hira. 2011. "Know Your Subject: A Gendered Perspective on Investor Information Search." *Journal of Behavioral Finance* 12:3, 117–130.

MacGregor, Donald G., Paul Slovic, Michael Berry, and Harold R. Evensky. 1999. "Perception of Financial Risk: A Survey Study of Advisors and Planners." *Journal of Financial Planning* 12:8, 68–86.

Madrian, Brigitte C., and Dennis F. Shea. 2001. "The Power of Suggestion: Inertia in 401 (k) Participation and Savings Behavior." NBER Working Paper No. 7682.

Markowitz, Harry. 1952. "Portfolio Selection." *Journal of Finance* 7:1, 77–91.

McKenzie, Craig R. M., and Michael J. Liersch. 2011. "Misunderstanding Savings Growth: Implications for Retirement Savings Behavior." *Journal of Marketing Research* 48:1, S1–S13.

Meier, Stephan, and Charles D. Sprenger. 2013. "Discounting Financial Literacy: Time Preferences and Participation in Financial Education Programs." *Journal of Economic Behavior & Organization* 95:3, 159–174.

Morris, Michael, Janice Nadler, Terri Kurtzberg, and Leigh Thompson. 2002. "Schmooze or Lose: Social Friction and Lubrication in e-mail Negotiations." *Group Dynamics: Theory, Research, and Practice* 6:2, 89–100.

Mullainathan, Sendhil, Markus Noeth, and Annette Schoar. 2012. "The Market for Financial Advice: An Audit Study." NBER Working Paper, w17929.

Patt, Anthony G., Hannah R. Bowles, and David W. Cash. 2006. "Mechanisms for Enhancing the Credibility of an Adviser: Prepayment and Aligned Incentives." *Journal of Behavioral Decision Making* 19:4, 347–359.

Pi, Shih-Ming, Hsiu-Li Liao, and Hui-Min Chen. 2012. "Factors That Affect Consumers' Trust and Continuous Adoption of Online Financial Services." *International Journal of Business and Management* 7:9, 108–117.

Price, Paul C., and Eric R. Stone. 2004. "Intuitive Evaluation of Likelihood Judgment Producers: Evidence for a Confidence Heuristic." *Journal of Behavioral Decision Making* 17:1, 39–57.

Riegelsberger, Jens, M. Angela Sasse, and John D. McCarthy. 2005. "Rich Media, Poor Judgment? A Study of Media Effects on Users' Trust in Expertise." *Proceedings of the HCI-05 Conference on People and Computers* 19:2, 267–284.

Sah, Sunita, George Loewenstein, and Daylian M. Cain. 2013. "The Burden of Disclosure: Increased Compliance with Distrusted Advice." *Journal of Personality and Social Psychology* 104:2, 289–301.

Shefrin, Hersh, and Meir Statman. 1985. "The Disposition to Sell Winners Too Early and Ride Losers Too Long: Theory and Evidence." *Journal of Finance* 40:3, 777–790.

Sillence, Elizabeth, and Pam Briggs. 2007. "Please Advise: Using the Internet for Health and Financial Advice." *Computers in Human Behavior* 23:2, 727–748.

Sniezek, Janet A., Gunnar E. Schrah, and Reeshad S. Dalal. 2004. "Improving Judgement with Prepaid Expert Advice." *Journal of Behavioral Decision Making* 17:3, 173–190.

Stigler, George J. 1961. "The Economics of Information." *Journal of Political Economy* 69:3, 213–225.

Tenney, Elizabeth R., Barbara A. Spellman, and Robert J. MacCoun. 2008. "The Benefits of Knowing What You Know (and What You Don't): How Calibration Affects Credibility." *Journal of Experimental Social Psychology* 44:5, 1368–1375.

Thaler, Richard. 1985. "Mental Accounting and Consumer Choice." *Marketing Science* 4:3, 199–214.

Thaler, Richard H., and Shlomo Benartzi. 2004. "Save More Tomorrow: Using Behavioral Economics to Increase Employee Saving." *Journal of Political Economy* 112:1, 164–187.

Thaler, Richard H., and Cass R. Sunstein. 2008. *Nudge: Improving Decisions about Health, Wealth, and Happiness*. New Haven, CT: Yale University Press.

Van Swol, Lyn M., and Janet A. Sniezek. 2005. "Factors Affecting the Acceptance of Expert Advice." *British Journal of Social Psychology* 44:2, 443–461.

Webb, Thomas, and Paschal Sheeran. 2006. "Does Changing Behavioral Intentions Engender Behavior Change? A Meta-analysis of the Experimental Evidence." *Psychological Bulletin* 132:3, 249–268.

17

Insurance and Risk Management

JAMES M. MOTEN JR., CFP®, CHFC®, RICP®, CRPC, CMFC
Assistant Professor of Finance
East Central University

C. W. COPELAND, CHFC®, RICP®, CLU
Assistant Professor of Insurance
The American College of Financial Services

Introduction

Economics is predicated on human decision-making processes. Traditional economic theory suggests that individuals make decisions that are in their own best interests and are consistent in their preferences. That is, they do not intentionally make decisions that would make them worse off. Individuals often seek assistance from advisors to help them accumulate assets for building wealth, thereby also improving their financial decision making. However, part of an advisor's responsibility is helping clients protect their accumulated wealth. This goal makes them better off financially, but is seldom communicated in such a manner.

This chapter explains how individuals make insurance purchasing decisions using risk management techniques within the constructs of behavioral finance. First, the chapter describes the types of risk, then surveys the most common types of insurance for individuals. Following is a brief survey of behavioral finance, leading to a discussion of the interactions of behavioral finance, insurance, and risk management. The chapter concludes with a summary and conclusions.

Insurance and Risk Tolerance

Insurance is a contract protecting against risk and containing four elements—offer and acceptance, consideration, competent parties, and a lawful purpose—that provides an individual or entity protection against financial losses caused by perils (Moten 2014). Purchasing insurance is based on the principle of *indemnification*, which involves compensating a party for a loss or damaged property to make the party whole again. To spread the cost of paying claims, insurance is also based on the law of large numbers. The *law of large numbers* is a statistical assessment stating that the larger the number of homogeneous exposure units independently exposed to loss, the greater is the probability that the actual loss occurred will equal the expected loss. The law of large numbers contrasts with the *law of small numbers*, which is a judgmental bias based on the belief that a sample population can be accurately predicted from a small number of observations. Insurance is a misunderstood commodity.

Later in this chapter, the topic of framing is discussed. At its core, *framing* concerns how to communicate with a client. Documentation shows that the perception of a problem not only depends on its presentation but also on the mindset of the decision maker. Advisors encounter people on an emotional roller-coaster desiring to achieve financial security. Insurance is rarely at the top of clients' lists, but when faced with their own mortality or that of a loved one, there's a shift in attention. Although insurance is relevant for all clients, its level of importance tends to increase with age. Advisors can guide clients seeking different types of insurance. Because clients differ, advisors need to improve their skills at presenting relevant information to different types of clients. When they frame insurance properly, its merits become clear to clients. As an economic tool, consumers can use insurance to build, protect, and pass on wealth. By framing insurance in this manner, consumers may better understand its benefits and not view it as a commodity.

THE NATURE OF RISK

Risk has different meanings to different people and varies with the individual (Yazdipour and Neace 2013). For example, Markowitz (1952), who developed modern portfolio theory (MPT), indicates that risk-averse investors attempt to develop a portfolio that maximizes their return for a given level of risk. Others view risk as a condition in which a possibility of loss exists. Insurance serves as a hedge against pure risk. *Pure risk* is a risk in which a chance of loss or no loss exists. No chance of gain exists, as there is the case of speculative risk; examples of speculative risk are playing the lottery and gambling.

The two primary types of risk that can affect an investment are systematic risk and unsystematic risk. *Systematic risk*, also called nondiversifiable risk, is the uncertainty inherent in the entire market. *Unsystematic risk*, also called diversifiable risk, is risk that is specific to a company. Diversification is useful in hedging against unsystematic or company-specific risk. For example, if workers of a company went on strike, the strike would only impact the company or possibly its industry; this is unsystematic risk. In contrast, a major terrorist attack such as the September 11, 2001, attack on Twin Towers in New York City or the Federal Reserve Bank's sudden raising of interest rates could affect the entire market, and hence are systematic risks (Moten 2014).

Risk can also be defined as possessing characteristics of objective risk and subjective risk. *Objective risk* has quantitative aspects that are numerical or statistical components and thus is well defined and measurable. *Subjective risk* has qualitative factors whereby the assessment of risk is based on perception, cognitive issues, and emotions, which are less defined and unmeasurable.

Insurance allows consumers to protect themselves from large losses for a relatively small premium. *Perils* are the causes of a possible loss resulting from such events as fires, lightning, explosions, aircraft damage, riots, smoke, and terrorism. *Hazards* are conditions that increase the likelihood that a loss will occur; the three primary types of hazards are physical, moral, and morale. *Physical hazards* are environmental conditions that affect or enhance the frequency and severity of a loss. *Moral hazards* involve dishonest behavior that causes loss. Morale hazards leads to attitudes of negligence and carelessness that dominate because of the existence of insurance.

The four primary responses to risk are risk avoidance, risk retention, risk reduction, and risk transfer. Of course, an individual may avoid the risk of loss by not engaging in an activity or owning property. Risk retention is the most common method of handling risk, however, and should be those risks that lead only to small losses. Risk reduction may be accomplished through loss prevention and loss control. When one party transfers the chance of loss to another party, that is a popular form of risk handling; purchasing insurance is a form of risk transfer.

BEHAVIORAL RESPONSES TO RISK

Insurance provides a framework for studying actual investor behaviors, such as rationality, bounded rationality, and prospect theory. *Rationality* refers to a decision in which the decision maker intentionally attempts to optimize utility. Alternatively, *bounded rationality* refers to limitations of the decision maker in access to information, cognitive ability, and available time (Copeland 2015). *Prospect theory* describes how real-world decisions involving risk can deviate from the rational decisions of expected utility theory. According to Simon (1955), individuals sometimes make decisions that appear to be irrational based on current information, situation, capability, and the environment in which they operate.

An individual typically *retains* a risk when both its severity and frequency are low. An example would be paying out of pocket to replace a Blu-ray disk; the cost of the disk has dropped substantially over time, and if damaged, is minimal to replace it. An individual typically *reduces* a risk when both the severity and the frequency are high. An example would be wearing a seatbelt while driving; auto accidents frequently happen and their results can be severe. The opportunity to avoid a risk is rare. Additionally, an individual typically *transfers* a risk if the severity is high and the frequency is low. An example is buying homeowners insurance to protect against catastrophic incidents; the cost of replacing a home is high, but the frequency of a fire is low, so consumers buy insurance when they want to transfer the risk of incurring placement costs from themselves to an insurance company.

Basic Types of Insurance

Five main types of insurance are available for individuals:

- **Disability**. This insurance replaces a portion of the insured's salary if the individual cannot work for a period of time owing to illness or injury.
- **Life**. This insurance protects a family or business from loss of income owing to the breadwinner's death.
- **Property and casualty**. This insurance protects against property losses to a business, home, or car and against the liability that may result from injury or damage to others.
- **Health**. This insurance pays for covered medical expenses.
- **Long-term care.** This insurance helps to pay for services such as assisted-living facilities, home healthcare, and/or nursing home stays.

The commonality among all these types of insurance is that they are designed to transfer risk and to protect income and/or assets.

DISABILITY INSURANCE

Disability insurance is intended to replace lost earnings owing to a disability, as defined by the policy. Choosing a disability policy requires considering the following parameters: (1) when coverage is triggered, (2) when benefits begin, (3) how much is paid, (4) when coverage ends, (5) what terms exist for policy renewal, (6) what is not covered, (7) what additional benefits and riders are available, and (8) how disability insurance income is taxed.

Disability coverage is a subform of health insurance and falls into four categories: total disability, partial disability, presumptive disability, and residual disability. *Totally disability* occurs when individuals cannot perform the duties of their "own occupation" for a specific period of time. Another version of total disability is "any occupation," and that is the form used by the Social Security Administration. *Partial disability* is the inability to perform one or more important duties of an insured's occupation. Partial disability benefits are usually 50 percent of the total monthly benefit. *Presumptive disability* involves the loss of sight, hearing, speech, or two limbs. The benefits for presumptive losses are usually provided and payable for a length of the benefit period or lifetime. *Residual disability* refers to an income replacement provision due to loss wages that result from a disability. *Residual disability* benefits provide a reduced monthly benefit in proportion to an insured's loss of income when he or she has been working again after a disability, but at reduced earnings (Moten 2014).

LIFE INSURANCE

Life insurance is a contract in which the insurer agrees to pay a stipulated amount to a designated beneficiary upon the occurrence of a contingency defined in the contract, usually that of death of the insured (Moten 2014). Among the various types of life insurance policies are term, permanent, and endowments. *Term life insurance* is a policy that provides protection for a limited number of years for a fixed premium. *Whole life insurance* provides permanent protection for an individual's life for a fixed premium. *Universal life insurance*, which is a variation of whole life insurance, provides permanent protection with a flexible premium. *Variable life insurance* is a form of permanent life insurance contract whereby the benefits vary with the investment performance of an underlying portfolio of securities, with fixed premiums or flexible premiums with a variable universal life. A *modified endowment contract* (MEC) is a life insurance policy whose premiums exceed what would have been paid to fund a similar type of life insurance policy with a given number of annual premium payments.

A traditional reason for purchasing life insurance is income replacement; consequently, it can be strategically positioned as a tool for retirement. A particular strategy of interest is *pension maximization*. This strategy is typically used to obtain more current pension benefit without denying the widow(er) future benefits. A *joint and survivor annuity* is an insurance product that continues regular payments as long as one of the annuitants is alive. Married couples who want to guarantee that a surviving spouse will receive regular income for life often select this type of annuity. Instead of taking the typical joint-and-survivor option, a couple can also choose to take the single life annuity option to get the higher pension benefit and use some of those gained resources to buy a life insurance policy to protect the surviving spouse once the other party dies. After evaluating the income needs of the surviving spouse and looking at available sources of income, having life insurance to replace the loss of income may be appropriate. This example can be considered a good application for a first-to-die policy, given that the need is income replacement for the remainder of the single spouse's life. One of the merits of life insurance that is often considered in wealthy households, but bypasses those with less money, is guaranteeing a legacy.

Some people spend too much of their assets, while others limit their spending. A common concern about over spending is that doing so may not leave a legacy to family members. When this is the case, guaranteeing a legacy by buying life insurance can free consumers to enhance their current lifestyle—possibly even providing more for their families both during their lifetimes and after death. For retirees with extra funds that they want to leave to children, grandchildren, or even a charity, the amount gifted can be leveraged by purchasing life insurance. Of course, the amount of the death benefits depends on the individual's age and health. Cash value life insurance also allows the retiree to retain flexibility, so that funds are still available to meet retirement needs, or as discussed previously, even be available for long-term care.

PROPERTY AND CASUALTY INSURANCE

The most prominent forms of property and casualty insurance are homeowners (HO) and automobile insurance. *Homeowners insurance* is a type of insurance that includes property and liability coverage. Regardless of the HO form, two sections of the contract are section I (coverages) and section II (liability). Section I of homeowners insurance covers the dwelling, other structures, personal property, and loss of use or damages. Section II of homeowners insurance covers personal liability and medical payments to others. *Automobile insurance* is a state requirement that typically provides a minimum amount of liability coverage (Moten 2014). The insurance satisfies a requirement needed to own and operate a motor vehicle. Insurance is also tied to the ability to register a vehicle. Factors influencing the cost of automobile insurance are the operator's age, gender, and driving record, as well as the vehicle's intended use. Automobile insurance covers six basic areas: (1) bodily injury liability, (2) medical payments or personal injury protection, (3) property damage liability, (4) collision, (5) comprehensive, and (6) uninsured and underinsured motorist coverage.

HEALTH INSURANCE AND LONG-TERM CARE INSURANCE

Health insurance and long-term care insurance are designed to provide protection in the event of a medical loss that could be short term, but catastrophic in nature or prolonged when a person is older and cannot perform at least two activities of daily living (ADLs) or is cognitively impaired. The six most common ADLs are (1) bathing, (2) dressing, (3) eating, (4) using the toilet, (5) transferring from a bed to a chair, and (6) caring for incontinence.

A Survey of Behavioral Finance

According to traditional finance or economics, individuals should behave in a rational manner. Investors can typically be placed in one of three different types of risk attitudes. Most investors are *risk averse*, which means that when faced with two investments with a similar expected return but different risks, the investor prefers the one with the lower risk. Investors with low risk aversion often prefer investing in money market mutual funds or certificates of deposit. Individuals who are *risk-seekers* are on the opposite end of the spectrum. Risk-seekers select investments with the highest level of risk for a chance at a high return. Even if a history of low returns exists, risk-seekers still invest in volatile or risky assets. By contrast, *risk-neutral* investors are in the middle, indifferent to the level of risk and concerned only with their desired rate of return.

These three risk attitudes explain the way rational investors react to risky situations. However, psychology and behavioral finance explain how consumers make purchasing decisions based on perceived risk. Specifically, behavioral finance explains why market participants make irrational systematic errors that are contrary to the way rational markets participants should behave. Some experts divide behavioral finance theory into three subcategories: biases, heuristics, and framing (Shefrin 2007).

BIASES

A *bias* is a tendency toward particular methods of thinking that can lead to bad judgment and irrational decision making. The following are biases, with a general example, a finance example, and an insurance example.

Excessive Optimism

Excessive optimism is the inclination to downplay the possibility of a negative outcome or to overemphasize the possibility of a positive outcome. Individuals with this bias think they are less likely than others to experience an unfavorable event.

- *General example*: "I don't have to wear a seatbelt when driving the short distance to my friend's house."
- *Finance example*: "The government bailed out Bear Stearns so we obviously don't have to follow Henry Paulson's advice to find a buyer for our firm."
- *Insurance example:* "I don't need life insurance now because I don't expect to die any time soon."

Overconfidence

Overconfidence is the propensity for individuals to believe their skills, knowledge, and abilities are better than they actually are. It also indicates a resistance to admit mistakes.

- *Simple example*: "I am smarter than everybody else so I don't need to study for my final exam."
- *Finance example*: "I know my calculations for the value of Apple stock must be correct, so I'll invest all my money in that company rather than diversify my portfolio."

- *Insurance example*: "Insurance is a 'rip-off.' I can do better by saving and investing my money in the market instead of giving it to the insurance company."

Confirmation Bias

Confirmation bias asserts that individuals look for data and information to verify their beliefs. Hence, they tend to ignore conflicting evidence. Thus, they tend to keep information that helps their case, but ignore information when it does not.

- *Simple example*: "Even though Sam bought me roses and diamond earrings for my birthday, he must not love me because I didn't get the new Mercedes I've been wanting."
- *Finance example*: "Despite economic sluggishness in China and Europe, the Federal Reserve should raise interest rates because the unemployment rate is near 5 percent."
- *Insurance example*: "I don't trust life insurance companies. My dad paid on his life insurance policy for year and it lapsed before he got a chance to benefit from it."

Illusion of Control

Illusion of control occurs when individuals tend to believe that they can control more than they actually can. In other words, people perceive that they have influence over things they do not.

- *Simple example*: When rolling dice in craps, which is a dice game in which the players make wagers on the outcome of the roll, or a series of rolls, of a pair of dice, evidence shows that people tend to throw harder for high numbers and softer for low numbers.
- *Finance example*: When investors use strategies such as limit orders to gain a sense of control over investments, even though the overall success of their portfolio is based on factors such as company performance, which are beyond their control.
- *Insurance example*: "I'll wait until I get closer to needing insurance before I buy it."

Status Quo Bias

Status quo bias occurs when individuals prefer to do nothing or maintain decisions they have made in the past. They tend to prefer the current state of affairs.

- *Simple example*: "I have always bought iPhones in the past so I guess I will buy another iPhone when it's time for my upgrade."
- *Finance example*: "My father told me that mutual funds were a safe investment so I plan to buy mutual funds."
- *Insurance example:* "I talked to my dad about his insurance and he felt that a burial policy was all I needed."

Hindsight Bias

Hindsight bias occurs when individuals unrealistically believe they would have predicted an event that occurred even though it would have been nearly impossible to foresee.

- *Simple example*: "I should have expected rain today because I washed my car yesterday."

- *Finance example*: "I had a feeling that the chief executive officer was embezzling money from the company."
- *Insurance example*: "Buying into the guaranteed insurability option would have been a waste of money because I've had this policy for 40 years and not been sick."

Recency Bias

Recency bias is the illogical tendency to make decisions based on what has happened in recent memory. Individuals think that what has been happening will continue.

- *Simple example*: "The football team has not lost a regular season game in more than nine years so I bet you $100 they will beat the next opponent."
- *Finance example*: "Because housing prices typically rise over time, we don't have to worry about buying a house that is out of our price range because we can always sell it if we have trouble making the payments."
- *Insurance example*: "Because the rate of returns on permanent insurance policies has been low, I would have been better off investing my money elsewhere."

Conservatism

Conservatism occurs when forecasters cling to prior beliefs in the face of new information (Byrne and Brooks 2008).

- *Simple example*: "That's the way that we have always done it."
- *Finance example*: "The efficient market hypothesis explains everything that we need to know about how the market works."
- *Insurance example*: "Single people shouldn't buy insurance because it is a waste of money."

Mental Accounting

Mental accounting is a method by which individuals allocate wealth using separate mental accounts while ignoring how they relate to other financial decisions.

- *Simple example*: "I have made big plans for my tax return!"
- *Finance example*: "I don't want my child to have to take out student loans so I am going to take the money from my 401(k) plan."
- *Insurance example*: "Since I have cash value in my life insurance policy, I will use that money instead of maintaining a savings account."

Regret Aversion

Regret aversion is a method in which individuals make decisions or refuse to make decisions so they can avoid feeling any emotional pain in the future due to making poor decisions.

- *Simple example*: "The best strategy for me is not to get involved."
- *Finance example*: "I lost money in the stock market in the past, so I'm going to keep my money in the bank."
- *Insurance example*: "I once had a permanent insurance policy, but it only earned 3 percent interest. I could have invested my money in a better opportunity."

HEURISTICS

A *heuristic* is a general rule or mental shortcut that helps increases the speed of decision making. These shortcuts present a problem when they hinder the ability to develop new ideas or when someone faces anomalous circumstances. The following biases are examples of heuristics, including representativeness, availability, and anchoring.

Representativeness

Representativeness is a way of thinking that places thoughts into categories. Individuals make judgments based on how well something fits into their preconceived notions based on categorization. This style of thinking closely resembles stereotyping.

- *Simple example*: "David is reserved, wears glasses, enjoys video games, and watches sci-fi movies. I bet he is a math or science major."
- *Finance example*: An investor who only owns oil-based stocks may believe the entire stock market is currently struggling. However, the reality is that his stocks are suffering because of falling oil prices.
- *Insurance example*: "Stock market returns are so good that buying term insurance and investing the difference has to be a good strategy."

Availability

Availability is the mental shortcut of relying on what most readily comes to mind when making decisions. Individuals mistakenly think that if they can recall something easily, it must be important and, therefore, serves as a good basis for decision-making.

- *Simple example*: "John is scared to ask Suzy to the prom because he still painfully remembers how Mary turned him down last year."
- *Finance example*: "Both producers and consumers hesitated to take advantage of record-low interest rates as the economy recovered because the memory of the financial crisis was fresh in their minds."
- *Insurance example*: "When a member of my church died, her family had to collect money to bury him; therefore, I am going to buy as much life insurance as I can afford."

Anchoring

Anchoring is the propensity to rely on the first number or piece of information (an anchor). Individuals then make subsequent judgments by adjusting the anchor to reflect new information. This heuristic can become a problem when they wrongly interpret new information through the lens of the original anchor.

- *Simple example*: Used car salesmen use anchoring to their advantage during negotiations. Once an initial price is given, any lower price sounds better to the buyer even if it is still more than the car is worth.
- *Finance example*: During the tech bubble of the late 1990s, investors continued to speculate and expect technology-based stocks to grow at a rapid rate although such growth was unsustainable in the long term.

- *Insurance example*: "My parents bought a permanent life insurance policy for me when I was young and by the time I was grown, it had considerable cash value. I am going to buy this type of policy for my children."

Affect Heuristic

Affect is the mental shortcut when individuals rely on their emotional response to a situation to make a decision. If they have positive feelings about the situation, they are more likely to perceive it as less risky. Affect is the "gut feeling" heuristic.

- *Simple example*: People are typically more afraid of airplanes than riding in automobiles because airplane crashes create a more emotional response.
- *Finance example*: "I believe that financial markets are more likely to increase on sunny days than on cloudy days because people generally have a more positive outlook."
- *Insurance example*: "My friend just died and his lack of a life insurance affected his family. I need to buy life insurance as soon as possible."

Causality

Causality occurs when individuals wrongly attempt to infer cause from an effect. For examples, individuals tend to associate correlation and causation.

- *Simple example*: "The amount of drowning deaths increases when ice cream sales also increase." It would be wrong to infer that rising ice cream consumption causes drowning deaths because the more likely explanation is that individuals eat more ice cream and swim more during the summer months.
- *Finance example*: "Increased economic growth in the United States causes more financial development." This relationship could easily be reversed: financial development could cause economic growth. Individuals need to be aware of reverse causality and third-part causes.
- *Insurance example*: "My health insurance was so expensive that I couldn't afford it, so I dropped the policy. Two weeks later, I had to go to the hospital. I bet if I had not dropped my health insurance, I wouldn't have had to go to the hospital."

Attribution Substitution

Attribution substitution occurs when individuals have to make a decision about something more complex and instead make a decision about a similar, easier substitute.

- *Simple example*: Someone who has been thinking about his relationships and then is asked about his happiness might substitute how happy he is with his relationships, rather than answer the question.
- *Finance example:* When domestic stocks are down, people often move their money into cash, as opposed to diversifying with international stocks or bonds or alternative investments.
- *Insurance example*: Anecdotal evidence suggests someone could be offered insurance against her death in a terrorist attack while on a trip to Europe, while another person could be offered insurance that would cover death of any kind on the trip. The first person is willing to pay more even though "death of any kind" includes

"death in a terrorist attack." The person is substituting the attribute of fear for the total risks of travel.

FRAMING EFFECTS

The *framing effect* is an example of cognitive bias in which people react to a particular choice in different ways depending on how it is presented, such as a loss or as a gain. Individuals tend to avoid risk when presented in a positive frame but seek risks when presented in a negative frame.

- *Simple example*: The glass is half-empty versus the glass is half-full.
- *Finance example*: Some people would rather risk doubling their money than losing half of their money, although the odds might be the same.
- *Insurance example:* Selling insurance to parents if a child to cover funeral costs is difficult because they do not want to think about their child's mortality and believe the odds are low for premature death. However, selling insurance to parents on their child is easier if it is to their child's future insurability and build cash value for the future and has a non-increasing premium.

Loss Aversion

Loss aversion occurs when individuals feel losses more strongly than they do gains. This situation becomes a problem when it causes them to go to irrational lengths to avoid taking risks. Another problem of loss aversion is that once people have invested time or money, they become irrationally risk tolerant to avoid feeling the loss (aversion to a sure loss).

- *Simple example*: Losing $20 that a person earned has a greater impact than losing $20 that the person found.
- *Finance example*: Risk-averse investors often choose low-risk investments despite offering lower expected returns than more risky investments.
- *Insurance example*: Most individuals buy the "state minimums" on auto insurance to save on premiums without thinking about the risk associated with being underinsured.

Herd Mentality

Herd mentality occurs when the behavior of others irrationally influences another. This bias is similar to "peer pressure." Individuals do not like to be left out, so they behave in ways contrary their normal behavior.

- *Simple example*: A non-coffee drinker may pour another beverage into a Starbucks cup because of the brand's popularity.
- *Finance example*: Bernie Madoff pulled off the largest Ponzi scheme in U.S. history because investors heard about his phenomenal returns from others and eagerly jumped on board.
- *Insurance example*: Insurance companies sometimes use celebrities to "sell" insurance in their commercials because they believe that the status and influence of celebrities convince many consumers to follow their example.

Disposition Effect

The *disposition effect* occurs when investors are less willing to recognize and acknowledge losses more quickly than gains. Similar to loss aversion, investors do not like to experience a loss so they may irrationally refuse to accept it.

- *Simple example*: A football player continues to play on an injured knee and causes permanent damage because he avoided taking adequate care of the injury.
- *Finance example*: Investors tend to sell stocks too early that increased in value and hold on to stocks too long that decreased in value.
- *Insurance example*: Some men are unwilling to buy insurance because they do not want "some other man living off their money" as opposed to being responsible and taking care of their family.

Money Illusion

Money illusion occurs when someone has difficulty factoring the effects of inflation into purchase decisions.

- *Simple example*: "Bread is now very expensive. I once could buy a loaf for a dollar."
- *Finance example*: "I previously could get enough interest from my money market account to pay my car note. Now the interest generated is too small to buy lunch."
- *Insurance example*: "My health insurance is 20 percent more than it was three years ago. I don't understand why it keeps increasing."

Behavioral Finance, Insurance, and Risk Management

Both traditional finance and the concept of rationality are based on the belief that when individuals receive new information, they make choices that follow normative decision-making techniques (Barberis and Thaler 2003). In traditional finance, these individuals are considered to be rational maximizers. A *rational maximizer* is an individual who rationally considers the pros and cons of a given purchase decision. Behavioral finance describes a different set of rules in which individuals sometimes make irrational decisions even when faced with seemingly rational choices. This irrationality leads them to make less than optimal decisions. Behavioral finance helps to explain biases that are inconsistent with rational behavior. Behavioral finance theories often serve as a framework for determining individual behavior in risk management decisions.

Belbase, Coe, and Wu (2015) study which behavioral finance theories explain an employee's decision to buy life insurance. They examined mental accounting, money illusion, and the role of defaults. The authors conducted 24 telephone interviews with employees who had to choose the amount of life insurance they wanted to buy. Specifically, their study examined employee perceptions about the threat of premature death, financial consequences of their premature death, and how to minimize the cost through mental accounting. Belbase et al. asked survey participants about their choice to buy voluntary supplemental life insurance benefits available to them through their workplace. Their objective was to determine how these benefits are presented to employees, what features are attractive, and what barriers exist for those who choose not to buy the insurance coverage.

The responses show that most respondents understand the purpose of life insurance but admitted that determining the proper amount of coverage needed was difficult. Over 40 percent of the respondents reported that they spent less than 30 minutes to determine the amount of insurance needed. The behavioral finance theory of mental accounting is the most widely used method for determining the proper amount. This preference occurs because mental accounting involves the tendency for individuals to separate money into distinct, separate accounts based on subjective criteria. The respondents' budget was the main factor used to find what amount of life insurance would be required to adequately replace the lost wages without regard to what was really necessary to maintain the family's current standard of living. The issue of affordability was more of an issue than an analysis of what they actually needed. The results identify the need to provide complementary education to help in making choices.

According to Fisher (1928), individuals sometimes think in terms of nominal rather than real monetary value. A nominal monetary view ignores inflation, which affects one's purchasing power. As Shafer, Diamond, and Tversky (1997) note, if this theory holds, then it contradicts the maximization paradigm that is prevalent in economic theory. They cite research in cognitive psychology suggesting that when faced with the same risky situation, multiple responses are available. When individuals only have a chance to gain more of an asset, they tend to choose the most risky proposition. However, consistent with loss aversion, when faced with the prospect of loss and gain, they prefer the safer bet. When individuals think in terms of monetary value, they demonstrate contradictory views of mental accounting when valuing their possessions. This narrow view could lead them to undervalue their possessions when determining the amount of property and casualty insurance or life insurance needed to maintain their current standard of living.

Liebman and Zeckhauser (2008) study the deficiencies in traditional economic models, which are very similar to traditional financial models when individuals face decisions to buy health insurance. The recent proliferation of healthcare choices has made this decision more difficult. Their study focused on two choices involving health insurance: (1) the type of insurance to select, and (2) when to buy insurance. They found that once customers decide to buy insurance, the more risk-averse individuals buy more insurance. This choice follows a rational decision-making model. Additionally, those expecting more health problems based on family medical history also tend to buy additional insurance. However, even when individuals identify that they need to buy more life and health insurance, they fail to conduct the proper analysis to adequately address the risk. The observed behavioral economics theory was "underestimation." Consumers who underestimate future events do not buy an adequate amount of health insurance because they concentrate on their present condition. Overall, Liebman and Zeckhauser found that underinsurance is a factor of inertia because of the complexity of coverage choices.

According to Kunreuther and Pauly (2014), consumers do not act rationally when making a decision to buy insurance. They also point out that individuals with insurance coverage act irrationally because they rely on intuition and emotions, rather than careful thought or proven research. Traditional economic theory suggests that risk-averse consumers should be willing to pay a small premium for a specified level of protection. However, Kunreuther and Pauly's empirical evidence suggests that even when facing low-probability and high-consequences scenarios, intervention is needed by public and private institutions to shape consumer behavior. The authors also find that many individuals select default options rather than actually assessing their risk management and insurance needs. Many consumers use intuition in the face of uncertainty, but this intuition is not based on research; rather, it is based on their narrow experience with purchasing insurance. When consumers take an active role and truly assess their needs, the benefits are widespread. Insureds suffer from underestimation.

Kunreuther and Pauly (2014) discuss an example involving the risk of terrorism. Even though actuaries and underwriters are mathematical experts, they underestimate the damage that could be caused by events such as the terrorist attack on the Twin Towers in New York City on September 11, 2001. This example further illustrates a company's failing to adequately account for low-probability and high-consequence events.

Two notable pieces of legislation that attempt to address the shortcomings in the decision-making process involve the purchase of insurance. Both the Biggert-Waters Act of 2012 and the Affordable Care Act of 2010 (ACA) attempt to address the issue of insurance shortfalls. The Biggert-Waters Flood Insurance Reform Act of 2012 extends the National Flood Insurance Program (NFIP) for five years, while requiring substantial program reform. The purpose of the Affordable Care Act (ACA) of 2010 is to make health insurance more affordable for those with little or no coverage. Many provisions of the ACA are meant to control the costs of insurance premiums and out-of-pocket costs for health care and access to insurance. The intent of both acts is to encourage or entice organizations and individuals to implement risk-reducing measures. Proposals for other forms of governmental intervention may reduce the risk to society at large.

Huber (2012) conducts a four-part study to determine the effects of contract elements, price presentation, company ratings, and consumer attitudes and perceptions on an individual's decision to buy certain levels of life insurance. The first part of the study tried to ascertain whether the decision to buy life insurance is based on guaranteed return or subjectivity willingness to pay, which is a financial pricing approach. The results suggest that even when faced with a guaranteed return, participants still deviate from the norm.

The second part of the study looked at the perceived value of life insurance based on different ways to buy insurance, including bundling, partial bundling, and unbundled. The results of the second part suggest that consumers do not alter their purchasing habits based on the bundling of the insurance product. Huber (2012) further suggests that the reason different individual decisions are not statistically significant is due to the complexity of the product and not the perception of an actual price difference.

The third part of the study examined the ratings of the insurance company and its effect on individual purchasing decisions. Huber (2012) studies whether individuals make purchasing decisions based on ratings and certifications of companies performed by third parties. The results suggest that company ratings and certification have a statistically significant impact on product evaluation and on risk perception.

The fourth part of the study focused on consumer attitudes and perceptions, and their influence on whether to buy or not to buy insurance. Huber (2012) tests the hypothesis using a unit-linked life insurance product without any guaranteed components. The results of study suggest that underlying attitudes significantly affect product perceptions. Huber (p. 169) points out that "risk avoidance presents a rather emotional component while uncertainty avoidance is rather analytical."

Summary and Conclusions

According to MPT, people have complete information about the likelihood of possible outcomes and can articulate their preferences about those possible outcomes. Hence, they should be able to maximize their expected utility. According to proponents of behavioral finance, individuals do not always operate rationally.

Regarding insurance, consumers often respond differently from what "makes sense." Stalwarts of the insurance industry advocate that individuals should buy life insurance if anyone associated with them would suffer financially if the individual were no longer around. The general thinking is that the income contribution being lost needs to be replaced and assets that have been accumulated need to be preserved. As related to insurance, behavioral finance helps explain why consumers' actions are different from what is expected, given the issues regarding risk. Behavioral finance stipulates that consumers exhibit behaviors that can be categorized as biases, heuristics, and framing references. Biases are a tendency toward particular methods of thinking that can lead to bad judgment and irrational decision making. Heuristics are general rules or mental shortcuts that help people make decisions faster. Framing effects are created by the way an idea is presented.

Each of these behavioral finance concepts helps provide a better understanding of the why, when, and how people buy insurance. Consumers are not motivated to buy insurance simply for protection. Their rationale (the "why") is largely due to status quo, the recent occurrence of an event, a desire to avoid a loss, and a lack of understanding of inflation or causality. Behavioral finance can also help provide understanding of the "when" in the purchasing decision. The "when" is often premised on the availability of a substitute option or how insurance fits into a predetermined category. The "how" of insurance decision making can be associated with confirmation of previous beliefs and/or the effect of emotion.

Generally, insurance sales have not decreased since 2009. By contrast, property and casualty insurance sales are up, owing to state law. Sales of health insurance have increased as a result of changes in federal law. Long-term care insurance has likely increased owing to more understanding of the preponderance of Alzheimer's cases and the frailty associated with longevity. Life insurance sales are actually down, even though the availability of information has increased several fold. Many use insurance as a risk management technique, but it cannot be confirmed that the reason is that consumers make smart buying decisions (LIMRA 2013).

DISCUSSION QUESTIONS

1. Explain the four primary responses to risk.
2. Discuss the three primary types of hazards associated with risk management.
3. Discuss the three most prevalent risk attitudes.
4. Identify and discuss the five main types of insurance for individuals.
5. Discuss three subcategories of behavioral finance theory.

REFERENCES

Barberis, Nicholas, and Richard Thaler. 2003. "A Survey of Behavioral Finance." In George M. Constantinides, Milton Harris, and René M. Stulz, *Handbook of the Economics of Finance, Volume 1*, 1052–1121. North Holland: Elsevier.

Belbase, Anek, Normal B. Coe, and April Wu. 2015. "Overcoming Barriers to Life Insurance Coverage: A Behavioral Approach." Working Paper, Center for Retirement Research, Boston College. Available at http://crr.bc.edu/wp-content/uploads/2015/06/wp_2015-5.pdf.

Byrne, Alistair, and Mike Brooks. 2008. *Behavioral Finance: Theories and Evidence*. Charlottesville, VA: Research Foundation of the CFA Institute.

Copeland, C. W. 2015. *Applications in Financial Planning II*. Bryn Mawr, PA: American College Press.

Fisher, Irving. 1928. *The Money Illusion*. Toronto: Longmans.

Huber, Carin. 2012. "Behavioral Insurance: Essays on the Influence of Ratings and Price Presentation on Consumer Evaluation, Risk Perception and Financial Decision-Making." Dissertation, University of St. Gallen, School of Management, Economics, Law, Social Sciences and International Affairs. Available at http://www1.unisg.ch/www/edis.nsf/SysLkpByIdentifier/3959/$FILE/dis3959.pdf.

Kunreuther, Howard, and Mark Pauly. 2014. "Behavioral Economics and Insurance: Principles and Solutions." Working Papers #2014-01, Wharton School, University of Pennsylvania. Available at http://citeseerx.ist.psu.edu/viewdoc/download?doi=10.1.1.645.8939&rep=rep1&type=pdf.

Liebman, Jeffrey, and Richard Zeckhauser. 2008. "Simple Humans, Complex Insurance Subtle Subsidies." NBER Working Paper 14330. Available at https://www.hks.harvard.edu/fs/rzeckhau/SimpleHumans_website_version.pdf.

LIMRA. 2013. "U.S. Retail Individual Life Insurance Sales (3Q2013)." Available at http://www.limra.com/Posts/PR/News_Releases/LIMRA__Individual_Life_Insurance_Sales_Experience_Strong_Fourth_Quarter_Growth.aspx.

Markowitz, Harry. 1952. "Portfolio Selection." *Journal of Finance* 7:1, 77–91.

Moten, James. 2014. *Introductory Financial Management: Theory and Application*. Second Edition. Redding, CA: Best Value Textbook (BVT) Publishing.

Shafer, Eldar, Peter Diamond, and Amos Tversky. 1997. "Money Illusion." *Quarterly Journal of Economics*, 12:2, 341–374.

Shefrin, Hersh. 2007. *Behavioral Corporate Finance: Decision that Create Value*. New York. McGraw-Hill Irwin.

Simon, Herbert A. 1955. "A Behavioral Model of Rational Choice." *Quarterly Journal of Economics* 69:1, 99–118.

Yazdipour, Rassol, and William P. Neace. 2013. "Operationalizing a Behavioral Finance Risk Model: A Theoretical and Empirical Framework." *Journal of Entrepreneurial Finance* 12:2, 1–32.

18

Psychological Factors in Estate Planning

JOHN J. GUERIN
Owner
Delta Psychological Associates, P.C.

L. PAUL HOOD JR.
Director of Planned Giving
The University of Toledo Foundation

Introduction

The dialogue between an estate planner and a client, whether from the legal or the financial planning profession, has a unique characteristic that distinguishes it from all other financial conversations. Regardless of the details of the consultation, there's a time when the results of the work will be tested. Alas, that testing will occur when the client is no longer present to rework the plan. That irrevocability of the estate plan thus creates a demand that the professional consider many possible resulting scenarios as a product of the planning process. Because all possible scenarios cannot be exhaustively anticipated, there's often room for error when developing an estate plan.

Along with the need to draft as comprehensive plan as possible, there is a substantial barrier also not present in many other forms of financial and life planning. That is, the formulation of an estate plan implicitly involves thoughtful consideration of the distribution of wealth. Along with this plan can be a statement of the feelings that accompany the distribution, or it can reflect a broad survey of the decedent's values, life stories, and worries. Such reflections are also sometimes contained in wills or in a separate document commonly known as an *ethical will* (Reimer and Stampfer 1991; Baines 2006).

This chapter explores the complexity inherent in the estate planning process, including its tentative relationship with behavioral finance. Included in this broad view is a discussion of common communication problems encountered in estate planning and a look at the effects in particular of discussions of mortality. This is followed by a review of models from clinical psychology that might be applied to estate planning, as well as some interview techniques that could facilitate planner–client discussions. Finally, the chapter ends with an overview of current and potential collaborations between the fields of psychology and financial planning.

Considerations for Estate Planning

Today, the process of estate planning has transmuted into a primary concern about being taxed on wealth for which taxes have already been paid. Therefore, the main issue in estate planning is one of tax avoidance, such that the issue of mortality actually often becomes a secondary consideration. Adding to this, the estate planner must acknowledge that most people have a low tolerance for discussions about their own mortality. Hence, both client and planner frequently "dance" around the issue, with the discussion characterized by euphemisms and with "gallows humor."

At the same time, there has been an evolution in the parlance of estates. The common term for arranging one's postmortem affairs has been called writing a "Last Will and Testament." This label suggests that not only does one distribute one's earthly possessions but also one provides a rationale for that distribution. That this framework may contribute to wealth stratification on a social level is usually not a consideration (Harrington 2012). The current focus of estate planning as tax liability avoidance and asset protection planning is not surprising, then, considering that the estate planning professional is usually an attorney. However, discussions about legacy and wealth transfer may also take place with a financial planner. But whether it happens in the office of an attorney or that of a financial planner, the practical and numerically definable nature of tax minimization makes it an attractive target for the work of an expert. This expert's input can offer a clear "value proposition," showing the impact of financial planning by demonstrating performance with and without such assistance.

Additionally, estate planning is an area of direct client service, yet it does not fit easily into a field of scientific research. For instance, psychologists and other mental health professionals may either consume or generate research that can apply to financial planning. Yet, borrowing the principles of human behavior in rendering these much-needed financial services requires that the planning professional select theories that seems to apply to direct services. This incorporates conceptual models from psychology that have varying degrees of credible research to support those ideas. The metaphor that aptly captures the situation is of service professionals attempting to construct an automobile while driving it.

Nevertheless, the rising interest in behavioral finance has made discussion of money and wealth a mainstream concern for psychologists and other mental health professionals. Although behavioral finance has established itself as a productive area of research, it is almost exclusively studied in academic and research settings. To date, mental health professionals are rarely adequately conversant with financial and/or legal issues to give any advice or direction that would impact financial and estate tactics.

For the service professional, there needs to be a clear link between psychology and finance. However, the nature of that link—or more precisely, the incorporation of that link into the practices of financial and psychological professionals—remains weak. Attorneys and financial planners know the importance of fuller, deeper, and more meaningful conversations about wealth, including an awareness that wealth is also measured in nonfinancial terms. Should the conversation take a turn toward emotional or psychological issues, or toward marital, family, or relationship dynamics, however, and the financial professional is beyond his or her sphere of expertise or competence. After all, this scenario risks professional liability exposure, as well as the loss of a client if the conversation deviates from a discussion of financial well-being. Indeed, the call to have more extensive discussions with clients adds a burden to the estate planner attorney, who has a formidable list of potential barriers with which to contend, including issues of confidentiality. A crisis may precipitate an individual's need for estate planning. Family dynamics may inhibit meaningful planning. Factors of jealousy, financial illiteracy, addictions, mental health issues, spending difficulties, and other barriers can restrict decision making and impair the client's judgment and cause discomfort for the planner (Foord and Ebersole 2007).

The estate planning attorney must also acknowledge the evolving nature of families (Allianz Insurance 2015). The traditional family has given way to blended families, single-parent households, same-sex partnerships/marriages, and older parents. According to Allianz, the number of traditional families has dwindled to about 28 percent of U.S. households. Some studies have considered the effects of these blended or modern families (Bernstein and Collins 1985; Hood and Bouchard 2012; Hood and Leimberg 2014). However, the vast majority of estate planners are still operating with a traditional model as their benchmark. Status quo bias or inertia may result because using the traditional family as the template for financial planning is simpler, requiring less effort and sophistication.

Recognizing such challenges, it is essential for an estate planner to understand the relationship dilemmas that can arise. Possessing some knowledge of the psychological research that may have studied client behavior is, therefore, important in the estate planning process. For example, clients may need to discuss matters that bear on mortality; knowing the extant clinical research on this can be of help. Furthermore, tools that psychologists use in other areas of clinical and consulting work may prove useful in discussions of planning. Of course, any research into behavioral issues in estate planning must consider the confidentiality owed to the client.

The Complexity of the Estate Planning Process

Because of the inherently sensitive nature of estate planning, the heightened emotional pitch of this discussion can have major therapeutic or anti-therapeutic effects. The estate planner has to be consistently aware of this possibility. Also, the meetings tend to be complex, given the many purposes of the process. Hood and Bouchard (2012) provide a list of some of these issues:

- The estate planner must gather a large amount of information, which may involve layers of complexity, such as when an estate involves partial or full interests in businesses, or families are blended or otherwise nontraditional. The information gathered must be both accurate and complete.
- In the service of completeness, issues often arise that need to be recognized as tangential, so a refocus may need to occur on multiple occasions.
- The estate planner must engender both a sense of comfort and of competence for the client.
- The estate planner must recognize and address the fact that estate planning involves a discussion of the client's mortality.
- If the client is more than one person, such as a couple, the estate planner must balance attention to both and attend to relationship dynamics as they arise. The complexity expands with the involvement of other family members.

- Client motivations have to be recognized. Both explicit and hidden agendas may be involved in the planning process.
- Family histories may be complex and delicate, particularly involving a blended family.
- The estate planner must gauge the client's mental status or competence to engage in planning. That assessment of mental status may include the possibility that another party could be attempting to exert undue influence.

Other considerations may be present as well, both at the outset and during the remainder of the planning process. First, since the planner's work is often billed on an hourly basis, the client may wish to move as quickly as possible, expressed directly or evident in some pressure applied. The planner sometimes sees this pressure as conflicting with a duty for completeness and adequate detail, and is obliged to inform the client of estimated costs, even though complexities may arise that affect the ultimate cost of the work. That is, checking the accuracy and/or completeness of the information supplied by the client sometimes calls for due diligence, and therefore affects the time estimates.

Second, an implicit imbalance exists in the planner–client relationship, given the planner's knowledge of and expertise in the process. This disparity can drive the planner into beginning to address the "how to" of an estate plan, rather than the "why" of the process.

Third, a potential for conflicts of interest arises in estate planning. The wealth holder is the client who must be served; however, the success of an estate plan is measured by the views of the beneficiaries. Thus, the estate planner must predict in the present how the plan will affect the beneficiaries later on, and whether the purposes and ideals of the benefactor will be served.

Although an estate planner may make a reasonable attempt to forecast the feelings of the client's survivors, the manner in which grieving takes place can be unpredictable. Conflicts can easily arise among beneficiaries over seemingly small matters, such as positive or negative feelings about the deceased or difficulties confronting their own mortality. Although these issues are daunting challenges in the process of estate planning, substantial evidence exists that a well-done estate plan can reinforce family cohesion and harmony, and that a well-conducted planning process can have a positive, growth-enhancing outcome for the client (Shaffer 1970; Glover 2012).

Planner–Client Communications

In part, as a result of the pressure to provide answers, the estate planner may assume the role of "expert," resulting in taking charge of the process and the conversation (Hood and Bouchard 2012). Especially among professionals who have constructed numerous estate plans, a tendency exists to "plug in the tape." That is, a professional may begin answering a question before the client has fully articulated it, in the belief that the question is already understood and a ready answer is appropriate. However, a client may read this behavior as a lack of understanding or concern. Remember, listening involves not just refraining from prematurely issuing advice but also employing concentration, inquisitiveness, acknowledgment, validation, summarization, and empathic concern.

Added to the complexity of listening and responding is the need to address emotional channels of communication, whether they are verbal, nonverbal, or paralinguistic. Indeed, the more important aspects of communication may be nonverbal. Where mixed do messages occur (i.e., where the nonverbal messages are incongruent with the verbal communication), the planner's attention to this discrepancy may open the door to deeper interaction.

THE EMOTIONAL CONTRACT

In psychotherapy, the initial stages may have an emotional contract focusing on the therapeutic relationship. This contract goes beyond elaborating the services that will be provided and covering issues such as confidentiality. However, the relationship dynamics in estate and financial planning are less likely to occur at the outset, yet they are an important part of managing the client's expectations that go beyond provision of the professional services. According to Hood and Bouchard (2012), some questions that are likely to arise for the estate planner are as follows:

- How available should the planner expect to be for any given client?
- What are the boundaries of the relationship?
- What are the client's expectations?
- What are the boundaries that the client expects the planner to honor in terms of spousal or family involvement?
- How much attention or "hand-holding" is the client going to need?
- Will the client allow work to be handled at a lower level of the organization, as in using clerks, paralegals, and junior associates?
- What are the specifics of confidentiality in this case?
- How educated or sophisticated is the client, and how will this drive client involvement in the process?
- Will the client suggest or demand services that compromise the planner's integrity or professional ethics?

Conversely, the client may be considering the following aspects of the emotional contract:

- Do I feel comfortable in the presence of and speaking with this planner?
- Does the planner appear to be competent to complete the work?
- Will the planner be loyal to my goals and needs?
- Will the planner be personally available when needed?
- Will the planner hear me out before advising?
- Does the planner pick up on nuances and nonverbal channels?
- Does the planner listen to me in a discerning manner?
- Is the relationship collegial rather than authoritative?
- Will the planner understand any questions that I haven't phrased in proper legal form?
- How long will the process take?
- How much will the plan cost?

COUNTER-TRANSFERENCE

As previously stated, the planner needs to listen on a deep level, and must be willing to enter into thorough discussions if the interaction goes in that direction. However, intensifying the interaction can move the planner into a discussion of matters he or she does not feel prepared for or trained to carry through. Additionally, emotional or psychological dynamics may insinuate themselves into the professional relationship. Such dynamics can arise on the planner's end of the relationship, on the client's end, or both.

For example, a conversation about mortality typically occurs at an intellectual level. However, if the client's deep engagement disarms the planner and disrupts that formal or strictly intellectual talk of mortality, the planner's own feelings on the matter may enter the discussion, whether consciously or not. This phenomenon occurs frequently in the field of psychotherapy and is labeled *counter-transference*, or the disruption of the therapeutic process based upon feelings toward the client or issues that the client's input or behavior evokes in the professional.

Counter-transference is generally viewed as an impediment to effective progress in therapy (Cerny 1985), whereas others view it as a potential tool (de Fries 2007). Still other researchers have sought to develop concepts of what qualities professionals need to possess or to develop so as to minimize the adverse impact or occurrence of counter-transference. Similarly, whether seen as a tool or impediment, these feelings may arise in both the client and the planner regarding mortality, but also may be evoked by those necessary discussions of using medical technology and life support, pain management, powers of attorney, advance directives, living wills, do not resuscitate (DNR) orders, and other relevant factors. The planner may indeed find aspects of the client's life that resonate with his or her own history or relationships, and will tend to view them from his or her own perspective. The estate planning context is especially vulnerable to the counter-transferential phenomenon, owing to the imbalance in knowledge leading to a quasi-parental positioning of the planner. The professional mandate for "zealous representation" of the client may also promote such reactions (Hamel and Davis 2008).

Researchers have extensively studied the phenomenon of counter-transference. Various attempts have also been made simply to understand what counter-transference is, what causes it, and how to integrate its various concepts (Rosenberger and Hayes 2002). Because of this complexity, the typical estate planner would probably be unable to remain current with the research; however, this should not discourage the estate planner from resolving to incorporate such basic understanding into the planning process (Scott 1973).

TRANSFERENCE

Along with counter-transference can come transference. *Transference* is the projection onto the professional of the feelings and attitudes the client has and had in an earlier relationship in life. This relationship is more likely to occur with a client whose experiences include having had a primary caretaker earlier in life, an authority figure, or a close sibling relationship. Some view the occurrence of a transferential reaction as an important event in psychotherapy, in that it enhances one's self-understanding. However, such insight is seldom helpful in the estate planning process. It is, in fact, more likely to be a disruptor, distorting the client's judgment. Nevertheless, the "expert" position of the planner increases the likelihood that the client will view him or her, consciously or not, as a parental or authority figure. Alas, because few estate planners are familiar with the phenomenon of transference, they are unlikely to notice when it occurs; consequently, a client's transferential reaction is likely to sidetrack or truncate the estate planning process, so it is best to be on guard.

Mortality and Other Client Fears

As mentioned earlier, the estate planning attorney needs to assess a client's competence to engage in the planning process. And this assessment may not be exclusive to the client's mental capacities at the time of developing the plan. Additionally, the liability of the attorney may extend to the client's beneficiaries. Despite the fact that a planner has a primary responsibility to the wealth-holding client, there is no clear starting line indicating where consideration of the interests of non-clients begins. Additionally, consideration of any ongoing capacity of the client to amend or adjust the estate plan over time should be addressed.

Some evidence indicates that judgment and decision-making capacity may vary in some settings, such as hospice care (Burton, Twamley, Lee, Palmer, Jeste, Dunn, and Irwin 2012). In those situations, systematic measurement apparently uncovers various deficits that are undetectable through clinical observation. Also, as a person ages, there are increasing levels of risk for undue influence (Peisah, Finke, Shulman, Melding, Luxenberg, Henik, and Bennett 2009). Similarly, the testamentary capacity of a dying person may be substantially compromised (Peisah, Luxenberg, Liptzin, Wand, Shulman, and Finkel 2014; Schneiderman 1983).

Many individuals consider themselves unique in their ability to be aware of their mortality. Yet, individuals have variable tolerances for their abilities to be aware of that mortality, on both intellectual and emotional levels. When estate planners consider their general obligation to assess a client's competence, there is recognition that doing purposeful planning with an engaged awareness of mortality will alter the quality of thinking that takes place, in terms of both process and outcome.

MORTALITY SALIENCE

Mortality salience (MS) is the general term used to describe the present awareness of mortality that a person has at any given time. As James (2013) notes, the defense against feelings of mortality can result in the "five D's": distraction, differentiation, denial, delay, and departure.

Distraction occurs when a client says that he is "too busy" to attend to estate planning. Differentiation takes place when the client thinks that confronting issues of mortality is not required at the time because she is in good physical health, has a genetic heritage of longevity, and sees himself well beyond the average range of life expectancy. Denial may take the form of believing that fears of mortality are overblown. The delay defense frequently occurs when the client says that he is going to tend to the planning at a later date. Finally, some clients "depart" from mortality discussions by simply discounting them off when they begin.

A body of research has examined the changes that take place for an individual as a result of MS. Chief among the considerations of MS is the contention that awareness of mortality may be a core motivator in human behavior (Kesebir and Pyszczynski 2011; Koca-Atabey and Oner-Ozkan 2014). Other investigators see mortality fears at the core of personality (Landau and Sullivan 2014). The centrality of the fear of death is also posited to lead to behaviors that reduce risk to the individual as an evolutionary mechanism (Leary and Schreindorfer 1997; Lerner 1997).

Some investigators, such as Bozo, Tunca, and Yeliz (2009), have examined the link between death anxiety and health-promoting behaviors. Anglin (2014) notes a shift in motivation to repair troubled relationships. Appeals for donations may also be more effective under conditions of heightened mortality salience (Cai and Wyer 2015). Dood and Handley (2007) also detect a tenacity in maintaining values. In some cases, emotional awareness and proximity to death can result in mood alterations that are reflective of depression, and goal-directed behavior may then be reduced (Hayes, Ward, and McGregor 2016). Long-held beliefs in an afterlife or mind–body dualism may promote comfort rather than depression (Ai, Kastenmüller, Tice, Wink, Dillon, and Frey 2014; Heflick, Foldenberg, Hart, and Kemp 2015). Lunn, Wright, and Limke (2014) discuss the role of attitudinal shifts in how MS affects perceptions of one's deity.

Still other investigators have found a link between enduring factors, such as self-certainty and uncertainty, in the emotional responses to MS (Hohman and Hogg 2015). Investigators also have noted that the contemplation of death enhances positive word use (Kashdan, DeWall, Schurtz, Dechman, Lykins, Evans, McKenzie, Segerstrom, Gaillot, and Brown 2014), and that MS increases personal optimism in people who have high self-control (Kelley and Schmeichel 2015). Others have found changes in social attitudes and perceptions (Khoo, See, and Hui 2014), as well as allocations of time and money (Lin and Ling 2014).

At the methodology level of many of these studies is some ambiguity about the effectiveness of measures taken to treat MS in an experimental setting (Mahoney, Saunders, and Cain 2014). Typically, researchers prime the subjects by introducing experiences that are presumed to raise MS on either a supraliminal or subliminal level. The effectiveness of this technique on the subliminal level has resisted operational definition, as well as in other areas of psychology where subconscious factors are presumed to play a role. As such, just how effective these methods are for inducing the experimental condition is unclear.

Given the variability that MS can introduce into a person's thoughts and feelings, those thoughts and feelings can apparently be a moving target when MS is introduced. This relationship may not affect legal definitions of competence, but it may influence the quality of the plan designed under those conditions.

TERROR MANAGEMENT THEORY

Linked to MS, *terror management theory* (TMT) (Solomon, Greenberg, and Pyszczysnki 2015) posits that the fear of death is at the core of one's personality and/or a wide range of decisions and behaviors, because the instinct for self-preservation is a basic, universal drive in life (Leary and Schreindorfer 1997). Some assume the centrality of TMT to be an evolutionary development, but others counter that this view is inconsistent with the tenets of evolutionary theory (Kirkpatrick and Navarette 2006). Still others see TMT in simpler terms—that MS evokes a basic need for control of outcomes (Snyder 1997), which extends the explanatory power of TMT to include voluntary suicide in terminal conditions. Regardless of whether TMT is an evolutionary development, its relationship to attitudes and behaviors has led to studies of its effect on one's defenses (Koca-Atabey and Oner-Ozkan 2014).

ADDITIONAL CLIENT FEARS

Additional sources of resistance and barriers exist that crop up in the planning process (Hood and Bouchard 2012). These issues have not been directly addressed in the psychological research literature, but they may make a regular appearance. In general, clients:

- Fear making a mistake in the plan.
- Experience trepidation about the future, whether in the realm of wealth or health, and that may paralyze the planning process.
- Worry or exhibit anxiety about hurting the feelings of their inheritors.
- Commit assets to the estate irrevocably and then outlast their ability to live well or pay their medical expenses.
- Have current estate plans that may have been solidified and then new laws may compromise that plan.
- Have a commitment to one plan that may engender feelings of a loss of flexibility to make future choices.
- Recognize that committing an estate plan to written documents requires disclosing financial and personal matters that may sacrifice privacy.

As a result of the client's heightened anxiety, worry, or fear, the estate planner can expect several emotional reactions. First, as discussed, the process of engaging in estate planning brings up the matter of mortality, which may affect cognitive capacity and judgment. This fear of death may be compounded by a concern with making poor decisions under conditions of emotional arousal (Glover 2012). The prospect of mortality may also bring separation anxiety about leaving one's loved ones.

Second, the client may procrastinate in concluding the estate work, as though finishing it might hasten his demise. This is similar to thinking that discussing suicide with a depressed person will precipitate a suicide attempt. A client may also avoid examining any life regrets by upgrading her view of her life to an ideal state. Alternatively, the client might move toward grandiosity in his self-perception. Still other clients may use the planning process to bargain with a higher power in eleventh-hour negotiations. This bargaining phenomenon is consistent with the stages of coping with mortality as described by Kübler-Ross (1969).

Expanded Complexity: Marital and Family Dynamics

As though the client's emotional responses to estate planning and mortality awareness were not enough, the estate planner should acknowledge that the planning takes place within a larger context that may include the client's spouse, children, close friends, and community. Perhaps as a result of that complexity, and the lack of well-developed tools in the professions, a natural and perhaps unconscious tendency exists to focus on the single client.

As Kingsbury (2013) notes, when a male client predeceases his wife, the woman changes financial planners more than 75 percent of the time. One observation taken from this statistic is that the woman has not felt included as a full partner in the planning process, and perhaps for a substantial amount of time. If one partner actively plans and the other is either silent or absent, the estate planner may draw the erroneous conclusion that the silence signals tacit approval.

When the greater complexity is acknowledged, orchestrating the input of an entire family in the estate planning process becomes quite difficult. There are no working models to accomplish this goal within the professional practice guidelines of the legal profession. So, adopting some knowledge gained in psychology is a natural move to consider.

Using Tools from Psychology

In using the field of psychology to inform the planning process, the estate planner will immediately encounter some difficulties, in that the most applicable is in clinical psychology. There have been substantial efforts to move toward practice models that are evidence and research based; still, many models focus on theory, assessment, and treatment in clinical practice.

SOME RECENT CLINICAL MODELS

Use of models became popular practice because they were so effective in clinical practice. Acceptance and commitment therapy (ACT) is a form of cognitive-behavior therapy or of clinical behavior analysis. The Gottman Method (Gottman and Silver 1999) and Imago Relationship Therapy (Hendrix and Hunt 1988) are just two of many extant models used for couples therapy. Family therapy uses more than a dozen models. If estate planning includes the disposition of a family business, some of organizational psychology's assessment and intervention methods may be pertinent or helpful.

For a clinical professional to be proficient in any given model, let alone a few different models, requires a fair amount of training and practice. It is clearly unrealistic to expect an estate planner to learn and become proficient with any of these models. There is a place for some inter-professional collaboration here, though coordinating the two professionals presents some other complexities that are addressed later in this chapter.

TOOLS FOR INDIVIDUAL ASSESSMENT

Although practitioners use many instruments for psychological assessment, other tools are available that focus on behavioral finance, financial style, and the fit between the financial styles of two or more people. With an enhanced awareness of the psychological aspects of the estate planning process, a financial planner or attorney can responsibly utilize these various tools to raise the quality of service. This goal can be accomplished while minimizing the possibility of going beyond one's scope of expertise.

Most of these instruments have been developed from the experience of the particular test developer. As such, they often have a high degree of *face validity*, which means that the assessment instrument seems to be measuring the desired outcome. Despite face validity being helpful, it is only one of many psychometric factors necessary to satisfy the psychometric conditions for a valid research instrument. Alas, very few of the available assessment tools on the market have been subjected to stringent examination.

At the same time, using these assessment instruments has strong appeal for both financial and estate planners because they can give some measure of insight into a person's financial style. This insight can then give the planner a basis for decision making, rather than relying on personal perceptions of the client.

For instance, using an assessment instrument can be a nonjudgmental means for approaching discussions about psychological and/or emotional barriers. It can also give the planner something to refer to when such encountering barriers, making the discussions nonconfrontational. For example, when a disagreement surfaces between the judgments of the planner and the client, the planner may well be able to refer to the results of the assessment instrument, presenting the situation as a difference in style, rather than one party being correct and the other incorrect.

Assessment instruments can also provide an intermediary function, so that the approach to sensitive and emotionally loaded discussions is eased by via the vehicle of test results. Discussions that bear on mortality, for example, may be initiated with a focus on a test's "objective" results.

Many valid and reliable instruments for assessing personality and interpersonal style are available. However, to apply any assessment findings to the planning process requires extrapolation from the intended purpose of the instrument, and that can extrapolation can lead to difficulties. Conversely, a few instruments have been developed specifically for use in fields involving financial style. The Financial DNA Assessment (FDNA) (Massie 2006) and the Fina Metrica assessment have not been reviewed in Carlson, Geisinger, and Janson (2015), but both have been developed in a psychometrically sound manner. Both instruments assess an individual's style, but they can also have a second administration to another person so as to compare results; consistencies between two individuals, such as marital partners, can then be evaluated. Additionally, the match or mismatch between a client and planner can be gauged. Both of these instruments consider the evolving field of behavioral finance, and this distinguishes them from most of the psychometrically robust instruments in common use for psychological assessment.

The FDNA describes traits that lie along a continuum running between two poles of a characteristic, with low, medium, and upper ranges. The instrument supposedly measures innate traits as opposed to learned behavior. The testing method is a forced-choice format and scores are computed for 12 main characteristics. The results can also be translated into suggested portfolio structures that are consistent with measures of both risk tolerance and loss avoidance. Conversely, Fina Metrica focuses more closely on issues of risk tolerance and loss avoidance, rather than on a wide range of characteristics. Both instruments have been widely used in both the United States and other countries, and both have been subjected to tests of validity and reliability to a greater degree than many similar instruments.

When using these instruments with a larger group, the estate planner should acknowledge the limits to conclusions drawn from a group scoring, because composite scores are averages of scores across participants; this dilutes the ability to detect outliers from the group, which in estate planning might be crucial knowledge to have. That is, knowing who may have tendencies that run contrary to the family norms may help the planner anticipate later disturbances in what is supposed to be a consensually validated plan.

An estate planner can use both instruments without having to rely on a psychologist to interpret the data, so long as he or she has familiarity with the instrument and its interpretations. Using the instrument can open up a discussion of how a client's personal style comes into play. This gives the client a perspective that allows him or her to step back from what is a natural tendency or inclination and make decisions that might be better informed.

TOOLS FOR FAMILY ASSESSMENT

Psychologists employ more than a dozen major schools or conceptual systems for family therapy, with each based on a different empirically developed model of family functioning. Each school or system has its own methods of assessment and practice, as well. When an estate planner is faced with the task of dealing with a family, there are few conceptual models to be followed, beyond one's own experience and instincts.

In this field of family assessment, some instruments are some useful tools, such as the FACES-IV, which takes a systems perspective and evaluates families along dimensions of cohesion and flexibility (Olson 2011). These instruments can assist a family with self-assessment in a manner that is integrated with its wealth, estate planning, and philanthropic goals. The Family Roadmap (Fowler 2002) is an inventory for assessing families along a number of dimensions bearing on family culture. Although it functions primarily as an assessment tool, it can prompt family members to reflect on their goals and arrive at a self-identity and definition.

Jaffe and Allred (2015) develop a family assessment system specifically targeting families who own businesses. The tool is specifically targeted toward wealth preservation across generations; hence, it offers an approach to matters of succession. Jaffe and Allred's tool also focuses on the personal motivations for wealth transmission across the generations, and so it can assist in establishing a meaningful rationale for the transfer of wealth.

Family assessment tools generally sidestep the issues of mortality salience and fears of death by focusing on continuity for the family and family business. Whether the values discussion will also awaken the mortality salience for the wealth creator is unclear.

LIMITATIONS ON THE USE OF PSYCHOLOGICAL TOOLS

One of the difficulties that estate planners often encounter when they want to use an assessment tool is an appearance of critical or negative judgments. In a clinical setting, some of the value of psychological testing is in targeting pathology. Unfortunately, this aspect of psychological assessment sometimes makes using such instruments undesirable in an estate planning context.

Instruments developed within the model of positive psychology, however, assess individuals from a strength-based perspective. *Positive psychology* is the scientific study of human flourishing and is an applied approach to optimal functioning. This branch of psychology uses scientific understanding and effective intervention to aid people in achieving a satisfactory life. Unlike some other frameworks in psychology, positive psychology focuses on personal growth, rather than on pathology.

As yet, there are no assessment instruments for wealth and financial style within the positive psychology community. Seligman (2002) has examined whether money contributes to happiness, and he found that increases in wealth do correlate with measures of happiness, but only to the point where one's wealth meets and slightly exceeds one's basic needs. That is, additional wealth does not increase one's happiness beyond that point. This finding can be useful in discussions of estate planning, giving perspective to clients when assessing the advisability of passing along wealth and making bequests (Bradley 2000).

Interview Methodologies from Psychology

The field of psychology has several methods of interviewing that can be considered by estate planners as ways to enhance discussion and encourage decision making.

APPRECIATIVE INQUIRY

Organizational psychology is a specialty that focuses on the organization, group, or company as the locus for development and change. Although pathology may be a factor, many aspects of the practice are strength-based, such as appreciative inquiry (AI). That is, AI follows a format that focuses on strengths rather than pathology. As an organizational tool, AI can be used in a group effort to construct a shared vision. Also, it can be an element of discussion for a family or family business discussion concerned with continuing the intention and vision of the wealth creator or present holder.

MOTIVATIONAL INTERVIEWING

The ambivalence toward discussions of mortality that has been mentioned earlier may open up interesting lines of inquiry. Good methods of interviewing will recognize and validate the inherent conflicts involved in the change process. Techniques such as motivational interviewing (MI) have emerged from the addictions and chemical dependency specialties of psychology, and has also been medical compliance issues, as well as other areas that are typically addressed in counseling and psychotherapy (Miller and

Rollnick 2013). Given that the change process often involves resistance or ambivalence, MI articulates a methodology that enhances discussion and decision making in the direction of change.

In clinical psychology, a common belief is that the decision and timing of change come from the client rather than the service provider. The technique recognizes that common conversations between an addict and either a professional or family member take the form of trying to convince the addict to change behavior. MI is a methodology that is somewhat counterintuitive, but it is both simple and sensible, guiding the addict to arrive at a decision to change. This procedure has proved more effective than attempts to push a person toward change. As a set of practical interviewing tools, MI may provide the estate planner with a set of techniques for mortality discussions that can overcome the ambivalence about mortality.

DIALECTICAL INTERVIEWING

A treatment modality from clinical psychology that recognizes the need to balance conflicting emotional forces is *dialectical behavioral therapy* (DBT). DBT is a well-structured approach that combines cognitive-behavioral therapy with mindfulness practice. The treatment targets specific areas of concern, such as self-harm or relationship difficulties, and combines individual treatment with psychoeducational group work. Although DBT was developed specifically to address problems encountered by clients with borderline personality disorder, a main tenet of the treatment involves enhancing the individual's ability to hold two opposing emotional states or emotions simultaneously (hence, the term "dialectic").

For the estate planner, the treatment focuses on mindfulness principles, requiring the observation of inner emotional experience in an observational manner, without judgment. The concept of holding two opposing emotional states at the same time may be applied in the financial setting when addressing conflicting desires to both discuss and avoid issues of mortality.

Looking Ahead: Collaboration Among the Professions

The current status of estate planning generally appears to be bifurcated into research and practice. The research is theoretical, emerging from psychoanalytic models that do not easily lend themselves to operationalization or clear outcome measurements. Yet, research in behavioral finance by Ariely (2008) and Kahneman (2011) possesses a field research quality that lends itself to both applied settings and outcome measures. The complications that emerge in designing useful research in the area of estate planning appear to result in part from the sensitivity that surrounds the issue of mortality. This distinguishes the estate planning effort from simple measurement of human decision making and its foibles. However, specific techniques from clinical practice reveal the merits of using different practices in the field. Indeed, there is a need to develop more scientific knowledge in the area of estate planning.

Along with the need to develop scientific knowledge in the study of estate planning, an inherently interdisciplinary nature of the practice presents ongoing challenges to service providers in psychology, law, finance, and business. The collaboration of these disciplines is an undertaking that has been developing only in recent decades, and involves setting guidelines of practice that serve the public while retaining the standards and integrity of each profession. Given the importance of money and finance in our lives, and the recognition that all of the involved disciplines deserve a voice, such a collaborative development is likely to continue into the foreseeable future.

In fact, holistic approaches to financial and estate planning uniformly endorse the collaboration of different professions and are viewed as necessary for rendering a high level of service to clients. This need to customize the estate planning service is partly a result of the proliferation of increasingly sophisticated computer- and Internet-based investment and planning services offered at greatly reduced costs. Rendering such highly individualized service is one way planners can reduce the impact of this commoditization of their services, where price competition has become a driving force.

A related issue is that each financial advisor has a professional perspective that is considered essential to the estate planning process. An element of competition can minimize the value of the aforementioned collaboration, whether recognized or not. Each professional desires to be the "most trusted advisor" to the client.

Nevertheless, cross-professional collaboration appears to be the wave of the future, although the details on how this will best take place remain unclear. Several inherent conflicts render the process of collaboration difficult. For example, distinct differences in practice exist between psychology and financial or estate planning. Professional standards differ between the fields. Additionally, the proper rendering of services in one profession can be unsettling to the client relationship in the other profession. For example, the discovery process in psychology may cause a surfacing of conflicts or emotional disruptions. An estate planner can see this development as potentially threatening the client relationship. Conversely, the psychologist may recommend, on the basis of psychological observations, that issues or items be included in an estate plan that are legally complex or even untenable. For example, the psychologist could recommend bequests that are conditioned upon future states, such as sobriety, or based on judgments of the differing psychological needs of the beneficiaries. The psychologist may make distinctions between what is an equal split of wealth and what might be a more equitable split, based on needs.

The models for this collaboration often appear to be those that will evolve over time among lawyers, financial planners, and mental health professionals. A philanthropy professional could also be in the mix. Already, several financial institutions and banks have formalized the organization of interdisciplinary collaboration within their organizations, usually to serve ultra-high net worth clients and client families. Under the umbrella of the firm, the orchestration of services could reduce competition among professionals. Additional models for collaboration could occur in the family office enterprises that provide varying levels of concierge services for financial, estate, philanthropic, and family dynamics and business issues, often oriented toward legacy planning.

The creation of forums for interdisciplinary collaboration among planners, attorneys, and mental health professionals has been occurring on a national and international level. Organizations such as the Purposeful Planning Institute, Family Firm Institute, Naz Rudin, and the Financial Therapy Association focus on the overlaps among law, psychology, and finance while employing a family dynamics perspective to research and development in what will be an ever-expanding body of knowledge in the field. No consensually accepted "best practices" are available in the field as models evolve over time.

Summary and Conclusions

This chapter explored the possibility of stronger connections between psychology and estate planning, first by discussing the psychology that underlies the planner–client relationship, and then by offering models for assessment and enhancement of the discussions that are so pertinent to estate planning. Lastly, the chapter opens the door to the future possibility of collaboration among the professions, leading to greater insights and enlarged service to clients in need of estate planning.

DISCUSSION QUESTIONS

1. Identify the issues that create differences between estate planning and other areas of financial planning that can impede or prevent progress.
2. Discuss the dimensions that differentiate estate planning from other areas of financial planning and wealth management in terms of the emotions accompanying decision making.
3. Explain why estate planning calls for collaboration between the planner and client, as well as between the client and inheritors.
4. Discuss how estate planning presents unusual challenges for the legal or planning professional.
5. Explain how transference or counter-transference might play a role in professional engagement.

REFERENCES

Ai, Amy L., Andreas Kastenmüller, Terrence N. Tice, Paul Wink, Michele Dillon, and Dieter Frey. 2014. "The Connection of Soul (COS) Scale: An Assessment Tool for Afterlife Perspectives in Different Worldviews." *Psychology of Religion and Spirituality* 6:4, 316–329.

Allianz Insurance. 2015. "Love Family Money." Available at http://www.allianzusa.com/lovefamilymoney.

Anglin, Stephanie. 2014. "From Avoidance to Approach: The Effects of Mortality Salience and Attachment on the Motivation to Repair Troubled Relationships." *Personality and Individual Differences* 66:August, 86–91.

Ariely, Daniel. 2008. *Predictably Irrational*. New York: Harper Collins.

Baines, Barry. 2006. *Ethical Wills: Putting Your Values on Paper.* Second Edition. Cambridge, MA: DaCapo Press.

Bernstein, Barton, and Sheila Collins. 1985. "Remarriage Counseling: Lawyer and Therapist Help with the Second Time Around." *Family Relations* 34:3, 387–391.

Bozo, Özlem, Ayča Tunca, and Šimšek Yeliz. 2009. "The Effect of Death Anxiety and Age on Health-promoting Behaviors: A Terror-management Theory Perspective." *Journal of Psychology* 143:4, 377–389.

Bradley, Susan. 2000. *Sudden Money: Managing a Financial Windfall.* New York: John Wiley & Sons, Inc.

Burton, Cynthia, Elizabeth Twamley, Lana Lee, Barton Palmer, Dillip Jeste, Laura Dunn, and Scott Irwin. 2012. "Undetected Cognitive Impairment and Decision-making Capacity in Patients Receiving Hospice Care." *American Journal of Geriatric Psychiatry* 20:4, 306–316.

Cai, Fengyan, and Robert J. Wyer. 2015. "The Impact of Mortality Salience on the Relative Effectiveness of Donation Appeals." *Journal of Consumer Psychology* 25:1, 101–112.

Carlson, Janet, Kurt Geisinger, and Jessica Janson (eds.). 2015. *Buros Mental Measurements Yearbook.* 19th Edition. Lincoln: University of Nebraska Press.

Cerny, Mary. 1985. "Countertransference Revisited." *Journal of Counseling and Development* 63:6, 362–364.

de Fries, Manfred. 2007. "Are You Feeling Mad, Bad, Sad or Glad?" Working Paper, INSEAD.

Dood, Tiffany, and Ian Handley. 2007. "Thoughts of Death Can Promote Resistance or Openness to Change." *Dissertation Abstracts International, Part B.* E189.

Foord, Elfrena, and Chuck Ebersole. 2007. "Roadblocks and Bridges in Estate Planning." *Journal of Practical Estate Planning* June-July, 35–40.

Fowler, Dean. 2002. *Love, Power & Money: Family Business between Generations.* Brookfield, WI: Glengrove.

Glover, Mark. 2012. "A Therapeutic Jurisprudential Framework for Estate Planning." *Seattle University Law Review* 35:2, 427–472.

Gottman, John, and Nan Silver. 1999. *Seven Principles for Making Marriage Work: A Practical Guide from the Country's Foremost Relationship Expert.* New York: Crown.

Hamel, Louis, and Timothy J. Davis. 2008. "Transference and Countertransference in the Lawyer-client Relationship: Psychoanalysis Applied in Estate Planning." *Psychoanalytic Psychology* 25:4, 590–601.

Harrington, Brooke. 2012. "Trust and Estate Planning: The Emergence of a New Profession and its Contribution to Economic Inequality." *Sociological Forum* 27:4, 825–846.

Hayes, Joseph, Cindy Ward, and Ian McGregor. 2016. "Why Bother? Death, Failure, and Fatalistic Withdrawal from Life," *Journal of Personality and Social Psychology* 110:1, 96–115.

Heflick, Nathan, Jamie Foldenberg, Joshua Hart, and Siri-Maria Kemp. 2015. "Death Awareness and Body-self Dualism: A Why and How of Afterlife Belief." *European Journal of Social Psychology* 45:2, 267–275.

Hendrix, Harville, and Helen Hunt. 1988. *Getting the l Love You Want.* New York: Henry Holt.

Hohman, Zachary, and Michael Hogg. 2015. "Fearing the Uncertain: Self Uncertainty Plays a Role in Mortality Salience." *Journal of Experimental Social Psychology* 57:March, 31–42.

Hood, Paul, and Emily Bouchard. 2012. *Estate Planning for the Blended Family.* Bellingham, WA: Self Counsel Press.

Hood, Paul, and Stephan Leimberg. 2014. *Tools and Techniques of Estate Planning for Modern Families.* Erlanger, KY: National Underwriter Company.

Jaffe, Dennis, and Stacy Allred. 2015. "Family Flash Points: Helping Families Resolve Conflict." Presented at *Purposeful Planning Institute Rendezvous,* August 7, Interloken, CO.

James, Russell. 2013. "Inside the Mind of the Bequest Donor." Self-published. ISBN: 1484197836.

Kahneman, Daniel. 2011. *Thinking, Fast and Slow.* New York: Farrar, Strauss and Giroux.

Kashdan, Todd, Nathan DeWall, David Schurtz, Timothy Dechman, Emily Lykins, Daniel Evans, Jessica McKenzie, Suzanne Segerstrom, Matthew Gaillot, and Kirk Brown. 2014. "More than Words: Contemplating Death Enhances Positive Emotional Word Use." *Personality and Individual Differences* 71:December, 171–185.

Kelley, Nicholas, and Brandon Schmeichel. 2015. "Mortality Salience Increases Personal Optimism among Individuals Higher in Trait Self-control." *Motivation and Emotion* 39:6, 926-931.

Kesebir, Pelin, and Tom Pyszczynski. 2011. "The Role of Death in Life: Existential Aspects of Human Motivation." In Richard M. Ryan (ed.), *The Oxford Handbook of Motivation*, 43–64. New York: Oxford University Press.

Khoo, Bernice, Ya See, and Michelle Hui. 2014. "Mortality Salience and Evaluations of In-group vs. Out-group Critics; The Role of Criticism Legitimacy and Perceived Threat." *European Journal of Social Psychology* 44:3, 242–254.

Kingsbury, Kathleen. 2013. *How to Give Financial Advice to Women*. New York: McGraw-Hill.

Kirkpatrick, Lee, and Carlos D. Navarette. 2006. "Reports of My Death Have Been Greatly Exaggerated: A Critique of Terror Management Theory from an Evolutionary Perspective." *Psychological Inquiry* 17:4, 288–298.

Koca-Atabey, Mulde, and Bengi Oner-Ozkan. 2014. "Loss Anxiety: An Alternative Explanation of the Fundamental Fears in Human Beings." *Death Studies* 38:10, 662–671.

Kübler-Ross, Elizabeth. 1969. *Death and Dying: What the Dying Have to Teach Doctors, Nurses, Clergy and Their Own Families*. New York: Scribner.

Landau, Mark, and Daniel Sullivan. 2014. "Terror Management at the Core of Personality." In Mario Mikulincer and Phillip R. Shaver (eds.), *APA Handbook of Personality and Social Psychology, Personality Processes and Differences*, Volume 4, 209–230. Washington, DC: American Psychological Association.

Leary, Mark, and Lisa Schreindorfer. 1997. "Unresolved Issues with Terror Management Theory." *Psychological Inquiry* 8:1, 26–29.

Lerner, Melvin. 1997. "What Does the Belief in a Just World Protect Us from: The Dread of Death or the Fear of Undeserved Suffering?" *Psychological Inquiry* 8:1, 29–32.

Lin, Chien-Wei, and I-Ling Ling. 2014. "A Good Defense Is the Best Offense: The Effects of Mortality Salience on Money and Time Allocations." *Conference of the Society for Consumer Psychology*, Miami, Florida, March 6–8.

Lunn, Michael, Ronald Wright, and Alicia Limke. 2014. "Thinking about My Death Affects How I Think God Sees Me." 15th Annual Meeting of the Society for Personality and Social Psychology, Austin, Texas, February 13–15.

Mahoney, Melissa, Benjamin Saunders, and Nicole Cain. 2014. "Priming Mortality Salience: Supraliminal, Subliminal and 'Double Death' Priming Techniques." *Death Studies* 38:10, 678–681.

Massie, Hugh. 2006. *Financial DNA: Discovering Your Unique Financial Personality for a Quality Life*. Hoboken, NJ: John Wiley & Sons, Inc.

Miller, William, and Steven Rollnick. 2013. *Motivational Interviewing: Helping People Change*. Third Edition. New York: Guilford Press.

Olsen, David. 2011. *Couple's Survival Workbook: What You Can Do to Reconnect with Your Partner and Make Marriage Work*. Oakland, CA: New Harbinger Publications.

Peisah, C., S. Finke, K. Shulman, P. Melding, J. Luxenberg, J. Heinik, and H. Bennett. 2009. "The Wills of Older People: Risk Factors for Undue Influence." International Psychogeriatric Association Task Force on Wills and Undue Influence, *International Psychogeriatrics* 21:1, 7–15.

Peisah, C., J. Luxenberg, B. Liptzin, A. Wand, K. Shulman, and S. Finkel. 2014. "Deathbed Wills: Assessing Testamentary Capacity in the Dying Patient." *International Psychogeriatrics* 26:2, 209–216.

Reimer, Jack, and Nathaniel Stampfer. 1991. *So That Your Values Live On: Ethical Wills and How to Prepare Them*. Woodstock, VT: Jewish Lights Publishing.

Rosenberger, Eric, and Jeffrey Hayes. 2002. "Therapist as Subject: A Review of the Empirical Countertransference Literature." *Journal of Counseling and Development* 80:3, 264–270.

Schneiderman, Gerald. 1983. "The Will: Guidelines for the Psychiatrist and the Attorney." *American Journal of Forensic Psychiatry* 4:3, 135–140.

Scott, James. 1973. "Psychological Aspects of Estate Planning" *Journal of Forensic Psychology* 5:December, 25–39.

Seligman, Martin. 2002. *Authentic Happiness: Using the New Positive Psychology to Realize Your Potential for Lasting Fulfillment.* New York: Simon and Schuster.
Shaffer, Thomas. 1970. *Death, Property and Lawyers: A Behavioral Approach.* Dunellen, NJ: Dunellen.
Snyder, Charles. 1997. "Control and the Application of Occam's Razor to Terror Management Theory." *Psychological Inquiry* 8:1, 48–49.
Solomon, Sheldon, Jeff Greenberg, and Tom Pyszczynski. 2015. *The Worm at the Core: The Role of Death in Life.* New York: Random House.

19

Individual Biases in Retirement Planning and Wealth Management

JAMES E. BREWER JR.
President, Envision Wealth Planning

CHARLES H. SELF III
Chief Investment Officer, iSectors

Introduction

People often live in the moment during most of their lives, including in regard to their money. *Present bias* is the tendency to overvalue immediate rewards at the expense of long-term intentions. For example, a child may want the "must have" toy. The parent may say no, focusing on paying the private school education, but the grandparent may choose to buy the toy to experience the immediate joy on that grandchild's face.

According to Statman (2011), an individual's relationship with money can take a utilitarian, emotional, or expressive form. Historically, the study of economics and finance has focused on the *utilitarian*, which is the ability for a service or good to satisfy needs and wants. Rapper Snoop Doggy Dogg (1993) says it this way: "I've got my mind on my money and my money on my mind." An *emotional* relationship focuses on achieving peace of mind, whereas an *expressive* relationship concentrates on the role money plays in defining an individual.

However, what about an individual's long-term best interests? In a fast-paced world, individuals often do not have the natural ability or the time to become experts in a topic and to execute the knowledge they possess. Recall the cardiologist who is overweight and smokes. Having someone to look out for the best interests of others and to provide a little nudge can promote better behavior.

Thaler and Sunstein (2009) introduce the concept of *nudging*, also known as *paternal libertarianism* (Thaler and Sunstein 2003). This concept describes how corporations, governments, or institutions can develop policies or tools to influence the behavior of individuals by changing their decisions toward outcomes that would not occur without the nudge. That is, the organization establishes the context in which people make decisions. For instance, financial planning policies based on nudging encourage people to save and invest more money. Howard and Yazdipour (2014, p. 195) provide an instance of this:

> In the example of a worker contributing to a defined contribution or 401(k) plan, the employee would be automatically enrolled to contribute the required amount to receive the maximum employer match. The employee could opt out by selecting an alternative contribution or by withdrawing from the plan.

Another example of nudging is the default settings for software—these choices are made for someone unless he or she selects a customized option. Nudging does not actually limit choice, but it suggests that someone with expert knowledge has already made the suitable choice.

Few people get a passing grade on the Financial Industry Regulatory Authority's (FINRA) financial literacy test. This finding is not surprising, considering that personal financial literacy is not a core curriculum subject in U.S. schools. Nevertheless, individuals benefit from a nudge toward making better choices about their financial decisions. In a *Forbes* interview with Peter Ubel (2015), Richard Thaler states, "A nudge, as we will use the term, is any aspect of the choice architecture that alters people's behavior in a predictable way without forbidding any options or significantly changing their economic incentives. To count as a mere nudge, the intervention must be easy and cheap to avoid." In the context of finance, working in someone's best interest takes on a legal status known as a *fiduciary*. Employers along with fiduciary financial planning and investment advisors can develop nudges, such as opting people into the company retirement plan and selecting professionally managed model portfolios for them.

Kinniry, Jaconetti, DiJoseph, and Zilbering (2014) estimate that working with a certain type of financial advisor using the Vanguard Advisor's Alpha Framework can add 3 percentage points (300 basis points) a year in net return. The framework includes suitable asset allocation using broadly diversified exchange-traded funds (ETFs), cost-effective implementation (expense ratios), rebalancing, behavioral coaching, asset location (tax-efficient investing), spending strategy (withdrawal order), and total return versus income investing. Vanguard attributes half of that return to behavioral coaching. Morningstar suggests that a financial planner can add 1.59 percentage points (159 basis points) in return from certain retirement planning advice (Blanchett and Kaplan 2013).

This chapter begins by examining some financial pitfalls, including people's all too common reliance on intuition, biases, and irrational behavior regarding their finances. These pitfalls create the individual's need for financial planning, which leads to evaluating whether to hire a professional, accept employer nudges, or utilize a combination of advice and nudges from a Certified Financial Planner™ (CFP®) or CFA professional. Then, the chapter highlights how nudges can enhance wealth, and concludes with a chapter summary.

Biases Create the Need for Financial Planning

RELIANCE ON INTUITION

According to Nobel Prize recipient Daniel Kahneman, people use two systems for thinking (Kahneman 2011): the fast system, which is intuitive and emotional, and the slow one, which is deliberate and logical. Given Kahneman's view, should people trust their intuition? The intuition of a child differs from the intuition of her parents. The education and greater life experience of parents should improve their intuition, but does the intuition of parents in their mid-years differ from the intuition of seniors?

Kahneman offers two basic conditions for evaluating the validity of an intuitive judgment: (1) there needs to be an environment sufficiently regular to be predictable, and (2) there needs to be an opportunity to learn these regularities through prolonged practice. When a situation meets both conditions, a person's acquired skills often serve as the basis for his or her intuition. Yet regardless of age, someone who has earned an academic degree or industry designation in investments is likely to be more skilled than someone who does not have that credential.

"UNBIASED" SELF-ASSESSMENTS

Many people attempt to assess their own financial needs. Often they simply rationalize the status quo, failing to see the biases in their thoughts:

- "I don't need an advisor." Often the bias is anti-accountability. An advisor may want to change a behavior the client enjoys. Another bias—*status quo* or *inertia*—is one in which the client does not want to change what is currently working. This bias, also known as the *ostrich effect*, is one in which a client keeps his head in the sand and avoids action of any type.
- "I'll think about retirement later. Just give me what I want today." This statement represents *present bias*. People who make such assertions think that the future will take care of itself by meeting their current needs.
- "I won't die." Spending money on life insurance premiums takes away from the pleasures of vacations and hobbies. Alternatively, focusing on financial obligations upon death saddens clients to think that they will not be young forever.
- "I won't get disabled." People do not want to think about becoming impaired and dependent on others. This statement also suggests that a person has control over undesirable events, known as the *illusion of control*. Further, burying one's head in the sand (ostrich effect) could be harmful to loved ones.
- "None of my friends are doing it." Although the herd may not be right, it offers a pleasant pack to emulate. Clients sometimes feel that their situation is not complicated and lends itself to self-diagnosis without specialized knowledge. Discovering additional complications might require an investment of both time and emotions to address them.
- "I save enough to get the employer's match in my retirement plan." People tend to focus on the match rather than calculating the needed amount to retire comfortably. Individuals prefer to focus on the most recognizable features: free money, which is a *salience bias*.

IRRATIONAL FINANCIAL BEHAVIORS

An individual's financial behavior often does not present a logical pattern of thought to the academic or financial professional, but it is perfectly coherent to the individual. This includes behaviors such as milestones, anchoring on names, money emotions, and money languages. These behaviors support the need for employer and advisor nudges, which are discussed later in the chapter.

Financial Milestones

Many people think in terms of a milestone-based, linear financial planning process: first secure a job, then get married, buy a house, start a family, plan for college education expenses for the children, and, finally plan for retirement. Individuals often associate with a peer group that holds similar views. When workers have a defined benefit pension plan, the employer contributes the most money; sometimes, the plan requires employee contributions or permits voluntary contributions. For workers with these plans, the pension system pays expected benefits when they are needed at a later time. Conversely, workers with elective plans or defined contribution plans, such as 401(k) plans, make their own contributions and investment decisions, following their peer group or hiring someone to help them. Even when they are proactive in these matters, there is great uncertainty about the amount of projected benefits upon retirement.

Anchoring on Investment Names

When venturing into unfamiliar territory, individuals often seek a familiar label, such as identifying themselves as conservative or aggressive investors. Not surprisingly, mutual funds include descriptors such as "conservative" or "aggressive" and some people are attracted to these funds because of those descriptors. However, the portfolio manager's notion of what is conservative may differ from that of investors'. Depending on the risk, return, and expenses charged by the fund, the fund might look conservative but its risk profile is actually aggressive. This situation can create anxiety if return volatility is present.

Some see the target-date fund strategy as the answer for all participants in 401(k) plans. A *target-date fund* is a mutual fund that automatically resets the asset mix of stocks, bonds, and cash equivalents in its portfolio according to a selected time horizon that is appropriate for particular investors. Participants and sometimes the employer's 401(k) decision makers believe that target-date funds promise a specific account balance on the date of the target-date strategy's name. Although called a target-date fund, the year does not refer to the adequacy of the account balance; it refers only to the fact that the fund becomes more conservative over time. Its returns do not contain a guarantee but, rather, depend on how the market performs. Some target-date funds are at the most conservative asset allocation at the target (stated) year. Yet, others could become the most conservative 15 or 20 years after the stated date, given that retirees may depend on the fund's balance for decades. Hence, the name "target-date fund" can be confusing.

Money Emotions

People have self-expressive desires. Both inexpensive and luxury automobiles provide a mode of transportation, but the impression they have on others differs. Saving money has little self-esteem appeal; others may be unaware that an individual has $5 million in the bank. Many people use consumer debt to obtain the appearance that they are wealthy; however, given the many sudden bankruptcies of high-profile figures, this image can be just an illusion. Individuals acting on the need for self-esteem disproves the notion of rational behavior.

Doctors, lawyers, and other highly skilled professionals often suffer from money shame. Brown (2012) discusses the physical and psychological tolls that shame can exact. These high-income earners fall prey to the same self-esteem and emotional challenges as experienced by less wealthy individuals. Their resources allow them to buy bigger homes in more affluent neighborhoods and to join exclusive clubs; their need to feed their self-esteem and keep up with their peers often drives their behavior. As Belsky (2010) notes, if these individuals find themselves subsequently teetering on a financial brink, they may ask, "How can I be in this situation? What does this say about me? I am smart so I can resolve this issue. Who can I trust to not expose my situation to my peers?" Although logical answers are available to these questions, individuals may lack the knowledge to recognize them or be unable to regulate their emotions and behavior. One option is to turn to a financial professional. According to Statman (2000), the true value of a financial planner or financial advisor lies in managing the investor, not the investments.

The word *smart* might result in detrimental financial decisions for clients. Everyone wants to be smart, yet people may label some children "dumb," at home or at school. The shame that these children feel about this labeling could last a lifetime, and certainly can affect their emotions about money. Away from those giving grades or critiques, they can now assess themselves as smart. Although they may be skilled in music, art, or some other talent for society, quantitative analysis may not be their area of expertise. When a predatory financial "professional" calls them "smart," these individuals receive affirmation based on what they want to hear. They may perceive that person as trustworthy and willing to accept their advice.

In fact, some investment providers like to incorporate the word *smart* into the names of their funds or analytic descriptors. Although *beta* refers to exposure to the broad market, these providers use the term "smart beta" to describe investing in securities that are highly correlated with a factor in the market such as low volatility or high dividend yield. These providers want investors to feel intelligent when investing in their products. Who would want a "dumb beta" when you could have "smart beta?"

Money Languages

Gender and marital status often contribute to money language. *Money language* is applied to how influences such as parental, ethnic, and religious cultures help shape our relationship with money. For example:

- "I'm a man; therefore, I'm good at numbers."
- "Women are the caregivers."
- "Our people's wealth comes from owning property. That's what our group does."
- Wife: "What's our retirement plan?" Husband: "Don't worry, it is under control, trust me."

Not surprisingly, men often exhibit overconfidence because they consider confidence a positive behavior. They do not want to be asked questions about the decisions they make. Some even want to play "stump the financial planner." This show of bravado behavior is an attempt to exhibit their masculinity to a spouse or significant other.

Some men say they are aggressive investors while actually being just as concerned about market swings as women. What they mean is that they want to earn better than average market gains when the market is up and want to switch to cash to avoid losses when the market is down. This market timing behavior is often very costly.

Additionally, men often do not want to think about either their mortality or an eventual decline in their health. Their partners are concerned about their mortality, however, if they count on the man's income for a large portion of household income. Men may reject purchasing more life insurance, using excuses such as: the advisor only wants to make money selling insurance, none of his friends carry that much insurance, or the family could be using that money for more productive purposes.

Women have the practical challenge of longer expected life spans than men have. This greater longevity means that women need to save more than men of the same age and income. In many married households, the husband rather than the wife drives the retirement planning decision. As these conversations are often emotionally charged, many couples want to avoid them.

Women may forgo investing in their 401(k) plans so as to invest in their spouse's retirement plan or to help pay for their children's education. If the couple is contributing to the spouse's 401(k) plan, a natural question is whether a different risk position appears in the portfolio that would be wise for the wife. If not, and divorce occurs, then she might receive less than what she otherwise would have received using a more moderate investing approach.

Anchoring and herd behavior influence individuals according to the norms of their race and culture. *Anchoring* is a cognitive bias that describes the tendency to rely too heavily on the first piece of information offered (the "anchor") when making decisions. *Herd behavior* describes how individuals in a group can act collectively without centralized direction. Although not obviously true in all cases, Dutch Americans have a reputation for being frugal, whereas African Americans often receive a label of being spenders. If African Americans anchor or believed these stereotypes, then they would spend. A person who does not follow cultural norms can be emotionally uncomfortable, feeling himself to be an outlier.

Another misconception is when African Americas choose to save, they are purposely conservative investors (Natella, Meschede, and Sullivan 2014). Prudential (2015) attributes conservative behavior to a lack of exposure, education, and information, which is availability bias. *Availability bias* refers to making decisions based on limited information. Thus, the relative lack of information and exposure of many African Americans may predispose them to more conservative investing behavior. According to Prudential, many financial services firms do not actively seek out African American investors, which could otherwise improve this group's risk taking ability.

Biases in Deciding Whether to Hire a Professional

The decision of whether to hire a financial professional should at least include evaluating the areas of someone's own financial literacy regarding the following current situation: (1) evaluating advisor competency and fiduciary status; (2) financial status, including the mix of credit and debt; (3) retirement planning; (4) college financing for children; (5) insurance policies; (6) tax management; (7) estate planning; and (8) investment strategy. Although most people elect to coordinate their own financial plans, research from the Financial Industry Regulatory Authority (FINRA 2013) reveals that 61 percent of U.S. respondents could not answer more than three of the following five questions correctly:

1. Suppose you have $100 in a savings account earning 2 percent interest a year. After five years, how much would you have?
2. Imagine that the interest rate on your savings account is 1 percent a year and inflation is 2 percent a year. After one year, would the money in the account buy more than it does today, the same, or less than today?
3. If interest rates rise, what will typically happen to bond prices? Rise, fall, stay the same, or is there no relationship?
4. True or false: A 15-year mortgage typically requires higher monthly payments than a 30-year mortgage, but the total interest over the life of the loan will be less.
5. True or false: Buying a single company's stock usually provides a safer return than a stock mutual fund.

There is much confusion about the term "financial advisor." No such professional designation exists. People who work with investments and insurance products might call themselves financial advisors because the term sounds better than "agent," "broker" or "financial salesperson." However, a working definition for a financial advisor would include those who provide advice in the best interests of the individual, which is legally known as a fiduciary; who holds an industry designation that minimally includes retirement planning, investment planning, and insurance planning; and who maintains an industry designation requiring continuing education. A CFP® professional fits this definition, having successfully completed extensive coursework and having practical experience in financial foundations, risk and insurance planning, retirement planning, investment planning, tax planning, and estate planning. The individual has also taken a fiduciary oath.

Beyond these particulars of training and knowledge, there are personal characteristics that people look for when considering a financial advisor.

TRUST

Trust for some people may reflect a good feeling about that person. In her TED talk, Onora O'Neill (2013) states: "I would aim to have more trust in the trustworthy but not in the untrustworthy. . . . Intelligently placed and intelligently refused trust is the proper aim." She provides a structure for evaluating trust that applies to the CFP® professional, indicating that the judgment of trust for professionals requires determining whether they are competent, honest, and reliable.

COMPETENCY

Most people have had no formal introduction to those involved in the financial planning industry. They often identify a financial advisor and financial planner as synonymous terms. Although commonly used, these may be self-appointed terms, as indicated earlier. That is why asking about registrations, licenses, and professional designations is important. Some who identify themselves as financial advisors may be mortgage agents or professionals who sell products, as oppose to offering advice. Many who call themselves a financial planner do not have the comprehensive planning competency of a CFP® professional.

Others mistake a professional's total assets under management (AUM) as an indicator of competency. The AUM is the total market value of the investments managed by a mutual fund, money management firm, hedge fund, portfolio manager, or other financial services company. Many firms in the financial services industry like to tout their size in terms of their AUM. They want investors to believe that because of the size of the assets they manage, they know what they are doing. But the AUM does not mean their clients are on track to reach their goals.

HONESTY

Most people prefer to hire people who will work in their best interests. Unless the professional is *required* to work in the client's best interests, such as is the case with a CFP® professional, potential clients should remain doubtful. The individuals who work in the client's interests can better frame a client's issues from a holistic financial standpoint, which includes the "Aspects of Financial Planning" explained in the next section.

RELIABILITY

As mentioned, the finance industry often touts AUM as an indicator of reliability and good results. However, there are better methods for evaluating the reliability of a financial profession. For example, a potential client could survey a few of the planner's clients on how the individual handles various situations. Those situations might be retirement income planning or education planning for blended families. Another assessment tool is the FINRA BrokerCheck, which provides the regulatory record of advisors.

Aspects of Financial Planning

Any categorization of the broad topic of financial planning will differ depending on one's perspective. The following are two major ones, helping to highlight the services of a CFP® or CFA charterholder. When taken together, these areas represent this chapter's definition of wealth management.

FINANCIAL STATUS AND STABILITY

The financial status of different individuals can vary dramatically. For example, some people do not have an emergency fund; perhaps they feel that emergencies will not happen to them. Others have large credit card balances, making their financial survivability difficult if they miss several paychecks. Some people's risk-management strategy is to hope that calamities do not happen to them. Car owners have auto insurance because it is legally required to drive an automobile, not because they want to hedge the financial risk of an accident. The rationale for these decisions is born of optimism and the ostrich effect. We all tend to create narratives concerning risk that is based on our intuition rather than deliberation.

Individuals take this intuitive framework with them when as employees they select options on their employer's health insurance or disability income protection. They have them in mind when they think about life insurance or an elective employer-sponsored defined contribution retirement plan. Although most people feel that health care is a necessity, they reject many other benefits because electing them will further reduce their take-home pay, another instance of present bias. Some people elect to continue with the health insurance plan they had the prior year, rather than investigate other options, revealing a status quo bias.

Many people do not like the high premiums of long-term care insurance. They typically focus on the premium, rather than the cost if they were to pay for nursing care completely out of pocket. In fact, most people do not have the cash for long-term care, or would rather risk the well-being of their loved ones to pay those costs. Some make incorrect, uninformed yet optimistic assumptions about the role of Medicare and Medicaid in covering long-term care. In short, people often create hopeful narratives that support their overall judgment, resulting in a denial of the facts in order to avoid negative emotions.

Narrow framing can seriously affect an individual's financial status. It especially becomes an issue when someone sees only part of the picture and not the whole. For instance, many people equate having $1 million in income to having $1 million in the bank. However, they have not calculated the taxes due, as well as other fees that may lower that amount. First-time recipients of large sums of money, such as lottery winners and athletes, often spend the money even before they receive the funds.

RETIREMENT PLANNING

Planning for retirement can be an emotional challenge. Many associate it with a loss of vibrancy and even impending death. Others see retirement as a time of financial freedom, a time to do the things they have been denying themselves while they were working. These people often have lived frugal lives and they leave their jobs at the earliest possible moment so they can enjoy themselves in their retirement.

Present bias has many people delaying their retirement planning until they reach their 50s or 60s. Their social groups and peers influence their thoughts about whether retirement planning is a priority. Additionally, in their considerations, they often discount the power of small savings and compounding interest, as research conducted by Ibbotson, Xiong, Kreitler, Kreitler, and Chen (2007) shows. Yet knowing the power of small savings could help them build their retirement funds.

Let's look at an example of the savings required for someone to live on 80 percent of a $60,000 gross income during retirement. Based on the Ibbotson et al. research, a 25-year-old would need to save 12 percent of her income until she retired at age 65. If she waits until age 50 to save, her savings rate should climb to 50 percent. These savings rates assume the investor will achieve certain investment returns, which may vary from those projected. Those returns may not be what the retirement investor actually earns. Obviously, a 25-year-old can more easily save a smaller percentage of income for a longer time than can a 50-year-old save a larger amount. Ibbotson et al. also show that as a person's income goes up, so does the rate of savings required to replace the same 80 percent of gross income.

Many individuals with access to workplace retirement savings plans do not participate in those plans. Because many of these plans offer some matching contribution from the employer, the workers are "leaving money on the table." Why would someone not take "free money?" Researchers at the National Bureau of Economic Research have concluded that employees often "follow the path of least resistance" (Choi, Laibson, Madrian, and Metrick 2015).

Some people view their 401(k) plans as a general savings account, rather than a tax-deferred, retirement savings account. They withdraw funds for current needs, without much thought about how that action will affect their retirement funds. In most cases, they would be better off using a simple savings account and reserving their 401(k) plan, thereby avoiding the early withdrawal penalty, income tax obligation, and potential market risk.

Similarly, many people are anxious to access their Social Security benefits as early as possible. They believe that they are simply receiving the money owed to them and some have concerns about their longevity. Unfortunately, maximizing a Social Security benefit is not a straightforward decision; delaying any claim for Social Security benefits can add $10,000s, if not $100,000s, over a lifetime. The reality is that more people will live longer than expected, as medicine and medical procedures continue to improve. Following a deliberate decision-making process for building one's retirement savings, rather than an intuitive or wishful one, may help people avoid poverty in old age.

People are prone to oversimplification, which leads to narrow framing or considering too few factors in making decisions. This bias emerges from a lack of time or information, leading to suboptimal decisions. Consider, for example, how some large financial institutions advertise that they can help people with 401(k) plan roll over the funds into their individual retirement accounts (IRAs). This assumes that an individual would be better off rolling over her 401(k) plan funds, rather than leaving them at her former employer. But is she moving her funds to a better investment? What makes that rollover better? And is the rollover consistent with her overall retirement plan? Additionally, is the ease of completing the paperwork the most important consideration? A slower, deliberative decision process might offer greater retirement benefits.

Earned income is taxable for Social Security purposes up to a set amount. Those who exceed this income cap often view the excess as "found" money (known as *mental accounting*), and not as an opportunity to save for retirement. This scenario is a framing situation: many people like the ego boost it provides and let others know they have exceeded the income cap. Others enjoy spending the money for fun pursuits or luxuries.

Investment Strategies

Investment planning comprises having an investment plan, asset allocation, value determination, selection of investments, market timing, regular review of investments, and tax planning. Let's consider the biases and typical investor behaviors that lead to faulty financial planning.

ONE-SIDED INVESTMENT PLANS

Investment planning is a multifaceted, often emotional pursuit. Based on mutual fund flows, the strategy followed by a majority of people is to chase investment returns and pursue market timing. Some find the pursuit of outperformance to be exhilarating; however, Portnoy (2014) points to the futility of attempting to pick funds that consistently outperform others.

Central to understanding and resolving the investor's paradox is recognizing that investing is a matter of choice as much as it is a matter of finance and statistics. As mentioned earlier, people prefer simple solutions. When they see their portfolio balance go down, references to dollar cost averaging and long-term investment strategies are not what they want to hear. Yet, an evidenced-based, optimal strategy uses broadly diversified asset allocation.

LIMITED DIVERSIFICATION

A basic tenant of Modern Portfolio Theory (MPT) is that the most efficient portfolios have the highest expected returns for the risks taken. According to Markowitz (1952), by knowing the assets' expected returns, volatility, and correlations, a set of portfolios will emerge that represents the most efficient available, known as the *efficient frontier*. Markowitz shows that efficient portfolios consist of low-correlated assets, which result in diversified portfolios.

Subsequent erroneous implementation of MPT led Markowitz (1959, 1991) to suggest enhancements to MPT. The creation of Post-Modern Portfolio Theory (Post-MPT), first devised by Rom and Ferguson (1993), addresses some of these errors by:

- Creating a set of investment choices having low correlations between them.
- Using 21st-century computational resources and statistical processes not dependent on historical returns, standard deviations, and correlations to generate efficient frontiers.
- Defining risk in more precise terms than volatility to reflect human behavior.
- Considering investment vehicles and trading costs when establishing portfolios.

Few individual investors can create these truly diversified portfolios on their own, however. They believe that investing in multiple mutual funds achieves full diversification. On the contrary, financial advisors often have access to tools and investment vehicles that can create such efficient portfolios for their clients.

CONFLICTING SOCIAL VALUES

Clients often hold strong social values, yet investing may take them outside those values. Do clients know the nature of their investments? Do they want to invest consistently within their social values to reach their financial goals? Are issues such as sustainability, religion, gender equality, or income gap important to them? As both Kinnel (2015) and Roberts (2015) show, there is a difference between the returns an investor receives and a comparable index return. Furthermore, investments in mutual funds, on average, fail to attain the funds' expected returns. Investor behavior accounts for much of this result. They often trade their account based on emotion. This leads to harmful behaviors such as buying high and selling low. However, working with an advisor that helps them invest in a values and goals based way can help calm their nerves. Investing in companies that are aligned with the investor's social and religious values could help these individuals stay with an investment strategy during volatile times.

FAULTY INVESTMENT SELECTION

Most people select their investments based on desired returns rather than a desire to avoid risk. Not all people who invest may realize that company cash flows vary over time, sales fluctuate, and demand for products can change, based on the general economic condition. Additionally, investors often listen to those who tell them what they want to hear, rather than those with opposing views. Some listen to con artists such as Bernie Madoff and have become victims, failing to question how he could deliver far higher returns than the market was producing.

Many investors watch pundits on television and listen to radio shows in search of forecasts and hot tips. Although some of the pundits are logical in their approach, others are not much more than entertainment. In contrast, companies such as Morningstar and Lipper use rating systems to help investors assess mutual funds. Many of these assessments employ historical data to base their ratings. Remember, though, that mutual funds carry a warning label saying that "past performance may not be indicative of future returns." Yet, historical performance is the basis that many people use when evaluating investment returns. Who has time to look at the small print, anyway?

Similarly, when investing in the company's retirement plan, many employees assume that the employer has carefully preselected the 401(k) menus. That is, a single person or investment committee has agreed with the company's selected providers. Yet the investment menu may reflect a profit incentive given to the selected provider and not be in the best retirement interests of the participants.

Many employees, 401(k) savers, make hasty selections because the process seem overwhelming. Some feel ashamed that they do not understand the complexity of the selection process. Others look for patterns of performance that often do not exist. They focus on the recent winners, take an equal percentage of each selection, or accept the default choice that could be a low return, cash equivalent fund. Others are overconfident in their ability to choose the funds. For many people, fund selection is based on historical performance; they want the past returns of the fund, not necessarily its future returns, which are uncertain.

STRESS ON MARKET TIMING

The pursuit of increasing returns via market timing comes loaded with an unending number of questions. Market timers focus on determining the optimal time to enter or exit the market, yet this decision hangs on predicting the answers to a variety of questions. Will the Federal Reserve change interest rates? Will investors listen to the pundit with his opinion on the matter? How will the foreign markets react? Will what happens in foreign markets that affect markets in the United States? What should we do and when should we do it?

Individuals want to appear smart, so they often quote various news sources. Without a solid background in economics or finance, though, these investors may not be able to evaluate what the experts are saying. They may discuss the news with peers who also want to show their intelligence and this cycle of groupthink can lead to unnecessary trading. Timing the market correctly can provide huge self-expressive benefits. The pundit gets bragging rights of saying "I told you so." And it can engender feelings of regret if one heard the advice and did not act on it.

Few investors understand the negative impact of management fees and trading costs on their returns. That is, trading costs decrease profits unless one can earn higher returns to overcome those costs. Nevertheless, frequent trading can give an investor feelings of empowerment, as in controlling one's own destiny. The evidence shows, however, that over the long-term, frequent traders lose more, on average, than they win (Barber and Odean 2000).

UNBALANCED INVESTMENT REVIEW

After creating their portfolios, many investors evaluate their performance based on whether the account balance has increased. The typical investment statement reports only present performance, without presenting the client's risk exposure. This type of presentation can lead an investor to trade on emotion. The most important evaluation of investment performance is whether it is consistent with the required returns in the financial plan, based on an individual's savings over a specific time period.

As mentioned, many retail investors use "expert" commentary from the media in making their financial decisions. The trustworthiness of these "experts" is based on being a media professional, rather than a credentialed financial professional. What is the real basis for their expertise? Asking that question requires research and deliberation, while interrupting the pleasure of satisfying of one's emotions.

Are these media "experts" actually investment advisors? They often speak in hyperbole, and they report the overall direction of a market index, such as the S&P 500. Yet some investors do not understand the implications of the S&P 500 index; they do not even know it is only a subset of the total investable universe. For example, if half of an investor's portfolio consists of bonds that track an intermediate bond fund index, then the S&P 500 index alone is not a good barometer of performance. Further, some experience positive or negative emotions based on the performance their investments compared to the S&P 500 index. Much of this stress would be avoided if they had knowledge of proper benchmarks for their holdings.

INADEQUATE TAX PLANNING

Tax planning is an often-overlooked area of financial planning. Unfortunately, many people mentally frame the matter as tax preparation versus tax planning. Moreover, they don't understand tax brackets in the U.S. tax system or capital gains taxes vs. income taxes. Decreasing the amount of those taxable dollars can increase one's wealth.

Unfortunately, most people do not think about taxes until April 15 is near. Their opportunity to save on their taxes mostly ended on December 31 of the prior year. The urgency of the tax deadline is a huge motivator, but procrastination is always looming. Few people pursue a knowledgeable tax professional who can help them find ways to save on their taxes, such as starting a 401(k) or health savings account.

Some individuals prefer a sense of control or think they can easily prepare their own tax returns. Many use a software program and/or online tax forms, believing they can do the work of a Certified Public Accountant (CPA). For others, their tax situation is simple and is merely an exercise in following directions. Yet a CPA can provide both tax planning and tax return preparation.

Most people prefer getting a tax refund rather than finding they owe the government a check. This attitude illustrates the concept of loss aversion. *Loss aversion* stems from an individual's strong desire not to take losses; typical investors feel a loss more emotionally than they do a gain.

Some people use their tax refund as a forced savings program. In many cases, that refund becomes more of a "slush fund," as it is put toward vacations and other pursuits. Many people overpay their taxes out of fear that they might owe at the time of their filing and not have sufficient funds to make the payment. Or, they may not give, insure, save, or invest the bonus, citing the unavailability of the funds to do so, even with refund in hand. Thus, an entire industry of tax preparers exists that has attached value to getting individuals a tax refund.

Enhancing Wealth Through Nudges

People need help in avoiding the self-expressive and emotional issues that can overwhelm their rational thinking. Qualified financial professionals can deliver this help. Yeske and Buie (2014, p. 195) point to the value of nudging as part of the financial planning process, that it is a method of reframing the conversation and drawing "the client's attention to a different aspect of the situation, one that transcends the present moment, or enlists client heuristics to nudge them into a healthy direction." Basically, there are two major types of professional nudges.

EMPLOYER NUDGES

Most employees have difficulty calculating their needed savings rates and returns, and then translating this information into retirement income. Benartzi (2012) highlights the importance of intelligent defaults to help employees with retirement planning. The most important is for employees to enroll automatically in a plan. Such a conclusion should not come as a surprise, given that most full-time employees experience automatic enrollment in Social Security. Another is to establish a default contribution rate, such as 6 percent, and then continue to increase it—to say, 10 percent—in annual increments. Given that employees typically know little about proper asset allocation, having a professionally managed portfolio is critical. An employer can provide the professional management through the qualified default investment alternative (QDIA) safe harbor.

According to U.S. Department of Labor regulations, if employers properly select and monitor their QDIA choice, they will receive relief (safe harbor) from liability for their employees' investment outcomes. The operative word is *properly*, as some employers have taken this to mean that all target-date funds qualify. But each potential QDIA fund needs to be analyzed separately to see if the QDIA definition is met.

Using that same thinking, employers should consider defaulting or nudging employees into the maximum health, disability, life, and long-term care insurance plans, if available. Rather than make employees become experts, employers should make the choice easy for them. New employees are unlikely to view these actions as reductions from their take-home pay (losses). Ideally, enrollment or benefits kick-off meetings can help inform employees about changes in the benefit selection and explain the philosophy behind the changes. This process can temper the emotions of people who may want to opt out.

At these meetings, employers can provide their employees with a retirement gap analysis or personalized retirement plan. Calculating the required savings rates and considering the inflation rates, expected returns, and time horizons are complicated. Besides being a cognitive challenge, this task can be emotionally draining; yet, people with a plan are more confident overall. Implementing such a program can reduce work disruptions, as well. Employees confident of their finances will spend less time thinking about and working on them during work hours. Employers can also offer employees the help of a financial professional through a workplace program.

FINANCIAL PLANNER NUDGES

The first task a financial planner should undertake when meeting with a prospective client is to establish trust, using O'Neill's (2013) three-factor model mentioned previously: competence, honesty, reliability. The planner should present how her credentials benefit the prospective client. She should educate the individual about the requirements of her various licenses, registrations, and designations. In the case of the Certified Financial Board of Standards, these requirements are passing college-level courses in financial fundamentals, retirement, tax, investments, and estate planning; passing a two-day exam; and delivering financial planning to clients for at least three years. Presenting a clean regulatory record with FINRA, the Securities and Exchange Commission (SEC), and the CFP board highlights a planner's honesty. Professionals can bolster their reliability by providing contacts that clients can access to check their experiences.

Financial professionals should use a meeting process that allows new clients to get to know them personally. Website and imagery showing the human side of the service can demonstrate how financial planning can help the client achieve his or her desired goals. Total wealth optimization (wealth management) is a multidisciplinary approach with priorities, trade-offs, emotions, and self-expressions. Its intention is to balance the many areas that can affect financial life.

The financial planner should ask questions that address the client's entire self: goals, interests, values, relationships, financials resources, and the desired number/type of planner contacts. These answers can uncover the underlying drivers for the client's expected outcomes or can establish needs. Are issues such as sustainability, religion, gender equality, and income gap important to the client? How might clients want to incorporate their social values into investments, giving, and activism?

After clarifying the client's goals, the financial planner should assess the client's resources and provide a plan based on standards that optimize the client's total wealth. Examples of these standards could be having a six-month cash reserve, maximum disability coverage (60 or 70 percent of current income), life insurance to cover human economic value, and Social Security benefits beginning at age 70, as well as consideration of the inflation rate, expected return targets for the time period, savings constraints, and if applicable, optimizing the use of employer-sponsored retirement plans.

Achieving these standards takes time. Part of the financial planning implementation is to help clients redirect their spending to areas that will help them advance toward their financial goals. The planner can reframe a cash-flow plan or budget from being a constrainer to becoming a tool that increases total wealth. For example, some budgets only support negative emotions, such as "I no longer can buy whatever I want." Instead, clients may experience positive emotions by associating a specific dollar amount with a desired client goal— "Save 10 percent of your earnings" does not have the same feel as "Save $600 a month so that you can confidently maintain your lifestyle after taking an early retirement at age 61." It is easier to change behavior when present happiness and future joy are equal concerns.

Most people seek to avoid immediate pain, such as obtaining negative investment returns. Investors often view these investment returns in isolation because they have not calculated the return needed to reach a specific goal. This tunnel focus can be at the expense of other areas of their financial plan. However, automating the income redirection helps address the loss of current discretionary spending and soothes the client's emotions accompanying this loss. Typically, employees view payroll deductions as forgone pain (passing up a bigger check) rather than an outright loss (paying into savings "out of pocket"). The planner should direct the client toward the joy of seeing all of his or her financial goals funded. The financial professional and the client can then celebrate the milestones reached along the way. Those milestones may include paying off existing debt, enrolling in the company's retirement plan, or achieving 20 percent of the client's retirement goal. These celebrations boost happy emotions and self-expression.

Planning professionals might reframe the retirement savings around the concept of "lifetime income smoothing." That is, would clients like to have an uninterrupted source of income that sustains their current lifestyle for the rest of their lives? In fact, like most defined benefit plan payments, this will be the default choice for most clients.

In making the investments, planners should focus on taking no more risk than is necessary to reach the client's goals. The choice should be minimum risk; heightened risk tolerance may not help the client reach her goals. Determining the client's tolerance of risk via a questionnaire can yield faulty results, based on her financial knowledge or emotional state at the time.

The financial planner needs to explain investment risk and expected investment return. The risk expectations are then used as guardrails for ongoing client reviews. And the reviews should be clear and useful. For example, it is more important for a client to understand that an equity portfolio's likely annual return range has been between −18 percent and +38 percent for the year than it is to know that the average rate of return has been 10 percent. Using analogies that resonate can enhance the client's understanding. For instance, people buy on performance and sell on risk. Therefore, the investment reviews should focus on the planner's investment process. Did the portfolio stay within the client's risk expectations?

Similarly, returns, either positive or negative, should be the reason a client considers making a change. As previously mentioned, Kinniry et al. (2014) highlight the 150 basis points of investor return that can be realized by helping the client stick with the plan through volatile markets. Ultimately, client behavior drives the returns they realize when undertaking the fiduciary investment process.

Summary and Conclusions

Emotions that arise from uncertainty and the need for immediate self-expression challenge the financial planning and investment process. FINRA and other research organizations have reported a general lack in people's financial literacy. Without such a foundation, people often let their emotions rule their behavior and find comfort in being part of the herd. This chapter has reviewed some of the emotion-charged behaviors that ill-serve investors. But, as suggested, carefully selecting and working with a qualified financial planner can help avoid such behaviors and ensure a stable financial life with a good retirement future.

Through nudging, employers can help create positive default choices for retirement, health, disability, life, and long-term care. Forward-thinking employers can provide one-on-one financial wellness support for their employees, as well. Similarly, financial advisors are most effective using a default option for corrective behavioral actions rather than having people opt in to benefits about which they know very little.

Behavioral finance in the financial planning process starts when an individual evaluates whether to change his or her current behavior. When the person realizes the need for change, the next question is whether to make the change personally or to seek professional help. A CFP® or, if the need is investment related, a Chartered Financial Analyst (CFA) represents a source of such help.

Especially, financial planners can help their clients by developing a default system designed to nudge them toward optimizing their total wealth. By assessing the client's knowledge, emotions, self-expressions, and resources, the financial planner can establish a deliberate process that helps them understand themselves and their financial needs holistically. Financial planning should be an ongoing process that celebrates milestone achievements.

More research needs to be done to address behavioral aspects of financial planning beyond investing. Federal and local policymakers should move toward bolstering high school and college education programs to include personal finance. This would benefit individuals and the market, as a whole.

DISCUSSION QUESTIONS

1. Discuss the biases individuals have when considering their need for financial planning.
2. Discuss the rationale for hiring and the criteria for selecting a financial professional.
3. Discuss several biases that individuals should overcome in the financial planning process.
4. Explain how employers can nudge employees toward financial security.
5. Describe how financial planners can nudge clients toward financial security.

REFERENCES

Barber, Brad, and Terrance Odean. 2000. "Trading Is Hazardous to Your Wealth: The Common Stock Investment Performance of Individual Investors." *Journal of Finance* 55:2, 773–806.

Belsky, Gar 2010. *Why Smart People Make Big Money Mistakes and How to Correct Them*. New York: Simon & Schuster.

Benartzi, Shlomo. 2012. *Save More Tomorrow: Practical Behavioral Finance Solutions to Improve 401(k) Plans*. New York: Penguin.

Blanchett, David, and Paul Kaplan. 2013. "Alpha, Beta, and Now . . . Gamma." Morningstar Investment Management. Available at http://corporate1.morningstar.com/uploadedFiles/US/AlphaBetaandNowGamma.pdf.

Brown, Brené. 2012. "Listening to Shame." TED Talk. TED.com. Available at https://www.ted.com/talks/brene_brown_listening_to_shame?language=en.

Choi, James, David Laibson, Brigitte Madrian, and Andrew Metrick. 2015. "Defined Contribution Pensions: Plan Rules, Participant Decisions, and the Path of Least Resistance." NBER Working Paper No. 8655. Available at http://www.nber.org/papers/w8655.

Financial Industry Regulatory Authority (FINRA). 2013. "Financial Capability in the United States." Available at http://test.financialbuildingblocks.com/assets/Financial%20Capability%20in%20the%20United%20States.pdf.

Howard, James, A., and Rassoul Yazdipour. 2014. "Retirement Planning: Contributions from the Field of Behavioral Finance and Economics." In H. Kent Baker and Victor Ricciardi (eds.), *Investor Behavior: The Psychology of Financial Planning and* Investing, 285–305. Hoboken, NJ: John Wiley & Sons, Inc.

Ibbotson, Roger, James Xiong, Robert P. Kreitler, Charles F. Kreitler, and Peng Chen. 2007. "National Savings Rate Guidelines for Individuals." *Journal of Financial Planning* April, 50–61.

Kahneman, Daniel. 2011. *Thinking, Fast and Slow*. New York: Farrar, Straus, and Giroux.

Kinnel, Robert. 2015. "Mind the Gap. Why Investors Get Less Than Their Funds' Total Return." *Morningstar News*. Morningstar.com, August 11. Available at http://www.morningstar.com/advisor/t/108179053/mind-the-gap-2015.htm.

Kinniry Jr., Francis M., Colleen M. Jaconetti, Michael A. DiJoseph, and Yan Zilbering. 2014. "Putting a Value on Your Value: Quantifying Vanguard Advisor's Alpha." Vanguard Research, March, 2–28. Available at http://www.vanguard.com/pdf/ISGQVAA.pdf.

Markowitz, Harry M. 1952. "Portfolio Selection." *Journal of Finance* 7:1, 77–91.

Markowitz, Harry M. 1959. *Portfolio Selection: Efficient Diversification of Investments*. New York: John Wiley & Sons, Inc.

Markowitz, Harry M. 1991. *Portfolio Selection: Efficient Diversification of Investments*. Second Edition. Cambridge, MA: Basil Blackwell.

Natella, Stefano, Tatjana Meschede, and Laura Sullivan. 2014. "Wealth Patterns among the Top 5% of African-Americans." *Impact Series*. Credit Suisse, November. Available at https://iasp.brandeis.edu/pdfs/2014/Top5.pdf.

O'Neill, Onora. 2013. "What We Don't Understand about Trust." TED Talk. TEDxHousesofParliament. Available at https://www.ted.com/talks/onora_o_neill_what_we_don_t_understand_about_trust?language=en.

Portnoy, Brian. 2014. *The Investor's Paradox the Power of Simplicity in a World of Overwhelming Choice.* New York: Palgrave Macmillan.

Prudential. 2015. "The African American Financial Experience." 2015–16 Prudential Research. Available at http://www.prudential.com/media/managed/aa/AAStudy.pdf?src=Newsroom&pg=AAFEStudy.

Roberts, Lance. 2015. "Dalbar: Why Investors Suck and Tips for Advisors." *AdvisorPerspectives,* April 8. Available at http://www.advisorperspectives.com/commentaries/20150408-streettalk-live-dalbar-why-investors-suck-and-tips-for-advisors.

Rom, Brian M., and Kathleen W. Ferguson. 1993. "Post-Modern Portfolio Theory Comes of Age." *Journal of Investing* 2:4, 27–33.

Snoop Doggy Dogg. 1993. *Gin and Juice,* Sony/ATV Tunes LLC, Walden Music Inc., Cotillion Music Inc., Longitude Music (Sherlyn), Suge Publishing, Snoop Doggy Dogg.

Statman, Meir. 2000. "The 93.6% Question of Financial Advisors." *Journal of Investing* 9:1, 16–20.

Statman, Meir. 2011. *What Investors Really Want: Know What Drives Investor Behavior and Make Smarter Financial Decisions.* New York: McGraw-Hill.

Thaler, Richard H., and Cass R. Sunstein. 2003. "Libertarian Paternalism." *American Economic Review* 93:2, 175–179.

Thaler, Richard H., and Cass R. Sunstein. 2009. *Nudge: Improving Decisions about Health, Wealth, and Happiness.* New York: Penguin.

Ubel, Peter. 2015. "Q & Amp; A With Richard Thaler on What It Really Means to Be a 'Nudge.'" *Forbes,* February 20. Available at http://www.forbes.com/sites/peterubel/2015/02/20/q-a-with-richard-thaler-on-what-it-really-means-to-be-a-nudge/.

Yeske, David B., and Elissa Buie. 2014. "Policy-Based Financial Planning: Decision Rules for a Changing World." In H. Kent Baker and Victor Ricciardi (eds.), *Investor Behavior: The Psychology of Financial Planning and Investing,* 191–208. Hoboken, NJ: John Wiley & Sons, Inc.

Part Five

THE BEHAVIORAL ASPECTS OF INVESTMENT PRODUCTS AND MARKETS

20

Traditional Asset Allocation Securities

Stocks, Bonds, Real Estate, and Cash

CHRISTOPHER MILLIKEN
Vice President, Portfolio Management
Hennion & Walsh Asset Management

EHSAN NIKBAKHT
Professor of Finance
Frank G. Zarb School of Business, Hofstra University

ANDREW C. SPIELER
Professor of Finance
Frank G. Zarb School of Business, Hofstra University

Introduction

Asset allocation is an investment strategy that selects different securities organized into mutually exclusive groups (i.e., asset classes), which exhibit different returns, risks, and pair-wise correlations (Securities and Exchange Commission 2009). In general, an asset class will have high intra-asset class correlation but low inter-class correlation. The objective of asset allocation is to achieve a balance between risk and return that meets an investor's goals, ability, and willingness to bear risk. Many view Harry Markowitz as the founder of the modern approach to asset allocation and the first to quantifiably measure the benefits of including asset classes that exhibit different return paths. He developed modern portfolio theory (MPT) during the 1950s and incorporated the relationships between expected risk, return, and correlation among securities. Markowitz's (1952) breakthrough led to Sharpe (1964), Lintner (1965), and Mossin's (1966) Capital Asset Pricing Model (CAPM), a linear equation that incorporates systematic risk that continues to be widely taught and extensively studied. Further discussion follows about the foundation of asset allocation and the pricing models that arose after the introduction of MPT.

Professional money managers use countless asset allocation models today, but all incorporate the core tenets of risk and return. A consistent characteristic of these models is an attempt to describe the optimal way to allocate assets to achieve the most desirable return distribution. These models vary widely and the principles upon which most are built are explored in more detail throughout the chapter. The inputs of these models all include some measure of standard deviation (risk), expected return, and the paired correlation of the individual securities. The less than perfect correlation of a portfolio's underlying holdings is the main factor that reduces the overall risk of a portfolio and the reason that the standard deviation of a multi-asset portfolio is not the weighted average of the individual securities' standard deviations. In simple terms, the firm-specific risk of individual securities offsets each other leaving only systematic (market) risk in a large portfolio. This concept is why asset allocation is said to be "the only free lunch in finance."

Extensive academic research has examined the importance of asset allocation and how much a portfolio's return can be attributed to it. Brinson, Hood, and Beebower (1986) attempt to quantify the portion of return for which the asset allocation decision is responsible and concluded that the mix of mutually exclusive asset groups explains 93.6 percent of a portfolio's return. Additional research has failed to reach clear consensus on this issue. Despite the continuing debate, the asset allocation decision appears at least partially responsible for the risk and return associated with a portfolio.

When building a portfolio and considering an asset allocation strategy, an investor must define the available asset classes and securities. The most common and perhaps fundamental building blocks are stocks, bonds, real estate, and cash. Other securities such as options, futures, and structured products can add diversification benefits and exhibit different risk and return characteristics, but these extend beyond the scope of this chapter and hence are not included in the discussion.

The basis of most decisions in finance rests heavily on balancing risk and reward, and the asset allocation decision is no different. An investor must decide on both a return objective and an overall level of risk. As related to the objective of the portfolio, the investor's target return mainly determines the portfolio's asset mix. For example, a portfolio created for the goal of wealth preservation typically contains a relatively higher percentage of assets that exhibit low volatility, such as fixed income and cash, and a relatively lesser percentage of volatile securities such as stocks. Conversely, a portfolio with the objective of capital appreciation uses a higher percentage of equities compared to relatively less risky fixed income and cash asset classes.

Real estate adds diversification benefits to both conservative and aggressive return objectives, and can be a stable allocation in most strategies. The relationships among stock, fixed income, and real estate returns historically exhibit low correlation, and combining all three, rather than viewing each in isolation, creates a more efficient risk and reward trade-off. Besides considerations of target return, both the ability and the willingness of an individual to assume risk play roles in determining an asset allocation strategy. The ability to tolerate risk is a function of several factors, including time horizon, wealth, and liquidity needs, whereas the willingness to take risk is a function of an investor's behavioral characteristics.

Current market conditions may also determine the asset allocation policy developed and maintained for a specific portfolio. This relationship results from the availability of certain assets and the fact that correlation, risk, and return expectations are nonstationary. That is, in certain periods, some assets may become illiquid, creating challenges for investment or divesture objectives. A prudent asset manager considers these factors and finds assets that can serve as suitable replacements.

This chapter offers a high level overview of asset allocation including several common asset allocation models and their benefits and drawbacks. A discussion of investor behavior considers the effects of both cognitive and emotional biases. This topic is an integral part of the allocation policy because the models reviewed assume rational investors who can operate with unbiased processing of information in addition to other constraints that affect the efficiency of the decision-making process.

Behavioral biases are both cognitive and emotional. In theory, cognitive errors are more easily corrected than emotional biases, which are ingrained in a person's emotional psyche. The research on the cognitive behavioral biases of individuals acknowledges that mental shortcuts such as heuristics, mental accounting, framing, and processing errors drive errors in the decision-making process. Errors are also driven by the investor's emotional state during the decision-making process. Thus, separating these two primary groups—cognitive and emotional—is appropriate when discussing the reasons individuals fall victim to these errors and when reviewing the impact on an investment policy and asset allocation strategy.

Whether intentional or unintentional, the initial asset allocation and structure of a portfolio greatly shapes the future distribution of returns. Although asset allocation is not the sole determinant of portfolio performance, it certainly is its largest determinant. For this reason, the methodology a portfolio manager chooses to use, such as mean-variance optimization or the Black-Litterman Model, is of utmost importance and drives the future realized risk and return.

A large amount of academic literature supporting traditional portfolio construction methods assumes a universe of rational, efficient decision makers. An increasing focus is on human behavior and inherent investment biases. The chapter thus begins by reviewing the building blocks of an asset allocation strategy, including stocks, bonds, real estate, and cash, and then examines the asset allocation models commonly used by portfolio managers before discussing behavioral biases and their implications on asset allocation.

As financial products continue to advance and change the medium used to deploy investment capital, the focus remains on models to determine the allocation across mutually exclusive groups of securities. Investment professionals can no longer ignore considerations of human behavior and flaws in decision making when developing a client's risk-return profile.

Asset Classes

In today's increasingly complex financial world, the number and variety of available asset classes is continually growing. In the early 1900s, an asset manager primarily chose among equities, debt (fixed income), and cash. These three mutually exclusive asset classes exhibit unique risk and return profiles with correlations that are less than perfect (+1), in some instances even less than zero, which provides for diversification potential. Today, however, asset managers have not only the traditional three asset classes but also numerous derivatives, such as futures, options, and swaps, as well as alternative investments that include real estate, hedge funds, private equity, and collectibles. This expanded universe of asset classes has greatly increased the ability of investors to find diversification opportunities and to improve a portfolio's risk-reward profile. Let's consider each of these asset categories.

EQUITIES

When the headline reads "GM Falls 5 Percent" the journalist is referring to the common equity issued by General Motors. *Equity* refers to an ownership claim in a publicly traded firm that can be bought or sold on a market with high liquidity and anonymity. *Private equity* involves investments in companies that are not publicly traded, but such an asset class is not discussed in this chapter.

Equity ownership includes voting rights and entitles the owner to a proportionate share of the profits. Investors can use blocks of equity to control a company by amassing a majority stake in its outstanding shares. For the retail investor, the benefits of equity ownership include participating in the profits and growth of the firm (McFarland 2002). For example, ownership of 10 percent of the equity shares of a company entitles an investor to both 10 percent of the company's votes and its profit or loss. Equity owners can also receive dividends, payments of cash, or additional shares.

Equities are exposed to higher risk than fixed-income securities, which are primarily concerned with return of principal and interest. Thus, the performance of equity securities is closely tied to a firm's profitability and exhibits the most variability. Additionally, equities have the lowest priority to receive payback or assets in the event of bankruptcy and come after creditors, employees, liens, and government claims. Often the shareholders of a bankrupt firm receive nothing. To summarize, the characteristics of the equity asset class are that they: (1) offer relatively higher expected risk and return, (2) provide capital appreciation and sometimes income, and (3) represent ownership in a company.

BONDS

Bonds, or fixed-income securities, are loans to corporations and other entities. When a corporation issues a bond, it asks for a loan from the investing community. The loan increases both cash (assets) and debt (liabilities) on the borrower's balance sheet. Fixed-income securities provide an investor with the opportunity to earn interest on the money loaned. The amount of capital and the payment schedule are predetermined, and the interest rate that is charged is typically quoted on an annual basis with semi-annual payments. At the end of the predetermined period, the investor receives the initial investment and the final interest payment (TD Ameritrade 2015).

Because fixed-income investors provide companies with funding, they are considered creditors and in most cases have a direct claim against a company's assets in the event of a bankruptcy. Fixed-income investments traditionally serve as a means of generating income and preserving principal. Consequently, investors view it as a more defensive security relative to stocks. For this reason, a heavier allocation to bonds is common in a portfolio with an objective of generating current income or reducing risk. Fixed-income investments have limited upside—the best case is the return of principal and interest on borrowed funds. To summarize, characteristics of fixed-income investments include (1) lower expected risk and return than stocks; (2) a focus on income, not capital appreciation: and (3) lower volatility than equities.

REAL ESTATE

Real estate in the framework of an individual investor's portfolio most commonly is the home in which the individual lives; and owing to the large relative value of homes for individuals, it often makes up the single largest holding in a portfolio. Some investors may also own additional real estate in the form of land, investment properties, vacation homes, and securities such as real estate investment trusts (REITs). To a lesser extent, individuals may have exposure to real estate through mortgage-backed securities (MBS) and other varieties of securitized debt, but these alternative frameworks are more common for institutional investors. The return structure of real estate holdings, whether physical assets such as homes and land or securities such as REITs and MBS, has historically been a low correlation with both stocks and bonds. This relationship is a great benefit to investors because it can theoretically lower the overall risk of the portfolio without sacrificing return potential.

However, real estate does pose challenges for individual investors. The primary challenge is the lack of acknowledgment that the home or other property is in fact an investment and should be considered part of the overall portfolio. This mental barrier is less common for holders of REITs and real estate securities, but must be overcome to fully comprehend the asset allocation in place and the risk–reward profile of the portfolio.

CASH

Cash refers to deposits that are considered risk free in a local currency that do not fluctuate in value. Technically, no asset is free of risk, but in the short term, inflation and liquidity concerns are ignored. Besides the physical notes, examples of cash alternatives include checking or savings account deposits, money market funds, and short-term U.S. Treasury bills (Morningstar 2015). Holding cash equivalents are most common for a portfolio manager because they earn a positive return.

Cash plays an important role in managing a portfolio when regular withdrawals are required. If the investment policy states that a fixed amount of funds must be withdrawn on a monthly basis, then holding a certain percentage of assets in cash offers flexibility for portfolio managers because they will not have to liquidate other investments to fulfill the distribution requirement. This strategy benefits the investor by minimizing capital gains taxes for positions that have appreciated in value and prevents the unnecessary liquidation of securities that have fallen in value in what potentially may be an inopportune time to liquidate. Because cash is a "risk free" asset, it has a zero correlation with stock, bond, and real estate holdings in a portfolio. Thus, increasing the allocation to cash serves to reduce a portfolio's risk.

During times of market stress, cash alternatives are often in high demand as traders seek to reduce exposure to risky assets such as stocks and low credit-quality fixed income. Certain portfolio management strategies also call for cash holdings when securities trading below intrinsic value cannot be found or identified. When opportunities present themselves, cash allows the manager the flexibility to purchase securities without the unnecessary liquidation of other assets ("buy on dips"). Although cash offers the aforementioned benefits, the downside to holding this asset is return drag. *Return drag* is the opportunity cost associated with the money's not being invested in other securities or assets during periods of increasing prices, which in turn lowers the portfolio's overall return. In summary, cash is a risk-free asset that reduces a portfolio's risk and offers flexibility, but has return drag reducing a portfolio's return.

THE RISK–RETURN TRADE-OFF

Risk and return are two key considerations in constructing a portfolio and finding the most efficient balance, is the major objective of asset allocation models. An investment policy statement (IPS) typically contains the risk and return parameters for the objectives of the invested funds outlined by the investor, as well as the investor's ability and willingness to take risk. Assessing the investor's risk tolerance is important because it could be less than the investor typically expresses. In a portfolio management context, a common measure of risk is a portfolio's standard deviation. This measure provides insight into how much invested capital could be lost relative to the average return of the market. A more detailed IPS could assign probabilities to the portfolio distribution.

When determining risk tolerance, a financial advisor typically profiles the client to gain insight into his or her investing experience, stage of life, comfort with swings in market value, and other important considerations. Investors who have less experience, are older or retired, or express discomfort with quick changes in market value often have a lower risk tolerance. Conversely, experienced, or younger investors who can accept significant changes in market value tend to have a higher risk tolerance.

Clarifying the distinction between portfolio risk and return is of paramount importance. The portfolio return calculation is intuitive, it involves taking the weighted average of the individual asset's return, usually on a historical basis. Calculating a portfolio's standard deviation is complicated and must explicitly incorporate paired correlations between all assets.

Return objectives within a portfolio contain two parts: (1) the frequency of cash flow distributions, and (2) the annualized total return. For example, income investors require a steady flow of dividends or interest payments, which they can use to cover expenses. By contrast, growth investors often have a longer investment time horizon and they focus more on the appreciation of an account's value and less on intermittent cash flows. Growth and income investing styles are not necessarily mutually exclusive.

Although MPT requires an investment manager to consider all the investable assets when designing the asset allocation strategy, many individuals exhibit a behavioral bias called *mental accounting*, which is the mental separation of assets into "buckets" to help keep their finances organized. Phung (2007) defines mental accounting as "the tendency for people to separate their money into separate accounts based on a variety of subjective criteria, like the source of the money and intent for each account."

In any case, whether investing for growth, income, or some combination, the earnings of the account are measured in percentage units and they estimate, on average, the capital growth on an annualized basis. To put this discussion on risk and return into context, consider the following example. If a manager invests $1,000 in a portfolio that follows a normal distribution with an expected rate of return of 4 percent, a risk (standard deviation) of 6 percent implies that at the end of the year the manager would expect earnings to fall between about −2 percent and +10 percent with a 68 percent probability.

Owing to the unique needs, preferences, and circumstances for each investor, there is no single objective measure that defines the appropriate return or risk level for all investors. However, the Sharpe ratio is the excess return per unit of risk as measured by a portfolio's standard deviation. It measures the efficiency of the risk–reward profile. This ratio divides the return of the portfolio less the return of the risk-free rate (i.e., excess return) by the portfolio's standard deviation. All else equal, investors prefer a higher Sharpe ratio because it points to a more efficient blend of risk and return. Sharpe (1994, p. 56) summarizes his measure:

> All the same, the ratio of expected added return per unit of added risk provides a convenient summary of two important aspects of any strategy involving the difference between the return of a fund and that of a relevant benchmark. The Sharpe Ratio is designed to provide such a measure. Properly used, it can improve the process of managing investments.

As this section shows, risk refers to the standard deviation of a portfolio's returns. Another measure of risk is systematic risk, or beta. *Systematic risk* is the aggregate risk associated with investing in the stock market and it cannot be diversified away. The first model to frame risk in the context of the overall market was the CAPM. Based on Markowitz's (1952) MPT, the developers of this model are Treynor (1999), Sharpe (1964), Lintner (1965), and Mossin (1966). Perold (2004, p. 16) discusses the CAPM: "It is the relationship between expected return and risk that is consistent with investors behaving according to the prescriptions of portfolio theory." Equation 22.1 represents the CAPM formula:

$$R = R_F + \beta(R_M - R_F) \tag{22.1}$$

where R_F is the risk-free rate, β is a measure of systematic risk, and R_M is the expected return of the market.

According to the CAPM, investors are compensated in two ways: time value of money and exposure to market risk. The risk-free rate represents the time value of money and compensates investors for investing capital over a given time period. The risk term, represented by $\beta(R_M - R_F)$, determines what the investor requires to take on additional systematic risk inherent in the asset.

According to the CAPM, the required return of an asset or portfolio is equal to the risk-free rate and a risk premium. If the expected or forecasted return is greater than the required return, the investment is undervalued and represents a bargain. The graphic representation of the CAPM for different betas is called the *security market line* (SML). The SML permits assessing the risk profile of individual securities or portfolios (Rosenberg 1981).

ALLOCATION MAINTENANCE

An important and perhaps underappreciated aspect of portfolio management is the procedures for and protocol to maintain and rebalance the investments. *Strategic asset allocation* (SAA) refers to the establishment of and adherence to a long-term target allocation among equity, fixed income, and cash. The allocation between stock and bond asset classes is determined based on a long-term expected return, risk, and pairwise correlations. For example, if equities have historically returned 10 percent a year and fixed income has returned 5 percent a year, a portfolio combination of 50 percent equities and 50 percent fixed income would yield an expected return of 7.5 percent a year over a full market cycle. These return, risk, and correlation estimates are referred to as *capital market assumptions* (or estimates) and they assume the average return when considering periods of expansion and contraction in the business, credit, and market cycle (Benz 2013).

Tactical asset allocation (TAA) represents a more active approach to weighting different asset classes. That is, TAA allows for a more flexible portfolio relative to SAA. The portfolio manager over-weights or under-weights the allocations based on an assessment of current and expected economic conditions. This process allows for potential outperformance relative to the benchmark if short- and intermediate-term opportunities arise that warrant an increased exposure to the asset class expected to outperform or a decreased exposure to the asset class expected to underperform. TAA allows the portfolio manager temporarily to unbalance or rebalance a portfolio to take advantage of these exceptional opportunities. This flexibility adds a market-timing component to the portfolio, which permits participation in those asset classes with favorable prospects. Investment professionals consider TAA to be a relatively active strategy that requires the willpower, discipline, and confidence to be able to return to the pre-set asset mix once the short-term opportunity has passed.

REBALANCING STRATEGIES

Several rebalancing strategies exist ranging from the very simple buy-and-hold to more sophisticated ones. The most simplistic approach is the *buy-and-hold strategy*, which does not rebalance the initial allocation. This asset allocation strategy is set at inception, but not adjusted. Thus, securities increasing in value represent a relatively larger portion of the account and securities decreasing in value represent a relatively smaller portion. Implementation is easy and increases exposure to investments that have performed well while reducing exposure to those that have not. Yet, a buy-and-hold strategy not only can alter the account's risk-return profile but also can lead to an eventual allocation inconsistent with the original IPS.

Calendar rebalancing is another rudimentary approach to rebalancing in which the investor simply sets a date, or several dates, throughout the course of the year that dictate when to place buy and sell orders to return the portfolio's allocation to its targets. One simple suggestion is to rebalance once a year on the investor's birthday. Although this approach maintains the target asset allocation, it may also force trades at what may be inopportune times while ignoring potentially beneficial trades in between rebalancing dates.

A more active rebalancing approach is the *constant mix strategy*. The constant mix strategy requires buying securities that have decreased in value and selling securities that have increased in value. This process forces the target asset allocation strategy to remain fixed, but often can incur large transaction costs and taxes if rebalancing is frequent. This strategy forms a contrarian strategy in which investors or portfolio managers buy during falling markets and sell during rising markets. For these reasons, most managers set bands around asset class weights so the rebalancing only needs to occur when allocations drift outside the initial target allocation.

Modern Portfolio Theory

As previously discussed, Harry Markowitz (1952) develops a theory of portfolio construction and eventually received the Nobel Memorial Prize in Economics for his seminal work in 1990. Although the basic tenets of MPT remain, the model has been expanded dramatically over time and has become more complex. The pioneering theory describes the steps a "rational investor" should use to build a portfolio that optimizes return based on a stated level of risk. It focuses on increased risk leading to higher return. According to Markowitz, forming an "efficient frontier" of optimal portfolios was possible that maximized the expected return for any level of risk.

MPT has served as the backbone of academic finance for decades, but it rests on unrealistic assumptions. The overarching assumption is that investors focus on optimizing the risk–reward trade-off for a given portfolio. The following assumptions are necessary for the MPT to hold:

1. Investors are rational, risk-averse, non-emotional beings, who solely focus on maximizing risk-adjusted return. MPT assumes that all investors are identically programmed computers that follow a pre-set action–reaction matrix. Day-to-day interactions with others indicate that this assumption is false, but it is required for the model to be internally consistent.
2. All investors have perfect and equal access to information and have accurately calculated, in advance, an asset's riskiness, and their perception of the return distribution forms a normal distribution. MPT assumes that asset prices reflect private and inside information and that risk can be accurately determined ex-ante. Again, although this assumption is false, it must be held for internal consistency.
3. All correlations between asset pairs are constant over time. MPT assumes that events do not change the relationships between assets. Observations of global markets show this assumption is also false because contagion occurs during market shocks and crises, and correlations often increase dramatically.
4. Returns are normally distributed and tail risk events occur no more frequently than expected from a normal distribution. In practice, returns tend to deviate from assumptions of normality based on observations. Tail risk events, or extremely low probability observations that lie in the "tails" of a bell curve, have historically occurred more than predicted by normal distribution.
5. Investors operate in a world of no transaction costs and taxes, and no minimum lot size exists for an investment. Contrary to these assumptions, all markets have transaction costs, including commissions and bid–ask spreads; also, investors face capital gains and/or income taxes as their investments produce income or appreciate in value. Furthermore, MPT assumes the ability to buy fractional shares, which is not a reasonable assumption for some investments.
6. Investors are price takers in the classic economic sense. That is, they can buy and sell any amount of shares without affecting the price. However, supply and demand have an effect on asset prices in the market.
7. Investors can lend and borrow unlimited amounts at the risk-free rate. This assumption is not literally true, as in comparing the return on savings deposits to mortgage rates from the same institution. Additionally, the cost and availability of risk-free

assets change during adverse market conditions or periods when the financial markets are under stress.

Clearly, the MPT is flawed and not directly applicable to the behavior and realities of capital markets. However, owing to a lack of alternatives, it has nevertheless formed the basis for many portfolio management strategies that attempt to correct or offer additional explanatory power using the same concepts as outlined in MPT. The most important assumption that needs to be discussed is that investors always behave rationally. The field of behavioral finance attempts to address this issue, but it has been unable to develop or adapt a universal solution.

MEAN-VARIANCE OPTIMIZATION AND THE BLACK-LITTERMAN MODEL

MPT sets forth the concepts that allow for the modeling of theoretically efficient portfolios. The actual mathematical framework for using risk, return, and correlation to create these portfolios is called *mean-variance optimization* (MVO). The complicated and time-consuming calculations necessary in MVO require using a computer to determine the optimal allocation. The inputs include risk and return data that are user-defined but typically ex-post in nature (i.e., they use historical data to suggest the future characteristics of each security).

A portfolio developed using MVO typically suffers from an overconcentration of assets into a few securities or asset classes and is highly input sensitive. Small changes in one or more of the risk, return, or correlation parameters can cause dramatic differences in the resulting allocations. Another drawback of this approach is the reliance on historical data. The historical returns and level of risk associated with each of the securities are unlikely to remain constant over the investor's time horizon. For these reasons, most portfolio managers use the MVO framework as a guide and incorporate constraints around asset classes that force the output to have a minimum or maximum investment in a set of asset classes. For example, the user forces the allocation to exhibit, say, a minimum of 40 percent and a maximum of 70 percent to equities. The ultimate allocation to stocks in this example falls inside the range and considers the most efficient level of equity exposure given the target return or level of risk. This result is tantamount to determining the optimal allocation mix under constrained optimization as opposed to unconstrained optimization, which is the MVO solution.

Perhaps the most accepted adjustment to MVO is the Black-Litterman Model (Idzorek 2004). This model addresses the input sensitivity assumption of the MVO model and changes the parameters to give a view that is not solely based on historical data, but also on the investors' views. The Black-Litterman Model overcomes the problem of high asset class concentration, input sensitivity, and estimation error associated with the traditional MVO model. By taking the market weights on the asset classes into consideration and using the CAPM, a reverse optimization calculation is performed to generate an expected return. Users of this model have the ability to express their views on asset classes by adjusting the returns calculated to suggest an over- or underperformance relative to the calculation. The resulting asset allocation strategy produced is a more diversified portfolio relative to MVO. Although the assumptions must continue to be held, the sensitivity of the inputs is greatly reduced, resulting in a more stable portfolio.

Behavioral Biases in Asset Allocation

The models and concepts discussed in the previous section fall under the category of traditional finance and assume that investors are rational. That is, investors make every decision in the context of their overall portfolios and goal of maximizing self-interests. Although some investors might be able to remove affective (emotional) biases from their decision making, others allow feelings, emotions, and moods to influence their investment decisions, often subconsciously. When investors make a decision based on an emotion, they suffer from an emotional behavioral bias. Other factors beyond emotions limit human decision making as well. Limitations in cognitive abilities and mechanical errors known as *heuristics* or *mental mistakes* also create behavioral biases that prevent investors from allocating assets efficiently.

A common example of this flaw to which investors fall victim is the *1/N heuristic*. This bias refers to the tendency for investors to allocate assets evenly across the investment choices that are available to them. To imagine this in practice, consider employees who have 10 investment options available in their 401(k) plan. In an attempt to diversify, they may place 10 percent of their funds in each security. Although Huberman and Jiang (2006) suggest that this type of allocation is not often followed to the specification in this example, the line of thinking is not uncommon. Morrin, Inman, Broniarczyk, Nenkov, and Reuter (2012) take this notion a step further and determined that a connection exists between the number of funds available to 401(k) participants and the tendency to allocate evenly. When investors face a large number of products from which to choose, they become overwhelmed by the decision and are more likely to simplify the process by allocating the investment dollars in small (often not equal) percentages across a large number of funds. This outcome is the result of a cognitive limitation.

Empirical evidence suggests that certain behavioral biases have a direct effect on aggregate asset pricing and can lead to excessively over- or undervalued asset classes (Baker and Ricciardi 2014). In the extreme, this collective behavior of investors can cause bubbles. Although researchers have identified many cognitive and emotional biases, this section of the chapter focuses on five that play an important role in the asset allocation decisions of investors. Familiarity, status quo, framing, mental accounting, and overconfidence biases all prevent investors from operating rationally and forming efficient portfolios.

FAMILIARITY BIAS

The familiarity bias occurs when investors place greater value, or expresses a preference for, holding securities they understand or with which they have a connection (Baker and Ricciardi 2014). Investors who hold a large percentage of their net worth in their employer's stock exhibit this bias because they are confident they know the company better than other investors and believe the stock is perpetually undervalued. Benartzi (2001) investigates the effects of past performance of company stock and the allocation of employee discretionary funds to company stock in 401(k) plans. He suggests that there is a positive correlation between strong recent stock performance and a greater allocation of employee 401(k) assets to company stock. This logic is also irrational from a concentration perspective, because an investor's total wealth, which includes labor income and financial wealth, now represents an even larger portion of his or her portfolio. Familiarity is also expressed through a preference for owning domestic stock over international stock, which is also called *home asset bias* (Stammers 2011).

Portfolios that are over-allocated to a single security carry unnecessary additional company-specific or nonsystematic risk. Enron is a tragic example of this flaw. By one estimate, Enron employees invested nearly 60 percent of their 401(k) assets in Enron stock. Enron's bankruptcy amid a massive accounting scandal subsequently wiped out this investment (Weinberg 2003). On a wider scale, familiarity with domestic securities prevents an investor from reaping the benefits of a portfolio with international diversification. As Figure 20.1 shows, international stocks are historically less than perfectly correlated with the U.S. stock market.

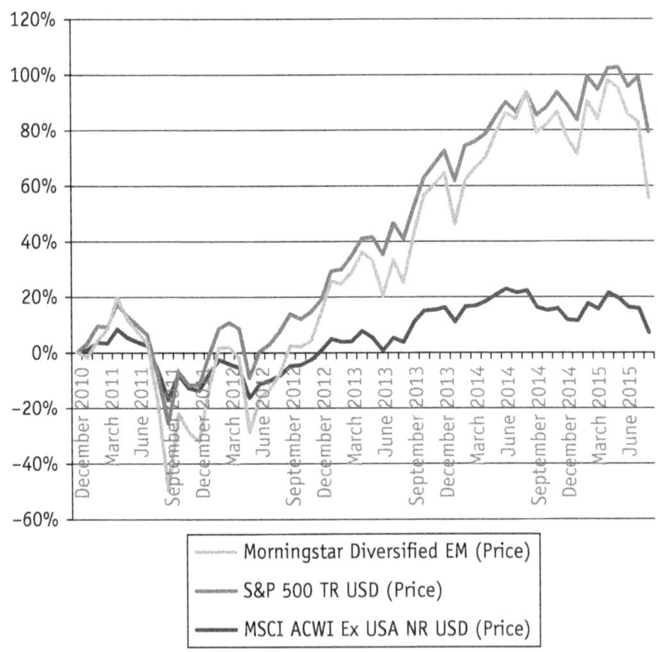

Figure 20.1 Performance of U.S., International, and Emerging Market Stock Indexes. This figure shows the historical relationship of monthly returns for domestic U.S. stocks (S&P 500 TR USD Price), developed international stocks (MSCI ACWI Ex USA NR USD Price), and emerging markets (Morningstar Diversified EM Price) from December 31, 2010 through August 31, 2015. Source: Bloomberg Terminal as of August 31, 2015.

Table 20.1 **Correlation Matrix of U.S., International, and Emerging Market Stock Indexes**

Index	*S&P 500 TR USD (Price)*	*MSCI ACWI Ex USA NR USD (Price)**	*Morningstar Diversified EM (Price)*
S&P 500	1.00		
MSCI ACWI Ex US	0.86	1.00	
Morningstar Diversified EM	0.73	0.90	1.00

Note: This table shows that the greatest diversification benefits come from assets exhibiting a negative correlation. However, including assets in a portfolio whose correlations are less than perfect (+1) also creates efficiencies in the risk and reward profile.

*MSCI ACWI Ex USA NR USD (Price) return taken from Bloomberg.

Source: Authors' calculations.

This type of relationship creates diversification opportunities and can improve a portfolio's Sharpe ratio by lowering the portfolio's standard deviation. For example, Table 20.1 considers the correlation matrix of the MSCI All Country World Index, the S&P 500 index, and the Morningstar Emerging Markets Index.

Familiarity bias is not unique to individual investors. Using survey data from Merrill Lynch, Strong and Xu (2003) studied fund manager sentiment in the United States, continental Europe, the United Kingdom, and Japan. They found that relative to equity markets, fund managers view domestic prospects more optimistically when compared to international counterparts. However, this result may not be a cognitive error but, rather, a conscious business decision. Parwada (2008) points out the informational advantage fund managers have when investing in domestic stocks versus international stocks. Choosing to hold a higher percentage of local versus international equities reduces research expenses.

At a high level, familiarity with broad asset classes can be an impediment to forming an efficient portfolio. Investors who have historically purchased equities but not fixed-income securities may be hesitant to invest in bonds because they may not understand how bonds function or see the benefits of introducing a fixed-income security to their stock portfolios. The opposite could also occur for investors who have only invested in fixed income and believe that stocks are too risky. In either case, the portfolio is unlikely to achieve the investor's long-term goals—certainly not as quickly or as safely as when using a proper asset allocation strategy.

STATUS QUO BIAS

Status quo bias affects investors who cannot build up enough momentum to change their asset allocation, even when doing so is in their best interests, because they exhibit high levels of inertia or procrastination. The reason for their inability to change may stem from *loss aversion,* which is the unwillingness to sell a position at a loss. A rational investor judges an investment based on its expected future performance, not its recent history, and can sell regardless of an investment's cost basis. Investors often comment that a loss is only a "paper loss" until a position is sold; this view is incorrect because a security is only worth its selling price at a given moment plus the opportunity cost of funding the investment. Thus this line of thinking can result in the poor decision of holding a security whose fundamentals suggest continued underperformance relative to the market.

The low number of trades in retirement accounts suggests that this bias exists on a broad scale. For example, Ricciardi (2012) reports that over a two-year period, about 80 percent of participants in his study made very few or no trades. Agnew, Balduzzi, and Sunden (2003) investigated retirement accounts over a four-year period from 1994 to 1998. They found that although trading activity varies depending on the characteristics of the participants, in aggregate the study's participants made fewer than one trade a year. To overcome the status quo bias, investors should ask themselves: "If I held cash instead of the security in question, would I buy it today?" This forces an analysis of expected return, rather than a view of the decline or appreciation in value. Another way to overcome this bias is to adopt a rebalancing approach that requires making trades either annually or after the portfolio has deviated from the target asset allocation strategy (Baker and Ricciardi 2014).

Besides there being a lower number of trades taking place within retirement accounts, many savers who are automatically enrolled in company 401(k) plans make no initial change away from the default fund in which they were placed at the outset. Madrian and Shea (2001) explored the status quo bias in this context and found that the majority of 401(k) participants, who were enrolled automatically, maintain the default asset allocation. Considering the default fund and the asset allocation are likely inappropriate for every participant, this status quo bias causes an inefficient allocation of both pretax income and the assets within the plan. Bilias, Georgarakos, and Haliassos (2010) find that in following large market downturns, participants do not reduce their equity holdings, suggesting that acquiring new information is not resulting in asset allocation adjustments owing to inertia.

FRAMING

Framing biases are common not only in asset allocation and behavioral finance but also in other aspects of human decision making. *Framing* is the tendency to behave differently depending on how information is presented (Barclays 2007). For example, consider presenting two portfolios, A and B, to an investor as follows: portfolio A has a 75 percent chance of returning 10 percent and a 25 percent chance of returning 0 percent, whereas portfolio B is expected to have a fixed return of 8 percent. An investor who chooses portfolio A makes the decision to do so because he perceives the high probability of earning 10 percent as more attractive than the lower 8 percent yield. Mathematically, portfolio B yielding 8 percent is more attractive from a risk–reward standpoint. Steul (2006) recognizes this type of behavior and goes further to describe how the type of distribution and the investor's own understanding of risk influence the framing effect. The author concludes that the effects of framing are present under both positively correlated portfolios and ambiguous risk. In other words, when the dispersion of returns of the individual securities that make up a portfolio are correlated, and when risk is ambiguous, framing is present.

Using a controlled experiment, Diacon and Hasseldine (2007) determined that the format used to present past performance to investors alters their view of the investment's potential risk and reward. Specifically, observers prefer viewing the return of an equity fund when expressed in an "index of fund values" format rather than a percent return format. Investors must not only be aware of the way projected future returns are presented but also the way past returns are expressed.

Investors who want to buy a stock or bond for their portfolios must also be aware of the way the relevant information about the security is presented. For example, before the issuance of an initial public offering (IPO), investment bankers and the company's management team go on a "road show" designed to generate interest in the company by brokerage houses. The investment bankers are likely to frame information about the company in the best light possible. Consequently, analysts and future investors might want to consider all available information, including filings to the Securities and Exchange Commission (SEC), and not simply rely on information presented by the parties with possible conflicts of interest.

This bias can alter a portfolio's asset allocation strategy by influencing investors to deviate from an efficient blend of stocks, bonds, real estate, and cash to a mix that appears attractive based on the presentation of the information. When investors receive a call from a financial advisor who describes a great stock or bond trade, they should make the buy decision in the context of their existing asset allocation strategy and not simply on the merits of the security alone. Investors should be aware of this flaw in decision making and avoid basing their investment decisions on information that presents securities in a positive light but neglects what may be their fundamental weaknesses.

MENTAL ACCOUNTING

Mental accounting refers to the cognitive organizational technique many investors employ by separating their investments into different buckets, without considering the overall asset allocation. More broadly, mental accounting can also be used in the context of a mental separation of personal finances and budgeting. For example, evidence shows that mental accounting plays a role in personal budgeting, not only in a monetary sense but also in terms of time and energy. For example, Heath and Soll (1996) discuss how individuals' labeling of expenses (i.e., for business or a personal hobby) affects the value they place on the expenditures, whether that value be money, time, or energy. Mental accounting affects a person's view of his or her current expenditures as it relates to monetary outlays. For instance, individuals have a tendency to separate expenses used for immediate consumption from those to be used later (Shafir and Thaler 2006).

Mental accounting in the context of asset allocation can potentially have a negative impact on a portfolio. For example, if an investor experiences an unrealized capital loss, but places too much importance on the dividend received, then the portfolio may be inefficiently allocated (Baker and Ricciardi 2015). Similarly, individuals who own real estate display mental accounting by not considering the real estate property as part of their overall portfolio. For this reason, individuals are more likely to sell property valued above its purchase price and less willing to sell when facing a loss (Seiler, Seiler, and Lane 2012).

In the context of asset allocation, mental accounting can cause investors to focus on the ratio of stocks to bonds in an account-by-account basis, without considering their entire exposure in stocks versus bonds. For example, an investor can structure his retirement account more aggressively with a 70 percent stock and 30 percent bond allocation, and a less risky nonqualified account with an asset allocation of 70 percent bonds and 30 percent stocks. Although the investor may feel good about having the aggressive funds in the retirement account and conservative funds in the taxable account, the reality is that the portfolio would have the same level of risk and return potential if the investor had both accounts with a single 50/50 portfolio (assuming equal dollar values of both accounts and ignoring taxes). Choi, Laibson, and Madrian (2009) investigated this issue empirically by comparing the asset allocation strategies of 401(k) participants' own contributions and their employer contributions. They found that when employers control the investment of their contributions, participants do not adjust their contributions (whose asset allocation is under their control) to reflect the employer's investment choices. This suggests that individuals do not incorporate the allocation of all their accounts when selecting investments. Simply focusing on the asset allocation in each account is inappropriate. Investors can overcome this bias by considering the asset allocation strategy associated with the overall portfolio, and not on an account-by-account basis.

OVERCONFIDENCE

According to Parker (2013), overconfidence has two components: overconfidence in the quality of the information received and overconfidence in one's ability to act on that information. The previously discussed asset allocation models assume that rational investors create theoretically correct portfolios. Overconfident portfolio managers and investors can rely too heavily on these models, and this bias can cause overreliance on the output the model produces. Relying too heavily on the inputs of these models is another source of overconfidence bias that negatively weighs on a portfolio's efficiency.

Overconfident investors can also have inefficient trading patterns, moving in and out of positions too quickly in the belief that they can outperform the market. This excessive trading incurs heavy transaction costs and potential taxable events, and can lower the portfolio's overall return (Koesterich 2013). For example, increases in trading activity are typical for individual investors following bull markets. The recent positive past performance of equities during a bull market cycle brings the individual investor's attention to the perceived opportunities that exist and leads to increases in trading activity (Chuang and Susmel 2011).

Certified Financial Planners (CFPs) also fall victim to overconfidence. Using survey data, Cordell, Smith, and Terry (2011) compared the confidence levels of financial professionals who only earned the CFP certificate with those held both the CFP and Chartered Financial Analyst (CFA) designations. They found that those only having the CFP designation are more confident in their overall abilities to give investment advice than are those with both designations. Individuals, arguably less skilled than either a

CFP certificate holder or a CFA charterholder, should take special note to approach investment decisions humbly.

Investor confidence must be balanced with an understanding of the limits of a given model or an investor's cognitive abilities. The latter is a much harder mental barrier for investors to overcome, but placing too much weight on the abilities of any one decision maker often leads to costly mistakes.

Summary and Conclusions

To create a model that incorporates the risk and return characteristics of securities, as well as the correlations between asset classes, Markowitz (1952) assumed that all investors are rational and emotionless. The pricing and asset allocation models that followed, including the CAPM and the Black-Litterman Model, also generate outputs that are theoretically sound according to Markowitz's world.

Behavioral finance attempts to incorporate human nature into capital market pricing and portfolio-level allocation decisions. Behavioral biases represent the emotional and cognitive errors that are so common in decision makers. Investors should take steps to identify and correct these often subconscious biases to avoid misallocating their capital. For instance, familiarity bias can directly lead to under-diversification. Status quo bias, which is a common problem with investors saving for retirement, can lead to an unusually low turnover in an investor's accounts. As a result, investors often fail to rebalance their portfolios. Framing can generate inefficient allocation of assets owing to this cognitive constraint. Mental accounting can be beneficial to investors who use it as a tool to keep funds organized; however, this bias can hurt investors who make asset allocation decisions on a "bucket-to-bucket" basis and do not consider the asset allocation of their entire portfolio. Finally, overconfidence has the potential to impact an investor's portfolio with negative side effects of placing too much faith in both historical data and the ability to make sound decisions with this data. Overconfident investors can rely too heavily on models that use traditional finance assumptions and trade too often, believing they can outperform the market.

The five behavioral biases reviewed in this chapter serve as an example of some of the most common errors in decision making. Although avoiding these mistakes on a subconscious level might be difficult, investors should make an effort to identify them and understand the effects they have on their overall asset allocation policy or trading behavior.

DISCUSSION QUESTIONS

1. Define tactical asset allocation (TAA) and discuss the advantages and disadvantages relative to strategic asset allocation (SAA).
2. Discuss the assumptions used in modern portfolio theory (MPT) and traditional finance models.
3. Discuss the shortfalls of mean-variance optimization (MVO) portfolios and how the Black-Litterman Model attempts to address these shortfalls.

4. Distinguish between cognitive and emotional errors, and provide an example of each.
5. Discuss the advantages and disadvantages to mental accounting and how investors can manage this cognitive error.

REFERENCES

Agnew, Julie, Pierlugi Balduzzi, and Annika Sunden. 2003. "Portfolio Choice and Trading in a Large 401(k) Plan." *American Economic Review* 93:1, 193–215.

Baker, H. Kent, and Victor Ricciardi. 2014. "How Biases Affect Investor Behaviour." *European Financial Review*. February, 2014. Available at http://www.europeanfinancialreview.com/?p=512.

Baker, H. Kent, and Victor Ricciardi. 2015. "Understanding Behavioral Aspects of Financial Planning and Investing." *Journal of Financial Planning* 28:3, 22–26.

Barclays. 2007. "What Is Framing?" Available at https://www.investmentphilosophy.com/us/behavioural-finance/decision-making-matters/what-is-framing.

Benartzi, Shlomo. 2001. "Excessive Extrapolation and the Allocation of 401(k) Accounts to Company Stock." *Journal of Finance* 56:5, 1747–1764.

Bilias, Yannis, Dimitris Georgarakos, and Michael Haliassos. 2010. "Portfolio Inertia and Stock Market Fluctuations." *Journal of Money, Credit and Banking* 42:4, 715–742.

Brinson, Gary, L. Randolph Hood, and Gilbert Beebower. 1986. "Determinants of Portfolio Performance." *Financial Analysts Journal* 42:4, 39–44. Available at http://www.cfapubs.org/doi/pdf/10.2469/faj.v42.n4.39.

Benz, Christine. 2013. "Find the Right Stock/Bond Mix." Morningstar. Available at http://news.morningstar.com/articlenet/article.aspx?id=619829.

Choi, James J., David Laibson, and Brigitte C. Madrian. 2009. "Mental Accounting in Portfolio Choice: Evidence from a Flypaper Effect." *American Economic Review* 99:5, 2085–2095.

Chuang, Wen-I, and Rauli Susmel. 2011. "Who Is the More Overconfident Trader? Individual vs Institutional Investors." *Journal of Banking and Finance* 35:7, 1626–1644.

Cordell, David M., Rachel Smith, and Andy Terry. 2011. "Overconfidence in Financial Planners." *Financial Services Review* 20:4, 253–263.

Diacon, Stephen, and John Hasseldine. 2007. "Framing Effects and Risk Perception: The Effect of Prior Performance Presentation Format on Investment Fund Choice." *Journal of Economic Psychology* 28:1, 31–52.

Heath, Chip, and Jack B. Soll. 1996. "Mental Budgeting and Consumer Decisions." *Journal of Consumer Research* 23:1, 40–52.

Huberman, Gur, and Jiang Wei. 2006. "Offering versus Choice in 401(k) Plans: Equity Exposure and Number of Funds." *Journal of Finance* 61:2, 763–801.

Idzorek, Thomas M. 2004. "A Step-by-step Guide to the Black-Litterman Model." Working Paper, Zephyr Associates. Available at https://faculty.fuqua.duke.edu/~charvey/Teaching/BA453_2006/Idzorek_onBL.pdf.

Koesterich, Russ. 2013. "Overcoming 3 Bad Investing Behaviors." February, 2013. Available at https://www.blackrockblog.com/2013/02/06/overcoming-3-bad-investing-behaviors/.

Lintner, John. 1965. "The Valuation of Risk Assets and the Selection of Risky Investments in Stock Portfolios and Capital Budgets." *Review of Economics and Statistics* 47:1, 13–37.

Madrian, Brigitte C., and Dennis F. Shea. 2001. "The Power of Suggestion: Inertia in 401(k) Participation and Savings Behavior." *Quarterly Journal of Economics* 116:4, 1149–1187.

Markowitz, Harry. 1952. "Portfolio Selection." *Journal of Finance* 7:1, 77–91.

McFarland, Margaret. 2002. "Final Rule: Amendment to Definition of 'Equity Security.'" Securities and Exchange Commission. Available at https://www.sec.gov/rules/final/33-8091.htm.

Morningstar. 2015. "Cash Equivalent." Available at http://www.morningstar.com/InvGlossary/cash_equivalent_definition_what_is.aspx.

Morrin, Maureen, J. Jeffrey Inman, Susan M. Broniarczyk, Gergana Y. Nenkov, and Jonathan Reuter. 2012. "Investing for Retirement: The Moderating Effect of Fund Assortment Size on the 1/N Heuristic." *Journal of Marketing Research* 49:4, 537–550.

Mossin, Jan. 1966. "Equilibrium in a Capital Asset Market." *Econometrica* 34:4, 768–783.

Parker, Tim. 2013. "4 Behavioral Biases and How to Avoid Them." Investopedia. Available at http://www.investopedia.com/articles/investing/050813/4-behavioral-biases-and-how-avoid-them.asp.

Parwada, Jerry T. 2008. "The Genesis of Home Bias? The Location and Portfolio Choices of Investment Company Start-Ups." *Journal of Financial and Quantitative Analysis* 43:1, 245–266.

Perold, Andre F. 2004. "The Capital Asset Pricing Model." *Journal of Economic Perspectives* 18:3, 3–24.

Phung, Albert. 2007. "Behavioral Finance: Key Concepts—Mental Accounting | Investopedia." Investopedia. Available at http://www.investopedia.com/university/behavioral_finance/behavioral5.asp.

Ricciardi, Victor. 2012. "Our 3-year Market Hangover." *MoneySense*. Available at http://www.moneysense.ca/invest/our-3-year-market-hangover/.

Rosenberg, Barr. 1981. "The Capital Asset Pricing Model and the Market Model." *Journal of Portfolio Management* 7:2, 5–16.

Securities and Exchange Commission. 2009. "Beginners' Guide to Asset Allocation, Diversification, and Rebalancing." Available at http://www.sec.gov/investor/pubs/assetallocation.htm.

Seiler, Michael J., Vicky L. Seiler, and Mark A. Lane. 2012. "Mental Accounting and False Reference Points in Real Estate Investment Decision Making." *Journal of Behavioral Finance* 13:1, 17–26.

Shafir, Eldar, and Richard H. Thaler. 2006. "Invest Now, Drink Later, Spend Never: On the Mental Accounting of Delayed Consumption." *Journal of Economic Psychology* 27:5, 694–712.

Sharpe, William F. 1964. "Capital Asset Prices: A Theory of Market Equilibrium under Conditions of Risk." *Journal of Finance* 19:3, 425–442.

Sharpe, William F. 1994. "The Sharpe Ratio." *Journal of Portfolio Management* 21:1, 49–58.

Stammers, Robert. 2011. "Three Behavioral Biases That Can Affect Your Investment Performance." *Forbes*, December 21. Available at http://www.forbes.com/sites/cfainstitute/2011/12/21/three-behavioral-biases-that-can-affect-your-investment-performance/.

Steul, Martina. 2006. "Does the Framing of Investment Portfolios Influence Risk-taking Behavior? Some Experimental Results." *Journal of Economic Psychology* 27:4, 557–570.

Strong, Norman, and Zinzhong Xu. 2003. "Understanding the Equity Home Bias: Evidence from Survey Data." *Review of Economics and Statistics* 85:2, 307–312.

TD Ameritrade. 2015. "Add Diversity and Stability to Your Portfolio with Fixed Income Securities." Available at https://www.tdameritrade.com/education/account-types-and-investment-products/bonds-and-cds.page.

Treynor, Jack L. 1999. "Toward a Theory of Market Value of Risky Assets." In Robert A. Korajczyk (ed.), *Asset Pricing and Portfolio Performance*, 15–22. London: Risk Books.

Weinberg, Ari. 2003. "The Post-Enron 401(k)." *Forbes*, October 20. Available at http://www.forbes.com/2003/10/20/cx_aw_1020retirement.html.

21

Behavioral Aspects of Portfolio Investments

NATHAN MAUCK
Assistant Professor
University of Missouri – Kansas City

Introduction

Traditional finance theory suggests that individuals entrust their investments to financial institutions in an effort to increase expected returns and/or to reduce risk. Although many individuals manage all or part of their wealth independently, they must still work with existing financial products. Furthermore, many individuals use the services of professional money managers. Indeed, the sheer volume of assets under management (AUM) by financial institutions signals their importance. According to the Organization of Economic Cooperation and Development (OECD 2014), mutual funds represent the largest such of this investment group as of 2014, with roughly \$30 trillion in AUM. Other important institutional investors and money-management products by size include exchange-traded funds (ETFs), hedge funds, and pension funds, with an estimated \$2.3 trillion, \$2.5 trillion, and \$20 trillion of AUM, respectively.

The relative importance of these institutions in the market has increased tremendously over time. Blume and Keim (2012) show that the proportion of U.S. publicly traded equity held by institutions increased from around 8 percent in 1950 to nearly 67 percent in 2010. On average, then, institutional investors should be more sophisticated, skilled, and rational than retail investors. In fact, although many reasons exist for the growth in absolute size and relative importance of institutional investors, one perceived benefit is professional asset management skills.

However, non-wealth-maximizing or irrational institutional investor behavior could explain outcomes that do not match these institutions' perceived rational superiority. The first such disconnect—that between the perceived benefits of institutions and reality—is the underperformance on average of those institutional investors. A potential driving force behind this underperformance may be behavioral biases of institutional investors. In short, an a priori expectation is that institutional investors are rational and wealth-maximizing investors, but this assumption may be incorrect. In truth, professional money managers demonstrate such biases as overconfidence, optimism, familiarity, home bias, herding, limited attention, disposition effect, and escalation of commitment, among others.

The second disconnect—that between investor expectations of institutions and reality—is related to the rationality, or lack thereof, of those individuals who are selecting the institutions. Specifically, regardless of the rationality of institutional investors, retail investors are likely to exhibit the usual biases whether they are selecting individual assets or products from institutions such as mutual funds and hedge funds. For instance, research has shown that retail investors chase the mutual funds and hedge funds with the highest returns. Yet, doing so appears suboptimal, based on the observation that fund returns are largely unpredictable. This trend-chasing may be attributed to behaviors such as a *representative bias*, which holds that investors over-weight recent experience when forming their expectations of future outcomes, leading them to chase high returns by seeking out recent high performers. Additional individual investor biases are documented in the context of specific money managers and their products, discussed in this chapter.

The rationales for forming mutual funds, ETFs, hedge funds, and pension funds differ, as do their respective levels of regulatory oversight. Such differences in products warrant a close examination of each type. Therefore, the purpose of this chapter is to explore the financial behavior of each of these important classifications of investments. For each type of money manager and/or product, the chapter presents evidence of the rationality of both its investor group and the retail investors who demand that service. Collectively, the evidence suggests that actual performance and practices of these investment instruments and their managers do not match the traditional finance expectations of wealth maximization and rational participation.

The first section of this chapter describes mutual fund size, performance, and rationality, followed by a discussion of the emergence of ETFs and evidence of their ability to enhance market efficiency. Then there is a section on the performance and investor biases for hedge funds, and a subsequent section on evaluating pension fund performance and the potential behavioral biases of pension fund managers. The chapter ends with a summary and conclusions.

Mutual Funds

The amount of AUM in mutual funds is impressive. According to the Investment Company Institute (ICI 2015), mutual funds control $16 trillion in U.S. assets alone as of year-end 2014. Table 21.1 displays the annual inflow/outflow of cash for U.S. mutual funds between 2000 and 2014, based on data from ICI. The average annual inflow is $196 billion, even with the net outflow period associated with the financial crisis that persisted between 2009 and 2011. Investor demand and the desire of investors to meet financial objectives, including return maximization and risk management, are driving forces underlying the huge size of mutual funds. According to ICI, roughly half of all mutual fund allocations are to publicly traded equity, with bond funds and money market funds making up about 40 percent of allocations.

Roughly 89 percent of mutual fund assets come from households. Based on the sources of mutual fund assets and the objectives of investors in mutual funds, the primary question of interest is whether the expectations of these households are being met.

Table 21.1 **Annual Cash Flows in U.S. Mutual Funds, Based on ICI Data**

Year	*Net New Cash Inflow (Outflow) in $Billions*
2000	388
2001	504
2002	75
2003	–48
2004	53
2005	254
2006	472
2007	879
2008	412
2009	–150
2010	–281
2011	–96
2012	198
2013	175
2014	102

Note: This table presents the yearly net new cash inflow or outflow of U.S. mutual funds between 2000 and 2014.

Source: ICI (2015).

ACTIVE VERSUS PASSIVE

One useful distinction to make in evaluating mutual fund performance is between active and passive management. Although overall AUM remains much larger for actively managed funds, passive funds such as index funds have increased in popularity. In particular, ICI data indicate that index funds account for roughly $2.1 trillion of the $16 trillion in U.S. mutual fund assets. Of particular note is that index funds added nearly $150 billion in 2014, compared to an overall inflow of only $100 billion for the industry overall in 2014. Thus, a net outflow of AUM in actively managed funds occurred in 2014, which was offset by an inflow into passively managed index funds. Table 21.2 displays the annual cash inflows into U.S. index mutual funds between 2000 and 2014. The relative increase in importance of index mutual funds is consistent with investors' becoming more interested in passively tracking the market versus attempting to pick money managers who beat the market.

Table 21.2 **Annual Cash Flows in U.S. Index Mutual Funds, Based on ICI Data**

Year	*Net New Cash Inflow (Outflow) in $Billions*
2000	26
2001	27
2002	25
2003	35
2004	40
2005	28
2006	33
2007	61
2008	35
2009	56
2010	58
2011	55
2012	59
2013	114
2014	148

Note: This table presents the yearly net new cash inflow or outflow in U.S. index mutual funds between 2000 and 2014.

Source: ICI (2015).

MUTUAL FUND PERFORMANCE

Much research is available on the performance of actively managed mutual funds, and this research typically documents underperformance. In a seminal study, Jensen (1968) examines 115 mutual funds and found that they were unable, on average, to outperform the market. In a particularly startling result, Jensen finds that mutual funds cannot recover their expenses. Thus, investors generally pay fees only to achieve lower performance than passively holding the market. More recent research, including Gruber (1996), French (2008), and Fama and French (2010) also documents the negative after-fee alphas for actively managed U.S. equity mutual funds. *Alpha* refers to risk-adjust returns (i.e., return not explained by risk).

Considerable debate surrounds the rationality of retail investor demand for actively managed mutual funds, which ultimately fail to outperform the market on a risk- and fee-adjusted basis. Investor demand is even more difficult to explain, considering the relatively large compensation and fees that accrue to financial intermediaries.

CHASING RETURNS

The literature is divided on whether it is rational for investors to pay mutual fund managers who fail to generate alpha. Yet, Gruber (1996) finds that investors chase performance, and that performance is partially predictable. These findings suggest that investors may be more rational than the initial evidence on mutual fund performance and return-chasing in particular would indicate. Similarly, Berk and Green (2004) developed a model showing that the observed characteristics of the mutual fund industry are mostly consistent with a rational and competitive market. A key insight gained from the model is that *competition* in the mutual fund industry is responsible for the failure of active fund managers to beat the market. In short, their model suggests that mutual fund managers have different levels of ability. Investors chase performance, and their influx of money ensures that future returns of successful managers will be competitive. Thus, investors cannot predict which managers will have the greatest skill.

Fama and French (2010) suggest that their empirical evidence contradicts the Berk and Green model. Specifically, they found that gross fund returns are zero, and that negative alpha is equal to the fees of the fund. Thus, investors do not earn zero alphas by investing in actively managed funds but, rather, earn negative alpha on average. Nonetheless, some interpret Fama and French as supportive of Berk and Green.

BEHAVIORAL ISSUES

Some researchers suggest that the underperformance of mutual funds may be due to behavioral biases and irrational investment choices on the part of fund managers. One of the first behavioral biases linked to mutual fund managers is *herding* (Wermers 1999), which is the tendency to follow others when trading. Herding could be rational if following others led to generating alpha, but the literature indicates that this is not the case. Another behavioral bias related to mutual fund performance is the *familiarity bias*, which also manifests itself in mutual funds through the home bias, or the tendency to invest in assets that are geographically close to fund headquarters (Baker and Nofsinger 2002).

LIMITED ATTENTION AND DISPOSITION EFFECT

Fang, Peress, and Zheng (2014) examined two behavioral explanations for mutual fund investment selection and performance, focusing on the role of media in mutual fund stock selection. Their first hypothesis relates to limited attention. As developed in Kahneman (1973), *limited attention* is a bias related to the observation that individuals' time is scarce and that this lack of unlimited attention may lead to certain biases. In the context of mutual fund managers, investors are more likely to notice and potentially select stocks that receive media coverage, regardless of whether doing so is wealth maximizing. Media attention may explain fund underperformance, given that the motivation for stock selection is not based on skill or superior information.

Similarly, fund managers may be less prone to the behavioral bias of limited attention and may instead exploit this bias among individual investors. In short, mutual fund managers would still trade in high media-coverage stocks, but their superior skill and ability to identify the mispricing caused by biased individual investors would result in superior performance. The results of Fang et al. are consistent with mutual fund managers' suffering from the same limited attention biases as do individual investors rather than with exploiting mispricing owing to retail investors' biases.

Others examine the disposition effect, which is related to prospect theory (Kahneman and Tversky 1979) in the context of mutual fund underperformance. The *disposition effect* is the tendency to gamble more with losses than with profits. Hence, investors tend to sell winners and hold losers. Lin, Fan, and Chi (2014) study the disposition effect in mutual fund managers and find that it negatively affects the performance of the funds. The observed escalation of commitment is related to self-attribution, optimism, and cognitive dissonance. *Self-attribution* suggests that individuals assign success to their skill and failure to bad luck. *Optimism* is related to individuals who are biased in their forecasts and overestimate their potential outcomes. *Cognitive dissonance* is the state of having inconsistent thoughts, beliefs, or attitudes, especially as relating to behavioral decisions and attitude changes. Collectively, this bias may lead to an escalation of commitment whereby a fund manager may stick to a losing investment strategy and thus could exacerbate underperformance. The survey evidence presented in Goetzmann and Peles (1997) is consistent with cognitive dissonance, as the authors find a positive bias involving mutual fund investors' memory of past returns.

BEHAVIORAL BIASES IN SELECTING MUTUAL FUNDS

Mutual funds tend to underperform on average, and some portion of the underperformance could result from behavioral biases. This observation leads to the second major theme of this chapter, which is the behavioral biases of individuals who select such funds. In particular, why it is that investors demand costly financial instruments that fail to beat passive strategies is a puzzle that has been addressed by the literature. Much early work in behavioral finance and individual investor biases has focused on stock picking rather mutual fund selection; however, two early results from the behavioral literature and mutual funds stand out. First, investors choose funds with high fees despite exacerbating underperformance (Gruber 1996; Barber, Odean, and Zheng 2005). Second, investors chase past performance when selecting mutual funds (Sirri and Tufano 1998; Bergstresser and Poterba 2002; Sapp and Tiwari 2004). As noted previously, Gruber (1996) documents this pattern, but interprets the relation as relatively rational, given that he finds mutual fund performance to be partially predictable. Subsequent literature, however, does not typically concur with the predictability conclusion. The behavioral literature instead suggests that return chasing in this context is irrational and the result of agency problems (Chevalier and Ellison 1997). Overall, this finding suggests that investors continue to demand actively managed mutual funds partly because they observe some funds outperforming passive strategies and they believe they can earn similar superior returns in the future by "chasing" these funds.

Bailey, Kumar, and Ng (2011) provide one of the few behavioral studies linking individual characteristics to mutual fund selection. They examined a wide range of the behavioral biases found in individual stock selection in the context of mutual fund selection, using thousands of brokerage accounts for U.S. retail investors. In particular, the authors focused on the disposition effect. Bailey et al. created a disposition effect proxy based on individual investors' actual realization of gains and losses. They also examined the role of narrow framing in mutual fund investing. *Narrow framing* is the tendency to focus on individual investments without considering the portfolio more generally. This tendency is measured by identifying investors with less clustered trades, which are more likely to suffer from framing. Another behavioral bias considered is *overconfidence*, which manifests itself in this case as the tendency to trade too frequently, but unsuccessfully. The authors proxied this bias using portfolio turnover and a dummy gender variable. Familiarity was measured by local bias, which was the distance between the investor's home and the fund's headquarters. The investor gambling preference was examined by identifying *lottery stocks*, which are low-priced stocks with both high idiosyncratic volatility and idiosyncratic skewness (based on Kumar 2009). Finally, they examined investor inattention to earnings news and macroeconomic news.

Bailey et al. (2011) find that behavioral factors are related to selecting investments. In particular, investors who exhibit biases tend to choose high-fee funds and avoid low-fee index funds. Mutual fund investors also trade more frequently and are more likely to chase trends. Given that this investment type exhibits particularly poor investment returns, the evidence is inconsistent with that indicating investors chase returns based on rational criteria. In short, behavioral biases of the individuals could explain the puzzling demand for underperforming active mutual funds.

Another possible explanation for the return-chasing observed in the retail investor selection of mutual funds is the hot-hand fallacy (Kahneman and Riepe 1998). Gilovich, Vallone, and Tversky (1985) examine the hot-hand fallacy in the context of basketball. They note that both basketball fans and players believe that players have periods in which they are particularly "hot," meaning their performance positively deviates from their long-term average performance. The authors conclude that this belief is an illusion, because the number of actual deviations from long-term averages is within the bounds of what should be expected based purely on chance. In the context of mutual fund selection, then, the *hot-hand fallacy* refers to investors' observing a "hot" streak by a given fund that has recently had strong performance and incorrectly inferring that the fund will continue to outperform in subsequent periods.

INDEX MUTUAL FUNDS

Although the popularity of actively managed funds despite their underperformance seems irrational, the index fund market presents another puzzle. Despite the fact that index mutual funds for a given asset should all have similar future returns (subject to tracking error), the fees of such funds vary widely. *Tracking error* is a measure of how closely a portfolio follows the index to which it is benchmarked. This observation appears to violate the law of one price (LOP), which states that identical goods should have identical prices. Choi, Laibson, and Madrian (2010) find that S&P index funds in the CRSP mutual fund database have fees ranging from 0 percent to 5.75 percent. As Elton, Gruber, and Busse (2004) show, high-fee passive funds still generate large fund inflows.

Although investors hold large positions in high-fee funds in general (Gruber 1996; Barber et al. 2005), the result is particularly striking in index funds. The literature has identified potential explanations that are generally behavioral, including financial literacy (Elton et al. 2004; Choi et al. 2010), return chasing (Sirri and Tufano 1998;

Sapp and Tiwari 2004; Choi et al. 2010; Bailey et al. 2011), search costs (Hortacsu and Syverson 2004), and marketing (Khorana and Servaes 2012).

Mauck and Salzsieder (2015) provide experimental evidence suggesting that the diversification bias could be partially responsible for investor selection of high-fee index funds. According to the *diversification bias,* which is based on Simonson (1990), people tend to diversify when making simultaneous choices. Read and Loewenstein (1995) coined the term diversification bias to describe this behavior, which others call the *diversification heuristic.* Thaler (1999) contends that though diversification may be rational, it is not necessarily utility maximizing.

An experiment conducted by Mauck and Salzsieder (2015) asks subjects to allocate a hypothetical portfolio among four different S&P 500 index mutual funds with fees and returns. The authors changed the fees and historical returns in various conditions. The results indicate that investors chase past returns that differ only due to reporting "since inception" returns, which do not correspond to the same time period for all funds and do not predict future differences in returns. However, even when holding historical returns constant for all four funds, investors do not focus their investments on the lowest-fee funds and instead diversify their holdings, even though doing so is suboptimal. In short, even in the absence of return-chasing, individuals do not minimize fees.

A possible explanation of the demand for money management services that fail to beat a passive strategy is that individuals are not solely interested in wealth maximization. As Gennaioli, Shleifer, and Vishny (2015, p. 92) note, "We . . . propose an alternative view of money management that is based on the idea that investors do not know much about finance, are too nervous or anxious to make risky investments on their own, and hence hire money managers and advisors to help them invest." In short, neither retail nor institutional investors are solely concerned with returns when selecting money managers (Lakonishok, Shleifer, and Vishny 1992).

Gennaioli, Shleifer, and Vishny (2015) use the analogy of medical doctors: patients need guidance on their treatment, and investors need guidance on their investments. Trust is an important component when selecting both doctors and financial advisors. As trust increases, the advisor can charge higher fees. Higher trust is likely required in higher-risk investments. According to this model, advisors are incentivized to cater to investors, leading money managers to adopt the biases of their clients. For example, fund managers had a strong incentive to reallocate to high-technology stocks during the late 1990s, despite the appearance of overvaluation resulting from the returns-chasing biases of their customers. Thus, the emotional and psychological needs and wants of individuals may partly explain the puzzling demand for both active and passive mutual funds.

Exchange-Traded Funds

Many exchange-traded funds (ETFs) are similar to index mutual funds, in that they are designed to track an underlying index or benchmark, and to provide a relatively low-fee product for investors. Most ETFs are similar to open-end funds, and many track indices such as the S&P 500. However, ETFs also allow exposure to commodities, currencies, and various strategy-based investments. ETFs differ from index funds in that investors

Table 21.3 **Annual Cash Flows and Total Assets of ETFs, Based on ICI Data**

Year	*Net New Cash Inflow (Outflow) in $Billions*	*Total Assets in $Billions*
2003	N/A	151
2004	75	226
2005	70	296
2006	112	408
2007	172	580
2008	–84	496
2009	207	703
2010	188	891
2011	48	939
2012	278	1,217
2013	394	1,611
2014	307	1,918

Note: This table presents the yearly net new cash inflow or outflow and total assets in ETFs between 2000 and 2014.

Source: ICI (2015).

can trade them directly on an exchange. Table 21.3 presents the annual cash flows into ETFs, as well as the overall size of ETFs between 2003 and 2014, based on data from the ICI (2015). The table indicates an average annual cash inflow to ETFs of $161 billion for the period, with nearly $2 trillion in total assets by the end of 2014. The annual average cash flow growth for E TFs compares similarly to mutual funds' average cash flow growth of $164 billion over the same period. Given that only $17 billion of the nearly $2 trillion in ETFs is actively managed, ETFs generally follow passive strategies, as suggested by proponents of market efficiency.

According to the literature, the introduction of ETFs is generally efficiency enhancing. For example, Kurov and Lasser (2002) have documented improved futures pricing efficiency in terms of both the size and the frequency of violations in price boundaries. Some view this relation as resulting from increased arbitrage trading (Hegde and McDermott 2004), and another possible explanation for the improved efficiency is the improved liquidity of the underlying stocks (Madura and Richie 2007). These results indicate that ETFs may be generally efficiency increasing. This conclusion is consistent with Gleason, Mathur, and Peterson (2004), who do not find evidence of investor herding in the ETF market. This result stands in contrast to the herding behavior that has been observed among institutional investors.

INVESTOR SENTIMENT

Although evidence shows that introducing ETFs has improved market efficiency, the literature also documents the presence of behavioral bias in ETF markets. In particular, investor sentiment has received much attention. *Investor sentiment* is the tendency of investors to have changes in risk tolerance or to become either optimistic or pessimistic with respect to future projections. Baker and Wurgler (2006, 2007) find that investor sentiment is related to future stock returns. Sentiment also appears to affect both individual and institutional investors (Edelen, Marcus, and Tehranian 2010). Chau, Deesomsak, and Lau (2011) study three large U.S. ETFs: the S&P 500 SPDR, the Dow Jones Industrial Average ETF "Diamond," and the Nasdaq-100 ETF "Cubes." Their results indicate that investor sentiment has a strong role in feedback trading (i.e., momentum) in ETFs. Furthermore, they found that this relation is stronger during bull markets than during bear markets.

OTHER BEHAVIORAL ISSUES

As Madura and Richie (2004) note, ETFs should be efficiency enhancing because they provide liquidity and opportunities to arbitrage away any mispricing. However, the tradability of ETFs may result in ETF price movements that are unrelated to price movements of the underlying assets. Consistent with this latter observation, Madura and Richie find that ETF prices overreact, and thus create inefficiency and opportunities for feedback traders.

Padungsaksawasdi and Daigler (2014) examine the return–volatility relation in the context of ETFs. Their study highlights an advantages of ETFs—namely, direct investability in both equity and commodity markets. Additionally, ETFs allow for a different perspective on existing behavioral theories. The authors relate representativeness, affect, and the extrapolation bias to the return–volatility relation. For instance, if investors with a representative bias observe a recent downward price movement, they may incorrectly believe the market is ready to decline. This conclusion may result in buying out-of-the-money put options as a hedge against price drops regardless of the cost of such puts, which would in turn create a higher VIX value. VIX is the ticker symbol for the Chicago Board Options Exchange (CBOE) Volatility Index, which shows the market's expectation of 30-day volatility. It is constructed using the implied volatilities of a wide range of S&P 500 index options. Similarly, affect created by the success or failure of a past trade could influence future investor decisions. If investors fear downward movements in the market, they may buy put options. A subsequent increase in the VIX, then, creates a negative return–volatility relation.

Finally, *extrapolation bias* describes a tendency of investors to treat past events as predictors of future events. Thus, when prices drop, these investors buy puts, which will bid up the price of insuring against downside risk. The empirical evidence indicates that these behavioral explanations best fit the negative return–volatility relation in commodity ETFs.

OVERALL ETF EFFICIENCY

Collectively, the evidence indicates that ETFs are generally efficiency enhancing. The prices of ETFs are subject to the behavioral biases of the investors selecting the ETFs, but compared to other investment types considered in this chapter, ETFs appear to be relatively efficient. Coupled with relatively lower fees and typically passive strategies, ETFs have increased in popularity. Given the relatively shorter period for the data, how longer-term performance of ETFs will manifest itself is unclear. Yet, early evidence indicates that ETFs are likely to continue to be an important investment option.

Hedge Funds

Hedge funds share some features with mutual funds, in that they invest in portfolios of assets and have discretion in selecting those assets. A major difference between the two fund types is that neither the Securities and Exchange Commission (SEC) nor any similar regulatory institution generally regulates hedge funds. As a result, the range of possible assets and strategies available to hedge fund managers is greater than that for mutual fund managers. Given the unregulated nature of hedge funds, data on such investments are more difficult to identify than for mutual funds. However, current estimates place the size of global hedge fund holdings at around $2.5 trillion (OECD 2014).

MISVALUATIONS

Although institutional investors potentially improve market efficiency, perhaps no group is more ascribed this ability than hedge funds. Given that hedge funds have a wider range of assets and strategies at their disposal, this circumstance should allow them to take advantage of any mispricing.

As Ritter (2004) notes, two general forms of misvaluation exist. One form is recurrent and can be arbitraged, whereas the other does not repeat and is longer term in nature. Hedge funds are often viewed as arbitrageurs. Regarding recurrent misvaluations, Ritter (2004, p. 433) comments that “Because of this, hedge funds and others zero in on these, and keep them from ever getting too big. Thus, the market is pretty efficient for these assets, at least on a relative basis.” Similarly, Brunnermeir and Nagel (2004, p. 2014) state that “Hedge funds are among the most sophisticated investors—probably closer to the ideal of ‘rational arbitrageurs’ than any other class of investors.”

Hedge funds can better exploit potential market inefficiencies than mutual funds owing to differences in the constraints faced by the funds. According to Fung and Hsieh (1997), mutual funds often face constraints on the number of assets, types of asset classes, use of leverage, and other strategies such as short selling. The authors further note that hedge funds differ from mutual funds with respect to these constraints; hedge funds can use more dynamic strategies with relatively fewer limitations.

One view of the hedge fund’s role in correcting mispricing is that it trades against mispricing. Consistent with this view, Kokkonen and Suominen (2015) find that hedge fund trading at least partially corrects market-wide mispricing. Yet, Brunnermeir and Nagel (2004) find that hedge funds followed the technology bubble rather than traded against it. Further, they find that hedge funds anticipated the eventual decline in technology stock prices and sold them accordingly. Overall, hedge funds were able to detect a bubble, presumably owing to investor sentiment rather than to rational forces, and they profited from this knowledge.

INVESTMENT PERFORMANCE

The research has documented that, similar to mutual funds, hedge funds typically underperform their benchmarks, or at least fail to generate positive alpha (Malkiel and Saha 2005). Hedge funds often fail to beat the market, but some evidence indicates that they outperform mutual funds (Ackermann, McEnally, and Ravenscraft 1999), although the difference may not be statistically significant (Griffin and Xu 2009). In fact, hedge funds that outperform benchmarks cannot generally repeat the effort (Brown, Goetzmann, and Ibbotson 1999). Yet, Fung, Hsieh, Naik, and Ramadorai (2008) find that hedge funds that generate alpha are more likely to survive than those that do not.

The actual returns realized by hedge fund investors are lower than those reported in raw hedge fund returns, owing to fees. After considering the fees, Dichev and Yu (2011) find that actual returns for hedge fund investors are between 3 and 7 percent lower than for a simple buy-and-hold benchmark. Early hedge fund fees typically followed the "2 and 20" structure, whereby investors pay a 2 percent fee for assets managed and a 20 percent fee on returns. French (2008) find that annual hedge fund fees from 1996 to 2007 averaged 4.26 percent of assets. Based on this high fee structure, hedge funds must generate significant annual abnormal returns to match a passively held portfolio. Furthermore, Garbaravicius and Dierick (2005) find that correlations between hedge funds and markets have increased, which Stulz (2007) partly relates to an observation that some hedge funds have become de facto mutual funds with higher fees.

In short, as with mutual funds, the continued and increasing popularity of hedge funds appears to challenge a rational view of investors who are seeking to maximize their wealth. Thus, why investors continue to invest in hedge funds despite their high fees and typical inability to beat the market is puzzling.

According to Agarwal and Naik (2004), hedge funds may provide investors with different risk exposures than do mutual funds, despite their investing in similar assets. The difference in risk is due to hedge funds' taking both long and short positions and sometimes using shorter investment horizons. Thus, investors may demand hedge funds owing to their individual risk preferences.

BEHAVIORAL ISSUES

Besides rational risk-based explanations, the literature contains behavioral explanations for the investor demand for hedge funds and their relatively high fees. As noted in the mutual funds section of this chapter, Gennaioli et al. (2015) develop a theoretical model that focused on trust as a determinant in the financial consumer's selection of funds. In particular, their study showed that investors are concerned with both wealth maximization and the anxiety that results from making risky decisions about a topic for which they lack understanding. Thus, investors are willing to pay fees for professional money management even when doing so results in underperformance. However, the role of trust is even more pronounced in higher-risk investments. In these cases of higher trust, fees are also expected to be higher, and this seems to explain the perplexing demand for hedge funds. In particular, hedge funds have both relatively high fees and high risk, yet they underperform passive strategies, particularly on an after-fee basis. The features of a hedge fund, particularly its high risk, mean that a relatively high degree of trust in the money manager is prerequisite for investing in that hedge fund.

Collectively, the evidence indicates that hedge funds may be efficiency enhancing, although this function does not serve to generate positive fee-adjusted alpha for hedge fund investors. Hedge funds differ from mutual funds mainly in the assets and strategies available to them, although some hedge funds are becoming de facto mutual funds with hedge fund fees.

Pension Funds

Employers typically establish pension funds for the purpose of investing employee retirement funds. Pension funds are the second largest group examined in this chapter, with current assets of around $20 trillion. Pension funds share characteristics with some sovereign wealth funds (SWFs) (Dewenter, Han, and Malatesta 2010). SWFs are government-owned investment vehicles often charged with the preservation of national wealth. However, this chapter excludes SWF research, which generally indicates that SWFs differ in both determinants and performance relative to other institutions (Kotter and Lel 2011; Knill, Lee, and Mauck 2012a, 2012b; Johan, Knill, and Mauck 2013; Bortolotti, Fotak, and Megginson 2015). Although the choice of omission is subjective, the implication is not trivial, because SWFs control an estimated additional $7 trillion (Bortolotti et al.).

Pension funds may invest in all the other investor groups covered in this chapter—namely, mutual funds, ETFs, and hedge funds. For instance, Agarwal and Naik (2004) note that pension funds such as CALPERS and Ontario Teachers have historically held both mutual funds and hedge funds in their portfolios. This allocation may be related to a desire for exposure to various risk premia. However, CALPERS discontinued its hedge fund program in 2014 (Aitken 2015). According to CALPERS's interim chief investment officer, hedge funds are no longer a viable option because of their complexity, cost structure, and inability to scale to size.

According to the OECD (2015), pension funds have 51.3 percent, 23.8 percent, and 9.6 percent of their assets in bills/bond, equities, and cash, respectively. The report also notes a shift to nontraditional investments beginning around 2012 in a search for greater yield, including hedge funds, private equity, and derivatives.

WINDOW DRESSING

As Lakonishok, Shleifer, Thaler, and Vishny (1991) note, some pension funds manage their investments in-house, but others use outside money managers. Regardless of which method is chosen, they note that pension fund managers face important annual performance reporting. Their evidence indicates that pension funds engage in "window dressing" by selling losers before the end of the year, so they are not forced to explain the inclusion of "loser" stocks in the portfolio. This end-of-the-year selling is not based on rational criteria but, rather, on the desire to avoid scrutiny. Lakonishok et al. (1992) find that outside managers who invest pension fund assets do not exhibit signs of herding, feedback trading, or passive trading. They conclude that such managers are "neither the stabilizing nor the destabilizing image" that is sometimes portrayed for such funds.

INVESTMENT PERFORMANCE

Andonov, Bauer, and Cremers (2012) study overall pension fund performance, including those with equity, fixed income, and alternatives. Importantly, unlike many prior studies that focus on the performance of outside managers, their sample included both internal and external managers. They note that pension funds have different motives from mutual funds—motives that could affect investment behavior. In particular, the mutual fund manager's pay is a function of the assets managed, which could in turn be strongly related to relative performance. In contrast, pension funds view actuarial factors as influencing fund inflows. The lack of incentive for short-term performance should lead to an ability to pursue less liquid investments relative to mutual funds. Yet, Andonov et al. note that the a priori relation between greater liquidity and subsequent return is unclear. Overall, they found that pension funds outperform the market, with positive abnormal returns of 89 basis points a year. This result is partly driven by the relatively greater exposure to alternatives, which are correspondingly associated with higher returns.

FEES AND PERFORMANCE

Bauer, Cremers, and Frehen (2010) document that pension funds achieve significantly lower cost levels than mutual fund fees. In particular, they estimate that pension fund fees are around 27 to 51 basis points a year, whereas mutual fund fees are roughly around 150 basis points a year, on average. Furthermore, pension funds outperform mutual funds despite not generating a positive alpha. Their analysis indicates that smaller pension funds, especially those with small-cap mandates, can beat their benchmarks.

RISK EXPOSURE

Andonov, Bauer, and Cremers (2015) compare U.S. public pension funds to private and public pension funds in the United States, Canada, and Europe. In particular, they noted that U.S. public pension funds can understate their liabilities by taking on riskier asset allocations. Their evidence shows that funds taking on greater risk for these purposes underperform other pension funds, which is mostly due to lower returns on the riskiest assets, specifically equities and alternatives. The authors conclude that the regulatory environment provides incentives for pension funds to act counter to the best practices recommended by financial theory.

PENSION FUND ACTIVISM

Another much discussed feature of pension funds is their tendency to be activist investors. Wahal (1996) examines firms targeted by shareholder activism on the part of the following pension funds between 1987 and 1993: California Public Employee Retirement System, California State Teachers Retirement System, Colorado Public Employee Retirement System, New York City Pension System, Pennsylvania Public School Employee Retirement System, State of Wisconsin Investment Board, College Retirement Equities Fund, Florida State Board of Administration, and New York State Common Retirement System. The results indicate that these pension funds are relatively successful at having their proposals adopted. However, the adoption of pension fund proposals is not associated with improved firm performance as measured by either the market response or long-term performance. Del Guercio and Hawkins (1999) find no evidence that pension funds are motivated by anything other than fund value maximization. An, Huang, and Zhang (2013) examine corporate sponsors of defined benefit pension plans. They note that such funds take on relatively low (or high) risk when they have low (or high) funding ratios and high (or low) default risk.

BEHAVIORAL BIASES

Overall, the literature documents some differences between pension funds and other classes of money managers. Collectively, the evidence suggests that pension funds generally underperform passive benchmarks, which is consistent with evidence on mutual funds and hedge funds. However, the literature also has explored potential sources of pension fund underperformance specific to pension fund managers. For example, Gort, Wang, and Siegrist (2008) find that Swiss pension fund managers are overconfident. In particular, the pension fund managers provided too narrow confidence intervals when asked to do so for past returns. However, the pension fund managers were less overconfident than the laypeople control group. Additionally, the authors find that younger and better-educated fund managers are less overconfident.

Overconfidence might also explain the belief of pension fund managers that they can either internally generate alpha or select outside managers who can do so (Barberis and Thaler 2003). Additionally, marketing efforts may influence pension fund managers to incorrectly believe they can pick alpha-generating outside money managers (Barber et al. 2005). However, given that Bauer et al. (2010) find that some pension funds, specifically smaller funds with small-cap mandates, can generate alpha, some classes of pension fund managers might have such skill. Foster and Warren (2015) develop a model that incorporates both rational and behavioral explanations for money management selection. They find that the optimism bias can lead to substantial losses when selecting money managers.

In summary, the literature indicates that pension funds can generally outperform mutual funds and have a much lower fee structure, but that pension funds still do not generate alpha. Additionally, pension fund managers exhibit similar biases as other investors, including overconfidence.

Summary and Conclusions

Professional money managers and products such as mutual funds, ETFs, hedge funds, and pension funds control a staggering amount of wealth, at approximately

$55 trillion as of the end of 2014. In general, these investors and products cannot produce alpha. Additionally, the fees charged for managing such investments range from modest (ETFs) to high (hedge funds). Combining the observed lack of alpha with the reality of investor fees makes the continued demand for such assets puzzling.

This chapter has documented the specific return characteristics and observed rationality of each investment group. The chapter also examined the rationality of those choosing to invest in such assets. Overall, both professional money managers and those paying for their services exhibit many behavioral biases that are seemingly at odds with a traditional view of wealth-maximizing financial theory. Perhaps in recognition of this observation, the observed trends in rising demand for these various assets seem to indicate a move toward more logical investor choices. In particular, the relative popularity of passive and low-fee assets such as index mutual funds and ETFs have increased tremendously since 2000.

DISCUSSION QUESTIONS

1. Explain the observed return performance of mutual funds, hedge funds, and pension funds.
2. Explain the similarities and differences between mutual funds and hedge funds.
3. Identify the behavioral biases demonstrated by fund managers.
4. Identify the behavioral biases demonstrated by those selecting money managers and related products.
5. Explain the trends in relative demand for active and passive strategies by both mutual funds and ETFs.

REFERENCES

Ackermann, Carl, Richard McEnally, and David Ravenscraft. 1999. "The Performance of Hedge Funds: Risk, Return, and Incentives." *Journal of Finance* 54:3, 833–874.

Agarwarl, Vikas, and Narayan Y. Naik. 2004. "Risks and Portfolio Decisions Involving Hedge Funds." *Review of Financial Studies* 17:1, 63–98.

Aitken, Roger. 2015. "Why Invest in Hedge Funds If They Don't Outperform the Market?" *Forbes.com.* January 21. Available at http://www.forbes.com/sites/rogeraitken/2015/01/21/why-invest-in-hedge-funds-if-they-dont-outperform-the-market/.

An, Heng, Zhaodan Huang, and Ting Zhang. 2013. "What Determines Corporate Pension Fund Risk-Taking Strategy?" *Journal of Banking and Finance* 37:2 597–613.

Andonov, Aleksandar, Rob Bauer, and Martijn Cremers. 2012. "Can Large Pension Funds Beat the Market? Asset Allocation, Market Timing, Security Selection, and the Limits of Liquidity." Working Paper, Maastricht University and University of Notre Dame. Available at http://papers.ssrn.com/sol3/Papers.cfm?abstract_id=1885536.

Andonov, Aleksandar, Rob Bauer, and Martijn Cremers. 2015. "Pension Fund Asset Allocation and Liability Discount Rates." Working Paper, Maastricht University and University of Notre Dame. Available at http://papers.ssrn.com/sol3/Papers.cfm?abstract_id=2070054.

Bailey, Warren, Alok Kumar, and David Ng. 2011. "Behavioral Biases of Mutual Fund Investors." *Journal of Financial Economics* 102:1, 1–27.

Baker, H. Kent, and John R. Nofsinger. 2002. "Psychological Biases of Investors." *Financial Services Review* 11:2, 97–116.

Baker, Malcolm, and Jeffrey Wurgler. 2006. "Investor Sentiment and the Cross-section of Stock Returns." *Journal of Finance* 61:4, 1125–1165.

Baker, Malcolm, and Jeffrey Wurgler. 2007. "Investor Sentiment in the Stock Market." *Journal of Economic Perspectives* 21:2, 129–151.

Barber, Brad M., Terrance Odean, and Lu Zheng. 2005. "Out of Sight, Out of Mind: The Effects of Expenses on Mutual Fund Flows." *Journal of Business* 78:6, 2095–2119.

Barberis, Nicholas, and Richard Thaler. 2003. "A Survey of Behavioral Finance." In George Constantinedes, Milt Harris, and René Stulz (eds.), *The Handbook of the Economics of Finance*, 1B, 1051–1121. North Holland: Elsevier.

Bauer, Rob, Martijn Cremers, and Rik Frehen. 2010. "Pension Fund Performance and Costs: Small Is Beautiful." Working Paper, Maastricht University, University of Notre Dame, and Tilburg University. Available at https://papers.ssrn.com/sol3/papers.cfm?abstract_id=965388.

Bergstresser, Daniel, and James Poterba. 2002. "Do After-tax Returns Affect Mutual Fund Inflows?" *Journal of Financial Economics* 63:3, 381–414.

Berk, Jonathan B., and Richard C. Green. 2004. "Mutual Fund Flows in Rational Markets." *Journal of Political Economy* 112:6, 1269–1295.

Blume, Marshall E., and Donald B. Keim. 2012. "Institutional Investors and Stock Market Liquidity: Trends and Relationships." Working Paper, University of Pennsylvania. Available at http://papers.ssrn.com/sol3/papers.cfm?abstract_id=2147757.

Bortolotti, Bernardo, Veljko Fotak, and William L. Megginson. 2015. "The Sovereign Wealth Fund Discount: Evidence from Public Equity Investments." *Review of Financial Studies* 28:11, 2993–3035.

Brown, Stephen J., William N. Goetzmann, and Roger G. Ibbotson. 1999. "Offshore Hedge Funds: Survival and Performance, 1989–95." *Journal of Business* 72:1, 91–117.

Brunnermeier, Markus K., and Stefan Nagel. 2004. "Hedge Funds and the Technology Bubble." *Journal of Finance* 59:5, 2013–2040.

Chau, Frankie, Rataporn Deesomsak, and Marco C. K. Lau. 2011. "Investor Sentiment and Feedback Trading: Evidence from the Exchange-Traded Fund Markets." *International Review of Financial Analysis* 20:5, 292–305.

Chevalier, Judith A., and Glenn D. Ellison. 1997. "Risk Taking by Mutual Funds as a Response to Incentives." *Journal of Political Economy* 105:6, 1167–1200.

Choi, James J., David Laibson, and Brigitte C. Madrian. 2010. "Why Does the Law of One Price Fail? An Experiment on Index Mutual Funds." *Review of Financial Studies* 23:4, 1405–1432.

Dewenter, Kathryn L., Xi Han, and Paul H. Malatesta. 2010. "Firm Values and Sovereign Wealth Fund Investments." *Journal of Financial Economics* 98:2, 256–279.

Del Guercio, Diane, and Jennifer Hawkins. 1999. "The Motivation and Impact of Pension Fund Activism." *Journal of Financial Economics* 52:3, 293–340.

Dichev, Ilia D., and Gwen Yu. 2011. "Higher Risk, Lower Returns: What Hedge Fund Investors Really Earn." *Journal of Financial Economics* 100:2, 248–263.

Edelen, Roger M., Alan J. Marcus, and Hassan Tehranian. 2010. "Relative Sentiment and Stock Returns." *Financial Analysts Journal* 66:4, 20–32.

Elton, Edwin J., Martin J. Gruber, and Jeffrey A. Busse. 2004. "Are Investors Rational? Choices among Index Funds." *Journal of Finance* 59:1, 261–288.

Fama, Eugene F., and Kenneth R. French. 2010. "Luck versus Skill in the Cross-Section of Mutual Fund Returns." *Journal of Finance* 65:5, 1915–1947.

Fang, Lily H., Joel Peress, and Lu Zheng. 2014. "Does Media Coverage of Stocks Affect Mutual Funds' Trading and Performance?" *Review of Financial Studies* 27:12, 3441–3466.

Foster, Douglas F., and Geoffrey J. Warren. 2015. "Why Might Investors Choose Active Management?" *Journal of Behavioral Finance* 16:1, 20–39.

French, Kenneth R. 2008. "Presidential Address: The Cost of Active Investing." *Journal of Finance* 63:4, 1537–1573.

Fung, William, and David A. Hsieh. 1997. "Empirical Characteristics of Dynamic Trading Strategies: The Case of Hedge Funds." *Review of Financial Studies* 10:2, 275–302.

Fung, William, David A. Hsieh, Narayan Y. Naik, and Tarun Ramadorai. 2008. "Hedge Funds: Performance, Risk, and Capital Formation." *Journal of Finance* 63:4, 1777–1803.

Garbaravicius, Thomas, and Frank Dierick. 2005. "Hedge Funds and Their Implications for Financial Stability." European Central Bank Occasional Paper 34. Available at https://www.ecb.europa.eu/pub/pdf/scpops/ecbocp34.pdf.

Gennaioli, Nicola, Andrei Shleifer, and Robert Vishny. 2015. "Money Doctors." *Journal of Finance* 70:1, 91–114.

Gilovich, Tom, Robert Vallone, and Amos Tversky. 1985. "The Hot Hand in Basketball: On the Misperception of Random Sequences." *Cognitive Psychology* 17:3, 295–314.

Gleason, Kimberly C., Ike Mathur, and Mark A. Peterson. 2004. "Analysis of Intraday Herding Behavior among the Sector ETFs." *Journal of Empirical Finance* 11:5, 681–694.

Goetzmann, William N., and Nadav Peles. 1997. "Cognitive Dissonance and Mutual Fund Investors." *Journal of Financial Research* 20:2, 145–158.

Gort, Christoph, Mei Wang, and Michael Siegrist. 2008. "Are Pension Fund Managers Overconfident?" *Journal of Behavioral Finance* 9:3, 163–170.

Griffin, John M., and Jin Xu. 2009. "How Smart Are the Smart Guys? A Unique View from Hedge Fund Stock Holdings." *Review of Financial Studies* 22:7, 2531–2570.

Gruber, Martin J. 1996. "Another Puzzle: The Growth in Actively Managed Mutual Funds." *Journal of Finance* 51:3, 783–810.

Hegde, Shantaram P., and John B. McDermott. 2004. "The Market Liquidity of DIAMONDS, Q's and Their Underlying Stocks." *Journal of Banking and Finance* 28:5, 1043–1067.

Hortacsu, Ali, and Chad Syverson. 2004. "Product Differentiation, Search Costs, and Competition in the Mutual Fund Industry: A Case Study of S&P 500 Index Funds." *Quarterly Journal of Economics* 119:2, 457–488.

Investment Company Institute (ICI). 2015. *Investment Company Factbook.* 55th Edition. Available at http://www.icifactbook.org/index.html.

Jensen, Michael C. 1968. "The Performance of Mutual Funds in the Period 1945–1964." *Journal of Finance* 23:2, 389–416.

Johan, Sofia A., April Knill, and Nathan Mauck. 2013. "Determinants of Sovereign Wealth Fund Investment in Private Equity vs Public Equity." *Journal of International Business Studies* 44:2, 155–172.

Kahneman, Daniel. 1973. *Attention and Effort.* Upper Saddle River, NJ: Prentice Hall.

Kahneman, Daniel, and Mark W. Riepe. 1998. "Aspects of Investor Psychology." *Journal of Portfolio Management* 24:4, 52–65.

Kahneman, Daniel, and Amos Tversky. 1979. "Prospect Theory: An Analysis of Decision under Risk." *Econometrica* 47:2, 263–291.

Khorana, Ajay, and Henri Servaes. 2012. "What Drives Market Share in the Mutual Fund Industry." *Review of Finance* 16:1, 81–113.

Knill, April M., Bong Soo Lee, and Nathan Mauck. 2012a. "Bilateral Political Relations and Sovereign Wealth Fund Investment." *Journal of Corporate Finance* 18:1, 108–123.

Knill, April M., Bong Soo Lee, and Nathan Mauck. 2012b. "Sovereign Wealth Fund Investment and the Return-to-Risk Performance of Target Firms." *Journal of Financial Intermediation* 21:2, 315–340.

Kokkonen, Joni, and Matti Suominen. 2015. "Hedge Funds and Stock Market Efficiency." *Management Science* 61:12, 2890–2904.

Kotter, Jason, and Ugur Lel. 2011. "Friends or Foes? Target Selection Decisions of Sovereign Wealth Funds and Their Consequences." *Journal of Financial Economics* 101:2, 360–381.

Kumar, Alok. 2009. "Who Gambles in the Stock Market?" *Journal of Finance* 64:4, 1889–1993.

Kurov, Alexander A., and Dennis J. Lasser. 2002. "The Effect of the Introduction of Cubes on the Nasdaq-100 Index Spot-futures Pricing Relationship." *Journal of Futures Markets* 22:3, 197–218.

Lakonishok, Josef, Andrei Shleifer, Richard Thaler, and Robert Vishny. 1991. "Window Dressing by Pension Fund Managers." NBER Working Paper No. 3617. Available at http://www.nber.org/papers/w3617.

Lakonishok, Josef, Andrew Shleifer, and Robert Vishny. 1992. "The Structure and Performance of the Money Management Industry." *Brookings Papers on Economics Activity: Microeconomics*, 339–391.

Lin, Yu-En, Whei-May Fan, and Hsiang-Hsuan Chih. 2014. "Throwing Good Money after Bad? The Impact of Escalation of Commitment of Mutual Fund Managers on Fund Performance." *Journal of Behavioral Finance* 15:1, 1–15.

Madura, Jeff, and Nivine Richie. 2004. "Overreaction of Exchange-Traded Funds during the Bubble of 1998–2002." *Journal of Behavioral Finance* 5:2, 91–104.

Madura, Jeff, and Nivine Richie. 2007. "Impact of the QQQ on Liquidity and Risk of the Underlying Stocks." *Quarterly Review of Economics and Finance* 47:3, 411–421.

Malkiel, Burton G., and Atanu Saha. 2005. "Hedge Funds: Risk and Return." *Financial Analysts Journal* 61:6, 80–88.

Mauck, Nathan, and Leigh Salzsieder. 2015. "Diversification Bias and the Law of One Price: An Experiment on Index Mutual Funds." *Journal of Behavioral Finance*. Forthcoming.

Organization for Economic Cooperation and Development (OECD). 2014. "OECD Institutional Investors Statistics 2014." Available at http://www.oecd-ilibrary.org/finance-and-investment/oecd-institutional-investors-statistics_2225207x.

Organization for Economic Cooperation and Development (OECD). 2015. "Pension Markets in Focus." Available at http://www.oecd.org/finance/private-pensions/globalpensionstatistics.htm.

Padungsaksawasdi, Chaiyuth, and Robert T. Daigler. 2014. "The Return-Implied Volatility Relation for Commodity ETFs." *Journal of Futures Markets* 34:3, 261–281.

Read, Daniel, and George Loewenstein. 1995. "Diversification Bias: Explaining the Discrepancy in Variety Seeking between Combined and Separated Choices." *Journal of Experimental Psychology: Applied* 1:1, 34–49.

Ritter, Jay R. 2004. "Behavioral Finance." *Pacific-Basin Finance Journal* 11:4, 429–437.

Sapp, Travis, and Aphish Tiwari. 2004. "Does Stock Return Momentum Explain the 'Smart Money' Effect?" *Journal of Finance* 59:6, 2605–2622.

Simonson, Itamar 1990. "The Effect of Purchase Quantity and Timing of Variety-Seeking Behavior." *Journal of Marketing Research* 28:2, 150–162.

Sirri, Erik R., and Peter Tufano. 1998. "Costly Search and Mutual Fund Flows." *Journal of Finance* 53:5, 1589–1622.

Stulz, René M. 2007. "Hedge Funds: Past, Present, and Future." *Journal of Economic Perspectives* 21:2, 175–194.

Thaler, Richard H. 1999. "Mental Accounting Matters." *Journal of Behavioral Decision Making* 12:3, 183–206.

Wahal, Sunil. 1996. "Pension Fund Activism and Firm Performance." *Journal of Financial and Quantitative Analysis* 31:1, 1–23.

Wermers, Russ. 1999. "Mutual Fund Herding and the Impact on Stock Prices." *Journal of Finance* 54:2, 581–622.

22

Current Trends in Successful International M&As

NANCY HUBBARD
Miriam Katowitz ('73) Endowed Chair in Management and Accounting
Goucher College

Introduction

Hubbard (2013) surveys financial executives from 162 companies who discussed their latest acquisitions. The nationalities of those companies included the United States, United Kingdom, Netherlands, France, Germany, Italy, Spain, Russia, Japan, China, India, Korea, Canada, and Brazil. Each country in the survey had at least one cross-border transaction for the studied period, for a total of 54 transactions. These transactions ranged in size from $75 million to $12.36 billion. The questionnaire asked the participants about the rationale for the acquisition, their synergy assessments, pricing valuations, due diligence, planning, any human resources issues that occurred after the transaction, and the overall success of the venture. The results of this survey will be explored in more depth in this chapter.

Hubbard (2013) conducts further in-depth interviews at 50 international companies, including their chief executives, board chairs, and senior directors, who discussed the issues, challenges, and successes involved in overseas expansion. The participants were from 16 countries, including the United Kingdom, France, Germany, Spain, Switzerland, Israel, Sweden, the United States, Caribbean, Brazil, South Africa, Nigeria, China, Japan, Australia, and India. They included executives from BP, Ford Motor Company, BT, Lafarge, Bank of China, JBS, Bayer, SAP, Sony, Hitachi, ABB, Santander, Cadbury Schweppes, Bae, Cargill, AB Group, and Teva. This chapter provides additional findings related to this research; the data are best understood in the context of current trends.

Current Trends: Economic Downturn Meets Global Risk Refocus

Four important business trends exist that are increasingly affecting international mergers and acquisitions (M&As): (1) the developing world's growth activity, (2) the resulting rise of the developing world acquirer, (3) the pursuit of lower degrees of integration with targets, and (4) global focusing. This chapter discusses each of these trends.

The economic tumult associated with the financial crisis of 2007–2008 brought with it an unexpected shift in M&A activity. Whereas previous acquisition activity, at least in large "mega deal" acquisitions of more than $1 billion, took place primarily in the developed world, the stagnation of those economies led organizations to turn instead to the rapidly developing economies for their growth opportunities. This situation, combined with infrastructure privatizations and a relaxing of overseas investment, created unprecedented opportunities in the nonindustrialized world (Chen and Findlay 2003), resulting in a dramatic increase in acquisition activity in these regions. In fact, by 2012 over one-third of all mega deals involved a developing world target, an acquirer, or both (Hubbard 2013).

Even within this arena, the demographics are changing. Organizations previously based in industrialized economies used to make acquisitions in the developing world. But transactions are increasingly occurring where both the target and the acquirer are in the developing world. The number of developing-world giants now actively acquiring in the industrialized world is also increasing, focusing on recognized brands and technology to supply both developed and emerging markets. Recent successful examples of this include acquisitions by JBS (Brazil) of Pilgrim's Pride, Lenovo (China) of IBM Personal Computers, Tata (India) of Jaguar, and Mittal (India) of Accelor. Even as economic growth slowly returns, the scope of activity in the developing world in terms of overall growth, consumer demand, and globalization means that this trend will continue for some time

A by-product of this activity has led to the second trend mentioned above: the growth of the developing-world acquirer. In fact, as of 2013 almost 20 percent of the world's largest companies now hail from nonindustrialized Europe, North America, and Japan, compared to 6 percent only 10 years ago (Hubbard 2013). Developing-world acquirers pose a new and considerable threat to Western industrialized companies, as these "new entrepreneurial giants" often operate their multi-billion-dollar behemoths as if they were a fraction of that size. They are familiar with the nuances of operating in the developing world, with its uncertainty and the flexibility that it entails, and they are innovative, able to do more with fewer resources. Yiu, Lau, and Bruton (2007) find that developing-world companies are more resourceful and able to stretch their technology further than their industrialized counterparts. For example, developing-world giants use technology and shallow organizational structures to facilitate fast decision making—a prerequisite for operating in the developing world's immature markets. This change has been borne out of necessity; previously, these companies did not have the resources to build bureaucratic systems, instead relying on their lean structures to reduce costs. They are more flexible in their partnering options, often pursuing "coopetition" (i.e., working with a competitor in one market only to compete in another), a concept often foreign to industrialized giants simply because it has never been required (Luo 2004).

When these developing-world globalizers make acquisitions internationally, they are forced to use existing target management, as their lean and flat organizational structures have not had employees to replace them. Thus, many of these businesses' integrations are highly decentralized, with a strong "hands off" approach. They target those few business areas for collaboration and investment, and leave the rest of the operations alone

(Luo and Tung 2007). The end result of this approach, known as *partnering*, is one in which acquired employees often feel they are in a joint venture with the acquirer, rather than acting as a subsidiary (Kale and Singh 2009). With lower degrees of integration and less cultural overlay between acquirer and target, the acquired company's employees are less affected by the acquisition and thus more likely to remain with the acquiring firm (Hubbard 2013).

Previously, some viewed this approach as a weakness. Now, when combined with sophisticated communication structures, this leanness promotes agility and innovation (Hubbard 2013). An increasing body of academics finds that emerging world entrepreneurial giants have used many characteristics of what had traditionally been a disadvantage—liability of newness—and transformed them into a competitive advantage (Autio, Sapienza, and Almeida 2000; Zahra, Sapienza, and Davidsson 2006; Wood, Khavul, Perez-Nordtvedt, Prakhya, Dabrowski, and Zheng 2011).

Some developing-world acquirers have begun adopting this approach with their increased market-entry activity. The end result is a marked shift toward using a "lighter touch" during acquisition implementation, as opposed to the traditional, immediately implemented integration plan. This shift is logical, because less opportunity exists for integration with existing operations when entering a new market. Some acquirers indicate that this approach is key to reducing any cultural conflict and for enhancing retention of target employees, which are the two primary concerns associated with international acquisitions. As will be discussed, the senior executives interviewed for this chapter identified using a lighter touch as the greatest reason for a successful acquisition.

THE RISE OF GLOBALFOCUSING

After losing their domestic divisional diversification, companies in the developed world began spreading their risk geographically, buying related businesses overseas. This trend is called *globalfocusing* (Meyer 2006). Starting in the mid-1980s, these companies also began a process of de-mergering, or dismantling and selling off their unrelated divisions. Repeatedly, diversified conglomerates with high-performing divisions were acquired by break-up specialists, who sold those divisions to related companies from which the acquirer could secure substantial operational synergies. These "Noah's Ark" acquisitions—where the combined organizations have two of everything, including finance departments, information technology (IT) systems, head offices, manufacturing locations, and branches—were ripe for rationalization and large cost savings. The divisional targets were worth more to their related companies because of these cost savings than their cash-generative value was to their previous parent company conglomerates. This trend continued through the 1990s, ushering in a new millennia of engulfing businesses with divisional diversification. In fact, by 2001, more than one-third of Britain's largest 100 companies were de-merging (Hubbard 2001). This trend continued domestically until only a handful of true industrialized conglomerates remained. Indeed, GE, a bastion of conglomerate performance, has only recently gone back to its industrial roots, eschewing much of its previous diversification (Krauskopf 2015).

Globalfocusing continues today both in the developed world and increasingly in the emerging economies. The large-scale de-merging process meant that highly attractive related targets were available—prestigious brands that simply did not fit into their divestor's industry. The Adams confectionary group, including the Chiclets gum brand, highlights this journey. Adams began the 1990s as a division of the pharmaceutical giant Pfizer. Pfizer's executives decided to concentrate on its core pharmaceutical business, and as a result divested Adams in 2003. In turn, Cadbury Schweppes bought Adams, adding a Latin American footprint that complemented Cadbury's U.K. coverage. Cadbury Schweppes then decided to focus on confectionary and de-merged their Schweppes division in 2008, which then became the Dr Pepper Snapple Group. Kraft ultimately acquired Cadbury in a hostile bid in 2010, thus globalfocusing themselves (Cadbury 2015).

Globalfocusing continues to offer organizations compelling opportunities that are capable of instantaneously enlarging that organization's geographic profile. These opportunities are called *transformational acquisitions* (Hubbard 2013). Hubbard finds as many as 15 percent of large multinational acquisitions are considered geographically transformational, propelling these organizations into new regions quickly and with substantial scale. While the extent of complementary geographic fit varies among organizations as they are juxtaposed, these often become target opportunities for more than one acquirer. As such, defensive acquisition of potentially transformational acquisitions for competitors has also become increasingly prevalent.

Interestingly, globalfocusing appears to be a Western multinational phenomenon, as Asian companies continue to pursue diversified business group profiles. *Chaebols* in South Korea and *kerietsus* in Japan—both representing the antithesis of globalfocusing—have existed for decades, and now government-sponsored business groups in China are increasingly becoming the norm (Lee and Jin 2009). Thus, no indication exists that Asian companies will follow the Western pattern of globalfocusing in the foreseeable future. Whether globalfocusing is a stage of corporate evolution or a proactively viable long-term business strategy is unknown at this point. But for now, it remains the norm rather than the exception.

The move toward globalfocusing partly explains the shift in what international acquisitions are seen to achieve. Since the 1990s, international expansion secured a reduced cost base primarily by lowering manufacturing costs or, in a few cases, creating economies-of-scale consolidations with an existing operation—an international version of the Noah's Ark acquisition (Kogat 1985; KPMG Management Consulting 1997). Since the mid-2000s, though, organizations have begun pursuing overseas acquisitions not for potential cost savings but to increase revenue, as they attempt to reach the developing world's potential consumers with their rapidly increasing purchasing power. Extending the work of Hubbard (2013), and based on her original survey, this chapter shows that almost half (48 percent) of cross-border acquisitions have been completed for market entry—findings supported by other researchers (Peltier 2004; Staples 2008).

The Attractiveness of Foreign Direct Investment Markets

The survey results (Hubbard 2013) has revealed what makes this new potential market so attractive. The responses included both financial and intangible measurements, which when combined offered an assessment of a market's attractiveness from which the respondents could rank opportunities. Some criteria, such as growth of gross domestic product (GDP) and overall potential customer market size, are obvious and self-explanatory. Others, such as maturity of the stock market and availability of local resources, are less apparent and measurable. Table 22.1 provides a comprehensive list of CEO responses in terms of their criteria for market attractiveness and is uniform across all those interviewed unless otherwise noted; as noted earlier, the respondents operate in a global capacity, although their relative importance differs per respondent.

To begin, several intangible indicators of market attractiveness warrant further clarification. Executives identified stock market maturity as important for two reasons: First, it provides an existing exit route via floatation if they consider divestment in the future. Second, and more important, it dictates the extent to which potential acquisition targets are available through public offering. In cases of immature or underdeveloped stock markets, few if any targets are available except through private purchase, thus greatly impeding the ability to acquire.

Table 22.1 **Financial and Intangible Factors for Market Attractiveness, According to Executives from 50 International Organizations**

Financial/Economic Factors	*Intangible Factors*
GDP size	Extent of nationalism
Growth of GDP	Difference in local country culture to existing operations
Cost and availability of raw materials	Necessary product tailorization for local differences
Size of local consumer market	Maturity of banks
Maturity and existing demand for product/local markets	Maturity of stock market
Existing competition	Complexity of local regulations, taxes and tariffs/bureaucracy of local governments/
Labor market cost and availability	Ability to acquire human capital (specific to Japanese respondents)
Infrastructure levels and cost	Supply chain availability
	Proximity to other potential export markets
	Corruption

Note: This table outlines the responses given by senior executives of 50 global businesses when asked, in an open-ended question: "What made a new international market attractive?" The answers are grouped into financially or economically based factors and intangible factors. Financial and economic factors are those considered to finite and measurable. Intangibles are more subjective in nature.

The executives also noted the maturity of the banking industry as critical for ensuring working capital. They also viewed unique local cultures as more challenging. In such cases, if the opportunity is great enough, executives enter markets despite local cultures, although modifying their mode of entry. In these cases, joint ventures and acquisitions are more attractive than greenfield investments. *Greenfield investment* involves entering a market organically with no partners while building new facilities and/or local relationships. Nationalism is a factor in certain jurisdictions and industries, especially energy, natural resources, and infrastructure delivery. Almost all Japanese company respondents mentioned the ability to acquire human capital as a key measure of a market's attractiveness. Interestingly, executives from no other nation mentioned this attribute as a factor.

Some factors that do not appear as important are somewhat surprising. In terms of economic and financial factors, the executives did not mention exchange rates and exchange restrictions as major impediments to entering a market. Neither is ownership restrictions seen as reducing market attractiveness; in fact, executives rarely ruled out a market's attractiveness because of an inability to own the operation outright. In fact, the opposite occurred: if a market was deemed attractive, the executives find a way in which to enter that market, whether or not by acquisition, joint venture, or greenfield investment.

As for intangible factors, the executives surveyed considered a corrupt government a minor barrier to investment, with the vast majority of respondents indicating that avoiding corrupt practices is just part of doing business globally. Similarly, respondents spoke of political instability in the same manner; with the increase in economic globalization comes the inevitable possibility of civil unrest—it is just part of doing business in less developed jurisdictions.

The Reasons for Acquisitions

For those companies choosing to expand internationally, acquisition remains the most preferred method over both joint ventures and greenfield investment when entering a new market (Hubbard 2013). Control was not identified as the greatest benefit but, rather, the ability to enter a market quickly with the requisite size, complete with intact supply and distribution chains. Indeed, control appeared to be a secondary benefit overall, albeit it was of primary concern in certain industries such as IT (Chen and Findlay 2003; Hubbard 2013). Although providing the same level of control, greenfield investment appears to be too slow, especially when entering fast-paced or changing markets. Similarly, some viewed joint ventures as slower than acquisitions, with the added concern of often not possessing clear control in many cases. Thus, as Chen and Findlay (pp. 25–26) suggest,

> For a latecomer to a market or a new field of technology, cross-border M&As can provide a way to catch up rapidly. With the acceleration of globalization, enhanced competition and shorter product life cycles, there are increasing pressures for firms to respond quickly to opportunities in the fast changing global economic environment. Cross-border M&As can provide a way to catch up rapidly.

Thus, the rationale for acquisition falls clearly into both meeting financial/strategic objectives and some irrational considerations. As discussed in the following sections, the research has shown that numerous acquisitions occur for irrational reasons. Included in this irrational behavior are activities such as overinflating the purchase prices and underestimating the potential synergies.

Figure 22.1 illustrates the rationales given by the surveyed executives for their last acquisition. The respondents offered both financial and intangible reasons, with market entry being the overwhelming one for cross-border acquisition. Combining market entry with transformational acquisitions—those transactions that instantly take the organization to the next level, with a substantial increase in geography—accounts for almost 60 percent of their rationale for acquisitions. Top-line growth, following a client into a new geography, takes the total of "revenue-enhancing acquisition objectives" to almost 70 percent. Cost-savings acquisitions, either through cheaper sourcing or economics of scale, account for only 8 percent. Although all respondents indicated that revenue-enhancing acquisition objectives factored into their decision making, only the

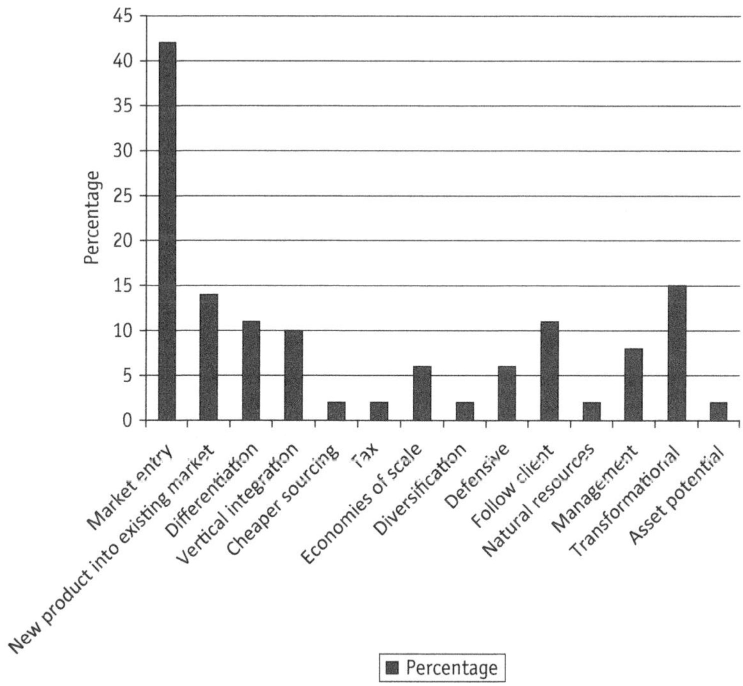

Figure 22.1 Reasons Given for Most Recent Acquisition from Executives of 50 International Companies. This figure highlights the reasons given by 50 senior executives for their last international acquisition. Respondents could provide more than one reason for an acquisition. The results demonstrate that market entry is the overwhelming reason given for most international acquisitions. When combined with other revenue-producing rationale, such as introducing a new product into an existing market and following a client, top-line growth is clearly the foremost acquisition strategy at present.

Japanese respondents indicated that cost savings factored into their decision-making process.

The intangible reasons for acquisition varied, especially among Japanese and developing-world respondents. In fact, every non-European and non-American respondent gave at least one intangible reason for an acquisition. These reasons include gaining access to new technology, natural resources, and management; diversification; and defensive acquisitions. Although executives from all nations indicated that acquiring new technology is an important reason for acquisitions, there were key differences mentioned in the other areas of intangibility, based on nationality. Japanese respondents were the only nationality represented to list acquiring key management resources as a major objective. They were also the only ones to indicate that differentiation from key competitors and diversification are key acquisition objectives. In fact, all the Japanese participants indicated differentiation factors in their decision making in some form, whereas no European or American firms indicated this factor in their decision making.

Despite its being important in understanding transformational acquisitions, only a small number of participants mentioned defensive acquisitions. As discussed previously, pending acquisitions could be transformational for more than one acquiring company. In these cases, securing the target for the acquisition not only serves to transform the acquiring business but also keeps a competitor from accomplishing the same.

IRRATIONAL REASONS FOR ACQUISITIONS

Although no respondents indicated irrational reasons for making acquisitions, other studies have painted a long and vivid history of irrational behavior in justifying acquisitions. Hunt, Lees, Grumbar, and Vivian (1987) find that irrational or nonstrategic reasons motivated well over half of U.K. acquirers, as illustrated in table 22.2. Subsequent research finds that managers instigated 26 percent of international acquisitions by U.S. firms for their own utility, as opposed to creating value for shareholders (Seth, Song, and Pettit 2000). Further research also supports this finding (Barclay and Holderness 1989; Hietala, Kaplan, and Robinson 2003; Gondhalekar, Sant, and Ferris 2004).

Several theories have been attempted to explain the irrational motivators behind this kind of behavior, including envy theory, free cash flow theory, defensive behavior, and the hubris hypothesis.

- *Envy theory.* Envy theory suggests that chief executives see their counterparts as conducting large transactions and getting greater remuneration for it. They in turn try to emulate that behavior (Goel and Thacker 2009), creating a manifestation of the principal–agent problem in which executives maximize their own utility and opportunity above that of shareholders (Seth et al. 2000; Zalewski 2001; Kummar 2006). Executives are rewarded primarily based on the size of their company, rather than by its profitability, further encouraging this behavior (Coeurdacier, De Santis, and Aviat 2009; Goel and Thacker 2009).
- *Free cash flow theory.* This theory suggests that executives may not want to relinquish funds to shareholders via dividends, instead opting to spend the money even on value-destroying acquisitions (Lang, Stulz, and Walkling 1991; Servaes 1991).

Table 22.2 **Irrational Reasons Cited for Acquisitions**

Irrational Reasons for Acquisition	*Dominant or Primary Motivation (%)*	*Secondary Motivation (%)*
Sending the right signals to the financial markets	20	40
Chairperson's insistence	8	35
Retrieve "face"	5	18
Rise in technology perception	0	15
Impress competition	3	8
Buying a tradition	0	8
Cash cow for other bids	3	5
Sort out another problem	0	3

Note: This table highlights the findings of Hunt et al. (1987) when they interviewed executives from large U.K. organizations as to their reasons for acquiring. In cases of both domestic and international acquisitions, Hunt et al. find that irrational—that is, nonfinancial or strategic— reasoning was given as a primary reason for almost 40 percent of acquisitions. Secondary motivations were even more prevalent when respondents were able to give more than one reason for acquiring. This evidence suggests that while financial and strategic reasoning for acquisitions dominates motivation, irrational motivations still need to be taken into account.

- *Defensive behavior.* Some executives engage in acquisitions to grow the business purely for personal defensive means—"eat or be eaten" or a "good defense is a strong offense" as the case may be (Gorton, Kahl, and Rosen 2009). Thus, executives acquire a target firm before it can buy their firm, which could otherwise result in executives subsequently losing their jobs.
- *Hubris hypothesis.* A long-established and much-tested theory of irrationality in acquisition objectives, this is otherwise known as chief executive overconfidence. First put forward by Roll (1986), the theory holds that chief executive officers (CEOs) overestimate their own abilities in achieving acquisition synergies and other financial objectives, leading them to complete the transactions even when presented with new and less favorable information and especially when it applies to potential cost savings and synergies (Bogan and Just 2009). As a result, the acquirer often pays too much for the target (Roll 1986; Eccles, Lanes, and Wilson 1999; Schmidt 1999; Lanes, Stewart, and Francis 2001; Cartwright and Schoenberg 2006).

Acquisition Success and Failure

No matter how the research is analyzed, the unavoidable truth is that acquisitions are not guaranteed to create value for internationalizing firms; in fact, it may be quite the contrary. Rostand (1994) finds that, at best, 45 percent fail to deliver their strategic objectives; at worst, between 60 and 70 percent do not reach their intended financial performance (Rostand 1994; Lasfer and Morzaria 2004; Stahl and Voight 2008). The majority of research agrees with countless studies finding the ability to generate value is inconsistent, with a 50/50 chance of being successful in creating shareholder value (Lubatkin, Srinivasan, and Merchant 1997; Brouthers, van Hastenburg, and van den Ven 1998; Agrawal and Jaffe 2000; Conn, Cosh, Guest, and Hughes 2001).

Figures 22.2 and 22.3 illustrate that, in the survey of 162 participants, respondents indicated they are more successful in acquiring than has been reported in previous surveys of both domestic and international acquisitions. Although self-reported success runs the risk of being more favorable than other forms of testing, previous research finds that self-reported responses are on a par with other forms of empirical testing (Hunt et al. 1987; KPMG 1999). This finding corresponds with the executive interviews, who also indicated greater levels of acquisition success (Hubbard 2013). Although such evidence bodes well for creating shareholder value via acquisition, it may be more related to how acquisitions are implemented than any deep lessons learned by acquirers.

The shift in the acquisition landscape toward market-entry objectives requires a different skill set for the acquisition success. In economies-of-scale acquisitions, success requires a systematic ability to implement complex operational integrations—combining systems and procedures, firing employees, retraining those who remain, and melding organizational cultures into a new, cohesive organization. Strong human

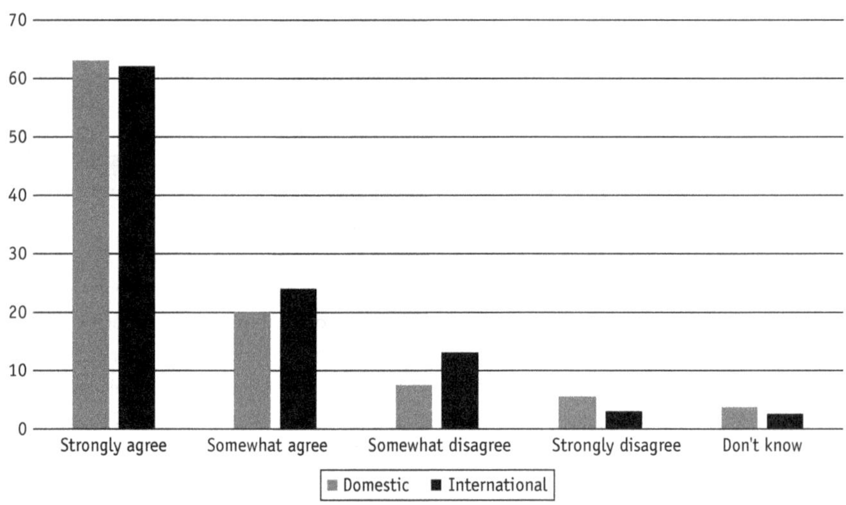

Figure 22.2 Views on Amount of Shareholder Value Gained from Most Recent Acquisition. The survey asked respondents about their most recent acquisition and whether it created shareholder value. The 108 domestic acquirers and 52 international acquirers indicated relatively uniformly that their latest acquisition did create value. More than 60 percent of both domestic and international acquirers strongly agreed that this is the case. The only area not seeing some differentiation is in the category of "somewhat disagreeing," in which international acquisitions were almost twice as likely to answer in this manner.

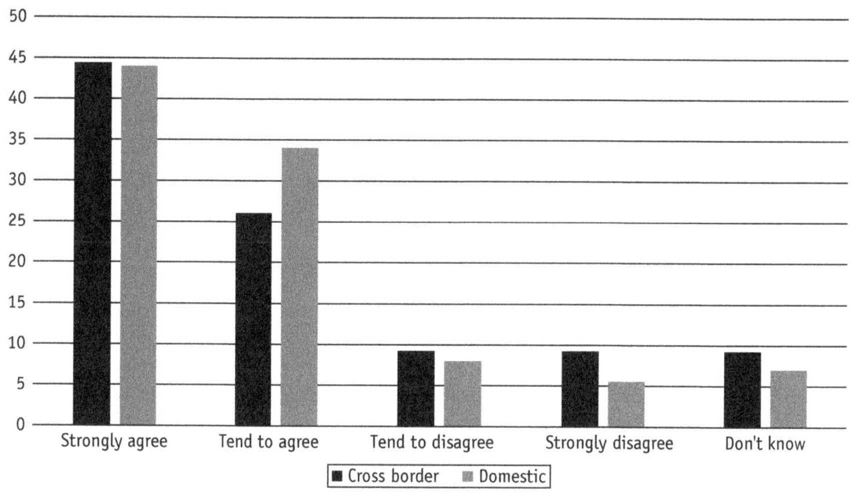

Figure 22.3 Views on Competitive Advantage Gained from Most Recent Acquisition This figure indicates the 160 respondents' answers when asked if their most recent acquisition made the company more competitive. Both the 108 domestic respondents and the 52 international respondents strongly agreed with that statement. More international respondents indicated that their acquisitions made their company more competitive compared to domestic acquirers, which had a higher percentage indicating that the acquisition did not make their company more competitive.

resource and IT departments, bolstered by program management expertise and often supported by specialist consulting firms who bring with them time-tested processes, are necessary for achieving the requisite organizational synergies. In the vast majority of cases, these gains simply fail to materialize as anticipated. Many examples exist in which the acquisition process not only failed to deliver its intended value but also damaged the acquirer's underlying business, owing to an overextension of resources. For example, Daimler's acquisition of Chrysler, Morrison's acquisition of Safeway, and Bank of America's acquisition of Countrywide all show how value-creating, economies-of-scale acquisitions destroyed value. As Fitzpatrick (2012) notes, the initial purchase price of Countrywide was $2.5 billion, but the estimated acquisition cost to Bank of America was more than $40 billion—to date. Acquisition success relies on a combination of financial rigor and human resource expertise for implementation; the sheer size and complexity of the process often makes success unachievable.

In this new world of international acquisitions, success is still derived from financial rigor and human resources (HR) expertise—it is the implementation of strategic objectives with a financial and human perspective. The areas being affected differ, however. Whereas managers achieved previous acquisition objectives through cost cutting, the current trend is for seeking gains in market share, not reductions in overlapping operations. Managers achieve their objectives through revenue growth opportunities, with synergies centered on creating value through intra-firm collaboration; this can be seen in cross-selling products in the new geographies and introducing new products into existing markets.

Little if anything exists to integrate economies-of-scale objectives, and the complex issues they bring are simply irrelevant today. Success relies on retaining existing expertise and using it throughout the organization, rather than on reducing costs. In other words, success depends on collaboration and retention, rather than reduction and harmonization. The skills are still financial in rigor and human resources and in IT for delivery, but they differ. Success depends on the acquired management remaining in place so as to achieve clear and measured organizational goals. These goals are achieved by managing the acquired unit's employees in a hands-off, almost partnering approach, supported by effective horizontal communication and decision-making channels. In other words, the acquiring companies achieve success by using a "lighter touch" in implementation. The next section provides a discussion of these elements.

Reasons for Acquisition Success

KPMG (1999) serves as an excellent template for understanding the complexities involved in achieving acquisition success internationally. The study conducted in 1999 asked executives at 107 large publicly traded companies what activities they undertook before acquiring internationally. The companies' performance was then tracked to ascertain performance differences versus their industrial peers.

As the transactions were large, they should have affected performance. Of those companies undertaking six key activities, all experienced increased performance versus their industrial peers. Only one of those that undertook some but not all of the six activities experienced an increase in relative performance. Those six activities were a combination of financially based and behaviorally oriented reasons. The three financially based activities were (1) conducting due diligence beyond financial and legal indicators, (2) having a rigorous pre-acquisition plan, and (3) undertaking thorough synergy papers. The three behaviorally oriented activities were: (1) having a process for dealing with cultural differences between the target and acquirer, (2) introducing strong internal communication process, and (3) deciding the top team early.

The types of acquisitions undertaken when this KPMG survey was conducted differ in intent from the majority of acquisitions being undertaken today. KPMG conducted the survey at the height of the economies-of-scale acquisition wave, whereas today most acquisitions are targeting top-line growth. Yet activities undertaken then are still relevant today. Following is an examination of these activities, with data provided by the Hubbard (2013) study of 54 international and 108 domestic survey respondents, as well as her 50 in-depth senior executive interviews.

FINANCIALLY BASED SUCCESS FACTORS

The three financially based activities undertaken by acquirers *before* the transaction that added value are: (1) conducting due diligence beyond financial and legal indicators, (2) having a rigorous pre-acquisition plan, and (3) undertaking thorough synergy papers. Synergy papers are pre-acquisition synergy analyses required for British acquisitions in publicly quoted transactions as a way of ensuring the cost-saving benefits are considered reasonable. Conducting due diligence before a transaction is normal, but successful acquirers conducted due diligence that went beyond purely financial and legal aspects. Successful acquirers also undertook extensive pre-acquisition planning often based on comprehensive synergy paper analysis. This process occurred even if the target was neither a publicly traded company nor located in a jurisdiction where this was legally required. Each activity will be discussed in turn.

Holistic Due Diligence

The KPMG (1999) survey finds a relationship between holistic due diligence and international acquisition success. Logic suggests that any additional knowledge gathered on the target before an acquisition would be beneficial in terms of both valuing the target and increasing the understanding of strategic fit. When asked about the key reasons for acquisition success in their last acquisition, the senior executives gave extensive due diligence as the equal highest response (Hubbard 2013). As seen later in this chapter, this suggests that those who pursue additional information appreciate its value.

Surprisingly, companies conduct little due diligence before international acquisitions in many cases. Table 22.3 displays findings from the large-scale survey, which asked the 54 cross-border respondents about the types of due diligence undertaken before the

Table 22.3 **Comparison of Due Diligence Undertaken by Domestic and Cross-border Acquirers**

	Domestic Acquisitions	*Cross-border Acquisitions (%)*
Financial	72	78
Commercial	61	63
Legal	56	57
Operational	57	52
Strategic	43	48
Information Technology	72	33
HR	47	19
Technological	1	4
Environmental	4	0
Tax	0	2
Other	3	7
None	3	4

Note: This table highlights the findings of a 162-company survey in which executives of 108 companies discussed their domestic acquisitions and 54 participants discussed their international acquisitions. Financial due diligence is the most common due diligence undertaken by both domestic and cross-border acquirers. Commercial, legal, operational, and strategic due diligence is also undertaken by roughly half of respondents in both domestic and international acquisitions. The biggest differences between domestic and international acquirers is revealed in their information technology and human resource due diligence. In both cases, domestic acquirers are far more likely to pursue due diligence when compared to their international counterparts.

transaction. Respondents reported that they completed 22 percent of overseas acquisitions without any financial due diligence, and 43 percent pursued no legal due diligence. Respondents reported conducting 7 percent of acquisitions with no due diligence.

Although almost all acquisitions should necessitate undertaking the financial and legal due diligence, KPMG (1999) finds an association between collecting information in other business functions and greater acquisition success. These areas include commercial due diligence, strategic due diligence, HR due diligence including information on the target middle and senior management, and IT due diligence. With the majority of international acquisitions pursuing top-line growth, the lack of commercial due diligence is surprising, although its dearth mirrors domestic due diligence activity. The two areas where the due diligence undertaken in overseas acquisitions differs substantially from domestic acquisitions involve HR and IT. International transactions are less than half as likely to have pursued this information when compared to their domestic counterparts. With "soft issues" being mentioned as key for cross-border acquisition success, the lack of due diligence in this area can be detrimental and these findings are paradoxical when overseas acquirers report greater acquisition success than before.

As many targets in the developing world are privately held, one relevant area of due diligence is an understanding of the expectations of the target's owners. In many cases, the owners are not selling to the highest bidder but, rather, to the organization that best meets its business philosophy and fit (Hubbard 2013). Regardless, their support is critical to completing the transaction; understanding their aspirations, expectations and concerns is paramount for ensuring the transaction is completed successfully.

Pre-acquisition Planning

Researchers repeatedly associate pre-acquisition planning with overall acquisition success (Buono and Bowditch 1989; Hubbard 1999; Lasfer and Morzaria 2004; Stahl and Voight 2008). Pre-acquisition planning was a key to their success, according to the senior executives interviewed (Hubbard 2013). Adequate planning provides the basis for virtually all other activities, including the synergistic fit with the acquirer's business; what, if any, of the target's assets are to be divested; key external and internal communication messages; top team selection; and pricing. It serves as the foundation for the synergy evaluations that follow.

The large-scale survey (Hubbard 2013) asked both domestic and international acquirers if they had a clear post-deal strategy before completion. As figure 22.4 shows, a combined 72 percent responded that they did, with 20 percent declining to answer the question and 8 percent responding that they did not. There was little differentiation between domestic and international acquirers. When the participants were asked when they began their planning, international acquirers indicated their planning was begun earlier than domestic acquirers, with 40 percent of the former beginning their planning at least five months before completing the transaction—over twice the percentage of domestic acquirers planning at that stage. In fact, almost 20 percent of international acquirers reported not planning until after completion of the transaction (a percentage also higher than among the domestic acquirers). This results is a residual effect delaying the synergy evaluation, communication, and other HR issues, and makes addressing such matters in a timely manner practically impossible.

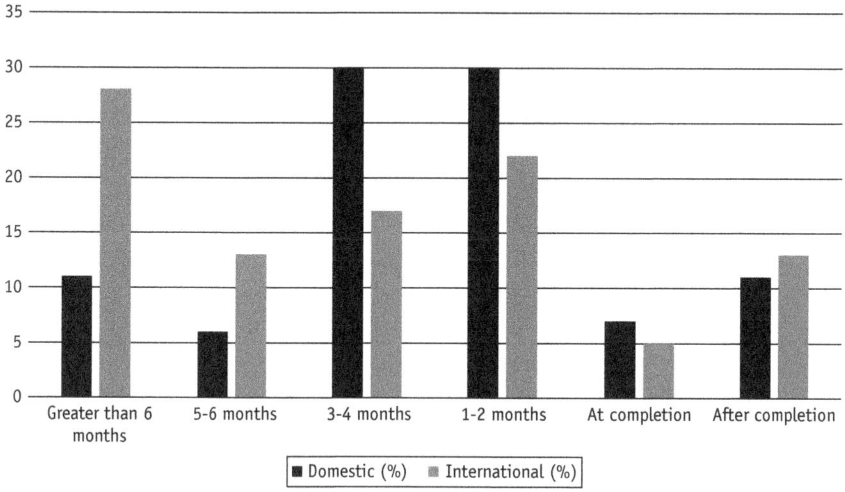

Figure 22.4 Advance Planning Time for Domestic and International Acquisitions. The figure reports the results of a survey asking 160 respondents when they began their planning before the acquisition completion. The 108 domestic acquirers and 52 international acquirers had differing approaches. A large percentage (28 percent) of international acquirers began their planning well in advance of the transaction's completion, compared to only 11 percent of domestic acquirers. In contrast, domestic acquirers were more likely to begin their planning in the four months before the transaction's completion. In both cases, a small but meaningful number of acquirers did not engage in planning before the acquisition.

Synergy

Understanding the financial costs and benefits to be derived by an acquisition is important for transactions of publicly held companies. Although not required for privately held company transactions, understanding the synergistic benefits, according to some researchers, considering the costs and time frames of a potential acquisition is critical for success (Lasfer and Morzaria 2004; Stahl and Voight 2008). With this in mind, the Hubbard survey asked both international and domestic respondents how much time they devoted to synergistic evaluations before completing the deals. As Figure 22.5 shows, almost half of all respondents reported investing little or no time in quantifying the synergies between the two organizations.

As previously discussed, recent international acquisitions have increasingly targeted top-line revenue opportunities—acquiring new markets and customers for existing products. The survey asked both domestic and international acquirers about what synergies they anticipated in their most recent acquisition. As Figure 22.6 shows, synergies being sought by international businesses focus on marketing (24 percent compared to none in domestic transactions), and less so on operations, back office, procurement, and property-cost reductions. Headcount reductions in which 60 percent of domestic acquirers anticipate synergies accounted for only 2 percent of international transactions. Thus, cost-reduction synergies across the board are less pursued in international acquisitions. This finding has a domino effect for HR. As discussed in the following

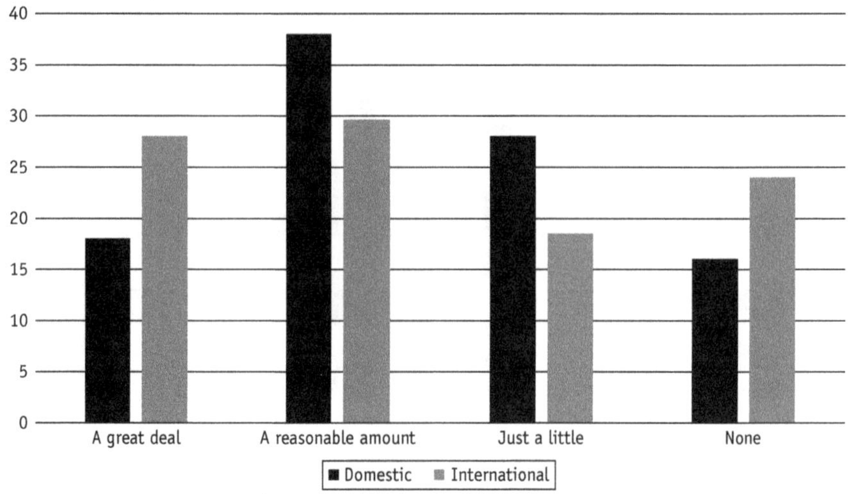

Figure 22.5 Comparison of Time Spent on Synergistic Evaluations, Domestic and International Acquirers. This figure highlights the different approaches taken by those acquiring domestically and internationally. Researchers asked respondents how much time they spent undertaking synergy evaluations. The 108 respondents undertaking domestic acquisitions were more likely to spend some time on synergy evaluation work, with almost two-thirds indicating they spent either a reasonable or just a little time on that activity. The 52 international acquirers, however, were more skewed at both ends of the spectrum, indicating they either spent a great deal or time or no time at all on synergy evaluations when compared to domestic acquirers.

section, the HR implications for top-line revenue synergies differ dramatically from cost-reduction synergies—retention and collaboration become paramount.

One opportunity that globalfocusing has provided internationalizing organizations is the ability to acquire sizable blue chip divisions that simply do not fit the divestor's new strategic direction. In many cases, the divested divisions were often starved of management time and resources, as they did not support the organization's core business thrust and as a result suffered from "orphan syndrome"—being unwanted and unappreciated by their parent company. If acquired in a transformational acquisition, these divisions immediately become integral to the acquirer's main business direction and can experience a radical rejuvenation. It is a golden opportunity for both the target and the acquirer.

BEHAVIORALLY BASED SUCCESS FACTORS

The KPMG survey (1999) reports three qualitative or behavioral elements considered critical to acquisition success: (1) having a process for dealing with cultural differences between the target and acquirer, (2) introducing a strong internal communication process, and (3) identifying the top team early. Additional research supports these activities as essential for acquisition success (Hubbard and Purcell 2001; Schweiger and Goulet

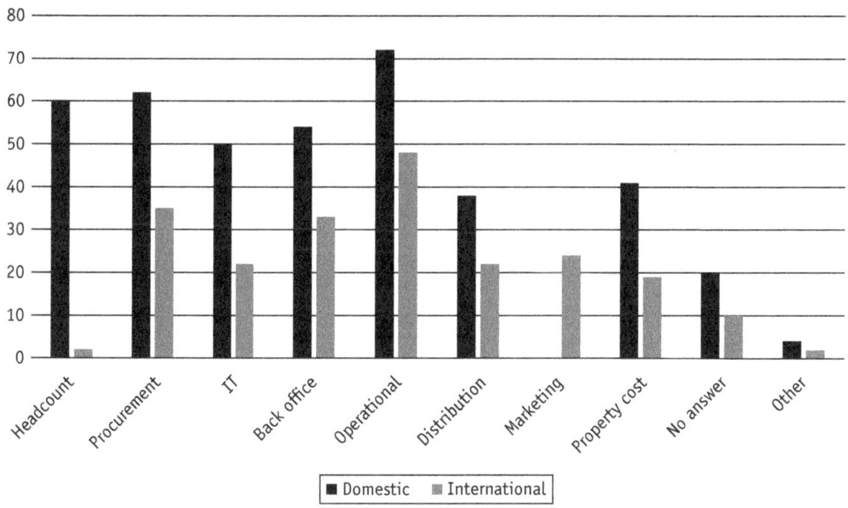

Figure 22.6 Anticipated Synergies for Domestic and International Acquisitions. This figure highlights the differences in anticipated synergies between domestic and international acquisitions. The survey asked the 108 domestic acquirers what synergies they expected upon completing their acquisition. They indicated they expected synergies in terms of headcount, procurement, and operations in at least 60 percent of domestic acquisitions. When asked the same question, only 2 percent of the 52 companies acquiring internationally foresaw headcount reductions, with substantially lower indications of other operationally based cost savings. Instead, almost one-fourth of them anticipated marketing savings, compared to none of the domestic acquirers.

2005; Cartwright and Schoenberg 2006; Lodorfos and Boateng 2006). Each of these findings is discussed in the following sections.

Cultural Differences

Culture can be defined as the systems and processes that lead to accepted behavior in an organization. Cultural differences exist between countries, organizations within the same country, and divisions and functions within one company.

Cultural differences, or "culture clashes" between the target and the acquirer, can be major impediments to acquisition success (Schmidt 1999; Applebaum and Gandell 2003; Weber and Camerer 2003; Badrtalei and Bates 2007). Walter (1985) suggests that culture conflicts account for as much as a 25 to 30 percent drop in performance after acquisition implementation. Other research finds that the performance drop does not result from the actual difference in culture, but from how the acquirer has addressed the cultural differences (Hubbard 1999; Hubbard and Purcell 2001; Applebaum and Gandell 2003; Rottig 2009). KPMG (1999) supports this position, suggesting that the cultural differences do not cause the problems, but that a lack of proactively managing those differences does. Companies acknowledging the cultural differences preemptively manage those disparities and experience success.

Recent research continues to highlight the perceived importance of culture, especially in cross-border acquisitions. The KPMB survey (1999) asked respondents to indicate their three biggest HR concerns post-acquisition. Figure 22.7 shows that for the Hubbard survey, almost 70 percent of cross-border acquirers reported that cultural differences are among their three top concerns, and was noted as the top response by almost twofold. Domestic acquirers were half as likely to indicate they felt cultural issues are a potential problem, suggesting that the acquisition's international aspect is the main cause of cultural concern.

Although cultural differences complicate cross-border transactions, the degree of integration can be a mitigating factor. Put simply, as the degree of integration decreases, cultural differences affect fewer employees. Conversely, as the degree of integration increases, more employees are exposed to the differences. In cases of high cultural dissimilarities, some acquirers opt for a lower degree of integration, thereby reducing the number of employees affected by the cultural difference. In doing so, they are borrowing the "partnering" approach previously discussed.

The increase in market-entry acquisition strategies reduces the frequency of fully integrated targets, again reducing potential cultural impact. Some organizations facing unavoidable cultural differences use more specialized coping tools, such as internal cultural facilitators who assist affected executives in operating in both organizations' cultures, introducing widespread cultural training tools, and employing culture audits—all designed to assist affected employees in becoming culturally "bilingual" (Hubbard 1999).

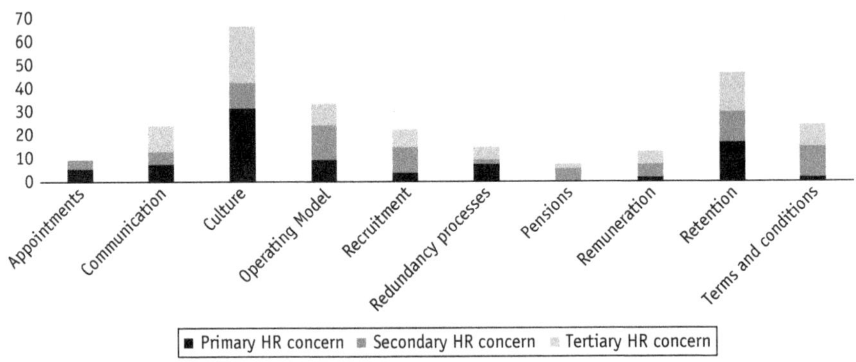

Figure 22.7 Top Three HR Concerns after-Acquisition by Cross-Border Company. This figure highlights the human resource concerns identified by international acquirers. The survey asked respondents to identify their three major HR concerns during the acquisition implementation. The top two responses of cultural differences and employee retention outpaced other responses, with the latter being the overwhelming primary concern. The operating model, communication, terms and conditions, and recruitment were also important concerns. Retention issues may be exacerbated, given the tardiness in achieving appointments at the department-head level.

Strong Internal Communication

Besides KPMG (1999), other studies have highlighted the role of internal communication in acquisitions (Piekkari, Vaara, Tienari, and Säntti 2005; Lodorfos and Boateng 2006; Stahl and Voight 2008). Yet, adequate internal pre-acquisition communication often is neglected, for several reasons. First, such communication relies on senior executives to craft and deliver the message at a time when they are usually involved in the deal negotiation and execution. Second, secrecy surrounding these transactions means that the executives often exclude all but a few insiders; thus, HR personnel are not given adequate time to prepare communications. Finally, and perhaps most important, accurate communication depends on pre-acquisition planning for its content. As previously mentioned, inadequate planning is endemic to various transactions. Without content, internal communications are ineffective.

International acquisitions bring with them other communication complications as well. For example, there is the need to translate key documents in a timely manner. Another is the potential of misunderstandings between colleagues when communicating in a language other than the native tongue. Also, those involved in the acquisition may be fluent in the language, but may not understand the cultural ramifications or linguistic nuances of what they are saying, let along how the other party interprets their communications (Piekkari et al. 2005). Finally, communication barriers can make cross-organizational collaboration more difficult unless organizations adopt a single corporate language (Ranft and Lord 2002).

After an acquisition, good communication serves two distinct purposes. From the acquiring company, effective communication can reduce the anxiety and ambiguity felt by employees of the acquired company, and in doing so, can create a sense of shared belonging (Buono and Bowditch 1989; Hubbard 1999; Ranft and Lord 2002; Schweiger and Goulet 2005). This relationship can aid in retention and productivity during a time when organizations are most vulnerable to their best employees leaving—those personnel who have the opportunities and potential motivation to move elsewhere. Second, effective communication can build the bridges that facilitate internal knowledge sharing (Ranft and Lord 2002). This intra-firm collaboration and knowledge sharing is what many revenue-enhancing acquirers want to achieve, yet it often remains elusive.

If intra-firm collaboration is critical for acquisition success, "rich communication" is fundamental for encouraging the necessary flow of information throughout the firm (Daft and Lengel 1986). Rich communication can be achieved by face-to-face meetings, cross-company project specific teams, site visits to and from the target and acquirer, social events, and cultural audits. Initial face-to-face meetings facilitate trust and encourage collaborators to use further technology to continue the ongoing communication. Yet, using technologically based communication without the initial personal interactions can be ineffectual (Ranft and Lord 2002). The geographic and cultural divide of international acquisitions can exacerbate a lack of communication and collaboration. Ranft and Lord (p. 438) suggest that "rich communications were not only helpful for establishing a favorable climate between the two organizations, but were essential for the actual exchange of knowledge across post-acquisition internal organizational boundaries, particularly when the acquired firms maintained substantial autonomy."

Top Team Selection

According to KPMG (1999), the final activity that successful acquirers undertake before the transaction's completion is to select the target's top team. Having the top team in place means that effective leadership is available to drive the implementation forward. This process is especially important in many developing-world economies, which are experiencing unprecedented growth and, therefore, have very competitive job markets. In markets where employees can switch jobs easily, securing key employees is even more important, as the ability to quickly leave a job for another is intensified.

Securing key employees does not seem to be a priority in many cross-border acquisitions, however. As Figure 22.8 shows, among the Hubbard survey respondents, more than one-fourth of international acquirers took three to six months to have a fully working management team in place at the department-head level, meaning that middle management appointments below that level took even longer to be finalized. This degree of management ambiguity can exacerbate employee retention issues, as affected managers leave the company in search of more concrete employment opportunities. Figure 22.7 shows that the survey evidence bears this out; retaining key staff is the second most often cited HR concern following acquisition.

As previously discussed, the increasing move toward partnering with the acquisition target can also improve retention rates among acquired employees. This partnership is

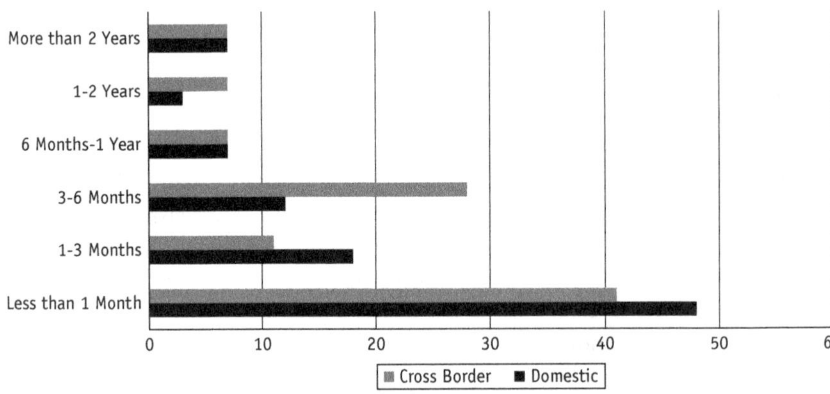

Figure 22.8 Time Needed to Appoint Senior Management after Company Acquisition. This figure outlines the amount of time needed for acquirers to place senior management into senior roles, in both domestic and international acquisitions. The survey asked respondents the amount of time needed to make appointments to the level of department head. The 103 domestic respondents indicated making about two-thirds of appointments to department-head positions within the first three months, with almost half of appointments occurring within one month. Although the 52 foreign respondents indicated that more than half of their appointments occurred in the first three months, almost 30 percent of appointments to department-head level took between three and six months. This delay in appointments means that middle management appointments take even longer, which may be exacerbating retention issues, especially in overheating international markets.

critical when the acquirers do not want to lose that imbedded knowledge. This observation can be especially important when entering a new and substantially different market. To lose those knowledgeable employees would heighten the acquirer's "liability of foreignness" in that market, thereby increasing its inherent risk (Johanson and Vahlne 2009).

OVERALL ACQUISITION SUCCESS FACTORS

Although the KPMG study was published in 1999, the pre-acquisition activities identified in that survey remain relevant today. When the Hubbard survey asked senior executives about the key factors for successful acquisitions, their responses, as shown in Figure 22.9, included many of the same responses as appeared in the KPMG survey, despite the passage of time. On the financial side, extensive due diligence, making strategic sense, clear planning, and a robust process are all important. On the behavioral front, the right leadership and dealing with cultural issues both figure prominently. Hubbard respondents viewed using a lighter touch in implementation as fundamental, which demonstrates the changed nature of cross-border market entry strategy and the

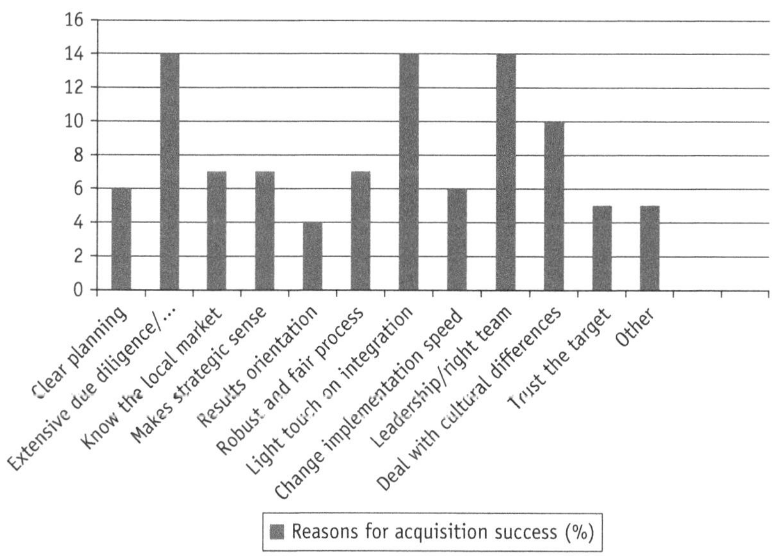

Figure 22.9 Stated Reasons for Acquisition Success. This figure indicates the reasons for success as given by executives from 50 global businesses when discussing acquisition. The survey asked executives to give three key factors for successful acquisitions. The respondents mentioned successes in both financial (due diligence) and people-based actions (right leadership), as well as in a strong process. Respondents identified a lighter touch on integration as being a top-three response, which contradicts previous research findings. Although management urged past acquirers to make changes immediately, a softer and slower integration was found to be more effective, especially when employee retention was mentioned as critical for future acquisition success.

lower degree of integration being undertaken. Even though international transactions have shifted from full integration to revenue-enhancing acquisitions, success continues to rely on a melding of financial and behavioral factors.

Summary and Conclusions

Investors interested in growth companies that are internationalizing their businesses by pursuing acquisition strategies should consider several key factors. First, transformational acquisitions, which represent opportunities to radically reshape an organization's geographic footprint, can uniquely and rapidly revolutionize an organization. Such acquisitions bode well for investors, because little overlap exists for integration issues to arise and subvert the organization's attention and efforts as it quickly gains global size. The opportunities are infrequent but attractive when they arise.

Second, some acquirers have built a track record in successfully acquiring overseas using a methodology that clearly works. As long as the type of acquisition remains consistent, those companies with proven track records warrant attention. Thus, companies that have pursued market-entry strategies with success should find that the process can be replicated across borders. Finally, those organizations that can articulate their strategic plans and demonstrate that they follow the six key activities previously discussed are far more likely to be successful than those that do not. In a changing world, nothing is foolproof. In the case of acquisitions, the merger of financial and behavioral processes greatly enhances the odds of success.

DISCUSSION QUESTIONS

1. Identify several irrational reasons for acquisitions.
2. Discuss how globalfocusing can reduce risk the way conglomeration did previously.
3. Explain how HR issues during acquisition have changed since 2000.
4. Explain the reasons the success rate of international acquisitions has improved.

REFERENCES

Agrawal, Anup, and Jeffrey F. Jaffe. 2000. "The Post-merger Performance Puzzle." In Cary Cooper and Alan Gregory (eds.), *Mergers and Acquisitions*. Amsterdam: JAI, 1–42.

Appelbaum, Stephen H., and Joy Gandell. 2003. "A Cross Method Analysis of the Impact of Culture and Communications upon a Health Care Merger: Prescriptions for Human Resources Management." *Journal of Management Development* 22:5, 370–409.

Autio, Erkko, Harry J. Sapienza, and James G. Almeida. 2000. "Effects of Age at Entry, Knowledge Intensity and Imitability on International Growth." *Academy of Management Journal* 43:5, 909–924.

Badrtalei, Jeff, and L. Donald Bates. 2007. "Effect of Organizational Cultures on Mergers and Acquisitions: The Case of DaimlerChrysler." *International Journal of Management* 24:2, 303–317.

Barclay, Michael J., and Clifford G. Holderness. 1989. "Private Benefits from Control of Public Corporations." *Journal of Financial Economics* 25:2, 371–395.

Bogan, Vicky L., and David R. Just. 2009. "What Drives Merger Decision Making Behavior? Don't Seek, Don't Find, and Don't Change Your Mind." *Journal of Economic Behavior and Organization* 72:3, 930–943.

Brouthers, Keith D., Paul van Hastenburg, and Joran van den Ven. 1998. "If Most Mergers Fail, Why Are They So Popular?" *Long Range Planning* 31:3, 347–353.

Buono, Ánthony, and James Bowditch. 1989. *The Human Side of Mergers and Acquisitions*. San Francisco: Jossey-Bass.

Cadbury. 2015. "The Story." Available at https://www.cadbury.co.uk/the-story#2000-Today.

Cartwright, Susan, and Richard C. Schoenberg. 2006. "Thirty Years of Mergers and Acquisitions Research: Recent Advances and Future Opportunities." *British Journal of Management* 17:S1, SI–S5.

Chen, Chunlai, and Christopher Findlay. 2003. "A Review of Cross-border Mergers and Acquisitions in APEC Economies." *Asian-Pacific Economic Literature* 17:2, 14–38.

Coeurdacier, Nicolas, Roberto A. De Santis, and Antonin Aviat. 2009. "Cross-border Mergers and Acquisitions and European Integration." *Economic Policy* 24:57, 55–106.

Conn, Robert L., Andy Cosh, Paul Guest, and Andy Hughes. 2001. "Long Run Share Performance of UK Firms Engaging in Cross Border Acquisitions." Working Paper No. 214. University of Cambridge, Centre for Business Related Research.

Daft, Richard L., and Robert H. Lengel. 1986. "Organizational Information Requirements, Media Richness and Structural Design." *Management Science* 32:5, 554–571.

Eccles, Robert G., Kersten R. Lanes, and Thomas C. Wilson. 1999. "Are You Paying Too Much for That Acquisition?" *Harvard Business Review* 77:4, 136–146.

Fitzpatrick, Dan. 2012. "B of A's Blunder: $40 Billion-Plus." *Wall Street Journal*, July 1. Available at http://www.wsj.com/articles/SB10001424052702303561504577495332947870736.

Goel, Anand M., and Anjan V. Thakor. 2009. "Do Envious CEOs Cause Merger Waves?" *Review of Financial Studies* 23:2, 487–517.

Gondhalekar, Vijay, R. Raymond Sant, and Stephen Ferris. 2004. "The Price of Corporate Acquisition: Determinants of Cash Takeover Premia." *Applied Economics Letters* 11:12, 735–739.

Gorton, Gary, Matthias Kahl, and Richard J. Rosen. 2009. "Eat or Be Eaten: A Theory of Mergers and Firm Size." *Journal of Finance* 64:3, 1291–1344.

Hietala, Pekka, Steven N. Kaplan, and David T. Robinson. 2003. "What Is the Price of Hubris? Using Takeover Battles to Infer Overpayments and Synergies." *Financial Management* 32:3, 5–31.

Hubbard, Nancy. 1999. *Acquisition: Strategy and Implementation*. Basingstoke: Macmillan.

Hubbard, Nancy. 2001. "Breaking up Is Hard to Do." In James Pickford (ed.), *Mastering Management 2.0: Your Single-source Guide to Becoming a Master of Management*, 121–124. London: Financial Times/Prentice Hall.

Hubbard, Nancy A. 2013. *Conquering Global Markets: Secrets from the World's Most Successful Multinationals*. Basingstoke: Palgrave.

Hubbard, Nancy, and John Purcell. 2001. "Managing Employee Expectations during Acquisitions." *Human Resource Management Journal* 11:2, 17–33.

Hunt, John W., Stan Lees, John J. Grumbar, and Philip D. Vivian. 1987. *Acquisitions: The Human Factor*. London: London Business School and Egon Zehnder International.

Johanson, Jan, and Jan-Erik Vahlne. 2009. "The Uppsala Internationalization Process Model Revisited: From Liability of Foreignness to Liability of Outsidership." *Journal of International Business Studies* 40:9, 1411–1431.

Kale, Prashant, and Harbir Singh. 2009. "Don't Integrate Your Acquisitions, Partner with Them." *Harvard Business Review* 87:12, 109–115.

Kogat, Bruce. 1985. "Designing Global Strategies: Comparative and Competitive Value-added Chains." *MIT Sloan Management Review* 26:4, 15–28.

KPMG Management Consulting. 1997. *Colouring in the Map: Mergers and Acquisitions in Europe*: Research Report. London.

KPMG Management Consulting. 1999. *Unlocking Shareholder Value: The Keys to Success: Mergers and Acquisitions:* Research Report. London.

Krauskopf, Lewis. 2015. "GE Seeks Sale of Asset Management Arm Amid Industrial Push." *Reuters*. Available at: http://in.reuters.com/article/us-general-electric-divestiture-idINKCN0RA 25920150910.

Kummar, Christopher. 2006. "Mergers and Acquisitions in the Pharmaceutical Industry in South America: Activity and Strategic Intentions." Paper presented at the 2006 Global Conference on Business and Finance, IBFR, Costa Rica. Available at http://www.imaa-institute.org/docs/kummer_mergers%20acquisitions%20m&a%20pharmaceutical%20industry%20south%20america%20activity%20strategic%20intentions%20strategy.pdf.

Lanes, Kersten, Richard Stewart, and Stephanie Francis. 2001. "What the Stock Market Wants to Know About a Merger." *Mergers & Acquisitions: The Dealermaker's Journal* 36, 5–46.

Lang, Larry, René Stulz, and Ralph A. Walkling. 1991. "A Test of the Free Cash Flow Hypothesis: The Case of Bidder Returns." *Journal of Financial Economics* 29:2, 315–335.

Lasfer, Meziane A., and Kirian Morzaria. 2004. "When Do Mergers and Acquisitions Create Value?" *International Finance and Law Review*. April, Supplement, 187–190.

Lee, Keun, and Xuehua Jin. 2009. "The Origins of Business Groups in China: An Empirical Testing of the Three Paths and the Three Theories." *Business History, Taylor and Francis Journals* 51:1, 77–99.

Lodorfos, George, and Agyenim Boateng. 2006. "The Role of Culture in the Merger and Acquisition Process: Evidence from the European Chemical Industry." *Management Decision* 44:10, 1405–1421.

Lubatkin, Michael, Narayanan Srinivasan, and Hermant Merchant. 1997. "Merger Strategies and Shareholder Value during Times of Relaxed Antitrust Enforcement: The Case of Large Mergers during the 1980s." *Journal of Management* 23:1, 59–82.

Luo, Yadong. 2004. *Coopetition in International Business.* Copenhagen: Copenhagen Business School Press.

Luo, Yadong, and Rosalie L. Tung. 2007. "International Expansion of Emerging Market Enterprises: A Springboard Perspective." *Journal of International Business Studies* 38:4, 481–498.

Meyer, Klaus E. 2006. "Globalfocusing: From Domestic Conglomerates to Global Specialists." *Journal of Management Studies* 43:5, 1109–1144.

Peltier, Stéphanie. 2004. "Mergers and Acquisitions in the Media Industries: Were Failures Really Unforeseeable?" *Journal of Media Economics* 7:4, 261–278.

Piekkari, Rebecca, Eero Vaara, Janne Tienari, and Risto Säntti. 2005. "Integration or Disintegration: Human Resource Implications of a Common Corporate Language Decision in a Cross-border Merger." *International Journal of Human Resource Management* 16:3, 330–344.

Ranft, Annette L., and Michael D. Lord. 2002. "Acquiring New Technologies and Capabilities: A Grounded Model of Acquisition Implementation." *Organization Science* 13:4, 420–441.

Roll, Richard. 1986. "The Hubris Hypothesis of Corporate Takeovers." *Journal of Business* 59:2, 197–216.

Rostand, Andre. 1994. "Optimizing Managerial Decisions during the Acquisition Integration Process." Paper presented to 14th Annual Strategic Management Society International Conference. Paris, France.

Rottig, Daniel. 2009. "Research on International Acquisition Performance: A Critical Evaluation and New Directions." *Academy Management Proceedings (Meeting Abstract Supplement)* 1, 1–6.

Schmidt, John, 1999. *Realising the Full Value of a Merger or Acquisition: A Risk Management Perspective.* Stamford. CT: Towers Perrin.

Schweiger, David M., and Philip K. Goulet. 2005. "Facilitating Acquisition Integration through Deep-level Cultural Learning Interventions: A Longitudinal Field Experiment." *Organizational Studies* 26:10, 1477–1499.

Servaes, Henri. 1991. "Tobin's Q and the Gains from Takeovers." *Journal of Finance* 46:1, 409–419.

Seth, Anju, Kean P. Song, and Richardson Pettit. 2000. "Synergy, Managerialism or Hubris? An Empirical Examination of Motives of Foreign Acquisitions of U.S. Firms." *Journal of International Business Studies* 31:3, 387–405.

Stahl, Günter K., and Andreas Voight. 2008. "Do Cultural Differences Matter in Mergers and Acquisitions? A Tentative Model for Examination." *Organization Science* 19:1, 160–176.

Staples, Clifford L. 2008. "Cross-border Acquisitions and Board Globalization in the World's Largest TNCS, 1995–2005." *Sociological Quarterly* 49:1, 31–51.

Walter, Gordon A. 1985. "Culture Collisions in Mergers and Acquisitions." In Peter J. Frost, Larry F. Moore, Meryl R. Louis, Craig C. Lundberg, and Joanne Martin (eds.), *Organizational Culture,* 301–314. Beverly Hills, CA: Sage.

Weber, Roberto, and Colin F. Camerer. 2003. "Cultural Conflict and Merger Failure: An Experimental Approach." *Management Science* 49:4, 400–415.

Wood, Eric, Susanna Khavul, Liliana Perez-Nordtvedt, Srinivas Prakhya, Raul Velarde Dabrowski, and Congcong Zheng. 2011. "Strategic Commitment and Timing of Internationalization from Emerging Markets: Evidence from China, India, Mexico, and South Africa." *Journal of Small Business Management* 49:2, 252–282.

Yiu, Daphne W., ChungMing Lau, and Garry D. Bruton. 2007. "International Venturing by Emerging Economy Firms: The Effects of Firm Capabilities, Home Country Networks, and Corporate Entrepreneurship." *Journal of International Business Studies* 38:4, 519–540.

Zahra, Shaker A., Harry J. Sapienza, and Per Davidsson. 2006. "Entrepreneurship and Dynamic Capabilities: A Review, Model and Research Agenda." *Journal of Management Studies* 43:4, 917–955.

Zalewski, David. 2001. "Corporate Takeovers, Fairness, and Public Policy." *Journal of Economic Issues* 35:2, 431–437.

23

Art and Collectibles for Wealth Management

PETER J. MAY
Independent Wealth Advisor

Introduction

This chapter explores the different aspects of buying and selling and collecting fine art and objects that are termed collectibles, viewed from a wealth management perspective. *Wealth management* in this context refers to the act of combining personal investment management, financial advisory, and planning disciplines directly for the benefit of high net worth (HNW) clients. The chapter opens with a review of the literature on behavioral aspects of collecting fine art and collectible objects. The section that follows identifies issues and items that collectors and wealth managers encounter in such wealth management, then expands to a section on the passion for acquiring, holding, and disposing of such assets. A discussion on fine art as an asset class follows. The chapter then moves into the effect of social media use and online aspects of wealth management and ownership, with a focus on education about art, global acquisition of art and collectibles, and give suggestions for how wealth managers can keep pace with developments in this rapidly changing arena. Finally, the chapter includes a summary and conclusions.

A Review of the Literature

Belk (1995) reports survey results based on 200 interviews with collectors that examined the advantages and drawbacks of the collecting process for individuals and households. The study found that, in severe cases, collecting items can be highly addictive and may cause dysfunction for the individual collector and his or her family. However, Belk notes that, overall, collecting is a favorable experience for individual investors.

Baker and Gentry (1996) interview groups of children about their collecting habits. The authors report that children collect items for the pleasure of experiencing the collection process, as a way to avoid boredom, to learn about the collecting field, to satisfy an emotional passion for certain items, to distinguish themselves from other people, and for connecting emotionally with family members and friends. Most adult investors develop a bias against viewing a collectible such as rare stamps as part of a diversification strategy. Instead, they view such collecting from a nonfinancial perspective. However, Grable and Xuan (2015, p. 78) report that "in general, collectible stamps do a relatively good job hedging inflation and declines in gold prices. . . . [Their] findings also suggest that those who invest in stamps need a very long time horizon and favorable market conditions in order to generate a profit."

AFFECTIVE REACTIONS IN THE COLLECTING PROCESS

Apostolou (2011) examines the role of collecting in eBay-based auctions for sales of fossilized dinosaur eggs, and found that collecting is largely based on the desirability of the item. The author reports that the desirability of the collectible piece is positively associated with its scarcity, size, and aesthetic pleasantness. Dimson and Spaenjers (2014) evaluate the long-term investment returns for collectibles, including fine art, stamps, and violins, and classified them as "emotional assets." They report that collectibles outperform gold, Treasury bills, and government bonds over the long investment horizon. Nevertheless, the expense of investing in rare collectibles is high and investors incur many potential risks. Dimson and Spaenjers (p. 20) report that "Emotional assets are particularly attractive to some high-net-worth investors. The need for vigilance makes it hard to justify the inclusion of emotional assets in the portfolios of most institutional investors."

McAlister and Cornwell (2012) examine the emotional role played by collectible toys, and how offering premiums connected with food purchases influences the food choices and eating habits of children. One part of their study examines the influence of toy collectibles offered as premiums with a food purchase. The findings reveal that these collectible toy premiums influence a child's viewpoint about unhealthy and healthy meal choices. They found that children prefer a healthy meal when it is accompanied by a toy collectible, but otherwise make an unhealthy food choice when there is no premium offered. Additionally, one could reflect on the impact on the purchasing parent. They may not care about the toy, yet the compromise was worth the healthy outcome.

Moods also influence the desire for collecting art. De Silva, Pownall, and Wolk (2012) investigated the role of mood changes on subjective risk and prices at art auctions in London between 1990 and 2007. De Silva et al. (p. 167) report the following results:

> Using a unique data set that includes presale estimates for paintings sold through Sotheby's and Christie's auction houses, as well as weather data for London from the British Atmospheric Data Centre, we find that the lower part of the price distribution is populated with paintings with a relative high private value, whereas in the upper part, prices are driven primarily by the common value characteristics.

Indeed, behavioral biases are often revealed in the collection of fine art. Beggs and Graddy (2009) demonstrate how both the price of a painting sold during an art auction and its pre-sale valuation by experts are anchored on the sold prices of other paintings with the same quality over the same time span. The study's major finding is the anchoring effect for buyers, sellers, and auctioneers. This can be based on either the "expecting anchoring" which is based on the buyer judgments or revealing anchoring biases in and of themselves.

The collection of fine art can also introduce agency problems. Mei and Moses (2005, p. 2409) evaluate the connection between auction house estimates of pre-sale values for art and the long-term returns for those art pieces:

> We find that the price estimates for expensive paintings have a consistent upward bias over a long period of 30 years. High estimates at the time of purchase are associated with adverse subsequent abnormal returns. Moreover, the estimation error for individual paintings tends to persist over time. These results are consistent with the view that auction house price estimates are affected by agency problems and that some investors are credulous.

Nordsletten and Mataix-Cols (2012) examine similar and different aspects of hoarding and collecting behavior. By reviewing the literature on collecting, they find that (p. 165) "for the majority of collectors, a diagnosis of Hoarding Disorder is likely to be effectively ruled out. For a minority of 'extreme' collectors, a diagnosis may potentially be adequate." According to McIntosh and Schmeichel (2004, p. 86), "collectors are drawn to collecting as a means of bolstering themselves by setting up goals that are tangible and attainable, and provide the collector with concrete feedback of progress."

SOME POPULAR TYPES OF COLLECTING

Carey (2008) indicates that people have an innate desire to collect items for both financial and nonfinancial reasons, so multiple reasons exist for building collections. Carey develops a model to explain how attempting to complete a set of collectibles influences a person's behavior; eventually, it brings higher value. For instance, a complete set of a collectible has greater value in the secondary market than the totaled value of the individual items. That is, the act of collection, when completed, brings additional value.

Art and Wine Collections

Agnello (2002) examines the relationship between risk and return for a sample of paintings by U.S. artists for sale at auction between 1971 and 1996. His findings reveal that total returns for investments in paintings are low, but large differences in annual performance exist. That is, paintings considered of higher quality post the largest gains, just behind equities, and returns are not compensated for higher risk. The author suggests that buying higher-quality paintings by famous artists is the best type of investment approach.

Wine may also serve as an option for return enhancement. Coffman and Nance (2009) note that wine as an investment has a long history in Europe, and is starting to emerge as an important asset class in the United States. To provide proper advice to clients, financial planners should be able to assess different types of investment-grade wines, understand the importance of the cellar log to make sure the wine has been appropriately stored and transported, identify highly regarded vendors to prevent counterfeit purchases, and value the different markets for collectible wine. Wine quality judgments and investment decisions are based on numerous factors: the geography where the grapes were grown and the year of harvest, the winery doing the aging and bottling, the vintage rating assigned by wine experts, and prices of prior vintages. The authors state that wine is an important asset within a client's portfolio for reducing volatility and a potential way to earn solid long-term returns.

Sports Cards, Especially Baseball

Baseball cards have merit in an investment portfolio. Haley and Van Scyoc (2010) examine the differences between book values and eBay prices for 30 1960s-era baseball cards that appeared on more than 870 auction listings. A general finding was that lower-quality baseball cards sell above their book values and higher-quality cards sell below their book values. Another finding was that when buyer insurance is offered by the seller, the number of bids on an item increases the price on eBay compared to the item's book value, and both the reputation of the seller and the number of bids increase the chances that the eBay item will be sold at a higher price than its book value.

Regoli, Primm, and Hewitt (2007) assess whether performance or race determined the numerical classification used by the baseball card manufacturer Topps to identify the top player baseball cards, also known as "royalty of the diamond," between 1956 and 1980. The authors conclude that player performance was the major determinant of the Topps baseball card numbering system. Additionally, Primm, Piquero, Regoli, and Piquero (2010a, p. 865) report that "card availability and, to a lesser extent, player performance is the most important factor affecting the value of a player's card, while importantly, a player's race is not a significant contributor to card value." In a related study, Primm, Piquero, Regoli, and Piquero (2010b, p. 129), who examined the role of race for cards of more than 1,200 white and black football players, report that "controlling for other factors, race has no effect on the value of players' rookie cards, whereas card vintage exerted the most influence on the value of players' cards."

Celebrity Possessions and the Death Effect

Newman, Diesendruck, and Bloom (2011) investigated the reasons individuals buy items that had previously been owned by celebrities: (1) direct association, (2) greater market demand, and (3) contagion (i.e., the belief that these objects contain some remnants of their previous owners). The items subsequently became collectibles. Market demand has a partial influence on price, but the contagion factor is the most important, influencing the value of possessions previously owned by celebrities.

Death may play a role in the value of certain art and collectibles. Matheson and Baade (2004) study how the value of a work of art or the memorabilia of celebrities increases after the death of the artist or celebrity. They point to previous literature identifying the "death effect." The basis for the "death effect" is the expectation of collectors that the supply is now limited, hence grows in desirability. However, this finding is based on the market for sports memorabilia. As Matheson and Baade (p. 1151) add, "the increase in prices is instead due to a 'nostalgia effect' as a result of the media attention that surrounds the death of a prominent public figure."

Seeing the Client's Passion from a Wealth Management Perspective

Passion often drives the acquisition of fine art and collectibles. Interest in a particular painting or admiration for a collectible baseball card often leads to the initial purchase. Subsequent purchases of similar items can then shape an individual into a collector. The competition among institutions to manage the assets of high net worth (HNW) and ultra-high net worth (UHNW) clients is fierce, as firms attempt to expand their services and evolve their platforms. A key question they face is how to further those relationships with value-added relationships and services. Art and collectibles may be the answer.

Introducing art and other collectibles to an investor may allow a manager to expand that client's investment options beyond the traditional choices. When taking this approach, however, wealth managers need to understand the nature of the markets involved and the various businesses surrounding them. It requires understanding the subject and the nature of the collector's passion: the who, what, where, why, and when. With this knowledge, though, wealth managers can better open the doors of an expanding relationship. The POV does shift for specific reason: the manager should consider introducing collecting, because it allows a conversation to take place that often does not. This conversation helps the client to make the best collection decisions from an investment viewpoint.

Introducing the idea of collecting as an investment option may ignite a passion for your clients. What are the client's investment needs? Who are the experts and third-party or family office service providers who can back up your recommendations? Acquiring this knowledge means working with the client in a close relationship. Online art markets enable individuals to more easily become acquirers and are proliferating on a daily basis. The financial manager should know that art acquisition, for example, and discussed later herein, is increasingly an important part of that world. Ideally, the wealth manager needs to integrate the client's collectible assets with his or her investments and wealth reality. Identifying and navigating the obstacles that get in the way a client's passion can sometimes be as simple as applying parental authority in a friendly and suggestive way such that the client will come to the wealth advisor more often than in the past when art and collecting was not part of the conversation. With sufficient knowledge and leadership skills, the wealth manager can guide the client along the best path, helping him or her make the best collection decisions from an investment viewpoint.

Collecting for Investment Value

How does the wealth manager integrate a client's collection into his or her financial balance sheet? The goal of wealth management is to keep a client's portfolio simple and concise. This includes creating a balance sheet and filling in the assets and liabilities. But what start as simple assets and liabilities can quickly become difficult to categorize. The asset side grows segmented, with current, short-term, and long-term assets. Personal tangible property and investments are only a few of the many category types.

Some clients buy art because they like collecting art. Others buy art because they consider art part of their investment portfolio. The difference between collecting art and investing in art is more a journey than an exact differentiation. For example, more than 30 million collectors worldwide enjoy collecting stamps, and they spend (invest) billions of dollars to assemble their collections. Because stamps do a relatively good job of hedging inflation, the evidence suggests that collectible stamps may be a useful alternative investment within a portfolio (Grable and Chen 2015). If collectors are acquiring art as a possible investment, how do wealth managers make sure they understand the client's needs?

Motivation is multifaceted, with collectors motivated primarily during the acquisition phase. So, identifying that motivational focus and the driving reasons for it should be foundational for wealth managers. There are conferences and seminars on this aspect of investing, as well as features of continuing education programs and business development courses. A simple Internet search points to articles, lectures, seminars, and events on the subject. Additionally, art advisors, collectors, and art consultants ask wealth managers to educate their clients on the nature of collecting, and they offer their services to incorporate art into their investment offering or investment platform. Family offices are often best positioned to integrate art into overall client's portfolio management, as it provides a way to preserve a family's collection. Applying the expertise of both internal and external teams to assess the future attractiveness and investment value of collectibles calls for a decision-making framework of sound governance (Zorloni and Willette 2014). Indeed, the financial industry as a whole, from wealth management to investment brokerage, is assuming a strategic view of art as an asset class. In addition to aiding individual clients and families, there are opportunities for expanding the industry conversation with additional methodologies for integrating art as an asset class into investment management. These areas include art lending, art philanthropy, and art in the context of estate planning. Especially, the art lending world continues to evolve and innovate, people increasingly buy fine art with the idea of borrowing money against its value.

Recently, art lending has become a "strategic focus," which implies that wealth managers are being asked to accommodate requests from important clients. Although many institutions, as part of their general marketing, indicate they now have more confidence in art as collateral, often the reality is that they merely extend client lines of credit. Nevertheless, as traditional lending institutions provide fewer loans and require additional collateral, art lending has surfaced as a financing vehicle without creating covenant-busting realities. Art lending is clean, simple, timely, and focused on providing value-added benefits.

Art philanthropy is another aspect calling for wealth management. Fine art may serve as a charitable gift, for example, that requires client discussions, including the recipient institution so that an art preservation plan can be created (Zorloni and Willette 2014). In a word, instead of selling their art, some investors find a charity, museum, or foundation to take it, display or store it until a later time when the institution can sell the art either privately or at public auction. Alternatively, a collector might consider transferring either part or all of a collection to a trust or foundation, which may call for review of state laws and disclosure requirements. Lastly, estate planning remains important as part of the wealth management process. Through all of these aspects of collecting as investment, wealth managers must consider the valuations, planning, and taxation.

Clients have personal, individual needs, and wealth managers must recognize these needs and see the means for meeting them as a business opportunity. Why should a traditional wealth management firm recognize and include art and collectibles in its portfolio management process? Because art represents a large part of the asset pool of some investors and as such affects their assets under management. The more an advisor knows about a client's interests and financial needs, the less likely he or she will be surprised to receive call from that client for an immediate transfer of funds to cover a recent art purchase.

As previously discussed, McAlister and Cornwell (2012) note the use of toys and other collectible objects as premiums for selling fast-food meals. The objects are highly sought after by children and often cause parents to alter or reconsider their choices or behaviors. If you extrapolate from that, you see that the possibilities are endless for wealth management. All aspects of art and collectibles should be integrated into client discussions, lest those conversations occur in the future at a competitor's office.

Additionally, entertainment and social events frequently center on art and collectibles, adding the emotional touch. Banks and wealth management firms have long supported the arts and offer events as part of corporate sponsorship and patronage. Frankly, these events both target the people with money to invest and are ways to show mutual interest. Wealth managers can create goodwill by inviting clients to events with an art theme. Art fairs and lectures with art historians or museum receptions with participating artists are similar examples of ways to solicit new clients and expand investment options for existing clients. Expanding the conversation, creating educational opportunities and innovative awareness for the client, and the client conversation continues to create value, which in the end is the wealth manager goal.

The Care, Management, and Disposition of Art Assets

ART LENDING

Lending is a mainstay of the banking side of wealth management. Loans and deposits are a natural and basic banking function. As a result, banking services should consider art lending. However, these transactions are complicated by the ability and/or capacity of the lending institution to take possession of the collateralized art. Works of art need careful transport, while the lending institution needs to be able to assume possession. With that possession comes responsibility for protected facilities with secure access and monitoring. These details of art lending create additional risks. An additional hurdle is that of the transfer of insurance liability, which can sometimes derail an acquisition.

ESTATE PLANNING AND ART ASSETS

Estate planning often overlooks the consequences that occur when a tax clause is not structured properly. Indeed, the wealth manager often does not pay attention to or get paid for anticipating "what could go wrong." Often, also, the client may not reveal his or her complete holdings to the attorney or wealth manager. Whether by accident or not, tangible personal property such as art sometimes disappears without a documented chain of ownership. In that case, conflict may arise among heirs.

Several key areas, including valuation, taxation, inheritance, and succession planning, need to be incorporated into the estate planning when art or collectibles are involved. For instance, the planning should consider a cost/benefit analysis of gifting options versus bequests. Valuations should be considered for successive generations when determining the possession and control of the art alongside the rest of the financial wealth. Each of these areas of expertise are well documented within the subject matter of income and estate taxes, yet too often wealth managers do not want to stretch the conversation with their clients to include these topics.

MANAGEMENT AND REPORTING

If the client is busy collecting art, then who takes responsibility for the management and reporting of those assets? The wealth manager could and should assume that role. The wealth manager then integrates the collection or collectibles into a comprehensive asset management and reporting structure. When performed correctly and in timely manner, the reporting structure can create dependency on the wealth manager; indeed, providing periodic and ongoing valuations should be on every wealth manager's task list.

Is the wealth manager in the best position for providing an unbiased service? Or, in the ever evolving and innovating world of online services, are dot.com providers more apt to provide this service? New tools are being created and improved for tracking inventory, pricing, and insurance. Are wealth managers prepared to evolve with the industry that is currently outside their regulatory bias? Can they remain current within the art world that compliance has yet to recognize? The core services of an art advisory might be best left to those with subject matter expertise. This area is one in which clients often come to the table with their own specialist or expert.

Art investment funds tend to be outside the traditional realm of wealth management, but they are an excellent option for those who want to own art, albeit indirectly. Much of the funding for the arts comes from non-U.S. sources. Many service providers and collectors believe that wealth management firms should be offering these funds, or at a minimum, be able to comment and advise on their suitability, as well as their strengths and weaknesses. Keeping abreast of developments within the art world should be a key job of wealth managers, if for no other reason than for basic business development.

ART AS AN ASSET CLASS

Should art be considered a separate asset class? Many say yes, although it does not fall within the guidelines of the Securities and Exchange Commission (SEC). Some wealth advisors avoid the subject for fear of not understanding how to assimilate art into a client's portfolio. Compliance issues such as the lack of regulatory oversight by the SEC are raised when an art balance sheet item is listed on the same page and is financially presented by a wealth manager in the context of a portfolio of traditional investments. Also, the art and art market continue to be unregulated. The risk of a wealth management firm dealing with a largely unregulated industry and products remains a major concern and seemingly a barrier to entry for purposes of advising clients.

However, for those willing to move into this field, there are numerous art indexes providing within their own parameters some estimates and measurements of the correlation of returns for purposes of financial decision making. The Mei-Moses index, which is available at www.artasanasset.com, is but one example. The question for wealth managers is "How does the client's art collection correlate with the current investment portfolio?" Most wealth managers have difficulty responding with a coherent answer.

The failure to provide a coherent response is not because no answer exists; rather, it is because internal compliance restricts their doing so. Art as investment is complex in nature. By its very nature, wealth managers must recognize the heterogeneity of the asset class. Yet, art can be an important consideration in any portfolio diversification strategy. For wealth managers to be able to present clients with a balanced portfolio, they must explain how art fits into that client's portfolio and the role it plays in an asset diversification strategy. As the value of fine art continues to increase, it has become an increasingly important portion of some clients' total net worth. Traditionally, assets are measured for their total return within acceptable levels of risk tolerance.

The Influence of Social Media on Wealth Management

Knowledge ownership has transitioned from research and text to Internet-based searches that are available to almost everyone. Technological advances have led to a shift in decision-making processes.

Knowledge, trust, and service are still critical components for the wealth management process, but they are being replaced by information on social media outlets. Such outlets have become a common commodity that can be easily acquired or searched. Knowledge, trust, and service have largely been relegated to another easily accessible "commodity." Pre-social media, those who taught, studied, and learned largely controlled the knowledge and had the subject matter expertise. Experts went to class, studied hard for long hours, earned a degree, and passed examinations. They got paid to share their knowledge with the public at large. In a similar fashion, trust was the product of long relationships, contacts, affiliations, and associations. People earned trust over time. Clients appreciated service, which was unique just like the delivery channel. Great service earned a star, a rating, and feedback.

This environment changed with the entry of social media. During a relatively short period, that knowledge or subject matter expertise was transformed from a protected, valued, and precious resource into a simple, easily obtainable commodity. The conversation and related research still takes place online, or may require multiple searches with coordinated follow-up. Think of the devices and services that can be done individually or with a smartphone. What started as a "simple" industry has exploded within the online world. The technologies are new and were virtually nonexistent five years ago. Transparency has improved and the opportunity for growth, expansion, and innovation is now largely limitless.

The most important aspects of this evolution, innovation, and revolution are the ability for increased awareness, access, and interest, as well as the passion for social media. When it comes to a desire to acquire art, most desires, addictions, and art afflictions are only a click away, and all are within the convenience of a smartphone, tablet, or computer. Clients today are finding, learning, and challenging what was unattainable only a few years ago. For example, even within the confines of social media websites such as LinkedIn, there are numerous discussion groups sharing information, posting articles, and allowing for member-to-member communications that can only continue the process of "shrinking the world" as it relates to online access, communication, and data retrieval.

So why do typical wealth advisors fail to use these sources of data to benefit their clients? Initially, the answer involved an issue of compliance and its related formalities. Compliance officers neither saw nor had a business-development reason to see a causal association between information on art and a lasting client relationship.

PREVIOUSLY LOCAL IS NOW GLOBAL—ART WORLDWIDE

Globalization is an often a misinterpreted and misunderstood term within the context of art and collectibles. Investments in one country may be unacceptable within the confines of another state or jurisdiction. Completing a transaction across geographical markets can increase the risk, and these risks can present themselves in forms including legal jurisdiction, title, and authenticity, not to mention rights and their enforcement. Such associated risks are similar to those that apply to the world of wealth managers and their related investment portfolio managers.

Current technology has increased people's access to art. What was once limited by geography, cost, and access is now practically attainable by all through technology. A need to see, touch, and discuss art in order to understand it remains, but the images, events, and experience can now be shared and used to educate the client experience. To stay ahead of the curve, wealth managers need to be even more knowledgeable—or at a minimum, be able to reach out to clients instead of waiting to react and respond to questions.

As the infrastructure and the tools of the Internet continue to increase at an fast pace, keeping up with globalization will become more difficult. Although the art market will always innovate and disrupt, it presents even better opportunities for wealth managers to show leadership in their client relationships. E-commerce now allows crossing borders with ease, but it also creates its own set of issues that existed with the local art dealer. The client can go from dealer to dealer "across the globe" with a point and click.

So how do wealth managers provide leadership for their clients? They do so by recognizing their needs and current reality as well providing guidance. Consider the issues of differing legal jurisdictions, authenticity, condition, defective title, rights, and enforcement. Additional issues include import, export, value added taxation, and the moving the art, which as mentioned earlier involves shipping, packing, and storing, as well as a cost-benefit analysis. Each of these items represents an opportunity to lead and guide the conversation through obtaining applicable knowledge, which creates a greater value added opportunity to service clients.

Online Art Education

With the continuing advancement and creation of online education, new and established art and collectible followers, just like those within the wealth management arena, can now be educated without limit. The key to success is the ability to be interactive, with an emphasis on media. Point-and-click solutions allow seemingly limitless possibilities. This change is positive, but can also be daunting. The only limit to what can be offered online is that which exists within and the constraints of current business models and regulators. Given the ability, intent, and interest of universities, museums, public institutions, and individuals to educate online, the initiative has great potential. The explosion of online tools will continue to strengthen the infrastructure used to supply information, including art information. Think of the number of art indexes, news sites, pricing databases, and analytical tools that already exist and continue to be created or discovered.

Individuals who travel to a website often observe a separate tab or page dedicated to "helpful links" or "useful tools" or some other descriptor. Build the connectors/links and they will follow. Wealth managers need to work more closely with outside/online information, subject to the requisite compliance limitations, and educational and industry experts so that their offering is the most complete offering. The only limitation is the self-imposed compliance-related restriction that the wealth management firm is not in that business. Wealth managers should no longer see themselves as product providers but as problem solvers, especially when it comes to art and collectibles.

Online Auctions and Other Marketplaces

As online auctions continue to receive increased investment attention, wealth managers should consider the thought process as part of their deliverable for investments and connectivity. If the investment world is attentive and the online auctions continue to grow, then the wealth client, especially the HNWs and UHNWs, will want to know more. The competition to provide data will increase.

New art marketplaces have been created out of the need for "virtual" brick and mortar sources. Online consumers need to acquire art from online stores. It was only a matter of time before the click-and-buy platform would be built in the art world. Yet, the online marketplace model is simply an intermediary. Go no further than to recall how Black Friday morphed into Cyber Monday.

IS C2C THE NEW B2B?

Although business to business (B2B) was a once a priority, consumer to consumer (C2C) has the potential to disrupt current business models. Entrepreneurs and traditional market players are now being left out of the discussion. C2C is the newest way to eliminate the proverbial middleman who has been the mainstay of how business was conducted previously.

C2C eliminates long-established relationships and enables consumers to work directly with other consumers. It basically reduces costs, so that the service or product can be exposed and introduced to the public. A community of participants thus is created that has been exposed to the opportunity to have limitless interactions and communications with the world at large.

This new the competitive landscape opens avenues to those previously at a disadvantage. The change may be good or bad depending on the side represented. Coupling the C2C and B2B environments results in a multidimensional thought process that can expand current thinking. Meanwhile, the B2B can fix and patch what the C2C may be unable to initially identify and make professional adjustments. For example, the business broker can expand on the transaction options where the initial consumer may not.

E-commerce

The role of e-commerce within the art community continues to evolve and expand similar to other businesses that are looking to expand their client base beyond the traditional geographic and connect-based models. The world is getting smaller but is also extending its reach. The Internet and online activity have become the general population's answer to "How do I get there?" Individuals are no longer limited by geography, finance, or even language. They can find, obtain, and explain almost anything within a category of subject matter by searching the Internet.

Better Tools Mean Better Data

Fee structure presents challenges for both wealth firms and innovative online ideas. For some services, such as consultation and information services, subscription fees for different levels of participation are possible. Wealth relationships should embrace the opportunity to know the location of such services, how they exist, and the best way to include them within their wealth platform offering. If a client can gain access to better tools for data management, wealth managers should become aware and begin to interact accordingly.

ONLINE BUSINESSES AND TRANSPARENCY

The online business world for markets and service providers is transforming the creation, delivery, and application of knowledge, as well as some services, into a commodity-based product that continues to lose its intellectual advantage. Entry of online businesses into business models that have been based on high profit margins and lack of transparency continues to grow, as evidenced by the innovative ways that new products and services such as inventory tracking are created and delivered. The online platform has less overhead and reduced transaction costs. This fact should enable this platform to compete with established businesses and models.

Increased transparency in the form of increased education and access is here to stay. More people are sharing more information about more art, especially at the lower and mid-ranges of the art market. This change does not mean that all information will become available to everybody all the time. The more expensive auction houses and private transactions will not become accessible to the general population.

As more information becomes available online by more people from more global geographies, additional information will be shared among people. Thus, wealth managers cannot cite lack of transparency as a limiting factor. This change continues to reinforce the need for wealth managers to grow past the biases and blockers that limit their participation with clients to bring art services and consulting into their wealth platforms.

COLLECTION MANAGEMENT TOOLS ARE REALLY WEALTH TOOLS

Given that liquidity is part of many business models, it should also be part of every art model or collection. Online services and access to information and data can only expand the reach to find and acquire new clients and new art. New clients would necessarily mean a growing market share and growing revenue.

Collection management tools such as inventory tracking and online education should be priority items or very soon to be items for integration into the wealth advisory service offering. Most tools are cloud based and are part of a quickly expanding art service, art support business model that can be used as a lead to other art related services or as a protector for current client based businesses. Helping clients collect and benefit from the accumulation and access to all information about everything he owns allows for greater prediction of the next steps with some relative ease.

Summary and Conclusions

To meet fiduciary approaches to the wealth management, wealth managers must determine how best to collect and disseminate information about art to their clients. Some may want to say that the fiduciary standard does not apply unless it falls within specific regulatory facts and circumstances. In today's world of social media overload and the accompanying ability to access almost anything at any time, wealth managers can no longer hide behind the curtain of convenient unintelligence when managing wealth, especially when the wealth includes art.

DISCUSSION QUESTIONS

1. Explain how passion plays in a portfolio containing art.
2. Elaborate on how a client might view adding art as an asset class to a current portfolio.
3. Discuss the role of risk mitigation for art investments.
4. Discuss the role of social media in information dissemination as related to art.
5. Justify the increasing use of "commodities" as a term to describe holdings.

REFERENCES

Agnello, Richard J. 2002. "Investment Returns and Risk for Art: Evidence from Auctions of American Paintings." *Eastern Economic Journal* 28:4, 443–463.

Apostolou, Menelaos. 2011. "Why Men Collect Things? A Case Study of Fossilised Dinosaur Eggs." *Journal of Economic Psychology* 32:3, 410–417.

Baker, Stacey Menzel, and James W. Gentry. 1996. "Kids as Collectors: A Phenomenological Study of First and Fifth Graders." *Advances In Consumer Research* 23:1, 132–137.

Beggs, Alan, and Kathryn Graddy. 2009. "Anchoring Effects: Evidence from Art Auctions." *American Economic Review* 99:3, 1027–1039.

Belk, Russell W. 1995. "Collecting as Luxury Consumption: Effects on Individuals and Households." *Journal of Economic Psychology* 16:3, 477–490.

Carey, Catherine. 2008. "Modeling Collecting Behavior: The Role of Set Completion." *Journal of Economic Psychology* 29:3, 336–347.

Coffman, Brett A., and Robert J. Nance. 2009. "Wine: The Illiquid Liquid Investment Asset." *Journal of Financial Planning* 22:12, 61–70.

De Silva, Dakshina G., Rachel A. J. Pownall, and Leonard Wolk. 2012. "Does the Sun 'Shine' on Art Prices?" *Journal of Economic Behavior and Organization* 82:1, 167–178.

Dimson, Elroy, and Christophe Spaenjers. 2014. "Investing in Emotional Assets." *Financial Analysts Journal* 70:2, 20–25.

Grable, John E., and Chen Xuan. 2015. "Collectible, Investment, or Both: Evaluating the Attractiveness of Collectible Stamps." *Journal of Financial Service Professionals* 69: 5, 78–87.

Haley, M. Ryan, and Lee Van Scyoc. 2010. "Adverse Selection, Seller Reputation and Buyer Insurance in Online Auctions for 1960s-Era Collectible Baseball Cards." *Applied Economics Letters* 17:13–15, 1341–1345.

Matheson, Victor A., and Robert A. Baade. 2004. "'Death Effect' on Collectible Prices." *Applied Economics* 36:11, 1151–1155.

McAlister, Anna R., and T. Bettina Cornwell. 2012. "Collectible Toys as Marketing Tools: Understanding Preschool Children's Responses to Foods Paired with Premiums." *Journal of Public Policy & Marketing* 31:2, 195–205.

McIntosh, William D., and Brandon Schmeichel. 2004. "Collectors and Collecting: A Social Psychological Perspective." *Leisure Sciences* 26:1, 85–97.

Mei, Jianping, and Michael Moses. 2005. "Vested Interest and Biased Price Estimates: Evidence from an Auction Market." *Journal of Finance* 60:5, 2409–2435.

Newman, George E., Gil Diesendruck, and Paul Bloom. 2011. "Celebrity Contagion and the Value of Objects." *Journal of Consumer Research* 38:2, 215–228.

Nordsletten, Ashley E., and David Mataix-Cols. 2012. "Hoarding versus Collecting: Where Does Pathology Diverge from Play?" *Clinical Psychology Review* 32:3, 165–176.

Primm, Eric, Nicole L. Piquero, Robert M. Regoli, and Alex R. Piquero. 2010a. "Racial Bias in Baseball Card collecting Revisited." *Social Science Journal* 47:4, 865–874.

Primm, Eric, Nicole L. Piquero, Robert M. Regoli, and Alex R. Piquero. 2010b. "The Role of Race in Football Card Prices." *Social Science Quarterly* 91:1, 129–142.

Regoli, Robert M., Eric Primm, and John D. Hewitt. 2007. "Where o' Where Did My Baseball Cards Go?: Race, Performance, and Placement in the Topps ERA, 1956–1980." *Social Science Journal* 44:4, 742–750.

Zorloni, Alessia, and Willette, Randall. 2014. "Managing Art Wealth: Creating a Single Family Office That Preserves and Protects the Family Art Collection." *Journal of Wealth Management* 16:4, 9–17.

Part Six

MARKET EFFICIENCY ISSUES

24

Behavioral Finance Market Hypotheses

ALEX PLASTUN
Associate Professor
Ukrainian Academy of Banking

Introduction

No single approach exists to explain the role of behavior in the financial markets. The existing concepts are not only contradictory but also based on different assumptions. For many years, the dominant economic theory that attempted to explain the behavior of financial markets was the efficient market hypothesis (EMH) (Fama 1965; Samuelson 1965). Fama (1965) points out that an efficient market is one in which the availability of information on current market prices corresponds with the intrinsic value of the asset. However, the many inconsistencies between the EMH and empirical observation led to the development of the behavioral finance market hypotheses. Behavioral finance does not assume the rationality of the investors, which is a basic assumption of the EMH, with empirical evidence to support this stance.

De Bondt and Thaler (1985) show that investors overvalue recent information and undervalue past information, resulting in market mispricing. Black (1985) introduces the concept of *noise traders*—irrational investors whose trades are not based on sound logic. These irrational investors can cause prices to deviate from their true value. Ijiri, Jaedicke, and Knight (1966) provide another reason for the irrationality: a habitual response to a familiar stimulus (termed functional fixation). As Mandelbrot (1972) shows, prices in the financial markets are not random, and he provides evidence of price persistence.

This chapter offers a synthesis of research on the behavior of financial markets and discusses the most popular behavioral finance market hypotheses. The first section explores the EMH, including its basic assumptions and key provisions, as well as presenting a short literature review. Also discussed is the random walk hypothesis, which serves as the basis for the EMH. The second section introduces behavioral financial market hypotheses and explores Lo's (2004) adaptive market hypothesis (AMH), with a view toward its basic assumptions and practical implications.

The third section presents the fractal market hypothesis (FMH), which is popular among practitioners. This theory denies the randomness of the price dynamics and general rationality of the investors; instead, it claims that financial markets are persistent and investors with different horizons are present in the markets. This section also provides comparative characteristics of the EMH and the FMH. The fourth and fifth sections then examine one of the most popular anomalies of the EMH and theories based on them—the overreaction and underreaction hypotheses. These sections present a brief description, supportive empirical evidence, and some theoretical explanations of these overreaction and underreaction effects. The sixth section deals with the noisy market hypothesis (NMH), which divides investors into rational and irrational investors, with noise explaining most of EMH anomalies. The final section explains the functional fixation hypothesis, which is based on a habitual response to a familiar stimulus, resulting in irrational actions and decisions.

The Efficient Market Hypothesis

The EMH is an economic theory that describes the behavior of financial markets. Work by Bachelier (1900) is the basis for this theory, and both Fama (1965) and Samuelson (1965) independently formulated the EMH hypothesis. Fama (1965) points out that an efficient market is one in which, owing to the availability of information, current market prices correspond to an asset's intrinsic value.

RANDOM WALK HYPOTHESIS

The random walk hypothesis (RWH) led to the emergence of the EMH. According to the RWH, an asset's price at a given moment does not depend on its earlier prices. As a result, the study of past price changes is not a way to determine the direction of future price movement.

Despite some controversy about this hypothesis (i.e., asset prices have a fundamental basis and are a monetary valuation of these factors), the RWH has found support on both practical and theoretical levels. Figure 24.1 models the dynamic process, using randomly generated prices. Figure 24.2 is a graph of daily gold prices. The two graphs are almost identical, yet such a situation is not unique. Similar examples can be found for other assets when comparing their price dynamics with randomly generated graphs. This indirect evidence offers support favoring the RWH.

Lo and MacKinlay (1987) reexamine the RWH, rejecting it for weekly indexes of U.S. stock returns from 1962 to 1985. Moreover, Lo and MacKinlay (1999) observe that after the publication of their research, several other studies also rejected the RWH.

EFFICIENT MARKET HYPOTHESIS: BACKGROUND

According to the EMH, all participants of financial markets are rational economic individuals who operate under conditions of free access to information that allows them to accurately predict future prices. The prices of assets under these conditions are fully consistent with their intrinsic values, a position which prevents abnormal profits in financial markets. Thus, markets in which prices of financial assets are equal to their intrinsic values are absolutely efficient.

As one of the founders of the EMH, Samuelson (1965) notes that in an informationally efficient market, price changes cannot be forecasted, assuming they fully incorporate the information and expectations of all market participants. According to Jensen

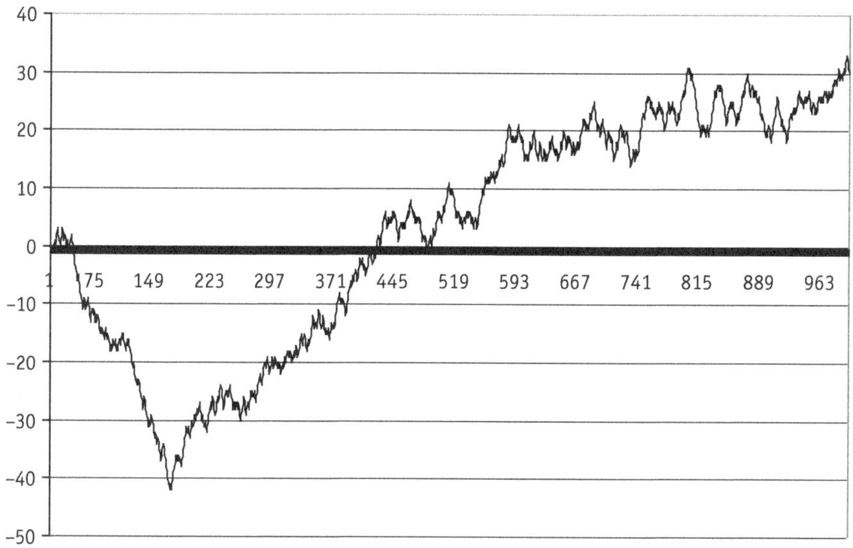

Figure 24.1 Randomly Generated Values. This figure shows the results of some randomly generated dynamics with a probability of 0.5. The horizontal axis displays the number of the experiment and the vertical axis shows the cumulative result of returns generation.

(1978), a market is efficient if, with respect to information set *N*, making economic profits by trading on the basis of information set *N* is impossible.

Thus, greater market efficiency implies that price changes are more randomly generated by the market. Indeed, the most efficient market is the one in which price changes are completely random and unpredictable. This conclusion is based on the fact that price is a direct result of many actions of market participants attempting to profit from information. That is, investors are constantly trying to use even the smallest informational advantages to gain profits. In doing so, they incorporate information into those market prices and quickly eliminate the profit opportunities that motivate their actions. If this situation occurs instantaneously, prices should always fully reflect all available information. Therefore, no profits can be obtained from information-based trading, because such profits have already been captured.

EFFICIENT MARKET HYPOTHESIS: ASSUMPTIONS AND PROVISIONS

The EMH is based on several key assumptions:

- All new market information is quickly and almost instantly reflected in the security prices.
- Only rational economic agents are acting in the financial markets.
- Financial markets exhibit perfect competition.

Figure 24.2 Gold Prices for Three-Month Period, 2006. This figure is a candlestick chart, which shows a portion of daily gold prices (vertical axis) during October and November 2006 (horizontal axis). The box is clear if the closing price is higher than the opening price, or is filled if the close is lower than the opening price. Source: MetaTrader Trading Platform. Available at http://www.metaquotes.net/en/metatrader4.

- Expectations of market participants are homogeneous (i.e., all investors evaluate the likelihood of future asset returns in the same way).
- Asset prices change according to the "law of a random walk."

Based on these EMH assumptions, the following key provisions can be formulated: (1) market prices equal the corresponding intrinsic values of assets; and (2) economic decisions that allow obtaining extra profits are impossible. Empirical observations in the financial markets do not universally support the assumptions that underlie the theory of efficient markets. The same applies to the main provisions of the EMH.

DIFFERENT FORMS OF THE EFFICIENT MARKET HYPOTHESIS

The presence of market anomalies and some practical inconsistencies in the basic theoretical assumptions of the EMH have led to the emergence of three forms of market efficiency—weak, semi-strong, and strong—based on different types of available information. The weak form of efficiency (past price and volume history) is freely available. The semi-strong form of efficiency (public information) results from all information that is publicly available, including past price and volume history of the market. The strong form of efficiency (private information) reflects all information from the previous groups, plus any inside information not available to most market participants.

EFFICIENT MARKET HYPOTHESIS: PROS AND CONS

According to Jensen (1978), no other proposition in economics exists that has more empirical support. Kothari and Warner (2007) study scientific publications that support the EMH. According to their analysis, more than 500 publications in top economic journals confirm rational investor behavior and the efficient response to new information. Nevertheless, empirical data from the financial markets show that the assumptions underlying the EMH do not always correspond with practice. For example, as Ball (2009) notes, the list of differences between observations and the EMH is long and includes both overreactions and underreactions to certain information; extreme volatility and seasonal increases in returns; and yield dependence on different variables, including market capitalization, dividend rate, and market rates. Although the EMH had been the dominant economic theory explaining the behavior of financial markets, many inconsistencies between the EMH and the empirical evidence led to the development of alternative concepts and theories.

The Adaptive Markets Hypothesis

Based on dissimilar preconditions and assumptions, behavioral finance and EMH view the financial markets differently. The major variance is the assumption of rationality on the part of market participants. EMH assumes participants are rational, whereby their financial decision is the optimal choice, whereas behavioral finance assumes that participants might exhibit semi-irrational behavior based on the notion of bounded rationality. *Bounded rationality* is the premise that individuals are influenced by their tastes, values, past judgments, and limits of their cognitive process, resulting in a satisfactory outcome.

Andrew Lo (2004) introduces a new theory that attempts to reconcile the EMH with behavioral finance, called the adaptive market hypothesis (AMH). According to Lo (2004), irrationality can be explained by the fact that individuals adapt to changing environments. The basic idea of the AMH is the application of evolutionary principles such as competition, natural selection, adaptation, and reproduction to financial markets.

This idea is consistent with trading activity in the financial markets. No trading strategy can constantly generate profits in the financial markets because those financial markets are always changing. For example, innovations such as Internet trading have dramatically changed the behavior of financial markets. As a result, investors need to constantly be searching for changes and evolve their strategies accordingly. The evolutionary idea of economic behavior is not new, however. For example, Wilson (1975) systematically applies the principles of competition, reproduction, and natural selection to human social interactions. Sociobiology is a field of scientific study based on the hypothesis that social behavior results from evolution, and it attempts to explain and examine social behavior within that context. According to Wilson, evolutionary processes, along with his sociobiology concept, depend on social behaviors such as altruism, aggression, fairness, religion, morality, and ethics..

Whereas Wilson (1975) uses sociobiology to explain social behaviors, Niederhoffer (1997) applies evolutionary theory to the behavior of financial markets. He considers financial markets as a unique ecosystem, with herbivores (dealers), carnivores (speculators), and decomposers (distressed investors). Similarly, Luo (1998) explores the implications of natural selection for futures markets. He argues that natural selection allows for long-term survival in the futures markets because the irrational traders lose their money and quickly leave the market. As a result, the best predictors of market movements generate better decisions and the markets gain efficiency.

THE SPECIES FOUND IN THE FINANCIAL MARKETS

Lo (2004) expands on the previous research by formulating the AMH to show that prices reflect as much information as are dictated by the combination of environmental conditions and number and nature of market participants, or species in the economy. *Species* in this context are distinct groups of market participants, each behaving in a common manner. For example, market makers, hedge funds, pension funds, and private investors can be thought of as separate species. These species are neither perfectly rational nor completely irrational; rather, they are bounded in their degree of rationality. They make choices based on past experience and their perception of what might be optimal in a given situation, based on the concept of bounded rationality. Lo (2004, p. 22) describes the behavior of market participants: "Individuals make choices based on experience and their best guesses as to what might be optimal, and they learn by receiving positive or negative reinforcement from the outcomes." Understanding of the environment, the nature of their species, and the prevailing species types helps investors comprehend the market.

A key insight provided by the AMH is that market equilibrium is neither guaranteed nor likely to occur at any point of time. This is because the relationship between risk and reward changes over time. Different factors can influence this relationship, including the relative sizes and preferences of various populations in the market, which may include ecology and institutional aspects such as the regulatory environment and tax law. Shifts in these factors over time are likely to affect any risk–reward relationship. For example, during periods of uncertainty and instability, investors usually reduce the amount of risky assets in search of "safe havens," and they act rationally. But then there are periods of collective greed or fear, when bubbles form and crashes occur and these are times when many investors act irrationally.

THE EVOLUTION OF THE FINANCIAL MARKETS

Neely, Weller, and Ulrich (2009) use the foreign exchange (forex) market as their example to demonstrate the evolutionary process of financial markets. The authors analyzed excessive returns in the forex market, and they show that the surplus returns of the 1970s and 1980s were real, not just the result of data mining. However, these profit opportunities disappeared by the early 1990s for models based on filter and moving-average rules. The investment landscape is also changing. Lo (2012) contends that the environment of the last decade is substantially different from that of the previous seven decades. He says that today's markets are larger, faster, and more diverse than at any other point in history.

The degree of market efficiency depends on conditions that characterize certain types of financial markets. If a large number of species fight for limited resources, the competition is high; in this case, markets such as the U.S. stock markets or forex will be efficient or at least reasonably efficient. Yet, if the number of species is small and the resources are abundant, some markets, such as emerging markets, can be inefficient. Environmental factors including the number of competitors in the market, adaptability of market participants, and magnitude of available profit opportunities influence market efficiency.

Another important aspect of the AMH is the presence of arbitrage or profit opportunities—the possibility to beat the market. Profit opportunities are the result of market changes and evolution; however, these opportunities are not constant and they disappear as traders exploit them.

The AMH recognizes the existence of different forms of market dynamics: trends, cycles, "flats," bubbles, and crashes. Each of these forms requires different investment strategies. As a result, investment strategies may perform well in some environments and poorly in others.

ADAPTIVE MARKET HYPOTHESIS: ASSUMPTIONS AND PRACTICAL IMPLICATIONS

The assumptions of the AMH are:

- Individuals act in their own self-interest, make mistakes, learn and adapt.
- Competition drives adaptation and innovation and natural selection shapes market ecology.
- Evolution determines market dynamics.

The main implications of the AMH include the following:

- A relationship between risk and reward exists, but it is unlikely to be stable over time because individual and institutional risk preferences are unlikely to be stable over time.
- Profit opportunities do exist occasionally.
- Investment strategies (based on technical or fundamental analysis) can perform well, but only in certain environments.
- Asset allocation can add value by exploiting the market's path dependence and systematic changes in behavior.
- Market efficiency is not an all-or-nothing condition, but is a characteristic that varies continuously over time and across markets.
- The primary objective of any market participant is survival, for which the catalysts are innovation and the ability to adapt to market changes.

One of the most crucial differences between the EMH and the AMH is return predictability. According to the EMH, return predictability is impossible, but the AMH accepts the possibility of it, based on empirical observations. Kim, Shamsuddin, and Lim (2011) find strong evidence that changing market conditions drive return predictability. Zhou and Lee (2013) cite similar conclusions that market conditions influence return predictability and that market efficiency varies over time. Charles, Darné, and Kim (2012) provide evidence favoring the AMH: the return predictability of foreign exchange rates occurs from time to time, depending on changing market conditions. Todea, Ulici, and Silaghi (2009) analyze the profitability of moving average strategies and conclude that their profitability is not constant in time; they also conclude that the degree of market efficiency varies through time, and this evidence supports the AMH.

More empirical research is required before the AMH can serve as a viable alternative to the EMH. Additional findings will determine the evolutionary dynamics of financial markets and investor behavior across time and circumstances. Nevertheless, the AMH helps to reconcile the EMH and behavioral finance, explaining different anomalies of the EMH while not denying its entire hypothesis. For example, Urquhart and McGroarty (2014) find that calendar anomalies support the AMH and that the AMH offers a better explanation of the calendar anomalies than the EMH.

The Fractal Market Hypothesis

A basic assumption of the EMH is the randomness of pricing processes, based on the RWH and the absence of memory in price movements. However, financial time-series patterns persist, including those of a short- and long-term nature.

Mandelbrot (1972) is among the first to provide evidence of the persistence of long memory in the financial markets. Later, Greene and Fielitz (1977) find long-term dependences in stock prices on the New York Stock Exchange (NYSE). Booth, Kaen, and Koveos (1982) also report that some financial series have long memories. Helms, Kaen, and Rosenman (1984) find long memory properties for the price of futures. As a result, Peters (1991, 1994) proposes an alternative nonlinear conception of financial

Table 24.1 **Comparative Characteristics of the Efficient Market Hypothesis and the Fractal Market Hypothesis**

Criterion	*EMH*	*FMH*
The rationality of market participants	Investors always act rationally and try to maximize their income.	Investors choose strategies within short-term or long-term horizons that are subject to psychological factors, but investors do not always act rationally.
The degree of competition in the market	None of the market participants can significantly affect prices, which equal the intrinsic value of assets.	Equilibrium prices are formed as a result of a combination of short-term technical trading and long-term fundamental valuation.
Price distribution	Prices are normally distributed and show Brownian motion.	Markets can demonstrate a positive price correlation (indicative of a trend), a persistent series (more often), and a negative correlation or anti-persistent series (rarely).
Assumptions about pricing	Price is the result of collective rational assessments and reflects the existing fundamental information.	Price reflects the "intrinsic value" only for the selected investment horizon and can be subjected to both fundamental and technical analysis.

markets, called the fractal market hypothesis (FMH). The basic assumptions of the FMH are the concept of fractals (presence of patterns in price movements) and the existence of different investment horizons, in which some investors make decisions based on short term horizons while others base them on long-term horizons.Table 24.1 presents the main differences between the FMH and the EMH.

THE IMPORTANCE OF PERSISTENCE

According to the FMH, a key characteristic of the financial time series is *persistence,* which is the characteristic of something that outlives the process that created it or the continuance of an effect after its cause is removed. Persistence means that prices may not be random and that trends are typical for a financial time series.

The EMH excludes the application of technical analysis, whereas the FMH operates numerous indicators that set the basis of its fractal technical analysis. Technical analysis, according to the FMH, can be an instrument to predict future prices. That is, it offers arbitrage opportunities for extra profits from trading in the financial markets.

One of the most applied aspects of the FMH is the presence of specific indicators for measuring the level of market efficiency, such as the fractal dimension and the Hurst exponent (Los 2003). It allows identifying markets with different levels of efficiency; an efficient market is a special case of the FMH.

Analysts have examined the persistence of financial data time series for different types of financial markets, such as stock markets, forex, and commodities, with mixed empirical results. For example, Greene and Fielitz (1977), Peters (1991), and Onali and Goddard (2011) found statistically significant evidence of long-term memory in the financial markets. However, Lo (1991), Jacobsen (1995), Crato and Ray (2000), and Serletis and Rosenberg (2007) all conclude that the price fluctuations are random, indicating the absence of long-term memory in the financial markets. Differences in methodology, time periods, and research objectives can explain these different conclusions. Two other aspects of these differences are the instability of both financial market behavior and a market persistence level (Mynhardt, Plastun, and Makarenko 2013; Caporale, Gil-Alana, Plastun, and Makarenko 2014b; Oprean, Tănăsescu, and Brătian 2014).

The Overreaction Hypothesis

The EMH states that prices in the financial markets are generated randomly. Yet, situations in the market occur that cannot be simulated by random generation. For example, figure 24.3 shows that random generation fails to display the patterns that took place between 2008 and 2010 in the U.S. stock market; this illustrates an example of overreaction.

Since the 1980s, researchers have paid more attention to overreactions in the financial markets. *Overreactions* are generally substantial deviations in prices of assets compared to their average (typical) values during certain time periods.

A REVIEW OF THE LITERATURE ON OVERREACTION

As De Bondt and Thaler (1985) show, investors overvalue more recent information and undervalue past information. This results in an anomaly in which portfolios with the worst (or best) dynamics during a three-year period show the best (or worst) results during the subsequent three years. This anomaly led to the formation of the overreaction hypothesis.

Various studies have examined the overreaction hypothesis. For example, Brown, Harlow, and Tinic (1988), who analyze NYSE data between 1946 and 1983, reached conclusions similar to De Bondt and Thaler (1985). Zarowin (1989) finds the presence of short-term market overreactions. Atkins and Dyl (1990) reported overreactions in the NYSE after significant price changes in one trading day, especially in the case of falling prices. Ferri and Min (1996) confirm the presence of overreactions by using S&P 500 Index data between 1962 and 1992. Larson and Madura (2003) use NYSE data between 1988 and 1998, and also show the presence of overreactions. Overreactions in other stock markets have been documented internationally, including those in Spain, Canada, Australia, Japan, Brazil, China, Greek, Turkey, and Ukraine (Mynhardt and Plastun 2013). According to Clements, Drew, Reedman, and Veeraraghavan (2009), the overreaction anomaly has not only persisted but also has increased since the 1990s.

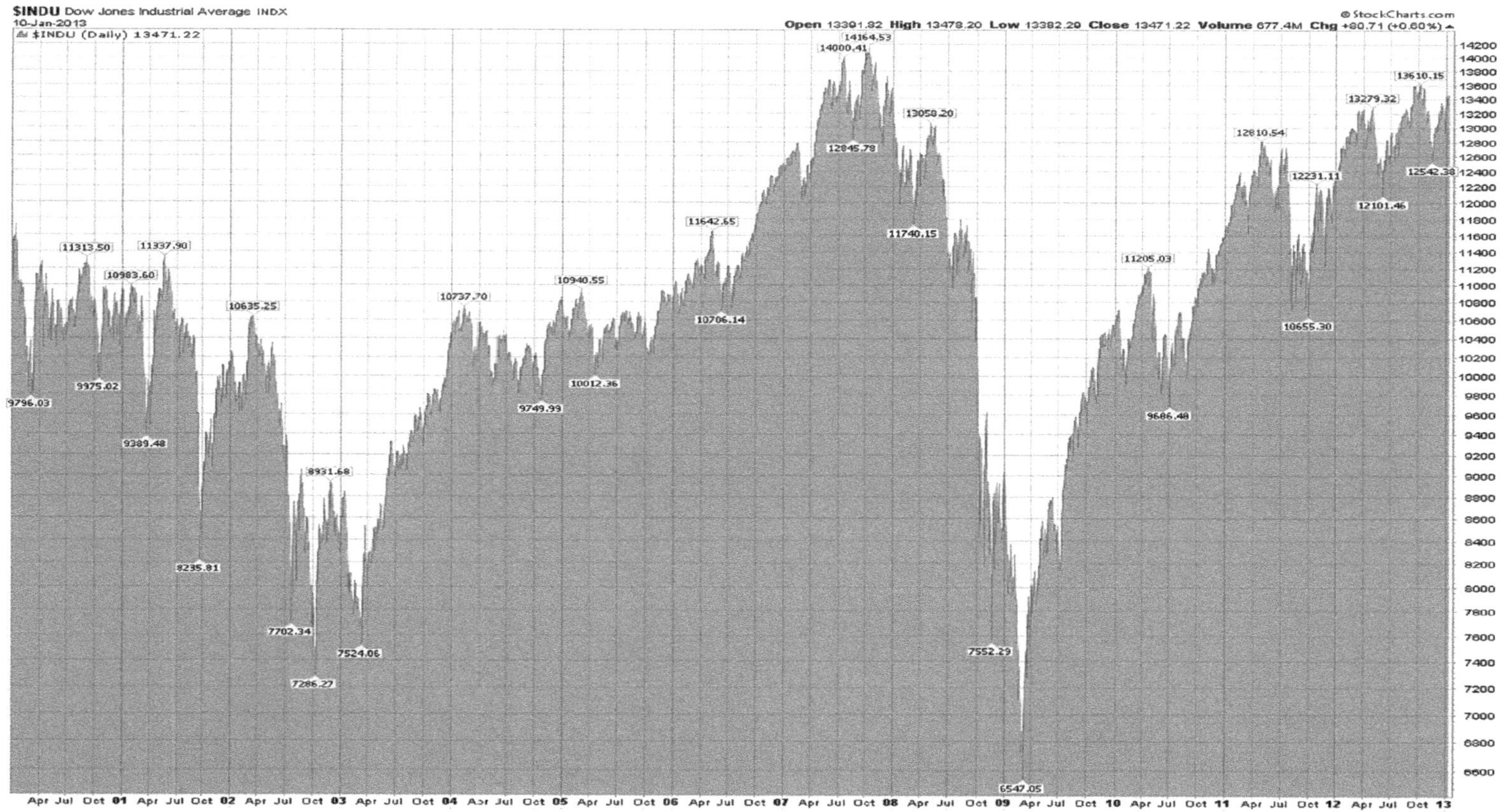

Figure 24.3 Movement of DJIA between 2000 and 2013. This figure shows the dynamics of the Dow Jones Industrial Average (DJIA) Index (vertical axis) between 2000 and 2013 (horizontal axis). Data between 2008 and 2010 illustrate an example of overreaction that took place in the U.S. stock market. Source: Historical Chart Gallery: Market Indexes. Available at http://stockcharts.com/freecharts/historical/djia2000.html.

REASONS FOR OVERREACTIONS

According to the overreactions theory, the irrational behavior of investors results as overreactions to new information. This leads to significant deviations in asset prices compared to their fundamental values. Table 24.2 shows the reasons for such overreactions, which can be psychological, technical, or fundamental in nature.

If an overreaction results from a combination of psychological, technical, and other nonrational factors, instead of being achievement of a new level of fair price, should those overreaction prices achieve equilibrium at the end of the overreaction? Bremer and Sweeney (1991) demonstrate that after a very strong negative price movement, there is a positive price movement, and this movement exceeds ordinary movements. Analyses of negative daily changes exceeding 10 percent have shown that the next day those prices increase by 1.77 percent, on average. This phenomenon can be explained by a fixation on profits (closing the opened positions generates profits) and a reassessment of the information by investors.

The overreaction hypothesis finds validity not only on the theoretical and empirical levels but also in the realm of real trading. Lehmann (1990) and Jegadeesh and Titman (1993) find that a strategy based on overreactions can generate abnormal profits. However, Caporale, Gil-Alana, and Plastun (2017), who analyzed different financial markets, find that a strategy based on counter-movements after overreactions does not generate profits in the forex and the commodity markets, but does remain profitable in the large-cap U.S. stock market. The authors identify a new anomaly based on the overreaction hypothesis, called the *inertia" anomaly,* in which on the day after an overreaction, prices tend to move in the same direction.

The Underreaction Hypothesis

As explained previously, the overreaction hypothesis deals with an unexpectedly strong investor reaction to certain events, with negative correlation in returns over the long run. Thus, contrarian movements appear after overreactions. However, an opposite situation could exist in which investors show little reaction to an event during its appearance but react actively in the next period. This phenomenon is a *positive autocorrelation,* by which a positive change today leads to positive changes tomorrow, and vice versa, in short-term returns; this is called the underreaction hypothesis.

Cutler, Poterba, and Summers (1991) and Bernard and Abarbanell (1992) both offer empirical evidence supporting underreaction. They find that stocks with announcements of higher earnings earned higher returns in the period after the announcements, which indicates that the market underreacts to earnings announcements (information wasn't incorporated at once—at the day of the announcement). Shleifer (2000, p. 427) states "the key idea that generates underreactions is that investors typically (but not always) believe that earnings are more stationary than they really are." Jegadeesh and Titman's (1993) study of the underreaction hypothesis find that stock returns are positively autocorrelated over a six-month horizon. They show that a strategy of buying a portfolio of stocks with the highest positive return in the previous months (winners), and selling those with the lowest returns (losers), can generate abnormal returns during

Table 24.2 **Reasons for Investor Overreactions**

Overreaction Cause	*Description*
Psychological reasons	• Investors act based on emotions (Griffin and Tversky 1992; Madura and Richie 2004). • Purely psychological characteristics of investor's behavior are panic and crowd effects. • **Representativeness effect:** If a particular market or market sector is growing rapidly over time, it forms a positive image among investors. Accordingly, investors begin to prefer assets of this sector. • **Overconfidence and biased attitude**: Investors often overestimate their ability to analyze the market situation.
Technical reasons	• Execution of stop-losses ("stops"). These are orders to close opened positions when reaching a certain level of losses (Duran and Caginalp 2007). Executing stop-loss orders acts as a movement catalyst or accelerator and leads to increases in the scale of basic movement and loss of control over its size. The most typical example of overreaction caused by stops execution is the collapse of the Dow Jones Industry Average (DJIA) in 1987 (Black Monday), when the DJIA lost 22.6 percent of its value. • **Margin-call theory**: In case of large and unexpected movement in the market, a margin-call mechanism often comes into action, closing the most unprofitable position of the client to release the margin (Aiyagari and Gertler 1999). • Technical analysis methodology is based on the previous price fluctuations in forecasts of future prices. A widely held belief is that current movement in asset prices can generate specific trading signals from various technical indicators that will lead to massive operations/trading in the current movement direction and will strengthen it causing overreaction
Fundamental reasons	• According to the price ratio hypothesis proposed by Dreman (1982), companies with low price/earnings ratios are undervalued. However, few investors want to buy stocks of these companies because investors still have strong memories of previous negative attitudes toward these companies. Nevertheless, when negative news of such companies ends and positive news becomes dominant, the demand for shares increases, leading to abnormal movements. The opposite situation is observed for overvalued shares.
Existence of noise traders	Irrational investors are those who make investment decisions on fragmentary information and current price fluctuations.
Other reasons	The lack of liquidity in the market can cause situations when even a small number and amount of transactions can lead to substantial price fluctuations (Jegadeesh and Titman 1993).

Source: Mynhardt and Plastun (2013).

the following months. The authors explain this phenomenon as investors' adapting to new information (positive or negative) too slowly; as the result, there is a momentum effect. Chan, Jegadeesh, and Lakonishok (1996) and Rouwenhort (1997) offer further evidence supporting the underreaction hypothesis.

REASONS FOR UNDERREACTION

A possible reason for the underreaction phenomenon is *conservatism bias*, which describes investors who are anchored to previous information about a company or financial asset. When there is new information, they view it in accordance with their prior stance. If this information is inconsistent with their earlier views, they may even ignore it. As a result, an inappropriate reaction to fundamentals occurs. A chance also exists that those investors might simply under-weight that new information, particularly a change in dividend policies or surprised earnings.

Another psychological reason for underreaction is *representativeness*, which describes how investors can see patterns in random processes. For example, investors might believe that earnings are more stationary than they really are (Shleifer 2000). They draw conclusions about new information such as an earnings announcements based on their interpretation of reality, which is not necessarily correlated with observation. A third possible reason for underreaction involves different types of investors. Some investors might make decisions based on fundamentals, whereas other investors might make decisions based on technical analysis. Some use a short-term perspective, but others use a long-term perspective. As a result, different investors make different investment decisions in the same situation: some might buy a certain asset because in the long run it will rise and fundamental factors provide evidence favoring this action; others might buy the asset because there are signs of a downtrend and the technical analysis indicators confirm this action.

Opportunities resulting from underreaction could generate profits or arbitrage, which is inconsistent with the EMH. For example, Bernard and Thomas (1989) show that a trading strategy based on underreaction generates positive returns. Frazzini (2006) builds an event-driven strategy based on underreaction. Jegadeesh, Chan, and Lakonishok (1996) provide a comprehensive analysis of investment strategies based on the underreaction and of evidence favoring the underreaction hypothesis.

The Noisy Market Hypothesis

A critical feature of the EMH is the assumption that all market participants are rational subjects. The FMH identifies at least two types of investors: those with a short-term orientation and those with a long-term perspective. These different investment horizons can lead to different decisions.

Black (1985) introduces the concept of *noise trading*. In the financial markets, rational investors trade on information, but noise traders do not. Shleifer and Summers (1990) further develop the concept. They explain that noise traders are not fully rational and they base their decisions on their own beliefs or sentiments. These beliefs and sentiments could be responses to pseudo-signals, such as following market gurus and forecasters, using technical analysis, believing they can identify price patterns, and other judgment biases such as extrapolating from past prices. Typical features of noise traders are over-optimism and overconfidence. If the beliefs of different noise traders correlate during a certain time, the aggregate demand for an asset can shift, resulting in a price change. These price changes can then produce deviations from fair (true) values. Summarizing the noise concept, Black (1985, p. 534) states: "Noise creates the opportunity to trade profitably, but at the same time makes it difficult to trade profitably."

Noise traders are important because they provide liquidity to the markets. The effects of noise trading generally are short term and possibly an increase in price volatility. If the number of noise traders is sufficiently large and the direction of their actions is the same, though, price bubbles may appear; in this case, the effect may become long term.

Siegel (2006) classifies market participants using a different decision-making basis: speculators and momentum traders, hedgers and insiders, institutional investors and banks, and others. Each of these participants has reasons for its decision making, such as diversification, asset management, tax optimization, speculation, and liquidity. As a result, many participants with different trading rationales can influence prices, which can then result in deviations from fundamental values during certain periods. Siegel (2006, p. A14) explains the noisy market hypothesis (NMH) as follows:

> Prices of securities are subject to temporary shocks that I call "noise" that obscure their true value. These temporary shocks may last for days or for years, and their unpredictability makes it difficult to design a trading strategy that consistently produces superior returns. To distinguish this paradigm from the reigning efficient market hypothesis, I call it the "noisy market hypothesis."

The NMH can explain some anomalies of the EMH, including the size and value of anomalies, overreactions, and underreactions.

One result of NMH development is a fundamental indexing investment strategy in which an investor forms a portfolio using one or more factors—such as book value, cash flow, revenue, sales or dividends—instead of a standard capitalization-weighted indexed approach where the weight of each stock in the index is proportional to the total market value of its shares (Arnott, Hsu, and Moore 2005). The NMH explains why prices cannot always be at their true value: they may contain pricing errors, caused by "noise." A lingering question is how to measure both of these pricing errors and noise.

The Functional Fixation Hypothesis

Behavioral finance maintains that investors cannot be fully rational. Irrationality is caused by many factors, with some clearly psychological in nature such as fear and greed, overconfidence, and anchoring. These factors might lead to nonrational behavior that results in price bubbles, overreactions, underreactions, and other anomalies.

Habit is certainly psychological aspect that can affect investor behavior. Habits are a result of an inability to change behavior, even when a situation has changed. In the academic literature, such a situation (termed a habitual response to a familiar stimulus) is called *functional fixation,* first documented by Ijiri et al. (1966, p. 194):

> People intuitively associate a value with an item through past experience, and often do not recognise that the value of an item depends, in fact, upon the particular moment in time and may be significantly different from what it was in the past.

Functional fixation can occur at all three stages of the decision-making process: input (source and form of the information available to decision makers), processing (acquiring information, evaluating the relevance of different items of information, and weighting the importance of specific items for the decision task), and output (decision stage) (Ghani, Laswad, Tooley, and Kamaruzaman 2009).

CAUSES OF THE FUNCTIONAL FIXATION

Functional fixation is a direct result of the habits formed by work experience, familiarity with the technologies used in the decision-making process, and personal characteristics such as gender, confidence and cognitive style (Nouri and Clinton 2006). Decision makers mentally acquire knowledge of similar or related information or situations, and they then tend to overlook information those situations. They also tend to assume that a particular interest or practice is always treated similarly (Ghani et al. 2009). Functional fixation also occurs when someone is unable to think in a different or adaptive way. Ambiguity is one of the more important cause of functional fixation.

Ijiri (1967) summarizes the main reasons for functional fixation as follows:

- Lack of knowledge about a change in accounting method.
- Lack of timely feedback that would enable individuals to infer that a change has occurred.
- No expectation of a different payoff.
- Response in a manner consistent with induced expectations of superiors.
- Habitual response to information.
- Presence of ambiguity about the object.

FUNCTIONAL FIXATION IN THE FINANCIAL MARKETS

Functional fixation can be applied to the financial markets as an inability of investors to change their decision-making process in response to a change in how the information they receive has been collected or presented. Empirical evidence suggests that financial analysts and investors fail to adjust fully when there have been changes in accounting methods that affect stock prices (Hand 1990; Sloan 1996; Maines and McDaniel 2000). This reluctance to adjust yields differences in their evaluations of the same results.

There has been extensive discussion of the phenomenon of functional fixation and its accounting implications in regard to investment (Hirst and Hopkins 1998; Maines and McDaniel 2000; Luft and Shields 2001; Libby, Bloomfield, and Nelson 2002; Ghani et al. 2009). Findings show that investors exhibit functional fixation when they compare financial statements of firms using different accounting policies. Many years ago, May (1932, p. 337) describes this situation as follows:

> We accountants know how varied are the methods commonly and legitimately employed, how great the effect of a difference of methods on the earnings of a particular period may be. . . . Investors give the same weight to profits of companies in the same business without knowing whether the profits to which their calculations are applied have been computed on the same basis or how great the effect of a difference in method might be.

Hand (1990), who proposes and tests the extended functional fixation hypothesis (EFFH), offers another view of the concept. For Hand, the EFFH states that investors might react to certain information in a manner consistent with the EMH (as a rational investor) *or* in a manner consistent with functional fixation.

POTENTIAL SOLUTIONS TO FUNCTIONAL FIXATION

Possible solutions to overcome functional fixation are as follows:

- Providing instructional learning (Luft and Shields 2001).
- Using an appropriate format for presenting information (Anderson and Kaplan 1992; Ghani et al. 2009).
- Using search-facilitating technologies (Hodge, Kennedy, and Maines 2004).

Functional fixation may lead to mispricing in the financial markets. As a result, investors who understand a company's real situation, and are not influenced by functional fixation, can trade better than those ones who are "functionally fixated." Functional fixation might also lead to anomalies in the financial markets, such as overreactions and underreactions.

Summary and Conclusions

The EMH was a dominant economic theory explaining financial markets for many years. It influenced the development of economic theory, such as modern portfolio theory, and the formation of financial markets, such as exchange-traded funds. Yet, restrictive assumptions and empirical inconsistencies have led to alternative hypotheses, and the most powerful among these is behavioral finance.

According to the EMH, investors are fully rational, yet a main postulate of behavioral finance is that investors can sometimes act irrationally. That irrationality leads to market anomalies and other situations that are inconsistent with the EMH. Various explanations these anomalies include differing investment horizons, presence of short- and long-term memory in the financial markets, noise traders, adherence to habit, and other purely psychological effects. The presence of anomalies has led to the development of different theories, concepts, and hypotheses to explain the markets and their behavior, including adaptive markets hypothesis, fractal market hypothesis, overreaction hypothesis, underreaction hypothesis, noisy market hypothesis, and functional fixation hypothesis.

These theories try to explain the empirical findings and cannot be viewed as a general theory of the financial markets. Refuting a theory such as the EMH involves exploring alternative frameworks. Although still popular, the EMH should be used only with great caution, because its assumptions and resultant anomalies are inconsistent with reality. Thus, a need exists to develop a general economic theory that explains financial market behavior.

Discussion Questions

1. Identify the necessary conditions for a market to be classified as efficient.
2. Discuss why no theory has emerged to fully replace the EFH.
3. Provide several examples to illustrate the evolution of the financial markets.
4. Discuss whether efficient markets exhibit return persistence and possible measures of market efficiency.
5. Explain whether the behavior of financial markets is consistent with the EMH.

References

Aiyagari, Rao, and Mark Gertler. 1999. "Overreaction of Asset Prices in General Equilibrium." *Review of Economic Dynamics* 2:1, 3–35.

Anderson, John, and Steven Kaplan. 1992. "An Investigation of the Effect of Presentation on Auditors' Non Investigation Region Judgments." *Advances in Accounting Information Systems* 1:1, 71–88.

Arnott, Robert, Jason Hsu, and Phil Moore. 2005. "Fundamental Indexation." *Financial Analyst Journal* 61:2, 83–99.

Atkins, Allen, and Edward Dyl. 1990. "Price Reversals, Bid-Ask Spreads, and Market Efficiency." *Journal of Financial and Quantitative Analysis* 25:4, 535–547.

Bachelier, Louis. 1900. "Théorie de la spéculation." *Annales scienifiques de l'École Normale Supérieure* 3:17, 21–86.

Ball, Ray. 2009. "The Global Financial Crisis and the Efficient Market Hypothesis: What Have We Learned?" *Journal of Applied Corporate Finance* 21:4, 8–16.

Bernard, Victor, and Jeffery Abarbanell. 1992. "Tests of Analysts' Overreaction/Underreaction to Earnings Information as an Explanation for Anomalous Stock Price Behavior." *Journal of Finance* 47:3, 1181–1207.

Bernard, Victor, and Jacob Thomas. 1989. "Post-Earnings-Announcement Drift: Delayed Price Response or Risk Premium?" *Journal of Accounting Research*, 27, 1–36.

Black, Fischer. 1985. "Noise." *Journal of Finance* 41:3, 529–543.

Booth, Geoffrey G., Fred R. Kaen, and Peter E. Koveos. 1982. "R/S Analysis of Foreign Exchange Rates under Two International Monetary Regimes." *Journal of Monetary Economics* 10:3, 407–415.

Bremer, Mark, and Robert J. Sweeney. 1991. "The Reversal of Large Stock Price Decreases." *Journal of Finance* 46:2, 747–754.

Brown, Keith C., W. V. Harlow, and Seha M. Tinic. 1988. "Risk Aversion, Uncertain Information, and Market Efficiency." *Journal of Financial Economics* 22:2, 355–385.

Caporale, Guglielmo Maria, Luis A. Gil-Alana, and Alex Plastun. 2017. "Short-term Price Overreactions: Identification, Testing, Exploitation." Computational Economics. Available at http://dx.doi.org/10.1007/s10614-017-9651-2.

Caporale, Guglielmo Maria, Luis Gil-Alana, Alex Plastun, and Inna Makarenko. 2014b. "Long Memory in the Ukrainian Stock Market and Financial Crises." *Journal of Economics and Finance* 40:2, 235–257.

Chan, Louis, Narasimhan Jegadeesh, and Josef Lakonishok. 1996. "Momentum Strategies." *Journal of Finance* 51:5, 681–713.

Charles, Amélie, Olivier Darné, and Jae H. Kim. 2012. "Exchange-rate Return Predictability and the Adaptive Markets Hypothesis: Evidence from Major Foreign Exchange Rates." *Journal of International Money & Finance* 31:6, 1607–1626.

Clements, Adam, Michael Drew, Evan Reedman, and Madhu Veeraraghavan. 2009. "The Death of the Overreaction Anomaly? A Multifactor Explanation of Contrarian Returns." *Investment Management and Financial Innovations* 6:1, 76–85.

Crato, Nuno, and Bonnie K. Ray. 2000. "Memory in Returns and Volatilities of Commodity Futures' Contracts." *Journal of Futures Markets* 20:6, 525–543.

Cutler, David, James Poterba, and Lawrence Summers. 1991. "Speculative Dynamics." *Review of Economics Studies* 58:3, 529–546.

De Bondt, Werner, and Richard Thaler. 1985. "Does the Stock Market Overreact?" *Journal of Finance* 40:3, 793–808.

Dreman, David. 1982. *The New Contrarian Investment Strategy*. New York: Random House.

Duran, Ahmet, and Gunduz Caginalp. 2007. "Overreaction Diamonds: Precursors and Aftershocks for Significant Price Changes." *Quantitative Finance* 7:3, 321–342.

Fama, Eugene. 1965. "The Behavior of Stock-Market Prices." *Journal of Business* 38:1, 34–105.

Ferri, Michael, and Chung-ki Min. 1996. "Evidence That the Stock Market Overreacts and Adjusts." *Journal of Portfolio Management* 22:3, 71–76.

Frazzini Andrea. 2006. "The Disposition Effect and Under-Reaction to News." *Journal of Finance* 61:4, 2017–2046.

Ghani, Erlane, Fawzi Laswad, Stuart Tooley, and Jusoff Kamaruzaman. 2009. "The Role of Presentation Format on Decision-makers' Behaviour in Accounting." *International Business Research* 2:1, 183–195.

Greene, Myron, and Bruce Fielitz. 1977. "Long-term Dependence in Common Stock Returns." *Journal of Financial Economics* 4:3, 339–349.

Griffin, Dale, and Alan Tversky. 1992. "The Weighing of Evidence and the Determinants of Confidence." *Cognitive Psychology* 24:3, 411–435.

Hand, John. 1990. "A Test of the Extended Functional Fixation Hypothesis." *Accounting Review* 65:4, 740–763.

Helms, Billy, Fred Kaen, and Robert Rosenman. 1984. "Memory in Commodity Futures Contracts." *Journal of Futures Markets* 4:4, 559–567.

Hirst, Eric, and Patrick Hopkins. 1998. "Comprehensive Income Reporting and Analysts' Valuation Judgments." *Journal of Accounting Research* 36:3, 47–75.

Hodge, Frank, Jane Kennedy, and Laureen Maines. 2004. "Does Search Facilitating Technology Improve the Transparency of Financial Reporting?" *Accounting Review* 79:3, 687–703.

Ijiri, Yuji. 1967. *The Foundations of Accounting Measurement*. Englewood Cliffs, NJ: Prentice-Hall.

Ijiri, Yuji, Robert Jaedicke, and Kenneth Knight. 1966. "The Effects of Accounting Alternatives on Management Decisions." In Robert Jaedick (ed.), *Research in Accounting Measurement*, 186–199. New York: American Accounting Association.

Jacobsen, Ben. 1995. "Are Stock Returns Long Term Dependent? Some Empirical Evidence." *Journal of International Financial Markets, Institutions and Money* 5:2/3, 37–52.

Jegadeesh, Narasimhan, and Sheridan Titman. 1993. "Returns to Buying Winners and Selling Losers: Implications for Stock Market Efficiency." *Journal of Finance* 48:1, 65–91.

Jegadeesh, Narasimhan, Louis Chan, and Josef Lakonishok. 1996. "Momentum Strategies." *Journal of Finance* 51:5, 1681–1713.

Jensen, Michael. 1978. "Some Anomalous Evidence Regarding Market Efficiency." *Journal of Financial Economics* 6:2/3, 95–101.

Kim, Jae H., Abul Shamsuddin, and Kian-Ping Lim. 2011. "Stock Return Predictability and the Adaptive Markets Hypothesis: Evidence from Century-Long U.S. Data." *Journal of Empirical Finance* 18:5, 868–879.

Kothari, S. P., and Jerold B. Warner. 2007. "Econometrics of Event Studies." In B. Espen Eckbo (ed.), *Handbook of Corporate Finance: Empirical Corporate Finance,* 3–36. Amsterdam/Oxford: Elsevier/North Holland.

Larson, Steven, and Jeff Madura. 2003. "What Drives Stock Price Behavior Following Extreme One-Day Returns." *Journal of Financial Research* 26:1, 113–127.

Lehmann, Bruce. 1990. "Fads, Martingales, and Market Efficiency." *Quarterly Journal of Economics* 105:1, 1–28.

Libby, Robert, Robert Bloomfield, and Mark W. Nelson. 2002. "Experimental Research in Financial Accounting." *Accounting, Organizations and Society* 27:8, 775–810.

Lo, Andrew. 1991. "Long-term Memory in Stock Market Prices." *Econometrica* 59:5, 1279–1313.

Lo, Andrew. 2004. "The Adaptive Markets Hypothesis: Market Efficiency from an Evolutionary Perspective." *Journal of Portfolio Management* 30:5, 15–29.

Lo, Andrew. 2012. "Adaptive Markets and the New World Order." *Financial Analysts Journal* 68:2, 18–29.

Lo, Andrew, and Craig MacKinlay. 1987. "Stock Market Prices Do Not Follow Random Walks: Evidence from a Simple Specification Test." *Review Financial Studies* 1:1, 41–66.

Lo, Andrew, and Craig MacKinlay. 1999. *A Non-Random Walk Down Wall Street.* Princeton, NJ: Princeton University Press.

Los, Cornelis A. 2003. *Financial Market Risk: Measurement & Analysis—Routledge International Studies in Money and Banking.* London: Taylor & Francis.

Luft, Joan, and Michael Shields. 2001. "Why Does Fixation Persist? Experimental Evidence on the Judgment Performance Effects of Expensing Intangibles." *Accounting Review* 76:4, 561–587.

Luo, Guo Ying. 1998. "Market Efficiency and Natural Selection in a Commodity Futures Market." *Review of Financial Studies* 11:3, 647–674.

Madura, Jeff, and Nivine Richie. 2004. "Overreaction of Exchange Traded Funds during the Bubble of 1998–2002." *Journal of Behavioral Finance* 5:2, 91–104.

Maines, Laureen, and Linda McDaniel. 2000. "Effects of Comprehensive-income Characteristics on Nonprofessional Investors' Judgments: The Role of Financial Statement Presentation Formats." *Accounting Review* 75:2, 179–207.

Mandelbrot, Benoit. 1972. "Statistical Methodology for Nonperiodic Cycles: From the Covariance to Rs Analysis." *Annals of Economic and Social Measurement* 1:3, 259–290.

May, George. 1932. "Influence of the Depression on the Practice of Accountancy." *Journal of Accountancy* 52:5, 336–350.

Mynhardt, Ronald H., and Alex Plastun. 2013. "The Overreaction Hypothesis: The Case of Ukrainian Stock Market." *Corporate Ownership and Control* 11:1, 406–423.

Mynhardt, Ronald. H., Alex Plastun, and Inna Makarenko. 2013. "Behavior of Financial Markets Efficiency during the Financial Market Crisis: 2007–2009." *Corporate Ownership and Control* 11:2, 473–488.

Neely, Christopher J., Paul A. Weller, and Joshua Ulrich. 2009. "The Adaptive Markets Hypothesis: Evidence from the Foreign Exchange Market." *Journal of Financial and Quantitative Analysis* 42:2, 267–488.

Niederhoffer, Victor. 1997. *Education of a Speculator.* New York, NY: John Wiley & Sons, Inc.

Nouri, Hossein, and Douglas B. Clinton. 2006. "Gender, Media Presentation, and Concern with the Correct Use of Words—Testing a Three-way Interaction." *Accounting Education* 15:1, 61–72.

Onali, Enrico, and John Goddard. 2011. "Are European Equity Markets Efficient? New Evidence from Fractal Analysis." *International Review of Financial Analysis* 20:2, 59–67.

Oprean, Camelia, Cristina Tănăsescu, and Vasile Brătian. 2014. "Are the Capital Markets Efficient? A Fractal Market Theory Approach." *Economic Computation & Economic Cybernetics Studies & Research* 48:4, 190–205.
Peters, Edward. 1991. *Chaos and Order in the Capital Markets: A New View of Cycles, Prices, and Market Volatility*. New York: John Wiley & Sons, Inc..
Peters, Edward. 1994. *Fractal Market Analysis: Applying Chaos Theory* to Investment and Economics. New York: John Wiley & Sons, Inc.
Rouwenhorst, Geert. 1997. "International Momentum Strategies." *Journal of Finance* 53:1, 67–84.
Samuelson, Paul. 1965. "Proof That Properly Anticipated Prices Fluctuate Randomly." *Industrial Management Review* 6:2, 41–49.
Serletis, Apostolos, and Aryeh Rosenberg. 2007. "The Hurst Exponent in Energy Futures Prices." *Physica A* 380:C, 325–332.
Shleifer, Andrei. 2000. *Clarendon Lectures: Inefficient Markets*. Oxford: Oxford University Press.
Shleifer, Andrei, and Lawrence H. Summers. 1990. "The Noise Trader Approach to Finance." *Journal of Economic Perspectives* 4:2, 19–33.
Siegel, Jeremy J. 2006. "The Noisy Market Hypothesis." *Wall Street Journal*, June 14, A14.
Sloan, Richard. 1996. "Do Stock Prices Fully Reflect Information in Accruals and Cash Flows about Future Earnings?" *Accounting Review* 72:3, 289–315.
Todea, Alexandru, Maria Ulici, and Simona Silaghi. 2009. "Adaptive Markets Hypothesis: Evidence from Asia-Pacific Financial Markets." *Review of Finance & Banking* 1:1, 7–13.
Urquhart, Andrew, and Frank McGroarty. 2014. "Calendar Effects, Market Conditions and the Adaptive Market Hypothesis: Evidence from Long-run U.S. Data." *International Review of Financial Analysis* 35:1, 154–166.
Wilson, Edward. 1975. *Sociobiology: The New Synthesis*. Cambridge, MA: Belknap Press of Harvard University Press.
Zarowin Paul. 1989. "Does the Stock Market Overreact to Corporate Earnings Information?" *Journal of Finance* 44:5, 1385–1399.
Zhou, Jian, and Jin Man Lee. 2013. "Adaptive Market Hypothesis: Evidence from the REIT Market." *Applied Financial Economics* 23:21, 1649–1662.

25

Stock Market Anomalies

STEVE Z. FAN
Associate Professor of Finance
University of Wisconsin Whitewater

LINDA YU
Professor of Finance
University of Wisconsin Whitewater

Introduction

Equity anomalies are empirical relations between stock returns and firm characteristics that cannot be explained by classical asset pricing models such as the capital asset pricing model (CAPM) (Sharpe 1964; Lintner 1965) or multi-factor models (Fama and French 1993; Carhart 1997). In other words, cross-sectional stock returns are predictable by different company characteristics. Return predictability has become the heart of the market efficiency debate and a focal point in asset pricing studies. In the traditional theory of market efficiency, in which investors are rational and security prices incorporate all relevant information, a security's price equals its fundamental value. Therefore, only "surprises" can move a security's price. Market efficiency predicts a lack of predictability in future stock returns, yet the discovery of equity anomalies directly contradicts the market efficiency theory. Not surprisingly, equity anomalies have become one of the most controversial topics in financial research, with widespread disagreement on the underlying reasons for this predictability.

Recent literature usually attributes the existence of anomalies either to an inadequacy in underlying asset pricing models or to market inefficiency. The inadequacy in asset pricing models is usually called the *rational explanation*. It builds on the traditional risk–return framework with assumptions that investors are perfectly rational and the market is efficient. Anomalies are the consequences of shortcomings in current pricing methods or of missing risk factors. Market inefficiency, then, attributes the existence of anomalies to investors' irrational behaviors and is referred to as the *behavioral explanation*. Within the framework of the behavioral explanation, investors do not collect and/or process available information rationally, because they suffer from cognitive biases that result in mispriced securities. The stock return predictability thus represents systematic mispricing in the equity market.

Understanding these anomalies has become increasingly important in asset allocation, security analysis, and other investment applications. Researchers have explored anomalies both in the United States and internationally. Hou, Xue, and Zhang (2015) examined 73 anomalies spread over six categories—momentum, value versus growth, investment, profitability, intangibles, and trading frictions—and compared their q-factor model to the Fama and French model. Their results show that their q-model outperforms the five-factor model (Fama and French 2014), especially in capturing price and earnings momentum and profitability anomalies. Fan, Opsal, and Yu (2015), who examined several anomalies in 43 countries, found that the anomalies exist in most equity markets over a long time period. Table 25.1 summarizes these anomalies around the world.

Because the scope of studies in anomalies is massive, this chapter focuses on two main objectives in making the topic manageable. First, the chapter reviews some well-known and widely accepted anomalies that have been documented in the finance literature. These anomalies include investment-related anomalies, value anomalies, momentum and long-term reversal, size, and accruals. Then, the chapter presents recent studies that attempt to explain the existence of these anomalies, including rational and behavioral explanations for their existence. The chapter ends with a summary and conclusion.

Equity Anomalies

An anomaly is typically discovered from empirical tests. With the rapid growth in the amount of data and computational power, there has been an explosion in discoveries of anomalies. Some researchers express concerns about the "over-discovery" of anomalies and data snooping (Lo and MacKinlay 1990). Although the concerns are legitimate, accumulated evidence seems to show that some anomalies are robust across equity markets and occur during different time periods.

In a typical empirical test, a long–short trading strategy using portfolios formed on different company-level characteristics would generate a positive abnormal return. This abnormal return could not be explained by current asset pricing models. The most frequently used models for anomaly empirical tests are the traditional asset pricing models such as CAPM (shown in equation 25.1), multi-factor models such as the Fama-French three-factor model (shown in equation 25.2), and four-factor models as shown in equation 25.3:

$$R_{it} - R_{ft} = \alpha_i + \beta_{0i} RM_t + \varepsilon_{it} \quad \textbf{25.1}$$

$$R_{it} - R_{ft} = \alpha_i + \beta_{0i} RM_t + \beta_{1i} SMB_t + \beta_{2i} HML_t + \varepsilon_{it} \quad \textbf{25.2}$$

$$R_{it} - R_{ft} = \alpha_i + \beta_{0i} RM_t + \beta_{1i} SMB_t + \beta_{2i} HML_t + \beta_{3i} MOM_t + \varepsilon_{it} \quad \textbf{25.3}$$

For each of these, $R_{it} - R_{ft}$ is the excess return from the long–short trading strategy.

In a test of anomalies, an abnormal return is usually represented by a significant α_i and RM_t, SMB_t, HML_t, and MOM_t stand for the market, size, value, and momentum factor, respectively. Given that summarizing all the discovered anomalies is a daunting task, the next section discusses only some well-known and well-established anomalies in the literature, including investment anomalies, value anomalies, momentum and long-term reversal, size, and accruals.

Table 25.1 **Summary Statistics for Abnormal Returns of Zero-cost Portfolios by Country and Anomaly**

Country	*AG*		*BM*		*IA*		*MOM*		*NSI*		*SIZE*		*TA*	
	H-L	*t-value*	*H-L*	*t-value*	*H-L*	*t-value*	*H-L*	*t-value*	*H-L*	*t-value*	*H-L*	*t-value*	*H-L*	*t-value*
Australia	0.978	3.62	1.081	4.56	0.383	1.32	0.884	3.75	0.532	2.02	2.098	6.36	–0.079	–0.19
Austria	–0.134	–0.31	0.837	1.98	0.246	0.58	0.938	4.16	0.438	1.58	0.09	0.32	0.44	0.76
Belgium	0.252	0.83	0.355	1.09	0.495	1.83	1.04	6.00	0.471	1.68	–0.222	–0.99	0.824	1.66
Canada	1.082	3.19	0.741	2.05	0.756	2.01	0.469	2.35	0.76	2.41	2.74	8.74	0.587	1.45
Denmark	0.666	2.60	0.875	2.91	0.528	1.91	1.057	4.96	0.428	2.00	0.835	3.39	0.578	1.97
Finland	0.617	1.41	0.858	1.86	0.088	0.23	0.814	2.67	0.269	0.87	0.549	1.77	0.115	0.31
France	0.942	3.48	1.044	3.71	0.329	1.01	0.815	4.07	0.419	1.84	0.716	3.81	0.468	1.40
Germany	0.936	2.71	0.73	3.48	0.818	2.31	0.932	4.30	0.579	2.54	0.564	2.34	0.926	3.05
Greece	0.725	1.81	1.103	2.56	–0.435	–0.73	1.212	2.57	0.336	1.15	1.203	2.10	0.444	0.37
Hong Kong	0.96	2.30	1.061	2.80	0.368	1.18	0.62	2.22	0.88	2.50	1.982	4.31	1.079	2.39
Ireland	0.485	0.99	0.68	1.52	–0.148	–0.31	1.018	3.34	0.115	0.22	0.545	1.19	-0.465	-0.57
Israel	0.006	0.01	1.57	2.06	0.259	0.50	0.725	1.75	0.91	1.37	1.685	4.04	0.066	0.12
Italy	0.058	0.24	1.234	4.79	–0.085	–0.29	0.844	3.66	0.414	2.67	–0.036	–0.14	1.098	2.69
Japan	0.303	1.71	0.607	3.28	0.064	0.37	0.033	0.15	0.309	2.12	0.631	2.59	0.111	0.51
Luxembourg	0.639	0.91	0.489	–0.84	0.761	0.83	0.447	1.44	–0.12	–0.24	0.073	0.17	–2.646	–1.83
Netherlands	0.334	1.01	0.628	1.88	–0.012	–0.04	0.953	4.30	0.888	3.43	–0.417	–1.91	–0.326	–0.65

New Zealand	0.14	0.30	0.581	1.10	0.057	0.16	1.055	2.70	0.069	0.17	0.44	1.09	0.449	0.93
Norway	0.088	0.23	0.823	1.95	–0.345	–0.88	1.047	3.81	0.55	1.73	0.523	1.53	0.41	1.05
Portugal	–0.059	–0.11	2.097	3.45	0.21	0.45	0.129	0.46	0.376	1.28	1.476	3.49	0.642	1.33
Singapore	0.363	1.01	0.541	1.62	–0.038	–0.14	0.223	0.67	0.238	0.93	0.88	2.11	0.242	0.70
South Korea	0.344	0.97	1.798	3.97	0.693	2.18	0.232	0.65	0.96	3.64	1.208	2.19	0.428	0.89
Spain	0.069	0.22	0.527	1.89	–0.064	–0.23	0.865	2.43	0.146	0.73	0.229	0.74	0.238	0.22
Sweden	0.868	2.24	0.66	1.74	0.322	0.94	0.709	2.59	0.699	1.91	–0.105	–0.43	0.106	0.31
Switzerland	0.232	1.01	0.559	2.20	0.348	1.35	0.742	4.25	0.374	2.06	–0.138	–0.70	0.16	0.65
Taiwan	0.115	0.24	0.861	1.47	–0.016	–0.05	0.065	0.18	0.509	1.45	0.486	1.01	0.328	0.93
United Kingdom	0.704	3.84	0.714	3.36	0.26	0.96	0.835	4.84	0.811	4.39	0.043	0.29	-0.151	-0.26
United States	1.305	2.19	0.936	2.07	0.13	2.19	1.036	4.67	2.686	1.70	2.44	7.17	2.16	1.76
Developed Countries	0.501	6.55	0.85	11.04	0.238	3.34	0.719	11.59	0.47	7.85	0.671	10.18	0.327	3.36
Argentina	1.336	2.10	1.548	2.13	0.186	0.35	-0.298	-0.40	0.329	0.60	0.964	0.67	0.947	1.07
Chile	0.462	1.31	0.709	2.17	-0.15	-0.60	0.706	2.75	-0.067	-0.26	0.081	0.20	0.006	0.02
China	0.005	0.01	0.618	0.66	–0.949	–1.24	0.129	0.22	–0.106	–0.20	1.482	2.06	0.745	2.02
Egypt	–0.88	–1.14	1.069	1.09	–1.40	–1.37	1.192	2.17	0.368	0.38	0.924	0.73	0.47	0.44
Hungary	1.824	1.53	3.929	2.73	1.669	1.40	0.526	0.88	1.069	1.10	3.101	2.42	–1.152	–1.01

(continued)

Table 25.1 **Continued**

Country	*AG*		*BM*		*IA*		*MOM*		*NSI*		*SIZE*		*TA*	
	H-L	*t-value*	*H-L*	*t-value*	*H-L*	*t-value*	*H-L*	*t-value*	*H-L*	*t-value*	*H-L*	*t-value*	*H-L*	*t-value*
India	1.231	2.33	1.474	2.52	1.224	3.38	0.482	1.03	0.242	0.66	1.319	1.65	0.419	1.23
Indonesia	−0.655	−0.78	0.998	1.14	0.073	0.14	0.021	0.04	1.061	1.80	0.164	0.23	0.161	0.19
Malaysia	−0.211	−0.78	1.173	3.37	0.219	0.95	0.463	1.26	−0.018	−0.07	1.045	2.33	0.088	0.11
Mexico	−0.191	−0.34	1.299	2.23	−0.436	−1.10	0.689	1.46	1.2	2.47	−0.351	−0.80	−0.729	−1.04
Pakistan	−0.304	−0.54	1.113	1.63	0.742	1.98	0.179	0.42	0.47	0.78	0.136	0.20	0.399	0.57
Peru	0.252	0.28	3.379	3.17	0.95	1.44	0.897	1.92	−0.277	−0.32	1.209	1.85	1.421	1.33
Philippines	0.757	1.24	2.193	3.38	1.109	2.23	−0.07	−0.14	0.36	0.81	2.13	3.06	−0.021	−0.03
Poland	1.016	1.33	2.183	1.93	1.365	2.94	1.523	1.68	−1.208	−0.60	−0.181	−0.19	1.237	1.64
South Africa	1.519	4.13	1.636	4.21	0.106	0.32	0.861	3.48	0.602	1.93	1.331	4.88	1.003	1.95
Thailand	0.471	1.30	2.028	4.66	0.197	0.79	0.101	0.29	0.014	0.04	1.334	2.99	1.307	2.91
Turkey	0.198	0.41	1.491	1.90	0.447	0.97	−0.571	−1.13	−0.199	−0.32	1.3	2.10	0.192	0.15
Emerging	0.375	2.45	1.608	8.80	0.316	2.38	0.43	3.34	0.271	1.67	1.051	5.34	0.346	1.76

Note: Table presents mean values of monthly abnormal returns and corresponding t values from the zero-cost strategy. In June each year t, we sorted all stocks in an ascending order from the most overvalued to the most undervalued into quintiles based on rankings of asset growth (AG), book-to-market (BM), investment-to-assets (IA), net stock issues (NSI), market equity (size), and total accruals (TA) in calendar year $t-1$. We calculated equal-weighted portfolio returns from July of year t to June of year $t+1$. Following Jegadeesh and Titman (1993), we used the "6/1/6" method to construct MOM portfolios. "H-L" denotes monthly returns of the zero-investment strategy (the high-minus-low portfolios—i.e., undervalued-minus-overvalued portfolios). The sample period was between 1989 and 2009.

Source: Adopted from Fan et al. (2015).

INVESTMENT ANOMALIES

Investment anomalies is a term referring to the stock return predictability from company characteristics related to its investment activities. Studies report that companies with high investment activities earn lower average returns than those with low investment activities. The *q*-theory (Cochrane 1991, 1996) provides a theoretical background of how investment can serve as a predictor for future stock returns. Many studies have used that test and verify that company-level measures of investment indeed have a power to predict future stock returns. These investment-related anomalies include asset growth (Cooper, Gulen, and Schill 2008), investment growth (Xing 2008), net stock issues (Fama and French 2008), investment-to-assets (Lyandres, Sun, and Zhang 2008), and abnormal corporate investment (Titman, Wei, and Xie 2004).

Cooper et al. (2008) discover that companies with high asset growth earn lower average returns than those with low asset growth. They show that standard risk–return models, including the conditional CAPM, do not explain the effect. They also find that investors overreact to past company growth rates and the asset growth effect is weaker in times of increased corporate oversight. Figure 25.1 shows the annual returns from a buy-and-hold trading strategy for both equal-weighted (panel A) and value-weighted (panel B) portfolios sorted by past asset growth rates. Watanabe, Xu, Yao, and Yu (2013) and Fan et al. (2015) both report similar asset growth effect in international equity markets.

In their influential study, Loughran and Ritter (1995) document that returns after stock issues, whether as an initial public offering (IPO) or a seasoned equity offering (SEO), are low. As Figure 25.2 shows, long-run returns of nonissuers outperform the long-run returns of IPOs and SEOs (Loughran and Ritter 1995).

Pontiff and Woodgate (2008) report that share issuance exhibits a strong cross-sectional ability to predict stock returns, and that its predictive power is more statistically significant than the predictive power of size, value, and momentum. Fama and French (2008) define *net stock issues* as the annual change in the logarithm of the number of shares outstanding. They find that companies issuing new equity underperform those with similar characteristics; according to Fama and French, net stock issues are one of the most pervasive anomalies. Daniel and Titman (2006) also show a negative relation between net stock issues and average returns.

VALUE ANOMALIES

Value anomalies refers to findings that ratios of value-related accounting measures to market value can predict future stock returns. The book-to-market (BM) ratio is one of the most studied value anomalies. Other value anomalies include earnings-to-price (E/P), dividends-to-price (D/P), and cash flow-to-price (CF/P) ratios. Many studies show that high BM stocks (or those using other measures) earn higher average returns than low BM stocks. Basu (1983) is among the first researchers to discover a value anomaly. He found that companies with a high E/P ratio earn greater positive abnormal returns than companies with a low E/P ratio. More recent studies of U.S. equities confirm that value stocks (i.e., stocks with a high BM ratio) on average outperform growth stocks (i.e., stocks with a low BM ratio) (Rosenberg, Reid, and Lanstein 1985; Fama and French 1992). Other studies find similar results in international equity markets (Fama and French 1998; Liew and Vassalou 2000).

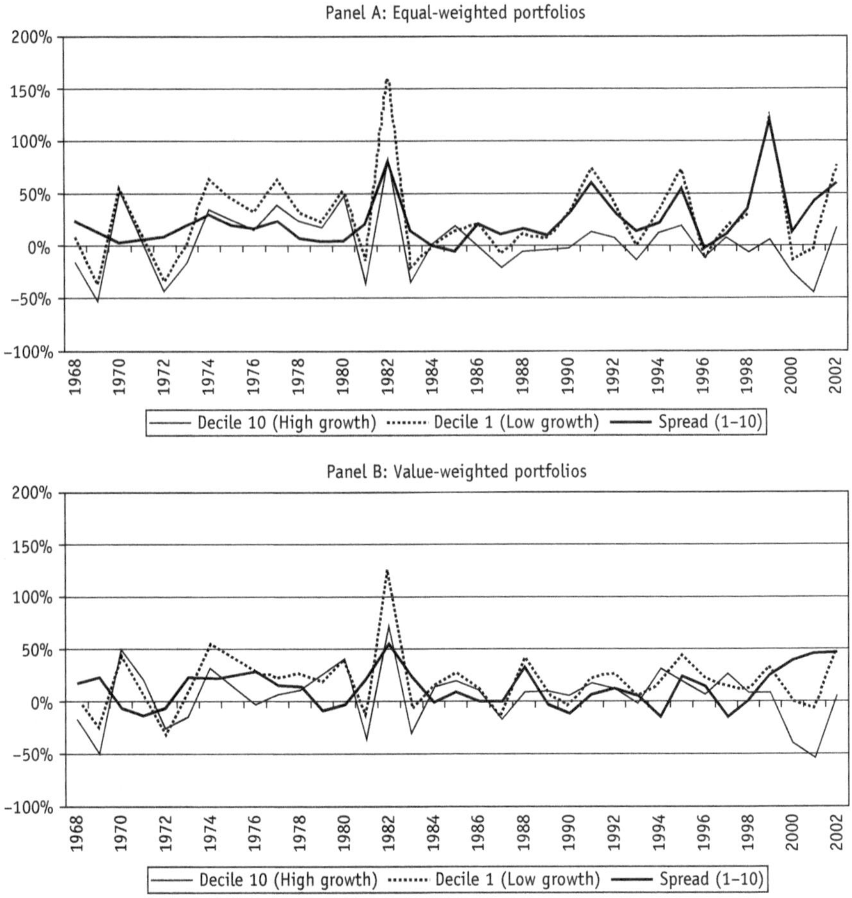

Figure 25.1 Time Series of Annual Return for Two Asset Growth Portfolios. In this figure, panel A plots the annual buy-and-hold returns for equal-weighted portfolios. Panel B plots the annual buy-and-hold returns for value-weighted portfolios. Portfolios are sorted by past asset growth rate, with decile 1 referring to firms with lowest rate and decile 10 referring to firms with highest rate. Source: Adapted from Cooper et al. (2008).

Fama and French (1992, 1993) contend that value (as measured by the value of common stock) and size are two risk factors missing from the CAPM. However, Daniel and Titman (1997) suggest that BM and size are not risk factors in an equilibrium pricing model, because these characteristics dominate the Fama-French size and BM risk factors in explaining the cross-sectional pattern of average returns.

MOMENTUM AND LONG-TERM REVERSAL

Momentum anomalies are perhaps the most famous in the equity market. Stocks that perform well in recent months continue to earn higher average returns in future months

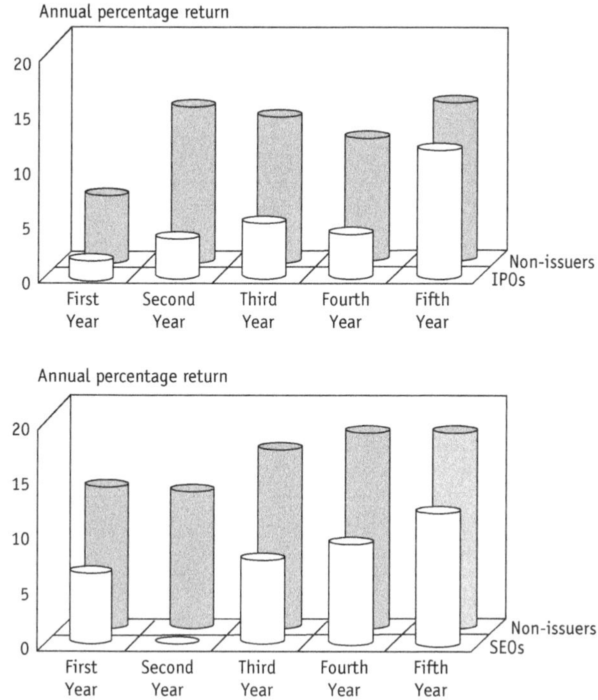

Figure 25.2 Comparison of IPO/SEO Annual Returns and Matching Annual Returns of Non-issuing Companies. This figure shows the annual returns of initial public offerings (IPOs) and their matching firms (non-issuers) (top) and the average annual returns of seasoned equity offerings (SEOs) and their matching non-issuing firms (bottom). The time period is from 1970 to 1990. All returns are calculated as the equal-weighted average buy-and-hold return during the next year.

than stocks that perform poorly. Jegadeesh and Titman (1993) present a trading strategy that simultaneously takes a long position in past winners and a short position in past losers to generate significant abnormal returns over holding periods of 3 to 12 months. The abnormal return is independent of market, size, or value factors. Table 25.2 shows the returns of portfolios formed based on past returns. As Jegadeesh and Titman (2001) show, the momentum effect continued into the 1990s after the anomaly's discovery. This later evidence suggests that their original results were not a product of data snooping bias.

As one of the most pervasive anomalies, momentum exists in most of the equity markets around the world and has persisted during different time periods (Rouwenhorst 1998; Hou, Karolyi, and Kho 2011; Fan et al., 2015). As Carhart (1997) shows, market, size, and value cannot be explained by the momentum factor. Since the Carhart study, this four-factor model has become a widely accepted model to test market efficiency and mutual fund performance. Table 25.2 demonstrates the momentum effect with the returns of the trading strategy proposed in Jegadeesh and Titman (1993). It presents the average monthly returns of portfolios formed based on previous six-month returns

Table 25.2 **Returns of Portfolios Formed Based on Previous Stock Returns**

	All	*S1*	*S2*	*S3*	*B1*	*B2*	*B3*
P	0.0079 (1.56)	0.0083 (1.35)	0.0047 (0.99)	0.0082 (2.22)	0.0129 (2.92)	0.0097 (2.01)	0.0052 (0.95)
P2	0.0112 (2.78)	0.0117 (2.29)	0.0102 (2.54)	0.0098 (3.08)	0.0140 (4.38)	0.0128 (3.37)	0.0086 (1.83)
P3	0.0125 (3.40)	0.0152 (3.23)	0.0125 (3.34)	0.0105 (3.53)	0.0132 (4.59)	0.0133 (3.77)	0.0102 (2.28)
P4	0.0124 (3.59)	0.0163 (3.59)	0.0130 (3.58)	0.0105 (3.66)	0.0134 (5.02)	0.0128 (3.82)	0.0110 (2.50)
P5	0.0128 (3.87)	0.0164 (3.74)	0.0134 (3.83)	0.0109 (3.85)	0.0135 (5.14)	0.0135 (4.15)	0.0121 (2.86)
P6	0.0134 (4.14)	0.0174 (4.08)	0.0146 (4.22)	0.0102 (3.66)	0.0135 (5.23)	0.0142 (4.38)	0.0122 (2.92)
P7	0.0136 (4.19)	0.0175 (4.13)	0.0143 (4.12)	0.0109 (3.90)	0.0136 (5.09)	0.0142 (4.43)	0.0126 (3.01)
P8	0.0143 (4.30)	0.0174 (4.11)	0.0148 (4.16)	0.0111 (3.86)	0.0143 (5.12)	0.0146 (4.44)	0.0132 (3.15)
P9	0.0153 (4.36)	0.0183 (4.28)	0.0154 (4.11)	0.0126 (4.17)	0.0165 (5.34)	0.0156 (4.56)	0.0141 (3.28)
P10	0.0174 (4.33)	0.0182 (3.99)	0.0173 (4.11)	0.0157 (4.41)	0.0191 (5.17)	0.0176 (4.53)	0.0160 (3.50)
P10 – P1	0.0095 (3.07)	0.0099 (2.77)	0.0126 (4.57)	0.0075 (3.03)	0.0062 (2.05)	0.0079 (2.64)	0.0108 (3.35)
F-statistic	2.83	2.65	4.51	4.38	2.51	1.99	1.69
p-value	(0.00)	(0.00)	(0.00)	(0.00)	(0.01)	(0.04)	(0.09)

Note: Table shows the average monthly returns of portfolios formed based on previous 6-month returns and held for 6 months. Portfolio P1 refers to an equal-weighted portfolio of stocks with the lowest past return decile. Portfolio P10 is the equal-weighted portfolio of stocks with the highest past return decile. S1, S2, and S3 stand for small, medium, and large firms, respectively. β_1, β_2, and β_3 stand for firms with small, medium, and large CAPM betas, respectively.

Source: Adapted from Jegadeesh and Titman (1993).

and held for six months for different sample groups. As the table shows, the winning portfolios outperformed the losing portfolios across all sample groups.

De Bondt and Thaler (1985, 1987) show that for portfolios of U.S. stocks formed based on returns for the past three to five years, losers outperform winners by 25 percent for the next three years. This phenomenon is called *long-term reversal*. Many studies corroborate the finding, such as Chopra, Lakonishok, and Ritter (1992).

SIZE

The *size anomaly* is among the earliest discovered anomalies. Banz (1981) and Reinganum (1981) show that small market capitalization companies earn higher average returns than those with large market capitalization. Fama and French (1992, 1993) report that the size combined with the BM ratio captures the cross-sectional return variation. Griffin (2002) find that the size anomaly also occurs in international equity markets. Hawawini and Keim (2000) report that researchers have observed the size anomaly during many sample periods and in most equity markets across countries.

ACCRUALS

The *accruals anomaly* refers to the negative relation between accounting accruals (the non-cash component of earnings) and subsequent stock returns. As Sloan (1996) shows, investors fixate on corporate earnings when valuing stocks. Owing to this bias, companies with high accruals earn lower average returns than those with low accruals. Figure 25.3 shows the returns of the accrual strategy for a sample of 40,679 company-year observations between 1970 and 2006, based on Sloan's (1996) study. Pincus, Rajgopal, and Venkatachalam (2007) extend Sloan's study to international equity markets, showing that the accruals anomaly exists in three other countries in addition to the United States (Australia, Canada, and the United Kingdom). They also found that the accruals anomaly is likely to occur both in common law countries and in countries allowing extensive use of accrual accounting and having a lower concentration of equity ownership. According to Hirshleifer, Hou, and Teoh (2012), the

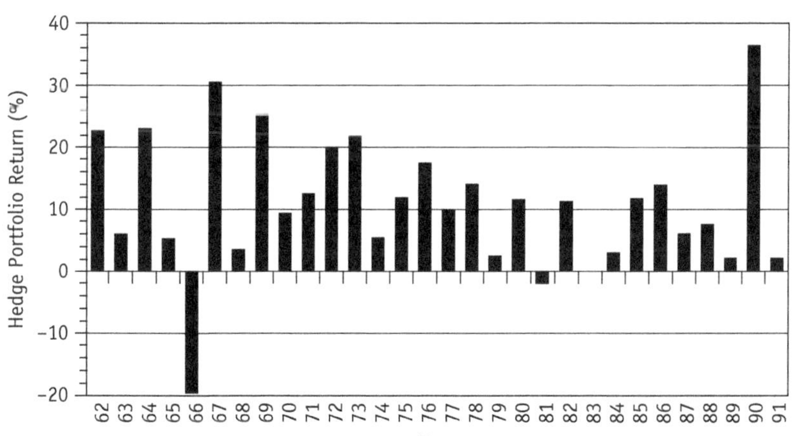

Figure 25.3 Returns of a Long–Short Portfolios Formed on Accruals. This figure shows the annual returns of a portfolio that takes a long position in the stocks of firms in the lowest decile of accruals and a short position in the stocks of firms in the highest decile of accruals. Source: Adapted from Sloan (1996).

accruals anomaly persists and, even more strikingly, its magnitude has not declined over time.

Why Anomalies Exist

The discovery of anomalies has generated numerous competing theories to explain their existence. Two main ideas have emerged in the literature. The first is the rational explanation, which builds on the foundation of traditional risk–return tradeoff theory. That is, a rational explanation explains these return patterns as resulting from shortcomings in the existing asset pricing models. Therefore, many studies strive to find better models or additional risk factors. The second theory attributes the return patterns to irrational investor behavior owing to human cognitive biases. Indeed, behavioral finance has become a main stream of thought in modern finance since its introduction more than 30 years ago. The remainder of this chapter summarizes the current research on these two types of theories.

THE RATIONAL EXPLANATION

Some notable models providing a rational explanation of the failure of the CAPM are the intertemporal capital asset pricing model (ICAPM) (Merton 1973); dynamic asset pricing models (Hansen and Richard 1987); consumption CAPM models (CCAPM) (Rubinstein 1976; Lucas 1978; Breeden 1979); and multi-factor models, including the Fama-French three-factor and four-factor models (Fama and French 1993; Carhart 1997), liquidity factor model (Pastor and Stambaugh 2003), and investment-based model (q-theory model) (Cochrane 1991, 1996; Hou et al. 2015).

The ICAPM (Merton 1973) extends the CAPM by using a different assumption about investor objectives. In the ICAPM, investors worry not only about their end-of-period payoff but also about the opportunities they will have to consume or invest the payoff. Maio and Santa-Clara (2012) apply ICAPM criteria to eight multi-factor models to test size and value effects. They show that only a small portion of their tests is consistent with the ICAPM theory.

Financial economists have criticized the CAPM for its incomplete description of asset prices due to its static nature, and consequently they have proposed a dynamic version of the CAPM. For example, Hansen and Richard (1987) show that a dynamic version of the CAPM could be valid. Gomes, Kogan, and Zhang (2003) develop a general equilibrium model that can capture the ability of the BM to describe the cross-sectional stock returns. Avramov and Chordia (2006) propose a framework that allows a stock's beta to vary with company-level size and BM, as well as with some macroeconomic variables. They apply the framework to test whether some well-known asset pricing models can explain the size, value, and momentum anomalies; their findings show that none of the models examined captures any of the market anomalies with a constant beta. However, when beta is allowed to vary, these models often explain the size and value effects, but not the momentum.

Chen, Roll, and Ross (1986) propose a model to describe the cross-sectional stock return with five macroeconomic factors. Since this influential study, many researchers have developed various multi-factor models. In general, these factor models can be roughly divided into models with macroeconomic factors and models with factors associated with company characteristics.

Pastor and Stambaugh (2003) investigate whether market-wide liquidity is a state variable that is important for asset pricing. They found that expected stock returns are related to liquidity after adjusting for exposures to market, size, value, and momentum factors. Sadka (2006) demonstrates that liquidity risk is important for asset pricing anomalies. The author decomposes company-level liquidity into variable and fixed price effects, and find that unexpected systematic (market-wide) variations of the variable component are priced within the context of momentum and post-earnings-announcement drift.

Fama and French (1993) suggest that cross-sectional differences in average returns are determined by company size and BM, in addition to market risk. Fama and French (1996) show that, except for the momentum effect, the impact of security characteristics on expected returns can be explained within a risk-based multi-factor model. According to Vassalou and Xing (2004), the size effect is, in fact, a default risk, and the BM effect is partially due to default risk. However, Daniel and Titman (1997) point out that uncertainty still exists about whether risk factors or non-risk company characteristics explain expected returns.

Zhang (2005) suggests that the value anomaly arises naturally in the neoclassical framework with rational expectations. Owing to the reversibility and countercyclical price of risk, value assets are riskier than growth options, especially when the price of risk is high. As Liu and Zhang (2008) show, temporarily higher industrial production loadings (a macroeconomic risk factor) on winners more than losers primarily drive the momentum anomaly.

Hou et al. (2015) develop an empirical *q*-factor model consisting of market, size, investment, and profitability factors. They found that this model largely summarizes the cross-sectional stock returns, showing that the model can explain about half of nearly 80 anomalies; the model outperforms the Fama and French (1993) three-factor and the Carhart (1997) four-factor models in explaining anomalies. Using dynamic investment-based models, Zhang (2005) captures the return patterns associated with the value anomaly. Wu, Zhang, and Zhang (2010) show that capital investment helps explain the accrual anomaly.

Despite great efforts and recent progress in the research, finding a rational risk-related explanation for anomalies has proved difficult, hence various researchers offer a behavioral explanation. For more than 30 years, behavioral finance has accumulated enough evidence to prove that human behavior is a key component in determining stock prices. The next section summarizes recent developments in developing a behavioral explanation of anomalies.

THE BEHAVIORAL EXPLANATION

Behavioral finance recognizes that investors have behavioral biases in collecting and processing financial information, as well as in making investment decisions. These behavioral biases are pervasive and persistent, and can introduce systematic mispricing in asset valuation. Because mispricing cannot be hedged away owing to the limits of arbitrage, various cross-sectional return patterns (anomalies) exist in the equity market. This section reviews the limits of arbitrage and then discusses several important behavioral biases and their impact on stock prices.

Limits of Arbitrage and Idiosyncratic Risk

The behavioral explanation acknowledges that mispricing is not due to missing risk factors in the CAPM model. Therefore, one would have to ask why these anomalies are not arbitraged away. Pontiff (1996, 2006) and Shleifer and Vishny (1997) suggest that arbitrageurs bear both systematic and idiosyncratic risk. *Systematic risk* is the risk attributable to market-wide risk sources. *Idiosyncratic risk* is risk that is specific to an asset. Because idiosyncratic risk cannot be diversified away, it presents a high cost to arbitrageurs. According to Shleifer and Vishny, rational investors do not drive away equity anomalies owing to this cost (i.e., the limits of arbitrage).

In a review of the limits of arbitrage, Gromb and Vayanos (2010) point out that the study of limits of arbitrage is evolving into an emphasis on the role of financial institutions and on agency frictions for asset prices. Theoretically, *arbitrage* is the risk-free exploitation of opportunities when some assets are overvalued relative to others. In a perfect market, these profit opportunities attract rational investors to correct the market mispricing, with no requirement for capital investment and risk. However, in reality, rational investors encounter constrains on implementing an arbitrage strategy.

Gromb and Vayanos (2002) study how leverage constraints prohibit arbitrageurs from eliminating the mispricings and they provide liquidity to outside investors. Some consider institutional money managers as the rational market corrector, but because of institutional constraints, most professional investors cannot sell short. Nagel (2005) investigates how this short-sale constraint on institutional investors affects cross-sectional stock returns, helping to explain cross-sectional stock return anomalies such as the value anomaly. Other studies such as Hirshleifer et al. (2011) also explain short-sale constraints.

Shleifer and Vishny (1997) suggest that idiosyncratic risk plays an important role in limiting arbitrage activities. Idiosyncratic risk is expected to be correlated with stock returns; however, considerable controversy exists about the empirical relation between idiosyncratic risk and expected return. Some studies report that the market does not price idiosyncratic risk (Bali, Cakici, Yan, and Zhang 2005; Huang, Liu, Rhee, and Zhang 2010). Other studies document both negative (Ang, Hodrick, Xing, and Zhang 2006, 2009; Guo and Savickas 2010) and positive relations (Goyal and Santa-Clara 2003; Malkiel and Xu 2006; Diavatopoulos, Doran, and Peterson 2008; Fu 2009).

Some studies suggest that idiosyncratic risk should be priced. Because the relative supply of the stocks that constrained investors cannot hold is high, the price of those stocks must be relatively low. Therefore, an idiosyncratic risk premium can be rationalized for such "unbalanced supply." Additionally, if constrained investors cannot hold all securities, the "available market portfolio" for unconstrained investors will automatically become less diversified (Malkiel and Xu 2006). The risk premium of the "available market portfolio" would be higher than the actual market portfolio in the traditional CAPM model; therefore, the market would price idiosyncratic risk.

Behavioral Finance

Many excellent survey articles are available on behavioral finance (Rabin 1998; Shiller 1999; Hirshleifer 2001; Daniel, Hirshleifer, and Teoh 2002; Barberis and Thaler 2003; Campbell 2006; Benartzi and Thaler 2007; Subrahmanyam 2008; Kaustia 2010). This section is not intended to provide a full review of behavioral finance; instead, it focuses on the impact of some well-documented human behavioral biases regarding stock returns. These biases include overconfidence and self-attribution, limited attention, disposition effect, and investor sentiment.

Overconfidence and Self-Attribution

People are usually overconfident about their own judgments, feeling they are right subjectively rather than objectively. De Bondt and Thaler (1995, p. 389) state that "perhaps the most robust finding in the psychology of judgment is that people are overconfident." Another human behavioral trait, self-attribution, is closely related to overconfidence. *Self-attribution* describes how people tend to credit themselves for past successes, but blame other factors for past failures. Researchers often use overconfidence and self-attribution to explain various anomalies.

As Daniel, Hirshleifer, and Subrahmanyam (1998) show, investors over-weight their private information (overconfidence) and underestimate their public information, owing to self-attribution. As a result, investors overreact to private information and underreact to public information. This asymmetric response of overconfident investors can explain momentum and long-term reversal in stock returns. As Odean (1998) reports, overconfidence influences the financial market and causes investors to trade more aggressively. Lakonishok, Shleifer, and Vishny (1994) provide evidence that value anomalies yield higher returns because contrarian investors bet against the overpriced "glamour" stocks created by the suboptimal behavior of typical investors (excessive extrapolation of past performance owing to overconfidence), and not because these value stocks are fundamentally riskier.

Daniel, Hirshleifer, and Subrahmanyam (2001) offer a model that includes both covariance risk and misperceptions of companies' prospects. In this model, some investors overestimate stock information owing to overconfidence; the overconfidence introduces pricing errors; the mispricing persists because arbitrageurs are risk averse. The authors show that their model can explain several well-known anomalies, including value and size.

As Hribar and Yang (2013) show, chief executive officer (CEO) overconfidence affects management forecasting, and this could be related to the accruals anomaly. Overconfidence tends to be stronger when uncertainty is higher. This then implies that overconfidence would be stronger in stocks having more valuation uncertainty. Jiang, Lee, and Zhang (2005) show that companies with high information uncertainty earn lower future returns and the momentum effects are much stronger for these companies. Their findings agree with theoretical models from Daniel et al. (1998). The evidence thus indicates that high information uncertainty exacerbates investor overconfidence and limits rational arbitrage.

Limited Attention

Limited attention is the tendency of people to neglect salient signals and to overact to relevant or recent news (Camerer, Ho, and Chong 2004). Hirshleifer and Teoh (2003) found that limited investor attention leads to market underreaction.

Because attention is a scarce cognitive resource (Kahneman 1973), investors have to be selective in processing information when they are making investment decisions, given the vast amount of information available and the inevitability of limited attention. As Peng and Xiong (2006) show, investors focus on market and sector-wide information more than on company-specific information, and this is known as *category thinking*. The authors model limited attention and study the impact of this limited attention on stock returns. Their model captures the return co-movement that is otherwise difficult to explain using standard rational expectations models.

Hong and Stein (1999) and Hong, Lim, and Stein (2000) show that limited attention can explain the momentum anomaly. They also find that momentum is stronger for low-attention stocks such as small stocks and stocks with low analyst coverage. Limited attention, such as neglecting the distinction between accruals and cash flows in earning components, could help to explain the accruals anomaly (Sloan 1996). As George and Hwang (2004) report, a 52-week high stock price affects the behaviors of the company and its investors, and it explains a large portion of the momentum anomaly. This finding is consistent with *framing theory*, a human behavior trait showing that the way a concept is presented in words or numbers affects the decision-making process of individuals. Hirshleifer and Teoh (2003) and Hirshleifer, Teoh, and Yu (2011) study the effect of limited attention on how investors process accounting information and its impact on stock returns. They conclude that both the value anomaly and the accruals anomaly result from limited attention more than from risks.

Disposition Effect and Prospect Theory

The *disposition effect* is the tendency of investors to sell assets that have risen in value rather than to sell those that have fallen (Shefrin and Statman 1985). According to Odean (1998), no conventional financial theories can fully explain the disposition effect. Thus, researchers have turned to prospect theory for an explanation. Kahneman and Tversky (1979) initially proposed prospect theory, and Tversky and Kahneman (1992) later extended it. *Prospect theory* describes investors' behaviors in such a way that they evaluate outcomes according to their perception of gains and losses relative to a reference point, typically the purchase price. Within the framework of prospect theory, investors are more sensitive to losses than to gains (*loss aversion*), and investors are risk-averse for gains and risk seeking for losses (*diminishing sensitivity*). Researchers use the loss-aversion component of prospect theory to explain the historical high equity premium (Benartzi and Thaler 1995; Barberis and Huang 2001, 2008a).

The disposition effect can generate price momentum because it creates a gap between a stock's fundamental value and its equilibrium price. Because this effect could lead stock prices to underreact to information (Grinblatt and Han 2005; Frazzini 2006; Birru 2015), recent past stock performance could continue in the short term. Barberis and Huang (2008b) study asset prices in a one-period economy within the framework of prospect theory. Their model generated a new prediction that the market prices a security's skewness in the distribution of its returns. They show that the skewness prediction from prospect theory can shed light on some well-known anomalies, such as net stock issues, described earlier in this chapter.

Sentiment

According to Baker and Wurgler (2006), *investor sentiment* is the propensity to speculate. More specifically, *market-wide sentiment* is the difference between the beliefs of sentiment-driven traders and correct objective beliefs (Delong, Shleifer, Summers, and Waldmann 1990). Baker and Wurgler (2006) find that the cross-sectional of future stock returns is conditional on beginning-of-period proxies for sentiment. When sentiment is low, small stocks, unprofitable stocks, nondividend-paying stocks, high-volatility stocks, extreme growth stocks, and distressed stocks tend to earn relatively high subsequent returns. Stambaugh, Yu, and Yuan (2012) explore the role of investor sentiment in 11 equity anomalies in cross-sectional stock returns. They find that each anomaly is stronger (i.e., its long–short strategy is more profitable) after high levels of sentiment.

Summary and Conclusions

Equity anomalies have become an increasingly important topic in asset pricing. This chapter discussed recent developments in this area and reviewed various investment-related anomalies, value anomalies, momentum, long-term reversal, size, and accruals. The discovery of anomalies has prompted the search for both new asset pricing models and additional risk factors. These efforts have dramatically improved our understanding of market efficiency and asset pricing. The discovery of anomalies has also prompted study of behavioral finance. As the ultimate executors in security trading, the behavioral biases of investors have a profound impact on security valuation. The many studies mentioned in this chapter show how investor behavior plays an important role in explaining stock return patterns. The findings suggest that an approach solely relying on either a rational or a behavioral explanation fails to produce a completely convincing result. Combining the approaches may be promising.

DISCUSSION QUESTIONS

1. Explain equity anomalies.
2. Discuss the major explanations of why equity anomalies exist.
3. Identify some behavioral biases of investors that can be attributed to anomalies.
4. Define an investment anomaly and identify some documented investment anomalies.

REFERENCES

Ang, Andrew, Robert J. Hodrick, Yuhang Xing, and Xiaoyan Zhang. 2006. "The Cross-Section of Volatility and Expected Returns." *Journal of Finance* 61:1, 259–299.

Ang, Andrew, Robert J. Hodrick, Yuhang Xing, and Xiaoyan Zhang. 2009. "High Idiosyncratic Volatility and Low Returns: International and Further U.S. Evidence." *Journal of Financial Economics* 91:1, 1–23.

Avramov, Doron, and Tarun Chordia. 2006. "Asset Pricing Models and Financial Market Anomalies." *Review of Financial Studies* 19:3, 1001–1040.

Baker, Malcolm, and Jeffrey Wurgler. 2006. "Investor Sentiment and the Cross-Section of Stock Returns." *Journal of Finance* 61:4, 1645–1680.

Bali, Turan G., Nusret Cakici, Xuemin Yan, and Zhe Zhang. 2005. "Does Idiosyncratic Risk Really Matter? *Journal of Finance* 60:2, 905–929.

Banz, Rolf W. 1981. "The Relationship between Return and Market Value of Common Stocks." *Journal of Financial Economics* 9:1, 3–18.

Barberis, Nicholas, and Ming Huang. 2001. "Mental Accounting, Loss Aversion, and Individual Stock Returns." *Journal of Finance* 56:4, 1247–1292.

Barberis, Nicholas, and Ming Huang. 2008a. "The Loss Aversion/Narrow Framing Approach to the Equity Premium Puzzle." In Rajnish Mehra (ed.), *Handbook of the Equity Risk Premium*, 199–236. Amsterdam: Elsevier.

Barberis, Nicholas, and Ming Huang. 2008b. "Stocks as Lotteries: The Implications of Probability Weighting for Security Prices." *American Economic Review* 98:5, 2066–2100.

Barberis, Nicholas, and Richard Thaler. 2003. "A Survey of Behavioral Finance." In George M. Constantinides, Milton Harris, and René M. Stultz (eds.), *Handbook of the Economics of Finance*, 1051–1119. Amsterdam: North-Holland.

Basu, Sanjoy. 1983. "The Relationship between Earnings Yield, Market Value, and Return for NYSE Common Stocks: Further Evidence." *Journal of Financial Economics* 12:1, 129–156.

Benartzi, Shlomo, and Richard H. Thaler. 1995. "Myopic Loss Aversion and the Equity Premium Puzzle." *Quarterly Journal of Economics* 110:1, 75–92.

Benartzi, Shlomo, and Richard H. Thaler. 2007. "Heuristics and Biases in Retirement Savings Behavior." *Journal of Economic Perspectives* 21:3, 81–104.

Birru, Justin. 2015. "Confusion of Confusions: A Test of the Disposition Effect and Momentum." *Review of Financial Studies* 28:12, 1849–1873.

Breeden, Douglas T. 1979. "An Intertemporal Asset Pricing Model with Stochastic Consumption and Investment Opportunities." *Journal of Financial Economics* 7:3, 265–296.

Carhart, Mark. 1997. "On Persistence in Mutual Fund Performance." *Journal of Finance* 52:1, 57–82.

Camerer, Colin F., Teck-Hua Ho, and Juin-Kuan Chong. 2004. "A Cognitive Hierarchy Model of Games." *Quarterly Journal of Economics* 119:3, 861–898.

Campbell, John Y. 2006. "Household Finance." *Journal of Finance* 61:4, 1553–1604.

Chen, Nai-Fu, Richard Roll, and Stephen A. Ross. 1986. "Economic Forces and the Stock Market." *Journal of Business* 59:3, 383–403.

Chopra, Navin, Josef Lakonishok, and Jay R. Ritter. 1992. "Measuring Abnormal Performance: Do Stocks Overreact?" *Journal of Financial Economics* 31:2, 235–268.

Cochrane, John. 1991. "Production-Based Asset Pricing and the Link between Stock Returns and Economic Fluctuations." *Journal of Finance* 46:1, 209–237.

Cochrane, John. 1996. "A Cross-Sectional Test of an Investment-Based Asset Pricing Model." *Journal of Political Economy* 104:3, 572–621.

Cooper, Michael J., Huseyin Gulen, and Michael J. Schill. 2008. "Asset Growth and the Cross-Section of Stock Returns." *Journal of Finance* 63:4, 1609–1651.

Daniel, Kent, David Hirshleifer, and Avanidhar Subrahmanyam. 1998. "Investor Psychology and Security Market Under- and Overreaction." *Journal of Finance* 53:6, 1839–1885.

Daniel, Kent, David Hirshleifer, and Avanidhar Subrahmanyam. 2001. "Overconfidence, Arbitrage, and Equilibrium Asset Pricing." *Journal of Finance* 56:3, 921–965.

Daniel, Kent, David Hirshleifer, and Siew Hong Teoh. 2002. "Investor Psychology in Capital Markets: Evidence and Policy Implications." *Journal of Monetary Economics* 49:1, 139–209.

Daniel, Kent, and Sheridan Titman. 1997. "Evidence on the Characteristics of Cross Sectional Variation in Stock Returns." *Journal of Finance* 52:1, 1–33.

Daniel, Kent, and Sheridan Titman. 2006. "Market Reactions to Tangible and Intangible Information." *Journal of Finance* 61:4, 1605–1643.

De Bondt, Werner F. M., and Richard H. Thaler. 1985. "Does the Stock Market Overreact?" *Journal of Finance* 40:3, 793–808.

De Bondt, Werner F. M., and Richard H. Thaler. 1987. "Further Evidence on Investor Overreaction and Stock Market Seasonality." *Journal of Finance* 42:3, 557–581.

De Bondt, Werner F. M., and Richard H. Thaler. 1995 "Financial Decision-Making in Markets and Firms: A Behavioral Perspective." In Robert A. Jarrow, Vojislav Maksimovic, and William Ziemba (eds.), *Handbooks in Operations Research and Management Science, Vol. 9: Finance*, 385–410. Amsterdam: North Holland.

De Long, Bradford J., Andrei Shleifer, Lawrence H. Summers, and Robert J. Waldmann. 1990. "Noise Trader Risk in Financial Market." *Journal of Political Economy* 98:4, 703–738.

Diavatopoulos, Dean, James S. Doran, and David R. Peterson. 2008. "The Information Content in Implied Idiosyncratic Volatility and the Cross-Section of Stock Returns: Evidence from the Option Markets." *Journal of Futures Markets* 28:11, 1013–1039.

Fama, Eugene F., and Kenneth R. French. 1992. "The Cross-Section of Expected Stock Returns." *Journal of Finance* 42:2 427–465.

Fama, Eugene F., and Kenneth R. French. 1993. "Common Risk Factors in the Returns on Stocks and Bonds." *Journal of Financial Economics* 33:1, 3–56.

Fama, Eugene F., and Kenneth R. French. 1996. "Multifactor Explanations of Asset Pricing Anomalies." *Journal of Finance* 51:1, 55–84.

Fama, Eugene F., and Kenneth R. French. 1998. "Value versus Growth: The International Evidence." *Journal of Finance* 53:6, 1975–1999.

Fama, Eugene F., and Kenneth R. French. 2008. "Dissecting Anomalies." *Journal of Finance* 63:4, 1653–1678.

Fama, Eugene F., and Kenneth R. French, 2014. "A Five-Factor Asset Pricing model." *Journal of Financial Economics* 116:1, 1–22.

Fan, Zaifeng, Scott Opsal, and Linda Yu. 2015. "Equity Anomalies and Idiosyncratic Risk around the World." *Multinational Finance Journal* 19:1, 33–75.

Frazzini, Andrea. 2006. "The Disposition Effect and Underreaction to News." *Journal of Finance* 61:4, 2017–2046.

Fu, Fangjian. 2009. "Idiosyncratic Risk and the Cross-Section of Expected Stock Returns." *Journal of Financial Economics* 91:1, 24–37.

George, Thomas, and Chuan-Yang Hwang. 2004. "The 52-Week High and Momentum Investing." *Journal of Finance* 59:5, 2145–2176.

Gomes, Joao, Leonid Kogan, and Lu Zhang. 2003. "Equilibrium Cross Section of Returns." *Journal of Political Economy* 111:4, 693–732.

Goyal, Amit, and Pedro Santa-Clara. 2003. "Idiosyncratic Risk Matters!" *Journal of Finance* 58:3, 975–1007.

Griffin, John M. 2002. "Are the Fama and French Factors Global or Country Specific?" *Review of Financial Studies* 15:3, 783–803.

Grinblatt, Mark, and Bing Han. 2005. "Prospect Theory, Mental Accounting, and Momentum." *Journal of Financial Economics* 78:2, 311–339.

Gromb, Denis, and Dimitri Vayanos. 2002. "Equilibrium and Welfare in Markets with Financially Constrained Arbitrageurs." *Journal of Financial Economics* 66:2, 361–407.

Gromb, Denis, and Dimitri Vayanos. 2010. "Limits of Arbitrage." *Annual Review of Financial Economics* 2:1, 251–275.

Guo, Hui, and Robert Savickas. 2010. "Relation between Time-Series and Cross-Sectional Effects of Idiosyncratic Variance on Stock Returns." *Journal of Banking and Finance* 34:7, 1637–1649.

Hansen, Lars P., and Scott F. Richard. 1987. "The Role of Conditioning Information in Deducing Testable Restrictions Implied by Dynamic Asset Pricing Models." *Econometrica* 55:3, 587–613.

Hawawini, Gabriel, and Donald B. Keim. 2000. "The Cross Section of Common Stock Returns: A Review of the Evidence and Some New Findings." In Donald B. Keim and William T. Ziemba,

Security Market Imperfections in Worldwide Equity Markets, 3–43. Cambridge: Cambridge University Press.

Hirshleifer, David. 2001. "Investor Psychology and Asset Pricing." *Journal of Finance* 56:4, 1533–1597.

Hirshleifer, David, Kewei Hou, and Siew Hong Teoh. 2012. "The Accrual Anomaly: Risk or Mispricing?" *Management Science* 58:2, 320–335.

Hirshleifer, David, and Siew Hong Teoh. 2003. "Limited Attention, Information Disclosure, and Financial Reporting." *Journal of Accounting and Economics* 36:1–3, 337–386.

Hirshleifer, David, Siew Hong Teoh, and Jeff Jiewei Yu. 2011. "Short Arbitrage, Return Asymmetry, and the Accrual Anomaly." *Review of Financial Studies* 24:7, 2429–2461.

Hong, Harrison, Terence Lim, and Jeremy C. Stein. 2000. "Bad News Travels Slowly: Size, Analyst Coverage and the Profitability of Momentum Strategies." *Journal of Finance* 55:1, 265–295.

Hong, Harris, and Jeremy C. Stein. 1999. "A Unified Theory of Underreaction, Momentum Trading and Overreaction in Asset Markets." *Journal of Finance* 54:6, 2143–2184.

Hou, Kewei, G. Andrew Karolyi, and Bong-Chan Kho. 2011. "What Factors Drive Global Stock Returns?" *Review of Financial Studies* 24:8, 2527–2574.

Hou, Kewei, Chen Xue, and Lu Zhang. 2015. "A Comparison of New Factor Models." Working Paper, Ohio State University. Available at https://fisher.osu.edu/~zhang.1868/Comparison2016June.pdf.

Hribar, Paul, and Holly Yang. 2013. "CEO Overconfidence and Management Forecasting." Working Paper, Singapore Management University. Available at http://ink.library.smu.edu.sg/cgi/viewcontent.cgi?article=2160&context=soa_research.

Huang, Wei, Qianqiu Liu, S. Ghon Rhee, and Liang Zhang L. 2010. "Return Reversals, Idiosyncratic Risk, and Expected Returns." *Review of Financial Studies* 23:1, 147–168.

Jegadeesh, Narasimhan, and Sheridan Titman. 1993. "Returns to Buying Winners and Selling Losers: Implications for Stock Market Efficiency." *Journal of Finance* 48:1, 65–91.

Jegadeesh, Narasimhan, and Sheridan Titman. 2001. "Profitability of Momentum Strategies: An Evaluation of Alternative Explanations." *Journal of Finance* 56:2, 699–720.

Jiang, Guohua, Charles M. C. Lee, and Yi Zhang. 2005. "Information Uncertainty and Expected Returns." *Review of Accounting Studies* 10:2, 185–221.

Kahneman, Daniel. 1973. *Attention and Effort*. Englewood Cliffs, NJ: Prentice-Hall.

Kahneman, Daniel, and Amos Tversky. 1979. "Prospect Theory: An Analysis of Decision under Risk." *Econometrica*, 47:2, 263–291.

Kaustia, Markku. 2010. "Disposition Effect." In H. Kent Baker and John R. Nofsinger (eds.), *Behavioral Finance: Investors, Corporations, and Markets*, 171–189. Hoboken, NJ: John Wiley & Sons, Inc.

Lakonishok, Josef, Andrei Shleifer, and Robert W. Vishny. 1994. "Contrarian Investment, Extrapolation and Risk." *Journal of Finance* 49:5, 1541–1578.

Liew, Jimmy, and Maria Vassalou. 2000. "Can Book-to-Market, Size and Momentum be Risk Factors That Predict Economic Growth?" *Journal of Financial Economics* 57:2, 221–245.

Lintner, John. 1965. "The Valuation of Risk Assets and the Selection of Risky Investments in Stock Portfolios and Capital Budgets." *Review of Economics and Statistics* 47:1, 13–37.

Liu, Xiaolei, and Lu Zhang. 2008. "Momentum Profits, Factor Pricing, and Macroeconomic Risk?" *Review of Financial Studies* 21:6, 2417–2448.

Lo, Andrew W., and A. Craig MacKinlay. 1990. "Data-Snooping Biases in Tests of Financial Asset Pricing Models." *Review of Financial Studies* 3:3, 431–467.

Loughran, Tim, and Jay Ritter. 1995. "The New Issues Puzzle." *Journal of Finance* 50:1, 23–51.

Lucas, Robert E. 1978. "Asset Prices in an Exchange Economy." *Econometrica* 46:6, 1429–1445.

Lyandres, Evgeny, Le Sun, and Lu Zhang. 2008. "The New Issues Puzzle: Testing the Investment-Based Explanation." *Review of Financial Studies* 21:6, 2825–2855.

Maio, Paulo, and Pedro Santa-Clara. 2012. "Multifactor Models and Their Consistency with the ICAPM." *Journal of Financial Economics* 106:3, 586–613.

Malkiel, Burton G., and Yexiao Xu. 2006. "Idiosyncratic Risk and Security Returns." Working Paper, University of Texas. Available at https://www.utdallas.edu/~yexiaoxu/IVOT_H.PDF.

Merton, Robert. 1973. "An Intertemporal Capital Asset Pricing Model." *Econometrica* 41:5, 867–887.

Nagel, Stefan. 2005. "Short Sales, Institutional Investors and the Cross-Section of Stock Returns." *Journal of Financial Economics* 78:2, 277–309.

Odean, Tettance. 1998. "Volume, Volatility, Price, and Profit When All Traders Are Above Average." *Journal of Finance* 53:6, 1887–1934.

Pastor, Lubos, and Robert F. Stambaugh. 2003. "Liquidity Risk and Expected Stock Returns." *Journal of Political Economy* 111:3, 642–685.

Peng, Lin, and Wei Xiong. 2006. "Investor Attention, Overreaction, and Category Learning." *Journal of Financial Economics* 80:3, 563–602.

Pincus, Morton, Shivaram Rajgopal, and Mohan Venkatachalam. 2007. "The Accrual Anomaly: International Evidence." *Accounting Review* 82:1, 169–203.

Pontiff, Jeffrey. 1996. "Costly Arbitrage: Evidence from Closed-End Funds." *Quarterly Journal of Economics* 111:4, 1135–1151.

Pontiff, Jeffrey. 2006. "Costly Arbitrage and the Myth of Idiosyncratic Risk." *Journal of Accounting and Economics* 42:1–2, 35–52.

Pontiff, Jeffrey, and Artemiza Woodgate. 2008. "Share Issuance and Cross-Sectional Returns." *Journal of Finance* 63:2, 921–945.

Rabin, Matthew. 1998. "Psychology and Economics." *Journal of Economic Literature* 36:1, 11–46.

Reinganum, Marc R., 1981, "Misspecification of Capital Asset Pricing: Empirical Anomalies Based on Earnings' Yields and Market Values." *Journal of Financial Economics* 9:1, 19–46.

Rosenberg, Barr, Kenneth Reid, and Ronald Lanstein. 1985. "Persuasive Evidence of Market Inefficiency." *Journal of Portfolio Management* 11:3, 9–16.

Rouwenhorst, K. Geert. 1998. "International Momentum Strategies." *Journal of Finance* 53:1, 267–284.

Rubinstein, Mark. 1976. "The Valuation of Uncertain Income Streams and the Pricing of Options." *Bell Journal of Economics* 7:2, 407–425.

Sadka, Ronnie. 2006. "Momentum and Post-Earnings-Announcement Drift Anomalies: The Role of Liquidity Risk." *Journal of Financial Economics* 80:2, 309–349.

Sharpe, William. 1964. "Capital Asset Prices: A Theory of Market Equilibrium under Conditions of Risk." *Journal of Finance* 19:3, 425–442.

Shefrin, Hersh, and Meir Statman. 1985. "The Disposition to Sell Winners Too Early and Ride Losers Too Long: Theory and Evidence." *Journal of Finance* 40:3, 777–790.

Shiller, Robert J. 1999. "Human Behavior and the Efficiency of the Financial System." NBER Working Paper No. 6375. Available at http://www.nber.org/papers/w6375.

Shleifer, Andrei, and Robert W. Vishny. 1997. "The Limits of Arbitrage." *Journal of Finance* 52:1, 35–55.

Sloan, Richard G. 1996. "Do Stock Prices Fully Reflect Information in Accruals and Cash Flows about Future Earnings?" *The Accounting Review* 71:3, 289–315.

Stambaugh, Robert F., Jianfeng Yu, and Yu Yuan. 2012. "The Short of It: Investor Sentiment and Anomalies." *Journal of Financial Economics* 104:2, 288–302.

Subrahmanyam, Avanidhar. 2008. "Behavioral Finance: A Review and Synthesis." *European Financial Management* 14:1, 12–29.

Titman, Sheridan, K. C. John Wei, and Feixue Xie. 2004. "Capital Investments and Stock Returns." *Journal of Financial and Quantitative Analysis* 39:4, 677–700.

Tversky Amos, and Daniel Kahneman. 1992. "Advances in Prospect Theory: Cumulative Representation of Uncertainty." *Journal of Risk and Uncertainty* 5:4, 297–323.

Vassalou, Maria, and Yuhang Xing. 2004. "Default Risk in Equity Returns." *Journal of Finance* 59:2, 831–868.

Watanabe, Akiko, Yan Xu, Tong Yao, and Tong Yu. 2013. "The Asset Growth Effect: Insights from International Equity Markets." *Journal of Financial Economics* 108:2, 529–563.

Wu, Jin, Lu Zhang, and X. Frank Zhang. 2010. "The q-Theory Approach to Understanding the Accrual Anomaly." *Journal of Accounting Research* 48:1, 177–223.

Xing, Yuhang. 2008. "Interpreting the Value Effect Through the q-theory: An Empirical Investigation." *Review of Financial Studies* 21:4, 1767–1795.

Zhang, Lu. 2005. "The Value Premium." *Journal of Finance* 60:1, 67–103.

26

The Psychology of Speculation in the Financial Markets

VICTOR RICCIARDI
Assistant Professor in Financial Management
Goucher College

Introduction

Throughout financial history, cognitive and emotional biases have driven investor behavior and influenced the financial markets in the form of bubbles. A stock bubble occurs when a substantial divergence exists between a financial asset's current market price and its intrinsic value. A *bubble* is distinguished by an extreme increase in the price or market of the financial security or asset, followed by a steep decline in price. These episodes of severe volatility and extreme risk-taking behavior within the financial markets have a detrimental impact on investment performance and economic conditions.

According to traditional finance, excessive speculation in the form of bubbles should not exist in the marketplace. Speculative behavior provides support against the efficient market hypothesis (EMH) espoused by traditional finance theory. The EMH is based on the premise that financial markets are efficient in the sense that investors in these markets process information instantaneously and that stock prices completely reflect all existing information (Ricciardi 2008a). Behavioral finance provides evidence for why speculative bubbles occur in the financial markets.

This chapter discusses major cognitive and affective issues of behavioral finance that influence the decision making of individuals and groups during times of speculation. The first section offers a brief presentation of aspects of speculative behavior in the financial markets. Next, the chapter examines several psychological issues prevalent during bubbles, including overconfidence, herd behavior, group polarization, groupthink, representativeness bias, familiarity bias, grandiosity, excitement, and overreaction and underreaction to market prices. The next section focuses on the aftermath of the financial crisis of 2007–2008 and the specific behavioral finance issues that investors exhibit for an extended time period after the catastrophe event, such as the influence of economic shocks, anchoring, recency bias, worry, loss aversion, status quo bias, and mistrust. The last section offers a summary and conclusions.

A Brief History of Speculation

Speculation, bubbles, manias, and crashes such as the Tulip Mania in the 1600s, the South Sea Bubble in the 1700s, the Panic of 1907, the stock market crashes of 1929 and 1987, the Nifty-Fifty stocks of the early 1970s, the Internet bubble (also called the dot. com bubble) of the late 1990s, and the financial crisis of 2007–2008 occur throughout financial history. For example, in reaction to the stock market crashes of 1929 and 1987, the Dow Jones Industrial Average (DJIA) fell almost 12 percent on October 29, 1929, and nearly 23 percent on October 19, 1987 (Schwartz 1995). These two stock market crashes illustrate the inefficiency of prices and the irrational group behavior of individuals.

Bubbles occur in financial markets when there are dramatic and unsustainable price increases as a result of overly optimistic and irrational excitement among investors. The circumstances surrounding bubbles happen in a similar fashion when markets have excessive price valuations above historical averages, such as the overvalued Internet stocks of the late 1990s. For the financial crisis of 2007–2008, the DJIA exceeded 14,000 in October 2007 and then declined to 6,600 in March 2009, representing more than a 50 percent decline in value. Throughout financial history, these speculative events often result when there is a new technology that people claim will change the world (Ricciardi 2017). For example, new inventions and innovations such as airplanes, automobiles, and radio underlay the stock market bubble of the 1920s. Another example is the Internet economy of 1990s, during which new investment approaches emerged to grant value to Internet stocks with no earnings profits or large losses. In the bubble stage of the Internet stocks, the investment approaches or tools of the past no longer apply such as earnings performance or stock valuation models based on dividends or earnings.

As Ricciardi (2010, pp. 143-144) points out, a major reason for the financial crisis of 2007–2008 was that traditional finance "embraced the complex innovations and exotic instruments of financial risk management . . . which contributed to the September/ October 2008 financial contagion." This historic episode demonstrates the imperfections in the assumptions and theories of traditional finance and contributes to the increased acceptance of behavioral finance. The tendency in financial markets for bubbles and crashes is evidence of the value of behavioral finance—because history often repeats itself.

Bubbles appear in academic studies involving laboratory experiments, not just in the real-world laboratory of financial markets. Laboratory experiments conducted with stock market stimulations demonstrate the misjudgments and irrational behavior of subjects during bubble and crash cycles, especially among novice investors and inexperienced traders (Smith, Suchanek, and Williams 1988). Bubble behavior also occurs among experienced traders and professional investors. Interestingly, there is a learning curve before subjects start to change their irrational bubble behavior. Caginalp, Porter, and Smith (2000) provide the following important finding from the academic literature on stock market bubble experiments:

> One of the replicable results from the experiments described earlier is that once a group experiences a bubble and crash over two experiments, and then returns for a third experiment, trading departs little from fundamental value.

Whether in a laboratory environment or in real-world financial markets, individual biases and crowd psychology are inherent in contributing to the repeated and frequent bad decision making that takes place during speculative times.

Behavioral Aspects of Speculation

The existence of speculative behavior in the form of bubbles happens based on a wide range of individual and group biases evident within the financial markets. This section focuses on overconfidence, herd behavior, group polarization, groupthink, representativeness bias, familiarity bias, grandiosity, excitement, and the overreaction and underreaction of market prices.

OVERCONFIDENCE

Overconfident behavior is an important bias that occurs during highly speculative times in the markets. Investors reveal overly positive views of their ability to control investment gains or forecast the performance of financial markets. Many investors believe they are above average in their intellect, overall judgment, and financial expertise (Ricciardi 2008b). According to Shefrin (2005, p. 6), "People who are overconfident about their abilities think they are better than they actually are. People who are overconfident about their level of knowledge think they know more than they actually know." For example, the historic bull market of the 1980s and 1990s created a long-term feeling of overconfidence, optimism, and euphoria in which it was felt that stock prices would continue to increase forever. Adams and Finn (2006, p. 48) state:

> From 1982 to 1999, the U.S. experienced an impressive bull market. Especially towards the latter half of that time period, much of the growth in market equity was due to the proliferation and rapid growth of technology and internet firms. As the Dow Jones Industrial Average increased ten-fold over 17 years, the NASDAQ composite index, teeming with tech stocks, increased thirty-fold.

A speculative case study of overconfident psychology is the Internet bubble of the late 1990s. First-time investors were unaware of the market valuation of initial public offerings (IPOs) of the Internet stocks and its connection with overconfidence, extreme enthusiasm, and the influence of crowd psychology (Ricciardi 2017). The major causes for this speculative bubble were the availability of online trading accounts, excessive margin loans balances, and the fascination of the general public and media with the fad of stock market investing (Ricciardi 2017). The Internet bubble burst and produced a severe bear market in the early 2000s. In October 2002, the value of the NASDAQ Composite fell below 1,200 from its historic high of 5,100 during the bubble only two and half years earlier. This change was the equivalent to more than a 75 percent downturn in stock prices during this period.

HERD BEHAVIOR

Another type of speculative financial behavior, herding or herd behavior explains how individuals in a group setting interact devoid of a premeditated or an intended outcome. That is, people like to join a crowd of investors who endorse their purchase and sell judgments for all types of financial assets, based on signals from the external marketplace. Herding occurs when a group of individuals such as novice investors and investment experts all make the same financial decisions based on a specific piece of information, while simultaneously ignoring other important data such as financial news or new earnings releases by corporations. Siegel (1998, p. 230) describes the herd urging as "it's better to fit in with the crowd—even if the crowd is wrong—than to risk being off on their own."

People who experience specific behavioral issues such as overconfidence, representativeness, excessive risk-taking behavior, anchoring bias, and negative emotions tend also to enhance the herding influence within groups (Ricciardi 2017). This herding behavior even amplifies the biases of individual investors to higher levels of extreme behavior. As Norton (1996, p. 43) states, "the herd minimizes risks and prevents loneliness. . . . [T]he result of herd behavior on stock prices is that they get bid higher or lower without regard to valuation." The size of the herd might eventually grow into many thousands of people trading the same security over a long period. External factors such as news coverage about a new investment philosophy or fad sometimes also lead to herd behavior. Rizzi (2014, p. 444) provides this additional perspective on herd behavior:

> *Herding* occurs when a group of individuals mimics the decisions of others. Through herding, individuals avoid falling behind and looking bad if they pursue an alternative action. Herding is based on the social pressure to conform and reflects safety by hiding in the crowd. In doing so, someone can blame any failing on the collective action and maintain his reputation.

Herd behavior often transpires over different time spans, ranging from weeks to years. Herding is a major psychological condition during a bubble, when investors buy investments on stock price momentum while disregarding other important issues such as financial data, historical stock valuations, and economic statistics. Investors experiencing herd behavior within the group also overstate or amplify the positive factors of price performance and develop incorrect assumptions about the upside potential of the markets. When the bubble ruptures or starts to deflate, panic ensures and individuals reveal their herding behavior by exiting and selling all the stocks in their portfolio, based on high levels of negative emotions (Ricciardi 2017). MacKay (1980, pp. ix–x) provides an example of speculation and crowd behavior in the historic bubble of Tulip Mania.

> Tulips, in the fourth decade of the seventeenth century in Holland, became the object of such insane and unreasoning desire that a single bulb—about the size and shape of an onion—could fetch a small fortune on any of the several exchanges that had sprung up to trade them.

Major trends in the financial markets start and finish with extreme periods of volatility based on emotion and the irrational behavior of investors. Over the entire market process, this herd behavior occurs on the upside of prices (overbuying of financial securities during bubbles) and on the downside (overselling of financial securities during crashes) because crowd psychology moves in the same direction when large groups of individuals drive investor sentiment. Financial history has a predisposition to repeat itself, with events of herding occurring during times of bubbles and crashes (Ricciardi 2017).

GROUP POLARIZATION

In the 1960s, Stoner (1961, 1967) first developed the concept of the *risky-shift effect,* in which people within a group often make judgments after extensive discussion that differ from the final decisions that someone would formulate on an individual basis. For example, many research studies in the social sciences show that groups in formal settings make riskier decisions than individuals; this is the risky-shift phenomenon. Stoner (1977, p. 333) provides the following perspective on the risky-shift effect:

> It is popularly assumed that groups are more conservative and cautious than individuals. Considerable evidence shows that in some situations groups make riskier decisions than individuals. In those situations group solutions tend to represent "risky shifts" from solutions that might be offered by individual group members. For example, in dealing with a hypothetical case in which an individual must decide whether to stay in a secure job or leave for one that is less secure but offers a higher salary, groups have been more likely than individuals to recommend the riskier option.

This risky-shift effect is associated with historic events such as NASA's decision to launch the space shuttle *Challenger* without testing the rubber O-rings, which then failed and caused the shuttle to explode; or the Soviet Union's invasion of Afghanistan without careful review of Mujahldeen insurgent activity.

Myers and Lamm (1976) modify the risky-shift phenomenon into a more general concept and named it group polarization. The *group polarization concept* is the notion that group conversation or debate results in shifts in the direction to more extreme opinions or views about final decisions among group members. However, research findings sometimes report that group discussion produces a change or shift in opinions of individual members that do not always result in greater risk-taking behavior. According to Wrightsman and Deaux (1981, p. 466), "It has been shown that, if the initial opinions of the group tend toward conservatism, then the shift resulting from group discussion will be toward a more extreme conservative opinion."

A premise of the group polarization concept is that groups can move in two different directions: groups may move either to extremely risky decisions or behaviors (known as the risky shift) or to very risk-averse decisions or behaviors (known as a cautious shift). The cautious shift demonstrates that some group judgments result in more conservative assessments than those of individuals. Yet, this finding contradicts the initial premise of Stoner's (1961) risky-shift effect. According to Stoner, group polarization takes place within a formal organizational structure, such as a nonprofit, government body, or corporation. The members of the group have specific management responsibilities, communicate with each other directly, and have a group size ranging from four to eight members (Ricciardi 2017).

A notable study from the area of behavioral accounting demonstrates how groups might shift in different risk-taking directions. Carnes, Harwood, and Sawyers (1996) investigate the influence of group discussion on the probability of tax professionals' taking tax return positions preferred by taxpayers as "gray areas" of the tax law. In the first experiment, the authors offer six ambiguous situations to 68 tax professionals. The researchers divide the participants into groups and instruct them to assess each situation before and after a group conversation. Generally, their findings confirm the premise that group dialogue leads to either risky or cautious shifts in tax professionals' judgment. In the first experiment, conversations led to a risky "pro-taxpayer shift" in all three high-probability cases and a cautious "pro-IRS shift" in two of three low-probability situations. Overall, then, group discussion results in higher, more risky tax return positions in situations defined as high probabilities of tax return position requested by the client. The evidence shows a cautious shift for lower, more conservative tax return positions in situations identified as having low probability.

The notion that groups sometimes make riskier decisions also occurs within the financial setting. Slovic (1972) discusses the risky-shift concept as a central aspect of group psychology within the investment management domain. The problem with a major change in judgment by group members is that the risk assessment often results in a problematic and irrational financial decision by the group. For instance, groups sometimes select an outcome that has a larger payoff but a lower chance of achievement. According to Ellis and Fisher (1990, p. 55), "If a group and its individual members were to place bets on a horse, for example, the group would more likely bet on 100-to-1 shot than would any of the individuals deciding alone."

Stephens and Silence (1981) examine the risky-shift effect among 35 commercial loan officers at five Texas banks. The authors provide the subjects with an imaginary loan application for an established bank customer who has a strong credit history at a time of economic uncertainty. They designed the loan application to raise "some concerns" but not so inappropriate as to be rejected immediately. The findings support the premise of the risky-shift effect, in that the loan officers rejected the loan application individually but approved it on a group basis or a committee level.

McGuire, Kiesler, and Siegel (1987) assess whether a difference in the type of communication delivery exists between face-to-face discussions and computer-mediated discussions about decision making on risky choices, on both individual and group bases. The authors evaluate 48 business managers individually and in three-member groups in which the subjects made risk assessments of investment alternatives. The authors place the subjects in both face-to-face discussions and real-time computer-oriented dialogues. In each setting, the task is to make two group decisions. McGuire et al. (p. 917) find that after face-to-face discussions, the groups "were risk averse for gains and risk seeking for losses, a tendency predicted by prospect theory and consistent with choice shift." In contrast, the computer-mediated group dialogues did not reveal a shift in decisions or the existence of prospect theory behavior.

Inferior group decisions occur in times of speculative behavior and bubble situations. Burton, Coller, and Tuttle (2006) find that investors who subsequently have the most excessive price valuations influence the market to a greater extent than do investors possessing the most conservative beliefs. As Burton et al. (p. 107) note, these results also imply "that participation in a market will accentuate risk preferences so that good news produces a cautious shift in prices (i.e., toward lower prices) whereas bad news produces a risky shift (i.e., toward higher prices)."

GROUPTHINK BEHAVIOR

The groupthink effect is an emerging topic within behavioral finance (Hayat 2015). In the early 1970s, Irving Janis first developed the idea of the groupthink effect (Sunstein and Hastie 2015). Groupthink behavior has been connected to several historical events in which members of a group do not have the desire to upset group consensus or harmony by stating an opposing view (Ricciardi 2017). Groupthink was first applied to President Kennedy's judgment to use military action by invading Cuba, known as the Bay of Pigs incident. Although President Kennedy's foreign policy advisors opposed his choice, they were highly tentative in expressing a contrary viewpoint about his decision. Janis (1971, p. 44) provides the following perspective of the groupthink effect:

> The symptoms of groupthink arise when the members of decision-making groups become motivated to avoid being too harsh in their judgments of their leaders' or their colleagues' ideas. They adopt a soft line of criticism, even in their own thinking. At their meetings, all the members are amiable and seek complete concurrence on every important issue, with no bickering or conflict to spoil the cozy, "we-feeling" atmosphere.

A major aspect of groupthink behavior is the notion of conformity. Regarding conformity in groups, Asch (1952) reports that differences of opinion cause people to search and find harmony in a final group decision that enables the individual decision maker to reduce the affective reactions of anxiety and fear. As Janis (1972, 1982) notes, the high levels of group pressure and feelings of anxiety among individuals to conform during a groupthink situation become overwhelming, resulting in a final group decision of consensus. Each person in the group experiences a personal aversion to depart from the final group's consensus opinion or majority outcome.

Groupthink events often occur within a formal setting among different types of organizations, such as nonprofits, government agencies, and corporations. In the field of behavioral corporate finance, Shefrin (2005) identifies the groupthink effect as a major cause of the past accounting scandals and corporate bankruptcies of WorldCom and Enron. Regarding the financial crisis of 2007–2008, Shefrin (2016) attributes the poor risk management practices and financial problems of AIG, Freddie Mac, and Fannie Mae to groupthink behavior. In particular, the organizational structure of many large organizations is faulty and bureaucratic, which stifles innovation (Schiller 1992, 2002). Schiller (1992, pp. 74-75) provides the following perspective about institutional investors:

> Group-decision difficulties . . . mitigated to some extent by the fact that their objective performance has always been observed on a regular basis . . . getting feedback on the success of their investment strategies. But, of course

> . . . the short-run immediate feedback on their quarterly investment performance may not awaken a bureaucracy to long-term strategic issues; there is room for "groupthink" to arise.

For many organizations, possible conditions exist for groupthink behavior because mistakes during the decision-making process influence all types of group behavior, especially financial issues. For example, Cici (2012) identifies this potential groupthink effect among investment management teams, and Puetz and Ruenzi (2011) point out the same behavior among mutual fund managers. For a research sample of 77 stock market professionals, Wright and Schaal (1988) report that these experts suffer from groupthink and that this behavior results in poor investment returns. All these expert groups suffer from groupthink behavior because the group's members arrive at absolute agreement without diligently evaluating financial recommendations or investment information. Additionally, a leader with an outgoing and assertive personality influences the group's overall risk-taking behavior (Shefrin 2008). The final outcome of the group is sometimes attributed to the risky-shift phenomenon (Ricciardi 2017).

Wright and Schaal (1988, p. 42) explain the association between individual and group decision makers in a finance setting:

> An investment committee will have a series of norms and attitudes that may be called "current policy." This includes views on economic conditions and the course of the markets. The more important the group is to the individual, the greater the likelihood each professional believes the policy is correct. He or she is not simply complying . . . but has internalized the committee policies so they are now the professional's own.

For the members of an investment committee, the majority position might change an individual's own opinion. A person might reveal a tendency to adhere to the current investment policy instead of stating any opposition, resulting in sustaining the status quo judgment and reinforcing groupthink behavior (Ricciardi 2017). Moreover, group members often respond to the people who challenge their viewpoints with disbelief and misgiving.

Groups applying groupthink use substandard financial strategies when making their final assessments and decisions. Groups might have access to too much information, inaccurate statistics, or flawed information that leads to inferior decision-making results. The typical behavior of a groupthink episode is that group members do not make a few minor mistakes in judgment; rather, the group tends to make catastrophic errors and decisions over an extended period. Ricciardi and Simon (2000) identify an example of potential groupthink in the mismanagement and bad financial decisions made by trustees at Eckert College. In August 2000, a news story read "Eyes Wide Shut: How Eckerd's 52 Trustees Failed to See Two-Thirds of Its Endowment Disappear." The theme of the news story concerned how Eckerd College's endowment fund fell from $34 million to $13 million, much to the dismay of the student body, faculty, administration, and trustees. As Pulley (2000, p. A31) notes:

> At Eckerd College here, those who have been trying to figure it out point to the Board of Trustees, whose own leaders concede that they didn't ask

> many questions, and allowed policies and practices that led to the financial fiasco. . . . Several trustees have likened the fiasco to the complex circumstances behind manmade disasters. . . . Over the years, Eckerd has suffered from poorly executed real-estate projects, questionable investments, an inability to provide the financial data needed to issue bonds to pay for capital projects, an understaffed financial office, antiquated accounting systems, and a college president who always seemed to have the answers.

The influence of group psychology is apparent in the history of finance as seen through the lens of speculative psychology: manias, bubbles, panics, and crashes, as well as herding, group polarization, and groupthink. All have some similar characteristics, because each involves an affective reaction within the group and aspects of crowd or mob psychology (Ricciardi 2017). Dreman (1977, p. 100) shows the association of groupthink to stock market psychology:

> The mindless conformity and the excessive risk taking that Janis describes in smaller groups are precisely the major symptoms that Le Bon pinpoints in larger crowds. Curiously enough, these symptoms, and the relaxed, chummy atmosphere often found in cohesive group decision making were also found to a significant degree in . . . speculative bubbles.

Dreman makes the point that a historical event can demonstrate a groupthink effect among a small group of investors, and then over time it broadens to a much larger group of individuals who start to follow a much larger herd (Ricciardi 2017). For instance, Nofsinger (2014, p. 135), who identifies the real estate bubble of 2001–2006 as a groupthink event, states: "Real estate became thought of as a speculative and tradable asset for some people, instead of an investment." The complete acceptance of all group members, the existence of extreme levels of overconfidence, and the presence of overly optimistic investors may lead to individuals' rejecting anything that might be considered evidence or beliefs contradictory to the final group judgment.

REPRESENTATIVENESS BIAS, FAMILIARITY BIAS, GRANDIOSITY, AND EXCITEMENT

An important bias that individuals reveal during the initial phase of a bubble is *representativeness bias,* which is a tendency to have an unrealistic view of a financial circumstance and then to over-weight how much this current situation is similar to past experiences. With this decision-making bias, investors incorrectly conclude that stock prices will continue to new highs based on a small sample of stocks. For instance, during a bubble, investors may see prices continuing to rise into the future. Representativeness bias accelerates the herd's risk-taking behavior to much higher levels, based on group psychology (Ricciardi 2017).

Familiarity bias is evident when people have a preference for and invest in familiar assets based on the name or reputation of the company. Investors prefer to invest in familiar local stocks (known as *local bias*) and over-invest in portfolios of domestic securities (known as *home bias*) (Baker and Ricciardi 2014a, 2014b, 2015). Investors also tend to underestimate and miscalculate the risk of familiar investments. For example, in the early 1970s, a bubble developed in a group of growth stocks known as the "Nifty-Fifty." These stocks consisted of 50 familiar large-cap blue chip stocks, such as IBM and Disney. The bubble eventually burst. Investors focused on blue chip stocks that received much media attention, which increased their familiarity and raised their prices. The investors incorrectly assessed these overpriced stocks as less risky and with producing a higher return, but the opposite was true.

Individuals experience high levels of greed when a stock market bubble is accelerating and investors want to join the crowd (Ricciardi 2017). They also suffer from extreme grandiosity. Lifton and Geist (1999, p. 24) describe this grandiosity as, "when prices continue to escalate, investors . . . feel like Icarus—they feel increasingly excited and capable of flying higher and higher." Indeed, the feeling of grandiosity makes investors feel invincible, coupled with extreme enthusiasm. As a result, they make irrational predictions of stock market performance returns and disregard risk and uncertainty (Ricciardi 2008a, 2008b).

The feeling of grandiosity that characterizes bubbles is connected with how excitement influences the speculative behavior in financial markets. Andrade, Odean, and Shengle (2016, p. 11) describe the role of excitement in bubble situations:

> We document, in an experimental setting, that magnitude and amplitude of bubbles is greater when, prior to trading, traders experience the high-intensity, positive emotion of excitement. . . . [T]he excitement generated by rapidly rising prices in real-world markets may trigger emotions that lead to larger asset pricing bubbles.

Individuals often disregard rational thinking and replace it with euphoric expectation, characterized by overconfidence and optimism about future investment performance. They focus on the short term and ignore the long-term investment horizon. The speculative bubble continues to expand until investors stop buying the stocks, in which case the market can no longer sustain the impracticable increase in price valuations and the bubble implodes.

OVERREACTION AND UNDERREACTION

During a bubble or crash, some investors overreact to new information while others underreact. Overreaction occurs when the stock price movement to the downside or upside happens too quickly (De Bondt and Thaler 1985). By contrast, underreaction occurs when the stock price movements to the downside or upside happen too slowly (Cutler, Poterba, and Summers 1991). There is a relatively short-term time horizon during which investors process new financial data—perhaps several hours, days, weeks, months, or even years. All types of investors over- or underreact to good or bad news which the market may perceive as positive (valuations increase) or negative (valuations decrease).

Investors often experience an exhilarated degree of overconfidence and optimism during a bubble, when stocks post strong increases in price. According to Dissanaike

(1997, p. 27), this overreaction occurs when "if stock prices systematically overshoot as a consequence of excessive investor optimism or pessimism, price reversals should be predictable from past price performance." For example, suppose a sector or industry repeatedly reports above-average earnings performance each quarter for an entire year. Investors overreact to this positive financial news, feeling excessively confident and optimistic about future earnings expectations; as a result, the stock prices are then mispriced or artificially overstated (Mynhardt and Plastun 2013). Eventually, those prices see a market sector correction and decline when there is news about industry groups such as below-average earnings performance. Negative sentiments take over. Conversely, when investors are overly negative about a sector or industry, its stock prices lead to excessive reactions to the downside, as happened with Internet stocks in the early 2000s and most all stocks during the financial crisis of 2007–2008 (Mynhardt, Plastun, and Makarenko 2013).

Other investors might underreact to financial news and respond too slowly (De Bondt and Thaler 1985). For example, investor sentiment is sometimes slow to change after a bubble bursts. Some individuals are slow to reacting to the change or fail to recognize that the market has moved from bull to bear market cycle. Further, some investors prefer to avoid the emotional pain of realizing an actual financial loss and suffer the accompanying regret of admitting an investment mistake.

Behavioral Biases Evident After the Financial Crisis

Every generation of investors has experienced a stock market bubble and a major bear market crash after the bubble bursts. This section examines behavioral finance issues in the aftermath of the financial crisis of 2007–2008.

After a bubble bursts, investors display several biases. In particular, the *collective memory hypothesis* suggests that recent economic shocks influence an individual's risk tolerance and change investor behavior (Rizzi 2014). Especially, the affective reactions of investors to recent economic distress have greater influence on investor judgment and decision making than do long-term historical investment performance data and other objective information. Although temporary, the change in expected long-term influence on risk tolerance and risk perception is likely to be lasting and negative. Nagel (2012) believes that younger individuals are more sensitive to recent negative performance than older investors, because the younger generation has a shorter investment history. For example, millennial clients are more prone to behavioral changes based on recent returns than are older investors such as baby boomers, who have had decades of experience. This was the case following the bear market of the early 2000s and the financial crisis of 2007–2008.

LASTING INFLUENCE OF ECONOMIC SHOCKS

Malmendier and Nagel (2011) examine the role of economic disruptions on individual investor and risk-taking psychology, using data from the Survey of Consumer Finances

(SCF) between 1960 and 2007. They find that investors who have experienced inferior stock market performance during their lifespan have a lower financial risk tolerance, are less willing to invest in common stocks, have a lower percentage of their overall portfolio in stocks, and are less optimistic about future stock performance. For safer assets such as bonds, people who experience lower bond returns are less likely to own bonds.

For instance, millennials are a younger generation that has suffered a severe economic downturn, making them more cautious toward risky securities. However, their reaction may not be as severe as the cohort group born after the stock market crash of 1929 known as the "Depression Babies" generation. In order to overcome these economic shocks, investors should take a long-term perspective of investing. Over the long-term asset classes performance are based on the concept known as *reversion to the mean*. This is the premise that prices and investment returns eventually move back toward their historical averages for each asset class.

Bricker, Bucks, Kennickell, Mach, and Moore (2011) examine the impact of the financial crisis of 2007–2008 on family households, using questionnaire data from the SCF before and after the crisis. Based on interviews done between mid-2009 and early 2010, the data reveals a transformation toward a more cautious financial psychology of the family unit after experiencing the financial shock. The families report a lower investment risk tolerance and a higher level of *precautionary savings* (i.e., a greater desire for safer cash instruments while reducing total household spending).

ANCHORING, RECENCY BIAS, AND WORRY

Individuals may suffer several biases after a bubble bursts, including anchoring bias and recency bias, as well as negative emotions such as worry or depression. *Anchoring* is the tendency to hold onto a belief and then apply it as a reference point for making future judgments. People often make judgments based on initial information and have difficulty altering or changing their viewpoints when they receive new information. In this way, many investors still employ a negative anchor after a financial crisis or stock market crash. Similarly, investor experience that focuses on recent financial performance has a strong impact on later judgments and decisions. This negative anchor is called *recency bias*. According to Rizzi (2014, p. 440), "Risk estimates become anchored on recent events. Overemphasis on recent events can also produce disaster myopia . . . as instruments are priced as if another crisis will occur."

As Ricciardi (2012) states, high levels of worry remain for years after a bubble or a crash. Consequently, investors tend to under-weight or avoid stocks within their portfolios because of extreme risk and loss aversion. They have strong negative emotions, including depression, anxiety, regret, or fear that affect their judgment. Based on an online questionnaire of more than 1,700 investors in 2010, Ricciardi (2011) finds that a much larger percentage of individuals associate the worry phrase with stocks (70 percent of respondents) than those who associate worry when compared to bonds (10 percent of respondents). Individuals who have higher levels of anxiety about investments in stocks tend to raise their risk perception and lower their risk tolerance. These higher levels of negative emotions and the anchoring effect caused by the financial crisis of 2007–2008 resulted in many investors avoiding individual stocks or stock mutual funds for several years.

LOSS AVERSION

Investors tend to focus on downside risk when they lose money after a stock market crash. When they experience this loss, the outcome not only results in an objective loss in dollar terms but also a subjective aspects as an emotional loss. In particular, when evaluating specific investment transactions, individuals allocate more importance to a loss than to earning an equivalent gain. This feeling of losing money can remain for a very long time. Many investors who realized severe losses during a financial crisis tend to avoid the riskier asset classes such as common stocks for an extended period.

STATUS QUO BIAS

After a bubble bursts, individuals suffer status quo bias, in which they no longer want to invest in stocks or avoid making decisions about their investment portfolios all together. The feeling of investment distress, which is based on other biases such as anchoring, worry, and loss aversion, further deepens the status quo bias by further delaying current financial decisions. Investors no longer want to manage their investments because they want to avoid reliving these bad experiences. After a financial crisis, many of these investors have portfolios that under-weight stocks and over-weight cash and bonds.

TRUST AND MISTRUST IN A FINANCIAL SETTING

Trust is a key element in society, needed to develop complicated social, psychological, and economic relationships. Trust and trustworthiness are functions of our dependence on or confidence in the truthfulness, accuracy, value, or worth of a person, organization, or matter. Trust is critical for establishing personal (e.g., a couple dating for the first time) and professional relationships (e.g., an individual investor and a financial advisor). For example, Joiner, Leveson, and Langfield-Smith (2002) evaluate the perceptions of trust between financial planners and their clients. Using 186 undergraduate business students, Joiner et al. investigate how trust factored into decisions to use expert language during the financial planning advisement process, as well as judgments on the quality of advice received, impressions of the planner's trustworthiness, knowledge and honesty, and prospects of consumers to seek such expert advice. Joiner et al. (p. 25) report the following:

> The results indicate that the overuse of technical language in a lay client consultation reduces clients' understanding of the advice offered. Lowered advice understandability negatively affects clients' perceptions of the professional adviser's expertise and trustworthiness and, subsequently, client's intention to seek the professional's advice.

Other aspects of trust are essential to fostering confidence in organizations (e.g., the credibility of government institutions) or markets (e.g., confidence in international stock markets). According to Doost and Fishman (2004, p. 623):

> Recent corporate scandals, fraud, and misuse of resources involving top executives and multi-billion dollar companies such as Sunbeam, Tyco,

> Medco, Enron, Worldcom, the NYSE and others—not to mention accounting giant, Arthur Andersen, threaten the viability and continued success of the U.S. economy, the global economy, and world-wide political stability. Stock markets, employees' pension funds, national employment rates, and the ability of citizens to trust in economic systems are all adversely affected.

People's overall trust in the private and public sectors began to decrease (i.e., a trend toward increased mistrust) in the late 1960s (Slovic 1993, 1999), and this extends to financial planning and advice. For example, the higher the level of mistrust individual possess in the financial experts, who may be informing the public about risky behavior, the more anxiety or worry people feel about the financial crisis or bursting bubbles. As Opdyke (2007, p. D1) comments, "a growing number of people who have spent years building a relationship with a trusted financial advisor are having to start over again with someone new." Olsen (2004, p. 190) relates this mistrust to the dot.com bubble of the late 1990s:

> First and foremost, the stability of the market was being undermined by conflicts of interest in the accounting and financial analysis professions. . . . Second, many stock option plans allowed managers to cash in their options after very short holding periods (less than a year). . . . [S]ome managers' behavior, while not overtly illegal or unethical, resembled gamblers playing with the "house money." That is, since they had not paid for their options, they behaved as if they had little to lose but a lot to gain by taking bigger risks with the firm's funds. Finally, trust in the official regulatory process was undermined by revelations of budget reductions among regulatory agencies and widespread public exposure of a cavalier and "public be damned" attitude on the part of many corporate executives and professional money managers.

Developing a strong level of trust takes a long time for investors. However, trust can quickly turn into mistrust, especially in the aftermath of a financial crisis. And once that mistrust takes hold, repairing and restoring trust can be difficult.

Summary and Conclusions

The speculative behavior associated with bubbles, manias, panics, and crashes are occasional, random, and severe events in financial history. Behavioral finance helps to explain that speculative behavior, based on cognitive processes and affective reactions that influence decision making. This chapter discusses various biases that influence the speculative psychology of investors during bubbles. These biases include overconfident behavior, herding, polarization, groupthink, representativeness bias, familiarity bias, grandiosity, excitement, and overreaction and underreaction to prices in financial markets. The chapter also presents a detailed overview of what happens in the aftermath of the financial crisis of 2007–2008 and the biases that influence some investors for an extended period, including the detrimental effect of repeated economic shocks, anchoring bias, recency effect, worry, loss aversion, status quo bias, and mistrust.

These are all important financial behaviors and characteristics about which financial professionals should be aware. By gaining such awareness, they can better understand and manage the behavior of their clients, because bad financial mistakes have a tendency to repeat themselves, especially during bubbles and crashes. In particular, some clients may experience negative long-term biases after market crashes that influence their overall judgment and decision making. The aftermath of the recent financial crisis resulted in many investors exhibiting lower levels of risk tolerance and higher levels of worry and risk perception, which in turn resulting in underinvesting in stocks and overinvesting in bonds and cash.

DISCUSSION QUESTIONS

1. Define the term *stock bubble*.
2. List and describe four major causes of speculative behavior.
3. List and explain four major biases that investors exhibit in the aftermath of the financial crisis of 2007–2008.
4. Discuss the influence of investor psychology in the aftermath of a financial crisis or when a bubble bursts.

REFERENCES

Adams, Brandon, and Brian Finn. 2006. *The Study of Behavioral Finance*. New York: iUniverse.

Andrade, Eduardo B., Terrance Odean, and Lin Shengle. 2016. "Bubbling with Excitement: An Experiment." *Review of Finance* 20:2, 447–466.

Asch, Solomon E. 1952. *Social Psychology*. New York: Prentice-Hall.

Baker, H. Kent, and Victor Ricciardi. 2014a. "How Biases Affect Investor Behaviour." *European Financial Review*, February-March, 7–10.

Baker, H. Kent, and Victor Ricciardi (eds.). 2014b. *Investor Behavior—The Psychology of Financial Planning and Investing*. Hoboken, NJ: John Wiley.

Baker, H. Kent, and Victor Ricciardi. 2015. "Understanding Behavioral Aspects of Financial Planning and Investing." *Journal of Financial Planning* 28:3, 22–26.

Bricker, Jesse, Brian Bucks, Arthur Kennickell, Traci Mach, and Kevin Moore. 2011. "Surveying the Aftermath of the Storm: Changes in Family Finances from 2007 to 2009." Working Paper, Federal Reserve Board. Available at https://www.federalreserve.gov/pubs/ feds/2011/ 201117/201117abs.html.

Burton, F. Greg, Maribeth Coller, and Brad Tuttle. 2006. "Market Responses to Qualitative Information from a Group Polarization Perspective." *Accounting, Organizations & Society* 31:2, 107–127.

Caginalp, Gunduz, David Porter, and Vernon L. Smith. 2000. "Overreactions, Momentum, Liquidity, and Price Bubbles in Laboratory and Field Asset Markets." *Journal of Psychology & Financial Markets* 1:1, 24–48.

Carnes, Gregory A., Gordon B. Harwood, and Roby B. Sawyers. 1996. "A Comparison of Tax Professionals' Individual and Group Decisions When Resolving Ambiguous Tax Questions." *Journal of the American Taxation Association* 18:2, 1–18.

Cici, Gjergji. 2012. "The Prevalence of the Disposition Effect in Mutual Funds' Trades." *Journal of Financial & Quantitative Analysis* 47:4, 795–820.

Cutler, David, James Poterba, and Lawrence Summers. 1991. "Speculative Dynamics." *Review of Economics Studies* 58:3, 529–546.

De Bondt, Werner, and Richard Thaler. 1985. "Does the Stock Market Overreact?" *Journal of Finance* 40:3, 793–808.

Dissanaike, Gishan. 1997. "Do Stock Market Investors Overreact?" *Journal of Business Finance & Accounting* 24:1, 27–49.

Doost, Roger K., and Teddi Fishman. 2004. "Beyond Arthur Andersen: Searching for Answers." *Managerial Auditing Journal* 19:5: 623–639.

Dreman, David. 1977. *Psychology and the Stock Market: Investment Strategy Beyond Random Walk.* New York: AMACOM.

Ellis, Donald G., and B. Audrey Fisher. 1990. *Small Group Decision*-Making: Communication and the Group Processes. New York: McGraw-Hill.

Hayat, Usman. 2015. "Investment Decisions: How to Avoid Groupthink." *CFA Institute Enterprising Investor Practical Analysis for Investment Professionals,* April 29. Available at https://blogs.cfainstitute.org/investor/2015/04/29/investment-decisions-how-to-avoid-groupthink/.

Janis, Irving. 1971. "Groupthink." *Psychology Today* 5:6, 43–46, 74–76.

Janis, Irving. 1972. *Victims of Groupthink: A Psychological Study of Foreign-Policy Decisions and Fiascoes.* Boston: Houghton Mifflin.

Janis, Irving. 1982. *Groupthink.* Boston: Houghton Mifflin.

Joiner, Therese A., Lynne Leveson, and Kim Langfield-Smith. 2002. "Technical Language, Advice Understandability, and Perceptions of Expertise and Trustworthiness: The Case of the Financial Planner." *Australian Journal of Management* 27:1, 25–44.

Lifson, Lawrence E., and Richard A. Geist. 1999. *The Psychology of Investing.* New York: John Wiley.

MacKay, Charles. 1980. *Extraordinary Popular Delusions and the Madness of Crowds.* New York: Crown.

Malmendier, Ulrike, and Stefan Nagel. 2011. "Depression Babies: Do Macroeconomic Experiences Affect Risk Taking?" *Quarterly Journal of Economics* 126:1, 373–416.

McGuire, Timonthy W., Sara Kiesler, and Jane Siegel. 1987. "Group and Computer-Mediated Discussion Effects in Risk Decision Making." *Journal of Personality and Social Psychology* 52:5, 917–930.

Myers, David G., and Helmut Lamm. 1976. "The Group Polarization Phenomenon." *Psychological Bulletin* 83:4, 602–617.

Mynhardt, Ronald H., and Alex Plastun. 2013. "The Overreaction Hypothesis: The Case of Ukrainian Stock Market." *Corporate Ownership and Control* 11:1, 406–423.

Mynhardt, Ronald H., Alex Plastun, and Inna Makarenko. 2013. "Behavior of Financial Markets Efficiency during the Financial Market Crisis: 2007–2009." *Corporate Ownership and Control* 11:2, 473–488.

Nagel, Stefan. 2012. "Macroeconomic Experiences and Expectations: A Perspective of the Great Recession." Paper Prepared for Academic Consultants Meeting of the Board of Governors of the Federal Reserve System, May 14.

Nofsinger, John R. 2014. *The Psychology of Investing.* Boston: Pearson.

Norton, Leslie P. 1996. "The Outliers: Refusing to Run with the Herd Can Be Dangerous, But Can Pay Off." *Barron's,* May 20, 43–44.

Olsen, Robert A. 2004. "Trust, Complexity and the 1990s Market Bubble" [Editorial Commentary]. *Journal of Behavioral Finance* 5:4, 186–191.

Opdyke, Jeff D. 2007. "Advisor Turnover Roils Investors." *Wall Street Journal,* October 9: D1, D4.

Puetz, Alexander, and Stefan Ruenzi. 2011. "Overconfidence among Professional Investors: Evidence from Mutual Fund Managers." *Journal of Business Finance & Accounting* 38:5/6, 684–712.

Pulley, John L. 2000. "Eyes Wide Shut: How Eckerd's 52 Trustees Failed to See Two-Thirds of Its Endowment Disappear." *Chronicle of Higher Education* 46:50, A31–A33.

Ricciardi, Victor. 2008a. "Risk: Traditional Finance versus Behavioral Finance." In Frank J. Fabozzi (ed.), *The Handbook of Finance, Volume 3: Valuation, Financial Modeling, and Quantitative Tools*, 11–38. Hoboken, NJ: John Wiley & Sons, Inc.

Ricciardi, Victor. 2008b. "The Psychology of Risk: The Behavioral Finance Perspective." In Frank J. Fabozzi (ed.), *The Handbook of Finance, Volume 2: Investment Management and Financial Management*, 85–111. Hoboken, NJ: John Wiley & Sons, Inc.

Ricciardi, Victor. 2010. "The Psychology of Risk." In H. Kent Baker and John R. Nofsinger (eds.), *Behavioral Finance: Investors, Corporations, and Markets*, 131–149. Hoboken, NJ: John Wiley & Sons, Inc..

Ricciardi, Victor. 2011. "The Financial Judgment and Decision-Making Process of Women: The Role of Negative Feelings." Third Annual Meeting of the Academy of Behavioral Finance and Economics, September. Available at www.ssrn.com/abstract=1936669.

Ricciardi, Victor. 2012. "Our 3-year Market Hangover." *MoneySense*. Available at: http://www.moneysense.ca/ 2012/05/09/our-3-year-market-hangover/.

Ricciardi, Victor. 2017. "The Role of Group Psychology in Behavioral Finance: A Research Starting Point for Banking, Economic, and Financial Historians." In Korinna Schönhärl (ed.), *Decision Taking, Confidence and Risk Management in Banks: From Early Modernity to the 20th Century.* Hampshire: Palgrave Macmillan.

Ricciardi, Victor, and Helen Simon. 2000. "The Case for Behavioral Finance: A New Frontier?" Presented at Northeast Business and Economics Association, 27th Annual Conference, October 7, St. John's University.

Rizzi, Joseph V. 2014. "Post-crisis Investor Behavior: Experience Matters." In H. Kent Baker and Victor Ricciardi (eds.), *Investor Behavior: The Psychology of Financial Planning and Investing*, 439-455. Hoboken, NJ: John Wiley & Sons, Inc.

Schwartz, Elaine. 1995. *ECON 101 ½*. New York: Avon.

Shefrin, Hersh. 2005. *Behavioral Corporate Finance: Decisions that Create Value*. New York: McGraw-Hill/Irwin.

Shefrin, Hersh. 2008. *Ending the Management Illusion*. New York: McGraw-Hill.

Shefrin, Hersh. 2016. *Behavioral Risk Management: Managing the Psychology That Drives Decisions and Influences Operational Risk*. New York: Palgrave Macmillan.

Shiller, Robert J. 1992. "Who's Minding the Store?" *The Report of the Twentieth Century Fund Task Force on Market Speculation and Corporate Governance*. New York: Twentieth Century Fund Press.

Shiller, Robert J. 2002. "Bubbles, Human Judgment, and Expert Opinion." *Financial Analysts Journal* 58:3, 18–26.

Siegel, Matt. 1998. "What Analysts and Cattle Have in Common." *Fortune* 138:4, 230.

Slovic, Paul. 1972. "Psychological Study of Human Judgment: Implications for Investment Decision Making." *Journal of Finance* 27:4, 779–799.

Slovic, Paul. 1993. "Perceived Risk, Trust, and Democracy." *Risk Analysis* 13:6, 675–682.

Slovic, Paul. 1999. "Trust, Emotion, Sex, Politics, and Science: Surveying the Risk-Assessment Battlefield." *Risk Analysis* 19:4, 689–701.

Smith, Vernon L., Gerry L. Suchanek, and Arlington W. Williams. 1988. "Bubbles, Crashes and Endogenous Expectations in Experimental Spot Asset Markets." *Econometric* 56:5, 1119–1151.

Stephens, David B., and Larry J. Silence. 1981. "Coping with 'Risky Shift' in the Loan Committee." *Journal of Commercial Bank Lending* 64:1, 50–57.

Stoner, James A. F. 1961. *A Comparison of Individual and Group Decisions Involving Risk*. Unpublished master's thesis, Massachusetts Institute of Technology, School of Industrial Management, Cambridge, MA.

Stoner, James A. F. 1967. *The Effect of General Values on Cautious and Risky Shifts in Group Decisions*. Unpublished doctoral thesis, Massachusetts Institute of Technology, School of Industrial Management, Cambridge, MA.

Stoner, James A. F. 1977. *Management*. Englewood Cliffs, NJ: Prentice-Hall.

Sunstein, Cass R., and Reid Hastie. 2015. *Wiser: Getting Beyond Groupthink to Make Groups Smarter*. Boston: Harvard Business Review Press.

Wright, John, and David Schaal. 1988. "Groupthink: The Trap of Consensus Investing." *Journal of Financial Planning* 1:1, 41–44.

Wrightman, Lawrence, and Kay Deaux. 1981. *Social Psychology in the Eighties*. Monterey, CA: Brooks/Cole.

27

Can Humans Dance with Machines?

Institutional Investors, High-Frequency Trading, and Modern Markets Dynamics

IRENE ALDRIDGE
Managing Director, Able Alpha Trading, Ltd. and Able Markets,
Director, Big Data Finance

Introduction

In October 2015, the U.S. Securities and Exchange Commission (SEC) counted 18 national security exchanges registered with the SEC under the Securities Exchange Act of 1934 (Securities and Exchange Commission 2015). The SEC-registered exchanges include the NYSE, NYSE Arca, NYSE MKT (formerly NYSE AMEX and the American Stock Exchange), BATS, BATS Y, EDGA, EDGX, BOX Options, Nasdaq, NASDAQ OMX BX, NASDAQ OMX PHLX, C2 Options, CBOE, Chicago Stock Exchange, ISE, ISE Gemini, Miami International Securities Exchange, and the National Stock Exchange.

The SEC-registered exchanges are often referred to as "lit" exchanges, in comparison with "dark" trading venues such as dark pools. According to Financial Industry Regulatory Authority (FINRA) Alternative Trading System (ATS) Transparency Data, the number of dark pools in the United States stood at 35 as of October 5, 2015, and included entities with names such as Aqua, Bids Trading, and Crossfinder. Several dark pools can be recognized as those operated by large banks, including Citi Cross, Barclays ATS, and JPM-X.

Perhaps not surprisingly, many institutional investors are concerned about innovations in the current market structure of the equity markets. For instance, D'Antona (2015) reports that 67 percent of U.S. and European buy-siders want natural blocks, which are the pools of liquidity where hedge funds, asset managers, and wealth managers can seamlessly execute large orders without retaining personnel or specialty firms to manage their order execution, as in the long-gone days when only one exchange existed.

This chapter discusses developments in today's equity markets, touching upon regulatory measures, competitive dynamics, and new entrants. Most important, the chapter shows that some of the fears surrounding modern microstructure may be true and require additional investigation. In particular, the chapter documents that institutional investors' fear of toxic liquidity may be warranted in today's equity markets.

Modern Market Structure and Liquidity

Despite the proliferation of trading venues, the market landscape is not necessarily a "Wild West," as there are many similarities among trading venues. Two types of orders facilitate the majority of trading across all exchanges: market orders and limit orders. A *market order* specifies the quantity of a given financial instrument that the trader desires to buy or sell, but not the price. The market order is then executed or filled immediately upon reaching an exchange at the best available price, provided the best price satisfies the *national best bid and offer* (NBBO) requirements, which is the best (lowest) available ask price and the best (highest) available bid price to investors when they buy and sell securities. A *limit order* is an order containing the price at which the trader would like to sell or buy a given quantity of stock. Unlike market orders, limit orders are executed only when they become the best-priced orders on the market, which happens when other better-priced limit orders are executed first or cancelled. Other, more complex order types tend to be aggregates of limit and market orders with various additional characteristics.

Furthermore, all U.S. equity trading venues deploy the centralized limit order book to record and match the orders. Also known as the double-sided continuous auction, the *limit order book* is a repository of orders organized by price levels. One limit order book typically exists for each financial instrument traded on a given exchange. The limit orders stored in the limit order book are "added" by traders much like the manufacturers of food may add their wares to the shelf of a grocery store. Some limit orders, known as *day limit orders*, expire at the end of the trading day, but others, the *good till cancel orders*, may last longer. Similar to a grocery supplier, the limit order trader specifies the size of the limit order and the desired trading price. By setting limit orders, traders add liquidity to the exchange. The resulting liquidity can be consumed by market order traders and other limit order traders who match the price of resting limit orders.

Liquidity is a complicated topic. *Liquidity* refers to the market's readiness to trade. The deeper the liquidity, the larger is the order the market can absorb immediately without noticeable market movement. Immediate market execution is accomplished using market orders. In order for a buy or sell market order to be fulfilled, the market order needs to be matched with one or more limit orders of the opposite direction—buy market orders being matched with sell limit orders and vice versa. As more limit orders are available for matching the arriving market order, the larger the market order can be. Thus, in technical terms, *liquidity* is the set of all available limit orders that can be used for immediate execution. Demsetz (1968) first defined *liquidity* as immediacy of execution. Figure 27.1 is a snapshot of a limit order book, containing "displayed" liquidity: resting buy orders ("bids") and sell orders ("offers"), aggregated by price from lowest to the highest. Besides displaying liquidity, most exchanges offer the opportunity to send in "hidden" limit orders that, similarly to traditional dark pools, are not revealed until they are executed.

According to folklore, modern liquidity has two subsets: "natural" liquidity and "toxic" liquidity. *Natural liquidity* is thought to consist of dependable limit orders ready to be matched with the incoming market orders or liquidity, for instance, placed by traders

Figure 27.1 Buy-side Available Liquidity Exceeding Sell-side Liquidity. The figure illustrates that an incoming market buy order faces a sparser limit order book, and hence a less certain execution, than an incoming market sell order.

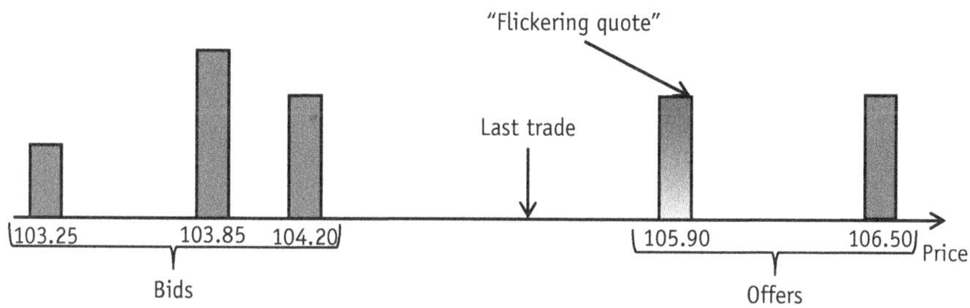

Figure 27.2 Example of impact of "Flickering Quotes" on Buy Offers This figure shows that a trader using a market buy order observes the best quote at price 105.90, but is filled at 106.50 because the 105.9 quote is canceled before the market buy order reaches the exchange, resulting in worse execution.

"who generally plan to hold the position for longer than one day" (Pragma 2011, p. 3). *Toxic liquidity,* also referred to as *opportunistic liquidity,* comprises the limit orders that are not dependable or stable. Just as the toxic market order flow leaves market makers at a disadvantage in a process referred to as adverse selection (Easley, Lopez de Prado, and O'Hara 2012), toxic liquidity can be disadvantageous to non-market-making participants such as institutional portfolio managers. Toxic limit orders are often cancelled, only to be promptly replenished by another set of identical limit orders. The goal of such on/off flickering is to be intentionally harmful to the markets along the following dimensions:

- Some market participants believe that flickering quote behavior is present to deceive market participants about the depth of the order book.
- Others believe that flickering quotes are used to prompt large traders into revealing their true position execution sizes. Such information mining on behalf of entities deploying flickering orders is known as "phishing" or "pinging."
- Overall, flickering or disappearing liquidity can to be toxic because it can exacerbate the market impact of incoming orders. Figure 27.2 shows an example of market toxicity.

Several researchers compare the toxicity of some exchange characteristics such as fee structure. Although all exchanges are obligated to observe the SEC Regulation National Market Systems (Reg NMS) that mandates all market orders to be executed only at NBBO prices or better quotes, owing to the competitive nature of the modern trading landscape, exchanges differentiate themselves by deploying different pricing and matching combinations. As Aldridge (2013a) discusses, some equity exchanges offer traders monetary incentives to provide liquidity in an attempt to attract limit orders, and thus to deepen available liquidity. Exchanges doing so are known as "normal" and offer "rebates" for providing liquidity (posting limit orders), while charging fees for taking liquidity (placing market orders). Other exchanges, known as "inverted," do the opposite. They charge for limit orders and pay for market orders. The NYSE is an example of a normal exchange and the Boston OMX is an inverted exchange.

A few exchange firms have offerings in each category. For example, BATS has normal and inverted exchanges in the firm's portfolio. According to Sofianos and Yousefi (2010), Aldridge (2013b), and Battalio, Corwin, and Jennings (2015), fees and other properties of exchanges affect the toxicity of their liquidity. For instance, Battalio et al. found that, on average, the fees across all the exchanges are in equilibrium, balancing the explicit fees with implicit costs, such as observed spreads. The lower the fee imposed on "liquidity makers" providing the limit orders, the higher is the observed spread on a given exchange, potentially implying higher toxicity levels. Aldridge found that order cancellation rates are lower on exchanges with lower liquidity maker fees (higher liquidity taker fees), also indicating lower toxicity levels.

Owing to the often-intense speed of flickering observed in toxic limit orders, some consider toxic liquidity to be generated by machines more so than humans, because of human traders' physical constraints in observing and clicking the orders. In contrast, human market makers and institutional market participants generate the most natural liquidity. As a direct consequence, the presence of toxic liquidity has prompted debates about the usefulness of high-frequency trading (HFT) as market making (Markets Media 2013). The next section discusses strategies deployed by high-frequency traders and their activities in the markets.

High-Frequency Trading

High-frequency trading (HFT) refers to a category of computer programs designed to process vast arrays of market information and trade the markets, typically in an intraday framework, only occasionally holding positions overnight. Aldridge (2013a) provides a detailed classification of HFT strategies. Broadly speaking, all HFT can be split into two large groups: aggressive HFT and passive HFT. The key difference between the two categories is their built-in impatience. Aggressive high-frequency traders (HFTs) tend to trade on time-sensitive information and typically prefer to use market orders that deliver immediate execution at the best available price. Most successful aggressive high-frequency traders require ultra-fast connectivity and speed of execution to reach the markets ahead of their competition. In contrast, passive high-frequency traders

Figure 27.3 Impact of Aggressive HFT Orders on Bid–Ask Spreads. This figure illustrates that an arriving aggressive order wipes out the best limit order(s) on the opposing side of the limit order book, widening spreads and increasing volatility through larger bid–ask bounce.

Table 27.1 **Average Aggressive HFT Participation in Equities on August 31, 2015**

Lowest Aggressive HFT, out of the S&P 500 Index	
	Percent (%)
ZNGA	7.4
VVUS	8.3
RAD	9.8
Highest aggressive HFT, out of the S&P 500 Index	
GOOGL	39.6
AMZN	38.1
GOOG	37.6

Note: This table shows the average proportion of aggressive HFT in the order flow of selected securities.

Source: AbleMarkets (2015).

engage in market making and other less time-sensitive strategies. As a result, passive high-frequency traders mostly use limit orders.

As a natural consequence of aggressive HFT market-taking activity, aggressive high-frequency traders tend to wipe out limit orders in the direction that they trade, increasing bid–ask spreads and resulting in higher realized volatility (defined by Andersen, Bollerslev, Diebold, and Labys 2002) from the bid–ask bounce. Figure 27.3 shows the basic mechanics of how aggressive HFT increases bid–ask spreads. The average proportion of aggressive high-frequency traders in stocks varies from stock to stock, but changes little over time.

Table 27.1 shows the daily average aggressive HFT participation in selected S&P 500 Index stocks on August 31, 2015. As table 27.1 shows, although the mechanics may follow all market-taking orders, two key issues pertaining to aggressive HFT behavior may particularly exacerbate available liquidity:

- Aggressive high-frequency traders tend to execute bursts of market orders at once, potentially deeply affecting the liquidity on one side of the limit order book.
- Aggressive HFTs often act in response to major market announcements, using their infrastructure to reach the markets just ahead of competing institutional traders, substantially worsening execution for the latter.

Several studies confirm the aggressive HFT impact on market volatility. For example, Zhang (2010) and Cliff, O'Hara, Hendershott and Zigrand (2011) find that aggressive HFTs are more active during the periods of high market volatility, potentially causing said volatility. Aldridge and Krawciw (2015) estimate that stocks with higher aggressive HFT display consistently higher volatility.

Conversely, passive HFTs tend to reduce volatility by propping up the limit order book and reducing spreads and the bid–ask bounce of prices. Of course, traders deploying passive HFTs can cancel their limit orders, as can everyone else placing limit orders. However, they cannot run away once their orders have been selected for matching by the exchange. In other words, just by placing a limit order, a passive HFT is committing to honor that order in the period of time before the order may be cancelled. No matter how soon the order cancellation may be sent, if the limit order is the best-priced order on the market, and if a market order arrives in the time span between the placement of the limit order and its cancellation, the limit order will be executed. Stated differently, any limit order always has a positive probability of execution. Figure 27.4 summarizes the actions of passive HFT's provision of liquidity.

Brogaard (2010) supports the passive HFT–lower volatility connection. Although other researchers find that HFT boosts liquidity (Linton and O'Hara 2011; Moriyasu, Wee, and Yu 2013; Jarnecic and Snape 2014), HFTs may be too quick to withdraw liquidity during uncertainty, resulting in extreme liquidity shortages and inducing crashes (Kirilenko, Kyle, Samadi, and Tuzun 2011; Linton and O'Hara 2011; Hasbrouck 2013).

A particular concern surrounding passive HFT has been a perceived rise in fast order cancellations and the resulting toxicity of liquidity in the markets. Hautsch and Huang (2011) and Hasbrouck and Saar (2013) document that 95 percent of all limit orders

Figure 27.4 Placement of Passive HFT Order Placement. This figure shows that an arriving passive limit order enhances liquidity, adding depth to the limit order book.

on the NASDAQ are cancelled, most within just one minute of order placement. Such unexplained behavior of limit orders has been troubling for traders, exchanges, and other market participants, resulting in claims that the observed cancellations are part of some market-manipulation schemes. Exchanges have experienced clogs in their networks, in which large portions of network bandwidths are taken over by order cancellations, delaying information transmittal for other orders, quotes, and trades. The sheer volume of the cancellations has baffled regulators, academics, and broker-dealers.

The remainder of this chapter closely examines the intraday limit order dynamics, including order-by-order analysis of the limit order book evolution. As the analysis shows, basic order-cancellation counts often erroneously incorporate activity by institutional investors in their estimates of the toxic liquidity.

A Limit Order Book Under a Microscope

A typical exchange may offer dozens of order types to traders of all categories, including institutions and HFTs. As of September 2015, the NYSE had 25 active order types, including six types of *immediate or cancel* (IOC) orders constituting variations of a market order, five types of displayed limit orders, and four types of non-displayed or hidden limit orders (Intercontinental Exchange 2015). Out of all the order types, the NYSE IOC market-order types make up 32.61 percent of all orders in aggregate, displayed limit orders of all stripes account for 41.51 percent of all orders, and non-displayed limit orders total just 2.46 percent of all orders. By comparison, the follow is the distribution of orders on BATS exchanges in September 2015: BATS IOC, including vanilla market orders, occurred 13.84 percent of the time, with displayed limit order variations submitted 48.91 percent of the time, and non-displayed orders accounting for 37.26 percent of the total order count (BATS Global Markets 2015). The differences in order prevalence by type may be a function of market structure divergences among exchanges. However, most exchange order types have at least one commonality: the structure of order transmission to and from the exchanges.

The commonalities in order transmission are not to be confused with the language of transmission, formally known as *transmission protocol*. As Aldridge (2013a) describes, many exchanges use FIX communication protocol to transmit messages. Yet, some other exchanges, such as the NASDAQ, have proprietary data transmission models that allow information exchange to be faster and more reliable than FIX. However, most protocols deploy a message structure that includes message additions, message cancellations, and message executions, with individual messages often linked by unique order identifiers to track the order arrivals and existing order modifications.

For instance, Table 27.2 shows a stylized excerpt from a message log recorded for GOOG on October 8, 2015, by BATS BYX exchange. The fields included in Table 27.2 are Unique Limit Order ID, used to identify all limit order additions and subsequent executions and revisions; the time the message was sent out by the exchange; the time when the original limit order was added; the size of the original limit order or revision; and the price of the original limit order. Table 27.2 shows two order types: "A" for a new limit order addition and "X" for a limit order cancellation. Additional order message

Table 27.2 **Sample from Level III Data (Processed and Formatted) for GOOG on October 8, 2015**

Unique Order ID	*Message Time (ET)*	*Symbol*	*Original Order Placement Time*	*Order Size*	*Limit Price*	*Order Type*
C91KT9003TDS	9:39:01.688	GOOG	9:39:01.688	100	637.33	A
C91KT9003TDS	9:39:02.790	GOOG	9:39:01.688	100	637.33	X
C91KT9003UU4	9:39:09.213	GOOG	9:39:09.213	100	629.23	A
C91KT9003UU4	9:39:10.212	GOOG	9:39:09.213	100	629.23	X
C91KT9003W7J	9:39:16.794	GOOG	9:39:15.799	100	648.45	X
C91KT9003OBR	9:39:19.967	GOOG	9:39:00.270	100	641.00	X

Note: This table presents a snippet of detailed order flow for GOOG recorded on October 8, 2015, by BATS. "A" messages represent limit order additions and "X" messages are limit order cancellations.

types may include partial or full executions of limit orders, market orders, and hidden order executions.

In the snippet of messages shown in Table 27.2, the first two messages pertain to order ID C91KT9003TDS. The first C91KT9003TDS message is an addition of the limit order with price 637.33 recorded at 9:39:01.688 AM ET. (The timestamp originally was reported in milliseconds following midnight, but was converted into regular time for reader convenience.) The second message pertaining to the same order ID—a cancellation—arrived just more than one second later. A similar pattern occurs with the next order ID, C91KT9003UU4. The message to add the 100-share order, this time with a price of 629.23, occurred at 9:39:09:213, while the exchange recorded the message to cancel the same order at 9:39:10:212, just 999 milliseconds later. The last two messages displayed in Table 27.2 are cancellations of orders placed earlier in the day and not shown in the table.

On October 8, 2015, GOOG had 50,274 messages that were of one of the following types: (1) limit order additions, (2) full or partial limit order cancellations, (3) regular limit order executions, and (4) hidden order executions. Of those messages, 24,824 (49.3 percent) were limit order additions, 24,750 (49.2 percent) were limit order cancellations, 139 (0.3 percent) were limit order executions, and 561 (1.1 percent) were records of hidden order executions. Table 27.3 summarizes the size properties of each category of orders. Of all the added limit orders, only 49 were greater than 100 shares, and the maximum order size was 400 shares. The posted limit orders exclude hidden or dark orders that are now available on most public exchanges ("lit" markets).

After a limit order is added (message type "A"), it can be cancelled or executed in part or in full, or it can remain resting in the order book until its expiry, typically at the end of the trading day or "until cancel." The trader who places the order completely determines the cancellation. The execution is a combination of factors: a resting limit order is executed when it becomes the best available order and a matching market order arrives, given that the order is not cancelled before the market order's arrival. A limit order may

Table 27.3 **Distribution of Order Sizes in Shares Recorded for GOOG on October 8, 2015**

	A	*E*	*P*	*X*
Average	94.27	87.37	68.50	94.21
Standard deviation	21.40	40.30	102.45	21.38
Maximum	400.00	300.00	2283.00	400.00
99%	100.00	207.56	138.79	100.00
95%	100.00	100.60	100.00	100.00
90%	100.00	100.00	100.00	100.00
75%	100.00	100.00	100.00	100.00
50%	100.00	100.00	86.50	100.00
25%	100.00	74.00	20.00	100.00
10%	80.00	37.30	5.00	80.00
5%	47.00	5.50	2.00	47.00
1%	2.00	3.00	1.00	2.00
Minimum	1.00	2.00	1.00	1.00
# Messages	24,824.00	139.00	561.00	24,750.00
Total Size	2,340,128.00	12,144.00	38,426.00	2,331,811.00

Note: This table illustrates distribution of order sizes for orders of different types. Order types are: "A"—add limit order, "E"—resting limit order executed, "P"—hidden limit order executed, and "X"—limit order cancellation.

cancelled all at once or in several cancellation messages, each message chipping away at the limit order's initial size. Similarly, a limit order may be executed in full if the matching market order size is greater or equal to that of the limit order. If the limit order is larger than the matching market orders, it will be partially executed.

Table 27.4 summarizes the distributional properties of time since the last record of each order appeared. For additions of limit orders, as well as for executions of hidden orders, the times are identically zero. Limit order cancellations average 8.3 seconds following the last action on the order ID: at the order placement or previous partial cancellation. The time distribution is highly skewed, with the median time between the last order action and the following order cancellation being just a half a second. Executions (order types "E") on average occur 18 seconds since the last order action, with the executions following limit order additions just 3 seconds at the median value.

Of 24,824 limit orders added to GOOG on October 8, 2015, 21,698 (87 percent) were cancelled in full with just one order cancellation. On average, single cancellations arrived just five seconds after the limit order was added to the limit order book. The

Table 27.4 **Distribution of Difference between Sequential Order Updates for All Order Records for GOOG on October 8, 2015**

	A	*E (ms)*	*P (ms)*	*X (ms)*
Average	0	17,932.87	0	8,299.75
Standard deviation	0	82,984.99	0	211,621.90
Maximum	0	687,989.00	0	18,326,189.00
99%	0	496,794.70	0	29,535.60
95%	0	33,518.00	0	11,545.15
90%	0	25,900.00	0	6,599.40
75%	0	10,049.00	0	2,237.00
50%	0	3,010.50	0	567.00
25%	0	626.00	0	68.00
10%	0	29.90	0	4.00
5%	0	0.00	0	1.00
1%	0	0.00	0	0.00
Minimum	0	0.00	0	0.00

Note: This table shows the duration of time (in milliseconds) since the last order update for each given order ID for various order types. Order types are: "A"—add limit order, "E"—resting limit order executed, "P"—hidden limit order executed, and "X"—limit order cancellation. "A" and "P" type orders are first recorded when added and executed, respectively.

median shelf life of a limit order with a single cancellation was even shorter: just more than half a second. Table 27.5 illustrates that most of the orders were 100 shares or smaller. As Davis, Roseman, Van Ness, and Van Ness (2015) first pointed out, there is little evidence to show that order cancellations are a result of single-share liquidity pinging—a "canary in a coal mine" theory that purports to describe some of the HFT activity. As Table 27.5 shows, most of the orders were in 100-share lots.

The limit orders not cancelled in full with a single order cancellation can be subsequently executed or cancelled at a later time. Figure 27.5 displays a histogram of the number of order messages for each added limit order when the order messages exceed two (typically, addition and cancellation, or addition and execution). As Figure 27.5 shows, some limit orders end up with as many as 50 limit order cancellations.

The most interesting part of the limit order dynamics could be in the intraday evolution of orders. Until 9:28 AM ET, limit orders arrive and are promptly cancelled, without any limit orders visibly resting in the limit order book for longer than five minutes. Displayed limit orders alternate between buys and sells and various price levels. Then, at 9:28:30.231 AM ET, two orders arrive—a buy at 596.57, order ID C91KT9000RU8; and a sell at 684.27, order ID C91KT9000RU9. The buy order is left untouched until 11:52:25.912 AM, at which point the buy order is modified through a simultaneous

Table 27.5 **Size and Shelf Life of Orders Canceled in Full, with a Single Cancellation for GOOG on October 8, 2015**

	Size	*Time Until Cancel (ms)*
Average	93.51	5,210.67
Standard deviation	22.56	154,922.70
Maximum	400.00	18,326,189.00
99%	100.00	27,946.44
90%	100.00	6543.00
75%	100.00	2284.00
50%	100.00	630.00
25%	100.00	97.00
10%	80.00	30.00
5%	47.00	1.00
1%	2.00	0.00
Minimum	1.00	0.00

Note: This table shows the summary statistics for limit orders canceled in full, as opposed to partial order cancellations.

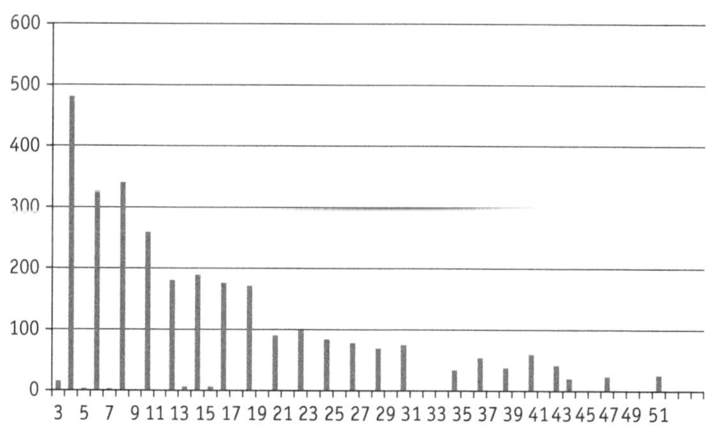

Figure 27.5 Histogram of umber of Order Messages per Each Added Limit Order. This figure shows the number of order messages for each added limit order excluding order additions, followed by single order cancellations. Addition of the limit order ("A" message) is included in the total order count, displayed on X axis. The Y axis shows the number of order IDs corresponding to each message count.

cancellation message and another added with the same order ID and size, at 590.16. At 14:59:30.895, the same order ID is in play again, this time receiving a simultaneous cancellation message and an "A" message with a price of 596.64. At 16:00:00, the limit order is finally cancelled. The sell order C91KT9000RU9 is updated via a simultaneous cancellation and an order addition at 9:49:44.619, when the price is reset to 677.88, and then 11:56:21.674, when the price is reset to 671.49, and then 14:39:58.082, when the price is changed to 677.95. This order, too, is finally cancelled at 16:00:00.000 by the exchange, probably because it was a day limit order.

When a limit order is adjusted, it is recorded not as a separate message but as a sequence of two messages with the same order ID: an order cancellation followed by an immediate order addition with revised characteristics. In GOOG data for October 8, 2015, 4,794 messages existed pertaining to limit order adjustments, making up 9.5 percent of the total message traffic. An average revision occurred 30 seconds after the last order update, indicating likely human direction. Of all the revisions, 99.0 percent occurred within 40 seconds of the original order addition or last revision. Table 27.6 summarizes the distribution of inter-revision times for limit orders on GOOG on October 8, 2015.

Of all order revision traffic messages, only 488 (10.2 percent) referred to singular order updates; the remaining (89.8 percent) of revised orders incurred several sequential revisions in a row. For example, the limit sell order C91KT9003EDZ was revised five times within six seconds from 9:38:05.139 to 9:38:11.424, with the limit sell price dropping with each consecutive order from 641.26 to 641.25, to 641.14, to 641.07, to 641.05. For the 3,244 messages pertaining to the sell order revisions, the price on 95 percent of the orders was revised downward (i.e., improved with each revision). Similarly, for the 1,550 buy order revision messages, the price was raised to be closer to the market in 96 percent of cases. In other words, the vast majority of the 9.5 percent of all limit order traffic comprising limit order revisions was beneficial: the limit order updates tightened spreads.

Unlike order revisions, 6,168 messages, or 12.3 percent of the 50,274 total order messages for GOOG recorded on October 8, 2015, were short-lived flashes of liquidity that can be considered "flickering liquidity." For example, a 100-share buy limit order C91KT9000W09 is placed at 9:30:02.763 for 632.55, only to be cancelled 678 milliseconds (ms) later without a simultaneous replacement. At 9:30:09.376, another buy limit order C91KT9000XZ0 arrives for a higher price of 638.01, and is held for a precise 1,000 ms, at which point it is also cancelled without an immediate replacement. Two more buy orders turn on and off sequentially, first for 636.55 at 9:30:11.403 for 1,001 ms, and then for 629.09 at 9:30:14.422 for 5,352 ms, before a hidden order execution trade print arrives: 23 shares at 642.27 executed at 9:30:47.035. A similar dance of short-lived quotes followed by hidden order executions continues throughout much of the trading day. Of the flickering orders, 1,622 message pairs (each flickering order comprises an order addition and an order cancellation) pertain to sell limit orders, and 1,462 pairs are on the buy side of the limit order book. Table 27.7 summarizes the distribution of the shelf life of orders that are cancelled without immediate replacement and can, therefore, be considered flickering.

Although the flickering orders identified in Table 27.7 are likely candidates for "pings" in the Pragma (2011) sense and "canaries" according to Davis et al. (2015), the

Table 27.6 **Distribution of Times between Subsequent Order Revisions for GOOG on October 8, 2015**

	Shelf Life of Limit Orders between Subsequent Revisions (ms)
Average	31,119.40
Standard deviation	469,658.70
Maximum	11,224,983.00
99%	40,072.72
95%	10,763.80
90%	5,458.00
75%	1,201.00
50%	45.00
25%	1.00
10%	0.00
5%	0.00
1%	0.00
Minimum	0.00
Message count	4794.00
% of all messages	95.36

Note: This table shows the distribution of time (in milliseconds) between subsequent order revisions.

results present a drastically different picture from that of some previous studies on the dynamics of limit orders, namely Hautsch and Huang (2011) and Hasbrouck and Saar (2013), who both find that 95.0 percent of limit orders are pings cancelled within one minute of their addition. At the same time, neither makes any mention of order revisions, potentially counting order revisions as simple order cancellations. Of course, possibly, order revisions may be treated differently in the dataset that Hautsch and Huang and Hasbrouck and Saar studied—NASDAQ TotalView. Either way, the results from the BATS data analysis presented in this chapter lead to a drastically different conclusion: only a small fraction (12.3 percent) of all message traffic had characteristics of potential pings, or toxic order flow—a far cry from the 95 percent reported in the earlier studies.

Of the remaining 78.2 percent of the entire message traffic not accounted for in order revisions and pings, only 700 orders (1.3 percent of the total daily message traffic) were order executions. Of those, only 139 orders (0.3 percent) were executions of limit orders displayed in the limit order book, message type "E." The remaining 561 executions (1.11 percent of total message traffic) were type "P" messages—matches of

Table 27.7 **Distribution of Duration of Limit Orders Canceled with an Order Message Immediately Following the Order Placement Message**

	Shelf Life of Flickering Limit Orders (ms)
Average	1,293.19
Standard deviation	7,682.14
Maximum	268,397.00
99%	11,430.36
95%	4,960.80
90%	2,633.70
75%	1,001.00
50%	196.00
25%	4.00
10%	0.00
5%	0.00
1%	0.00
Minimum	0.00
Message count	6,168
% of all messages	12.27

Note: This table shows the distribution of visibility of flickering limit orders.

market orders with hidden limit orders, or special order types that do not appear in the centralized limit order book.

The finding that most order executions are accomplished with hidden limit orders is not entirely surprising. Yao (2012) studies NASDAQ data in 2010 and 2011, and finds that hidden orders accounted for 20.4 percent of all executions. This percentage has probably increased, as "lit" exchanges are moving toward structures akin to dark pools.

Order-Based Negotiations

According to Yao (2012) and other recent research, market participants may use "lit" limit orders to signal their willingness to buy and sell at specific prices. Most of the execution, however, happens in the interaction with hidden or dark liquidity that cannot be directly observed in the limit order book. A swift negotiation may follow an indication of interest, resulting in a hidden order execution. An alternative, less positive, yet popular hypothesis can be that the institutions and other market-order and hidden-order traders are influenced by flickering, suboptimal liquidity provided by high-frequency traders. This section presents simple tests of the quality of the orders in today's markets.

To test the interaction of various order types, each order message within the data set is first separated and labeled as one of the following categories: a message revision, a ping, a regular limit order addition, and a regular limit order cancellation. The message revision orders are picked out by matching the limit order IDs of sequential orders where the order addition follows the order cancellation with slightly different parameters. Pings are identified as order cancellations following order additions with the same order ID without subsequent order additions. All order types are assigned indicator functions with $\{0, 1\}$ set of outcomes, depending on which subset of order types the order messages belong. Finally, 10-message and 300-message moving average series are created for each order type to serve as dependent variables in the analysis of those order type impacts on "lit" and hidden order execution.

The observed impact of various order types appears to change considerably from high frequency to lower frequency. On average throughout the day, 10 exchange messages were timestamped every five seconds, with a median time of two seconds and the lowest decile of sixty-seven milliseconds. Conversely, 300 messages were processed every 2.5 minutes, on average, with a median processing time falling to 1.8 minutes and 10 percent of all 300-message blocks crowding into 1 minute. Although a human trader can theoretically follow every 10 trading messages in just two seconds, a more likely scenario is that actions at that speed are processed by a machine, whereas human traders would more likely observe data at a minute scale (i.e., 300-message horizon).

At 10-message frequencies, both regular market order executions and hidden order executions exhibit dependence on the dynamics of other order types. Using the indicator functions to denote the occurrences of market order and hidden order executions, and regressing the obtained values on prior 10-order moving average proportions of other order occurrences, a statistically significant relation can be deduced of the following nature:

1. At high frequencies, flickering orders bear little impact on the execution of hidden orders. However, they have a negative impact on the execution of market orders, potentially deterring market order traders from sending in the market orders.
2. At high frequencies, limit order revisions have no impact on market order execution, but have a positive impact on hidden order execution. Potentially, limit order revisions serve to identify hidden order locations and approach hidden order locations faster, resulting in matching.
3. At high frequencies, regular limit order placement and cancellation has the greatest impact on the execution of both market orders and hidden orders. Surprisingly, in the cases of market orders and hidden orders, the impact of new limit order arrivals and cancellations is negative: the more regularly (non-revision, no-flicker) that limit order arrivals and cancellations are observed in the limit order book, the fewer market orders and hidden orders are executed. Potentially, new limit orders are alternative actions to market orders, with traders choosing limit orders whenever the impending market movement is not perceived as urgent. Similarly, additions and cancellations of regular limit orders may delay hidden order discovery, reducing the hidden order cancellation rates.

Table 27.8 **Market Order Executions (Message Type "E") and Other Order Type Dynamics at 10-Message Frequency**

	Model 1	*Model 2*	*Model 3*	*Model 4*
Intercept	0.0026 (10.279)	0.0033 (10.523)	0.0397 (20.043)	0.0367 (18.650)
Limit order revisions, 10-order MA of indicator function, preceding limit order execution	0.0021 (0.904)	–	–	–
Flickering orders, 10-order MA of indicator function	–	–0.0024 (–1.739)	–	–
Regular limit order additions, 10-order MA of indicator function	–	–	–0.0735 (–18.469)	–
Regular limit order cancellations, 10-order MA of Indicator function	–	–	–	–0.0676 (–17.051)
Adjusted R^2	–0.0000	0.0000	0.0086	0.0073

Note: This table shows the results of regressions examining prevalence of market order executions following limit order revisions (Model 1), flickering orders (Model 2), regular limit order additions (Model 3), and regular limit order cancellations (Model 4) within the following 10 messages (median time of 2 seconds).

Tables 27.8 and 27.9 summarize the statistical results of analyses of the impact of order types on hidden and "lit" order executions at the 10-order message horizon. As these tables show, at the 10-message frequency both hidden and "lit" order execution are significantly determined by factors unrelated to the order messages immediately preceding execution. This finding is indicated by the statistical significance of the intercept in all models shown. The findings serve to illustrate the relative importance that market participants place on the occurrence of flickering limit orders.

At the 300-message frequency, there is a much stronger dependency of order execution on the preceding pings and order revisions. Specifically, Tables 27.10 and 27.11 show the following:

- At lower frequencies, flickering orders have a strong impact on market and hidden order execution. Specifically, an increase in pings leads to an increase in market orders and hidden order executions with 99.9 percent confidence. This finding starkly contrasts with findings about the flickering order impacts at higher frequencies when the execution of market orders declines with increases in flickering quotations.
- At lower frequencies, limit order revisions present a much stronger influence on increased market order and hidden order execution than at higher frequencies.

Table 27.9 **Hidden Limit Order Executions (Message Type "P") and Other Order Type Dynamics at 10-Message Frequency**

	Model 1	*Model 2*	*Model 3*	*Model 4*
Intercept	0.0107 (20.789)	0.0118 (18.399)	0.1219 (30.932)	0.1269 (32.516)
Limit order revisions, 10-order MA of indicator function, preceding limit order execution	0.0079 (1.708)	–	–	–
Flickering orders, 10-order MA of indicator function	–	0.0035 (1.259)	–	–
Regular limit order additions, 10-order MA of indicator function	–	–	–0.2187 (–27.624)	–
Regular limit order cancellations, 10-order MA of Indicator function	–	–	–	–0.2299 (–29.199)
Adjusted R^2	0.0000	0.0000	0.0190	0.0212

Note: This table shows the results of regressions examining prevalence of hidden order executions following limit order revisions (Model 1), flickering orders (Model 2), regular limit order additions (Model 3), and regular limit order cancellations (Model 4) within the following 10 messages (median time of 2 seconds).

- At lower frequencies, the impact of regular order addition on market and hidden order executions is present, but it is less statistically significant than that observed at higher frequencies.

The divide in how market participants perceive and interpret flickering quotes is informative on many levels. First, it could reveal a weakness in the centralized quotation system, known as Securities Information Processor (SIP), administered by the SEC. The routine operation of SIP involves gathering quotes from various trading venues, finding the best bid and the best offer among the quotes, and then redistributing the best quotes back to market participants. Trading venues might use SIP to determine which exchange to forward a market order in the absence of best quotes on a given exchange.

The presence of flickering quotes on a particular exchange could cause SIP to post the flickering order as the best nationwide quote, and cause a spike in market order routings to that exchange. As a result, the routed market orders may or may not be filled up at best prices. Alternatively, human traders watching market data on screens could perceive the flickering quotes as the true available liquidity and attempt to execute against the quotes using either market or hidden orders. Finally, flickering orders could be pure pings seeking to identify pools of hidden liquidity within the spread in a given limit

Table 27.10 **Market Order Executions (Message Type "E") and Other Order Type Dynamics at 300-Message Frequency**

	Model 1	*Model 2*	*Model 3*	*Model 4*
Intercept	0.0021 (7.159)	0.1275 (330.659)	0.1511 (8.348)	0.1413 (9.395)
Limit order revisions, 10-order MA of indicator function, preceding limit order execution	0.0141 (3.644)	–	–	–
Flickering orders, 10-order MA of indicator function	–	0.0429 (40.443)	–	–
Regular limit order additions, 10-order MA of indicator function	–	–	–0.2997 (–8.157)	–
Regular limit order cancellations, 10-order MA of Indicator function	–	–	–	–0.2809 (–9.165)
Adjusted R2	0.0002	0.0349	0.0017	0.0021

Note: This table shows the results of regressions examining prevalence of market order executions following various order types at 300-message frequency (median time of nearly 2 minutes).

order book. In this case, a small match of a flickering order with a hidden order establishes the location of a potential liquidity pool in the limit order book.

In the context of signaling, both hypotheses postulated at the beginning of this section appear to hold true: (1) machine traders identify and filter behavior of other machines, disregarding issues such as flickering quotes or pings; and (2) lower-frequency traders appear to interact with flickering liquidity. Although the results presented here are a case study of an individual stock—GOOG, on just one trading day, October 8, 2015—the results are easily extended to a larger stock universe where similar conclusions hold.

Summary and Conclusions

As this chapter shows, contemporary equity markets are evolving to best meet institutional investors' needs. Some issues, however, particularly those pertaining to the collaboration of human and machine traders, remain unresolved. Most regulated ("lit") exchanges are accommodating the demand for block trading by converging to a model that supports large hidden block orders, producing substantial liquidity readily available to execute institutional investors' mandates. In BATS data, for instance, the vast majority of order executions are conducted with hidden limit orders and just a small fraction are carried on with market orders.

Table 27.11 **Hidden Limit Order Executions (Message Type "P") and Other Order Type Dynamics at 300-Message Frequency**

	Model 1	*Model 2*	*Model 3*	*Model 4*
Intercept	0.0076 (13.019)	0.0030 (2.993)	0.6243 (17.651)	0.4465 (15.167)
Limit order revisions, 10-order MA of indicator function, preceding limit order execution	0.0725 (9.440)	–	–	–
Flickering orders, 10-order MA of indicator function	–	0.0671 (10.204)	–	–
Regular limit order additions, 10-order MA of indicator function	–	–	−1.2402 (−17.271)	–
Regular limit order cancellations, 10-order MA of Indicator function	–	–	–	−0.8824 (−14.710)
Adjusted R2	0.0018	0.0023	0.0076	0.0055

Note: This table shows the results of regressions examining prevalence of hidden order executions following various order types at 300-message frequency (median time of nearly 2 minutes).

Furthermore, the chapter has demystified HFT activity and shows that the kind of HFT market-making, often considered the worst owing to the "flickering" liquidity it delivers, comprises only a small fraction of available liquidity. Although not as copious as previously thought, flickering liquidity appears to have a dual impact at distinct frequencies. At high frequencies, the flickering liquidity is mostly detrimental to itself, as it is readily observed and avoided by other high-frequency market participants. At lower frequencies, however, the flickering liquidity appears to attract execution of both market and hidden orders, potentially causing order routing toward flickering order books by the SEC's consolidated tape via SIP and thus disadvantaging human traders.

This chapter also has presented the first study of the impact of limit order revisions on market activity. Like flickering liquidity, limit order revisions appear to have a dual impact on order executions, depending on the frequency at which the orders are observed. At high frequencies, visible limit order revisions appear to credibly signal a willingness to negotiate and are followed by a higher number of hidden order executions than other order types. At lower frequencies, however, limit order revisions appear to stem market and hidden order executions.

Finally, the chapter has shown that regular limit order additions and, separately, cancellations appear to deter the execution of market and hidden orders. The observed negative impact of order additions and order cancellations is more statistically significant at higher frequencies. Traders observing the markets may want to be aware of the market's responses to individual orders and reconsider their processing of market data, as well as their placement of orders, with the market signaling context in mind.

DISCUSSION QUESTIONS

1. Discuss the main differences among various equity exchanges operating in the United States.
2. Discuss the key types of HFT.
3. Explain how exchanges distribute market information.
4. Describe how exchanges record various order types.
5. Identify the liquidity considerations that market participants need to consider.

REFERENCES

AbleMarkets. 2015. "Tracking Aggressive HFT in Commodities Helps Investors Predict Volatility, Hedge Their Exposures." Available at http://www.ablemarkets.com/AbleMarkets/load.php?-f=TrackingAggressiveHFTinCommoditiesHelpsInvestorsPredictVolatility20151021.pdf.

Aldridge, Irene E. 2013a. *High-Frequency Trading: A Practical Guide to Algorithmic Strategies and Trading Systems.* Second Edition. Hoboken, NJ: John Wiley & Sons, Inc.

Aldridge, Irene E. 2013b. "Market Microstructure and the Risks of High-Frequency Trading." Working Paper, Able Alpha Trading, LTD. Available at http://ssrn.com/abstract=2294526.

Aldridge, Irene E., and Steve F. R. Krawciw. 2015. "Stocks with Higher Aggressive HFT Are More Volatile." *Traders' Magazine*, July, 12.

Andersen, Torben G., Tim Bollerslev, Francis X. Diebold, and Paul Labys. 2002. "Modeling and Forecasting Realized Volatility." *Econometrica* 71:2, 529–626.

BATS Global Markets. 2015. "Order Type Usage Summary." Available at http://www.batstrading.com/market_data/order_types/.

Battalio, Robert H., Shane A. Corwin, and Robert H. Jennings. 2015. "Can Brokers Have It All? On the Relation between Make-Take Fees and Limit Order Execution Quality." Working Paper, University of Notre Dame. Available at http://ssrn.com/abstract=2367462.

Brogaard, Jonathan A. 2010. "High-Frequency Trading and Its Impact on Market Quality." Working Paper, Northwestern University.

Cliff, Dave, Maureen O'Hara, Terrence Hendershott, and Jean-Pierre Zigrand. 2011. *The Future of Computer Trading in the Financial Markets.* U.K. Government Office for Science.

Davis, Ryan L., Brian S. Roseman, Bonnie F. Van Ness, and Robert A. Van Ness. 2015. "Canary in a Coal Mine? One-Share Orders and Trades." Working Paper, University of Mississippi. Available at http://ssrn.com/abstract=2508352.

D'Antona, Jr., John. 2015. "67 Percent of U.S. and European Buysiders Want Natural Blocks, Tabb Reports." *Traders Magazine*, October 20. Available at http://www.tradersmagazine.com/news/buyside/67-of-us-and-european-buysiders-want-natural-blocks-tabb-reports-114554-1.html.

Demsetz, Harold. 1968. "The Cost of Transacting." *Quarterly Journal of Economics* 82:1, 33–53.

Easley, David, Marco Lopez de Prado, and Maureen O'Hara. 2012. "Flow Toxicity and Liquidity in a High-frequency World." *Review of Financial Studies* 25:5, 1414–1493.

Hasbrouck, Joel. 2013. "High-Frequency Quoting: Short-Term Volatility in Bids and Offers." Working Paper, New York University.

Hasbrouck, Joel, and Gideon Saar. 2013. "Low-latency Trading." *Journal of Financial Markets* 16:4, 646–679.

Hautsch, Nicholas, and Ruihong Huang. 2011. "The Market Impact of a Limit Order." *Journal of Economic Dynamics and Control* 36:4, 501–522.

Intercontinental Exchange. 2015. "NYSE—Order Type Usage (Percentage of Matched Volume)." Available at https://www.nyse.com/publicdocs/nyse/markets/nyse/NYSE-Order-Type-Usage.pdf.

Jarnecic, Elvis, and Mark Snape. 2014. "The Provision of Liquidity by High-Frequency Participants." *Financial Review* 49:2, 371–394.

Kirilenko, Andrei A., Albert S. Kyle, Mehrdad Samadi, and Tugkan Tuzun. 2011. "The Flash Crash: The Impact of High-Frequency Trading on an Electronic Market." Working Paper, Massachusetts Institute of Technology.

Linton, Oliver, and Maureen O'Hara. 2011. "The Impact of Computer Trading on Liquidity, Price Efficiency/Discovery and Transaction Costs." U.K. Government Foresight Project.

Markets Media. 2013. "Liquidity: The Good, the Bad, and the Ugly." Available at http://marketsmedia.com/liquidity-the-good-the-bad-and-the-ugly/.

Moriyasu, Hiroshi, Marvin Wee, and Jing Yu. 2013. "The Role of Algorithmic Trading in Stock Liquidity and Commonality in Electronic Limit Order Markets." Working Paper, University of Western Australia.

Pragma. 2011. "OnePipe 3.0: The Next Generation Dark Liquidity Aggregator." Available at http://www.pragmatrading.com/sites/default/files/one_pipe_3.0_2011_0.pdf.

Securities and Exchange Commission. 2015. "Investor Information: Exchanges." October 27. Available at http://www.sec.gov/divisions/marketreg/mrexchanges.shtml.

Sofianos, George, and Ali Yousefi. 2010. "Smart Routing: Good Fills, Bad Fills and Venue Toxicity." *Goldman Sachs Equity Execution Strategies Street Smart* 40: 1–9.

Yao, Chen. 2012. "Hidden Agendas: A Study of the Impact of Concealed Orders." Working Paper, University of Illinois at Urbana-Champaign.

Zhang, X. Frank. 2010. "High-Frequency Trading, Stock Volatility and Price Discovery." Working Paper, Yale School of Management. Available at http://ssrn.com/abstract=1691679.

Part Seven

THE APPLICATION AND FUTURE OF BEHAVIORAL FINANCE

28

Applications of Client Behavior

A Practitioner's Perspective

HAROLD EVENSKY, CFP
Chairman, Evensky & Katz/Foldes Financial
Professor of Practice, Texas Tech University

Introduction

Advising clients about their investments is a challenging endeavor. The investment universe involves many complexities and often counter-intuitive aspects. Additionally practitioners often misapply various behavioral finance concepts. Understanding the behavioral errors of clients and knowing the techniques that might help mitigate such errors forms a useful knowledge base for the financial advisor. The purpose of this chapter is to discuss various behavioral concepts and strategies that can help clients avoid behavioral errors, with the result of increasing the probability of a successful plan design and implementation.

The chapter begins with a discussion of the importance of client education in establishing a long-term relationship. Next, the chapter explains the value of framing the planning process, followed by a section on behaviorally based client management. The final section offers a summary and conclusions.

Aspects of Client Education

Educating the new client about the advisor's planning and investment philosophy is a critical step in establishing a sound, long-term relationship. The following section provides examples that have proved successful in practice.

FRAMING THE PROCESS: ANCHORING ON THE EFFICIENT FRONTIER

Many practitioners used to introduce the planning process by presenting the classic Markowitz efficient frontier graphics, accompanied by a high-level discussion of the optimization process, including such concepts as standard deviations, correlations, and nonlinear programming. Advisors were so entranced with their knowledge that they failed to see their clients' eyes glaze over as they tuned out of the presentation. One day,

Deena Katz, a founder of Evensky & Katz/Foldes Financial (hereafter called "the firm"), observed that "when you go to the doctor, you don't expect . . . a lecture on the development of the medicine . . . prescribed for you." Given that insight, the firm recognized that it was misframing the discussion. Instead of a formal and intimidating technical presentation, advisors at the firm now frame the educational process in an informal, nonthreatening way using the following approach.

Current practice is to work in teams, whereby an associate supports a senior advisor in the client meetings. After completing the "meet and greet" ceremonies, the senior advisor starts the meeting with an introduction such as "Okay, let's get started, I'm going to give you a quick overview on modern portfolio theory and explain how we're going to help you figure out how you should be invested to enjoy your retirement. This is going to be fun." The advisor then turns to the associate and says "Have you got an extra sheet of paper?" At which point the associate tears a page from a notepad and gives it to the senior advisor. The advisor then draws the simple graph illustrated in Figure 28.1 and explains: "This is a picture of possible investments showing the balance between risk and return. Down on the lower left corner is cash or money market instruments with minimal risk and minimal return. High up on the right is an all-stock portfolio with high risk and high potential return, and somewhere in the middle is an all-bond portfolio with moderate risk and moderate return."

Even with just three investment choices, the advisor can design many portfolios. For example, one portfolio could consist of 1 percent bonds and 99 percent stocks; 99 percent bonds and 1 percent stocks; 20 percent cash, 40 percent bonds, and 40 percent stocks, and so forth. Figure 28.2 illustrates various combinations of investment choice.

Figure 28.2 illustrates the *efficient frontier*, which is a set of theoretically optimal portfolios that offer the highest expected return for a given level of risk, or the lowest risk for

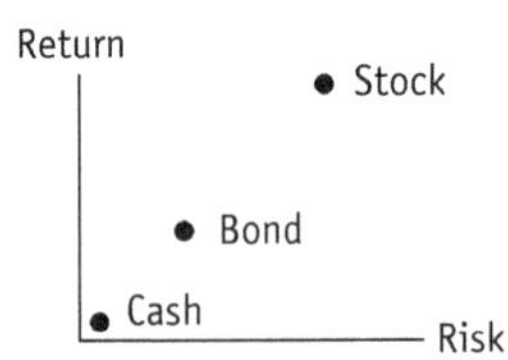

Figure 28.1 The Relation Between Risk and Return. This figure shows the relation between risk and return in a way that investors can easily understand.

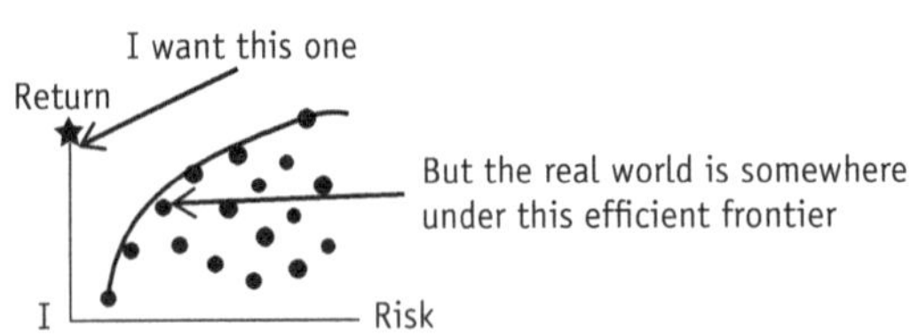

Figure 28.2 The Efficient Portfolio. This figure shows a large number of possible portfolios within a constrained universe of possibilities.

a given level of expected return. Investors desire a portfolio that will give them a high return with as little risk as possible, but the actual projected performance results fall somewhere along and under that curve. The importance of the curve is to show that no one "best" portfolio exists for everyone. The best portfolio depends on the risk–return preference of each investor. A major responsibility of the advisor is to assist in determining the most appropriate portfolio for an investor by using two criteria: (1) the long-term return needed to supply the funds necessary to achieve client goals; and (2) an assessment of personal *risk tolerance,* which is the degree of variability in investment returns that an investor is willing to withstand.

When financial planners mention risk, they are generally referring to the potential loss in an investment portfolio that often results from a market downturn. Unfortunately, similar to many terms in the financial world, "risk" has numerous meanings. *Risk capacity* describes how much investment risk clients might take based on their financial resources (i.e., how severe a financial loss clients might sustain and still have the financial resources to meet their goals). Many investors have ample financial resources and can afford to take considerable market risk, but that does not necessarily mean they are emotionally prepared to live with that risk. *Risk requirement* is the level of return that clients need to meet their financial goals. Although a financial planner considers both risk capacity and risk requirement, risk tolerance is also a critical element in developing an allocation recommendation. As Guillemette, Finke, and Gilliam (2012, p. 42) note,

> In such times as these [global financial crisis] . . . the assessment of how clients will react to a severe market downturn will be critical in determining whether they continue to follow his planner's recommendations. If a risk tolerance questionnaire fails to accurately measure a client's portfolio allocation preference, it is more likely that client will want to shift his or her portfolio to cash during market downturns.

Unfortunately, no universal agreement exists on the definition of "risk tolerance" or its measurement (Roszkowski, Dalaney, and Cordell 2009). Despite considerable discussion and debate about the differences in risk tolerance, risk perception, risk aversion, and loss aversion, no practical guidance is available for choosing the appropriate asset allocation for clients. From a practitioner's perspective, as Guillemette et al. (2012) imply, the only useful definition of *risk tolerance* is the threshold for emotional pain—that point at which a client calls the advisor during a painful bear market and says, "I can't stand it. Sell the securities in my portfolio and place the funds in cash." The advisor's goal is to design a portfolio that will keep the risk below that threshold.

During the initial educational process, the advisor explains the importance of using a computer-based analysis know as a *capital needs analysis* to determine the unique return required to achieve a client's goals with a high probability. This analysis takes into consideration: (1) the client's unique goals, such as caring for aging parents, funding grandchildren's' college, and/or paying off a mortgage; (2) the timing and costs of reaching those goals; (3) the importance and priority of each goal; (4) where the money is invested, such as in personal accounts and tax-deferred accounts; and (5) taxes, investment expenses, and inflation. With this information, a financial advisor can estimate a required portfolio return.

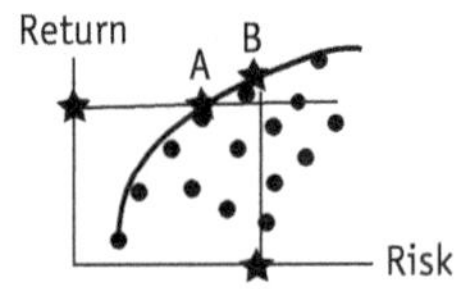

Figure 28.3 Anchoring on the Efficient Frontier: Risk Tolerance Exceeds Risk Need. This figure demonstrates that when a client's risk tolerance exceeds his or her risk need, two possible "best" portfolios are available. One portfolio provides the best return for the client's risk tolerance and another provides the return that the client needs at the lowest risk.

With an estimate of the client's return requirement and risk tolerance, the advisor can then determine the most appropriate portfolios. In describing viable options, the advisor adds two lines to the risk-return graph. Figure 28.3 shows that one line reflects the risk required to achieve a required portfolio return and the other reflects the client's risk tolerance.

Next, the advisor explains that, based on this information, two "right" answers are available: one reflects a portfolio with an acceptable risk and the other reflects a portfolio with the required return. A major cognitive bias that the financial professional likely employs is called *anchoring*, which is when an investor holds on to a belief and then applies it as a subjective reference point for making future decisions. The advisor applies this anchoring bias to identify the client's risk tolerance.

Portfolio B seems most appropriate because it provides the highest return for its level of risk; however, Portfolio A, which is the portfolio that provides the client with the return needed to achieve his goals, has lower risk. Although both are correct answers, the next step is to determine the more appropriate option to recommend to the client. This choice depends on the advisor's professional experience and philosophy. An advisor who is less confident in the accuracy of the risk tolerance estimate might opt to recommend Portfolio A, with a lower return, because the advisor expects it to meet the client's return needs and provide some cushion for risk tolerance. An advisor who is more confident in estimating the client's risk tolerance might recommend Portfolio B, in the belief that the higher the return, the more financial flexibility the client will have over time.

If an advisor believes that the client should be encouraged to consider Portfolio A, the advisor may introduce the concept of Pascal's wager, a classic philosophical construct devised by the seventeenth-century French philosopher, mathematician, and physicist Blaise Pascal. The following scenario illustrates how an advisor might present this concept to clients.

"Suppose you were told that the probability God exists is only 20 percent. You could decide that with those odds you would ignore morals and ethics and live a guilt-free immoral life. Of course, despite the low odds that God exists, you would face fire and brimstone if that were wrong. Conversely, if you choose to live a moral life and God does not exist, you will have had a nice life, but if God does exist, you would have a wonderful afterlife."

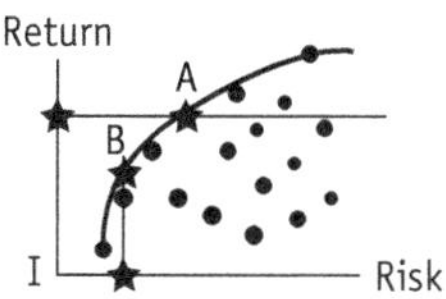

Figure 28.4 Anchoring on the Efficient Frontier: Risk Need Exceeds Risk Tolerance. This figure demonstrates that when the client's risk need exceeds his or her risk tolerance, two suboptimal choices are available. One choice provides the return the client needs at a risk exceeding his tolerance, and another offers a return below that needed to meet all the client's goals at a risk within the level of tolerance.

What's the point? People often focus on probabilities and forget to look at consequences. Even if a high probability exists that the advisor identifies the correct risk tolerance and invests accordingly but is wrong, the client might panic and sell everything in a severe bear market and never recover. Or, if the advisor invests at a lower stock exposure based on meeting the client's goals, the client's heirs might receive less money but the client will have enjoyed achieving those personal financial goals.

Figure 28.4 shows another possible result: the client's return objective requires a stock exposure higher than what is compatible with the identified risk tolerance. If this is the case, the client has two choices: eat less well or sleep less well. When markets are reasonably stable, clients can easily think, "Well, okay, I'll take a bit more risk so I can do everything I want." Unfortunately, if the portfolio later drops precipitously in a bad market, the client is likely to forget that resolve to weather the storm and might sell (Lowenstein 2000). Again, the potential consequences may far outweigh the possible benefits.

THE BASICS OF CLIENT EDUCATION

Given that the client has been introduced to the concept of anchoring on the efficient frontier, the advisor can then discuss some basic investment concepts in a manner that a nonprofessional can understand so as to build a strong foundation for professional investment recommendations.

Modern Portfolio Theory

According to Markowitz (1952), risk is as important as return in designing an investment portfolio. Figure 28.5 shows two alternative investments. Although both investment A and investment B are highly volatile, their return patterns are opposites of each other, though both trend upward over time. In this simple example, allocating 50 percent to each investment results in the effective canceling out of portfolio volatility. This simple chart demonstrates why combining two risky investments can result in a safer portfolio, although achieving this goal is difficult in practice.

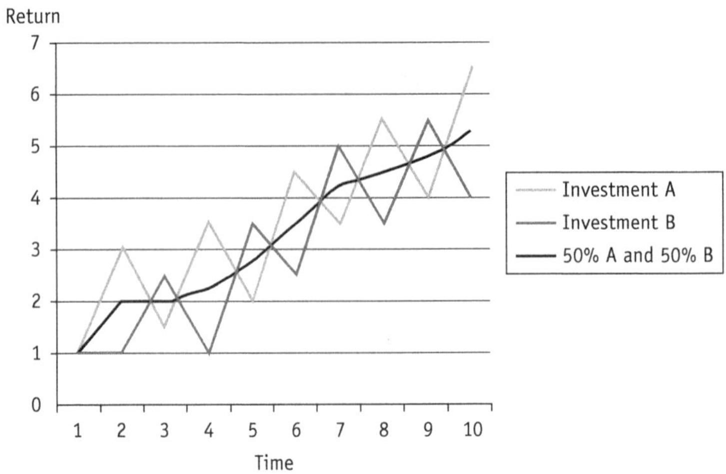

Figure 28.5 Risk Reduction through Diversification. This figure shows two volatile investments, A and B. Although they both trend up over time, their peaks and troughs tend to be in opposite directions. By placing half of a portfolio's assets in each investment, the variation in the portfolio's value is substantially reduced because the volatility of the individual investments tends to cancel each other out.

Capital Asset Pricing Model

Next, the advisor might introduce the concepts of systematic and unsystematic risk, as well as the capital asset pricing model (CAPM) (Sharpe 1964). Investing in a single company may result in a total loss because of such factors as mismanagement or the company's being in the wrong place at the wrong time. In both cases, the result might be potential bankruptcy. A useful example is an investment in the rental of a single-family house versus a 10-unit apartment complex, with all units having the same monthly rental. A vacancy in the home means a 100 percent loss of income; the vacancy in an apartment means a 10 percent loss.

The critical point is that an individual investment is subject to *unsystematic risk*, also called diversifiable risk, which is risk that is specific or unique to the company. Unsystematic risk cannot be anticipated; One example includes the Tylenol scare in the early 1980s, when Tylenol capsules laced with potassium cyanide killed seven people in the Chicago area. This incident almost put Johnson & Johnson, the manufacturer of Tylenol, out of business. That tampering incident then inspired hundreds of copycat incidents. Another example is the Deepwater Horizon oil spill, which began April 20, 2010, in the Gulf of Mexico on the BP-owned Transocean-operated Macondo Prospect. After the explosion and sinking of the Deepwater Horizon oil rig, a sea-floor oil gusher flowed for 87 days, until being capped on July 15, 2010. As of February 2013, criminal and civil settlements, and payments to a trust fund, has cost the company $42.2 billion (Fontevecchia 2013). A discussion of unsystematic risk leads to a discussion of diversification as a risk management solution for reducing unsystematic risk.

After the advisor educates the client on the importance of diversification to reduce unsystematic risk, the advisor can then introduce the concept of *systematic risk*, also known as undiversifiable risk, which is the risk endemic to the entire market or market segment. These risks include market risk, interest rate risk, reinvestment risk, and inflation risk. *Market risk* is the risk that the entire market, or a particular market segment, will experience an economic downturn. For example, a client might invest in the S&P 500 Index, which is a U.S. stock market index of 500 large company stocks listed on the NYSE or NASDAQ. Many regard this index as the best single gauge of performance for large-cap U.S. equities. When the market is down, this means that an investment included in the S&P 500 Index is also down.

A typical response from self-styled conservative investors is "That's why I avoid stocks and invest in bonds." If so, the advisor can ask what happens to the "conservative" portfolio of bonds when interest rates rise. Many investors realize that rising interest rates lead to a decline in the value of their bond portfolios. The client has now been introduced to *interest rate risk*, which is the chance that an increase in interest rates will negatively affect the value of a fixed-income investment such as bonds. The naïve investor's default response is to suggest managing that risk by investing in short-term bonds. In a low-interest-rate environment, the client recognizes that is a "solution" with a low return; the risk in a high-interest-rate environment is less obvious. In this case, a brief history lesson on reinvestment risk is in order.

In 1981, the return on U.S. Treasury bills was 14.7 percent. One year later, it decreased 30 percent to 10.5 percent. By 1987, the return fell to 5.5 percent. Those changes meant the income on a $100,000 investment dropped from $14,700 in 1981 to $5,500 in 1987, which is a loss of $9,200 in income. This scenario is a classic example of confusing "certainty" with "safety." That is, the client's corpus was protected, but that did not ensure safety because his standard of living may have been negatively affected.

As the client absorbs that lesson, the advisor can then introduce the concept of *purchasing power risk*, which is the risk that inflation will erode the value of the dollar. Even the most conservative retiree investors are aware of this inflation risk. The advisor might conclude the discussion by noting that no single investment will protect the client from these multiple systematic risks, and that the only "safe" strategy is to diversify among the asset classes.

Asset Allocation

The advisor can begin a discussion of portfolio selection by explaining that the three most important considerations in managing an investment portfolio are asset allocation, security selection, and market timing. According to a study by Brinson, Hood, and Beebower (1995) and Ibbotson (2000), asset allocation is a critically important factor driving portfolio performance. Their findings help to explain why financial advisors develop an asset allocation that is best suited to the client's circumstances and "anchor" the client on the efficient frontier.

Framing the Planning Process

In behavioral finance, the *framing effect* is an example of cognitive bias, in which people react to a particular choice in different ways depending on how it is presented, such as a loss or a gain. Attention focuses, then, on how to appropriately anchor risk through risk coaching and on anchoring the return through a capital needs analysis. However, clients who engage in improper anchoring become fixated on past information, and they use that information to make inappropriate investment decisions. Instead, their ideas and opinions should also be based on relevant and correct facts so as to be considered valid. However, this is not always so. The concept of anchoring draws on the tendency of investors to attach or "anchor" their thoughts to a reference point, even though it may have no logical relevance to the decision at hand. In the financial world, investors who base their decisions on irrelevant figures and statistics can experience mistakes because of this cognitive bias (Phung 2015).

ANCHORING THE RISK: RISK COACHING

As previously noted, the concept of risk tolerance is still being debated. In fact, some challenge the possibility of determining, in advance, a client's risk tolerance in a bear market. Such debates are irrelevant for the financial advisor. As mentioned earlier, the only relevant risk measure is that threshold of emotional pain just before the client calls the advisor and says "I can't stand it anymore. Sell my portfolio [and put me in cash]!" Having the ability to predict that threshold with certainty is unrealistic. Practitioners are aware that when the markets are trending up, a client's risk tolerance is higher; and when they are trending down, the client's risk tolerance decreases. Unfortunately, advisors cannot simply throw up their hands and say, "It's impossible to determine a client's risk tolerance."

Planning for a client's long-term financial health requires making asset allocation recommendations. Although financial planners might be unable to predict a client's risk tolerance with certainty, they must do the best they can. Over the years, using lessons from behavioral finance, Evensky & Katz/Foldes Financial developed a risk-coaching questionnaire to assist the firm's advisors in estimating a client's risk tolerance. The term *coaching* is not used in the sense of guiding clients' responses but, rather, to describe a process that includes both educational and framing concepts that assist in arriving at a credible result. The following discussion offers some examples.

Advisors emphasize that investing requires a long-term horizon. The discussion focuses on funds that the client is unlikely to need for at least five years. A major aspect of the risk coaching process is to obtain client buy-in by stressing this long-term concept. The discussion and questionnaire starts by clarifying what the client considers to be a retirement investment nest egg. Specifically, the questionnaire asks:

- What is the approximate value of this investment portfolio?
- What percentage of your total investments is represented by this portfolio?
- Is there an immediate or near term (i.e., within five years) need for income from this portfolio? If yes, when will it become needed?
- Approximately how much will be needed in after-tax dollars annually?
- "Do you plan to make substantial cash withdrawals over the next five years?

If the client answers yes to either of the last two yes/no questions, the advisor then adjusts the answer to the approximate value of the investment portfolio.

For example, suppose the client originally indicated that the investment portfolio was $1 million. If the client needs $50,000 next year to relocate a parent to a new house, the advisor then explains that he will allocate the $50,000 needed into a cash flow reserve account (to be discussed later) and adjust the investment portfolio base from $1 million to $950,000. If the client indicates that "We also need about $10,000 in three years for a special anniversary trip," the advisor takes $10,000 for the cash flow reserve and adjusts the investment portfolio base to $940,000.

The next question also emphasizes a long-term strategy asking, "What is the portfolio's investment time horizon?" *Investment time horizon* refers to the number of years the client expects the portfolio to be invested before dipping into the principal. An alternative question is "How long will the goals for this portfolio continue without substantial modification?" The advisor asks the client to indicate the number of years of the investment time horizon. If the time horizon is less than 10 years, the advisor then asks the client to explain when the funds will be needed.

Next, the advisor presents the client with a list of investment attributes, as shown in Table 28.1. These attributes are not moral issues. They are neither good nor bad, but simply investment attributes. The point is to discover how important the client considers each attribute. The client can answer with all 6s (most important), all 1s (least important), or any combination of scores. The advisor instructs the client to answer these questions assuming that over the next 20 to 30 years, the client achieves those long-term investment goals.

Clients typically answer the attribute "capital preservation" by marking either 5 or 6. A ranking of high importance is expected. In 30 years of practice, Evensky & Katz/Folds Financial has never had a client state a goal of losing the corpus, so this allows the client to forcefully document long-term preservation of capital as a primary concern. Regarding "growth," almost all clients, including very conservative investors, typically

Table 28.1 **Attributes of Investing**

Attribute	*Most*					*Least*
Capital preservation	6	5	4	3	2	1
Growth	6	5	4	3	2	1
Low principal volatility	6	5	4	3	2	1
Inflation protection	6	5	4	3	2	1
Current cash flow	6	5	4	3	2	1
Aggressive growth	6	5	4	3	2	1

Note: This table assists in engendering a discussion with a client about the difference in investment attributes, such as capital preservation and principal volatility, and the contradictory nature of goals, such as the desire for both capital preservation and inflation protection. For each of the following attributes, circle the number that most correctly reflects your level of concern. The more important, the higher is the number. You may use each number more than once.

pick a number between 4 and 6. The advisor explains to the client that this is a "gotcha" question. The client quickly recognizes that investments in cash, money market instruments, or Treasury bills, which are the only investments that ensure the preservation of the corpus, will not result in long-term growth. This response emphasizes the client's conflicting goals.

The response to "low principal volatility" helps distinguish between loss of corpus and interim volatility. If a client selects 4, 5, or 6 for this, the advisor continues the discussion so that the client understands that such a short-term volatility constraint may have a large negative impact on being able to achieve those long-term goals. The "inflation protection" attribute is another "gotcha" question. Again assuming that the client neither adds nor withdraws from the portfolio, this question helps identify the importance that the value of the investments would enable the client to buy a specific amount of goods and services in today's dollars. This question tests the client's sensitivity to inflation. Even the most conservative retirees generally select a 5 or 6 because they recognize that "safe" investments such as certificates of deposit and short-term bonds, subject to inflation erosion, will be insufficient in the long term to meet financial goals.

For "current cash flow," the only correct answer is 1. If the client selects any other number, the advisor asks "What did we miss?" Responding to the quizzical look on the client's face after this response, the advisor reminds the client that earlier he had been asked about his short-term need for both cash flow and lump-sum expenses. The advisor has moved these funds out of the investment portfolio, allocating funds to the cash flow reserve portfolio. If something has been missed, the opportunity is now available to increase the allocation to the cash flow reserve and reduce the allocation to the investment portfolio. The client can then comfortably select 1 as the answer.

The attribute "aggressive growth" does not mean high growth such as in emerging markets but, rather, strategies such as using naked puts and buying on margin. A *naked put*, also called an *uncovered put*, is a put option whereby the option writer or seller may not have sufficient liquidity (cash) to cover the contracts in case of assignment. *Buying on margin* refers to using borrowed money to purchase securities, which increases both the client's leverage and potential risk and return. Most clients select 1, which is fine, because the firm does not recommend such strategies. The idea behind the question is that the client has been able to select 6 for capital preservation and 1 for aggressive growth, helping to frame and establish his comfort level with the overall process.

The questionnaire also asks several redundant questions, such as "What percent of your investments are you likely to need within five years?" "Up to what percentage of this portfolio can be put into long-term investments?" By this point, the client recognizes that the answers of 0 percent and 100 percent, respectively, anchor their commitment to long-term investing.

To frame the client's risk and return balance, the advisor asks him to select the portfolio that best represents his comfort level. The first column in Table 28.2 describes portfolio risk. The first term (i.e., low, moderate, and high) describes short-term risk of less than five years, and the second describes long-term risk of over five years. The second column is the firm's projected return for the portfolio. An inflation assumption is included to provide the basis for a discussion about the difference between nominal and real return.

Table 28.2 **Projected Return and Risk Exposure under Different Risk Levels**

Overall	*Projected*	*Hypothetical Risk Exposure*	
Risk Level	*Total Return (Inflation = 3%)*	*"Worst Case"* (12 months)*	*Bear Market** (10/07–2/09)*
Low/Low	6.0%	–4.0%	–10.6%
Low/Low	6.8	–7.0	–14.5
Moderate/Low	7.2	–9.0	–16.2
Moderate/Low	7.4	–10.0	–20.1
Moderate/Low	7.6	–11.0	–22.9
Moderate/Low	7.8	–13.0	–25.7
High/Moderate	8.0	–14.0	–29.1
High/Moderate	8.3	–16.0	–32.4
High/Moderate	8.6	–20.0	–35.2
High/High	8.8	–22.0	–40.8
High/High	9.0	–24.0	–45.9
High/High	9.4	-–27.0	–50.9

Note: This table allows the client to select a portfolio that meets his comfort level where the return expectations and portfolio risks are related and explicitly displayed. Several portfolio performance projections are listed below, including hypothetical potential losses for these portfolios. In the right column, check the portfolio that most nearly reflects the goal of your portfolio.

* A two standard deviation estimate.

** The Great Recession.

The third column is the theoretical "worst case" risk over a 12-month period. It is actually the loss estimate based on the firm's two standard deviation estimate. Unfortunately, the experience of the financial crisis of 2007–2008 demonstrates that reality may be far greater than two standard deviations, which prompted adding a column to reflect the actual loss during the bear market of the financial crisis. The advisor explains that he knows the client would like to select diagonally for low risk and high return, but reality requires that he look horizontally, thus helping frame the relationship between risk and return. This discussion is based on one of the few quantifiable questions that helps establish an acceptable bond-to-stock ratio.

The final question deals with the behavioral aspects of prospect theory and loss aversion (Kahneman and Tversky 1979; Tversky and Kahneman 1992), but the advisor presents it in a less formal manner. The advisor gives the client the following scenario:

"You've just stepped through the door of a huge gambling casino and a band strikes up a rocking medley. Thousands of people surround you hollering and cheering, and balloons and confetti stream down from the ceiling. As you stand there bewildered, a gentleman in a tuxedo walks up to you and says 'Congratulations! You're our 10 millionth customer and you win! Now this is Vegas, so you have a choice.' He points to his outstretched right arm holding what looks like bills going to the ceiling and says, 'This is $800,000. Point to my right arm and it's yours! But, because this is Vegas you have a choice. In my left hand I have a brown bag with 10 Ping-Pong balls, 8 white and 2 black. Put your hand in and pick a white ball and you win $1 million. Pick a black ball and you win nothing. What will it be?' "

This question has been used for over a decade, and less than 5 percent of clients select taking a chance. The follow-up scenario is, "Sorry, I made a mistake, you're not in Vegas, but you're in Hell. The devil walks up to you and says 'No surprise but you lost; however, I'm a gambling man so you have two choices.' He holds out his right arm and says 'See, it's empty. Point to that arm and you owe me $800,000. In my left hand I have a brown paper bag with 10 ping-pong balls, 8 white and 2 black. Put your hand in and pick a black ball and you owe me nothing, pick a white ball and you owe me $1 million. What will it be?' " The results are consistently just the opposite, in that more than 90 percent of clients say they will take a chance.

Advisors use these scenarios to frame the difference between risk aversion and loss aversion. As an example, the advisor at a brokerage firm might view a client's portfolio as too conservative and suggest moving half the funds into the market to earn a higher return. In that case, the "conservative" client might leave. Evensky & Katz/Foldes Financial might make the same recommendation, but for a different reason. If an advisor recommends increasing the stock allocation, the reasons are not to make the client richer but, rather, to avoid a client's losing his standard of living in retirement. A conservative investor gains a new perspective and now understands and reconsiders revising his investments to increase the stock allocation.

ANCHORING THE RETURN: CAPITAL NEEDS ANALYSIS

Given that the first anchor has been applied to the client's risk tolerance, the next anchor is an estimate of the required return necessary to accomplish the client's goals. The capital needs analysis considers the four primary elements of each goal: cost, timing, priority, and importance. For example, if a client wants to provide for a grandchild's college education, the advisor would need to determine the year the expenditure would begin, number of years to be funded, annual cost, expected tuition inflation, and priority of that goal relative to all other client goals. Although these seem easy questions to answer, a client often has difficulty providing the necessary information without guidance. The traditional solution is to provide the client with a data-gathering questionnaire that lists various goals. An example is the form for a college funding goal from Pie Technologies MoneyGuide Pro (https://cdn.moneyguidepro.com/Pdf/ClientTools/College_Zoomer.pdf).

Unfortunately, clients often find a comprehensive data-gathering package overwhelming and either return an incomplete package to the advisor or simply decide that the process is too intimidating and terminate their planning efforts at this stage. To deal with this potential planning barrier, Bob Curtis, principal of PIEtech, developed the Goal Card Game. Reframing the data-gathering process as a fun card game is a simple but effective strategy.

To reframe the data-gathering process as a positive experience, the advisor introduces the card game with "Let's have fun and play cards." The advisor offers the client a deck of cards, each with a picture reflecting a possible goal, such as funding college, travel, purchasing a second home, providing support for a friend or family member, starting a new business, or replacing a car. The presentation continues with the advisor saying:

"We are going to develop a plan for the rest of your life. This is really exciting, but to ensure the life you want to live, we need to determine when and where you will need to use your financial resources. So what I want you to do now is take this deck of cards and make two piles. Those goals that have nothing to do with your future go into the first pile. In the second pile, I want you to put the cards that may resonate with you."

The process is interactive, especially when a couple is involved, because envisioning their future with pictures of possible goals in front of them engenders a lively discussion. For example, one person might pick up the home remodeling card and aggressively slap it into the "no interest pile," only to have the other grab the card and move it to the "We need this" pile, commenting, "You promised I could remodel the kitchen!"

After sorting all the cards, the advisor and client focus on the cost, timing, and importance of the goals selected. The advisor then gives the client a set of the selected goal cards along with the data-gathering questionnaire to complete as time permits. This process not only reframes the potentially unpleasant experience to one that is fun but also results in the client's emotional ownership of the outcome.

When the client returns the completed questionnaire, the advisor, using capital needs software, can integrate that information with his capital market expectations and determine the portfolio allocation necessary for the client to achieve the unique goals. The advisor can then provide a definitive recommendation for the client's investment policy statement (IPS).

Behaviorally Based Client Management

Advisors often believe that their clients are at risk of making bad decisions. In such cases, techniques and responses based on behavioral theory can be effective tools in guiding those clients to better decisions. The following are examples that can lead to successful conclusions.

MARKET TIMING

The client may believe that he or a selected advisor can accurately predict when to exit the equity market before a major correction. Although academic research suggests the unlikelihood of this strategy over an extended period, referencing that research often fails to persuade an investor enamored with his own ability (Sharpe 1975; Chang and Lewellen 1984: Jeffrey 1984; Malkiel 2004). The following framing technique can be successful in having the client reconsider his commitment to a market timing strategy.

The client is asked if he can name the top 10 artists of all time or the top 10 movies or the top 10 songs, or if a sports fan, the top 10 athletes. A client typically responds "Of course." The advisor follows up with the observation that although some disagreement might exist about who belongs on the list, coming up with the 10 names should not be a problem. The advisor then asks, "Name the top 10 market timers of all time." The typical response is silence. The follow-up question is, "Well, name the top five." Again, the client does not respond. The advisor concludes with, "Name one top market timer." With a final no response, the advisor has clearly made his point. If successful market timers were available, people should know their names. Because the person draws a complete blank, the client realizes that the strategy may not be as obvious a solution as the individual previously believed. Hence, the person is likely to reconsider whether to engage in market timing.

WOULD YOU BUY THAT STOCK TODAY?

A client might present a portfolio to an advisor that has a large position in a stock with a substantial unrealized loss. If the advisor determines that the position is inappropriate for the client's portfolio, then the advisor should recommend selling the stock. The client often responds that he plans to sell the stock as soon as the price recovers to the point that the individual does not face a sizable loss. Despite the advisor's explanation of why holding the stock is inadvisable, the client often remains unwilling to sell. The following framing technique is often successful in getting the client to reconsider.

With this strategy, the advisor asks the client, "Would you buy that stock today?" The response is frequently no. The advisor then explains that if the client gives his permission to sell, the proceeds of that sale would be in the client's account the next morning. Therefore, by keeping the stock, the client is actually making a decision to buy the stock at today's price. When reframed as a purchasing decision instead of a sale decision, the client often elects to sell.

A HOT INVESTMENT

In this scenario, the client approaches the advisor anxious to buy an investment recommended by his neighbor, a family member, or friend or based on a story in the media. If the advisor believes the investment is inappropriate, the financial professional might provide a thoughtful and fundamentally sound explanation about the potential risk of the investment, the inappropriateness of the investment as a part of the total portfolio, and a lack of information the client has about the investment or other sound objections. Unfortunately, the client is often so excited and enamored about this hot tip that he disregards the advisor's wise counsel. In this case, several framing techniques might prove useful.

The first technique recognizes that the client may discount what the advisor says and thus transfers control to the client. "That sounds like a very exciting investment, but I am unfamiliar with that investment. Tell me more about it." This strategy allows the client to share his excitement and to expound on all the possible benefits of the investment. The advisor then follows up with, "As I said, I am unfamiliar with that investment so I was wondering what might go wrong?" This question triggers the client's mind to focus on risk, not just potential return. This novice investor may say, "Well, government approvals are needed that might not come through and the firm needs to get its financing in place that might also fall through." By the time the client has refocused his attention on what might go wrong instead of solely on the excitement of everything going right, he may elect to pass on the investment or at least reduce his commitment.

Another technique is also based on reframing the client's attention from the upside to the consequences. "Your idea sounds like a very exciting and potentially rewarding one, so I updated your financial plan to see what such an investment might do for you. I found that if successful, you can not only take that expensive two-week Caribbean cruise you and your wife have been planning but also take the three-month world cruise. However, if it fails, I estimate you would have to continue working two years past your current planned retirement date." This strategy prevents many clients from making inappropriate investments with a substantial portion of their retirement savings.

The prior examples are based on reframing a client's focus from the expected positive outcome to the potential negative result. This strategy can be a powerful tool in many circumstances and is based on Pascal's wager, discussed previously. An advisor might also use such a strategy as a framing device for his longevity assumption. It can be presented in this manner.

"When developing your retirement plan, a critical factor is estimating how long you are likely to live. Based on the fact that you are a nonsmoker, your current health and your parents' and siblings' health history, I might recommend planning until age 93." If the client responds, "No, that's too long. I don't think I'll make it past my mid-80s," the advisor then reminds the client about Pascal's wager as follows: "Although you could die by 85, if you plan to that age and you live until 93, the quality of your life for those last eight years is likely to be greatly compromised." Discussing the concept of Pascal's wager with clients can be a powerful educational and framing tool in many aspects of the client relationship, helping the client to look beyond probabilities, avoid behavioral errors, and make rational decisions in the retirement planning process.

BEHAVIORAL THEORY IN PRACTICE: AN EXAMPLE

A major risk facing retirees is known as *sequence of return risk*, which is the relations between the order in which investment returns occur, the timing of withdrawal of funds in retirement, and the impact on portfolio value. As Bengen (1994) demonstrates, even if returns average out in the long term, early market declines combined with ongoing withdrawals can result in a client's retirement spending shortfall.

For financial advisors, managing this risk has both practical and behavioral components. The design of an implementation plan that mitigates the sequence of return risk is an example of a practical component. The management of client emotions and actions in a volatile market environment is an example of a behavioral component. These issues and an investor's tendency to think in terms of *mental accounts* (which refers to the tendency for individuals to mentally separate their money into distinct accounts based on subjective criteria such as the source or use of funds [Shefrin and Thaler 1988]) led Evensky to develop the Evensky & Katz Cash Flow Reserve strategy in the early 1980s (Evensky 1997), which was updated in 2013 (Pfeiffer, Salter, and Evensky 2013). Today, this plan would be described as a two-bucket strategy. Implementation of the strategy involves bifurcation of the client's total portfolio into a cash flow reserve portfolio (the short-term portfolio) and an investment portfolio (the long-term portfolio).

The cash flow reserve portfolio is funded for two possible short-term client goals. The first funding goal is any lump-sum expenditures the client anticipates within the next five years. The basis for the five-year time frame for lump-sum needs is the historical market record. The risk of investment loss for short periods is substantial. For known short-term needs, the client's goal is to have a specific dollar payout available. Although a market investment may result in a higher return, it may also result in providing inadequate funds when the short-term goal requires funding. As an example, this need for funding might include college funding for a grandchild, a special anniversary trip, or home remodeling. The second potential reserve would be one year's worth of funds required for the client's annual living expenses. For example, a client anticipating a need for a gross cash flow of $100,000, including taxes with an annual income from Social Security and pension of $70,000, would fund the cash flow reserve with the $30,000 shortfall. This amount would not generally exceed 4 percent of the total portfolio. Although 4 percent is consistent with Bengen's 4 percent rule (Bengen 1994), the firm's recommended maximum withdrawal is not based on any arbitrary rule; rather, it is limited to an amount that a capital needs analysis concludes can be sustained over the client's life span. The balance of the assets would fund the long-term investment portfolio.

The basis for the one-year cash flow allocation is both behavioral and practical, whereas the five-year lump-sum allocation is primarily related to the practical management of withdrawal risk. Although an obvious opportunity cost exists for the funds allocated to the cash flow reserve portfolio, the investment portfolio's equity allocation may be modestly increased to offset this opportunity cost.

Before retirement, most clients are used to receiving a consistent salary income, the "paycheck syndrome." In retirement, when that consistent cash flow stream disappears, this often results in angst on the retiree's part. To simulate his prior experience, the advisor would arrange with the portfolio custodian to provide the client monthly payments equal to 1/12 of the supplemental cash flow reserve. The custodian makes the payment to the client's personal checking account thus replacing the "paycheck." Typically, custodians do not charge for the service

Having separated out short-term cash flow needs, the investment portfolio can be designed and managed as a long-term, total return portfolio. As time passes and the investment portfolio requires rebalancing, the advisor takes the opportunity to refill the cash flow reserve portfolio to its original target amount. For example, assume the following:

Initial Allocations

Total portfolio	$1,000,000
Cash flow reserve (supplemental living expenses)	$40,000
Investment policy	50 percent fixed income/50 percent equity
Investment portfolio	$960,000
Fixed income	$480,000
Equity	$480,000

18 Months Later (Bear Market)

Total portfolio	$910,000
Cash flow reserve (supplemental living expenses)	$30,000
Investment policy	50 percent fixed/50 percent equity
Investment portfolio	$880,000
Fixed income	$500,000
Equity	$380,000

At this stage, the advisor would rebalance the portfolio, selling fixed income and buying equity. If no cash flow reserve is available, that would entail selling $60,000 of fixed-income securities and buying $60,000 of equity. In this example, in which a need exists to fund the cash flow reserve, the advisor would sell $65,000 of fixed income, buy $55,000 of equity, and transfer $10,000 to the cash flow reserve portfolio.

Rebalanced Portfolio

Total portfolio	$910,000
Cash flow reserve (supplemental living expenses)	$40,000
Investment portfolio	$870,000
Investment policy	50 percent fixed income/50 percent equity
Fixed income	$435,000
Equity	$435,000

The result is a portfolio balanced in accordance with the investment policy statement and a fully funded cash flow reserve account, all without having to sell equities at a substantial loss.

According to Evensky (1997), this approach is useful tool. The practical benefits of this strategy are as follows:

- Providing substantial control over the timing of investment liquidations can eliminate most cash flow related volatility drain.
- Making an investment portfolio for the long term can improve tax and expense efficiency.
- Having a large reserve of liquid funds provides flexibility in meeting the unique and changing needs of clients.

Besides these practical benefits, the most important benefits are behavioral:

- Having a consistent and dependable cash flow, independent of market volatility and changing dividend and interest rates, enables effectively managing the paycheck syndrome by providing comfort to the client during turbulent markets.

- Having the source of the client's short-term cash flow needs visible and reliable in bear markets enables clients not to panic because they know that their "paycheck" will continue and they will not have to sell investments at a sizable loss.
- Knowing that the strategy was in place and has been tested during the October 1987 Black Monday crash, tech bust, and financial crisis of 2007–2008, and has been uniformly successful, enables clients to remain fully invested and weather these turbulent market periods.

REPORTING

One final application of behavioral management involves reporting. Although advisors generally encourage their clients to focus on long-term performance, client reporting typically focuses on performance and includes performance metrics for the last quarter and year-to-date, typically benchmarked to some index such as the S&P 500. As an alternative, advisors should consider revising their standard reports to frame the information provided to clients in a manner consistent with long-term planning. Asset allocation primarily determines a client's long-term investment success (Brinson et al. 1995). Thus, the first element of the report should be the policy, not the performance.

Portfolio performance should also focus the client on the long term. Improperly framing performance by providing short-term return metrics encourages investors to react in the short term, ultimately undermining their long-term goals. Therefore, the shortest time period reflected in the report should be one year. Finally, the goal of clients' investment portfolio as reflected in the IPS is to help them provide the real cash flow necessary to accomplish their goals, not to beat the market. As a result, performance should be benchmarked to the consumer price index (CPI), not the S&P 500 Index. Individual managers should be benchmarked to an investable index, such as exchange-traded funds, reflecting the manager's investment style.

Summary and Conclusions

Behavioral finance provides a rich source of insights into client behavior, enabling practitioners to empower their clients to make better decisions. The use of these concepts begins with framing and the new client's education, plus introduction to the concept of anchoring on the efficient frontier. The advisor continues with tools such as the MoneyGuidePro Card game to help capture the complexity of client goals and evaluate the client's risk tolerance, such as the Evensky & Katz Risk Coaching process. Before implementation, preparing a thoughtful IPS helps frame the client's expectations and provides a road map for the actual implementation and ongoing management. Introducing clients to behavioral concepts such as overconfidence and anchoring helps them manage their tendency to make behavioral errors. Revising quarterly reports to properly emphasize the long-term nature of investing and appropriate benchmarking keep clients focused on the important aspects of their investment returns. Finally, behavioral based strategies such as the Cash Flow Reserve enable clients to weather unpleasant volatile markets.

DISCUSSION QUESTIONS

1. Distinguish between risk capacity and risk requirement.
2. Discuss the meaning of risk tolerance.
3. Explain how to present the various elements of a client's quarterly report.
4. Describe framing and how a financial advisor might use it.

REFERENCES

Bengen, William P. 1994. "Determining Withdrawal Rates Using Historical Data." *Journal of Financial Planning* 7:4, 171–180.

Brinson, Gary P., L. Randolph Hood, and Gilbert L. Beebower. 1995. "Determinants of Portfolio Performance." *Financial Analysts Journal* 51:1, 133–138.

Chang, Eric C., and Wilbur G. Lewellen. 1984. "Market Timing and Mutual Fund Investment Performance." *Journal of Business* 57:1 Part 1, 57–72.

Evensky, Harold. 1997. *Wealth Management—The Financial Advisor's Guide to Investing and Managing Client Assets*. New York: McGraw-Hill.

Fontevecchia, Agustino. 2013. "BP Fighting a Two Front War as Macondo Continues to Bite and Production Drops." *Forbes*, February 5. Available at www.forbes.com/sites/afontevecchia/2013/02/05/bp-fighting-a-two-front-war-as-macondo-continues-to-bite-and-production-drops/.

Guillemette, Michael A., Michael Finke, and John Gilliam. 2012. "Risk Tolerance Questions to Best Determine Client Portfolio Allocation Preferences." *Journal of Financial Planning* 25:5, 36–44.

Ibbotson, Roger G., and Paul D. Kaplan. 2000. "Does Asset Allocation Policy Explain 40,90, or 100% of Performance?" *Financial Analysts Journal* 56:1, 26–33.

Jeffrey, Robert H. 1984. "The Folly of Stock Market Timing: No One Can Predict the Markets Ups and Downs over a Long Period, and the Risks of Trying to Outweigh the Rewards." *Harvard Business Review* July-August, 102–110.

Kahneman, Daniel, and Amos Tversky. 1979. "Prospect Theory: An Analysis of Decision under Risk." *Econometrica* 47:2, 263–291.

Lowenstein, George. 2000. "Emotions in Economic Theory and Economic Behavior." *American Economic Review* 90:2, 426–432.

Malkiel, Burton. 2004. "Models of Stock Market Predictability." *Journal of Financial Research* 27:4, 445–459.

Markowitz, Harry. 1952. "Portfolio Selection." *Journal of Finance* 7:1, 77–91.

Pfeiffer, Shaun, John Salter, and Harold Evensky. 2013. "The Benefits of a Cash Reserve Strategy in Retirement Distribution Planning." *Journal of Financial Planning* 26:9, 49–55.

Phung, Albert. 2015. "Behavioral Finance: Key Concepts—Anchoring." *Investopedia*. Available at http://www.investopedia.com/university/behavioral_finance/behavioral4.asp?he.

Roszkowski, Michael J., Michael M. Delaney, and David Cordell. 2009. "Intraperson Consistency in Financial Risk Tolerance Assessment: Temporal Stability, Relationship to Total Score and Effect on Criterion-related Validity." *Journal of Business Psychology* 24:4, 455–467.

Sharpe, William. 1964. "Capital Asset Prices—A Theory of Market Equilibrium under Conditions of Risk." *Journal of Finance* 19:3, 425–442.

Sharpe, William. 1975. "Likely Gains from Market Timing." *Financial Analyst Journal* 31:2, 60–69.

Shefrin, Hersh, and Richard Thaler. 1988. "The Behavioral Life-Cycle Hypothesis." *Economic Inquiry* 26:4, 609–643.

Tversky, Amos, and Daniel Kahneman. 1992. "Advances in Prospect Theory: Cumulative Representation of Uncertainty." *Journal of Risk and Uncertainty* 5:4, 297–323.

29

Practical Challenges of Implementing Behavioral Finance

Reflections from the Field

GREG B. DAVIES
Founding Partner, Centapse, London
Associate Fellow, Oxford, Säid Business School

PETER BROOKS
Behavioral Finance Transformation Director
Barclays, London

Introduction

Taken in isolation, the ideas and concepts that make up the field of behavioral finance are of limited practical use. Indeed, many of the attempts to apply these ideas amount to little more than a trite list of biases and pictures of human brains on PowerPoint slides. Talking a good game in the arena of behavioral finance is easy, which often leads to the misperception that it is superficial. Indeed, making behavioral finance work in practice is challenging: it requires integrating these ideas with working models, information technology (IT) systems, business processes, and organizational culture.

This chapter reviews some of the common misperceptions of applied behavioral finance and the problems of implementing behavioral ideas, based on experience gained in leading a functioning corporate behavioral finance team for nearly a decade. The chapter is intended to be neither an academic discussion on methodological rights and wrongs of human behavior nor an instruction kit for practical application—the range of environments and applications is too broad. Instead, the goal is to provide an overview of themes that result in poor implementation or outcomes, or in misguided applications to commercial problems.

The first section addresses some misconceptions commonly held by aspirant practitioners, including more than a few academics trying their hand at commercial applications, about the nature of behavioral finance. The second section looks at some of the common problems or barriers to successful utilization of behavioral principles in practice. The third section offers some constructive principles on how to approach application. The final section concludes with some more practical suggestions on how to bring this rich body of knowledge to life within an organization.

Misconceptions in Commercial Practice About Behavioral Finance

Before discussing the difficulties of practical implementation, it is often necessary to persuade practitioners of the need to consider behavioral approaches at all. This task has become much easier since the turn of the century, as terms such as *behavioral finance, behavioral economics,* and *decision science* are now much more familiar and less daunting. This change has been helped considerably by the explosion of accessible popular science books on various aspects of the field, as well as by various mainstream journalists covering the ideas in news stories. The sharing of the Nobel Memorial Prize in Economic Sciences in 2002 by Daniel Kahneman and Vernon Smith dramatically increased public awareness. The financial crisis of 2007–2008 further enhanced the credibility of behavioral finance, as it provided a painful reminder that emotion and psychology are fundamental to how the financial system functions. This increased credibility was particularly true in contrast to other areas of economic research—behavioral economics was about the only field of economics that came out of the financial crisis with more credibility than it had going in. The attention paid to the field of behavioral economics by governments, particularly in the United States and the United Kingdom following the publication of the book *Nudge* (Thaler and Sunstein 2008), and regulators, with the United Kingdom's Financial Conduct Authority (FCA) leading the way, has further increased its acceptance.

The commercial world is now much more open to behavioral thinking. This openness can lead to misconceptions and skepticism, sometimes to the point where it risks appearing a management fad rather than a serious body of academic knowledge. Most unfortunate among these misconceptions is the notion that behavioral finance consists of nothing more than a list of psychological biases. This perception is unfortunate because the thoughtful categorization of a complex field into a number of distinct heuristics and biases, each accompanied by compelling examples, has helped to make the field more understandable, accessible, and popular.

THE "BIAS" BIAS

Today, extremely long lists of biases are available, which do little to convey the underlying sophistication, complexity, and thoroughness of more than half a century of highly robust experimental and theoretical work. These lists provide no real framework for potential practitioners to deploy when approaching a tangible problem. And many of these biases appear to overlap or conflict with each other, which can make behavioral finance appear either very superficial or highly confused.

The easily accessible examples that academics have used to illustrate these biases to wide audiences have sometimes led to the impression that behavioral economics is an easy field to master. This misrepresentation then leads to inevitable disappointment when categorizing biases proves not to be a panacea. A perception of the field as "just anecdotes and parlor games" reduces the willingness of the commercial world to put substantial investments of time and resource into building applications grounded on the underlying ideas. Building behavioral finance ideas into commercial applications requires both depth and breadth of understanding of the theory and, in many cases, large resource commitments. Having broad guiding frameworks, such as the notion of "two systems of reasoning" (Sloman 2002) enables users to approach the somewhat chaotic multitude of behavioral findings in a practical way, rather than to have a lengthy list that provides no conceptual framework with which to apprehend the complexity.

BEHAVIORAL IS NOT IN CONFLICT WITH TRADITIONAL

A second misconception is that behavioral finance necessarily conflicts with traditional finance (also called classical or standard finance). This concern raises barriers to acceptance, particularly among those who have built their careers on understanding and deploying the tools, models, and ideas of traditional finance, and has often been perpetuated by behavioral proponents seeking to advance their ideas by focusing on areas where traditional finance is deficient. Again, these "anomalies" have been an effective way of demonstrating that any attempt to understand financial systems without considering behavioral aspects is incomplete, but have sometimes led to the impression that behavioral approaches are entirely antagonistic to traditional financial models.

This combative approach and academic debate of the two schools of financial thought is not useful when trying to solve practical problems: it is off-putting to those in industry and risks entire systems being dismissed based on problems with specific details. Implementation of behavioral ideas requires building on what already exists by understanding traditional financial theory and frameworks. Couching language in terms that those in the industry can easily understand and accept is essential. Recognizing that behavioral finance is not in opposition to traditional finance but, rather, a generalization of it, is crucial. The tools and models of traditional finance in many ways provide the "right" answer. The descriptive inadequacy of *Homo economicus* does not mean dismissing all the normative models of classical finance but, rather, requires thinking about how to adapt them for the complex reality of real people and multifaceted environments. Behavioral finance should help to make traditional finance more relevant, because it shows how to relax the overly narrow normative assumptions to adapt these models to the real world, providing better solutions for real people.

THE COST OF "LABELS"

A final source of misconception comes largely from within the academic field itself: the endless debates about what it is and what it is not; continual attempts to define and label subsets of research findings as "behavioral finance" or "behavioral economics", "social psychology", or "decision science"; and methodological debates about what should be excluded. This labeling and quarreling may be of academic interest, but it leads to considerable confusion among practitioners and makes the field as a whole look disconnected and internally inconsistent. This situation, in turn, leads to concerns that, whatever it is called, behavioral finance is not sufficiently developed and coherent to be practically useful.

Among these debates are those about whether deviations from the normative models should be classified as "biases", or whether heuristics are reasonable responses to complex choice environments, including the concern as to whether they are "ecologically rational" (Todd and Gigerenzer 2012). The purist interpretations often lead to straw-man definitions of what is "in" and "out" of the broad field, drawing artificial boundaries and divisions and casting doubts on potentially valuable tools and ideas as being somehow outside the fold.

A commonly expressed concern, at least in the mainstream press, is that there exists no grand unified theory of behavioral economics, and that the field is thus merely a chaotic collection of unconnected and often contradictory findings. For the purpose of practical implementation, the notion that this is, or needs to be, a clearly defined field should be eliminated, reducing the desire to erode it with arbitrary labels and definitions. Human behavior operates at multiple levels, from the neurological to complex social interactions. Any quest for a grand unified theory to mirror that of physical sciences may well be entirely misguided, together with the notion that such a theory is necessary for the broad field to be useful. Much more effective is an approach of treating the full range of behavioral findings as a rich toolbox that can be applied to, and tested on, a range of practical concerns.

Challenges of Applying Behavioral Finance

The use of behavioral finance often falls prey to superficial approaches or inappropriate applications of financial theory. This section explores concerns with the practical implementation of behavioral finance by both industry practitioners and academic consultants, who often resort to a "lift and drop" of techniques between different domains of choice with little understanding of the context of those choice domains. The section includes examples of recent successes in applying behavioral finance.

SUPERFICIAL APPROACHES

The first major challenge is that behavioral finance is not particularly effective if applied superficially. Yet, superficial attempts are commonplace. Some seek to do little more than offer a checklist of biases, hoping that informing people of poor decision making can solve the problem. Instead, a central theme of decision science is the consistent finding that merely informing people of their adverse behavioral proclivities is very seldom effective in combating them.

Because behavioral finance is both topical and fascinating to many people, it attracts "hobbyists" who can readily recite a number of biases, but who have neither the depth of knowledge of the field overall nor a solid grasp of the theoretical underpinnings of the more technical aspects of the field. For example, some refer to the behavioral concepts of *loss aversion* or *prospect theory*, without truly understanding the foundations and shortcomings. Even Cumulative Prospect Theory (CPT) (Tversky and Kahneman 1992), a framework containing many powerful insights central to behavioral research and arguably the most accepted alternative to the traditional Expected Utility Theory, is frequently both misunderstood and misstated outside, and sometimes inside, academia. CPT is further discussed in the next section.

This chapter is not an attempt to erect barriers to entry among behavioral practitioners and claim that only those with advanced degrees in the field should be taken seriously. On the contrary, the effect of greater academic training can cause its beneficiaries to hold on too closely to narrow and technical interpretations of the field to make them effective practitioners. Indeed, some of the most effective practitioners do not have an extensive academic background in the field. However, they have invested considerable time and effort in getting to know and deeply understand the breadth and depth of the field. They understand how new insights intersect with traditional theory and approaches, and reflect on how this body of knowledge applies to a wide range of practical problems and decision environments.

Limited study of behavioral finance through reading the popular books on the topic may equip one to sound knowledgeable and appear convincing. However, as this field is a relatively new one, the purchasers of behavioral expertise are seldom equipped to know the difference and may be unable to tell a superficially convincing approach from approaches that embody true understanding. This leaves the field open to consultants peddling "behavioral expertise" but having in their toolkit little more than a list of biases that they apply sequentially and with little variation to each problem encountered. Warning flags should go up whenever the proposal rests heavily on catalogues of behavioral biases or contains a preponderance of pictures of brains.

Superficial application of behavioral finance leads to a particular tendency to take a behavioral principle or "bias" in isolation and then implement something based on this process, without considering the broader complexities of the environment. A specific problem may arise in part from a particular identified bias, but it does not necessarily follow that resolving this bias will either resolve the problem or that the intervention itself will not cause additional unforeseen problems of its own. Human behavior is complex and is influenced by a multitude of simultaneous effects—some internal, some social, and some environmental. These multiple factors all interact. Trying to understand and change behavior by going through a list of "biases" one by one in isolation fails to account for this complexity.

Many examples exist of nudges that have effectively addressed a specific problem, often by focusing on a particular behavioral finding. However, many examples of unsuccessful nudges are also available. Changing behavior in a desired direction often requires a sophisticated program of experimentation and testing to see what works and what does not. It requires thoughtful consideration of all the aspects of the environment and behavior that requires substantially more depth and breadth than simply ticking off a list of biases. For example, the recently launched incomeIQ test from Schroders (2015) assesses respondents' propensity to display a number of behavioral biases indicating areas of improvement. Although customers may appreciate the helpful tips, this test may do little to alter anyone's behavior.

By contrast, the Save More Tomorrow program for increasing pension contribution rates is an example of a good behavioral design (Thaler and Benartzi 2004). This behavioral approach has been developed through sophisticated and thoughtful understanding of many aspects of human behavior. It shows a clear understanding of both the environment in which the strategy will be deployed and the objective the nudge is trying to achieve.

An example of a behavioral intervention, seemingly used without fully weighing up the associated costs, is the design of the default pension solutions in the UK's National Employment Savings Trust (NEST). To encourage those new to pension contributions to participate over time and stay invested, the default solutions are invested at reduced risk levels early on to ensure that the investors' early experiences with investing are comfortable and they do not get put off by experiencing too much market volatility early in the process. Superficially, this seems like a good idea because emotional comfort with investing decisions plays a huge role in long-term investing success, and bad experiences early on may have long-term harmful consequences. However, this approach reduces risk at exactly the time when investors are most financially capable of taking risk. That is, their investment portfolios are small and their time horizons are long, which limits the long-term effects of early losses. Although this strategy has emotional benefits, it also has considerable financial costs. As a result, this strategy should be used only in those circumstances and for those investors for whom the benefits outweigh the costs. It might, for example, make sense for nervous investors with regard to their regular investments, but pension investments are the one area in which investors tend not to pay much attention to short-term performance. Thus, the strategy is very likely to commit investors to expected financial costs in a set of circumstances with few compensating emotional benefits.

Fidelity recently announced the launch of a "people like me" approach to investing, in which investors can enter personal details such as their age and the value of their holdings as a basis of comparison for investment decisions that have been taken by others with similar characteristics. This approach can have powerful effects on behavior in many domains, leading people to reduce energy usage or exercise more. In the field of investing, however, it primarily encourages investors to copy other people's poor investment decisions.

ACADEMIC "LIFT AND DROP"

The flip side of superficial approaches from untrained commercial practitioners, which usually occur in the consulting field, is that of applications marketed by highly trained academics who often fail to consider the realities of commercial life outside the laboratory. Academics tend to build what they consider to be real-world applications within academe and then seek to "lift and drop" these into commercial or policy applications. A core concern is that those in the commercial world seeking behavioral solutions frequently have little expertise by which to evaluate the proposals and can be easily won over by impressive-sounding academic credentials.

Academic findings are not always easily transferable, at least not without substantial effort to tailor them to be effective in a real-world environment. There are often confounding environmental variables or unintended consequences from well-intentioned behavioral interventions. Three particular types of misguided attempts to implement academic behavioral ideas are (1) to base an implementation on a single behavioral tendency that is valid when observed in controlled experimental conditions, but which has potential costs in a real-world setting; (2) to deliver highly technical solutions, which are over-engineered and thus not suitable to the practical problem they are trying to address; and (3) to offer behavioral alternatives to how things are already done without truly understanding the traditional approaches or the language and beliefs of existing practitioners.

Many of the suggested behavioral approaches to goals-based investing and attempts to build this into practical investment tools exemplify the first type of a misguided attempt (Das, Markowitz, Scheid, and Statman 2010). Goals-based investing is frequently justified using the notion of mental accounting, arguing that individuals do not typically see money as completely fungible, but instead compartmentalize their financial situation into mental accounts (Thaler 1999). A valid implication of this framework is that investors find financial decision making easier and more comfortable if they can conceive of their wealth in "pots." Furthermore, investors tend to be more motivated if they are pursuing specific goals for which they are saving. The recommendations of this strand of the literature generally lead to the suggestion that investments should be managed in a series of "buckets," each connected to a specific future goal and each with its own time horizon and risk profile.

Mental accounting brings benefits to investors insofar as it makes decision making easier and more contained. However, this approach also largely fails to consider the concomitant costs. Mental accounting reduces financial and psychological flexibility, tying investors to a particular structure of goals and preferences that may be spuriously precise reflections of their actual fuzzy aspirations. As a result, investors are relatively less able to adapt to changing circumstances and preferences over time. In short, this strategy commits the naturalistic fallacy of deriving "ought" from "is." Much of the academic research in behavioral finance is descriptive in that it describes how people actually behave, not how they should behave. This approach of goals-based investing delivers both the benefits and the costs of mental accounting. By contrast, a method truly designed to address the problem would seek to build systems that incorporate the benefits while minimizing the costs (Davies and Brooks 2014).

An example of over-engineered technical solutions is in the area of portfolio optimization. The behavioral literature shows that investors do not exhibit expected utility theory preferences when making decisions. Instead, their decision making is more closely approximated by non-expected utility models such as CPT (Tversky and Kahneman 1992). Optimizing a portfolio for CPT preferences is not an easy task because the optimization is non-convex. However, He and Zhou (2011) address the issue and find that computing a portfolio that would be optimally held by an individual whose preferences are described by CPT is possible. Although this process is possibly an interesting mathematical exercise, why would any investor ever want to hold this portfolio? Investing is a long-term activity. Yet, this process incorporates within portfolio solutions the very features that arise from behavioral responses to the immediate context (e.g., reference dependence and loss aversion), extrapolating them to portfolio choices influencing long-term outcomes of the investor's total portfolio. In short, CPT as a practical implementation commits the naturalistic fallacy: it confuses descriptive preferences for normative preferences, and thus commits investors to all sorts of choices that in the long term they are likely to wish they had not made. Observed human choice in small frames is certainly not always optimal in broader long-term frames.

At least two other problems exist with this approach to portfolio optimization. First, it assumes that an individual investor's preferences can be specified precisely using a sophisticated model such as CPT. This model can have up to five parameters to be estimated—one governing loss aversion, two relating to the value function curvature in gains and losses, and two associated with some specifications of the probability distortion function. Moreover, the behavioral parameters, calibrated on immediate revealed preferences or hypothetical choices, are assumed to be stable over time and appropriate to long-term preferences for total wealth. Insofar as emotional responses to the current context, environment, emotional state, and frame induce behavioral proclivities, they are unlikely to be stable. Rather, they will exhibit large fluctuations in strength depending on whether the decision maker is reflecting calmly on broader frames and longer horizons or anxiously focused on narrow problems. So, even if applying a descriptive model to a normative solution were appropriate, accurately fixing this model becomes unlikely. Hence, users might exhibit spurious confidence and precision in a solution inappropriate to the problem at hand.

Yet, such approaches are increasingly available in commercial applications: systems putting investors through a sequence of questions that aim to elicit specific individual revealed preferences for risk attitudes, time preferences, ambiguity aversion, loss aversion, probability distortion—sometimes among other features. Advisors then use these results to calculate recommended individually tailored portfolio recommendations that somehow "optimize" the portfolio for all these "revealed preferences."

This sort of approach is fundamentally misguided. It begins with spuriously precise measurements of descriptive features of an investor's point in time decision pattern, which are likely to be highly unstable, or at the least to evolve over time. The approach then applies these preferences from one specific decision frame to another one entirely. However, the biggest problem with this approach is the notion that these descriptive features of someone's choices are those that should be applied to a recommended solution. Thoughtful investors should repudiate many of these revealed preferences as being inappropriate for their long-term wealth outcomes. For example, it is near impossible to rationalize why any investor would logically choose to use distorted probabilities when selecting an optimal investing strategy. The same goes for any specifications that are frame dependent, as are most of the features of CPT.

A similar difficulty faces those goals-based portfolio construction approaches that use aspiration-based preferences such as Shefrin and Statman (2000). These approaches assume that an investor's ability to specify a target outcome for an individual goal today should be taken as an accurate expression of long-term preferences. Such preferences would imply that the goal is fixed, certain, and absolute, so that investors would give up substantial upside rather than accept any reduction in the chance of reaching this goal. However, the goal may instead simply be an easy way for an investor to express something that is in reality fuzzy and uncertain. Treating such preferences as "optimal" or accurate is likely to incur a large potential cost for little gain.

The essential problem with all these approaches is that they take a descriptive academic model that explains choice behavior with reasonable accuracy in specific circumstances, and then apply it much more broadly than can be reasonably justified to quite different real-world situations. Normative models should be used if the goal is to help guide behavior. The goal of practical implementations of behavioral insight should be to help decision makers mitigate deviations from these normative theories, within the constraints imposed by the human need for immediate emotional comfort with situations and decisions (Davies and Lim 2014).

End users of such tools often have little experience that would enable them to evaluate whether a particular approach is fit for a specific purpose or over-engineered. This problem is exacerbated in academic "lift and drop" applications relative to the superficial approaches discussed in the previous section. That is, the academic pedigree and apparent sophistication and precision can give a strong illusion that the approach is at the cutting edge of behavioral science, rather than a spurious application of unstable solutions that could lead to investors' locking short-term emotional preferences into important long-term choices.

The fact that many behavioral practitioners are critical of existing traditional approaches, without truly understanding them, makes this concern more problematic. They also often arrive without understanding the assumptions, knowledge base, and common language of the commercial world and as such fail to communicate effectively, potentially resulting in considerable misunderstanding. Offering the commercial world an alternative to an established approach requires the ability to communicate the new ideas in terms that those in the industry clearly understand.

LACK OF TAILORING TO FIT THE PROBLEM AND ENVIRONMENT

Effective behavioral implementation needs to be highly tailored and attuned to the precise environment and the practical realities of the problem at hand. This requires considering both the increased complexity and noise of decision making outside the laboratory, as well as the organizational realities of getting the solutions implemented, accepted, and used. Tailoring the design and organizational deployment are at least as important as the behavioral aspects if the implementation is to be effective.

The process of achieving these goals often fails on several levels. First, the implementation is frequently unsuccessful because it is not accepted into the organization at the outset, leading to skepticism and low usage. Gaining acceptance requires senior sponsorship. Acceptance also requires extensive efforts to ensure that the proposed approach fits into the organizational structure, existing processes, technology and systems, and regulatory requirements. Additionally, educating, preparing, and training the users are essential to ensure both initial acceptance and continued usage, which in turn requires ongoing support. Consideration of an organization's culture is a vital part of this process.

Second, some devote insufficient thought to user experience (UX) design and ease of use, often adding steps or elements to existing processes. These may lead to better outcomes if used, but can also make employee or client tasks more time-consuming or difficult. Poor user experience hampers both acceptance and use of a behavioral tool, and also often makes the behavioral insights themselves less effective. A clever behavioral intervention is of no value if not used.

This limitation is particularly true for both technology and software-based implementations, but also of other behaviorally designed processes such as client profiling and fact-finding tools, sales processes, and product-approval processes. An example of such a limitation is the deployment of decision journaling systems to help individuals document the rationale behind their decisions to combat hindsight and confirmation biases, and thus to facilitate improved decision making. This approach is widely advocated by the behavioral literature and should be a feature of any good decision support tool or system. However, unless well designed to fit with the specific needs of the user, the details of the decisions they make, and the organizational environment in which they operate, decision makers will simply fail to use the tool effectively. They may also reject outright the broader behavioral system of which it is a component. For many decision makers, the additional task of having to document even a one-sentence rationale for frequent decisions can be perceived as too onerous, regardless of how effective it might be.

Perhaps a better initial approach is twofold: (1) automate the capture of as many features of the decision as possible, and (2) design a series of questions that the individual can quickly answer and which capture some essential features of the decision maker's emotional state at the time, to be used later to combat hindsight bias. For example, simple multiple-choice response scales capturing the decision maker's level of confidence and emotion when making the decision may provide useful data at very low effort. The crucial element of the process is that the design is intimately linked to the needs of the decision maker and his or her willingness to engage.

EXECUTIVE RELUCTANCE

A final concern with practical implementation is that many executives are reluctant to fully embrace behaviorally grounded approaches, even given considerable evidence supporting their effectiveness. Fortunately, this discomfort with novelty is no longer as prevalent as it was, but other sources of reluctance persist, forming barriers to adoption.

Some of this reluctance is related to the perceptions of superficiality previously noted. Many sophisticated executives have read popular books and articles in the field. They are rightly suspicious of others overselling simplistic approaches that offer no deeper insights than methods currently used. Another perception is that behavioral approaches are useful only for trite or trivial problems. Discussions with senior executives should start by pointing out the many failings of superficial approaches, and being deliberately critical is often necessary to get sufficiently over their skepticism to move forward.

A related problem is that many successful executives assume that implementing behavioral ideas is simple and does not need to be tackled systematically and deeply. This attitude is an example of overconfidence that also leads to perceptions that behavior can be changed simply by reading about or discussing biases, without the need to laboriously build this knowledge into tools and organizational design.

A particular reluctance in the finance industry lies in openness to behavioral findings on framing of information and data design. Reframing financial information to align the frame to broader objectives, rather than narrow details and myopic horizons, can lead to substantially better decision making. Lower complexity is usually beneficial. Benartzi (2015) offers an approachable recent summary of our behavioral knowledge with regard to digital design. However, the finance industry is typically quantitative in nature. This creates great reluctance to genuinely believe that shielding ourselves, employees, or clients from too much information and reducing the detail and frequency of data are things that should be pursued.

A final area of executive reluctance is an often surprising unwillingness to engage with experimentation, and with testing behavioral approaches using randomized control trial (RCT) designs, which deploy rigorous application of scientific methods to truly establish what works and what does not. Some of this reluctance comes again from overconfidence. In the commercial world, individuals are usually rewarded for having a clear idea, believing in it, and pushing it to implementation. This mindset is not conducive to admitting a lack of conviction or to design through experimentation.

The corporate world is certainly becoming more open to RCT approaches, but currently these are often used to test relatively small aspects of design, such as the placing of design elements on the screen or the use of different fonts or colors. Such aspects are worth testing and can sometimes make a surprisingly large difference. Yet, even more valuable would be testing larger aspects of behavioral design that require executives to admit they do not know which path to take. This admission requires considerable courage, and being able to generate sufficiently interesting solutions, filter them, and then design alternatives for testing requires considerable effort, knowledge, creativity, and commitment. It also requires substantial investment in resources to build prototypes and rapidly deploy and test them. RCT approaches are more expensive than fiddling with numerous shades of blue on a web page, but the potential upside of transcending the limits of traditional corporate innovation is also substantially greater.

THE GOOD NEWS

Despite drawing attention to the challenges of implementation, over the last decade industry and policymakers have become more open to behavioral insights, with many examples of good implementation and good behavioral design. These successes include automatic enrollment in pensions in various parts of the world, which has led to millions saving for their retirement that would not have otherwise been doing so. The United Kingdom's Behavioural Insights Team has, among others, used RCT designs to increase tax compliance and the effectiveness of job centers. In the United Kingdom, the FCA has been pioneering behavioral approaches to financial regulation to improve outcomes for customers, and many companies and start-ups are using gamification techniques to encourage better health and financial behaviors. A small number of sophisticated behavioral consultancies are also helping companies and governments address commercial and social problems with substantial rigor and credibility. Barclays has spent nearly a decade building behavioral approaches into IT systems, sales process, profiling tools, investment solutions, and many other ways of helping people to make better financial decisions, including a recent launch of a behavioral framework to encourage impact investing and philanthropy (Davies 2015).

Behavioral findings are more widely known and accepted than they were previously. They are being piloted and explored in an ever-wider range of industries and applications. Furthermore, advances in digital technology and data analytics are opening up new vistas for application and making personalization, testing, and delivery cheaper and easier. With that said, industry and government are still only in the initial stages of building the decades of robust academic behavioral research into practical applications. Much still needs to be learned and tried.

Applying Behavioral Finance

The previous section presented illustrations of good and bad applications of behavioral finance. This section offers a set of principles that should be considered when applying behavioral finance.

PRINCIPLE 1: BEHAVIORAL FINANCE IS ALMOST ALWAYS USELESS IN ISOLATION

Consider the most isolated application of behavioral finance: simply educating people about their biases. Awareness may lead to a small improvement in actions and decisions, but any effect is likely to be short-lived, as the stimuli for the biased action have not been changed or removed. Successful applications of behavioral finance require an approach to people, processes, and technology. They also require an acknowledgment that the traditional approach to any scenario may not be wrong. Corporate executives and others should not repudiate traditional thinking but, rather, embrace and augment it with an understanding of behavior.

The financial crisis of 2007–2008 brought much criticism of traditional portfolio management practices. This required organizations to reexamine their asset allocation techniques to evaluate possible improvements. Using volatility as a portfolio risk measure is computationally convenient, but is incongruous with how individual investors think about risk, and it leads to unreasonable conclusions about the preferences of investors (Egan, Davies and Brooks 2011). Is there a way of measuring portfolio risk that better reflects how individuals think about risk—that is, that is focused on the downside and allowing for better than expected outcomes to reduce portfolio risk? Along with quantitative financial analysts, Davies and De Servigny (2012) create a behavioral measure of portfolio risk that can be included in a traditional risk and return optimization framework with the objective function of minimizing behavioral risk subject to a given level of return. This Behavioral Modern Portfolio Theory recognizes that behavioral finance is part of the solution, but not the whole solution. In their model, the departure from the traditionally used form of modern portfolio theory (MPT) is relatively small. It still allows investment practitioners to talk about efficient frontiers and asset allocation in a manner that is consistent with their professional training, and yet is linked to client measures of risk tolerance (Davies and Brooks 2014) that are stable and do not suffer from false precision or over-engineering. The importance of ingrained knowledge should not be underestimated when trying to drive adoption of behavioral finance in a large organization. This belief leads to a second principle.

PRINCIPLE 2: BEHAVIORAL FINANCE IS A COMPANION TO TRADITIONAL APPROACHES

A recommended mindset is to start with the belief that there are probably good reasons for why things are as they are, but to understand traditional approaches deeply enough to challenge the status quo. The implication is that behavioral finance is only ever part of the solution and needs to complement traditional approaches. Today, successful behavioral finance practitioners need to be specialists in behavioral finance and generalists in many other areas. They cannot operate in isolation from other specialists within an organization.

PRINCIPLE 3: BEHAVIORAL FINANCE IS NOT JUST NUDGES

Although all behavioral finance applications attempt to change behavior in some way, the wide array of tactics tend to align to a few broad options: educate people about their biases; rely on decision inertia with passive nudges such as changing the default option; and go beyond passive nudges by critically assessing how to present an active choice. Simply educating people about their biases is ineffective. As a result, there has been an increase in nudge techniques because evidence shows them to be effective at changing behavior in many situations (Thaler and Sunstein 2008). However, a nudge is a blunt tool and may not always result in good individual decisions. Furthermore, although nudges may be effective in addressing specific, isolated behaviors, they are not particularly useful in helping people make confident, informed choices in complex decision environments.

Returning to the example of auto-enrollment in company pension plans, such a program may or may not lead to better outcomes. By auto-enrolling employees in a pension scheme, the total amount of pension savings will increase within society. Yet, are people saving more appropriately for their retirement? This is far from certain. The nudge takes one decision away from savers—whether or not to join the company pension plan—but it does so by making one-size-fits-all assumptions on other decisions. The bluntness of this nudge comes from the employees' likely perception that all decisions related to their pension savings have been addressed. The default rate of contribution and the default fund selection act as safety nets for those who would not make a decision for themselves. Rather than employees' reviewing their contribution rate and investment fund, which are much more difficult assessments for novice investors, most succumb to inertia and contribute the default amount into the default fund with no assessment of whether this is appropriate for their type of retirement. A single default, no matter how well chosen to be approximately right for most, is always going to be precisely wrong for many. In effect, a valuable nudge on one decision has created more questionable nudges on two additional decisions. Although people are saving more for retirement in the United Kingdom, it is unlikely that most are saving the appropriate amount for their retirement as a result of auto-enrollment.

This assessment is not a criticism of auto-enrollment; it is an effective nudge. But more should be done to engage people with the choices that they still need to make. Although debate continues about whether the libertarian paternalistic approach of manipulating choice through nudges is an affront to free choice, this debate misses a more important concept of *asymmetric paternalism*, which refers to policies designed to help people who can't or won't behave so as to advance their own interests—for example, by constraining options or nudging toward default options while encouraging more active engagement and less fettered choice for those who are willing and able to decide themselves.

Under asymmetric paternalism, practical applications of behavioral finance focus equally on those who cannot or will not make a decision, and those who could or would engage with making their own choices given an accessible opportunity to do so. Practical applications of nudges have tended to be overly focused on those who would not otherwise do something that is in their better interests, often to the detriment of those who are capable of making the decision. Behavioral finance practitioners need to do more to apply their skills toward engaging decision makers and helping them make confident and informed decisions in complex environments, as much as to finding defaults that work well for the passive majority.

PRINCIPLE 4: ASYMMETRIC PATERNALISM SHOULD BE A GUIDING PRINCIPLE

In practice, this principle means using a full toolbox of behavioral approaches. For example, if the goal is confident and informed decision making, then the individual needs three things at the point of decision: (1) the knowledge required to make the decision, (2) engagement with the decision, and (3) the emotional comfort to enact it. Table 29.1 reflects how effective various approaches are at achieving these three requirements.

Simple information disclosure and traditional education accomplish little with respect to these approaches (Fernandes, Lynch, Jr., and Netemeyer 2014). Nudging can change behavior, but may actually have a harmful effect on knowledge and engagement because the comfort that knowing someone has thought about the problem is also an invitation for people to disengage. Only by bringing the full behavioral toolkit to bear can a fully engaged, informed, and confident choice emerge.

Table 29.1 **Effect of Approaches to Behavioural Change on Knowledge, Engagement, and Emotional Comfort**

	Knowledge	*Engagement*	*Emotional Comfort*	*Examples*
Disclosure	Little or none	None	None	Disclaimers Caveat emptor
Traditional Education	Little or none	Little or none	Little or none	Seminars Classes
Nudges	None or negative	None or negative	Some	Auto-enrollment Defaults
Engaged Choice	Yes	Yes	Yes	Just in time education Gamification

Note: This table shows how different behavioral tools contribute to the forming confident and engaged decision makers.

PRINCIPLE 5: GOOD APPLICATIONS OF BEHAVIORAL FINANCE SHOULD COMBINE AN UNDERSTANDING OF HOW PROCESSES AND PEOPLE INTERACT TO INDUCE BETTER DECISIONS

Many people fail to make decisions because they feel they do not understand the complexity of what they need to consider, or because arriving at and enacting any decision are just too difficult. Applications of behavioral finance that take advantage of these individuals reflect dishonorably on the discipline. Sadly, the finance industry has a large number of examples of failures in this regard. The use of teaser rates on credit cards and savings account products are among the most pervasive.

A common practice in the United Kingdom and the United States credit card industry is to offer an extended period of zero percent interest for individuals who transfer an existing balance from another credit card and pay a small percentage as a transfer fee. This opportunity can be advantageous for those who are disciplined in their finances. However, the way that people and process interact in this example means that many are set up to fail.

At the end of the interest-free period, the interest rate reverts to a level much more typical of unsecured lending. If the borrower fails to remember that the interest-free period is coming to an end and does not clear the debt, either by making regular payments or by transferring to a new interest-free deal, the rate the borrower ends up paying is typically punitive compared to the most competitive standard rates. Although banks now have a responsibility to alert customers to the end of teaser rate deals, ample opportunity to profit from the inertia of ill-disciplined customers remains.

The central role of behavioral finance should be to reinforce good behaviors and help people make better financial decisions. It should not be used to profit at the hands of customers who do not recognize their own behavioral biases. Thus, behavioral finance fits well with the growing emphasis banking regulators are giving to *conduct risk*, which can loosely be defined as any commercial conduct that causes customer detriment.

Behavioral finance provides the insights and toolkit to ensure that customers are treated fairly, but this requires understanding how people interact with the processes that are put in front of them. The following are some examples to ponder of whether some specific decision frames are designed to account for potential behavioral bias.

- When a user interface designer recommends shortening the number of available lines on an investment fund selection document so that it fits on fewer pages, is the designer aware that the form is providing a subtle nudge to customer choices and that this might limit portfolio diversification (Benartzi and Thaler 2007)?
- Can customers be expected to read and understand a lengthy exclusions and disclosures document on a travel insurance policy without any information on the typical costs of obtaining medical treatment abroad to help judge the value of the policy? The framing of maximum limits on policy payouts does not describe the risk the insured customer still carries. Insurance policies often suffer intangible information asymmetries that make judging good value very difficult for consumers.
- What is the best way to inform pension savers whether they are on track for the kind of retirement they want? Can monetary forecasts be translated into lifestyle

desires? Is showing the current lifestyles that the pensions are forecast to be able to provide a better way to frame the information, and can it spur workers to raise their contribution rates?

- Why do online investment platforms often show customers their daily returns and returns since purchase for each investment when displaying the portfolio? Daily return is not aligned to the typical customer's time horizon and increases perceptions of risk, and return since purchase creates an irrelevant performance anchor that can trigger the disposition effect. Both can result in detrimental customer decision making. Is a better approach to broaden the frame to show portfolio-level past performance measured over an appropriately long time horizon?

Behavioral finance practitioners need to accept a role in helping people make better decisions, and not simply identify biases or promulgate those biases for corporate profit. This goal requires the integration of behavioral finance within organizations.

How to Make Behavioral Finance Work in an Organization

The practical application of behavioral finance within an organization is tricky, particularly in large organizations. How can an organization start to take knowledge that is concentrated in a few individuals and make it usable by all?

The FCA's focus on using behavioral finance has been beneficial, but also arguably somewhat harmful to the practical application of behavioral finance in UK financial institutions. Beneficial, because it highlights and legitimizes a body of academic knowledge that has rarely been applied in the real world. However, as a consequence, the first areas in financial institutions to become awakened to behavioral finance have often been the regulatory control functions, which have typically scrambled to learn something so that they are not behind their regulator in knowledge. Although any application of the field should be encouraged, trying to convince senior decision makers of the value of behavioral finance by focusing on lowered compliance risk has the effect of limiting the perceived scope of benefits and applications. Hiring specialists is necessary, but to be truly effective in changing the organization they need to be part of business strategy, customer insight, and proposition design teams, and not just within control functions.

Putting practical applications of behavioral finance in the hands of nonspecialists requires an assessment and redesign of tools and processes, and widespread adoption of behavioral finance within large organizations requires thoughtful design. For example, the Behavioural Insights Team, which was formerly part of the UK Cabinet Office, published their EAST (easy, attractive, social, and timely) framework for using behavioral insights (Behavioural Insights Team 2014). Behavioral interventions should be:

- Easy (E): includes harnessing the power of defaults, reducing the "hassle factor" of taking up a service, and simplifying messages.
- Attractive (A): includes attracting attention and designing rewards and sanctions for maximum effect.

- Social (S): includes showing that most people perform the desired behavior, using the power of networks, and encouraging people to make a commitment to others.
- Timely (T): includes prompting people when they are most likely to be receptive, considering the immediate costs and benefits, and helping people plan their response to events.

Examples that cohere to this framework include pension auto-enrollment, which uses the power of defaults; donating a set amount to charity via a text message, which provides a default donation and removes the hassle of finding someone's bank card details; and providing the details of average household energy usage with utility bills, which prompts people to use less.

The EAST framework provides a useful guide for nonspecialists when thinking about how to harness behavioral finance. However, it should not be construed as reducing behavioral finance to a checklist of biases and actions that, if avoided or implemented, mean that someone has done a good job. These tools of the behavioral specialist are not a substitute for that specialist's knowledge. The Behavioural Insights Team also recognizes that "it cannot be applied in isolation from a good understanding of the nature and context of the problem." A trained behavioral finance specialist should be involved in the "behavioral audit" of existing and new processes to determine areas of possible improvement. This forms a final principle to consider when applying behavioral finance.

PRINCIPLE 6: ATTEMPTS TO MODIFY BEHAVIOR USING BEHAVIORAL FINANCE TOOLS REQUIRE A DEEP UNDERSTANDING OF THE OBJECTIVE AND CONTEXT OF THE DECISION PROBLEM

Digital services are growing in importance and popularity in various industries. This growth represents the next frontier for behavioral design and excellence. Benartzi (2015) provides a description of the challenges of influencing behavior on small-screen devices. These challenges provide not only an opportunity to make behavioral excellence a priority but also a strong position from which behavioral finance can influence other offline areas of organizations.

Striving for behavioral excellence takes time. While a team is establishing itself and its influence in an organization, senior management must support the initiative for it to be effective.

A second element of necessary senior management support is their acceptance that behavioral finance is as much art as it is science. Some behavioral interventions are likely to fail. These failures should not be seen as a weakness of the practical application of the discipline but, rather, as an additional opportunity to learn in an empirical setting. Marketing strategies typically embrace an experimental approach in which theories are tested and adapted. Behavioral finance needs the same approach. Well-intentioned behavioral interventions could lead to unexpected customer responses. As conduct risk increases the focus on customer detriment, demonstrating strong behavioral rationale for an intervention is critical, despite the possibility that it fails to assist disadvantaged customers. Regulated organizations need to be confident that they will not be sanctioned because of failed experimentation aimed at helping customers make better decisions.

Summary and Conclusions

Great potential exists for behavioral finance approaches to improve the financial decision making of individuals, groups, and organizations. However, harvesting this potential must include an asymmetric paternalistic approach. Most important, this requires more knowledge of the field than can be garnered through reading popular science books. Untrained practitioners are driving an overreliance on nudge as a technique to the detriment of clients and customers. In our example of a behaviorally motivated alternative to modern portfolio theory, understanding how clients behave is deeply embedded in the portfolio optimization. These kinds of implementations require specialist knowledge and are the true vanguards of the discipline. If organizations are serious about making the fullest use of behavioral finance, they need a core team of specialists within the business that has enough support from senior management to effect improvements at all levels of organizational teams and processes. An organization can achieve this in many ways, but many examples are available of both failed and successful attempts to embed behavioral finance. Although no perfect model of applied behavioral finance exists, the discipline still has many opportunities to grow and mature, and there are many commercially valuable untapped insights in the decades of rigorous academic research that underpins the field.

DISCUSSION QUESTIONS

1. Explain how nudging alone constitutes a narrow use of behavioral finance knowledge.
2. Discuss the features of good and bad applications of behavioral finance.
3. Discuss an example of behavioral finance supplementing traditional approaches.
4. Explain asymmetric paternalism.

REFERENCES

Behavioural Insights Team. 2014. *EAST: Four Simple Ways to Apply Behavioural Insights*. London: Behavioural Insights Team.

Benartzi, Shlomo (with Jonah Lehrer). 2015. *The Smarter Screen: What Your Business Can Learn from the Way Consumers Think Online*. London: Piatkus.

Benartzi, Shlomo, and Richard H. Thaler. 2007. "Heuristics and Biases in Retirement Savings Behavior." *Journal of Economic Perspectives* 21:3, 81–104.

Das, Sanjiv, Harry Markowitz, Jonathan Scheid, and Meir Statman. 2010. "Portfolio Optimization with Mental Accounts." *Journal of Financial and Quantitative Analysis* 45:2, 311–334.

Davies, Greg B. 2015. *The Value of Being Human: A Behavioural Framework for Impact Investing and Philanthropy*. London: Barclays–Wealth and Investment Management.

Davies, Greg B., and Antonia Lim. 2014. "Managing Anxiety to Improve Financial Performance: Don't Let the Best Be the Enemy of the Achievable." In Andrew Rudd and Stephen Satchell (eds.), *Quantitative Approaches to High Net Worth Investment*, 69–98. London: Risk Books.

Davies, Greg B., and Arnaud De Servigny. 2012. *Behavioral Investment Management: An Efficient Alternative to Modern Portfolio Theory*. New York: McGraw-Hill Professional.

Davies, Greg B., and Peter Brooks. 2014. "Risk Tolerance: Essential, Behavioural and Misunderstood." *Journal of Risk Management in Financial Institutions* 7:2, 110–113.

Egan, Daniel, Greg B. Davies, and Peter Brooks. 2011. "Comparisons of Risk Attitudes Across Individuals." In James J. Cochran, Louis Anthony Cox, Jr., Pinar Keskinocak, Jeffrey P. Kharoufeh, and J. Cole Smith (eds.), *Wiley Encyclopedia of Operations Research and Management Science*, 1–13. Hoboken, NJ: John Wiley & Sons, Inc.

Fernandes, Daniel, John G. Lynch Jr., and Richard G. Netemeyer. 2014. "Financial Literacy, Financial Education and Downstream Financial Behaviors." *Management Science* 60:8, 1861–1883.

He, Xue Dong, and Xun Yu Zhou. 2011. "Portfolio Choice under Cumulative Prospect Theory: An Analytical Treatment." *Management Science* 57:2, 315–331.

Schroders. 2015. "Schroders incomeIQ." Available at http://incomeiq.schroders.com/en/uk/investor/.

Shefrin, Hersh, and Meir Statman. 2000. "Behavioral Portfolio Theory." *Journal of Financial and Quantitative Analysis* 35:2, 127–151.

Sloman, Steven A. 2002. "Two Systems of Reasoning." In Thomas Gilovich, Dale Griffin and Daniel Kahneman (eds.), *Heuristics and Biases: The Psychology of Intuitive Judgment*, 379–396. New York: Cambridge University Press.

Thaler, Richard H. 1999. "Mental Accounting Matters." *Journal of Behavioral Decision Making* 12:3, 183–206.

Thaler, Richard H., and Shlomo Benartzi. 2004. "Save More Tomorrow: Using Behavioral Economics to Increase Employee Saving." *Journal of Political Economy* 112:1, 164–187.

Thaler, Richard H., and Cass R. Sunstein. 2008. *Nudge: Improving Decisions about Health, Wealth, and Happiness*. New Haven, CT: Yale University Press.

Todd, Peter M., and Gerd Gigerenzer. 2012. *Ecological Rationality: Intelligence in the World*. New York: Oxford University Press.

Tversky, Amos, and Daniel Kahneman. 1992. "Cumulative Prospect Theory: An Analysis of Decision under Uncertainty." *Journal of Risk and Uncertainty* 5:4, 297–323.

30

The Future of Behavioral Finance

MICHAEL DOWLING
Associate Professor in Finance
ESC Rennes School of Business

BRIAN LUCEY
Professor of Finance
Trinity Business School, Trinity College Dublin

Introduction

The future of behavioral finance requires understanding more about its philosophy, gaining a deeper understanding of the drivers of financial behavior, and ensuring rigorous research. This field of study is just at its beginning stages when it comes to understanding the influences of human behavior as applied to an individual, firm, groups, or institutions making financial decisions. The initial anomalies in traditional finance that inspired the birth of behavioral finance in the 1980s have given way to the current sampling of clearer behavioral biases from the literature on decision making and psychology. The next step of deeper engagement in more complex behavioral understanding will be more difficult, but the path is well established in many other business fields. This chapter provides a potential roadmap for this development of behavioral corporate finance and investor psychology.

Behavioral corporate finance is perhaps the most obvious candidate to begin this journey. The current focus in behavioral corporate finance is on chief executive officer (CEO) traits and sometimes chief financial officer (CFO) or board of director characteristics as the primary means for introducing behavioral biases into the firm's financial decision making. This focus should be replaced by a more comprehensive understanding of top management teams and the institutional influences on financial decision making within corporations. New research approaches, such as grounded theory and other qualitative tools, are necessary for this development to progress.

In research on asset pricing investor psychology, an area of behavioral finance subject to heavy criticisms of data mining, a need exists for much richer models of investor behavior and the social psychology of groups of investors. The current research on behavioral asset pricing has allowed that prices can predictably move in pricing patterns owing to widely experienced decision-making biases. However, these patterns are based on rather simple models of the drivers of behavior and are heavily restricted as to how these biases must be proxied, owing to data restrictions. The future of behavioral asset pricing needs researchers to be more comfortable using the rich new behavioral and social datasets that online media offer for building a more holistic and targeted understanding of the drivers of investment behavior. There is also a need to work closely with experimental finance and data science researchers to design, model, and measure the behavior of groups of investors so as to form realistic representations of how groups of investors in a market make investment decisions and how this influences pricing. A particular "prize" for investor psychology is in understanding sentiment as an overall measure of psychological influence on asset pricing.

Although this chapter focuses on behavioral corporate finance and investor psychology, it broadens to include the philosophical underpinnings of behavioral finance and the need for ensuring robust investigations of behavioral patterns. The chapter begins with an evaluation of the philosophical development of behavioral finance and it extrapolates, based on other fields, the next steps in this development of an overall philosophical approach to behavioral finance research. The, the chapter discusses the reliability of behavioral finance research in the context of research methods in psychology and economics, referencing the rigor and replicability of findings in those areas.

The Philosophy of a Future Behavioral Finance

Frankfurter (2007) remarks on the general disdain for philosophical discussion in finance. He relays the story of a former student who attempted, in a PhD seminar, to discuss the philosophical implications of the ubiquity of utility theory in finance and was told that "this is a finance course and not a philosophical course" (p. 49). Such a comment would be anathema to researchers in other disciplines, even those closely aligned with finance such as management or mathematics. Also, a disdain for philosophical discussion does not preclude the influence of philosophical perspectives on the conduct of finance and behavioral finance research.

Guba and Lincoln (1994, p. 105) argue for the primacy of philosophical perspective in conducting research because "questions of method are secondary to questions of paradigm." This perspective generally acknowledges that the research perspective influences the selection of methods and problems. Before commencing any empirical inquiry, researchers must address their ontological and epistemological assumptions and, indeed, consider how such assumptions align with their research question and their methodological choices. Ontology describes reality, whereas epistemology is the relation between reality and the investigator, with the methodology being the technique used to discover such relationship.

This point is crucial in beginning any exploration of the future of behavioral finance. By understanding the philosophy of research in behavioral finance, the researcher can learn more about the development of the behavioral finance research paradigm, how theory should be built, and how research questions fit into the paradigm and research program. Researchers can then extrapolate how the "knowing" in behavioral finance will progress, based on how the research philosophy has developed. This section starts with a brief summary of the philosophy of science perspectives of Thomas Kuhn and Imre Lakatos, and then places behavioral finance within these frameworks.

Thomas Kuhn popularized the commonly used terms "paradigm," "paradigm shift," "normal science," and "anomalies" in the discussion of how science is conducted and progresses. According to Kuhn, science is conducted within paradigms, with a paradigm being a collection of core frameworks, terminology, and methodologies that researchers use to solve problems within a particular area (Kuhn 1970). Bird (2013), in his analysis of Kuhn's contribution, gives the function of a paradigm as that of supplying puzzles for scientists to solve and providing the tools for their solution.

Working within a paradigm, scientists can engage in *normal science,* which is the everyday process of solving problems in an area of research. As anomalies, or counter-examples, arise, scientists attempt to place these within the confines of the paradigm. Sometimes the anomalies are just ignored, as the importance of normal science is considered paramount to paradigm rejection, or scientific revolution. Only when an anomaly arises that cannot be explained and that threatens the core methods or rejects the core theories can a paradigm rejection or paradigm shift occurs. Kuhn (1970, p. 68) terms this a "crisis." The anomaly makes normal science impossible, and thus a change must occur. If researchers do move to a new paradigm, this new paradigm must not only have the explanatory and problem-solving power of the old paradigm but must also offer new and exciting research opportunities.

Lakatos (1978) proffers a similar perspective to that of Kuhn, but focuses more on how research progresses. His views are insightful for determining a plausible future philosophy for behavioral finance. Lakatos prefers the term "research program" to "paradigm." He views a *research program* as a collection of theories used by researchers in a particular area of study. These theories are divided into a "hard core" and "auxiliary hypotheses." The hard-core theories are the deeply held beliefs shared by researchers involved in a particular research program. The auxiliary hypotheses emanate from hard-core theories. Auxiliary hypotheses represent the "work in progress," the testable hypotheses, and the less firmly held beliefs of the researchers. The auxiliary hypotheses also serve as protection against attacks on the hard core from those outside the research program. Auxiliary hypotheses can be adjusted, or even rejected, in order to protect the hard core.

Lakatos (1978) addresses the issue of theory succession by dividing research programs into two categories: progressive and degenerative. A *progressive research program* offers exciting research opportunities and appears to offer new findings. In contrast, a *degenerative research program* is one that researchers constantly have to defend from attack (perhaps, by adjusting the auxiliary hypotheses) and one that is unable to generate new and exciting findings. Eventually, researchers in a degenerative program switch into more exciting research programs.

These perspectives on the philosophy of science allow the charting of the development of a philosophy for the behavioral finance research program. The anomalies literature of the 1980s represented an initial criticism of the traditional finance assumptions of rational investors and efficient markets. Traditional finance responded by making increasing adjustments to their theories, as predicted by Kuhn (1970) and Lakatos (1978). For example, the single-factor capital asset pricing model (CAPM) has evolved into a five-factor model (Fama and French 2015) and a wide range of competing models, most of which fail to adhere to the rigorous statistical tests for data mining (Harvey, Liu, and Zhu 2015).

Moving beyond the initial phase of identifying anomalies in traditional finance, behavioral finance can be described as a research program in its own right. A key feature of this new research program is a clear focus on using the concepts of *bounded rationality,* in which people's cognitive constraints impose limits on the extent to which they can be "rational" in their decision making and the influence of psychology to develop

Table 30.1 **Scopus Article Count for "Behavioral Finance" and "Investor Psychology" Keywords**

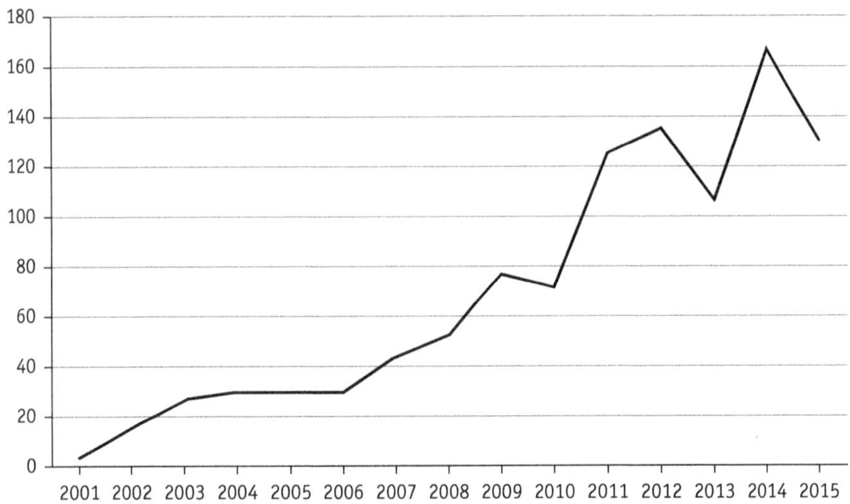

Note: This table tracks the annual number of articles appearing in Scopus-covered economics and finance journals that have "behavioral finance" or "investor psychology" keywords.

Source: The author's work using the Elsevier Scopus database.

testable hypotheses of financial decision making. There is now a reduced focus on criticizing traditional finance. Researchers in behavioral finance are increasingly debating the most appropriate behavioral theories to explain financial behavior. That it is a progressive research program is evident from the rise in behavioral finance research being published. Table 30.1 provides a time series of articles published in Scopus-covered economics and finance journals since 2001 with the keywords "behavioral finance" and "investor psychology." Table 30.2 is a count of working papers appearing in the Social Science Research Network (SSRN) Behavioral & Experimental Finance eJournal, also suggesting a vibrant research area with the upward trend indicating its progressive nature.

Given the recent nature of this rise in behavioral finance research, as opposed to research on anomalies in traditional finance, which began in the 1980s, this field seems clearly to be in the early stages of becoming a progressive research program. The challenge for the future of behavioral finance is that work must continue to be both theoretical and empirically progressive. That is, researchers in behavioral finance must advance new theories and be able to empirically investigate and continue to develop these theories.

Normal behavioral finance research as it currently exists usually investigates confirmed theories from the field of psychology, examining their applicability to financial behavior. Researchers usually make adjustments to these theories to make them suitable from a finance perspective. However, this process is, at best, just the beginning of how a core theory of behavioral finance should appear. The future will require much richer

Table 30.2 **Count of Articles in SSRN Behavioral and Experimental Finance eJournal**

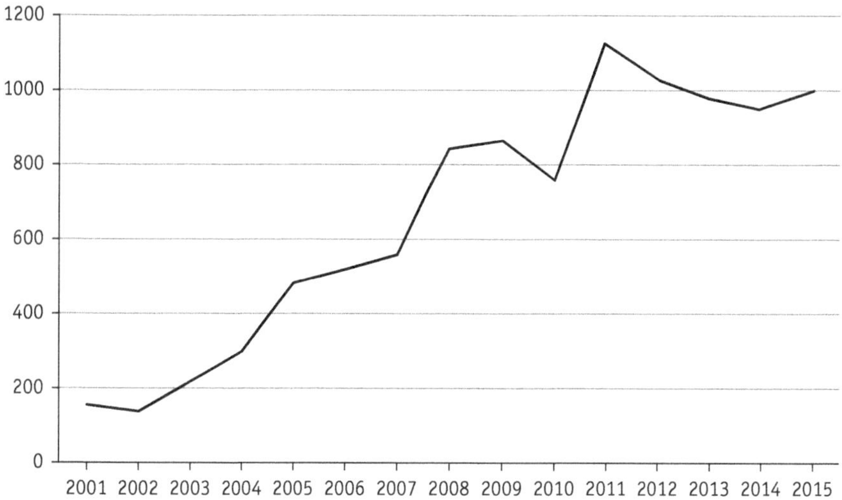

Note: This table counts the number of yearly submissions to the SSRN Behavioral and Experimental Finance eJournal, which is the primary depository for working papers and accepted paper abstracts in this area.

Source: The author's work using SSRN Behavioral and Experimental Finance eJournal data.

finance-specific behavioral theories. One key issue, however, is how few outlets exist for publishing pure theoretical research on behavioral finance, or even more generally on finance, unlike the economics or business fields. Being a primarily empirical field means there is a limited section in each research paper devoted to small theoretical development. A progressive research program will need more cognizant of the importance of rewarding purely theoretical research so as to have a solid core of theories upon which to draw. Both the *Journal of Behavioral & Experimental Finance* and the *Journal of Behavioral Finance* welcome theoretical papers, albeit neither of these journals is particularly highly ranked at present. Higher-ranking finance journals do not normally publish behavioral finance theory papers. The rare, purely theoretical papers that have been published, such as Mehra and Sah (2002), need to find a home in economic journals.

Empirical work also needs to have the right tools to appropriately investigate theories of behavioral finance. However, the profession is currently hampered by an almost exclusively positivist quantitative approach to research. A move away from these purely positivist quantitative methodologies is likely to feature in the future of behavioral finance, as it will be necessary to investigate the validity of new behavioral theories.

Two epistemological paradigms that are the focus of scientists' view of reality are the positivist and the interpretivist perspectives. The *positivist perspective* is based on a scientific principle consisting of an objective social reality that can be identified. Thus, quantitative approaches, but not limited to quantitative, can effectively enable identifying patterns of this assumed social reality. The *interpretivist perspective*, by contrast, assumes that reality is a social construct that cannot be studied outside of the social actors who create that reality. Therefore, a focus is on methodologies that enable an understanding to be built of the social actors' view, role, and influence in this social world (Livesey 2006). The methodologies most appropriate to this interpretivist perspective tend to be qualitative, but qualitative methodologies are largely ignored in finance, including behavioral finance.

Interpretivist methodologies start as close as possible to the idea of no theory, and then use appropriate methodologies to build theories based on data. This approach is in contrast to positivist research, which largely focuses on testing theory (Walsham 2006). If behavioral finance is to continue to develop into a progressive research program, it needs interpretivist methodologies that allow rich theories to be built and new testable hypotheses to be developed. Sample interpretivist methodologies applied in the analogous field of management include ethnographic, action research, and grounded theory, where the researcher is directly involved in the group being studied, and indirect methods such as building case studies through, for example, interviews.

There has been strong philosophical progress in advancing from anomalies-based attacks on traditional finance to the beginnings of a vibrant progressive research program in behavioral finance. The next steps call for developing a core of theory rather than borrowing one from another discipline. Integrating more interpretivist methodologies allows these theories to be developed and appropriately tested.

The Future of Behavioral Corporate Finance

Baker and Wurgler (2012) outline the two main current perspectives of behavioral corporate finance as (1) focusing on rational managerial actions to account for the biases of investors, and (2) investigating whether behavioral biases influence managerial financial decisions. In the first perspective, the firm is a relative bastion of financial rationality that times financing decisions based on an understanding of investor psychology and frames decisions with this same psychology in mind. The second perspective allows managers to run firms with some of the same behavioral biases as investors, and these biases influence an organization's financial decision-making process.

Both approaches have some validity but also some problems. A reasonable assumption is that managers can rationally use their superior information and expertise to efficiently finance the firm and better frame financing decisions than a group of investors with limited time for analysis and bounded rationality, and when an individual firm is just one of a portfolio of investments. Ikenberry, Lakonishok, and Vermaelen (1995) show that when companies repurchase their own shares in the market, those repurchased shares outperform in subsequent periods compared to benchmark indices and to similar firms. Thus, companies presumably can use their superior internal information to better identify intrinsic firm value than can investors and they use this to make positive financial decisions that benefit overall shareholder value.

This first rationalist perspective of behavioral corporate finance is very much wedded to a traditional behavioral finance perspective of noise traders versus smart money (Black 1986). Managers are positioned as smart money, whereas investors are positioned as noise traders allowing identifiable mispricing to exist in stock prices. Various problems exist with this perspective that suggests it will not play a strong role in the future of behavioral corporate finance research. One problem is that this research largely rests on very minimal investigation of a company's motivations to undertake this type of behavior. Single-question anonymous surveys of company executives, usually the CFO, are the most common source of claims that companies react to their perception of market over- or undervaluation of their stock (Graham and Harvey 2001). Yet, little is known about how companies identify mispricing or what valuation models are used and how these differ from those of investors. Thus, researchers cannot know if executives' motives are truly rational.

A second, more fundamental issue is the lack of knowledge about whether management is reacting to investor behavioral bias–driven irrationality or just investor mispricing. Rational management responses to investors making fundamental errors of valuation is not "behavioral" in the sense that it does not use psychological theories to advance understanding of financial decision making. Although richer information on how firms make these decisions can overcome the first problem of a lack of knowledge about managerial motivations, the second problem restricts the potential for behavioral insights to play a role in the future of this aspect of modern behavioral corporate finance.

The second perspective, whereby managers might be subject to behavioral biases that influence their financial decision making, offers a more productive avenue for the future development of behavioral corporate finance. The research to date has largely investigated the overconfidence and optimism of CEOs with various approaches for measuring overconfidence, and links the presence of overconfidence to risk taking in the company's financial decisions. For example, Malmendier and Tate (2005) measured overconfidence by the holding of in-the-money, own-company options by CEOs. The premise is that CEOs who hold undiversified portfolios through large own-company investments or unexercised in-the-money options are overconfident. Recent research has developed this further by refining the measurement of overconfidence. For example, Huang and Kisgen (2013) draw on the greater likelihood of males being overconfident to show that males make more acquisitions. Graham, Harvey, and Puri (2013) used psychometric testing to determine the optimism of CEOs, and they link this to their attitudes on risk taking. Other research, beyond the scope and purpose of this chapter, has expanded the range of CEO characteristics investigated, such as humility (Ou, Waldman, and Peterson 2016) and narcissism (Aktas, De Bodt, Bollaert, and Roll 2012).

An issue with the current primary focus on the behavioral influence of the CEO is that much management research contends the CEO plays only a small role in the overall direction of the firm. Quigley and Hambrick (2015) report that CEO influence accounts for about 20 percent of the variability in performance of U.S. companies in recent years. This variability is measured by variability in profit as a percentage of sales, profit as a percentage of assets, and market-to-book ratios. This finding represents an increase from about 10 percent influence on variability in performance from the 1950s, so CEOs have apparently become more influential over time. Still, CEOs only explain about one-fifth of performance, and a natural question arises as to whether behavioral finance is focusing too narrowly by concentrating on a person who explains a relatively small percentage of performance. In the same analysis, general company characteristics explain about 30 percent of performance variability and 50 percent of the explanation for performance variability is simply "unknown."

A further issue is that current behavioral corporate finance studies of the CEO seek to identify single behavioral facets of those CEOs, so researchers are not capturing much of these individuals' decision-making perspective. The influence of the CEO on company direction in other countries differs from that which happens in the United States. Crossland and Hambrick (2007) find that the influence of the CEO is much less in Germany and Japan compared to the United States, which raises questions as to the international applicability of the U.S. behavioral corporate finance focus on the CEO.

Continuing with Hambrick's body of research, the seminal paper by Hambrick and Mason (1984) contends that CEO characteristics matter, but that focusing on the wider top management team (the "upper echelons") is probably more important, and the modern focus of research on strategic corporate decision making takes place here. In a later review of his 1984 article, Hambrick (2007, p. 334) summarizes the impact of the paper as creating a consensus of "attention to executive groups, rather than to individuals, often yield[ing] better explanations of organizational outcomes." Papadakis and Barwise (2002) offer an example of this research, having investigated whether CEO characteristics or top management team characteristics matter more in explaining 70 strategic decisions made by Greek firms across different strategic areas. Their results show that focusing on the top management team is a much more useful clue in explaining such decisions.

Thus, behavioral corporate finance research needs to become more familiar with the influence of not just the CEO and maybe the CFO but also the rest of the top management team if researchers want to move in line with accepted management wisdom on how companies actually make strategic decisions. This seems particularly important for strategic corporate finance decisions that are not purely financial, such as acquisitions, but probably of less importance for more core financial decisions on how to finance the company.

Ultimately, the future of behavioral finance also needs to become more familiar with *organizational theory*, which is the holistic view of how the company is organized and how this influences its decision making. DiMaggio and Powell (1983) provide the classic reference on the sociology of the corporation, arguing that three institutional factors—coercive, mimetic, and normative isomorphism—work together to determine decision making and create similarity between companies. *Coercive isomorphism* refers to external cultural influences on the company; *mimetic isomorphism* is the imitation of other companies' practices in the face of uncertainty; and *normative isomorphism* is based on standards and norms that influence company behavior. Imagining how these factors would influence corporate financial decisions is easy; yet, the actual implementation of this theory is far from straightforward. As mentioned earlier, implementation requires researcher familiarity with interpretivist qualitative methodologies, such as action research and grounded theory.

A final large gap in modern behavioral corporate finance research needing to be addressed is a greater understanding of how cultural differences and behavioral biases interact to influence corporate financial decisions around the world. Behavioral corporate finance is largely U.S. based at the moment. Unlike research in similar disciplines such as management, researchers have not yet made a sufficient effort to focus on cross-cultural differences in behavior. Evidence shows there are cross-cultural differences in a wide range of corporate finance behaviors, such as dividend pay-outs (Fidrmuc and

Jacob 2010), corporate governance (Bushman, Piotroski, and Smith 2004), and cash holdings (Ramirez and Tadesse 2009). However, the interaction between culture and psychological theories is complex.

Lucey and Dowling (2014), using emerging markets as an example, examined each of the main psychological theories and how they differ across cultures, and they found significant cultural influences. A summary of the analysis in that work suggests that of the three main psychology fields applied in finance (cognitive, emotion, and social), social psychology is the most likely to vary across countries owing to their strong cultural influence. Emotional effects are largely universal, and cognitive biases need to be individually assessed, because there is an important interaction between actual cognitive biases and levels of experience that differs across countries. These findings suggest much more work needs to be done to make behavioral corporate finance have international relevance. International studies need to determine appropriate interactions between cultural effects and psychological influences on corporate financial decision making.

The Future of Investor Psychology and Asset Pricing

Investor psychology involves the application of cognitive, emotion, and social psychology theories to an understanding of investor decision making (Hirshleifer 2001). The field of cognitive psychology provides decision-making biases that can explain how investors might make suboptimal investment decisions. *Emotion psychology* explains the role of feelings in investor decision making, whereas *social psychology* offers some explanation for how collectives of investors might make jointly influenced and biased investment decisions that are priced in the cross-section of asset prices.

One fundamental issue that needs to be addressed for the future of behavioral asset pricing is the evident failure of the field to develop productive research. The limited evidence suggests that many identified asset pricing findings are just not real, using robust statistics. The influential Sullivan, Timmerman, and White (1999) study, for example, finds that most technical trading rules simply have no statistical support after making appropriate robustness adjustments. More recently, Harvey et al. (2015) claim that most asset pricing models do not stand up to scrutiny after applying a different, but similar, set of robustness checks for data mining, The models checked were predominantly based on traditional finance principles rather than on behavioral ones, suggesting a wider problem with the entire field of asset pricing. These findings are likely to be only a small indication of a wider problem, as the robustness adjustment techniques usually take account only of published research. A known bias in publishing exists toward accepting papers with statistically significant findings.

If the asset pricing researchers continue to produce large volumes of research that is, at least indirectly, a product of data mining, then it will necessarily become a degenerative research program. This situation is a challenge for researchers in investor psychology, but also an opportunity because advances are possible in understanding investor psychology and its influence on asset pricing. The remainder of this section contains potential ways for the field to reverse its current downward trajectory.

The first, large opportunity is in sentiment modeling. There has been a proliferation of sentiment models in recent years as new approaches to, and data for, measuring investor sentiment have become available. These models range from the fundamental data approach of Baker and Wurgler (2006) to modern attempts to capture the emotions of groups of investors through social media sources, such as the Twitter sentiment model of Bollen, Mao, and Zeng (2011). The exponential growth of competing models suggests that understanding sentiment is in its infancy, with new models appearing on the market on a daily basis that are touted as the latest cure-all for understanding sentiment. Yet, sentiment modeling does offer the best potential for behavioral asset pricing to integrate both psychological influences on investors and the social psychology group effect of many investors experiencing those influences.

An issue at the moment is the theoretical nature of the current sentiment measures. Even the seminal Baker and Wurgler (2006) model uses six variables without strong justification for how the authors selected those six variables out of an almost infinite universe of possible sentiment measures. The authors put these six variables in a principal component analysis to extract factors, thus involving more judgment as to what the factors actually represent. Finally, they made an adjustment for what they consider "rational" sentiment and "irrational" sentiment. Once again, the authors do not seriously explore what rational sentiment might mean or consider whether rational and irrational sentiments can possibly be disentangled from an investor perspective, even if a statistical tool technically allows the procedure to be done. Such a data-driven exercise imbued with judgment at each stage is unlikely to offer a core theory for sentiment models going forward.

In the future, investor sentiment models need to have a core of fundamental theory to guide the building of the model. Otherwise, this area of study runs the risk of having a wide range of competing models that are simply statistically compared, often using very limited datasets, rather than fundamentally coherent models. Two possible ways for developing this fundamental theory include (1) understanding the nature of sentiment better through experimental finance, and (2) collaborating with computer science researchers to better capture the data needed to measure sentiment and advance sentiment theories.

Sentiment is the residual influence of groups of investors making trading decisions based on shared opinions. Although those shared opinions are likely to be predominantly rational expectations about the prospects for investment, there's also a role for feelings such as optimism and pessimism. Overconfidence and other cognitive biases might likewise be important if decision makers widely experience their heuristic influence. Experimental finance probably offers some of the best potential to model the real influence and nature of sentiment, and it already has a wide range of studies in this area, such as Smith, Suchanek, and Williams (1988) and Haruvy, Lahav, and Noussair (2007). Yet, a need exists for such experimental studies to create more realistic market environments, perhaps in a field setting, and to focus more on the nature of sentiment. This should foster greater understanding of the complexity of how sentiment is seeded and evolves, including the foundational psychological and financial factors that interact to create and drive sentiment. Behavioral finance researchers in the sentiment area need to collaborate with experimental finance teams to create such models.

Collaboration with data scientists from the computer sciences is necessary to understand how to model the data that is now available to measure sentiment, such as data from Twitter and other social media sources. Researchers have been largely content to keep such data analysis reserved for behavioral finance researchers, despite this not being an area of obvious expertise. Sharing the analysis with researchers who are experts in handling the data and determining its meaning is a necessary next step. Expecting behavioral finance researchers to be as familiar with interrogating what is often multiple terabytes of social data as they are with developing behavioral theories is unrealistic. This shift means more behavioral finance research will need to find a home in computer science journals as a way of demonstrating that the data approaches are considered valid within computer science.

Experimental finance in general offers strong potential to inform theory building in asset pricing. Indeed, it already performs this role to some extent, such as the aforementioned sentiment models. However, barriers exist between experimental finance and behavioral finance that limit idea sharing. Noussair (2016) speaks to these issues in his Presidential Address to the Society for Experimental Finance in 2015, suggesting it is something about which experimental finance exhibits awareness. The first issue that Noussair raised was that experimental finance emerged from experimental economics and so it did not explicitly originate to work within behavioral finance. This origin is not a problem with experimental finance but, rather, speaks to potentially different motivations within the two disciplines of experimental and behavioral finance. The second issue is that experimental finance researchers do not sufficiently collaborate with researchers in other finance subdisciplines. A similar comment could easily be made about the need for behavioral finance researchers to collaborate with experimental finance researchers in order to build valid behavioral finance theories. The fact that some researchers bypass experimental finance research and go straight to psychological theories that might be inapplicable in a finance context seems perverse. According to Noussair, about half the research presented at the 2015 Society for Experimental Finance annual conference was on asset pricing, and another 36 percent of the papers involved investor characteristics, so the current lack of deep integration between experimental finance and behavioral asset pricing is surprising, given the similarity of interest.

Other approaches to improve robustness involve researching outside of equity pricing in the application of behavioral theories. Cummins, Dowling, and Lucey (2015) applied behavioral principles to the pricing of nonferrous metals, representing a first study in these markets. The fact that researchers conducted in 2015 the first investor psychology study of the huge aluminium, nickel, copper, tin, lead, and zinc financial markets suggests the discipline is confined to equity pricing. To what other markets might sets of behavioral theories apply? Expanding behavioral asset pricing research outside of equity pricing is likely to be a feature in the future, and is already under way.

The potential to explore historic datasets for evidence of behavioral influences on asset pricing figures prominently in future research efforts. In recent years, researchers have constructed retrospective stock prices for the eighteenth and nineteenth centuries that are broadly uninvestigated from an investor psychology perspective. For example, the Global Financial Data database provides stock price data as far back as 1693 and commodities pricing data as far back as the thirteenth century. Investigating cognitive biases on such historical data is likely to be of limited use, owing to the fact that modern investors are not cognitively comparable to investors in those previous eras. However, such data offer the potential for research into the influence of emotional and social psychology on investing, given that emotional and social psychology influences are likely to be innate factors in investor behavior (Lucey and Dowling 2014).

One recent feature of markets—the increase in cross-market contagions owing to the "financialization" of markets (Flassbeck, Bicchertti, Mayer, and Rietzler 2011)—also offers new potential for behavioral asset pricing researchers, in a context similar to that of exploring new financial markets. The rise of financialization should increase the contagion of behavioral principles across markets and thus offers a rationale for exploring new markets with which behavioral equity market researchers currently lack familiarity.

Another issue that may become more prominent in the future of investor psychology research is the need to incorporate culture into investor behavior models. This issue is similar to the need in behavioral corporate finance. With a cultural behavioral asset pricing perspective, investor psychology research largely dominated by the study of Anglo-Saxon culture countries is likely to be increasingly viewed as merely regional studies of phenomena that probably differ across countries. Asset pricing behavioral patterns such as momentum are culturally determined. For example, Ji, Zhang, and Guo (2008) find that Chinese investors are more likely to predict a reversal from short-term price patterns, whereas Canadian investors are more likely to predict a momentum pattern.

Improving the Reliability of Behavioral Finance Research

Much of behavioral finance research relies on survey or experimental evidence. Many other papers rely on proprietary or otherwise "secret" data. In common with much of finance and economics, concerns about replicability and reproducibility are increasing, albeit from a low base. Cochrane (2015), who is a leading empirical financial economist, has recently breathed new life into this debate. Mapping Cochrane's arguments to a behavioral and experimental perspective appear worthwhile.

One item of note is the apparent lack of concern with reliability in current behavioral finance research. A Scopus search for "replication" or "replicability" combined with "behavioral finance" or "experimental finance" yields few results. At a high level, that of publication, a dearth of interest exists in the issue. Counter this with psychology, in which there has been a very active debate on reliability and replication for several years. As psychology is a contributing founding paradigm of behavioral finance, this gap is all the more worrisome. One wonders whether behavioral finance researchers are even aware of the replicability of theories selected from psychology. This section explores three issues: (1) the debate started by Cochrane (2015) from a behavioral perspective, (2) the psychology debate, and (3) a proposal drawn from areas including behavioral science as to how to improve the reliability of behavioral finance research.

Cochrane is one of the most cited and respected economists of his generation. Yet, he clearly has felt uneasy for some time about the proliferation of papers that are, to all intents and purposes, not replicable. He commences with a discussion of data errors and data fragility, noting, for example, the coding errors in the influential Reinhart and Rogoff (2010) paper, the highly sensitive nature of many other papers to data or coding specification, and the challenges of identification. He adds that the absence of data and code accompanying published research makes true replication of reported results impossible. Particularly problematic are *secret data*, which are confidential or proprietary data. Cochrane advocates various solutions, but all distill to the proposition that what is valued matters. Unless and until finance research values explicitly the reproducibility and replicability of empirical results, via the editorial, tenure, and hiring processes, little incentive exists to be open.

Within economics, a widespread reason exists to be concerned about the lack of replication and robustness. Yet, a recent set of studies suggest a widespread lack of interest in the same. Vlaeminck and Herrmann (2015) find that even when journals are nominally committed to having a data-sharing or data-openness policy, enforcement is inconsistent and unreliable. Duvendack, Palmer-Jones, and Reed (2015), who presented the results of a large-scale study on the issue, report that only 27 of 333 economics journals regularly (i.e., defined as over 50 percent of papers published in a journal) publish data and methods files alongside published papers, and only 10 explicitly welcome replication studies. Indeed, replication is not a consideration for most journals, editors, or authors. The Goettingen University replication network (Replication Wiki 2016) lists several hundred replication studies, but few are pure replications in a narrow sense. Researchers have not carried out similar studies in finance, suggesting that the finance field has not even started to contemplate applying these issues as a central research design approach.

Researchers are only beginning to ask whether economics, and by extension finance, has a replication crisis. Based on an examination of 13 leading journals and 60 papers, Chang and Li (2015) conclude that replication is generally impossible. Brodeur, Le, Sangnier, and Zylbergerg (2016) raise the issue of "p-hacking" in which researchers use different models to obtain ideal results and fail to disclose the full set of tests. Harvey (2015, p. 37) contends that "many of the factors discovered in the field of finance are likely false discoveries." The latter arises from poor inferential statistics—in particular, the failure to control for false discovery rates and multiple hypotheses.

What of behavioral finance? Little sense of urgency exists in the field, as in much of economics and finance. Clemens (2015) indicates that a standard metric for measuring a paper's reliability or replicability does not exist. Although the foundations of behavioral finance are situated in psychology, the same degree of concern does not follow. This is evident from the publication of the Open Science Collaboration study (Open Science Collaboration 2012), which sought to systematically replicate all papers published in three leading psychology journals in 2008. The study shows that the results in terms of replicability are essentially the same as reported in Chang and Li (2015).

The first section of this chapter identified behavioral finance as being at the beginning stages of a progressive research program but in need of a solid core of theory and appropriate methodologies in order to continue to grow. The reliability of behavioral finance research is, therefore, critical at this stage of its development. Reliable research requires reliable theories; otherwise an excessive number of theories emerge and valid research has to compete with research that cannot stand up to rigorous replication. This situation distracts researchers from pursuing the most fruitful avenues for future research. Now is the time to create a social norm for methodologies that incorporate method and data openness so as to encourage replication.

Next, there are three broad solutions for ensuring reliable behavioral finance research. The first is institutional. Cochrane's (2015) arguments on the need for schools and institutes to take seriously data issues in their hiring and promotion process are worthwhile, but such a culture change is likely to take a long time. Journals also need to make changes. Harvey (2015) offers an interesting perspective on the three main finance journals, in which he describes a frustrated attempt by the editors to enforce a degree of replicability. Apart from the argument on proprietary, or what Cochrane calls "secret" data, there is a fear even at the top-tier journals that this replication standard would damage the comparative reputations of the journals, in that some would not have such a policy, making their papers less citable and less "notable."

First, in the interests of research, journals need to insist that their authors make available their datasets and clear methodology files. Researchers should welcome such transparency, because it promotes the robustness of the field. If data cannot be made available, then perhaps editors can publish papers accompanied by a note stating that some results involve some degree of "trust." Editors could possibly place such papers in a separate section of their journals. Calling the section "Non-Replicable Research" presumably would rapidly overcome even the most fervent researcher protests. Second, consideration is needed for pre-experiment research protocols and registered replication reports. These studies would be multi-unit in nature, following the same template as to how to proceed, the results of which would be published simultaneously, allowing comparison and a sense of the "true" effect. This framework is currently being rolled out in psychology.

Third, there also needs to be consideration of improving the communications infrastructure of behavioral and experimental finance. For good or ill, the double-blind peer review for a journal remains the dominant paradigm. The relatively few journals that focus on behavioral and experimental areas could consider a degree of hybrid reviewing. In some open-access areas, reviews are done post-publication, as well. Opening up the behavioral finance journals to an explicit aim of open-post replication review might yield benefits. Although scientists are sensitive to replication that fails (Fetterman and Sassenberg 2015), it would be a greater loss not to be open to identifying potential failures. Another approach would be to integrate meta-analysis and structured literature reviews with replication issues. Structured reviews in medical and cognate disciplines lay the foundation for further research; these are known as Cochrane Reviews in the medical sciences. Examples of this approach are increasing in medicine (Pharoah, Tsai, Ramus, Phelan, Goode, Lawrenson, and Buckley 2013) and psychology (Nieuwenstein, Wiergenda, Wicherts, Blom, Wagenmakers, and van Rijn 2015), in which the meta-analysis is the first stage that informs the subsequent replication. Finally, a newly developed bibliometric tool, the R-Index (Schimmack 2012, 2014), could provide "a doping test for science" (in the words of its creator) in the form of a statistical test for bias in a series of studies. A behavioral finance equivalent of this would allow insight into which subareas are most likely to provide the potential for fruitful future research.

Summary and Conclusions

This chapter has offered a personal view of the future concerning many aspects of modern behavioral finance and has attempted to unify this perspective around a common core. That is, behavioral finance needs to recognize that it is just beginning to be a progressive research program in a philosophical sense. That perspective necessitates a strong focus now on developing a robust common core of theory and reaching agreement on the nature of valid methodologies. Borrowing theory from psychology and methods from traditional finance were a necessary compromise in developing behavioral finance as a discipline. However, ignoring the core parts of a vibrant research program is unacceptable as the field becomes more established.

The issues these compromises raise can be viewed from the selected focus of both the behavioral corporate finance and investor psychology sectors. Behavioral corporate finance currently rests on the "rational manager/irrational investor" perspective, which is both poorly specified from a behavioral theory view and unlikely to offer progressive research. The other main focus—CEO characteristics—is out of touch, in that management research has taken a more holistic view of organizational decision making. The influence of investor psychology on asset pricing is probably the weakest part of modern behavioral finance. Its main potential contribution—the modeling of sentiment—is mired in competing theoretical approaches that only offer confusion, owing to a proliferation of measurements. There is a need in investor psychology research to collaborate with disciplines that complete the skillsets needed to appropriately investigate asset pricing phenomena such as sentiment; this is primarily accomplished by working with researchers in the computer sciences and experimental finance to build theory and test new complex datasets.

Although this chapter is critical of the current state of behavioral finance, behavioral finance has undeniably made astonishing progress from its start in the 1980s, when it primarily involved checking for different returns at different times of the week, month, and year. Most behavioral finance research now considers theory as a building block for any quality empirical paper. The problem is to make sure the most appropriate theories and the most informed empirical approaches are used.

DISCUSSION QUESTIONS

1. Discuss the extent to which behavioral finance has progressed philosophically since the 1980s anomalies literature, and how it might develop in the future.
2. Discuss problems with the "rational managers/irrational investors" research stream in behavioral corporate finance.
3. Discuss whether characteristics of top management teams are likely to be featured in future research on the drivers of corporate financial behavior.
4. Identify and explain key issues that need to be resolved concerning current measures of investor sentiment.

REFERENCES

Aktas, Nihat, Eric De Bodt, Helen Bollaert, and Richard Roll. 2012. "CEO Narcissism and the Takeover Process: From Private Initiation to Deal Completion." AFA 2012 Chicago Meetings Paper.

Baker, Malcolm, and Jeffrey Wurgler. 2006. "Investor Sentiment and the Cross-Section of Stock Returns." *Journal of Finance* 61:4, 1645–1680.

Baker, Malcolm, and Jeffrey Wurgler. 2012. "Behavioral Corporate Finance: A Current Survey." In George M. Constantinides, Milton Harris, and René M. Stulz (eds.), *Handbook of the Economics of Finance*, vol. 2, 357–424. New York: Elsevier.

Bird, Alexander. 2013. "Thomas Kuhn." In Edward N. Zalta (ed.), *The Stanford Encyclopedia of Philosophy*. Available at http://plato.stanford.edu/archives/fall2013/entries/thomas-kuhn/>.

Black, Fischer. 1986. "Noise." *Journal of Finance* 41:3, 528–543.

Bollen, Johan, Huina Mao, and Xiaojun Zeng. 2011. "Twitter Mood Predicts the Stock Market." *Journal of Computational Science* 2:1, 1–8.

Brodeur, Abel, Mathias Le, Marc Sangnier, and Yanos Zylberberg. 2016. "Star Wars: The Empirics Strike Back." *American Economic Journal: Applied Economics* 8:1, 1–32.

Bushman, Robert M., Joseph D. Piotroski, and Abbie J. Smith. 2004. "What Determines Corporate Transparency?" *Journal of Accounting Research* 42:2, 207–252.

Chang, Andrew C, and Phillip Li. 2015. "Is Economics Research Replicable? Sixty Published Papers from Thirteen Journals Say "Usually Not." FEDS Working Paper No. 2015-083.

Clemens, Michael A. 2015. "The Meaning of Failed Replication: A Review and a Proposal." *Journal of Economic Surveys*. Forthcoming.

Cochrane, John. 2015. "Secret Data" *Grumpy Economist*. Available at: http://johnhcochrane.blogspot.com/2015/12/Secret-Data.html.

Crossland, Craig, and Donald C. Hambrick. 2007. "How National Systems Differ in Their Constraints on Corporate Executives: A Study of CEO Effects in Three Countries." *Strategic Management Journal* 28:8, 767–789.

Cummins, Mark, Michael Dowling, and Brian M. Lucey. 2015. "Behavioral Influences in Non-Ferrous Metals Prices." *Resources Policy*, 45, 9–22.

DiMaggio, Paul, and Walter W. Powell. 1983. "The Iron Cage Revisited: Collective Rationality and Institutional Isomorphism in Organizational Fields." *American Sociological Review* 48:2, 147–160.

Duvendack, Marek, Richard Palmer-Jones, and Bob Reed. 2015. "Replications in Economics: A Progress Report." *Econ Journal Watch* 12:2, 164–191.

Fama, Eugene F., and Kenneth R. French. 2015. "A Five-Factor Asset Pricing Model." *Journal of Financial Economics* 116:1, 1–22.

Fetterman, Adam K., and Kai Sassenberg. 2015. "The Reputational Consequences of Failed Replications and Wrongness Admission among Scientists." *PLoS one* 10:12, e0143723.

Fidrmuc, Jana P., and Marcus Jacob. 2010. "Culture, Agency Costs, and Dividends." *Journal of Comparative Economics* 38:3, 321–339.

Flassbeck, Heiner, David Bicchetti, Jorg Mayer, and Katja Rietzler. 2011. "Price Formation in Financialized Commodity Markets: The Role of Information." United Nations Conference on Trade and Development (UNCTAD).

Frankfurter, George M. 2007. "Still Autistic Finance." In George M. Frankfurter (ed.), *Theory and Reality in Financial Economics: Essays Toward a New Political Finance*, 47–62. Hackensack: World Scientific.

Graham, John R., and Campbell R. Harvey. 2001. "The Theory and Practice of Corporate Finance: Evidence from the Field." *Journal of Financial Economics* 60:2, 187–243.

Graham, John R., Campbell R. Harvey, and Manju Puri. 2013. "Managerial Attitudes and Corporate Actions." *Journal of Financial Economics* 109:1, 103–121.

Guba, Egon, and Yvonna S. Lincoln. 1994. "Competing Paradigms in Qualitative Research." In Norman Denzin and Yvonna S. Lincoln (eds.), *Handbook of Qualitative Research,* vol. 2, 105–117. London: Sage.

Hambrick, Donald C. 2007. "Upper Echelons Theory: An Update." *Academy of Management Review* 32:2, 334–343.

Hambrick, Donald C., and Phyllis A. Mason. 1984. "Upper Echelons: The Organization as a Reflection of its Top Managers." *Academy of Management Review* 9:2, 193–206.

Haruvy, Ernan, Yaron Lahav, and Charles N. Noussair. 2007. "Traders' Expectations in Asset Markets: Experimental Evidence." *American Economic Review* 97:5, 1901–1920.

Harvey, Campbell R. 2015. "Reflections on Editing *The Journal of Finance*, 2006–2012." Available at http://ssrn.com/abstract=2191787.

Harvey, Campbell R., Yan Liu, and Heqing Zhu. 2015. ". . . And the Cross-Section of Expected Returns." *Review of Financial Studies*. Forthcoming.

Hirshleifer, David. 2001. "Investor Psychology and Asset Pricing." *Journal of Finance* 56:4, 1533–1597.

Huang, Jiekun, and Darren J. Kisgen. 2013. "Gender and Corporate Finance: Are Male Executives Overconfident Relative to Female Executives?" *Journal of Financial Economics* 108:3, 822–839.

Ikenberry, David, Josef Lakonishok, and Theo Vermaelen. 1995. "Market Underreaction to Open Market Share Repurchases." *Journal of Financial Economics* 39:2, 181–208.

Ji, Li-Jun, Zhiyong Zhang, and Tieyuan Guo. 2008. "To Buy or to Sell: Cultural Differences in Stock Market Decisions Based on Price Trends." *Journal of Behavioral Decision Making* 21:4, 399–413.

Kuhn, Thomas S. 1970. *The Structure of Scientific Revolutions.* Second Edition. Chicago: University of Chicago Press.

Lakatos, Imre. 1978. "The Methodology of Scientific Research Programmes, Vol. 1." *Philosophical Papers*. Cambridge: Cambridge University Press.

Livesey, Chris. 2006. *The Relationship between Positivism, Interpretivism and Sociological Research Methods*. London: AS Sociology.

Lucey, Brian M., and Michael Dowling. 2014. "Cultural Behavioral Finance in Emerging Markets." In Mohamed Hedi Arouri, Sabri Boubaker, and Duc Nguyen (eds.), *Emerging Markets and the Global Economy*, 327–346, Amsterdam: Elsevier.

Malmendier, Ulrike, and Geoffrey Tate. 2005. "CEO Overconfidence and Corporate Investment." *Journal of Finance* 60:6, 2661–2700.

Mehra, Rajnish, and Raaj Sah. 2002. "Mood Fluctuations, Projection Bias, and Volatility of Equity Prices." *Journal of Economic Dynamics and Control* 26:5, 869–887.

Nieuwenstein, Mark R., Tjardie Wierenga, Richard D. Morey, Jelte M. Wicherts, Tesse N. Blom, Eric-Jan Wagenmakers, and Hedderik van Rijn. 2015. "On Making the Right Choice: A Meta-Analysis and Large-Scale Replication Attempt of the Unconscious Thought Advantage." *Judgment and Decision Making* 10:1, 1–17.

Noussair, Charles. 2016. "Society for Experimental Finance Presidential Address 2015." *Journal of Behavioral & Experimental Finance*. Forthcoming.

Open Science Collaboration. 2012. "An Open, Large-Scale, Collaborative Effort to Estimate the Reproducibility of Psychological Science." *Perspectives on Psychological Science* 7:6, 657–660.

Ou, Amy Y., David A. Waldman, and Suzanne J. Peterson. 2016. "Do Humble CEOs Matter? An Examination of CEO Humility and Firm Outcomes." *Journal of Management*. Forthcoming

Papadakis, Vasilis M., and Patrick Barwise. 2002. "How Much do CEOs and Top Managers Matter in Strategic Decision-Making?" *British Journal of Management* 13:1, 83–95.

Pharoah, Paul DP, Ya-Yu Tsai, Susan J. Ramus, Catherine M. Phelan, Ellen L. Goode, Kate Lawrenson, Melissa Buckley, et al. 2013. "GWAS Meta-Analysis and Replication Identifies Three New Susceptibility Loci for Ovarian Cancer." *Nature Genetics* 45:4 362–370. Available at http://www.nature.com/ng/journal/v45/n4/abs/ng.2564.html#author-information.

Quigley, Timothy J., and Donald C. Hambrick. 2015. "Has the 'CEO Effect' Increased in Recent Decades? A New Explanation for the Great Rise in America's Attention to Corporate Leaders." *Strategic Management Journal* 36:6, 821–830.

Ramirez, Andres, and Solomon Tadesse. 2009. "Corporate Cash Holdings, Uncertainty Avoidance, and the Multinationality of Firms." *International Business Review* 18:4, 387–403.

Reinhart, Carmen M., and Kenneth S. Rogoff. 2010. "Growth in a Time of Debt." *American Economic Review* 100:2, 573–578.

Replication Wiki. 2016. Available at http://replication.uni-goettingen.de/wiki/index.php/Main_Page.

Schimmack, Ulrich. 2012. "The Ironic Effect of Significant Results on the Credibility of Multiple-Study Articles." *Psychological Methods* 17:4, 551–566.

Schimmack, Ulrich. 2014. "Quantifying Statistical Research Integrity: The Replicability-Index." Available at http://ww.r-index.org/.

Smith, Vernon L., Gerry L. Suchanek, and Arlington W. Williams. 1988. "Bubbles, Crashes, and Endogenous Expectations in Experimental Spot Asset Markets." *Econometrica* 56:5, 1119–1151.

Sullivan, Ryan, Allan Timmermann, and Halbert White. 1999. "Data-Snooping, Technical Trading Rule Performance, and the Bootstrap." *Journal of Finance* 54:5, 1647–1691.

Vlaeminck, Sven, and Lisa-Kristin Herrmann. 2015. "Data Policies and Data Archives: A New Paradigm for Academic Publishing in Economic Sciences?" *EconStor Open Access Articles* 145–155.

Walsham, Geoff. 2006. "Doing Interpretive Research." *European Journal of Information Systems* 15:3, 320–330.

Discussion Questions and Answers (Chapters 2–30)

Chapter 2 The Financial Psychology of Players, Services, and Products

1. **List and explain some fundamental issues of behavioral finance.**
Four major tenets of behavioral finance are loss aversion, heuristics, overconfidence, and status quo bias. Loss aversion is when people evaluate specific financial choices in which they allocate more importance to a loss than to earning a gain. Heuristics are mental shortcuts people use to process information because of too much data, time limits, or other pressures. Overconfidence is the inclination to overrate one's level of expertise, skills, or abilities in order to predict investment returns. Status quo bias is when people suffer from inertia by defaulting to the same decision or accepting the current circumstance. Adjusting such behavior often requires major incentives.

2. **Provide an overview of the behavioral finance perspectives of risk.**
The behavioral finance viewpoint of risk is based on both the objective issues and the subjective factors in assessing risk for a specific financial service or investment product. A major premise is the notion of loss-averse behavior, in which individuals allocate more weight to losses than to gains. Consequently, they may select satisfactory rather than optimal outcomes. An emerging subject in behavioral finance concerns an inverse (negative) relation between perceived risk and return.

3. **Define the heuristic biases of representativeness, anchoring, and mental accounting.**
Representativeness is a bias in which individuals have an instinctive tendency to develop a viewpoint about a specific experience and over-weight how much this circumstance reminds them of other familiar decisions. Anchoring is the inclination for individuals to latch on to a piece of information or past experience as a reference point for making judgments and final decisions. Individuals frequently make a financial judgment on the first information they are presented and have problems

changing their assessment to new data. Mental accounting is a decision-making approach in which individuals split their financial assets into different mental categories or compartments.

4. **Define and describe the process of worrying within the finance domain.**
The process of worrying is a regular and widespread human experience, especially about finances. Financial worries induce past memories and mental pictures of future episodes that can influence decision making. An individual may have negative feelings, such as high levels of worry toward risky investments, which may result in avoiding certain types of financial securities. This behavioral perspective of financial worry is how an individual might respond to a specific condition or judgment that results in higher levels of depression, dread, regret, or unhappiness about their personal finances.

Chapter 3 Individual Investors

1. **Discuss the main differences between the traditional and the modern finance paradigm in understanding the behavior of individual investors.**
The traditional finance paradigm assumes that individual investors make rational decisions and respond only to economic incentives. However, the modern finance paradigm takes a more holistic approach by recognizing the complexity of individual decision making and its collective influence on financial markets and firm decisions. In the modern paradigm, biological roots, personal life experiences, psychology, nonstandard preferences, and behavioral context such as social norms and culture shape individual investors' behavior.

2. **Explain the broad implications of studies of genetics, neural roots, and personal life experiences for understanding the behavior of individual investors.**
Studies show that investor behaviors and preferences have biological roots and life-course determinants. Although many tend to describe behavioral biases or nonstandard preferences as suboptimal, such behavioral traits and preferences may be the result of optimal learning in evolutionary ancient times or in personal life. Thus, studies of genetics, neural roots, and life experiences in finance offer powerful insights for understanding the existence and heterogeneity of behavioral traits among individual investors.

3. **Discuss the disposition effect and the proposed explanations for this effect.**
The disposition effect refers to the tendency of investors to sell winner stocks more readily than loser stocks. Some experts propose that the dual-risk attitude embedded in prospect theory generates risk aversion in the main domain and risk seeking in the loss domain, leading to a greater tendency to realize capital gains. Others suggest that investors experience realization utilities, which promote the realizing gains more than the realizing losses. Some show that cognitive dissonance is partly responsible for the disposition effect. When investors can blame their investment managers, they exhibit no disposition effect in mutual fund redemption decisions.

4. **Identify the social factors that influence individual investor decisions and discuss the importance of considering the social context when making investment decisions.**
Every individual belongs to social networks from which they acquire information, process information, and reference their own behavior. Thus, the group members, group norms, and societal cultures influence investor decision making. Social interaction may facilitate wiser investment decisions. However, when information sharing among groups is incomplete, biased, or distorted, suboptimal decisions may prevail. Culture has a distinct, powerful, and long-lasting impact on investor decision making. Understanding these social factors can help provide a better understanding of group investing behavior, societal trends about investing platforms, and the role of fashion and fads in investment ideas.

Chapter 4 Institutional Investors

1. **Discuss whether institutional investors are subject to behavioral biases to the same extent as individual investors.**
Empirical evidence suggests that individual investors are much more likely to trade based on behavioral biases. Some evidence suggests that institutions are subject to the disposition effect and overconfidence, but generalizing this evidence is limited due to small sample sizes.

2. **Explain whether mood, not directly related to financial fundamentals, affects institutional investors.**
Institutional investors seem to be less subject to mood, unrelated to market fundamentals, compared to individual traders. However, some mood-based trader behavior seems to exist among institutions. For example, a study of weather patterns shows that relative overpricing of securities on the Dow Jones Industrial Average increases on cloudier days at the same time as does institutional investors' selling propensities of the securities. A stock-level mood proxy from institutional investors' holdings is positively related to a stock's returns, especially in more difficult to arbitrage securities.

3. **Discuss whether evidence showing that institutions herd with their trades supports irrational (market destabilizing) or rational (market stabilizing) reasons for institutional herding.**
Empirical evidence documents a strong tendency of institutions to herd. Various behavioral reasons could drive such herding. In the case of the institutional traders, herding appears information based. For cascading, evidence shows that institutions follow each other's trades because they infer information from each other. Because institutions trade on the same information from the underlying fundamentals, herding occurs unintentionally. Both cascading and investigative herding speeds up incorporating fundamentals into security prices and thus increases market efficiency.

4. **Identify how institutions can exploit behavior biases of individual investors' in their trading choices.**
Institutions can exploit individual investors' behavioral biases by being on the winning side of the trades. For example, institutions could take advantage of market underreaction to earnings announcements. Earnings surprises, both positive and negative, are followed by a drift because of the market's initial underreaction to the surprise. Institutional investors are aware of the drift and profit from it in their trades.

5. **Discuss how institutional agents can use behavioral finance to benefit their clients.**
Understanding basic behavioral characteristics can help financial advisors construct financial plans and portfolio allocations for their clients. For example, financial advisors could administer a simple questionnaire to better understand if their clients are likely to suffer from overconfidence or loss aversion. Using the tools from behavioral finance, advisors can educate their clients, construct and customize clients' portfolios to fit their investment personalities, and guide clients during periods of market turmoil.

Chapter 5 Corporate Executives, Directors, and Boards

1. **Identify and explain three psychological factors that differentiate CEOs in the agency and stewardship frameworks.**
Three factors differentiating CEOs are motivation, identification, and use of power. The motivation of agent CEOs comes from an economic self-interest and leads to behaviors and decisions that they perceive as improving their economic being. Alternatively, steward CEOs are motivated by intrinsic rewards and acts to enhance their achievements and self-efficacy. Identification refers to taking responsibility and blame within an organization. Agent CEOs externalize the company's problems to avoid blame and may exacerbate them by not taking responsibility. The steward CEO views the problems as an opportunity to work toward the common goals and earn achievements. Finally, the use of power in a company in the agency framework is institutional in nature to control and influence the CEO. In the stewardship framework, power is on a personal level and derives from expertise, respect, and loyalty.

2. **Discuss how CEO optimism might lead to poor capital investments.**
Optimistic managers overestimate an investment's cash flows and underestimate its risk. Thus, some projects may appear to have a positive net present value when they really do not. This bias leads to investing in poor projects.

3. **Explain how a CEO might become overconfident.**
Managers tend to over-credit their own role for successes and blame bad luck for poor outcomes. This self-attribution bias leads to overconfidence through experience. This overconfidence leads to being more likely to apply for higher-level management positons, so overconfident managers are promoted more often.

4. **Identify and explain group dynamic biases that might affect a board of directors.** Groups sometimes suffer from social loafing, poor information sharing, and groupthink. Social loafing, or the free-rider problem, occurs when board members fail to put in a high level of effort and still get credit for the successes of the group. They believe others will do their portion of the work. Poor information sharing occurs when a board member has specialized knowledge but fails to share it because of the power of knowing something that others do not. Also, a board member may fail to share information that is contradictory to the consensus belief as a confirmation bias. Groupthink is a failure to explore alternative options by not seriously discussing them in an effort to achieve consensus.

Chapter 6 Financial Planners and Advisors

1. **Explain the various regulatory regimes that encompass financial planners and advisors, and identify when a particular advisor would fit under each regime.** Financial planners and financial advisors are not regulated as distinct professions. Instead, they are regulated depending on the functions they perform. Financial advisors who are compensated for providing investment advice are typically regulated as Investment Advisor Representatives (IARs) and are affiliated with a Registered Investment Advisor (RIA). IARs are held to a fiduciary standard of care, where their recommendations must be in the best interests of their clients. The Securities and Exchange Commission (SEC) oversees large RIAs and state securities regulators oversee small RIAs. Financial advisors who are compensated for helping individuals buy and sell financial products are typically regulated as a registered representative of a broker-dealer (BD). As such, they are held to a suitability standard of care, in which the products they sell must be suitable for their customers. The Financial Industry Regulatory Authority (FINRA) is a self-regulatory organization (SRO) that oversees broker-dealers, and the SEC oversees FINRA. State insurance commissions regulate financial advisors who sell insurance products.

   Financial advisors may be licensed to provide multiple services for clients. As a result, they may fall under multiple regulatory regimes. For example, an advisor may be an IAR, a registered representative of a BD, and an insurance agent. As such, FINRA, the SEC (and/or state securities regulators), and the state insurance commissions of any state where the advisor does business would oversee the advisor.

2. **Discuss the agency costs involved in receiving professional financial advice and how to mitigate those costs.** Agency costs include monitoring costs, bonding costs, and residual losses. Monitoring costs involve a principal managing the work performed by an agent. In financial planning, this arrangement involves a client managing the work of his or her financial advisor. This monitoring can be achieved through regulation by relying on knowledgeable regulators to oversee the work of financial advisors. Bonding costs that advisors typically incur can include the standard of care to which an advisor is held, such as the fiduciary or suitability standard. Bonding costs can also include rigorous certifications that can serve as a public signal that an advisor has acquired

adequate financial knowledge to be considered a competent professional and is willing to abide by a particular ethical code of conduct. Residual losses include any additional losses that may be incurred, despite the best efforts of the principal.

Individuals can mitigate agency costs by using an advisor who is willing to incur adequate bonding costs. They can also check public records to ensure that no regulators or certifying organizations have disclosed any disconcerting information about the advisor or the advisor's firm.

3. **Describe the common compensation structures used by financial advisory firms, and identify potential conflicts of interest within each compensation structure.**
Financial advisory firms can be compensated through commissions, a percentage of assets under management (AUM), an hourly rate, a retainer fee, project-based fees, or some combination of these methods. Commission-based compensation may entice an advisor to buy and needlessly sell financial products or to recommend products with larger commissions. Advisors with AUM-based compensation may seek ways to increase the amount of managed assets, either by incurring more investment risk than is optimal or by discouraging withdrawals from the portfolio of managed assets. Charging an hourly rate may encourage advisors to spend unnecessary time working on a particular client's situation, while retainer fees may encourage the opposite, in which advisors may shirk in their responsibilities. Lastly, project-based compensation may entice advisors to overestimate the time and other resources that a project requires or to short-change the resources actually used. Although conflicts of interest may exist regardless of the compensation structure, ethical and competent financial advisors can operate within any form of compensation.

4. **Discuss the characteristics of individuals who typically employ the services of financial planners and advisors.**
Individuals who use a financial advisor tend to be wealthier and have more income. They also are prone to have better financial behaviors with proactive attitudes about retirement. Such individuals are more likely to be older and have more education than those who do not use a financial advisor. Women are also more likely than men to report using a financial advisor.

5. **Discuss empirical evidence about the value of financial advice.**
The value of financial advice can include both quantitative and qualitative factors. Regarding quantitative factors, individuals with a financial advisor tend to have more diversified portfolios with more asset classes. They also tend to have higher portfolio turnover, incur more fees, and experience lower portfolio returns. The negative impacts of using a financial advisor may result from misaligned incentives between the client and the advisor and may be avoided by mitigating agency costs.

Qualitatively, financial advisors may help clients acquire adequate insurance protection and favorable tax-sheltered accounts. Financial advisors may also help clients maintain a long-term focus, which can be particularly beneficial during recessions. Some estimate the value of using a financial advisor to be between 1.5 and 3 percentage points (150 and 300 basis points).

Chapter 7 Financial Analysts

1. **Discuss whether regulation solves the problem of bias in analysts' reports.**
   Regulation solves the problem of bias in analysts' reports only to the extent that the regulations remove bias driven by conflicts of interest. If the bias also results from behavioral factors, such as confirmation bias or the leniency heuristic, then regulation can only reduce but not eliminate bias. Information uncertainty fills the environment in which financial analysts form their forecasts and recommendations. As such, the possibility of behavioral biases driven by this uncertainty is high.

2. **Identify two incentives or environmental factors that increase analyst bias.**
   Incentives to curry favor with the firm managers the analysts are following to get better information can increase analyst bias. The incentives to please firm managers to increase trading and investment banking business for their brokerage house can also increase bias. Each of these responses should also lead to increased compensation for the analyst.

3. **Identify analyst characteristics that reduce analyst bias.**
   Some studies show that experience in forecasting may reduce analyst optimism. Additional research finds that analysts who follow fewer companies and those who forecast more frequently are less optimistic in their forecasts.

4. **Discuss whether the market recognizes and adjusts for the bias in analysts' reports.**
   Much evidence finds that optimism in analysts' reports harms smaller and less sophisticated investors. Several studies show that larger investors understand and adjust for the bias in analysts' reports.

Chapter 8 Portfolio Managers

1. **Describe the primary steps of the portfolio management process.**
   The first step in the portfolio management process is to establish the fund's goals along with its constraints. Next, the manager develops and implements the portfolio strategy, which includes determining an investment strategy to undertake and select the fund's investments. The last step is to monitor and adjust the portfolio, which is an ongoing process to ensure that the fund continues to follow the established objectives.

2. **Compare the structure of traditional and alternative asset management firms and identify biases that may arise as a result of their differences.**
   Traditional asset management firms manage relatively straightforward, traditional financial products and are compensated based on a percentage of their assets under management (AUM). Alternative asset managers receive both a fee based on AUM and a performance fee for returns above their high-water mark. Because hedge fund managers receive both management and performance fees, they may be incentivized to engage in risk-taking behavior to maximize their potential compensation.

3. **Describe the disposition effect and how it affects portfolios based on an investor's utility.**
The disposition effect is a phenomenon where investors feel more strongly about losses than they do gains. That is, a gain followed by an equal-size loss generates negative utility. Therefore, investors hold onto losing investments because they do not want to realize a loss (risk-seeking behavior), but quickly sell winning investments to ensure that any gains are not eliminated (risk-avoidance behavior). In a portfolio context, portfolio managers tend to sell winners too early and hold losers too long.

4. **Contrast the different biases displayed by male and female portfolio managers and the consequences of each on their respective portfolios.**
Female portfolio managers are less likely to display overconfidence bias than are male portfolio managers, which has ramifications on trading activity and concentrated positions. Women also have a greater ability to admit mistakes and to sell losing investments. Further, women are less likely to engage in herding behavior and their portfolios have differentiated return patterns as a result.

Chapter 9 Financial Psychopaths

1. **Identify the distinguishing characteristics of a traditional psychopath.**
The distinguishing characteristics of a traditional psychopath include a pervasive, life-long pattern of problematic behavior, deceitfulness, impulsivity, irritability and aggressiveness, reckless disregard for the safety of self or others, consistent irresponsibility, lack of moral compass, and absence of remorse. Psychopaths usually present a charming demeanor.

2. **Explain how traditional and financial psychopaths differ.**
Financial psychopaths are a subset of corporate psychopaths. As such, they display most of the traits of traditional psychopaths, but tend to be "passive" in nature. That is, financial psychopaths prefer to manipulate and exploit others through tactics other than physical violence. Financial psychopaths have control over financial resources rather than managing entire companies. As such, they use financial instruments and financial transactions to inflict damage on others in pursuit of financial gains for themselves, experiencing no remorse for the consequences of their actions.

3. **Discuss the key changes in the economic and financial environment that facilitated an increase in the psychopathic-like behavior exhibited by financial professionals.**
The biggest factor that changed the financial environment is the continued and rapid advancement in computer technology. Other key factors include more mathematicians and computer-skilled people employed in the financial sector, shifting the personality profile of the sector, transition to off-exchange trading platforms, less relationally based trading venues, financial theories that emphasize maximizing financial returns, and loosening of regulations governing financial markets.

4. **Explain why correctly identifying financial psychopaths is important.**
Correctly identifying financial psychopaths is important because they have the potential to topple the financial system if left unchecked. Successful financial psychopaths, such as Bernie Madoff and Lee B. Farkus, can operate over long periods without detection. Operating in this manner enables them to build up enormous liabilities from their financial schemes, which are usually linked to nonexistent securities so nothing is backing the liabilities. At the same time, the financial psychopath appears to be prospering with excess money. The increased linkage of financial systems globally makes this situation even more precarious.

Chapter 10 The Psychology of High Net Worth Individuals

1. **Define HNWIs and discuss the demographic trend.**
HNWIs, or high net worth individuals, are individuals or households with more than $1 million in net worth, which is investable assets excluding primary residence, collectibles, consumables, and consumer durables. The global number of HNWIs and their total wealth has grown substantially. Wealth is not only concentrated to the top 1 percent of the world population; it also enjoys the highest growth rate at the very top. Asia-Pacific and North America drive the majority of growth. China and India are expected to drive global HNWI growth over the next few years.

2. **Identify the key players in the wealth management industry in the United States.**
The key players in the wealth management industry in the United States are full-service broker-dealers (wirehouses), independent broker-dealers (IBDs), independent Registered Investment Advisors (RIAs), private banking, and multi-family offices (MFOs).

3. **Discuss the different assumptions and approaches of behavioral vs. traditional finance.**
Behavioral finance recognizes real human behaviors and focuses on cognitive biases and heuristics. The behavioral finance model combines psychology with financial theory to understand the interplay between markets and human emotions, personality, and reason. The behavioral approach is evidence based. The traditional finance model assumes a "perfect" market for capital where investors are completely rational, emotionless, self-interested maximizers of expected utility with stable preferences. The traditional approach is normative.

4. **Describe goal-based wealth management and holistic investing.**
Goal-based wealth management considers the short, intermediate, and long-term personal theme of HNWIs to help them prioritize their goals holistically. Success is measured by how clients are progressing toward reaching their personalized goals against the broad range of needs and concerns, versus the traditional approach of measuring performance based on relative returns against benchmark market indices. Holistic investing is characterized by personal relationships, frequent human

interactions, and customized advice. HNWIs are offered integrated financial planning and wealth management advice and solutions encompassing investment, credit, tax, estate planning, insurance, philanthropy, and succession planning, both for businesses and for personal wealth.

Chapter 11 The Psychology of Traders

1. **Define overconfidence and give some examples of how overconfidence affects trading strategy.**
   Overconfidence is one of the most severe biases affecting trader behavior. Formally, overconfidence is the tendency for someone, such as a trader, to perceive his or her knowledge and skills better than they actually are. In practice, overconfidence induces traders to believe that they possess superior information than other market participants (the better-than-average effect) or to underestimate the actual riskiness of their portfolios (miscalibration). This misperception is popular especially among male traders, leading them to hold undiversified portfolios and to trade more than advisable. Overtrading implies a higher amount of transaction costs and thus a reduction in the trader's net performance.

2. **Describe the main differences between gregarious and contrarian investment strategies.**
   A gregarious investment strategy is the tendency of traders to follow others' beliefs instead of their own. This behavior can be both rational and irrational. The former situation appears when traders prefer to follow the decisions of those whom they believe are more informed or possess superior trading skills. Herding behavior can also be irrational when investors follow the group's beliefs, even when they clearly seem erroneous. In this situation, the approach is to reduce potential mental discomfort deriving from wrong individual trading decisions. As several studies suggest, only a low percentage of traders are profitable. Thus, even though gregarious behaviors (i.e., momentum-type strategies) perform well when markets are trending, investors should revise their strategies and use an approach that is the opposite of the majority of investors before the market cycle changes. But employing a contrarian strategy does not mean systematically moving in the opposite direction to the trend in all market conditions. Thus, traders who want to profitably adopt a contrarian strategy have to identify areas where high uncertainty can lead most investors to make wrong decisions. This usually happens when stock market prices substantially differ from their fundamental values (e.g., close to market tops or bottoms). Identifying those areas in practice can be difficult because emotions play a critical role in influencing trading decisions. Hence, following a profitable contrarian strategy requires strong mental discipline.

3. **Explain the meaning of investor sentiment and provide some examples.**
   Investor sentiment is the attitude of traders toward the market not justified by changes in fundamentals. Sentiment is clear as markets approach tops (or bottoms) when most traders are optimistic (or pessimistic). Yet, the prevalent market feeling can be difficult to determine when prices do not show a defined trend.

Two broad categories of sentiment indicators are available: the opinion-style and the action-style indicators. The former group collects all indexes based on surveys or judgments of specific categories of investors about future market scenarios. An example of an opinion-style indicator is the University of Michigan Consumer Sentiment Index, which surveys consumers to gather expectations about the overall economy. Action-style indicators include all indicators describing the actual behaviors put in practice by market participants. Examples of action-style indicators are the Commitments of Traders (COT), which details the positioning of investors on different futures markets, and the CBOE Volatility Index (VIX), which measures the 30-day implied volatility priced into S&P 500 index options.

4. **Define possible solutions to mitigate opportunistic behavior in trading simulations.**
   Trading simulations are useful tools to increase experience and improve the knowledge and skills of novice traders. Unfortunately, participants can also be induced to adopt opportunistic behaviors just to win the competition, such as investing only in high-volatile assets and concentrating their portfolios. To mitigate unrealistic behaviors that participants can exhibit, several options can make trading challenges more realistic. These options include having participants share their profits and losses with the subject promoting the competition and not allowing participants to directly observe other teams. Such actions could improve the quality of investment simulations and help overcome cognitive errors affecting novice traders.

Chapter 12 A Closer Look at the Causes and Consequences of Frequent Stock Trading

1. **Explain why frequent stock trading is bad for investor returns.**
   Although academic researchers may not all agree on what drives frequent stock trading, they do agree that frequent trading is detrimental to returns. The inferior performance of frequent traders is largely due to their paying more commissions and generally spending more on transaction costs. In fact, the more often frequent traders trade, the more it costs them.

2. **Identify the major factors that might drive frequent trading.**
   Research indicates that various factors might drive some people to trade more often than others, including high risk seeking, overconfidence, gambling addiction, and emotional issues. Of these factors, risk seeking seems to have the most evidence as a factor contributing to frequent trading. Research suggesting that frequent trading may be a form of compulsive gambling is more recent.

3. **Differentiate among recreational, aspirational, and sensation-seeking motives for investing and explain which of these motives leads to the greatest trading frequency.**
   Recreational or leisure motives treat active investing as a source of fun. Investors motivated mainly by this purpose actually enjoy investing. The aspiration for riches motive views investing similar to a lottery, providing a very small chance for

possibly huge payoffs. These investors may not enjoy investing, but they are very focused on the potential outcome. Basically, they are hoping to become wealthy. The sensation-seeking motive focuses on how the act of trading, with all its uncertainties, provides the stimulation and novelty some people may feel they need to keep their life exciting. The thrill of both the potential gain and the potential loss drives investors motivated by sensation seeking. Two of these groups—the recreational and sensation-seeking investors—trade for emotional rather than rational reasons. However, only the sensation-seeking, risk-taking motive actually predicts frequent trading. In other words, only investors who enjoy gambling (the third group) turn over their portfolios at a much higher rate than other investors.

4. **Identify and explain the gender differences that exist in investing and gambling behavior.**
Males generally trade more frequently than females, resulting in men having lower returns than female investors. Women are more fiscally conservative than men and tend to invest in less risky assets. Both risk seeking and overconfidence are more common in men than in women. Overconfidence and risk seeking are also correlated with more frequent stock trading. Of course, different types of risk and overconfidence exist. Compared to women, men seek greater risk both financially and otherwise. Men tend to be more impulsive. Compared to women, men are more likely to be overconfident in terms of believing their skills are better than average across domains.

In terms of gambling, males are more likely than females to suffer from gambling disorder. Males start gambling at a younger age and tend to develop gambling disorder at a younger age than females, who are more likely to begin gambling at an older age and to develop gambling disorder in a shorter time frame. Among those with gambling disorder, females seek treatment sooner than men. This is also true of other psychological disorders.

5. **Discuss whether mobile technology is likely to affect frequent trading.**
The rapid increase in mobile device adaptation and usage continues to affect the global economy. The global proliferation of smartphones and other mobile devices is likely to increase the pervasiveness of frequent stock trading. Researchers find that compulsive gamblers gamble more when new gambling platforms become available to them. Thus, the widespread use of the Internet and mobile devices is likely to also increase the tendency of some investors to indulge in overtrading. However, in the context of investing in stocks, additional research is needed to understand the effect of mobile usage on trading frequency.

6. **Discuss the prevalence of frequent stock trading.**
Frequent trading is a common problem. In fact, some consider investor overtrading as an epidemic. To illustrate, the turnover rate on the New York Stock Exchange (NYSE) reached nearly 100 percent in 2004. Moreover, researchers find that rational reasons, such as portfolio risk-rebalancing needs, do not explain this high rate of turnover. The problem is particularly serious for the most active traders, who trade much more than the average trader and realize even larger losses for trading too often.

Chapter 13 The Psychology of Women Investors

1. **Explain how men and women view the topic of investing differently and why advisors should know this.**
   Historically, women have been raised without having much knowledge about money and have deferred to men in the household to make decisions. Some females may be cautious about taking control of finances; women often want security and a sense of belonging. Men view investing as a competitive endeavor, in which high risk to reward is acceptable. Understanding the motivations of clients can help advisors better serve their clients.

2. **Explain why women often lack confidence about financial matters and how this may affect their financial decisions.**
   Women are not raised to have high financial confidence, due to societal pressures that allow the men in their lives to control the financial decisions. This negatively affects women's comfort and understanding about investing, as well as other financial matters. Sometimes, women's preference for low risk or "safe" investments can negatively affect their ability to accumulate wealth.

3. **Identify several important financial concerns of women.**
   Women have several important financial concerns. For example, many women struggle to balance their careers with their family responsibilities and feel overwhelmed, overextended, and overworked. Many are concerned about being able to provide for their loves ones in the long term, even after retirement.

4. **Discuss how the caregiver role affects investing.**
   As the traditional caregiver, women look for lower-risk investments that allow long-term returns with smaller upfront investments. They spend short-term monies as part of their caregiver roles. Women have to fund longer time frames in retirement with a shorter work history. Their shorter work history or gaps in employment often result in smaller defined-pension benefits and smaller retirement plan balances.

5. **Discuss how advisors should treat women.**
   Women need their advisors to be able to connect with them. Women also need to know that they are heard and understood. Women want someone to work with them to understand the impact that one decision may have on other areas of their financial lives.

Chapter 14 The Psychology of Millennials

1. **Explain why Millennials are distrustful of the financial services industry.**
   Millennials came of age in financially unstable times and many saw their parents' financial situation compromised. They witnessed the dot-com and housing bubbles burst, the Enron and Bernie Madoff scandals, and the financial crisis of 2007–2008, as well as the subsequent recession and prolonged economic recovery. A 2016 Facebook white paper reports that half of Millennials feel they have no one they can trust for financial guidance and fewer than 10 percent trust financial institutions for this guidance.

2. **Explain how Millennials differ from Baby Boomers other than age.**
   One key generational difference between millennials and baby boomers is that Millennials have always had access to the Internet. Although Boomers are "the TV generation," Millennials are not restricted to just one screen. They are taking the lead in integrating mobile technology and the Internet into their lives and thus are changing the way they consume entertainment, shop, bank, and invest. Millennials who do not use a financial advisor use these tools and resources to educate themselves about money management and financial planning.

3. **Discuss how financial advisors can engage Millennials.**
   Millennials are now the largest generation to date, surpassing Baby Boomers at 80 million strong. Although Boomers currently hold the greatest amount of wealth, Millennials are poised to become the wealthiest generation. Financial advisors must communicate using the language and the tools that Millennials use, which means having a vital social media presence and a user-friendly website, blogs, videos, and content aimed at demystifying wealth management and investing.

4. **Explain how money habits of Millennials disprove the stereotype that they are a lazy and an entitled generation.**
   Several studies indicate that the unique financial challenges Millennials face, such as student debt, have compelled them to adopt responsible money habits. Millennials are opting to save and invest their money rather than overspend. Millennials are not only contributing to employer-sponsored retirement plans but also using online tools to track their expenses, live within their means, and control their wants.

Chapter 15 Psychological Aspects of Financial Planning

1. **List the six steps of the financial planning process as defined by CFP Board of Standards and Financial Planning Standards Board.**
   The six steps in the financial planning process are: (1) developing and defining the client-planner relationship, (2) collecting client data including goals, (3) analyzing and evaluating the client's current financial status, (4) developing and providing recommendations and/or different options, (5) implementing the recommendations, and (6) monitoring the recommendations.

2. **Explain why financial planning clients tend to rely on secondary markers of quality when judging the advice they receive from their advisors.**
   Financial planning has high credence properties, meaning consumers have difficulty judging the quality of the service even after being rendered. To minimize cognitive dissonance, clients look to things they can directly observe, such as all forms of communication.

3. **Discuss how the availability heuristic can affect a financial planning client's perception of financial planning recommendations and/or propensity to act on them.**
Availability refers to the propensity to be biased by information that is easier to recall such as highly impactful or more recent memories. For instance, a client's willingness to buy long-term care insurance often depends on whether this individual personally knew someone who had received home health care assistance or lodging at a skilled nursing facility. Personal experience of long- or short-lived relatives could influence the willingness to plan for a long retirement.

4. **Describe how the mental biases of overconfidence, anchoring, and loss aversion can interact to cause financial planning clients to make suboptimal decisions.**
Anchoring bias, overconfidence, and loss aversion can result in poor decisions and outcomes. Overconfidence often results in employees holding too much in employer stock or options, believing they have insider insights that are superior to market signals. Loss aversion and the anchoring bias can influence these employees to continue to hold employer stock and options even when a reversal in the company's fortunes or those of its industry causes its stock price to decline, confirming the wisdom of broad diversification.

Chapter 16 Financial Advisory Services

1. **Explain the difference between financial advisors and brokers.**
Brokers often represent the firms whose products they recommend and sell, whereas financial advisors operate independently of these firms. Furthermore, unlike salespeople and brokers, financial advisors in most countries are required by law to put their clients' interests ahead of their own. Although financial advisors may receive some commissions based on sales of certain financial products, the variable earnings of brokers consist entirely of commissions.

2. **Discuss the purpose of financial advice to consumers.**
Financial advisors help their clients articulate their financial goals and implement steps to achieve these goals by providing advice on saving, credit, taxation, the choice of financial products from different providers, investment opportunities, and various wealth and income risks. Also, consumers may delegate management of their investments and pensions to financial advisors.

3. **Describe the types of consumers who are more likely to look for financial advice.**
Women are more likely to seek out financial advice than men. In laboratory settings, less financially literate consumers are more likely to look for financial advice, although those actually receiving financial advice outside of the laboratory are typically richer, older, better educated, and more experienced investors. People who are more future oriented and anxious are also more likely to use financial advice.

4. **Explain why high-quality financial advice may not reach those who would benefit the most from it.**
Financial advisors may find providing high-quality advice only to well-informed and wealthy consumers because these advisors believe that (1) less sophisticated consumers could have a lower willingness to pay for advice because they are unable to distinguish between good and bad advice, and (2) poorer consumers are less profitable due to their smaller portfolios and less wealth. When consumers pay for financial advice with upfront fees and not by commissions, those with less experience and financial sophistication might be reluctant to pay before they can see the benefits.

5. **Describe characteristics of financial advisors that affect the degree to which consumers follow their advice.**
Consumers value financial advisors with more experience, but they prefer advisors who use less technical language and investment jargon. Although confidence is important, advisors who admit some uncertainty about their recommendations tend to be more persuasive. Consumers take more advice from advisors deemed trustworthy, which is also related to a degree of tailoring and personal involvement in the advice process. Consumers are also more likely to be persuaded by advisors similar to them in terms of gender, education, age, region, and political affiliation.

Chapter 17 Insurance and Risk Management

1. **Explain the four primary responses to risk.**
The four primary responses to risk are risk avoidance, risk retention, risk reduction, and risk transfer. Risk avoidance is a response to risk in which individuals avoid the activity altogether. Risk retention is a form of self-insurance in which individuals retain the risk and pay for some of the loss themselves. Risk reduction is a response to risk in which individuals take precautionary measures to reduce the likelihood or severity of a loss. Risk transfer is a response to risk in which individuals transfer a portion of potential risk to a third party.

2. **Discuss the three primary types of hazards associated with risk management.**
The three primary types of hazards are physical, moral, and morale hazards. Physical hazards arise from the condition or use of the property itself. An example of a physical hazard is ice on a stairway. Moral hazards involve dishonest behavior in which the individual causes the loss intentionally. A morale hazard involves attitudes of negligence and carelessness. An example of a morale hazard is when an individual leaves a spare key under the door mat because he knows he has insurance.

3. **Discuss the three most prevalent risk attitudes.**
The three most prevalent attitudes toward risk are risk neutral, risk adverse, and risk seeking. Risk-neutral investors are more concerned about the expected return from an investment regardless of the risk. Risk-adverse investors require a higher return when taking a higher level of risk. Risk-seeking investors accept higher levels of risk even when uncertainty about the return exists.

4. **Identify and discuss the five main types of insurance for individuals.**
The five main types of insurance for individuals are:
    - *Disability*: Some disability policies guarantee income replacement of 50 to 60 percent of the policyholder's income. The cost of disability insurance is based on many factors, including age, occupation, and health.
    - *Life*: This type of insurance protects a family or business from loss of income due to death.
    - *Property causality*: This type of insurance protects against property losses to a business, home, or car and against the liability that may result from injury or damage to others.
    - *Health insurance*: This type of insurance pays for covered medical and surgical expenses. The insured can be reimbursed for expenses or the care provider can be paid directly to the care facility.
    - *Long-term care*: These policies reimburse policyholders a daily amount for services to assist them with activities of daily living, such as bathing, dressing, continence, transferring from bed to chair, or eating. The cost of the policy depends on an individual's age, benefits chosen, and health at the time the policy is issued.

5. **Discuss the three subcategories of behavioral finance theory.**
The three subcategories of behavioral finance theory are biases, heuristics, and framing references. Bias is a tendency toward particular methods of thinking that can lead to bad judgment and irrational decision making. Common behavioral finance biases include chasing trends, overconfidence, and a limited attention span. Heuristics are mental shortcuts that help people make decisions faster. Commonly used heuristics include availability and representativeness. Framing is an example of cognitive bias in which people react to a particular choice in different ways depending on how it is presented, such as a loss or a gain. Individuals tend to avoid risk when presented with a positive frame, but seek risk when presented in a negative frame. Some common framing effects are regret aversion, disposition effect, and anchoring.

Chapter 18 Psychological Factors in Estate Planning

1. **Identify the issues that create differences between estate planning and other areas of financial planning that can impede or prevent progress.**
Several differences between estate planning and other areas of financial planning can affect progress. For example, estate planning involves a discussion of mortality, which is an uncomfortable discussion for both planners and clients. The effectiveness of an estate plan is often measured after the demise of the client.

2. **Discuss the dimensions that differentiate estate planning from other areas of financial planning and wealth management in terms of the emotions accompanying decision making.**
Several dimensions involving emotions that accompany decision making differentiate estate planning from other areas of financial and wealth management. For example, discussions involving mortality are very difficult for many people. Family and marital dynamics can also influence the planning process. Clients may have

difficulty relinquishing their wealth, even after death, and may consider plans that attempt to control their wealth after death.

3. **Explain why estate planning calls for collaboration between the planner and client, as well as between the client and inheritors.**
   Although an attorney has an obligation to represent his client, estate planning requires considering the impact of the estate on beneficiaries, and the planning process may require involving family members and others who may serve as inheritors. This consideration is necessary to address issues related to legal issues and tax-related planning.

4. **Discuss how estate planning presents unusual challenges for the legal or planning professional.**
   Estate planning presents several unusual challenges for the legal or planning professions. For example, the planner may need to include other parties in the planning process, which may produce difficulties around issues of confidentiality and privilege. Including other parties may also require a level of skill in managing the emotional dynamics of a family, which may be beyond the planner's sphere of professional competence.

5. **Explain how transference or counter-transference might play a role in professional engagement.**
   Transference or counter-transference could affect the professional engagement in several ways. Whether or not the professional has dealt with his own issues of mortality, any of that individual's unresolved conflicts may play a role in the interaction, on either a conscious or an unconscious level. Additionally, discussing an estate plan could mobilize feelings about the relationship of the client to his family and touch on feelings the planner has for the people in his life.

Chapter 19 Individual Biases in Retirement Planning and Wealth Management

1. **Discuss the biases individuals have when considering their need for financial planning.**
   Individuals exhibit many biases when assessing whether they need financial planning. For example, they often rationalize their status quo and feel that they are fine handling their money. However, this can be a consequence of wanting to use money for emotional and self-expressive pursuits. Even when feeling that the current situation is not optimal, they choose to keep their head in the sand, exhibiting the ostrich effect. Planning involves thinking about the future, which contrasts with the present bias, which focuses on living for today. Often, people follow the herd. If their friends are managing their finances in a certain manner, then they may conclude that the herd is right. Additionally, people often suffer from the bias of available information when determining the best financial course of action. Discovering more complications might require an investment of both time and emotion.

Many people spend to boost their self-esteem. Friends can own their cars and houses, but may have low bank balances. Some of the need for greater self-esteem may emerge from one's culture or race. Stereotypes often exist about gender and marital status. Not following these expectations can be emotionally taxing. Thus, following the herd is often easier than going against it.

2. **Discuss the rationale for hiring and the criteria for selecting a financial professional.**
Many people think in terms of a milestone-marked, linear financial planning process: secure a job, get married, buy a house, start a family, plan for children's college, and finally, plan for retirement. Individuals often associate with a peer group that holds the same view. For example, when teachers join a school system with a defined-benefit pension plan, the employer is the predominant contributor. Sometimes, the plan requires employee contributions or permits voluntary contributions. For these and many other public employees, the pension plan is designed to pay expected benefits when needed. Workers with elective plans, such as 401(k) plans, however, must make their own contribution and investment decisions, follow their peer group's action, or hire someone to help them. Even when they are proactive in these matters, these workers face great uncertainty concerning projected benefits upon retirement.

The decision whether to hire a professional should at least include evaluating the following areas of financial literacy: (1) ability to evaluate an advisor, (2) financial status, including the mix of credit/debt, (3) retirement planning, (4) college planning, (5) insurance planning, (6) tax planning, (7) estate planning, and (8) investment planning.

Much confusion exists over the term "financial advisor." Because no professional financial advisor designation exists, a wide range of professionals who sell investment and insurance products call themselves financial advisors. Financial advisor sounds better than agent, financial recommender, or financial salesperson. A professional financial advisor:

- Acts as fiduciary and gives advice in the best interests of the individual.
- Holds an industry designation that includes retirement planning, investment planning, and insurance planning.
- Maintains an industry designation requiring continuing education.

Choosing a trusted advisor is important. Unfortunately, individuals often base this choice on limited information or without delving into the advisor's credentials. Some advocate that trust should be based on credentials, honesty, and reliability. Others focus on a financial professional's claim of large assets under management and ascribe talent or fiduciary oversight (working in their best interests) to this claim. This leads people to assume, rather than confirm, that their financial professional is working as a fiduciary.

3. **Discuss several biases that individuals should overcome in the financial planning process.**
Many individuals would rather spend money on fun today than think about their future. This requires them to change from a completely present bias to one that

considers their long-term financial health. Money saved for a potential future emergency or insurance that may or may not be used reduces the available cash to spend today. People often underestimate the probabilities of realized adverse events and assume negative incidents will not occur. Proper risk-planning techniques lead clients to recognize their mortality and that they do not fully control their lives.

In determining how much to contribute to a retirement plan, some workers believe that they can retire comfortably if they match the maximum employer contribution. Many pursue beating the market with their retirement money rather than considering the risk reduction of a broad asset allocation, which is indicative of an overconfidence bias. The media gives investors overconfidence in their ability to outperform the market.

4. **Explain how employers can nudge employees toward financial security.**
Employers can use intelligent defaults to facilitate increasing the retirement savings of their employees. Most important, all employees should be defaulted into participating in the plan. Inertia will work toward the benefit of having most employees stay in the plan. Employers engaging qualified financial professionals to provide employees a retirement gap analysis could also help promote retirement. Most employees do not have the ability to calculate the required savings and rate of return targets to retire comfortably. A financial professional not only can help them with these calculations but can also act as a coach during the plan's implementation, which may last 20 to 40 years. Employers can also expand guidance on all employee benefits including health, disability, life, and long-term care insurance.

5. **Describe how financial planners can nudge clients toward financial security.**
Much confusion exists about the various registrations and designations of retail financial professionals. CFP professionals represent one of the few accredited designations, according to the Financial Industry Regulatory Authority (FINRA). Using the FINRA website and other tools, CFP professionals can educate clients about the kind of financial professional best matching the needs of the individual investor. Similar to an engaged doctor, CFP professionals listen to symptoms, ask questions, and perform diagnostic tests to get a better indication of an individual's true goals and needs. This process can be overwhelming to some. The planner can turn all this information into clear specific financial goals to attain and create a mutually agreed-upon priority list.

Many individuals have difficulty changing their spending habits. A financial planner can thoroughly analyze a client's spending pattern to see ways to reallocate expenses that may not be apparent to the individual. The greatest value for many individuals is having an accountability partner who can empathize with their situation. Many individuals have no formal knowledge of investing. Investment risk is known to be one of the more emotional issues faced by individuals. A financial professional using a risk and reward evidence-based methodology can educate clients on the available options for managing investment risk. Finally, in knowing that financial management is an emotional process, the advisor helps the client celebrate attaining certain milestones, providing positive reinforcement.

Chapter 20 Traditional Asset Allocation Securities: Stocks, Bonds, Real Estate, and Cash

1. **Define tactical asset allocation (TAA) and discuss the advantages and disadvantages relative to strategic asset allocation (SAA).**
   TAA allows for greater flexibility in deviating from target weights over the short to intermediate term. These deviations usually result from a change in risk and/or return assumptions due to the economic or market environment. Because of the deviation from the target weights, a portfolio that uses TAA has the potential to outperform the benchmark if the assumptions are correct and the adjustments are executed properly. If, however, the assumptions are incorrect and/or the execution is poor, the portfolio may underperform the benchmark.

2. **Discuss the assumptions used in modern portfolio theory (MPT) and traditional finance models.**
   Traditional finance describes a theoretical market environment in which the participants act solely for their own benefit and maximize economic utility. The assumptions that must be upheld for MPT include the following: (1) all investors have perfect and equal access to information; (2) correlations between assets remain constant over time; (3) returns are normally distributed; (4) no transaction costs or taxes are applicable; (5) investor buying and selling does not affect price; and (6) investors can borrow and lend unlimited amounts at the risk-free rate.

3. **Discuss the shortfalls of mean-variance optimization (MVO) portfolios and how the Black-Litterman model attempts to address these shortfalls.**
   The shortfalls of the MVO model are its high sensitivity to inputs and overreliance on historical data. The resulting asset allocation strategies are usually heavily concentrated in only a few assets or securities. The Black-Litterman model uses CAPM and a reverse-optimization process with market weights to generate forward-looking assumptions, rather than relying on historical returns. The result is less reliance on historical data in isolation and portfolios with more diversified asset allocation strategies.

4. **Distinguish between cognitive and emotional errors, and provide an example of each.**
   Cognitive errors are based on heuristics, which are mental shortcuts. They result from imperfections in human decision making. For example, the decision to hold an equal weight of all securities in a portfolio because an investor assumes this creates a diversified portfolio is called the 1/N heuristic. Emotional biases are mistakes that investors make based on their feelings toward a decision. An example of an emotional bias is familiarity in which investors place greater value on or express a preference for holding securities they understand or have a connection, such as a common stock inherited from a family member.

5. **Discuss the advantages and disadvantages of mental accounting and how investors can manage this cognitive error.**
Mental accounting is the act of allocating capital to different buckets based on the end use. For example, an individual may have a savings account for a family vacation and an investment account to fund retirement. In the context of asset allocation, an investor may have multiple accounts with different allocations to stocks, bonds, and cash. Each account appears properly allocated, but deviates from the overall portfolio level. This deviation might cause an over-concentration in one or more securities and an inefficient blend of capital. Mental accounting can help an investor separate funds for his designated purposes and increase the investor's likelihood of achieving long-term savings goals. The key to mental accounting's successful use is not to follow this strategy unintentionally. Although an investor can use multiple accounts, he should pay attention to the asset allocation of the overall portfolio.

Chapter 21 Behavioral Aspects of Portfolio Investments

1. **Explain the observed return performance of mutual funds, hedge funds, and pension funds.**
Evidence shows that mutual funds, hedge funds, and pension funds earn, on average, non-positive alphas. Although hedge funds and pension funds outperform mutual funds, hedge fund outperformance is less clear on an after-fee basis.

2. **Explain the similarities and differences between mutual funds and hedge funds.**
Mutual funds and hedge funds are both portfolios of assets designed to provide investors with places to deploy their capital and earn returns. Mutual funds are regulated, face relatively strict reporting requirements, and are limited in terms of assets and strategies available. Hedge funds are generally unregulated, face little to no reporting requirements, and have a much broader range of assets and trading strategies available, including short sales, leverage, and derivatives.

3. **Identify the behavioral biases demonstrated by fund managers.**
Fund managers demonstrate herding bias by which they follow the trades and trends of others in the market, even when doing so does not generate alpha. Additionally, fund managers demonstrate overconfidence and optimism in how they believe they know things with greater precision than they do and also expect outcomes to be better than they are. Other biases of fund managers include familiarity, home bias, limited attention, disposition effect, and escalation of commitment.

4. **Identify the behavioral biases demonstrated by those selecting money managers and related products.**
Investors selecting money managers exhibit the same biases as professional fund managers, including herding, overconfidence, optimism, familiarity, home bias, limited attention, disposition effect, and escalation of commitment. Herding is the tendency to follow other investor actions. Overconfidence describes a bias in decision

making in which individuals believe they know something with greater certainty than is actually the case. Optimism relates to biased in forecasts that overestimate potential outcomes. Familiarity bias is the tendency to invest in companies or funds that are known to an individual. Home bias is the tendency to invest in assets that are geographically close to fund headquarters. Limited attention is a bias related to the observation that individuals' time is scarce and that this lack of unlimited attention may lead to certain biases. Disposition effect describes the tendency to gamble more with losses than profits. Escalation of commitment may result in a fund manager's remaining in a losing investment strategy, which in turn could exacerbate underperformance.

Individuals also exhibit the representativeness bias, hot-hand fallacy, financial illiteracy, search costs, diversification bias, affect, and extrapolation bias. Representativeness bias holds that investors over-weight recent experience when forming expectations of future outcomes. The hot-hand fallacy is the illusion of short-term outperformance, which in reality is within the bounds of expected performance. Financial illiteracy describes a lack of understanding about personal finance and investing concepts. Search costs refer to the time and effort required to identify investments. Diversification bias is the tendency to diversify even when doing so is suboptimal. Affect is an emotional association with a decision. Extrapolation bias is a tendency of investors to treat past events as predictors of future events.

5. **Explain the trends in relative demand for active and passive strategies by both mutual fund and ETFs.**
   Between 2000 and 2014, the demand for passive strategies increased relative to that for active strategies. In particular, demand for index mutual funds, which follow passive strategies, disproportionately drives the net cash inflow into all mutual funds. The growth of ETFs has been impressive, with average annual cash inflows roughly equal to that of mutual funds between 2003 and 2014.

Chapter 22 Current Trends in Successful International M&As

1. **Identify some of the irrational reasons for acquisitions.**
   Four main reasons exist for irrational acquiring: (1) envy theory, (2) free cash flow theory, (3) defensive behavior, and (4) the hubris hypothesis. Envy theory suggests that executives see their cohorts acquiring and getting greater benefits. They then engage in acquisitions to seek the same benefits. Free cash theory suggests that executives spend net income to acquire companies rather than return funds to shareholders. Defensive behavior research suggests executives acquire other firms to keep from being acquired themselves. Finally, the hubris hypothesis suggests that executives perceive that their skills are better than they really are. Consequently, they continue to make unwise acquisitions believing that they can be successful despite a low likelihood of that occurring.

2. **Discuss how globalfocusing can reduce risk the way conglomeration did previously.**
   Organizations previously reduced risk by pursuing a diversification strategy. Thus, by being in multiple industries within a given geographic area, organizations reduced the impact of seasonal and industrial fluctuations. With globalfocusing, organizations lost that ability by taking on a narrower industrial focus. To counter that and to reduce risk, these organizations internationalized, thus spreading their country exposure and reducing risk.

3. **Explain how HR issues during acquisition have changed since 2000.**
   Previously, the majority of acquisitions occurred for economies-of-scale synergies. The acquisition process required combining organizations, reducing staff numbers and harmonizing systems, management styles, and organizational cultures. Carrying out this process required HR departments that were strong in organizational structuring, terminations, training, and harmonization. Acquisitions now take place for marketing entry where little integration with current operations exists. The necessary HR skills are retention and facilitation of horizontal cross-company communication, and intra-company collaboration.

4. **Explain the reasons the success rate of international acquisitions has improved.**
   Acquisitions previously occurred for economies of scale, which created considerable organizational upheaval. Few acquirers could fully capitalize on those cost savings. Recent acquisitions rely more on enhancing revenue through geographic expansion. Consequently, a prolonged and disruptive implementation phase has less impact on organizations. Instead, acquirers use lighter touch integration. Consequently, employees feel less change with success coming through intra-organizational cooperation and increased market coverage for existing products.

Chapter 23 Art and Collectibles for Wealth Management

1. **Explain how passion plays in a portfolio containing art.**
   Passion can be a driving force behind an art collection. Understanding that the passion can become problematic is critical for wealth managers. Such knowledge equips them to better relate to the "I gotta have it" mentality that can grip a collector. This allows managers to empathize with their clients and provide better leadership with their wealth and collection.

2. **Elaborate on how a client might view adding art as additional asset class to a current portfolio.**
   Portfolio objectives related to risk and return must be assessed in conjunction with investor constraints. Next, asset allocation choices can consider the role of art in a potential portfolio. The client and the wealth manager must recognize that art should be viewed through a different lens. Like many alternative assets, an active secondary market does not exist for art, which may present a challenge for clients with higher liquidity needs. If art is included in the asset allocation mix, wealth

managers need to benchmark art appropriately and understand that the art is not a silo on the balance sheet.

3. **Discuss the role of risk mitigation for art investments.**
   Risk mitigation is the ability to spot, identify, and quantify any decision that may affect financial status. Understanding and integrating art and finances requires a client to look beyond the obvious and identify the collateral issues that others may miss. Inadequate liability insurance can put an art collection at risk because the investment portfolio does not consider art as a separate asset class.

4. **Discuss the role of social media in information dissemination as related to art.**
   The social media have moved art and collectible investing beyond the local level as potential art investors now have access to outline outlets. Despite lacking a formal secondary market, a wider exposure to art creates a marketplace where art can be more readily compared and proxies for fair market value can be better determined.

5. **Justify the increasing use of "commodities" as a term to describe holdings.**
   Knowledge has become accessible at levels never foreseen. The days of the knowledge-based classroom and brick and mortar are becoming limited. Wealth managers who invest their time in listening and leading are likely to be better equipped to attract more clients, assets, and opportunities. As art becomes a more readily accepted asset choice, and as trading outlets become more numerous, art begins to resemble more conventional commodity assets. Such assets are increasingly being considered part of the portfolio holdings of investors.

Chapter 24: Behavioral Finance Market Hypotheses

1. **Identify the necessary conditions for a market to be classified as efficient.**
   A market would be classified as efficient if it exhibits absolute equality of information, including a total absence of insider information, full rationality of market participants, market liquidity, perfect competition in the financial markets, and the same investment horizons and expectations for all market participants.

2. **Discuss why no theory has emerged to fully replace the EMH.**
   Financial markets are too complicated to be described with a single theory containing highly restrictive assumptions. Such assumptions lead to inconsistencies with empirical observations. As a result, the EMH remains only a theoretical model. Additional theories are needed that are more consistent with empirical observation.

3. **Provide several examples to illustrate the evolution of the financial markets.**
   An example of the evolution of financial markets is technological leaps, including advances in computer capabilities, Internet trading, and high-frequency trading. Another example is the appearance and development of the new economic theories such as the EMH. Additionally, changes in securities regulation and changes in economic systems, such as the evolution from an industrial to a post-industrial and information economy, can act as drivers for the evolution of the financial markets.

4. **Discuss whether efficient markets exhibit return persistence and possible measures of market efficiency.**
Efficient markets should not exhibit persistence if evidence supports that they random walk. Persistence implies the presence of price memory, implying that previous prices influence current values. If so, trends can exist in the financial markets. This possibility gives opportunities for price prediction, which is impossible in efficient markets because prices changes are random and unpredictable. In theory, market efficiency can be measured using the level of persistence. If no persistence exists in prices, the market can be treated as efficient. The reasons for persistence focus on the irrationality of the investors, existence of noise traders, and technical and fundamental analysis.

5. **Explain whether the behavior of financial markets is consistent with the EMH.**
The behavior of financial markets is generally consistent with the EMH. Predicting future prices and generating profits from trading is difficult. Nevertheless, situations exist that the EMH cannot explain. Empirical observations, called market anomalies, provide arguments against the EMH. Because behavioral finance explains these anomalies well, providing a synthesis of these theories is important to give a fuller explanation of the financial market behavior.

Chapter 25 Stock Market Anomalies

1. **Explain equity anomalies.**
Equity anomalies are empirical relations between future stock return and company characteristics that cannot be explained by classical asset pricing models such as the CAPM or multi-factor models. In other words, cross-sectional stock returns are predictable by different company characteristics.

2. **Discuss the major explanations of why equity anomalies exit.**
Recent literature usually attributes the existence of anomalies to either an inadequacy in underlying asset pricing models or market inefficiency. The inadequacy in asset pricing models is usually called the rational explanation. It builds on the traditional risk–return framework under assumptions that investors are perfectly rational and the market is efficient. Anomalies are the consequences of short-comings of current pricing methods or missing risk factors. Market inefficiency attributes the existence of anomalies to the irrational behavior of investors and is usually called a behavioral explanation. Under the framework of the behavioral perspective, investors do not collect and/or process available information rationally because they suffer from cognitive biases, so securities are mispriced. The stock return predictability represents systematic mispricing in the equity market.

3. **Identify some behavioral biases of investors that can be attributed to anomalies.**
The behavioral biases include overconfidence and self-attribution, limited attention, disposition effect, and investor sentiment. People are usually overconfident about their own judgments being right subjectively rather than objectively. Self-attribution refers to when people tend to credit themselves for past successes, but blame other

factors for failures. Limited attention is the tendency of people to neglect salient signals and overact to relevant or recent news. The disposition effect is the tendency of investors to sell assets that have risen in value rather than to sell those that have fallen. That is, investors tend to sell winners and hold on to losers. Investor sentiment is the propensity to speculate. Researchers often use these behavioral biases to explain various anomalies.

4. **Define an investment anomaly and identify some documented investment anomalies.**
   An investment anomaly refers to the stock return predictability resulting from company characteristics that relate to its investment activities. Studies report that companies with high investment activities earn lower average returns than those with low investment activities. The q-theory provides a theoretical background of how investment can serve as a predictor for future stock returns. The following studies test and verify that company-level measures of investment indeed have power to predict future stock returns. These investment-related anomalies include asset growth, investment growth, net stock issues, investment to assets, and abnormal corporate investment.

Chapter 26 The Psychology of Speculation in the Financial Markets

1. **Define the term *stock bubble*.**
   A stock bubble occurs when market participants drive stock prices considerably above their intrinsic values. Thus, a bubble is an unexpected and dramatic increase in the price of the financial asset or investment ultimately resulting in an extreme decline in price.

2. **List and describe four major causes of speculative behavior.**
   Four major causes of speculative behavior are overconfidence, herding, representativeness bias, and familiarity bias. Overconfidence is the tendency of an investor to overestimate his level of skills, expertise or accuracy when forecasting future stock market performance. Herding is exhibited when a group of investors makes the same investment judgments about a specific piece of information and decides this information is likely to lead to increased stock prices. Representativeness bias is when people are inclined to develop a belief about a current experience and overweight the importance of this information. During a bubble, investors conclude that stock prices are likely to continue to increase based on a small sample of initial stock price data. Familiarity bias is evident when investors demonstrate a preference for and invest in familiar securities. During a bubble, investors perceive familiar stocks as being less risky with the possibility of achieving higher returns.

3. **List and explain four major biases that investors exhibit in the aftermath of the financial crisis of 2007–2008.**
   Four major investor biases evident in the aftermath of the financial crisis of 2007–2008 were anchoring, loss aversion, status quo bias, and mistrust. Anchoring is the

inclination to hold a viewpoint and then apply it as a reference point for determining future decisions. Investors often apply a negative anchor after a stock market bubble bursts. Loss aversion is evident when investors assign more importance to a loss than to achieving an equivalent gain when assessing specific financial transactions. The experience of investors' losing money might remain for an extended period. Often individuals who realize losses during a financial crisis tend to avoid investing in the stock market. After a financial crisis, investors may suffer from status quo bias, no longer wanting to invest in common stocks or avoid managing their investment portfolios. After a financial crisis, the public often exhibits mistrust of financial institutions and markets. Considerable time may elapse before this trust is restored.

4. **Discuss the influence of investor psychology in the aftermath of a financial crisis or when a bubble bursts.**
   After a financial crisis, some investors may exhibit negative long-term biases that affect their overall assessment and decisions about financial markets. In the aftermath of a stock market bubble, this situation results in investors' experiencing lower levels of risk tolerance and higher degrees of negative emotion and perceived risk. Consequently, they tend to under-invest in risky assets such as common stocks and over-invest in safer assets such as cash and bonds.

Chapter 27 Can Humans Dance with Machines? Institutional Investors, High-Frequency Trading, and Modern Markets Dynamics

1. **Discuss the main differences among various equity exchanges operating in the United States.**
   Equity exchanges in the United States differentiate themselves by fee structure. Some exchanges charge fees for using market orders to take away liquidity. Such exchanges are often referred to as "normal" exchanges and provide rebates to traders using limit orders to add liquidity. The NYSE is an example of a normal exchange. Another class of exchanges, known as "inverted," do the opposite by rewarding traders bringing in market orders with rebates and charge traders adding liquidity.

2. **Discuss the key types of HFT.**
   All HFTs are either aggressive or passive. Aggressive HFTs tend to use market orders to capture short-lived arbitrage opportunities. Passive HFTs use limit orders to provide liquidity in market-making strategies.

3. **Explain how exchanges distribute market information.**
   Exchanges distribute trading information via messages. Each exchange decides how to communicate with its market participants. Some exchanges follow a standardized FIX trading message protocol, whereas other exchanges develop their own proprietary communication protocols.

4. **Describe how exchanges record various order types.**
Typically, all exchanges send at least one message for each of the following market occurrences: limit order addition, limit order cancellation, and order execution. The messages typically contain an order id, timestamp, security traded, order size, and order price.

5. **Identify the liquidity considerations that market participants need to consider.**
Analysis shows that traders at various frequencies respond differently to a wide range of market dynamics, such as flickering limit orders, limit order revisions, and order additions and cancellations. For example, HFTs appear to disregard flickering quotes, while lower-frequency traders appear drawn in by flickering quotes. Order revisions also appear to polarize traders. For example, HFTs seem to view limit order revisions as credible negotiation signals, while low-frequency traders avoid trading when limit order revisions occur in the markets.

Chapter 28: Applications of Client Behavior: A Practitioner's Perspective

1. **Distinguish between risk capacity and risk requirement.**
Risk capacity describes how much investment risk a client might take based on his financial resources (i.e., how severe a financial loss a client might sustain and still have the financial resources to meet his goals). *Risk requirement* is the level of return a client needs to meet his financial goals.

2. **Discuss the meaning of risk tolerance.**
Risk tolerance is the amount of risk that an investor is comfortable taking, or the degree of uncertainty that an investor can handle. Risk tolerance is often related to a client's demographic characteristics, such as age, gender, employment, and net worth. As investors tend to feel optimistic during bull markets and pessimistic during bear markets, some contend that a client's risk tolerance varies with market performance. The risk of basing recommendations on demographic factors is that a client may not be representative of a specific demographic profile. The advisor's goal is to recommend an allocation that a client will maintain during turbulent times. A variable measure of risk tolerance would be counterproductive because it might incorrectly reflect the client's risk tolerance at a major market correction, resulting in the client's liquidating financial assets at the wrong time.

3. **Explain how to present the various elements of a client's quarterly report.**
Typically, a client's quarterly report is solely performance focused, including short-term performance such as the last quarter and year to date. Performance is also often measured against a market benchmark, such as the S&P 500 Index. Given the importance of asset allocation to achieving long-term returns, having an allocation graph or table showing both policy and current allocations would be an important element in a quarterly report. To focus a client on long-term vs. short-term

performance, the report could delete information of less than 12 months. Because portfolios are rarely 100 percent invested in equity, a market benchmark could provide a misleading guide. Furthermore, a client's plan and resultant allocation recommendation are based on an estimated real return needed, so benchmarking against the CPI could be more appropriate than using the S&P 500 Index.

4. **Describe framing and how a financial advisor might use it.**
Framing is a behavioral heuristic recognizing that people tend to reach conclusions based on how information in the form of words and numbers are presented. By reframing issues, an advisor can assist clients in avoiding behavioral errors and making better decisions. For example, asking questions such as "Would you buy that stock today?" and "What might go wrong?" are potential framing questions that might affect client behavior.

Chapter 29: Practical Challenges of Implementing Behavioral Finance: Reflections from the Field

1. **Explain how nudging alone constitutes a narrow use of behavioral finance knowledge.**
The success of nudging by using smart defaults in pension auto-enrollment and organ donation, or through social comparisons in energy consumption, suggests that nudging can be the panacea for a wide range of decision problems. This process excludes more creative uses of behavioral finance that rest on features such as simplifying the decision, encouraging engagement, reducing the frictions between deciding and implementing a decision, and pre-commitment to future actions. Nudging is just one part of the behavioral finance toolkit and should not be the sole, or default, tool. Successful applications of behavioral finance require a root and branch approach to understanding the possible improvements to how decision makers interact with organizational processes.

2. **Discuss the features of good and bad applications of behavioral finance.**
A misconception exists that behavioral finance is nothing more than a list of biases, and that it is therefore "easy" to do. As a result, many attempts to apply behavioral finance seek to do little more than offer a checklist of biases. This process assumes that problems can be largely solved by informing people of how they make poor decisions. Merely informing people of their biases is very seldom effective in combating them. Approaches that are not easily transportable between domains can lead to overly engineered solutions.

The best approaches to behavioral finance demonstrate a highly tailored approach to the problem. The program Save More Tomorrow is one such example. This program deals with the inertia or procrastination that stops many people from joining their company's pension plan by keeping initial contribution rates low. Save More Tomorrow also addresses the loss aversion associated with raising contribution rates by getting the participant to pre-commit to future contribution increases out of future pay rises. Although most effective in a period of rising wages, this process is still a highly tailored application of behavioral finance that has led to demonstrable success in raising retirement saving.

3. **Discuss an example of behavioral finance supplementing traditional approaches.** A criticism of modern portfolio theory for individual investors is that optimizing with volatility as a risk measure is not behaviorally justified. The implication that deviations away from the expected return, both positive and negative, add to risk does not reflect how individuals either do, or should, think about risk. Investors rarely state that getting more than they expect feels like a risk. Simply switching the risk measure to something that can be behaviorally justified shows how an understanding of individual behavior can supplement an ingrained traditional approach to investing.

4. **Explain asymmetric paternalism.** Asymmetric paternalism is a dual-focused approach to help people make better decisions. Making major financial decisions is difficult for many people. As a consequence, they typically make no decision at all. The application of smart defaults for this group can be helpful. The default may not be a perfect solution, but if well chosen, it can lead to a better financial outcome. However, many are capable of making their own decisions and this should not be forgotten by simplistically applying a default for all. They need to be actively engaged with financial decisions and helped to make the best choice for their circumstances. Most individuals require some blend of paternalism and engagement to suit their specific capabilities and circumstances. Asymmetric paternalism involves default choices for those who would not or could not make their own decisions, but involves actively engaging those who would or could make their own decisions (or, in practice, some blend of nudges and active engagement for each decision-making, according to their need). This asymmetric approach protects the most vulnerable financial decision makers while assisting the less vulnerable to make the best decisions possible.

Chapter 30: The Future of Behavioral Finance

1. **Discuss the extent to which behavioral finance has progressed philosophically since the 1980s anomalies literature, and how it might develop in the future.** In a Thomas Kuhn philosophy of science perspective, the initial anomalies literature was firmly within the traditional finance paradigm. Defenders of the core paradigm could dismiss the anomalies using the tools and methodologies of traditional finance. Behavioral finance can now be categorized as a separate research paradigm that has its own core theory and some of its own methodologies. It is also clearly a progressive research program based on the growth in publications. The challenge now is to strengthen the core theory and utilize methodologies appropriate to these theories.

2. **Discuss problems with the "rational managers/irrational investors" research stream in behavioral corporate finance.**
The idea that financial decision making in a company is rational, but financial decision making outside a company is not rational seems like an odd compromise. Minimal evidence exists that financial decision making within organizations is rational and unbiased. This view assumes that companies understand when investors are being irrational, even though this view has not been developed based on case studies or other qualitative research of the companies making these decisions. More fundamentally, if companies successfully engage in market timing of equity and debt issues, are they responding to fundamental mispricing by investors or to investor irrationality?

3. **Discuss whether characteristics of top management teams are likely to be featured in future research on the drivers of corporate financial behavior.**
The chief executive officer (CEO) influences perhaps 20 percent of the variability of a company's performance. Thus, ignoring the drivers of the other 80 percent of variability occurring in current behavioral corporate finance seems perverse. Modern strategic management research prefers to focus on the top management team as drivers of strategic decisions, and this focus should include corporate finance decisions. Thus, behavioral corporate finance may start to emulate this practice. A move toward integrating more organizational theory into behavioral corporate finance entails greater emphasis on the wider firm outside of the CEO, including the top management team.

4. **Identify and explain key issues that need to be resolved concerning current measures of investor sentiment.**
Because a multitude of measures exist in investor sentiment, a greater cross-comparison of these is needed moving forward to identify the most suitable measures. A dearth of understanding exists about the fundamental drivers of investor sentiment—issues such as cultural influences and the extent to which sentiment influences different types of investors. New data opportunities are on the horizon to develop better measures of sentiment, but this development requires working with researchers in other disciplines and not purely keeping the theory building and testing within the domain of behavioral finance.

Index

(Page numbers in *italics* refer to tables (*t*) and figures (*f*) within the text.)

Printed in the USA/Agawam, MA
January 2, 2018

666763.059